Lecture Notes in Computer Science   12673

Formal Methods

Subline of Lectures Notes in Computer Science

More information about this subseries at http://www.springer.com/series/7408

Aaron Dutle · Mariano M. Moscato ·
Laura Titolo · César A. Muñoz ·
Ivan Perez (Eds.)

NASA
Formal Methods

13th International Symposium, NFM 2021
Virtual Event, May 24–28, 2021
Proceedings

 Springer

Editors
Aaron Dutle
NASA Langley Research Center
Hampton, VA, USA

Laura Titolo
National Institute of Aerospace
Hampton, VA, USA

Ivan Perez
National Institute of Aerospace
Hampton, VA, USA

Mariano M. Moscato
National Institute of Aerospace
Hampton, VA, USA

César A. Muñoz
NASA Langley Research Center
Hampton, VA, USA

ISSN 0302-9743   ISSN 1611-3349   (electronic)
Lecture Notes in Computer Science
ISBN 978-3-030-76383-1   ISBN 978-3-030-76384-8   (eBook)
https://doi.org/10.1007/978-3-030-76384-8

LNCS Sublibrary: SL2 – Programming and Software Engineering

This Springer imprint is published by the registered company Springer Nature Switzerland AG
The registered company address is: Gewerbestrasse 11, 6330 Cham, Switzerland

Preface

The NASA Formal Methods (NFM) Symposium is a forum to foster collaboration between theoreticians and practitioners from NASA, academia, and industry, with the goal of identifying challenges and providing solutions to achieve assurance in mission-critical and safety-critical systems. Examples of such systems include advanced separation assurance algorithms for aircraft, next-generation air transportation, autonomous rendezvous and docking of spacecraft, on-board software for unmanned aerial systems (UAS), UAS traffic management, autonomous robots, and systems for fault detection, diagnosis, and prognostics. The NASA Formal Methods Symposia welcome submissions on cross-cutting approaches that bring together formal methods and techniques from other domains such as probabilistic reasoning, machine learning, control theory, robotics, quantum computing, and many more.

The topics covered by NFM 2021 included

- Advances in formal methods:

  - Formal verification, model checking, and static analysis techniques
  - Theorem proving: advances in interactive and automated theorem proving (SAT, SMT, etc.)
  - Program and specification synthesis, code transformation and generation
  - Run-time verification
  - Techniques and algorithms for scaling formal methods
  - Test case generation
  - Design for verification and correct-by-design techniques
  - Requirements generation, specification, and validation

- Integration of formal methods techniques:

  - Use of machine learning techniques in formal methods
  - Integration of formal methods into software engineering practices
  - Integration of diverse formal methods techniques
  - Combination of formal methods with simulation and analysis techniques

- Formal methods in practice:

  - Experience reports of applications of formal methods in industry
  - Use of formal methods in education
  - Verification of machine learning techniques
  - Applications of formal methods in the development of

    - autonomous systems,
    - safety-critical systems,
    - concurrent and distributed systems,
    - cyber-physical, embedded, and hybrid systems,
    - fault-detection, diagnostics, and prognostics systems, and
    - human-machine interaction analysis

This volume contains the papers presented at NFM 2021, the 13th NASA Formal Methods Symposium, held virtually during May 24–28, 2021, and organized by the Formal Methods group at the NASA Langley Research Center. NFM 2020 was also held virtually and was organized by the Formal Methods group at the NASA Ames Research Center. Previous symposia were held in Houston, TX (2019), Newport News, VA (2018), Moffett Field, CA (2017), Minneapolis, MN (2016), Pasadena, CA (2015), Houston, TX (2014), Moffett Field, CA (2013), Norfolk, VA (2012), Pasadena, CA (2011), Washington, DC (2010), and Moffett Field, CA (2009). The series started as the Langley Formal Methods Workshop, and was held under that name in 1990, 1992, 1995, 1997, 2000, and 2008.

Papers were solicited for NFM 2021 under two categories: regular papers describing fully developed work and complete results, and short papers describing tools, experience reports, or work-in-progress with preliminary results. The symposium received 66 submissions for review out of which 24 were accepted for publication. Among these papers, 21 are full papers and 3 are short papers. The submissions went through a rigorous review process where each paper was first independently reviewed by at least three reviewers and then subsequently discussed by the Program Committee. In addition to the refereed papers, the symposium featured five invited speakers: Erika Abraham (RWTH Aachen University, Germany), Cristina Cifuentes (Oracle Labs, Australia), Matthew B. Dwyer (University of Virginia, USA), Azadeh Farzan (University of Toronto, Canada), and Rob Manning (NASA Jet Propulsion Laboratory, USA). In addition to the main program, the symposium also had one affiliated workshop, The 6th Workshop on Formal Integrated Development Environment (F-IDE 2021), held virtually during May 24–25, 2021.

The organizers are grateful to the authors for submitting their work to NFM 2021 and to the invited speakers for sharing their insights. NFM 2021 would not have been possible without the collaboration of the outstanding Program Committee and additional reviewers, the support of the Steering Committee, the efforts of the staff at the NASA Langley Research Center and at the NASA Aeronautics Research Institute (NARI), and the general support of the NASA Formal Methods community. The NFM 2021 website can be found at https://shemesh.larc.nasa.gov/nfm2021.

May 2021

Aaron Dutle
Mariano M. Moscato
Laura Titolo
César A. Muñoz
Ivan Perez

Organization

General Chairs

César A. Muñoz   NASA, USA
Ivan Perez   National Institute of Aerospace, USA

Program Committee Chairs

Aaron Dutle   NASA, USA
Mariano M. Moscato   National Institute of Aerospace, USA
Laura Titolo   National Institute of Aerospace, USA

Steering Committee

Julia Badger   NASA, USA
Aaron Dutle   NASA, USA
Klaus Havelund   NASA Jet Propulsion Laboratory, USA
Michael Lowry   NASA, USA
Kristin Yvonne Rozier   Iowa State University, USA
Johann Schumann   SGT Inc./NASA Ames Research Center, USA

Program Committee

Erika Abraham   RWTH Aachen University, Germany
Mauricio Ayala-Rincón   Universidade de Brasília, Brazil
Julia Badger   NASA, USA
Nikolaj Bjørner   Microsoft Research, USA
Jasmin Blanchette   Vrije Universiteit Amsterdam, Netherlands
Sylvie Boldo   Inria, France
Alessandro Cimatti   Fondazione Bruno Kessler, Italy
Misty Davies   NASA, USA
Gilles Dowek   Inria/ENS Paris-Saclay, France
Catherine Dubois   ENSIIE-Samovar, France
Alexandre Duret-Lutz   LRDE/EPITA, France
Gabriel Ebner   Vrije Universiteit Amsterdam, Netherlands
Marco A. Feliu   National Institute of Aerospace, USA
Jean-Christophe Filliâtre   CNRS, France
Pierre-Loïc Garoche   ENAC, France
Alwyn Goodloe   NASA, USA
John Harrison   Amazon Web Services, USA
Klaus Havelund   NASA Jet Propulsion Laboratory, USA
Marieke Huisman   University of Twente, Netherlands

Brian Jalaian	ARL/Virginia Tech, USA
Susmit Jha	SRI International, USA
Michael Lowry	NASA, USA
Panagiotis Manolios	Northeastern University, USA
Paolo Masci	National Institute of Aerospace, USA
Anastasia Mavridou	SGT Inc./NASA Ames Research Center, USA
Stefan Mitsch	Carnegie Mellon University, USA
Yannick Moy	AdaCore/Inria, France
Natasha Neogi	NASA, USA
Laura Panizo	University of Málaga, Spain
Corina Pasareanu	CMU/NASA Ames Research Center, USA
Zvonimir Rakamaric	University of Utah, USA
Camilo Rocha	Pontificia Universidad Javeriana Cali, Colombia
Nicolás Rosner	Amazon Web Services, USA
Kristin Yvonne Rozier	Iowa State University, USA
Johann Schumann	SGT Inc./NASA Ames Research Center, USA
Cristina Seceleanu	Mälardalen University, Sweden
Natarajan Shankar	SRI International, USA
J. Tanner Slagel	NASA, USA
Mariëlle Stoelinga	University of Twente, Netherlands
Cesare Tinelli	University of Iowa, USA
Caterina Urban	Inria, France
Virginie Wiels	ONERA, France

Additional Reviewers

Arielly de Lima, Thaynara	Lewis, Robert
Backeman, Peter	Mayero, Micaela
Balachandran, Swee	Melquiond, Guillaume
Desharnais, Martin	Merz, Stephan
Dureja, Rohit	Popescu, Andrei
Geatti, Luca	Reynolds, Andrew
Graham-Lengrand, Stephane	Rubbens, Bob
Gu, Rong	Şakar, Ömer
Joosten, Sebastiaan	Traytel, Dmitriy
Kumar, Ankit	van der Wal, Djurre
Larraz, Daniel	Volk, Matthias

Abstracts of Invited Talks

SMT Solving: Past, Present, and Future

Erika Abraham

RWTH Aachen University

Abstract. Since the development of the first computer algebra systems in the '60s, automated decision procedures for checking the satisfiability of logical formulas gained more and more importance. Besides symbolic computation techniques, some major achievements were made in the '90s in the relatively young area of satisfiability checking, and resulted in powerful SAT and SAT-modulo-theories (SMT) solvers. Nowadays, these sophisticated tools are at the heart of many techniques for the analysis of programs and probabilistic, timed, hybrid and cyber-physical systems, for test-case generation, for solving large combinatorial problems and complex scheduling tasks, for product design optimisation, planning and controller synthesis, just to mention a few well-known areas. In this talk we give a historical overview of this development, describe our own solver SMT-RAT and discuss some fascinating new developments for checking the satisfiability of real-arithmetic formulas.

The Flavour of Real-World Vulnerability Detection and Intelligent Configuration

Cristina Cifuentes

Oracle Labs

Abstract. The Parfait static code analysis tool focuses on detecting vulnerabilities that matter in C, C++, Java and Python languages. Its focus has been on key items expected out of a commercial tool that lives in a commercial organisation, namely, precision of results (i.e., high true positive rate), scalability (i.e., being able to run quickly over millions of lines of code), incremental analysis (i.e., being able to run over deltas of the code quickly), and usability (i.e., ease of integration into standard build processes, reporting of traces to the vulnerable location, etc). Today, Parfait is used by thousands of developers at Oracle worldwide on a day-to-day basis.

In this presentation, we'll sample a flavour of Parfait — we explore some real world challenges faced in the creation of a robust vulnerability detection tool, look into two examples of vulnerabilities that severely affected the Java platform in 2012/2013 and most machines since 2017, and conclude by recounting what matters to developers for integration into today's continuous integration and continuous delivery (CI/CD) pipelines. Key to deployment of static code analysis tools is configuration of the tool itself - we present our experiences with use of machine learning to automatically configure the tool, providing users with a better out-of-the-box experience.

Distribution-aware Validation of Neural Networks

Matthew B. Dwyer

University of Virginia

Abstract. Neural networks (NN) are trained to produce a statistically accurate function approximation for data drawn from a target data distribution. The data distribution can be thought of as an implicit precondition on the use of the network. As with traditional software, the validation process need only focus on inputs satisfying the precondition – attempts to invoke a function outside of its precondition constitute errors that should be mitigated at runtime.

In this talk, we advocate for the modeling of the data distribution and describe how it can be exploited for NN testing, verification, and falsification. Incorporating such a model into NN validation processes can reduce their cost and increase their effectiveness. We demonstrate this by speeding up the process of generating valid NN test inputs while completely avoiding the generation of invalid test inputs.

Contents

Balancing Wind and Batteries: Towards Predictive Verification of Smart Grids

Thom S. Badings[1](✉)⬤, Arnd Hartmanns[2]⬤, Nils Jansen[1], and Marnix Suilen[1]

[1] Department of Software Science, Radboud University, Nijmegen, The Netherlands
thom.badings@ru.nl
[2] University of Twente, Enschede, The Netherlands

Abstract. We study a smart grid with wind power and battery storage. Traditionally, day-ahead planning aims to balance demand and wind power, yet actual wind conditions often deviate from forecasts. Short-term flexibility in storage and generation fills potential gaps, planned on a minutes time scale for 30–60 min horizons. Finding the optimal flexibility deployment requires solving a semi-infinite non-convex stochastic program, which is generally intractable to do exactly. Previous approaches rely on sampling, yet such critical problems call for rigorous approaches with stronger guarantees. Our method employs probabilistic model checking techniques. First, we cast the problem as a continuous-space Markov decision process with discretized control, for which an optimal deployment strategy minimizes the expected grid frequency deviation. To mitigate state space explosion, we exploit specific structural properties of the model to implement an iterative exploration method that reuses precomputed values as wind data is updated. Our experiments show the method's feasibility and versatility across grid configurations and time scales.

1 Introduction

Electricity grids need to constantly maintain a balance between power supply and demand; imbalances result in frequency deviations, which ultimately lead to critical events like blackouts [23]. The increasing deployment of renewable energy sources such as solar and wind power—which react sharply to hard-to-predict weather conditions—makes maintaining the balance increasingly difficult. In day-to-day operation, the balancing is managed at two time scales. One day ahead, the transmission system operator (TSO) schedules conventional generators to match the predicted demand minus the expected renewable generation based on weather forecasts. During the day, the TSO fills potential gaps introduced by any mismatch between forecast and actual weather conditions by *ancillary services*, which run on a short-term schedule that is updated every few minutes.

On the supply side, the most prominent ancillary service are *spinning reserves* from generators, which compensate for contingencies (such as generator failures)

This research has been partially funded by NWO grants OCENW.KLEIN.187 and NWA.1160.18.238, and by NWO VENI grant no. 639.021.754.

and deviations from the predicted demand. To free capacity for spinning reserves, some generators operate below their rated capacity, making them a costly service. The TSO's day-ahead plan thus makes a tradeoff between allocating sufficient reserves to mitigate any potential imbalance and minimizing unused generator capacity [36]. *Demand-side flexibility* [3], on the other hand, is provided by various assets connected to the grid, including batteries [19] and HVAC systems [12,40]. They can reduce or increase the overall power consumption at some time point by injecting or withdrawing electricity into or from the grid. Such flexibility-based services *shift* power consumption in time rather than changing the total [22]. Examples today include the ODFM service in the UK [27] and various applications of *demand response* worldwide [1]. In this paper, we approach the fundamental challenge of short-term scheduling for flexibility-based ancillary services:

> Given a power grid with significant uncertain wind power generation, optimally schedule the deployment of the available ancillary services over a finite horizon to minimize the expected total grid frequency deviation without violating any hard constraints on grid stability and operation.

Hard constraints include a maximum frequency deviation (we use $\pm 0.1\,\mathrm{Hz}$) as well as all generation, transmission, battery, and ramping capacities. Repeating the optimization every few minutes with new wind measurements leads to a model predictive control (MPC) loop covering a full day of short-term scheduling.

The task can be expressed as a semi-infinite nonconvex stochastic optimization problem, with the potential deviation of wind conditions from the forecast given by some stochastic process. Already a finite version of this problem is NP-hard and infeasible to solve in practice [8,26]. Previous work instantiated the stochastic process by a black-box discrete-time Markov chain (DTMC) and then resorted to a sampling-based *scenario optimization* approach [24,35], which linearizes the nonconvex constraints and solves the resulting linear (but still semi-infinite) stochastic optimization problem up to some statistical confidence and error. The drawbacks of this approach are the *approximation error* introduced by the linearization step and the *statistical error* due to the use of sampling [10].

Our Contribution. To overcome the need for both sampling and linearization, we model the problem as a Markov decision process (MDP) [32]. MDPs combine probabilistic choices, which we use to follow a white-box DTMC for the wind errors, and nondeterminism, which we use to capture the service deployment decisions to optimize over. A direct cast of the problem into an MDP would yield continuous state and action spaces: state variables would represent continuous quantities (e.g., grid frequency), and control decisions would range over real-valued intervals (e.g., charge current applied to a battery). We thus (i) discretize the controllable values into finitely many control *actions*. Since control decisions are only made every few minutes, (ii) the model is discrete-time. Further, wind conditions at the current time are known, so (iii) there is a single initial state for every (iv) finite horizon. In combination, (i)–(iv) entail that we can only reach a finite subset of the continuous state space. Thus we can build an MDP with finitely many states and actions. We use the original (non-linearized) continuous dynamics of the power grid to compute the successor state following an action. A cost function penalizes frequency deviations; violations of hard constraints lead to absorbing non-goal states. An action selection strategy that minimizes the expected accumulated cost to reach the time horizon then defines an optimal deployment of ancillary services. We track the time, making the MDP a directed acyclic graph in theory and a tree in practice. In the MPC loop, we only need the action selected in the initial (current) state; when time advances to the next control decision, we get a new initial state (based on measured wind conditions in reality and sampled from the wind error DTMC in our experiments) from which to repeat the procedure. Thus a large part of the new iteration's MDP can be reused from the previous iteration; we only need to add one more layer for the advanced time horizon. We present the continuous-state dynamics of the power system in Sect. 3, explain the formal and technical details of our MDP-based approach in Sect. 4, and report on an experimental evaluation in Sect. 5.

Our approach has three key advantages: We (1) obtain a *strategy that is sound* w.r.t. the physical constraints, i.e. it is guaranteed to satisfy the battery, generator, and ramping capacities (but not necessarily the frequency and transmission limits). The same cannot be guaranteed with scenario optimization due to the linearization and statistical error. We (2) *exploit the tree structure* of the MDP to speed up computations in the MPC loop; and (3) by relying on existing probabilistic model checking technology, the approach is *easy to extend*, for example with multiple objectives, unreliable communication, or demand uncertainty. Its main drawbacks are that, while sound and optimal for the discrete MDP, the computed strategy is sound but *may not be optimal for the continuous model*: an optimal strategy in the continuous model may require a control input that lies between the discrete options of the MDP. Moreover, the MDP's *state space grows exponentially* with the time horizon and precision of the discretization. We investigate the effects of varying degrees of discretization and time horizons on the quality of the schedule and the tractability of the problem in our experimental evaluation.

Related Work. Previous studies of demand-side flexibility consider, for example, *vehicle-to-grid* [19,42] and *buildings-to-grid* integration [21,33,34,40]. As renewable generation is primarily decentralized, regional congestion is an issue [7,31]; congestion management under uncertain generation was studied in [15,18,28]. The majority of the previously cited works use continuous-state models. Several also apply the MPC pattern [20,35,40] and generally state the optimization as an *optimal power flow* problem [23]. As mentioned, scenario optimization [9,10,24] is sampling-based; in a different approach to sampling, [2] uses Monte Carlo tree search for optimal power flow in the presence of many distributed energy resources.

When it comes to Markov models, [16] uses MDPs for optimal storage scheduling, while [13] computes MDP-based optimal charging strategies for electric vehicles. Probabilistic safety guarantees have been formally verified on DTMC models [30,38], i.e. MDPs where a fixed control strategy is embedded in the model.

[17] studies decentralized protocols in solar panels to stabilize grid frequency. Finally, we mention that our way of deriving the MDP is similar to the approach of the StocHy tool [11] and its predecessor FAUST^2 [39], which however lack support for costs/rewards and do not implement our efficient MPC loop.

2   Preliminaries

A *discrete probability distribution* over a finite set X is a function $\mu\colon X \to [0,1]$ with $\sum_{x \in X} \mu(x) = 1$. The set of all distributions over X is $Dist(X)$. We write $|X|$ for the number of elements in X. Notation $x_{1:n}$ introduces a vector $[x_1, \ldots, x_n]$.

Definition 1. *A Markov decision process (MDP) is a tuple* $\mathcal{M} = (S, A, s_I, T, c)$ *where S is a finite set of states, A is a finite set of actions, $s_I \in S$ is the initial state, $T\colon S \times A \rightharpoonup Dist(S)$ is the (partial) probabilistic transition function, and $c\colon S \to \mathbb{R}$ is the state-based cost function. We assume deadlock-free MDPs.*

A *discrete-time Markov chain* (DTMC) is an MDP with only one action at every state. For DTMCs, we omit the set of actions A by simply typing the transition function $T\colon S \to Dist(S)$. To define an expected cost measure on MDPs, the nondeterministic choices of actions are resolved by *strategies*. A memoryless deterministic *strategy* for an MDP is a function $\sigma\colon S \to A$. For other types of strategies, we refer to [6]. Applying strategy σ to an MDP $\mathcal{M}$ resolves all nondeterministic choices and yields an *induced DTMC* $\mathcal{M}^\sigma$. The expected cost of reaching a set of goal states $G \subseteq S$ in this induced DTMC is denoted by $\mathrm{EC}^{\mathcal{M}^\sigma}(\lozenge\, G)$. The goal is to compute a strategy that minimizes the expected cost.

3   Continuous-State Power System Modelling

The continuous power system model is a system of nonlinear differential equations. We explain its setup and components in this section. We then discretize the model w.r.t. time, obtaining continuous-state dynamics as a set of nonlinear equations.

3.1   Grid Model Dynamics

We model a power grid as an undirected graph of interconnected nodes, to which generators and loads are connected. The example grid in Fig. 1 has one generator, three nodes with connected loads, plus one wind farm and one battery. We adopt the grid model dynamics proposed in [5,35]. The dynamics in every node are given by the *active power swing equation*, which describes the balance between electrical and kinetic energy at that node in the grid [41]. The state at time t for node n is determined by the voltage angle and frequency, yielding the dynamics:

$$m_n\ddot{\delta}_n(t) + d_n\dot{\delta}_n(t) = \bar{P}_n(t) - \sum_{p \in \mathcal{N}} b_{n,p}\sin(\delta_n(t) - \delta_p(t)) \tag{1}$$

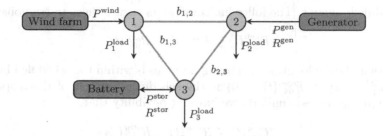

Fig. 1. 3-node example electricity grid.

where $\delta_n(t)$, $\dot{\delta}_n(t)$, $\ddot{\delta}_n(t) \in \mathbb{R}$ are the voltage angle, angular velocity (frequency), and angular acceleration of node n, and m_n and d_n are inertia and damping coefficients, respectively. $\bar{P}_n(t) \in \mathbb{R}$ is the power balance at node n, and is given by the sum of the generation and loads at that node. The power flow between node n and all connected nodes $p \in \mathcal{N}$ is assumed to be purely reactive and characterized by the line susceptance, $b_{n,p}$, and the difference in voltage angle between the connected nodes. A detailed description is available in [3,35].

3.2 Grid Frequency Control

The *grid frequency deviation* for node n, denoted $\omega_n(t)$, is the difference between the absolute frequency, $\dot{\delta}_n(t)$ in Eq. 1, and the desired frequency (for example, 50 Hz in Europe). The value of $\omega_n(t)$ can be controlled by the injection or consumption of electrical energy; any mismatch between power supply and demand results in a deviation of the frequency. As shown in Fig. 1, we distinguish five power generating or consuming assets:

- $P^{gen}(t)$ is the *conventional power dispatch*. Conventional generators are subject to ramping limits, so the derivative $\dot{P}^{gen}(t)$ is restricted to certain bounds.
- $P^{load}(t)$, the *consumer load*, represents the known and uncontrollable demand. We can readily extend the model to controllable or uncertain demand.
- $R^{gen}(t)$ is the deployment of *spinning reserves*. It is a control variable in the optimal power flow problem.
- $P^{wind}(t)$, the *wind power generation*, is a random variable [29] due to its limited predictability. We define $P^{wind,fc}(t)$ as the forecast wind power at time t; then the *forecast error* is $\Delta P^{wind}(t) = P^{wind}(t) - P^{wind,fc}(t)$.
- A *battery* is an energy storage buffer whose *state of charge* (SoC) $q(t)$ follows the injection or consumption of energy. $P_{stor}(t)$ is the uncontrollable power input variable, known from the day-ahead plan, and $R_{stor}(t)$ is the demand-side flexibility power rate, which is a control variable in the power flow problem.

3.3 Ancillary Service Deployment

Ancillary service deployment is subject to two restrictions: reserves and storage flexibility must be scheduled a day ahead, and the deployment can never exceed the scheduled amount. The following constraints ensure these restrictions:

$$- R_{\text{ds}}^{\text{gen}}(t) \leq R^{\text{gen}}(t) \leq R_{\text{us}}^{\text{gen}}(t) \tag{2}$$

ensures that the deployment of spinning reserves is within the scheduled bounds, where $R_{\text{ds}}^{\text{gen}}(t) \geq 0$ ($R_{\text{us}}^{\text{gen}}(t) \geq 0$) is the scheduled amount of down-spinning (up-spinning) reserves. Similarly we have for flexibility that

$$- R_{\text{dd}}^{\text{stor}}(t) \leq R^{\text{stor}}(t) \leq R_{\text{id}}^{\text{stor}}(t), \tag{3}$$

where $R_{\text{dd}}^{\text{stor}}(k) \geq 0$ and $R_{\text{id}}^{\text{stor}}(k) \geq 0$ are the scheduled decreased- and increased-demand flexibility, respectively.

3.4   Discrete-Time Storage-Integrated Power System Model

We discretize the continuous dynamics with respect to time to render the problem of optimal frequency control tractable. The resulting model is a set of nonlinear equations, which albeit discretized w.r.t. time are still defined on continuous state and control spaces. They describe the transition from one continuous state and control input to the resulting continuous state one discrete time step later.

Consider a power grid with n_t nodes, n_g generators, n_f wind farms, and n_s batteries for storage. Its continuous dynamics are given as a system of $2n_t + n_g + n_s$ first-order differential equations. The features of the continuous state space are given by the voltage angles $\delta_{1:n_t}$ and frequencies $\omega_{1:n_t}$ for all n_t nodes, the power generation $P_{1:n_g}^{\text{gen}}$ for all n_g generators, and the state of charge $q_{1:n_s}$ of all n_s batteries. The vector of control variables contains the *change* in generator dispatch $\dot{P}_{1:n_g}^{\text{gen}}$ and the reserve deployment $R_{1:n_g}^{\text{gen}}$ for all n_g generators, plus the flexibility deployment $R_{1:n_s}^{\text{stor}}$ for all n_s batteries. We discretize w.r.t. time via the first-order backward Euler implicit method [37] to obtain the nonlinear function

$$x(k+1) = f\big(x(k), u(k), v(k), w(k)\big), \tag{4}$$

- with $f(\cdot)$ reflecting the dynamics of the considered power system, which are nonlinear due to the sinusoid, $\sin(\delta_n(t) - \delta_p(t))$, in Eq. 1,
- $x(k) = [\delta_{1:n_t}, \omega_{1:n_t}, P_{1:n_g}^{\text{gen}}, q_{1:n_s}] \in \mathbb{R}^{2n_t + n_g + n_s}$ the state vector,
- $u(k) = [\dot{P}_{1:n_g}^{\text{gen}}, R_{1:n_g}^{\text{gen}}, R_{1:n_s}^{\text{stor}}] \in \mathbb{R}^{2n_g + n_s}$ the vector of control variables,
- $v(k) = [P_{1:n_t}^{\text{load}}, P_{1:n_f}^{\text{wind,fc}}, P_{1:n_s}^{\text{stor}}] \in \mathbb{R}^{n_t + n_f + n_s}$ the uncontrollable known inputs, and
- $w(k) = [\Delta P_{1:n_f}^{\text{wind}}] \in \mathbb{R}^{n_f}$ the vector of uncontrollable random variables.

We omit further details for the sake of brevity and refer the interested reader to [5] and [40] for the full derivation and discretization of similar grid models.

Power Balance and Control Variables. The day-ahead generator power dispatch is scheduled such that generation plus wind power forecast matches the consumer load pattern. We impose the following constraint at every time point k:

$$\sum_{i=1}^{n_g} P_i^{\text{gen}}(k) + \sum_{m=1}^{n_f} P_m^{\text{wind,fc}}(k) = \sum_{n=1}^{n_t} P_n^{\text{load}}(k). \tag{5}$$

Since $P_m^{\text{wind,fc}}$ and P_n^{load} are known, imposing this equality constraint yields $n_g - 1$ independent control variables. Hence, in a single-generator grid, the day-ahead planning is fixed by the wind forecast and consumer load, while in a grid with multiple generators, the required total dispatch must be divided between the different units. In a similar manner, during the day itself, the reserve power and storage flexibility can be deployed together to restore the mismatch in the power balance caused by forecast errors at any time point:

$$\sum_{i=1}^{n_g} R_i^{\text{gen}}(k) + \sum_{m=1}^{n_f} \Delta P_m^{\text{wind}}(k) = \sum_{n=1}^{n_s} R_n^{\text{stor}}(k), \tag{6}$$

where ΔP_m^{wind} is a random variable, and both R_i^{gen} and R_n^{stor} are control variables. Hence, imposing Eq. 6 yields $n_g + n_s - 1$ independent control variables.

Power System Constraints. The discrete-time power system model in Eq. 4 is subject to a number of constraints. First of all, the equality constraints in Eqs. 5 and 6 are imposed to enforce the balance between power supply and demand. Second, power lines have limited transmission capacity, and generators have limited generation capacity and ramping capability. Third, the deployment of reserve power and storage flexibility is limited by their scheduled values, as described in Eqs. 2 and 3. Finally, the electrical storage units have a limited capacity, and can only be charged or discharged at a given maximum rate. For the explicit formulation of the constraints we refer the interested reader to [35].

4 Discrete-State Receding Horizon Control Problem

Our goal is to overcome the need for sampling and linearization to optimize ancillary service deployment. Directly using the model presented in Eq. 4 would require dealing with continuous state and action spaces. Our approach is to discretize the actions, then explore the resulting finite number of (continuously-valued) successor states up to a given exploration depth. In this way, we obtain a finite MDP that can be solved iteratively using a receding horizon principle. This approach is a discrete-state model predictive control technique. We now present the wind error DTMC, followed by the details of our exploration procedure and the formal definition of the finite-horizon MDP.

4.1 Stochastic Wind Power Model

Recall that the wind power forecast error, $\Delta P_m^{\text{wind}}(k) \in \mathbb{R}$, of every individual wind farm $m \in \{1, \dots, n_f\}$ is a continuous random variable in Eq. 4. Exploiting the time discretization of Sect. 3.4, we construct a DTMC for the forecast error of every wind farm with time resolution equal to the discretization level of the

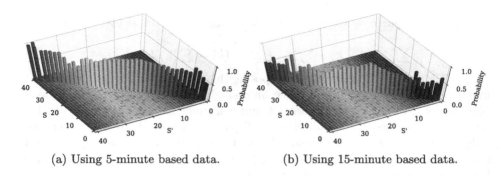

(a) Using 5-minute based data.   (b) Using 15-minute based data.

Fig. 2. Transition probability function of the wind error DTMC.

dynamics. For this section, we assume the presence of only one wind farm to simplify notation. Let S be the finite state space of the DTMC, and let function $M \colon \mathbb{R} \to S$ map the wind power forecast error $\Delta P^{\mathrm{wind}} \in \mathbb{R}$ to a state $s_w \in S$: every value of the continuous random variable ΔP^{wind} is approximated by the value of a discrete state $s_w \in S$. The DTMC's transition function $T \colon S \to Dist(S)$ describes the probability that a transition occurs from one state s_w at any time k to another state s'_w at time $k+1$ with probability $T(s_w)(s'_w)$.

Historical Wind Power Data. We follow the method proposed in [25,29] to construct the DTMC based on the historical wind power forecast error. The states S are based on a uniform discretization of the historical forecast error. The transition probabilities in T are determined using a maximum likelihood estimation, by counting the number of transitions from one state s_w at time k to a successor state s'_w at time $k+1$. We use five years (2015–2019) of on-shore wind power data measured every 15 min from the TenneT region of the German transmission grid, obtained from the *ENTSO-E Transparency Platform* [14]. We interpolate the data to a 5-min basis, to match the time resolution we employ in the numerical demonstration in Sect. 5. The data set contains the wind power forecast, $P^{\mathrm{wind,fc}}$, and the actual power, P^{wind}, thus providing a five-year time series of the observed wind power error, ΔP^{wind}. M then maps every continuous value of ΔP^{wind} to one of 41 discrete states, i.e. $S = \{s_w^1, \dots, s_w^{41}\}$, as in [25]. We show the resulting transition matrices in Fig. 2 for the original 15-min and the interpolated 5-min data. The matrix is diagonally dominant, reflecting the strong auto-correlation of the forecast error.

4.2 State Space Exploration Procedure

Next, we present our method to explore the continuous state space of the model up to a given exploration horizon. We discretize the continuous control variables such that their potential values define a set of actions for an MDP, then a priori eliminate those actions that lead to states violating the constraints of Sect. 3.4.

Let $X_k = (x(k), s_w)$ denote the continuous state vector $x(k)$ at time k, and the DTMC state s_w associated with the current wind power forecast error. To define an initial state, we use a concrete measurement at the first time step. Then, we use the dynamics in Eq. 4 in combination with transitions of the wind error DTMC to compute the possible successor states for each time step. At time step k we select a control input $u(k)$ and, based on the dynamics in Eq. 4, receive a set of successor states with different $x(k+1)^1, \ldots, x(k+1)^n$, one associated with every possible wind error successor state, $s_w^1, \ldots, s_w^n$ with $T(s_w)(s_w^i) > 0$ for all $1 \leq i \leq n$. The features in $x(k+1)^i$ related to power generation $(P_{1:n_g}^{\mathrm{gen}})$ and battery SoC $(q_{1:n_s})$ are equal for all $1 \leq i \leq n$, while the grid features $(\delta_{1:n_t}, \omega_{1:n_t})$ depend on the wind successor state, s_w^i. As the probabilities to reach these successor states depend exclusively on the probabilities defined by the DTMC, we reach state $X_{k+1} = (x(k+1)^i, s_w^i))$ with probability $T(s_w)(s_w^i)$.

Feasible Control Space. Under the two balance constraints in Eqs. 5 and 6, the vector of control variables $u(k)$ in Eq. 4 contains $2n_g + n_s - 2$ independent variables. Since the dynamics in Eq. 4 and the constraints imposed on the system are known, we can determine the continuous subset of control inputs $u \in \mathcal{U}_{X_k} \subset \mathbb{R}^{2n_g + n_s - 2}$ that do not lead to a violation of any of the constraints at time $k + 1$. Note that this set depends on the state X_k at time k. Given the subset of feasible continuous control inputs, we apply a grid-based discretization in all $2n_g + n_s - 2$ dimensions, to obtain a set A_{X_k} of *feasible and discrete actions* at time k, where the subscript denotes the dependency on X_k. From this discretization of the control actions, an important property follows. Given the current state X_k at time k, every action $a \in A_{X_k}$ has a different set of *discrete successor states* X_{k+1} at time $k + 1$. By only exploring the continuous state-space for the feasible actions in A_{X_k}, we minimize the size of the resulting finite-state model.

A schematic example of this procedure for two state features (one node frequency and one battery SoC) is shown in Fig. 3. The blue dot corresponds to current state X_k at time k, and the straight arrows show the discrete actions $a \in A_{X_k}$. The curved arrows show the effect of the forecast error to the grid frequency, which depends directly on the actual successor state in the DTMC. Because all successor states of a_1 violate the maximum SoC constraint $(q(k) \leq q^{\mathrm{max}})$, this action can be *eliminated a priori*. Similarly, all successors for a_5 violate the maximum frequency deviation limit $(\omega(k) \leq \omega^{\mathrm{max}})$. Actions a_2 and a_3 will not lead to any violation, and are, therefore, included as feasible discrete actions. Action a_4 may or may not violate the constraints depending on the wind power forecast error. Therefore, this action cannot be eliminated a priori.

Exploration. The finite exploration horizon with starting time k and look-ahead of K_h steps is the set $\{k, \ldots, k + K_h\}$. The exploration procedure can be performed recursively for all discrete actions $a \in A_{X_k}$ for every k, until the desired horizon is reached. We obtain a tree-structured model as in Fig. 4, where the *branching factor* depends on the number of actions and possible wind successor states, and the *depth* is given by the horizon length. For brevity, the

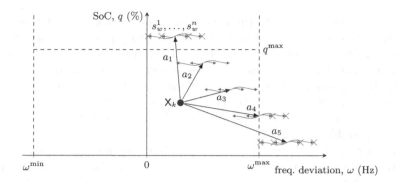

Fig. 3. Discrete actions $a_1, \ldots, a_5$ and their mapping to two continuous state-space features: a battery SoC and the frequency in one node. Curved arrows show the effect of wind successor states, and dashed lines are system constraints.

dependency of the set of discrete actions on the current state is omitted in this figure.

Recall that we consider only those states $X_k = (x(k), s_w)$ of the continuous state space that are visited during the exploration. We provide the full definition of the MDP $\mathcal{M} = (S, A, s_I, T, c)$ with exploration horizon $\{k, \ldots k + K_h\}$, where

- every state $s \in S$ is associated with an X_k from the continuous state space;
- the set of actions A is the union of all feasible action sets A_{X_k} for all X_k;
- the initial state s_I is given by a concrete measurement (x_0, s_w);
- the partial probabilistic transition function $T\colon S \times A \rightharpoonup Dist(S)$ maps state-action pairs to the corresponding distributions over successor states according to the wind error DTMC;
- the cost function $c\colon S \to \mathbb{R}$ assigns the immediate cost given by the sum of the absolute value of the frequency deviation in every grid node.

Finally, we define the set $G \subseteq S$ of *goal states* as the states that are reached at the end of the horizon $k + K_h$ and satisfy the constraints.

Receding Horizon and Tree Structure. We compute the strategy σ that induces the minimal expected cost $\mathrm{EC}^{\mathcal{M}^\sigma}(\lozenge G)$ for the MDP with horizon $\{k, \ldots k + K_h\}$. Using this strategy, we implement the (first) optimal action $a_0 = \sigma(s_0)$ where s is associated with X_k. Having executed the optimal action at time k, we then apply the so-called *receding horizon principle*, meaning that we *shift* the exploration horizon one step forward in time. We update the MDP for the shifted horizon, which is now given as $\{k + 1, \ldots k + K_h + 1\}$, and again compute an optimal strategy. Hence, with every shift of the exploration horizon in time, we *reveal small bits of new information* near the end of the horizon.

As an example, consider an initial exploration horizon defined as the time frame between 9:00–9:15 AM. Computing an optimal strategy for the corresponding MDP means that we take all the information within that time frame into

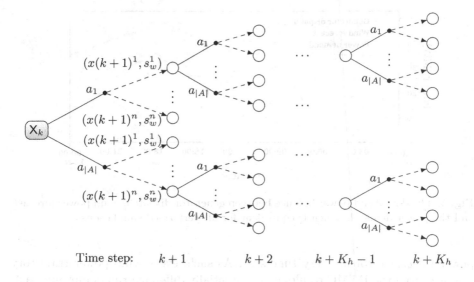

Time step: $k+1$ $k+2$ $k+K_h-1$ $k+K_h$

Fig. 4. Visualization of the state-space exploration procedure, with initial measurement X_k at time k, and finite horizon with end time $k + K_h$. Solid edges represent discrete actions, whereas dashed lines reflect different successor states.

account, i.e. we have perfect knowledge within the horizon. However, a possible change in the power demand (or any other uncontrollable input) that is forecast at 9:30 AM is not revealed to the model, until the exploration horizon also spans that time step. Defining an adequate length of the exploration horizon reflects a trade-off between model size and the optimality of the solution.

When we shift the exploration horizon from $\{k, \ldots, k+K_h\}$ to $\{k+1, \ldots, k+K_h+1\}$, another layer is added to the MDP. As the starting time of the horizon also shifts, we gain new information via a new measurement at $k + 1$, and then obtain a single new initial state for the MDP with the new horizon. By exploiting the tree structure of the MDP, we extend the current MDP with a new layer of successor states and take the subtree starting at the newly found initial state at time $k + 1$. Simultaneously, we shrink the layer at the top, by pruning all states that cannot be reached anymore from the new initial state.

The approach of iteratively solving and updating the MDP for shifting horizons is similar to a discrete-state model predictive control technique. This iterative method is applied until a desired simulation horizon is reached (such as 24 h).

5   Numerical Study

We demonstrate the performance of our approach on multiple variants of the 3-node example grid already introduced in Fig. 1. To this end, we *simulate the wind error DTMC*, and apply our method to build the MDP using the sampled wind

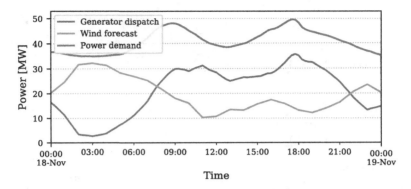

Fig. 5. The day-ahead power balance between generator dispatch, wind power forecast, and the power demand, which is equivalent for all performed simulations.

power forecast error at every time step. As such, every wind power trajectory sampled from the DTMC results in a (potentially different) run of our approach. We solve the MDP to obtain the first action in the sequence of optimal decisions over the exploration horizon, which is then executed to obtain the initial state at the next time step. By applying the receding horizon principle, we iteratively follow this procedure, until a final simulation horizon of 24 h is reached.

5.1   Experimental Setup

We consider a simulation time resolution of 5 min, and a full simulation horizon of 24 h. Using the receding horizon exploration procedure, this means that $\frac{60}{5} \cdot 24 = 288$ MDPs are solved to obtain the results over one 24-h run. The same demand and wind power forecast are used for every simulation, resulting in the day-ahead power dispatch shown in Fig. 5. This figure shows that under the forecast conditions, the power supply and demand are perfectly balanced, leading to a stable grid frequency in the absence of forecast errors. Both the power demand and wind power forecast are based on historical data obtained from the *ENTSO-E Transparency Platform* [14], and are scaled appropriately for the simulation study. The scheduled flexibility deployment limits per battery are set to ± 2 MW, while the scheduled reserve limits per generator are ± 0.25 MW.

Simulation Cases. Simulations are performed on three variants of the example grid in Fig. 1. In the simplest case, we aggregate the three nodes into one, resulting in a grid where all assets are connected to the same node. The second variant is the exact network shown in Fig. 1. The third variant is an extension of the second, where a second storage unit is connected to node 1.

Then, we perform simulation studies for different values of: a) the *exploration horizon* (300, 600, and 900 s), and b) the *levels of discretization for the actions* denoted by λ (with values between 3 and 25 steps). To evaluate the quality of the solution of our technique, we perform a statistical analysis on every case, by repeating every experiment 100 times. Note that this Monte Carlo type simulation is merely used to evaluate the quality of the obtained solutions, and not required to apply our technique in practice.

Data Availability. The code and data needed to reproduce the results presented below are archived at DOI 10.4121/14185139 [4]. Our prototype implementation is written in Python version 3.8.3, and allows the user to run the cases defined above or simulate with any other parameter setting. Our simulations ran on a Windows laptop with Intel Core i7-1065G7 CPU (1.3–3.0 GHz) and 16 GB RAM.

5.2   Results

Run Times. The observed run times are approximately proportional to the number of MDP states, and grow exponentially with the exploration horizon. For the 3-node system with 1 battery, an action discretization level of $\lambda = 5$ steps, and exploration horizon of 300 s, the average run time *per iteration* of the receding horizon (i.e. for solving one MDP) is 0.01 s, resulting in around 3.51 s per 24 h run. For the same case with longer exploration horizons of 600 and 900 s, average run times are 0.14 and 2.09 s, respectively, per receding horizon iteration.

The strongest increase in run time is observed for the 3-node, 2 battery case, where the average observed times were 0.03, 1.03, and 223.59 s for exploration horizons of 300, 600, and 900 s, respectively. This steeper increase is explained by the exponential growth of the model size with respect to the number of actions, which is higher for the case with 2 batteries.

Failed Runs. As visualized before in Fig. 3, a discrete action can lead to a successor state that violates one of the system constraints. In total, 4.2% of the performed iterations for all cases combined resulted in a violation of either the frequency limits or the power line transmission capacity. No significant differences in the percentage of failed runs is observed across the different cases. Since these runs are incomplete and not representative for the simulated cases, they are not reported for further analysis. Nevertheless, the number of failed runs provides an empirical indication of the adequacy of the scheduling limits for the reserve and flexibility deployment. A high percentage of failed runs means that the ancillary service scheduling limits might be insufficient, and should be enlarged.

Solution Quality. The cost function of the MDP penalizes the sum of the absolute value of the frequency deviations in all grid nodes. Therefore, the quality of the obtained solution can be evaluated by taking the integral of the total observed frequency deviation over the simulation horizon:

$$J = \int_{k_0}^{k_{\text{end}}} |\sum_{n=1}^{n_t} \omega_n(k)| dk,$$

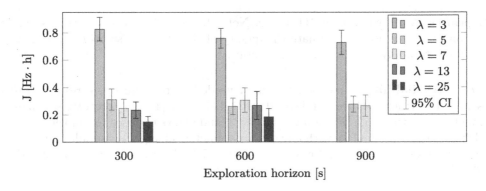

Fig. 6. Average total frequency deviations for the 3-node case for different λ.

where k_0 and k_{end} cover the full 24-h simulation time. The lower the value of J, the better the quality of the solution in terms of total frequency deviations.

A comparison of the value for J between multiple cases on the 3-node network from Fig. 1, with different levels of $\lambda \in \{3, \ldots, 25\}$, is shown in Fig. 6. Every bar shows the average results and the 95% confidence interval (CI) of the 100 iterations performed for that case. Due to infeasible run times, simulations for the cases with exploration horizon of 900 s and $\lambda \geq 13$ were omitted.

We observe that (1) a *longer exploration horizon does not improve the quality of the solution* in terms of frequency deviations significantly. On the other hand, (2) *increasing the number of discrete actions* in every dimension yields a significantly better solution quality. This observation suggests that it is more beneficial to have a more fine-grained discretization of the continuous control space, than to invest in a longer optimization horizon.

MDP Model Size. In Fig. 7, the average number of states and actions per MDP are compared for different network configurations, all with $\lambda = 5$. All cases were simulated for 100 runs, except for the case with 2 batteries, which was only simulated for 1 run, due to a too long run time. We see that the number of states and actions is *independent of the number of grid nodes*. The intuition behind this is that an increased number of state features does not yield a larger MDP. In fact, the branching factor of the applied exploration procedure only depends on the number of actions and successor states in the wind error DTMC, and is independent of the number of state features. As expected, increasing the number of batteries to 2 yields a significant increase in the number of MDP states and actions, especially for a longer exploration horizon, due to the additional dimension of the continuous control space.

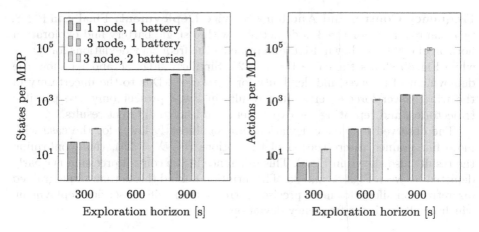

Fig. 7. Average MDP states (left) and actions (right) for cases with $\lambda = 5$, and varying numbers of nodes and batteries (plotted in log scale).

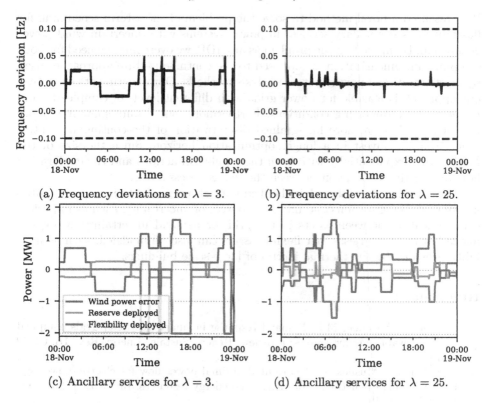

(a) Frequency deviations for $\lambda = 3$.   (b) Frequency deviations for $\lambda = 25$.

(c) Ancillary services for $\lambda = 3$.   (d) Ancillary services for $\lambda = 25$.

Fig. 8. Results for two runs for the 3-node case with 1 battery, for different λ.

Frequency Control and Ancillary Service Deployment. Finally, in Fig. 8, two example runs for the 3-node network with a single battery and exploration horizon of 600 s are shown. Figure 8a presents the frequency deviations for $\lambda = 3$, while Fig. 8b shows the same for $\lambda = 25$. Similarly, Figs. 8c and 8d show the deployment of reserves and flexibility for both cases. Due to the uncertainty in the wind power forecast error, the results in Fig. 8 present only two possible trajectories, and repeating the experiment can lead to different results.

The observed frequency deviations are significantly lower for the case with more fine-grained discretization of the actions (i.e. $\lambda = 25$), thus confirming the results also shown in Fig. 6. This difference in the control precision is clearly depicted between Figs. 8c and 8d. The intuition behind this is that a fine-grained discretization allows for more precise control of the ancillary service deployment, which results in lower frequency deviations.

6 Concluding Remarks

We presented a novel method to solve the problem of short-term scheduling for flexibility-based ancillary services in power systems with uncertain wind power generation. By modelling the problem as an MDP, we overcome the need for both sampling and linearization, as opposed to the continuous-state approaches used by most traditional power system analysis methods. Our experiments show that our approach is feasible for power grids with different levels of complexity and under realistic operating conditions. Furthermore, our results show it is more beneficial to have a more fine-grained discretization of the continuous control space, than to invest in a longer optimization horizon. Since the size of the MDP grows exponentially with both the number of actions and the exploration horizon, making a trade-off between the two is necessary.

In the future, we will exploit the flexibility of our model to incorporate alternative grid configurations and multiple sources of uncertainty, such as imperfect communication between assets in the grid, or demand uncertainty. Moreover, instead of the batteries, other flexible assets can also be modeled, such as flexibility provided by the thermal inertia of large-scale buildings.

References

1. Aghaei, J., Alizadeh, M.I.: Demand response in smart electricity grids equipped with renewable energy sources: a review. Renew. Sustain. Energy Rev. **18**, 64–72 (2013)
2. Al-Saffar, M., Musílek, P.: Distributed optimal power flow for electric power systems with high penetration of distributed energy resources. In: CCECE 2019, pp. 1–5. IEEE (2019)
3. Badings, T.S.: MSc Thesis. Buildings-to-Grid Integration for Demand-Side Flexibility in Power Systems with Uncertain Generation. University of Groningen (2019)
4. Badings, T.S.: Balancing wind and batteries: towards predictive verification of smart grids (artifact). 4TU.ResearchData (2021). https://doi.org/10.4121/14185139

5. Badings, T.S., Rostampour, V., Scherpen, J.M.: Distributed building energy storage units for frequency control service in power systems. IFAC-Pap. OnLine **52**(4), 228–233 (2019)
6. Baier, C., Katoen, J.P.: Principles of Model Checking. MIT Press, Cambridge (2008)
7. Bertsch, J., Hagspiel, S., Just, L.: Congestion management in power systems: long-term modeling framework and large-scale application. J. Regul. Econ. **50**(3), 290–327 (2016)
8. Boyd, S.P., Vandenberghe, L.: Convex Optimization. Cambridge University Press, Cambridge (2014)
9. Calafiore, G.C., Campi, M.C.: The scenario approach to robust control design. IEEE Trans. Autom. Control. **51**(5), 742–753 (2006)
10. Campi, M.C., Garatti, S.: The exact feasibility of randomized solutions of uncertain convex programs. SIAM J. Optim. **19**(3), 1211–1230 (2008)
11. Cauchi, N., Abate, A.: StocHy: Automated verification and synthesis of stochastic processes. In: Vojnar, T., Zhang, L. (eds.) TACAS 2019. LNCS, vol. 11428, pp. 247–264. Springer, Cham (2019). https://doi.org/10.1007/978-3-030-17465-1_14
12. Chertkov, M., Chernyak, V.: Ensemble of thermostatically controlled loads: statistical physics approach. Scientific reports **7**(1), 1–9 (2017)
13. Ding, T., Zeng, Z., Bai, J., Qin, B., Yang, Y., Shahidehpour, M.: Optimal electric vehicle charging strategy with Markov decision process and reinforcement learning technique. IEEE Trans. Ind. Appl. **56**(5), 5811–5823 (2020)
14. ENTSO-e: Transparency Platform - Generation Forecasts for Wind and Solar, Control area Germany (2020)
15. Gerard, H., Rivero Puente, E.I., Six, D.: Coordination between transmission and distribution system operators in the electricity sector: a conceptual framework. Utilities Policy **50**, 40–48 (2018)
16. Grillo, S., Pievatolo, A., Tironi, E.: Optimal storage scheduling using Markov decision processes. IEEE Trans. Sustain. Energy **7**(2), 755–764 (2016)
17. Hartmanns, A., Hermanns, H., Berrang, P.: A comparative analysis of decentralized power grid stabilization strategies. In: Winter Simulation Conference, pp. 158:1–158:13. WSC (2012)
18. Hemmati, R., Saboori, H., Jirdehi, M.A.: Stochastic planning and scheduling of energy storage systems for congestion management in electric power systems including renewable energy resources. Energy **133**, 380–387 (2017)
19. Kempton, W., et al.: A test of Vehicle-to-Grid (V2G) for Energy Storage and Frequency Regulation in the PJM System. Results from an Industry-University Research Partnership (2008)
20. Liu, Y., et al.: Coordinating the operations of smart buildings in smart grids. Appl. Energy **228**(July), 2510–2525 (2018)
21. Lymperopoulos, I., Qureshi, F.A., Nghiem, T., Khatir, A.A., Jones, C.N.: Providing ancillary service with commercial buildings: the Swiss perspective. IFAC-Pap. OnLine **28**(8), 6–13 (2015)
22. MacDougall, P., Roossien, B., Warmer, C., Kok, K.: Quantifying flexibility for smart grid services. In: 2013 IEEE Power Energy Society General Meeting, pp. 1–5. IEEE (2013)
23. Machowski, J., Dong, Z.Y., Member, S., Zhang, P.: Power System Dynamics: Stability and Control. Wiley, Hoboken (2006)
24. Margellos, K., Goulart, P., Lygeros, J.: On the road between robust optimization and the scenario approach for chance constrained optimization problems. IEEE Trans. Autom. Control. **59**(8), 2258–2263 (2014)

25. Margellos, K., Haring, T., Hokayem, P., Schubiger, M., Lygeros, J., Andersson, G.: a robust reserve scheduling technique for power systems with high wind penetration. In: Proceedings of PMAPS, pp. 870–875 (2012)
26. Murty, K.G., Kabadi, S.N.: Some NP-complete problems in quadratic and nonlinear programming. Math. Program. **39**(2), 117–129 (1987)
27. NG ESO: Optional downward flexibility management (ODFM) service documents. National Grid ESO (2020)
28. Nguyen, D.B., Scherpen, J.M.A., Bliek, F.: Distributed optimal control of smart electricity grids with congestion management. IEEE Trans. Autom. Sci. Eng. **14**(2), 494–504 (2017)
29. Papaefthymiou, G., Klöckl, B.: MCMC for wind power simulation. IEEE Trans. Energy Convers. **23**(1), 234–240 (2008)
30. Peruffo, A., Guiu, E., Panciatici, P., Abate, A.: Safety guarantees for the electricity grid with significant renewables generation. In: Parker, D., Wolf, V. (eds.) QEST 2019. LNCS, vol. 11785, pp. 332–349. Springer, Cham (2019). https://doi.org/10.1007/978-3-030-30281-8_19
31. Pillay, A., Prabhakar Karthikeyan, S., Kothari, D.P.: Congestion management in power systems - a review. Int. J. Electr. Power Energy Syst. **70**, 83–90 (2015)
32. Puterman, M.L.: Markov Decision Processes: Discrete Stochastic Dynamic Programming. Wiley Series in Probability and Statistics, Wiley, Hoboken (1994)
33. Razmara, M., Bharati, G.R., Shahbakhti, M., Paudyal, S., Robinett, R.D.: Bilevel optimization framework for smart building-to-grid systems. IEEE Trans. Smart Grid **9**(2), 582–593 (2018)
34. Rostampour, V., Badings, T.S., Scherpen, J.M.A.: Buildings-to-grid integration with high wind power penetration. In: CDC, pp. 2976–2981. IEEE (2019)
35. Rostampour, V., Badings, T.S., Scherpen, J.M.A.: Demand flexibility management for buildings-to-grid integration with uncertain generation. Energies **13**(24) (2020)
36. Rostampour, V., Ter Haar, O., Keviczky, T.: Distributed stochastic reserve scheduling in ac power systems with uncertain generation. IEEE Trans. Power Syst. **34**(2), 1005–1020 (2018)
37. Sincovec, R.F., Erisman, A.M., Yip, E.L., Epton, M.A.: Analysis of descriptor systems using numerical algorithms. IEEE Trans. Autom. Control. **26**(1), 139–147 (1981)
38. Soudjani, S.E.Z., Abate, A.: Aggregation and control of populations of thermostatically controlled loads by formal abstractions. IEEE Trans. Control. Syst. Technol. **23**(3), 975–990 (2015)
39. Soudjani, S.E.Z., Gevaerts, C., Abate, A.: FAUST[2]: formal abstractions of uncountable-state stochastic processes. In: TACAS. LNCS, vol. 9035, pp. 272–286. Springer (2015)
40. Taha, A.F., Gatsis, N., Dong, B., Pipri, A., Li, Z.: Buildings-to-grid integration framework. IEEE Trans. Smart Grid **10**(2), 1237–1249 (2019)
41. Trip, S., Bürger, M., Persis, C.D.: An internal model approach to frequency regulation in inverter-based microgrids with time-varying voltages. In: CDC, pp. 223–228. IEEE (2014)
42. Wang, J., Liu, C., Ton, D., Zhou, Y., Kim, J., Vyas, A.: Impact of plug-in hybrid electric vehicles on power systems with demand response and wind power. Energy Policy **39**(7), 4016–4021 (2011)

nnenum: Verification of ReLU Neural Networks with Optimized Abstraction Refinement

Stanley Bak$^{(\boxtimes)}$ (ID)

Stony Brook University, Stony Brook, NY 11794, USA
`stanley.bak@stonybrook.edu`

Abstract. The surge of interest in applications of deep neural networks has led to a surge of interest in verification methods for such architectures. In summer 2020, the first international competition on neural network verification was held. This paper presents and evaluates the main optimizations used in the nnenum tool, which outperformed all other tools in the ACAS Xu benchmark category, sometimes by orders of magnitude. The method uses fast abstractions for speed, combined with refinement through ReLU splitting to increase accuracy when properties cannot be proven. Although the abstraction refinement process is a classic approach in formal methods, directly applying it to the neural network verification problem actually reduces performance, due to a cascade of overapproximation error when using abstraction. This makes optimizations and their systematic evaluation essential for high performance.

Keywords: Neural network verification · ReLU · ACAS Xu

1 Introduction

Deep neural networks are powerful machine learning methods that can provide accurate approximations to functions learned from data. One downside of neural networks is that they are often unexpectedly sensitive to small targeted changes in the inputs. This is most well-known in the context of perception systems, where changes that a human cannot see can sometimes cause the systems to misclassify an image [13]. Such adversarial examples attacks [24] can also be applied to decision-making networks, where the system can fail due to what could essentially be sensor noise [15].

In order to apply neural networks to safety-critical and even mission-critical systems, stronger assurances are usually desired. One approach to do this involves developing algorithms to reason formally over the function computed by a neural network. The *open-loop neural network verification problem* tries to prove properties over the inputs and outputs of a network. For example, given interval bounds on each input, can you prove the maximum output of the network does not change?

© Springer Nature Switzerland AG 2021
A. Dutle et al. (Eds.): NFM 2021, LNCS 12673, pp. 19–36, 2021.
https://doi.org/10.1007/978-3-030-76384-8_2

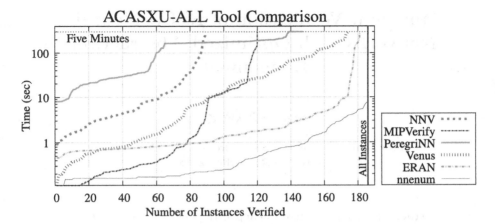

Fig. 1. At VNN-COMP 2020, the `nnenum` tool verified each ACAS Xu benchmark in under 10 s. (image from competition report [16]).

The most studied version involves neural networks with ReLU activation functions, for which many algorithms tools have been proposed. The biggest problem with these methods is often scalability, where networks cannot be verified in a timely manner. Analysis speed also affects the size of networks that can be analyzed in a reasonable amount of time. Speed improvements to a verification algorithm will mean that analysis of larger networks becomes more feasible.

This last summer in July 2020, the first international competition on neural network verification, VNN-COMP 2020, was held [16]. There were two categories of benchmarks evaluated: (i) image classification benchmarks that have generally larger numbers of inputs and network sizes, and (ii) control benchmarks which have less inputs and are generally smaller. The second category consisted of 184 benchmarks taken from the well-studied ACAS Xu system [18].

The results from the control category are shown in the cactus plot in Fig. 1. The `nnenum` tool was the fastest for this category, sometimes by orders of magnitude (note the y-axis is log scale). Although the comparison is imperfect—the participants each ran their own tool on their own hardware—the performance difference cannot be explained by hardware alone. Several new algorithmic optimizations were necessary to achieve `nnenum`'s performance.

This paper outlines and evaluates the main optimizations used in `nnenum`. Although `nnenum` also performed well on the image classification category, we focus our measurements in this paper on the ACAS Xu benchmarks, as a different set of optimizations was used for the larger perception networks. The next section provides a brief description of the high-level algorithm used for neural network verification of ReLU networks and the ACAS Xu benchmarks. A presentation, evaluation, and tool implementation of several optimizations is the main contribution of this work, and is presented in Sect. 3. The paper finishes with related work and a conclusion.

2   Overview

In this section, we provide an overview of the verification problem, benchmarks, and algorithm used in our evaluation in the next section.

2.1   Verification Problem

Our goal in this work is to efficiently solve the open-loop neural network verification problem. In this problem, we assume we are given a set defined with linear constraints over the network inputs $\mathcal{I}$ and a second set of unsafe states defined with linear constraints over the outputs $\mathcal{U}$. The network we analyze consists of fully connected layers with rectified linear unit (ReLU) activation functions, although the method has also been extended to work with convolutional layers, max pooling layers, and others [33,35]. ReLU activation functions are defined as $ReLU(x) = \max(x, 0)$, so that the neural networks compute a piecewise linear function. The verification problem is to find an input $i \in \mathcal{I}$ which when executed on the neural network produces an unsafe output $u \in \mathcal{U}$, or prove no such input exists. The execution semantics of fully-connected neural networks is well-known and reviewed in many papers [3], so we do not restate it here.

2.2   ACAS Xu Benchmarks

In this work, we focus our evaluation on the well-known ACAS Xu benchmarks [18]. These benchmarks provide several open-loop specifications for neural networks that are intended to compute a lossy compression of a large lookup table containing actions to prevent collisions among aircraft [17]. Each of the 45 neural networks has 300 neurons arranged in six fully-connected layers with ReLU activation functions. There are five inputs corresponding to the aircraft states, and five outputs corresponding to possible commands of the ownship aircraft to avoid collisions. Each property is defined using linear constraints over the inputs and outputs, matching the problem description in Sect. 2.1. The first four of these properties are applicable to all 45 networks, and we use these 180 benchmarks for our evaluation throughout this paper. In the original work with Reluplex [18], analysis times for these properties ranged from seconds to days, with some unsolved instances that presumably ran for days without producing a verification result. The ACAS Xu benchmarks are thus a mix of easy and difficult problems, some of which are SAT and some are UNSAT. Although the networks are small compared with image classification neural networks, they are similar enough to neural networks used in decision making and control to make them good benchmarks for verification algorithms.

2.3   Set Representations

The basis of our implementation is a reachability algorithm [34] based on the linear star set data structure [10], which we just call *star sets* in this paper.

Star sets are way to represent a set of states in some Euclidean space $\mathbb{R}^n$. They are defined using two parts: (1) a half-space polytope ($\mathcal{H}$-polytope) in some m-dimensional space, and (2) an affine transformation that takes the m-dimensional $\mathcal{H}$-polytope to the n-dimensional space. Star sets are efficient for (i) Computing high-dimensional affine transformations of sets (ii) Taking intersections with arbitrary linear constraints and (iii) Optimizing using linear programming (LP). These are all the operations needed to analyze neural networks with fully-connected ReLU layers [3].

The algorithm we describe in the next subsection also makes use of zonotope over approximations to improve efficiency. Zonotopes are a representation of a set of states in some Euclidean space $\mathbb{R}^n$ that encode an affine transformation of a *box* from some k-dimensional space. Zonotopes are efficient for affine transformations and very fast for linear optimization using a simple loop, but unlike star sets they cannot encode general intersections with linear constraints. Note that star sets are also efficient for linear optimization, but this requires invoking an LP solver so is often orders of magnitude slower than optimization with zonotopes.

2.4   Verification Algorithm Overview

We next provide a brief overview of the verification algorithm. A more complete description of the problem and algorithm are provided in an earlier work [3], where systematic analysis of optimization for *exact* analysis was performed. In the next section we will continue this approach of systematically analyzing optimizations, but instead for a modified version of the algorithm that uses abstractions to compute overapproximations of the set of possible outputs of a neural network. When the abstract system fails to verify the property, refinement is performed and the process repeats with a finer abstraction, all the way down to exact analysis if necessary.

The algorithm first represents the input set $\mathcal{I}$ using *both* a star set and a zonotope (called a prefilter zonotope in the earlier work). Each layer is then iterated over in the network, with an inner loop that iterates over each neuron in the layer. To go from the n_i values (dimensions) from one layer to the n_{i+1} values (dimensions) at the next layer, an affine transformation is performed on the sets, defined by the $n_{i+1} \times n_i$ weights matrix and n_{i+1} bias vector in the neural network at layer i. At each neuron within a layer, the sets are optimized over to check the lower and upper bound of the possible inputs to the neuron. If the lower bound is greater than zero or the upper bound is less than zero—for which we say the input or neuron is *one-sided*—then the nonlinear ReLU activation function is equivalent to a linear transformation and can be directly performed on the star set and zonotope. For efficiency, the optimization is first done using the zonotope rather than the star set, which can sometimes prove the input is one-sided without using LP. If the input is not one-sided, for exact analysis, the set can be split in two along the boundary where the input to the neuron is equal to zero, using an intersection operation. For the zonotope, since intersections are not supported, the operation is generally ignored resulting in a strictly larger set (an overapproximation), although some accuracy control can be performed through *zonotope domain contraction*. Zonotope domain contraction is the process of reducing the size of the box domain in the zonotope definition, so that it is a tighter overapproximation of the exact set represented by the star set. Since the affine transformations in the star set and zonotope are identical, zonotope contraction can be done by computing box bounds on the star set whenever an intersection is taken. When the sets are split in two, the algorithm proceeds recursively, performing the appropriate linear operation on the sets for the current neuron and proceeding to the next one. In the worst case, if splitting is done at every neuron, this can result in an exponential number of sets, which is not surprising as exact analysis for ReLU neural networks is NP-complete [18]. In practice, the problem is sometimes tractable, which means the choice of benchmarks is essential to evaluate an algorithm's practicality. This is a bit similar to how SAT solving is an NP-complete problem, but annual competitions since 1992 have pushed the limits of what is achievable in practice [6].

In the abstraction refinement version of the algorithm developed here, rather than immediately splitting the star set when neurons are not one-sided, we first overapproximate the ReLU region using the best convex relaxation in the neuron's input-output plane, sometimes called the triangle relaxation [12], which can be efficiently represented using a star set. This overapproximation is shown later in Fig. 3 (top-left), and has been formally described in other work [34]. Use overapproximation rather than splitting has the advantage of avoiding worst-case exponential splitting, but also has trade offs. The overapproximation adds a dimension to the domain of the star set as well as extra constraints, which makes future optimizations using LP slightly slower computationally. Also, the result is an overapproximation, which means that future neurons analyzed may look like they split whereas in reality they are one-sided, leading to even more error that takes even longer to analyze. Error can cascade through the network in this way leading to what we call an *error snowball*. Further, once the set is propagated through all the layers, it is possible that the output set intersects the unsafe set $\mathcal{U}$, whereas the real set does not; there can be spurious counter-examples due to the overapproximation in the abstraction.

In the previous work with star sets [34], cases where the abstraction intersected the unsafe set $\mathcal{U}$ produced a verification result of UNKNOWN. Here, we instead propose to go back and perform a split on the first neuron where overapproximation was used—a refinement step. The process then proceeds recursively, again trying overapproximation at each remaining neuron that is not one-sided and then checking for intersection with the unsafe set $\mathcal{U}$. If there is still an intersection, refinement is performed again on a second neuron, and so on, until either the property is proved, an unsafe counter-example is found, or no remaining neurons exist where an overapproximation was done. Since the algorithm eventually reverts to exact analysis, it is sound and complete. It also has the potential to be faster, when abstractions can prove there is no intersection with $\mathcal{U}$. However, as will be shown in the next section, a direct implementation can actually be slower in many cases.

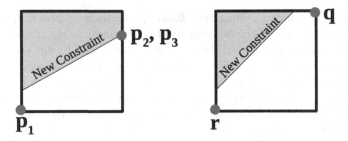

Fig. 2. The new zonotope domain contraction algorithm computes new box bounds by finding points p_1, p_2, and then p_3, requiring only three LPs instead of four (left). In the best case, computing bounds with the new approach only requires two LPs, regardless of the number of dimensions n, instead of $2n$ with the old approach (right).

3   Optimizations

We now present and evaluate several key optimizations that are essential to the performance of nnenum. We run each optimization on all the 180 ACAS Xu benchmarks described in the Sect. 2.2. We use a timeout of one minute for each benchmark and report the number of timeouts encountered as well as the total runtime. For lack of a better option, we count a timeout as one minute of total runtime, but keep in mind that the number of timeouts should weigh much more heavily when comparing approaches; some ACAS Xu benchmarks have been known to run for hours or days in other work. All measurements in this paper were done on a laptop running Ubuntu 20.04 with an Intel Xeon E-2176M CPU running at 2.70GHz containing 32 GB RAM. Our implementation of the algorithm is available online as part of the nnenum tool[1], including Dockerfile and scripts to run all the ACAS Xu benchmarks.

3.1   Zonotope Domain Contraction

As mentioned in the algorithm overview in Sect. 2, zonotopes are used to provide quick outer approximation of the bounds of the possible inputs to each neuron. If these are accurate, many neurons can be proven to be one-sided without needing to do linear programming in the star sets, which is significantly more efficient. For abstract analysis later, we will also consider using zonotopes, so the tightness of the zonotope is even more important.

Although zonotopes do not support intersections when splitting sets, their box domains can be reduced to contain the set after intersection which improves accuracy and reduces runtime. The problem of determining the tightest box domain can be solved using linear programming on the exact set represented by the star set. The most direct algorithm is to minimize and maximize along every input, so that a neural network with n inputs will require solving $2n$ LPs. In our

---

[1] https://github.com/stanleybak/nnenum.

earlier work on optimizing exact analysis [3], we compared this direct approach, which we call Old LP here, with a Single Loop approach for zonotope domain contraction. In the Single Loop method, a single constraint was analyzed to see if it reduced the box bounds of the zonotope's domain. This does not produce tight box bounds, but it was shown to be faster overall as it did not require LP solving.

Here we re-examine domain contraction using a few further optimizations. First, rather than solving $2n$ LPs to determine box bounds, we leverage additional information available to the problem. Namely, we take advantage of the box bounds on the zonotope domain that are available prior to taking the intersection. The problem becomes to determine if adding one additional constraint to the star set's domain (an $\mathcal{H}$-polytope) changes its bounding box, given the original bounding box.

Our new zonotope contraction approach, called New LP, uses LP to optimize over the star set's $\mathcal{H}$-polytope with an optimization direction vector of all -1 values, to try to simultaneously find the lower bounds of all the variables in a single LP. In the best case, this point will have a value equal to the minimum value of each dimension in the old bounding box, and we can proceed to find upper bounds in the same fashion but using a vector of all 1 values. If only some of the variables achieved their earlier lower bound, the process repeats, setting to 0 in the optimization direction vector all of the variables that matched their earlier lower bound. To process stops when no new variables in the result get to their earlier lower bound, after which each variable that did not achieve their earlier lower bound is minimized individually using LP.

An example of this algorithm is shown in the 2-D case in Fig. 2. In the figure, the box domain is intersected with a linear constraint, so that the upper grey region should be excluded from the resultant set. On the left side of the figure, the algorithm would first maximize in the direction of $\langle -1, -1 \rangle$ (minimizing the sum of x and y) finding point p_1, which matches the previous bounding box, so that we know that the lower bounds of both x and y are unchanged. Next, we maximize $\langle 1, 1 \rangle$ finding point p_2, which matches the old upper bound of x. The next maximization direction is $\langle 0, 1 \rangle$, which gives point p_3, which proves that the upper bound of y should be reduced, because the vector we optimized over only had a single non-zero entry. In this case, we found the box bounds using three LPs, whereas the original approach needed four.

In the best case, the algorithm can reduce the number of LPs to solve in an n-dimensional problem, corresponding to a neural network verification problem with n inputs, from $2n$ to 2. Such as case is shown in Fig. 2 on the right, where one LP would first find point r and then a second LP would find point q, which is sufficient to show the box bounds have not been updated due to the new constraint. For this reason we expect the benefit to be greatest for this new zonotope domain contraction algorithm when the input space is high dimensional, such as in image recognition adversarial example verification benchmarks. Even in ACAS Xu, however, there are five inputs and so the savings can be beneficial.

Table 1. Domain contraction optimizations with exact analysis.

Optimization	Timeouts	Runtime [sec]
No contraction	50	3471.2
Single loop	32	2778.8
Old LP	44	3220.9
Old LP + Witnesses	31	2680.1
New LP	31	2743.8
New LP + Witnesses	28	2549.0

A second optimization we consider for zonotope domain contraction is to track the witnesses of the box bounds. Whenever we compute box bounds, we can store the witness points in the set that exhibit the lower and upper bounds. When a new constraint is added, if the new constraint does not exclude the witness point from the set, which can be checked with simple dot product, then the bound for that variable/direction is unchanged. This witness approach can be applied to both the old contraction algorithm (Old LP + Witnesses) and new proposed contraction algorithm (New LP + Witnesses). For example, consider again the right side of Fig. 2. If p and r are the witness points exhibiting the box bounds, then we can quickly check that the new constraint does not eliminate p or r from the set. Thus, we can prove the box bounds have not changed, without any need for LP solving.

The results for the various zonotope domain contraction options, in addition to a No Contraction approach, are shown in Table 1. Both the newer algorithm and tracking witnesses improve performance. Although the Single Loop approach is faster than the Old LP method, using the New LP method, especially when tracking witnesses is even faster. All zonotope contraction methods outperform No Contraction. For the remaining optimization in this paper, we use zonotope domain contraction with the New LP + Witnesses approach.

3.2 Direct Abstraction Refinement

We next examine direct abstraction refinement approaches. As described earlier, these algorithms first use an abstraction to try to prove the property by overapproximating all the ReLU functions when individual neurons are not one-sided. If the property cannot be proven, the computation backtracks to the first ReLU that was an overapproximation and the set is instead split. Each of the two sets is then processed recursively, again trying overapproximations at the next neuron which could split.

If the ith neuron in a layer has an input with lower bound $l_i < 0$ and upper bound $u_i > 0$, various overapproximations are possible for the output of the neuron which do not require splitting. Figure 3 shows four possibilities, where the input to the neuron is on the x axis and the output is on the y axis. The triangle overapproximation (top-left) is the best convex relaxation on the

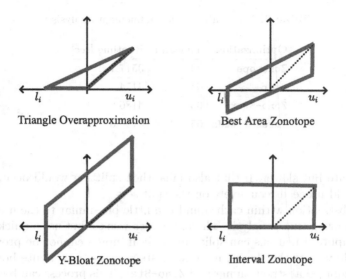

Fig. 3. When the inputs to some neuron i are bounded between l_i and u_i, many overapproximations can provide efficient abstractions of the nonlinear ReLU activation function, $ReLU(x) = \max(x, 0)$. In each plot, the x axis is the input to the neuron, and the y axis is the output.

single neuron input-output plane and is possible to represent with star sets [34]. Although better linear overapproximations are possible by bounding multiple neurons at once [28], it is unclear so far if this improves overall performance, so we focus on the single neuron case in nnenum. Although the star set triangle overapproximation approach, which we call Star, is the most accurate, it can sometimes be slow as optimization over star sets uses linear programming. It can be actually beneficial to use a less accurate zonotope abstraction, which can compute bounds of subsequent neurons more quickly. With zonotopes, actually multiple abstractions are possible, which can be parameterized by the slope of the zonotope [29]. Three choices are shown in Fig. 3 (top-right and bottom row). While the best-area zonotope generally has less overapproximation error, all the zonotopes are actually incomparable from a set perspective. Each zonotope type has points in the neuron input-output plane that are excluded in one of the other zonotope abstractions, and so none is better in all cases. The Zonotope approach uses the best-area zonotope abstraction for each neuron that can split.

In addition to using individual abstractions, nnenum also makes use of two new ideas in the context of neural network verification: (i) *multi-round abstractions* and (ii) *multi-abstraction analysis within each round*.

Multi-round analysis proceeds by first trying one abstraction and then trying another one before proceeding to split. For example, multi-round analysis with two rounds could first try to prove the property using the best-area zonotope abstraction, which is fast but less accurate. If that does not succeed, analysis would then try to use the triangle overapproximation with star sets, which is

Table 2. Direct abstraction refinement analysis.

Optimization	Timeouts	Runtime [sec]
Zonotope	29	3517.1
Star	64	4174.3
Zono-Star	63	4186.8
Three rounds	65	4190.0

more accurate but slower. If that also fails, then splitting would occur and the process would proceed recursively on the split sets.

Multi-abstraction within each round is a little bit similar to the use prefilter zonotopes during exact analysis. There, the idea was to first use a quick abstraction to compute if neurons can split, and only if inputs cannot be proven to be one-sided do we use the slower, more accurate star set to compute bounds. We call this combined abstraction method Zono-Star. This process can be extended to an arbitrary list of abstractions, and towards the problem of computing the lower and upper bounds of each neuron rather than just rejecting splits. The approach works by using each abstraction to compute the lower and upper bounds of the next neuron's input, stopping if any of the abstractions shows it is one-sided. Since all abstractions are overapproximations, even when splits cannot be rejected we can still use the greatest lower bound and the least upper bound from all of the abstractions. Then, for constructing the overapproximating zonotopes or star sets for the next neuron, these tighter bounds are used for all of the abstractions. For example, we could consider all three zonotope abstractions *at the same time*. Since zonotope analysis is quick, this multi-abstraction method offers a way to improve accuracy with little cost. A similar concurrent multi-abstraction approach has been used in the context of parallelotope bundles [8] for reachability analysis of dynamical systems [9,20] where it was called "all-for-one" analysis.

Multi-round and multi-abstraction can also be combined. For example, in the first round could try to prove the property using just the best-area zonotope abstraction, and if that fails a second round could use all three zonotopes together, and then if that fails we could do a third round with all three zonotopes as well as the triangle overapproximation with star sets. This approach is called Three Rounds.

The measurements for the various abstractions are shown in Table 2. From the analysis, the Zonotope methods looks better than the more accurate abstractions, even with multi-round and multi-abstraction analysis. The main reason is that the other three levels of abstraction have star sets that use LP solving to determine bounds, which turns out to be a bottleneck.

However, even the `Zonotope` abstraction refinement method is slower than the `New LP + Witnesses` exact analysis method described earlier in Sect. 3.1. This would seem to imply that abstraction refinement is a losing strategy for high-performance neural network verification, unless we can find further optimizations to improve the approach. In the next subsection, we discuss the cause for this unintuitively poor performance, and propose and evaluate further optimizations to the abstraction refinement algorithm.

3.3 Abstraction Refinement Improvements

In the worst case, the abstraction refinement approach will revert to exact analysis. However, performance in these cases is much worse than directly doing exact analysis, as time must be spent at each abstraction phase to propagate abstract sets and check if the final sets are unsafe. Upon examining the performance of various phases of the algorithm, it turned out that propagating abstract sets can sometimes be very slow. The cause of this was determined to be the *error snowball* effect described in Sect. 2.4. Basically, an overapproximation is less accurate, and so it is more likely that neurons analyzed will look like they may split, causing a further reduction in accuracy. The splitting processes adds variables to the LPs needed to compute neuron bounds using star sets, and adds generators to the zonotope abstractions, slowing down analysis of neurons further in the network. Worse, after all the slow computation completes, the set at the end of the network has lots of error and very rarely can prove the safety specification. The computation has taken a long time and its result was useless. To speed up performance, then, we need methods that prevent error snowballs, reduce their impact, or detect them before they get out of hand.

We consider different ways to adjust the computation time / error trade off when using star sets. If we can increase the analysis speed for a slight reduction in accuracy, this may reduce the computation time when error snowballs occur during abstract analysis. The first method we look at to do this we call `Quick Star`. Here, the bounds for each neuron are computed only using zonotopes, like with a multi-abstraction round, but these bounds are also used to construct a star set overapproximation. This star set is only used to check for intersection with the unsafe set, rather than for computing the bounds on the neuron inputs. Only a single LP is used at the end to check for intersection with the unsafe set, as the bounds computations are all done with zonotopes. The approach we use with `Quick Star` uses the `Three Rounds` abstraction which uses three zonotopes in the final round to get the tightest bounds possible without LP.

A second way to speed up star set analysis with a slight accuracy reduction deals with the bounds computation process. Rather than computing two bounds for each neuron, we consider only computing a single bound in order to try to prove the neuron is one-sided, and use the zonotope bounds for the other side if this fails. The side to choose (lower or upper bound), is selected by leveraging a quick concrete execution of the neural network. In this way, for example, we will never compute the upper bound for a neuron's input if the concrete execution has a positive input value for that neuron, as the upper bound could not be less than concrete input value. This method, which uses a single LP per bounds computation, is a bit of a compromise between direct star set abstraction, which use two LPs to compute the lower and upper bounds, and Quick Star, which uses zero LPs. We evaluate this approach using the combined zonotope-star abstraction and refer to it as One Sided Zono-Star.

One way we investigate to try to prevent error snowballs, rather than just reducing their effect, is called Execution-Guided Overapproximation (EGO). EGO works by changing the order in which abstractions are constructed. Rather than first trying abstract analysis and then splitting if the abstraction fails, EGO first splits as much as possible essentially proceeding as if it were exact analysis. Upon succeeding to verify one branch of the search space after many splits, the method backtracks like a normal depth-first search, but now starts to try abstract analysis. This continues further and further up the search tree, until abstract analysis no longer succeeds in proving the property, causing the method to again switch to exact analysis and repeat. Essentially, rather than starting from an abstract system and performing refinement, EGO analysis starts with a concrete set and iteratively constructs more and more abstract systems. This avoids costly abstraction analysis near the root of the search tree that often result in error snowballs. More details on EGO are available in a online report [1]. For the EGO method, we use the Zono-Star abstraction, as well as the Three Rounds abstraction which we call EGO Three Rounds.

Instead of EGO, there are other methods we try to use to prevent and detect error snowballs. One method, called Split Limit, tracks the number of splits that occurred whenever an abstraction successfully verified a portion of the search tree. When backtracking and continuing abstract analysis, if the number of splits using zonotopes exceeds some factor multiplied by the previous number of splits, this method directly splits without trying abstract analysis. The intuition for this approach comes from the observation that error snowballs often have a huge number of neurons that split, much more than previous successful analysis. We analyze different multiplication factors in the context of the Split Limit method. For example Split Limit 1.5 would mean that if the last successfully verified abstraction had 10 neurons that split, and the current zonotope-only abstraction has more than 15 splits, abstraction analysis with star sets would not even be attempted.

A second idea to reduce the impact of error snowballs is to directly use timeouts for the abstraction analysis (Abs Timeout). These methods again have a parameter that we tune which is the number of seconds abstraction analysis runs before it is stopped.

The third way to improve performance creates a threshold for when Split Limit should be used. We noticed when the number of splits is very small in successful abstract analysis, using a simple multiplicative factor may give up on abstract analysis too quickly. For example, if an abstraction with two splits succeeds, having a Split Limit of 2 would reject any system with more than four splits in zonotope analysis. In the Split Min methods, we enforce a minimum on the number of splits before we consider the Split Limit multiplicative factor.

Table 3. Optimized abstraction refinement analysis.

Optimization	Timeouts	Runtime [sec]
Quick star	43	3802.8
One sided	26	2998.5
EGO	2	1469.2
EGO 3 rounds	2	1467.1
Split Limit 1.1	31	3090.2
Split Limit 1.2	32	3288.4
Split Limit 1.3	31	3247.7
Split Limit 1.4	31	3215.4
Split Limit 1.5	28	3229.9
Split Limit 1.6	32	3291.1
Split Limit 1.7	30	3184.8
Abs Timeout 0.02	0	274.8
Abs Timeout 0.04	0	371.7
Abs Timeout 0.06	0	451.5
Abs Timeout 0.08	0	520.7
Abs Timeout 0.1	0	577.7
Split Min 10	3	1236.4
Split Min 20	0	485.5
Split Min 30	0	298.6
Split Min 40	0	224.7
Split Min 50	0	191.5
Split Min 60	0	178.4
Split Min 70	0	173.6
Split Min 80	0	175.7
Split Min 90	0	188.7

For example, we could set a Split Min threshold of 30, where any abstraction where the zonotope analysis split on less than 30 neurons will always be analyzed abstractly with star sets. Again the minimum value is a parameter that we tune through measurements.

The result of each of the optimizations run on all the ACAS Xu benchmarks is shown in Table 3. Using Quick Star reduced the number of timeouts from 63 with Zono-Star down to 43. The One Sided approach made a bigger difference, reducing the number of timeouts from 63 with Zono-Star to 26. For the rest of the optimizations we continue to use the one-sided optimization. EGO was even faster, where analysis now only had 2 benchmarks that exceeded the one minute timeout. The additional abstraction rounds in EGO 3 Rounds no longer slowed the method down as with the direct abstraction refinement approaches from

Table 2. We noticed this was generally the case when there were few error snow-ball cases, so we continue to use the three-round abstraction in the remaining measurements.

Although EGO and Quick Star methods both improved performance by reducing the effect of error snowballs, it was difficult to think of ways to fur-ther improve their speed. The goal of the remaining three optimizations, Split Limit, Abs Timeout, and Split Min, was to be able to get closer to the accuracy of using star set overapproximation without the large runtime.

Using Split Limit, we improve upon the Three Rounds result which had 65 timeouts, although the method is still slower than EGO. The method is not too sensitive to the parameter used, and we use Split Limit 1.5 for the remaining measurements.

Adding in Abs Timeout, we finally achieve a method where every benchmark finishes within one minute (no timeouts occur). Generally, smaller values of the abstraction timeout parameter seem to be faster. We used an Abs Timeout 0.04 when evaluating the Split Min parameter (we also tried 0.02 and 0.06, but they was slightly slower when used with Split Min).

Finally, adding the Split Min optimization further reduces the total com-putation time to run all the ACAS Xu benchmarks. The Split Min 70 method analyzed all 180 benchmarks using a runtime sum of 173 s.

We also tried many optimization options individually that were not reported in detail in the tables. For example only using Abs Timeout without Split Limit was also fairly fast, but still had a few timeouts. Doing things like turning off zonotope domain contraction also severely hurt performance of the overap-proximation methods. Overall, the best performance we found was achieved using a combination the presented optimizations, with Split Limit, Abs Timeout, and Split Min used in combination to prevent error snowballs with star set analysis.

4   Related Work

Many additional methods for verification of neural networks have been pro-posed [21,38], including methods based on mixed integer-linear programming (MILP) [22,32], symbolic interval propagation [36,37], SMT-based approaches based on modifications to the Simplex linear programming algorithm [18,19], and MILP methods with local search [11].

Linear star sets have been explored in the context of other problems. In par-ticular, efficient high-dimensional reachability analysis of hybrid systems with linear differential equations is possible with star sets [2,4], where the primary operations needed are the same as in the neural network verification case: affine transformation, intersection with linear constraints, and optimization. Other names for essentially the same data structure as linear star sets include affine forms [14], constrained zonotopes [23,27] and $\mathcal{AH}$-Polytopes [26].

Other optimizations may provide further improvements to performance, such as using the spurious region to guide refinement [40], similar to counter-example guided abstraction refinement [7]. We did not find a way to use this in our algorithm without hurting overall performance, although it may be an avenue for further investigation.

Another critical choice in the algorithm is the ordering of neurons when performing splitting. We tried several heuristic orderings within each layer, with only minor impact on performance. In nnenum, we always visit the neurons layer by layer, but rearrange the order of neurons so that they are sorted in decreasing order of their L_∞ norm distance of the zonotope bounds estimates, which only slightly outperforms just visiting the neurons in the original order. More computationally advanced methods, such as those that track gradient information [37], compute output sensitivity [39], perform dependency analysis [5] or use information from LP shadow prices [25] could further improve efficiency.

In the future, we may also consider other abstractions such as symbolic intervals [36, 37] or using single upper and lower bounds (called DeepPoly [30]) which could offer different accuracy / performance trade offs.

5 Conclusion

We presented an abstraction refinement algorithm for verification of neural networks based on the star set data structure. Importantly, we showed that several optimizations are possible and necessary with the approach in order to create a highly efficient algorithm—abstraction refinement is actually slower than directly using exact analysis without the optimizations presented. While optimizing an algorithm might be seen as an engineering problem, we believe such optimization is necessary to guide the appropriate place to develop new theory. It is difficult to really evaluate an algorithm and know which bottlenecks are worth improving without an optimized implementation.

In this paper, we showed that the fully optimized version of nnenum verified all 180 ACAS Xu benchmarks from properties 1 to 4 using a sum total runtime of 178 s. During the VNN-COMP 2020 competition, the *single* ACAS Xu benchmark consisting of property 2 and network 4-2 required 240 s for ERAN [31] and 648 s for Venus [5], the two next fastest tools. The performance of nnenum would not be possible without the methods presented in this paper.

References

1. Bak, S.: Execution-guided overapproximation (EGO) for improving scalability of neural network verification (2020). http://stanleybak.com/papers/bak2020vnn.pdf
2. Bak, S., Duggirala, P.S.: Hylaa: a tool for computing simulation-equivalent reachability for linear systems. In: Proceedings of the 20th International Conference on Hybrid Systems: Computation and Control. HSCC 2017 (2017)
3. Bak, S., Tran, H.-D., Hobbs, K., Johnson, T.T.: Improved geometric path enumeration for verifying ReLU neural networks. In: Lahiri, S.K., Wang, C. (eds.) CAV 2020. LNCS, vol. 12224, pp. 66–96. Springer, Cham (2020). https://doi.org/10.1007/978-3-030-53288-8_4

4. Bak, S., Tran, H.D., Johnson, T.T.: Numerical verification of affine systems with up to a billion dimensions. In: Proceedings of the 22Nd ACM International Conference on Hybrid Systems: Computation and Control, pp. 23–32. HSCC 2019, ACM, New York, NY, USA (2019). http://doi.acm.org/10.1145/3302504.3311792

5. Botoeva, E., Kouvaros, P., Kronqvist, J., Lomuscio, A., Misener, R.: Efficient verification of relu-based neural networks via dependency analysis. Proc. AAAI Conf. Artif. Intell. **34**(04), 3291–3299 (2020). https://doi.org/10.1609/aaai.v34i04.5729, https://ojs.aaai.org/index.php/AAAI/article/view/5729

6. Buro, M., Büning, H.K.: Report on a SAT Competition. Fachbereich Math.-Informatik, Univ. Gesamthochschule, Zurich (1992)

7. Clarke, E., Grumberg, O., Jha, S., Lu, Y., Veith, H.: Counterexample-guided abstraction refinement. In: Emerson, E.A., Sistla, A.P. (eds.) CAV 2000. LNCS, vol. 1855, pp. 154–169. Springer, Heidelberg (2000). https://doi.org/10.1007/10722167_15

8. Dreossi, T., Dang, T., Piazza, C.: Parallelotope bundles for polynomial reachability. In: Proceedings of the 19th International Conference on Hybrid Systems: Computation and Control, pp. 297–306 (2016)

9. Dreossi, T., Dang, T., Piazza, C.: Reachability computation for polynomial dynamical systems. Formal Methods Syst. Des. **50**(1), 1–38 (2017). https://doi.org/10.1007/s10703-016-0266-3

10. Duggirala, P.S., Viswanathan, M.: Parsimonious, simulation based verification of linear systems. In: Chaudhuri, S., Farzan, A. (eds.) CAV 2016. LNCS, vol. 9779, pp. 477–494. Springer, Cham (2016). https://doi.org/10.1007/978-3-319-41528-4_26

11. Dutta, S., Jha, S., Sankaranarayanan, S., Tiwari, A.: Output range analysis for deep feedforward neural networks. In: Dutle, A., Muñoz, C., Narkawicz, A. (eds.) NFM 2018. LNCS, vol. 10811, pp. 121–138. Springer, Cham (2018). https://doi.org/10.1007/978-3-319-77935-5_9

12. Ehlers, R.: Formal verification of piece-wise linear feed-forward neural networks. In: D'Souza, D., Narayan Kumar, K. (eds.) ATVA 2017. LNCS, vol. 10482, pp. 269–286. Springer, Cham (2017). https://doi.org/10.1007/978-3-319-68167-2_19

13. Goodfellow, I.J., Shlens, J., Szegedy, C.: Explaining and harnessing adversarial examples. arXiv preprint arXiv:1412.6572 (2014)

14. Han, Z., Krogh, B.H.: Reachability analysis of large-scale affine systems using low-dimensional polytopes. In: Hespanha, J.P., Tiwari, A. (eds.) HSCC 2006. LNCS, vol. 3927, pp. 287–301. Springer, Heidelberg (2006). https://doi.org/10.1007/11730637_23

15. Huang, S., Papernot, N., Goodfellow, I., Duan, Y., Abbeel, P.: Adversarial attacks on neural network policies. arXiv preprint arXiv:1702.02284 (2017)

16. Johnson, T.T.: International verification of neural networks com- petition (vnncomp) (2020)

17. Julian, K.D., Lopez, J., Brush, J.S., Owen, M.P., Kochenderfer, M.J.: Policy compression for aircraft collision avoidance systems. In: 2016 IEEE/AIAA 35th Digital Avionics Systems Conference (DASC), pp. 1–10. IEEE (2016)

18. Katz, G., Barrett, C., Dill, D.L., Julian, K., Kochenderfer, M.J.: Reluplex: an efficient SMT solver for verifying deep neural networks. In: Majumdar, R., Kunčak, V. (eds.) CAV 2017. LNCS, vol. 10426, pp. 97–117. Springer, Cham (2017). https://doi.org/10.1007/978-3-319-63387-9_5

19. Katz, G., et al.: The marabou framework for verification and analysis of deep neural networks. In: Dillig, I., Tasiran, S. (eds.) CAV 2019. LNCS, vol. 11561, pp. 443–452. Springer, Cham (2019). https://doi.org/10.1007/978-3-030-25540-4_26

20. Kim, E., Duggirala, P.S.: Kaa: a python implementation of reachable set computation using bernstein polynomials. EPiC Ser. Comput. **74**, 184–196 (2020)
21. Liu, C., Arnon, T., Lazarus, C., Barrett, C., Kochenderfer, M.J.: Algorithms for verifying deep neural networks. arXiv preprint arXiv:1903.06758 (2019)
22. Lomuscio, A., Maganti, L.: An approach to reachability analysis for feed-forward relu neural networks. arXiv preprint arXiv:1706.07351 (2017)
23. Raghuraman, V., Koeln, J.P.: Set operations and order reductions for constrained zonotopes. arXiv preprint arXiv:2009.06039 (2020)
24. Rauber, J., Brendel, W., Bethge, M.: Foolbox: A python toolbox to benchmark the robustness of machine learning models. arXiv preprint arXiv:1707.04131 (2017)
25. Royo, V.R., Calandra, R., Stipanovic, D.M., Tomlin, C.: Fast neural network verification via shadow prices. arXiv preprint arXiv:1902.07247 (2019)
26. Sadraddini, S., Tedrake, R.: Linear encodings for polytope containment problems. In: 2019 IEEE 58th Conference on Decision and Control (CDC), pp. 4367–4372. IEEE (2019)
27. Scott, J.K., Raimondo, D.M., Marseglia, G.R., Braatz, R.D.: Constrained zonotopes: a new tool for set-based estimation and fault detection. Automatica **69**, 126–136 (2016)
28. Singh, G., Ganvir, R., Püschel, M., Vechev, M.: Beyond the single neuron convex barrier for neural network certification. In: Advances in Neural Information Processing Systems, pp. 15098–15109 (2019)
29. Singh, G., Gehr, T., Mirman, M., Püschel, M., Vechev, M.: Fast and effective robustness certification. In: Advances in Neural Information Processing Systems, pp. 10802–10813 (2018)
30. Singh, G., Gehr, T., Püschel, M., Vechev, M.: An abstract domain for certifying neural networks. Proc. ACM Program. Lang. **3**(POPL), 1–30 (2019)
31. Singh, G., Gehr, T., Püschel, M., Vechev, M.: Boosting robustness certification of neural networks. In: International Conference on Learning Representations (ICLR) (2019)
32. Tjeng, V., Xiao, K., Tedrake, R.: Evaluating robustness of neural networks with mixed integer programming. arXiv preprint arXiv:1711.07356 (2017)
33. Tran, H.-D., Bak, S., Xiang, W., Johnson, T.T.: Verification of deep convolutional neural networks using ImageStars. In: Lahiri, S.K., Wang, C. (eds.) CAV 2020. LNCS, vol. 12224, pp. 18–42. Springer, Cham (2020). https://doi.org/10.1007/978-3-030-53288-8_2
34. Tran, H.D., et al.: Star-based reachability analysis of deep neural networks. In: ter Beek, M.H., McIver, A., Oliveira, J.N. (eds.) FM 2019. LNCS, vol. 11800, pp. 670–686. Springer, Cham (2019). https://doi.org/10.1007/978-3-030-30942-8_39
35. Tran, H.D., et al.: NNV: the neural network verification tool for deep neural networks and learning-enabled cyber-physical systems. In: Lahiri, S.K., Wang, C. (eds.) CAV 2020. LNCS, vol. 12224, pp. 3–17. Springer, Cham (2020). https://doi.org/10.1007/978-3-030-53288-8_1
36. Wang, S., Pei, K., Whitehouse, J., Yang, J., Jana, S.: Efficient formal safety analysis of neural networks. In: Advances in Neural Information Processing Systems, pp. 6367–6377 (2018)
37. Wang, S., Pei, K., Whitehouse, J., Yang, J., Jana, S.: Formal security analysis of neural networks using symbolic intervals. In: 27th USENIX Security Symposium, pp. 1599–1614 (2018)

38. Xiang, W., et al.: Verification for machine learning, autonomy, and neural networks survey. arXiv preprint arXiv:1810.01989 (2018)
39. Xiang, W., Tran, H.D., Johnson, T.T.: Output reachable set estimation and verification for multilayer neural networks. IEEE Trans. Neural Netw. Learn. Syst. **29**(11), 5777–5783 (2018)
40. Yang, P., et al.: Improving neural network verification through spurious region guided refinement. arXiv preprint arXiv:2010.07722 (2020)

Minimum-Violation Traffic Management
for Urban Air Mobility

Suda Bharadwaj[1]([✉]), Tichakorn Wongpiromsarn[2], Natasha Neogi[3],
Joseph Muffoletto[1], and Ufuk Topcu[1]

[1] The University of Texas at Austin, Austin, TX 78712, USA
{suda.b,stevencarr,utopcu}@utexas.edu
[2] Iowa State University, Ames, USA 50011
nok@iastate.edu
[3] NASA-Langley Research Center, Hampton, USA
natasha.a.neogi@nasa.gov

Abstract. Urban air mobility (UAM) refers to air transportation services in and over an urban area and has the potential to revolutionize mobility solutions. However, due to the projected scale of operations, current air traffic management (ATM) techniques are not viable. Increasingly autonomous systems are a pathway to accelerate the realization of UAM operations, but must be fielded safely and efficiently. The heavily regulated, safety critical nature of aviation may lead to multiple, competing safety constraints that can be traded off based on the operational context. In this paper, we design a framework which allows for the scalable planning of a UAM ATM system. We formalize safety oriented constraints derived from FAA regulations by encoding them as temporal logic formulae. We then propose a method for UAM ATM that is both scalable and minimally violates the temporal logic constraints. Numerical results show that the runtime for our proposed algorithm is suitable for very large problems and is backed by theoretical guarantees of correctness with respect to given temporal logic constraints.

1 Introduction

1.1 Problem Significance

Recent years have seen increased urbanization, economic expansion, underinvestment in infrastructure, and the rise of ride hailing services and e-commerce. These changes have led to an increase in transportation delays, vehicle congestion during peak times, and environmental impacts resulting in escalating mobility challenges in urban areas. The emerging Urban Air Mobility (UAM) aviation market is being catalyzed by advances in increasingly autonomous systems, electric propulsion, and novel business models such as on-demand, aerial ride sharing, thereby helping to address congestion issues in urban areas [5].

UAM has the potential to be a safe, functional solution to the air transportation problem for passengers and cargo in and around a densely populated

© Springer Nature Switzerland AG 2021
A. Dutle et al. (Eds.): NFM 2021, LNCS 12673, pp. 37–52, 2021.
https://doi.org/10.1007/978-3-030-76384-8_3

urban area. An air traffic management system that governs a large number of these novel UAM operations over a small geographical area in a safe and efficient fashion is key to the realization and deployment of the UAM vision.

1.2   Scalable and Verifiable Safety for UAM

The scale and density of projected UAM operations will far exceed the safe workload capacity of human controllers, necessitating the deployment of increasingly autonomous solutions for functions like aircraft management (e.g., managing flightpath and altitude requests, managing airborne and ground based holding times, etc.) and aircraft separation.

Currently, there is no established infrastructure for air traffic management of a scalable UAM concept of operations. Under current aviation paradigms, air traffic management is carried out in a centralized fashion by air traffic controllers. The U.S. National Airspace System (NAS) is comprised of 5.3 million square miles of domestic airspace and 24 million square miles of oceanic airspace. There are approximately 5,000 flights airborne at any given moment. Over 14,000 air traffic controllers manage these aircraft and perform multiple safety-critical functions, such as air traffic separation which guarantees that a minimum spacing between aircraft is maintained [7]. In contrast, for UAM operations to deploy at scale for profit, it will be necessary to have hundreds (or even thousands) of UAM aircraft aloft over an urban airspace under 500 square miles [9]. The sheer number of vehicles, along with the necessary reduced separation criteria between them in order to achieve the required densities, will require the development of increasingly autonomous capabilities for aircraft clearance, separation, and flow management in the UAM ecosystem.

Deploying increasingly autonomous systems in the US airspace is a challenge. Commercial aviation is among one of the most safety-critical systems in the world and has stringent standards for the design, deployment, and operation of aircraft and air traffic control systems. These regulations are detailed in Chap. 14 of the Code of Federal Regulations (14 CFR). The ability to assure increasingly autonomous systems to aviation grade standards is thus crucial for their acceptance. Safety-critical functions such as aircraft separation must provide strict guarantees on their behavior and the correctness of their outcomes. Thus, increasingly autonomous air traffic management systems will have to tackle the dual issues of scalability and verifiable safety in order to be deployed in the NAS.

1.3   Setting

In this paper, we employ a hierarchical decomposition of the UAM operations space motivated by the physical and geographical infrastructure required to field the system. Such an architecture has been studied in [2,3] and allows for scalable air traffic management. UAM vehicles take off and land from a landing pad, called a vertipad, which includes the final approach and takeoff (FATO) area. A vertiport is comprised of several vertipads, the respective vertipad FATOs, and charging and maintenance facilities. A vertihub is comprised of several vertiports. Vertihubs provide air traffic control services (i.e., real time control of aircraft movement) between vertiports under their control and air traffic management services (i.e., strategic and long term planning of aircraft movement and flows) for vehicles transiting between adjacent vertihubs. Figure 1 provides a visual representation of vertiports and vertihubs. We focus on a synthesis strategy for vertihubs, each of which is responsible for assuring the safety of all vehicles in its airspace.

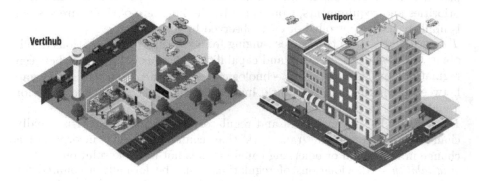

Fig. 1. Vertihub and vertiport depiction

In general, it is not always feasible to guarantee the satisfaction of all safety constraints under all conditions. Such scenarios are explicitly accounted for in 14 CFR §107.21, which allows for emergency deviation from regulations if required as long as the deviation is reported. For example, a vehicle may have to make an emergency landing if it is about to run out of fuel, even if violates separation requirements. Thus, there is a need for an air traffic management approach that allows for *formally justifiable* violation of safety constraints if necessary. In this paper, we study the synthesis of control strategies for automated air traffic management for UAM while obeying safety regulations. In particular, we focus on the case where all safety regulations cannot be feasibly satisfied, as is allowed for small, cargo-carrying UAS under emergency operation. We present a decentralized, scalable synthesis approach that provably *minimally violates* the given safety requirements. Note that if it is possible to satisfy all safety properties for the duration of the flight, the approach yields a solution with zero violations (i.e., all safety requirements are guaranteed for the duration of the flight).

1.4   Contribution and Innovation

We present the first decentralized approach to minimum violation planning. We use temporal logic for a formal representation of safety regulations and guarantee that these regulations are minimally violated across the global system. Furthermore, we establish a *framework* in this paper for minimum-violation for the small UAS cargo-carrying application over urban areas. Our framework has the following properties:

- *Scalability* - UAM operations are envisioned to occur at a scale well beyond the capabilities of current air traffic management approaches, as current day approaches are typically labor-intensive. It is crucial to safely guarantee operations of increasingly autonomous vehicles at scale in order for UAM to be commercially viable.
- *Decentralization* - The environment is likely to encompass multiple service providers and stakeholders. Each stakeholder will have potentially competing priorities and requirements. Consequently, the full state of the entire system is unlikely to be controlled or even observed by a single entity.
- *Transparency* - With companies ranging from startups to corporations developing UAM vehicles, services, and capabilities, there is a disconnect between regulation and the pace of technological development. Bridging the gap between regulation and real-world implementation practices is necessary for a viable path to deployment.
- *Flexibility* - The technological and regulatory landscape of UAM is rapidly changing. Any proposed framework that cannot efficiently incorporate a change in regulation or emerging capabilities is not a viable solution.
- *Auditability* - All violations of regulations must be formally accounted for and reported. Our proposed method implicitly allows for such an analysis, as it not only synthesizes a control strategy for air traffic management but also the associated violation.

1.5   Path to Deployment

Assessing the safety of an increasingly autonomous system relies on being able to bound the behavior and interactions of the components of the system as well as its interfaces with its operational environment. Performance-based regulation is employed in aviation to specify explicit properties that must be evinced by a component or element of the system (and/or operational environment) in order for the system safety claims to be met. For example, 14 CFR §107.49 (d) states that: "If the small unmanned aircraft is powered, ensure that there is enough available power for the small unmanned aircraft system to operate for the intended operational time". This fuel requirement forms a temporal logic constraint on the vehicle during its flight. The controller synthesis method for the vertihubs must adhere to this constraint, in order to demonstrate compliance to 14 CFR §107.49. The minimum violation guarantees provided by the presented synthesis process help to demonstrate that this regulation will be satisfied as much as possible throughout the flight process. Thus, the guarantees provided by the synthesis method presented in this paper may serve as a partial means of compliance to the regulation—supplemented with the generation of test and design analysis artifacts as well as operational procedures.

The presented synthesis framework provides a path to deployment of these increasingly autonomous systems in safety-critical contexts. Air traffic management services, such as aircraft separation, may then be offered in a UAS Traffic

Management (UTM) inspired framework, which interfaces with today's traditional Air Traffic Management framework [17]. In this framework, authority may be delegated by the FAA to provide select air traffic management services such as low-altitude weather information, congestion management, terrain avoidance, route planning, re-rerouting, separation management, and contingency management [13,15]. One of the main attributes of the UTM system is that it does not require human operators to monitor every vehicle continuously, as in the traditional ATM system, thereby enabling increasingly autonomous realizations of specified air traffic management functions. We believe that integration of the approach in this paper into a UTM-like construct provides a path to deployment for UAM operations, as the provided safety guarantees will greatly enhance the assurance case for higher-risk operations currently not supported by UTM (e.g., operations in dense urban environments with UAS exceeding 55 lbs).

1.6   Related Work

Some preliminary work is being done in cooperative ATM for next generation air traffic management [16], but this work considers a scheduled approach for large passenger aircraft and cannot handle management for on-demand flights. Similarly, there is work done on distributed control for ATM of small unmanned aerial systems (UAS) [8], but this work relies on cloud based architectures that do not currently satisfy strict aviation safety requirements. Hybrid control approaches have been applied [19], however scalability proves to be an issue. To the best of our knowledge, this is the first approach implementing minimally violating controller synthesis for large-scale UAM ATM operations. Formally verified tools such as DAIDALUS [14] provide safety guarantees at lower levels of operations, however, it does not handle the fleet-level operations. Another approach called *runtime enforcement* [6,18] aims to guarantee a specified property by detecting and altering the behavior of the system at runtime. An existing approach called shielding [4,12] uses reactive synthesis and assumes that the shield has full knowledge and control of the whole system—in this case the entire UAM system and the vehicles it handles. A technique for synthesizing quantitative shields for multi-agent systems in a fully centralized manner was presented in [1]. However, all these approaches are only applicable if a feasible solution exists. If it is not possible to satisfy all safety requirements, no solution is possible. In contrast, in the approach presented in this work, if no feasible solution exists, we can still synthesize a controller that minimally violates safety.

Our approach is based on minimum-violation planning [20,21] for systems that are subject to potentially infeasible safety requirements. Given a prioritized safety specification, which specifies the priority and weight of each safety requirement, minimum-violation planning computes a plan that minimally violates the requirements. In particular, we propose a novel *decentralized approach* to minimum-violation planning in order to handle large-scale systems that cannot be handled by current state-of-the-art approaches.

2   Notation and Setting

In this section, we present the relevant technical notation for the minimum violation synthesis problem in the UAM setting.

2.1   Operating Environment

Recall that the environment is divided into smaller regions called vertihubs. Each vertihub is governed by a *vertihub controller* that has radio line of sight to all vehicles in the region denoted as T_i as shown in Fig. 2. A vertihub controller is responsible for managing *requests* by UAM vehicles (henceforth referred to as vehicles) to either *land at* or *take off from* a desired vertiport in its region or *pass through* to a neighboring region.

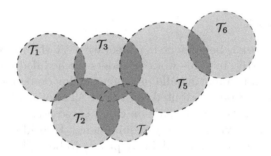

Fig. 2. Example UAM operating environment. Green circles correspond to the regions of vertihub controllers.

Requests. We define a request as a tuple $O = (r, T, c)$ where

- $r \in \mathcal{R}$ is the request class from a predefined set of classes $\mathcal{R}$. Request classes include *landing at a particular vertiport in the region, pass-through region, take-off from vertiport in the region*. Depending on the nature of the problem, $\mathcal{R}$ can be defined to capture all types of desired outcomes for vehicles.
- $T \in \mathbb{N}$ is the amount of time left before the request *must* be granted. t can function as an analogue for fuel reserves as vehicles requesting to land cannot hover indefinitely.
- $c \in C$ is the class of UAM vehicle from a predefined set of vehicles C.

At any given timestep t the vertihub is managing requests from multiple vehicles. We define the initial set of requests as the *request allocation* and denote it as $\mathcal{O}^{\text{init}}$. We model the *vertihub controller* that is responsible for managing these requests as a *labeled weighted finite transition system*.

Example 1. Tower T_1 is given a set of N requests to handle $\mathcal{O}^{\text{init}} = \{O_1^{T_1} \ldots O_N^{T_1}\}$. For example, $O_1^{T_1} = (port\,A, 5, passenger)$ corresponds to a request by a *passenger vehicle* trying to land at port A in *at most* 5 time steps.

Transition System Model for Vertihub Controller. A vertihub controller is modeled as a tuple referred to as a labeled weighted finite transition system $\mathcal{T}_i = (S_i, s_{\text{init}_i}, \Delta_i, \text{AP}_i, L_i)$ where

- S_i is a finite state space. It is the set of all currently unapproved requests. Formally, if there are currently m unapproved requests, we write $S_i = \{O_{i,1} \dots O_{i,m}\}$. We note that the state space can also include additional features of interest such as number of vehicles in the airspace, their landing/take-off statuses, and others. However, for notational simplicity we do not include these in the definition presented in this paper. In practice, these features, alongside the relevant modifications to the transition function, are straight-forward to include.
- $s_{\text{init}_i} \in S_i$ is the initial set of requests $\mathcal{O}_i^{\text{init}}$.
- $\Delta_i \subseteq S_i \times S_i$ is the deterministic transition function that governs how requests evolve. We have $(S_i^t, S_i^{t+1}) \in \Delta_i$ if:
  - all *approved* requests at timestep t, denoted $\mathcal{O}_{i,a}^t \subseteq S_i^t$, are not present in S_i^{t+1}, i.e., if $O_{i,j} \in \mathcal{O}_{i,a}^t$ then $O_{i,j} \notin S_i^{t+1}$, and
  - all *unapproved* requests at timestep t, denoted $S_i^t \setminus \mathcal{O}_{i,a}^t$, have their time remaining decremented, i.e., for all $O_{i,j} = (r, T, c)$ and $O_{i,j} \in S_i^t \setminus \mathcal{O}_{i,a}^t$, we will have $O_{i,j} \in S_i^{t+1}$ and $O_{i,j} = (r, \max(T - 1, 0), c)$. Informally, if request is not approved Δ_i decrements the remaining timer on the request by 1.
- AP is a set of atomic propositions.
- $L : S \rightarrow 2^{\text{AP}}$ is the labeling function.

At every timestep, the decision problem for the controller is to choose a set $O_{i,a}^t \subseteq S_i^t$ of requests to approve. The controller will also have the option to reroute the request to neighboring controllers. We discuss this process formally in Sect. 3.

Example 2. Consider vertihub controller $\mathcal{T}_1$ with two pending requests $O_1^{\mathcal{T}_1} = (port\ A, 5, passenger)$ and $O_2^{\mathcal{T}_1} = (port\ A, 3, passenger)$. In this case, at time step t we have $S_1^t = \{O_{1,1}, O_{1,2}\}$ where $O_{1,1} = O_1^{\mathcal{T}_1}$ and $O_{1,2} = O_2^{\mathcal{T}_1}$. Let us assume at time step t that the controller approves request $O_{1,2}$. We denote this as $\mathcal{O}_{1,a}^t = \{O_{1,2}\}$ and we will have $S_1^{t+1} = \{O_{1,2}\}$ where $O_{1,1} = (port\ A, 4, passenger)$.

A finite trace of $\mathcal{T}_i$ is a finite sequence of states $\tau_i = s_{i,0} s_{i,1} \dots s_{i,n}$ such that $s_{i,0} = s_{\text{init}_i}$ and $(s_{i,j}, s_{i,j+1}) \in \Delta_i$, for all $j \in \mathbb{N}_{\leq n-1}$. A finite trace $\tau = s_0 s_1 \dots s_n$ produces a finite word $w(\tau) = L(s_0) L(s_1) \dots L(s_n)$. For any $s \in S$, we let $\text{Traces}(\mathcal{T}, s)$ represents the set of all finite traces of $\mathcal{T}$ that ends with s.

The aim of the transition system $\mathcal{T}_i$ is to reach a *goal state* denoted $s_{\text{final}} \in S_i$. Since the hub controller needs to eventually grant all requests, s_{final} corresponds to the state with no more pending requests. Formally, we have $s_{\text{final}} = \emptyset$.

The goal of this approach is to synthesize a trace for each vertihub such that requests are accepted in a manner that satisfies all regulations. However, if this is not possible, it must approve requests in a way that minimally violates regulations. We employ linear temporal logic due to its ability to formally express a wide array or requirements.

We employ finite linear temporal logic (FLTL) to precisely describe the safety-oriented regulations. We note this FLTL has been used in the context of autonomous driving to formally represent road safety laws for planning [20,21].

Finite Linear Temporal Logic. An FLTL formula is built up from (a) a set of atomic propositions; (b) the logic connectives: negation ($\neg$), disjunction ($\vee$), conjunction ($\wedge$), and material implication ($\implies$); and (c) the temporal operators: next ($\bigcirc$), always ($\square$), eventually ($\diamond$), and until ($\mathcal{U}$). We refer the reader to [11] for full FLTL semantics.

An FLTL formula ψ over a set AP of atomic propositions is interpreted over a finite word $w = l_0 l_1 \ldots l_n \in (2^{AP})^{n+1}$, and we write $w \models \psi$ if w satisfies ψ. In particular, consider $p \in AP$. Then, $w \models p$ if and only if $p \in l_0$. Also, $w \models \square p$ if and only if $p \in l_i$ for all $i \in \{0, \ldots, n\}$.

Example 3. 14 CFR §107.49 (d) requires the vehicle to have enough power for its operations and hence, a vertihub cannot force a vehicle to loiter for too long. We can capture this as a specification $\psi = \square\{\neg fuel\_too\_low_i\}$ where $fuel\_too\_low_i$ is an atomic proposition that is true when request $O_i = (r, T, c)$ has $T = 0$.

Prioritized Safety Specification. A *prioritized safety specification* is a tuple $\mathcal{P} = (AP, \Omega, \Psi, \varpi)$ where AP is a set of atomic propositions, Ω is a set of FLTL formulas over AP, $\Psi = (\Psi_1, \Psi_2, \ldots, \Psi_N)$, $\Psi_i \subseteq \Omega$ for all $i \in \{1, \ldots, N\}$, and $\varpi : \Omega \to \mathbb{N}$ is the priority function that assigns the weight to each $\psi \in \Omega$.

Example 4. A potential prioritized safety specification $\Psi = \{\Psi_1, \Psi_2\}$ for a vertihub to satisfy is $\Psi_1 = \{\psi_{1,1}\}, \Psi_2 = \{\psi_{2,1}, \psi_{2,2}, \psi_{2,3}\}$ where

- $\psi_{1,1} =$ Never allow the timer on a request to expire.
- $\psi_{2,1} =$ Do not land vehicles past a vertiport's capacity.
- $\psi_{2,2} =$ Do not allow more than M vehicles in the vertihub's airspace at a time.
- $\psi_{2,3} =$ Do not land a vehicle at a vertiport it did not request.

Note that the requirements at level i are strictly more important than those at level i+1, i.e., the system first attempts to minimize the amount of violation of level-1 requirements. Then among all the policies that minimize the violation of level-1 requirements, it attempts to minimize the amount of violation of level-2 requirements, and so on. In Example 4, the first specification is the highest priority and the remaining specifications are all of equal priority. We use this example in the case study detailed in the Experimental Results section.

Lack of Safety. Consider an FLTL formula ψ over AP and a finite word $w = l_0 l_1 \ldots l_n \in (2^{\mathrm{AP}})^{n+1}$. The *lack of safety* of w with respect to ψ is defined as

$$\lambda(w, \psi) = \min_{I \subseteq \mathbb{N}_{\leq n} | \mathsf{vanish}(w, I) \models \psi} |I|, \tag{1}$$

where for any given finite sequence $w = l_0 l_1 \ldots l_n$ and a set $I \subseteq \mathbb{N}$, $\mathsf{vanish}(w, I)$ is defined as a subsequence of w obtained by removing all l_i, $i \in I$.

Let $\mathcal{P} = (\mathrm{AP}, \Omega, \Psi, \varpi)$ be a prioritized safety specification where $\Psi = (\Psi_1, \Psi_2, \ldots, \Psi_N)$. We define the *lack of safety* of w with respect to $\mathcal{P}$ as

$$\lambda(w, \mathcal{P}) = (\lambda(w, \Psi_1), \ldots, \lambda(w, \Psi_N)) \in \mathbb{N}^N, \tag{2}$$

where for each $i \in \{1, \ldots, N\}$,

$$\lambda(w, \Psi_i) = \sum_{\psi \in \Psi_i} \varpi(\psi) \lambda(w, \psi). \tag{3}$$

Note that there are two mechanisms to address the unequal importance of safety specifications. Namely, the prioritization of specifications by Ψ and the weighting function $\varpi(\psi)$. The weights ϖ indicates the importance among different requirements within the same level.

The lack of safety of a trace τ of a finite transition system with respect to $\mathcal{P}$ is defined based on its produced word, i.e., $\lambda(\tau, \mathcal{P}) = \lambda(w(\tau), \mathcal{P})$. The standard lexicographical order is used to compare the lack of safety between different traces.

Remark 1. There are two mechanisms to specify the unequal importance of different specifications, the hierarchy $(\Psi_1, \Psi_2, \ldots, \Psi_N)$ and the weights captured by ϖ. As the standard lexicographical order is used to compare the lack of safety between different traces, the algorithm first minimizes the lack of safety with respect to the specifications in Ψ_1. Then, among all the traces that minimizes the lack of safety with respect to Ψ_1, it minimizes the lack of safety with respect to the specifications in Ψ_2, and so on. The weights ϖ only matter for the specifications within the same level of hierarchy.

3 Problem Formulation

Global System. We define the global system as the composition of the vertihub controllers. Assume we have N vertihub controllers $\mathcal{T}_1 \ldots \mathcal{T}_N$. We define a connectivity graph $G_{\mathcal{T}}$ as a directed graph with each vertex corresponding to a controller. We say two controllers are *connected* if they share an edge in the graph. Let $connect(\mathcal{T}_i)$ be the set of hub controllers $\mathcal{T}_j$ where $i \neq j$, that share an edge with $\mathcal{T}_i$. For example, in Fig. 2, overlapping hub regions share an edge in the corresponding directed graph in Fig. 3, and therefore the corresponding controllers are connected.

Formally, we define the global system as a tuple $(\mathcal{O}^{\mathrm{init}}, \Phi, \mathcal{T})$ where $\mathcal{O}^{\mathrm{init}} = \{O_1, \ldots, O_M\}$ is the global set of requests across all vertihubs, $\Phi : \{\mathcal{T}_1, \ldots, \mathcal{T}_N\} \rightarrow$

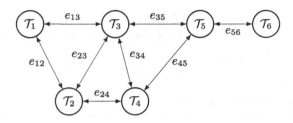

Fig. 3. The connectivity graph G_T of the UAM hub controllers T depicted in Fig. 2. Each edge e_{ij} corresponds to T_i and T_j being connected, i.e., the outputs of T_i are inputs to T_j and vice versa.

$2^{|\mathcal{O}^{init}|}$ is the *request allocation function* such that $\Phi(T_i)$ is the request set allocated to hub T_i, and $T = (S, s_{init}, \Delta, \text{AP}, L)$ is a networked composition of N hub controllers $T_1, \ldots, T_N$ such that:

- $S = (S_1, S_2, \ldots, S_N)$ where S_i is the set of all currently unapproved requests assigned to hub T_i. Note, however, that due to possible reallocation of requests, it is not necessary that S_i only contains the requests in s_{init_i}. Instead, it contains requests in $\bigcup_i s_{init_i}$ such that each request is assigned to at most one hub, i.e., $S_i \cap S_j = \emptyset$ for all i, j.
- $s_{init} = (s_{init_1}, s_{init_2}, \ldots, s_{init_N})$
- $\Delta \subseteq S \times S$ such that $(S^t, S^{t+1}) \in \Delta$ if for each unapproved request $O_i = (r, T, c) \in S_i^t$ at each hub T_i,
  - it remains unapproved with its time remaining decremented and either assigned to the same hub, i.e., $O_i = (r, T-1, c) \in S_i^{t+1}$, or a connected hub, i.e., $O_i = (r, T-1, c) \in S_j^{t+1}$ for some $T_j \in connect(T_i)$, or
  - it is approved by hub T_i or a connected hub $T_j \in connect(T_i)$, i.e., $O_i \in \mathcal{O}_{i,a}^t \cup \mathcal{O}_{j,a}^t$, in which case the request is not present in $\bigcup_k S_k^{t+1}$.
- $\text{AP} = \text{AP}_1 \cup \text{AP}_2 \cup \cdots \cup \text{AP}_N$
- $L : S \to 2^{\text{AP}}$ such that $L(s_1, \ldots, s_N) = \bigcup_i L_i(s_i)$.

Put simply, we construct the transition function Δ as the composition of *intra-hub* transitions and *inter-hub* transitions. Since vehicles can only move between neighbouring hubs, *inter-hub* transitions are limited to occurring only between those hubs that are connected in the graph G_T.

Vertihub Violation Cost. Each vertihub T_i is given a prioritized safety specification $\mathcal{P}_i$ and request allocation $\Phi(T_i) = s_{init_i}$. Given a request allocation function Φ, the *violation cost* of vertihub T_i executing a finite trace $\tau_i \in \text{Traces}(T_i, s_{final})$ is denoted $\lambda_{\Phi(T_i)}(\tau_i, \mathcal{P}_i)$. We denote the *optimal* violation cost of T_i for a request allocation function Φ as $\lambda_{\Phi(T_i)}^* = \min_{\tau_i \in \text{Traces}(T_i, s_{final})} \lambda_{\Phi(T_i)}(\tau_i, \mathcal{P}_i)$.

The cost of the global system T is dependent on the conjunction of the prioritized specifications $\mathcal{P} = \mathcal{P}_1 \wedge \mathcal{P}_2 \wedge \cdots \wedge \mathcal{P}_N$, global requests $\mathcal{O}^{init}$, and request allocation function Φ. Formally, we define

$$\lambda_\Phi = \sum_{i=1}^{N} \lambda_{\Phi(\mathcal{T}_i)}^*. \tag{4}$$

3.1 Problem Statement

Given a set of N hub controllers $\mathcal{T}_1 \dots \mathcal{T}_N$, a connectivity graph $G_{\mathcal{T}}$ and a prioritized safety specification for each controller $\mathcal{P}_1, \dots, \mathcal{P}_N$ with $\mathcal{P} = \mathcal{P}_1 \wedge \cdots \wedge \mathcal{P}_N$, construct a request allocation function Φ and corresponding trace $\tau^* = \{\tau_1, \dots, \tau_N\}$ where $\tau_i \in \text{Traces}(\mathcal{T}_i, s_{\text{final}})$ that minimizes the lack of safety for the entire system. Formally,

$$\tau^* = \underset{\tau \in \{\text{Traces}(\mathcal{T}, s_{\text{final}})\}}{\arg\min} \lambda(\tau, \mathcal{P}). \tag{5}$$

4 Solution Approach

4.1 Overview

Motivated by the cost structure in (4), we decompose the traffic management problem into two subproblems:

1. Compute an optimal request allocation Φ^* such that

$$\sum_{i=1}^{N} \lambda_{\Phi^*(\mathcal{T}_i)}^* \leq \sum_{i=1}^{N} \lambda_{\Phi(\mathcal{T}_i)}^*,$$

   for any request allocation Φ. Informally, the optimal request allocation Φ^* will have a lower or equal cost compared with any other allocation.
2. Given a request allocation Φ, compute an optimal trace τ_i^* for each vertiport $\mathcal{T}_i$ such that

$$\lambda_{\Phi(\mathcal{T}_i)}(\tau_i^*, \mathcal{P}_i) \leq \lambda_{\Phi(\mathcal{T}_i)}(\tau_i, \mathcal{P}_i),$$

   for any trace $\tau_i \in \text{Traces}(\mathcal{T}_i, s_{\text{final}_i})$.

The second problem can be solved using minimum-violation planning as in [20, 21]. To solve the first problem, we need to find the globally optimal request allocation for all the vertihubs. This is a combinatorially hard problem. To solve the problem in a distributed manner, we propose an auction-based algorithm. In each round, each vertihub identifies potential requests to be reallocated and offers each of these requests to other connected vertihubs. The request with highest cost is then selected, and a connected vertihub accepts this request if it can accommodate the extra request with less cost than the original vertihub. Finally, the request will be reallocated to the vertihub that can accommodate the request with the lowest cost. This auction-based request allocation ensures that the overall cost decreases in each round and terminates when no more requests can be reallocated without extra cost.

Algorithm. Given a request allocation Φ, we define the cost of vertihub $\mathcal{T}_i$ accommodating a request O as

$$C_i^{\Phi}(O) = \min_{\tau_i} \lambda_{\mathcal{O}_O^i}(\tau_i, \mathcal{P}_i) - \min_{\tau_i} \lambda_{\mathcal{O}_{\emptyset}^i}(\tau_i, \mathcal{P}_i), \tag{6}$$

where $\mathcal{O}_O^i = \Phi(\mathcal{T}_i) \cup \{O\}$ is the set of requests allocated to $\mathcal{T}_i$ together with the request O, and $\mathcal{O}_{\emptyset}^i = \Phi(\mathcal{T}_i) \setminus \{O\}$ is the set of requests allocated to $\mathcal{T}_i$ without the request O.

The algorithm initializes Φ based on the desired location associated with each request. Then, it updates Φ iteratively as follows.

(a) Initialize the set $\mathbb{O}$ of potential requests to be reallocated in this iteration as the empty set.
(b) Each vertihub $\mathcal{T}_i$ computes the cost $C_i^{\Phi}(O)$ for accommodating each request $O \in \Phi(\mathcal{T}_i)$. It then adds each request as well as its associated cost $(O, C_i^{\Phi}(O))$ to $\mathbb{O}$ for all requests O with $C_i^{\Phi}(O) > 0$.
(c) If $\mathbb{O}$ is empty, then the algorithm terminates and outputs Φ. Otherwise, we let O^* be the request with the highest cost in $\mathbb{O}$ and C^* be its associated cost.
(d) Each vertihub $\mathcal{T}_i$ computes the cost $C_i^{\Phi}(O^*)$ for accommodating O^*. Consider two possible cases.
  – $C_i^{\Phi}(O^*) \geq C^*$ for all $\mathcal{T}_i$, i.e., no other vertihub can better accommodate this request. Then, the request O^* is removed from $\mathbb{O}$ and the algorithm goes back to step (c) to attempt reallocating the next worst request.
  – $C_i^{\Phi}(O^*) < C^*$ for some $\mathcal{T}_i$. Then, Φ is updated so that the request O^* is allocated to $\mathcal{T}_{i^*}$ that minimizes the cost of accommodating O^*, i.e., $C_{i^*}^{\Phi}(O^*) \leq C_i^{\Phi}(O^*)$ for all $\mathcal{T}_i$. This iteration finishes and the algorithm starts the new iteration with step (a). In the case where there are multiple vertihubs with equal lowest cost C^*, a tie breaker heuristic, e.g., based on tower id and priority, can be used.

As the number of requests is finite, the cost is non-negative and strictly decreases in every iteration except the last iteration. Thus, the algorithm is guaranteed to terminate and output a request allocation that is at least as good as the initial allocation. This is formally stated as follows.

Proposition 1. *Let Φ^{init} be the initial request allocation. Then, the algorithm terminates with request allocation Φ such that $\lambda_{\Phi} \leq \lambda_{\Phi^{init}}$.*

We remark that for ease of presentation the algorithm assumes the vertihub network is fully connected. In implementation, it is straightforward to modify the algorithm to directly incorporate the network constraints.

5   Experimental Results

In this section, we detail the results of a case study implementing the presented algorithm[1]. All experiments were run on an AMD Ryzen 5 3600x processor with

---

[1] The code for the implementation can be found at https://github.com/JoeMuff999/Automata-Testing.

6 cores @ 4.3 Ghz and 16 GB RAM. For the purposes of this demonstration, we use the prioritized safety specifications given in Example 3. We use the toolbox TuLiP [22] to compute minimally violating traces. We randomly generate vehicle requests in a format compatible with the Mission Planner Algorithm [10] developed at NASA Langley. The data contains simulated, timestamped on-demand requests for origin-destination trips corresponding to vertiports in particular vertihubs. We then run our algorithm to minimally violate the regulations described in Example 3.

Scalability. Figure 4 shows the runtime per iteration per vertihub for different numbers of total vertihubs as well as the number of iterations until the algorithm converges.

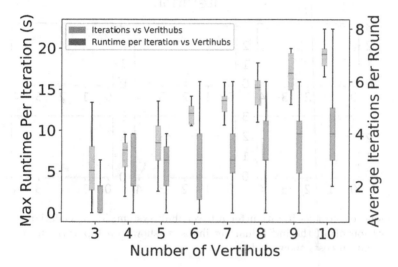

Fig. 4. Worst case runtime per iteration per vertihub (blue) and iterations until convergence (green). (Color figure online)

It is clear that the average runtime scales efficiently as the number of vertihubs increases. In general, the total number of iterations before convergence also stays relatively constant albeit with a higher variance as the system size increases. However, since the overall violation of the system's safety decreases with every iteration, in practice, we can always terminate the algorithm after a certain number of iterations and still have reduced the total violation cost. We note that even the smallest instance of the problem, i.e., 3 vertihubs with a maximum of 5 requests was unable to be solved in under 10 min using the centralized method in [20]. Furthermore, these results are a worst-case analysis as we assume the vertihubs are fully connected, i.e., all vertihubs can transfer requests to any other vertihub. In practice, the pool of vertihubs that can accept requests from other vertihubs will be smaller and this will limit the number of computations needed.

Violation Cost. To demonstrate the decreasing violation cost, we run our algorithm on the specific case of a 6 vertihub system with 10 requests. As shown in Fig. 5, the initial request allocation has a cost of 11 for the highest priority regulation. After 4 iterations, the cost has decreased to 0 while the cost for the second priority regulation stays at 2.

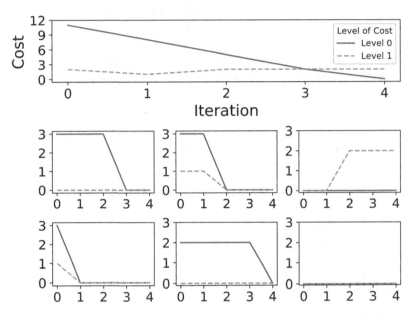

Fig. 5. Violation cost vs iteration for a 6 vertihub system. Total violation, i.e., sum of the violation of all the individual vertihubs, is shown on top with the individual vertihub violation costs shown below.

Batch Processing. The presented method in this paper relies on processing batches of requests at a time. However, in practice, requests arrive sequentially in real time. In most cases however, the requests are known in advance and hence can be planned for. In this result, we demonstrate the effect of different batch sizes on overall violation cost. The data used in the simulation was generated by NASA Langley in conjunction with partners performing UAM demand studies. We divide incoming requests into batches of 5, 10, and 15 requests at a time. Each batch is then processed before moving on to the next batch. We then sum the total violation cost across all batches for the entire data set. We note that we only report the level 1 violation cost as the level 0 violation cost is 0 in all cases.

As seen in Table 1, violation cost reduces as the batch size increases. This result is expected as the smaller batch sizes typically result in myopic plans that can cause violations down the road. However, it is not necessarily feasible to plan with large batch sizes as it requires a large look-ahead which may not be possible in practice.

Table 1. Level 1 violation cost and corresponding average synthesis time per batch per tower for different batch sizes.

Batch size	Violation cost	Computation time (s)
5	71	6.6
10	63	32.5
15	56	161.9

In this paper, we focus on the decentralization of the minimum violation planning procedure. Looking forward, we plan to extend the work in this paper to a *real-time* planning framework that can resynthesize plans at runtime as batches of requests arrive in order to avoid violations resulting from myopic planning.

6   Conclusion

The work in this paper is the first to consider a decentralized minimum violation planning approach for UAM traffic management. The method is generalizable and flexible, as it is agnostic to the design of the underlying vehicles being controlled, and it can handle any changes in the safety constraints and still provide guarantees. Empirical results show the practical viability of our approach and is able to handle large numbers of connected vertihubs and requests. For future work, we aim to incorporate online re-planning in order to react to incoming vehicle requests in real-time and still satisfy regulations as much as possible.

Acknowledgements. This work was partially supported by grants NSF 1652113, NASA 80NSSC21M0087, and AFOSR FA9550-19-1-0005.

References

1. Bharadwaj, S., Bloem, R., Dimitrova, R., Konighofer, B., Topcu, U.: Synthesis of minimum-cost shields for multi-agent systems. In: 2019 American Control Conference (ACC), pp. 1048–1055 (2019)
2. Bharadwaj, S., Carr, S.P., Neogi, N.A., Topcu, U.: Decentralized control synthesis for air traffic management in urban air mobility. IEEE Trans. Control Netw. Syst. 1–1 (2021)
3. Bharadwaj, S., Carr, S., Neogi, N., Poonawala, H., Chueca, A.B., Topcu, U.: Traffic management for urban air mobility. In: Badger, J.M., Rozier, K.Y. (eds.) NFM 2019. LNCS, vol. 11460, pp. 71–87. Springer, Cham (2019). https://doi.org/10. 1007/978-3-030-20652-9_5
4. Bloem, R., Könighofer, B., Könighofer, R., Wang, C.: Shield synthesis: In: Baier, C., Tinelli, C. (eds.) TACAS 2015. LNCS, vol. 9035, pp. 533–548. Springer, Heidelberg (2015). https://doi.org/10.1007/978-3-662-46681-0_51
5. EmbraerX: Flight plan 2030: An air traffic management concept for urban air mobility. EmbraerX (2019)

6. Falcone, Y.: You should better enforce than verify. In: Barringer, H., et al. (eds.) RV 2010. LNCS, vol. 6418, pp. 89–105. Springer, Heidelberg (2010). https://doi.org/10.1007/978-3-642-16612-9_9
7. Federal Aviation Administration: Fact Sheet - Facts about the FAA and Air Traffic Control
8. Foina, A.G., Sengupta, R., Lerchi, P., Liu, Z., Krainer, C.: Drones in smart cities: overcoming barriers through air traffic control research. In: 2015 Workshop on Research, Education and Development of Unmanned Aerial Systems (RED-UAS), pp. 351–359 (2015)
9. Goyal, R.: Urban air mobility (UAM) market study (2018)
10. Guerreiro, N.M., Butler, R.W., Maddalon, J.M., Hagen, G.E.: Mission planner algorithm for urban air mobility-initial performance characterization. In: AIAA Aviation 2019 Forum, p. 3626 (2019)
11. Gunter, E., Peled, D.: Temporal debugging for concurrent systems. In: Katoen, J.-P., Stevens, P. (eds.) TACAS 2002. LNCS, vol. 2280, pp. 431–444. Springer, Heidelberg (2002). https://doi.org/10.1007/3-540-46002-0_30
12. Könighofer, B., et al.: Shield synthesis. Formal Meth. Syst. Des. 51(2), 332–361 (2017). https://doi.org/10.1007/s10703-017-0276-9
13. Moore, A., et al.: Testing enabling technologies for safe UAS urban operations. In: Proceedings of the 2018 Aviation, Technology, Integration, and Operations Conference. No. AIAA-2018-3200, Atlanta, Georgia, June 2018
14. Muñoz, C., et al.: Daidalus: detect and avoid alerting logic for unmanned systems. In: 2015 IEEE/AIAA 34th Digital Avionics Systems Conference (DASC), pp. 5A1-1-5A1-12, September 2015
15. Neogi, N., Cuong, C., Dill, E.: A risk based assessment of a small UAS cargo delivery operation in proximity to urban areas. In: Proceedings of the 37th Digital Avionics Systems Conference (DASC). London, England, UK, September 2018
16. Prevot, T., et al.: Co-operative air traffic management: a technology enabled concept for the next generation air transportation system. In: 5th USA/Europe Air Traffic management Research and Development Seminar, Baltimore, MD, June 2005
17. Prevot, T., Rios, J., Kopardekar, P., Robinson, J.E., Johnson, M., Jung, J.: UAS traffic management (UTM) concept of operations to safely enable low altitude flight operations. In: Proceedings of the 2018 Aviation, Technology, Integration, and Operations Conference. No. AIAA-2016-3292, Washington, DC, June 2016
18. Schneider, F.B.: Enforceable security policies. ACM Trans. Inf. Syst. Secur. 3(1), 30–50 (2000)
19. Tomlin, C., Pappas, G., Lygeros, J., Godbole, D., Sastry, S., Meyer, G.: Hybrid control in air traffic management systems. IFAC Proc. Vol. 29(1), 5512–5517 (1996)
20. Tumova, J., Castro, L.I.R., Karaman, S., Frazzoli, E., Rus, D.: Minimum-violation LTL planning with conflicting specifications. In: 2013 American Control Conference. pp. 200–205, June 2013
21. Tumova, J., Hall, G.C., Karaman, S., Frazzoli, E., Rus, D.: Least-violating control strategy synthesis with safety rules. In: Proceedings of the 16th International Conference on Hybrid Systems: Computation and Control, pp. 1–10. HSCC 2013, ACM, New York, NY, USA (2013). https://doi.org/10.1145/2461328.2461330
22. Wongpiromsarn, T., Topcu, U., Ozay, N., Xu, H., Murray, R.M.: Tulip: a software toolbox for receding horizon temporal logic planning. In: Proceedings of the 14th International Conference on Hybrid Systems: Computation and Control, pp. 313–314 (2011)

Integrating Formal Verification and Assurance: An Inspection Rover Case Study

Hamza Bourbouh[1], Marie Farrell[3]([✉]) [ID], Anastasia Mavridou[1] [ID],
Irfan Sljivo[1] [ID], Guillaume Brat[2], Louise A. Dennis[4] [ID], and Michael Fisher[4] [ID]

[1] KBR/NASA Ames Research Center, Mountain View, USA
[2] NASA Ames Research Center, Mountain View, USA
[3] Department of Computer Science, Maynooth University, Maynooth, Ireland
marie.farrell@mu.ie
[4] Department of Computer Science, University of Manchester, Manchester, UK

Abstract. The complexity and flexibility of autonomous robotic systems necessitates a range of distinct verification tools. This presents new challenges not only for design verification but also for assurance approaches. Combining the distinct formal verification tools, while maintaining sufficient formal coherence to provide compelling assurance evidence is difficult, often being abandoned for less formal approaches. In this paper we demonstrate, through a case study, how a variety of distinct formal techniques can be brought together in order to develop a justifiable assurance case. We use the AdvoCATE assurance case tool to guide our analyses and to integrate the artifacts from the formal methods that we use, namely: FRET, COCOSIM and Event-B. While we present our methodology as applied to a specific Inspection Rover case study, we believe that this combination provides benefits in maintaining coherent formal links across development and assurance processes for a wide range of autonomous robotic systems.

1 Introduction

The adoption of formal methods in industry has been slower than their development and adoption in research. One of the main pitfalls is the difficulty in integrating the results from formal methods with non-formal parts of the system development process. A central stumbling block is the formalisation of the (informal) natural language descriptions needed to perform the formal analysis, as well as the analysis and interpretation of the formal verification results.

Work supported by NASA ARMD System-Wide Safety Project, UK Research and Innovation and EPSRC Hubs for "Robotics and AI in Hazardous Environments": EP/R026092 (FAIR-SPACE), and the Royal Academy of Engineering.
The authors thank Dimitra Giannakopoulou for her valuable feedback on this work.
M. Farrell—Majority of Farrell's work took place at the Universities of Liverpool & Manchester.

© Springer Nature Switzerland AG 2021
A. Dutle et al. (Eds.): NFM 2021, LNCS 12673, pp. 53–71, 2021.
https://doi.org/10.1007/978-3-030-76384-8_4

The integrated formal methods approach relies on various tools cooperating to ease the burden of formal methods at various phases of system development. This often involves facilitating the use of one tool/formalism from within another (e.g. Event-B∥CSP [41]), the development of a tool/formalism that incorporates multiple others (e.g. Why3 [20]), or the construction of systematic translations between tools/formalizms (e.g. EventB2JML [40]). Recent work argues that, for autonomous robotic systems, the use of multiple formal and non-formal verification techniques is both beneficial and necessary to ensure that such systems behave correctly [19,30]. Notably, the usually modular nature of robotic systems makes them more amenable to an integrated verification approach than monolithic systems [8]. The inherent modularity in robotic systems usually stems from the use of a node-based middleware such as the Robot Operating System (ROS) [39]. However, other middlewares such as NASA's core Flight System (cFS) [36] also support the development of similarly complex, modular systems.

In this paper, we study the support for integrating formal verification results at both system- and component-level in the design, implementation and assurance of a critical system, namely, an autonomous rover undertaking an inspection mission. In contrast to usual approaches to integrating formal methods, such as those described above, we use an assurance case as the point of integration rather than building bespoke tools or defining mathematical translations between specific formal methods. In this way, we harness the benefits of an integrated approach to verification without the usual overheads. Specifically, we use AdvoCATE [16] to perform safety engineering and assurance, FRET [23] to elicit and formalize requirements, and COCOSIM [6] with Kind2 to perform compositional verification of the system-level requirements. Further, we use Event-B [2] and Kind2 for the component-level formal verification. AdvoCATE facilitates the integration of the artifacts/evidence produced from these tools.

In summary, we contribute an inspection rover case study that demonstrates:

- how these tools can be linked via an argument in an assurance case.
- the benefit of using distinct tools due to their limitations (e.g. Kind2 would time out on certain properties that were verified in Event-B).
- how developing with formal methods in mind from the outset can influence the design of the system, making it more amenable to formal verification.

2   Tool Support

Assurance Case Automation Toolset (AdvoCATE) [16] supports the development and management of assurance cases, which are composed of all of the assurance artifacts that are created during system development. To enable automation, AdvoCATE is built with a formal basis where all of the assurance artifacts can be defined and formally related. Some artifacts can be created directly in AdvoCATE (e.g., hazard log, bow tie diagrams), while others, such as formal verification results, can be imported. AdvoCATE uses the Goal Structuring Notation (GSN) [1] to document assurance cases in the form of arguments.

Formal Requirements Elicitation Tool (FRET) [23,24] is an open source framework [22] for the elicitation, formalization and understanding of requirements. FRET helps understanding and review of semantics by utilizing a variety of forms for each requirement: natural language description, formal logics, and informal diagrams. System requirements are defined in a hierarchical fashion using structured natural language with a precise meaning, and can be exported in a variety of forms to be used by formal analysis tools such as COCOSIM [34,35].

Contract-based Compositional Verification of Simulink Models (COCOSIM) [6] is an open source framework [12] for Simulink/Stateflow formal verification. COCOSIM translates a Simulink model into Lustre code [26], which can then be verified using the Kind2 model-checker [9]. COCOSIM annotates the model with assume-guarantee contracts. Verification can then be performed in a compositional way or by checking the contracts against component behavior.

Event-B [2] is a formal method that is used in the verification of cyber-physical systems [4,31,37]. Event-B uses a set-theoretic modelling notation and supports formal refinement. Event-B models are composed of machines, which model the dynamic components of a systems' specification, and contexts, which model the static components. Event-B has tool support via the Rodin Platform, an Eclipse-based IDE, which generates proof obligations for a given specification and provides support for automatic and interactive proof with the Atelier-B prover [3].

3   Assurance-Based Formal Methods Integration

The objective of this work is *to study the integration of formal verification results via the development of an assurance case, as applied to a robotic system, using a tool palette that includes the three NASA Ames tools* FRET, COCOSIM, *and AdvoCATE, as well as Event-B*. To this end, we provide a step-by-step methodology that builds on top of existing NASA guidelines [18,27] that can be used in the design and development of mission-critical systems. In particular, existing guidelines [27] suggest the following phases: 1) characterization; 2) modeling; 3) specification; 4) analysis; and 5) documentation. Each phase consists of constituent processes and the overall process is iterative rather than sequential.

Our methodology focuses on the application of formal methods and connects it to parts of a greater system safety assurance methodology [13] needed to perform and assure the application of formal methods. Our methodology is guided by the need to devise a detailed assurance case that integrates verification results from a number of distinct tools. The steps that we followed are the following:

Step 0: Characterize initial system.
Step 1: Create initial system model.
Step 2: Perform preliminary hazard analysis.
Step 3: Define mitigations and safety requirements.
Step 4: Refine system model according to mitigations.
Step 5: Formalize requirements and create formal specification(s).
Step 6: Perform verification and simulation at system- and component-levels.
Step 7: Document verification results and build safety case.

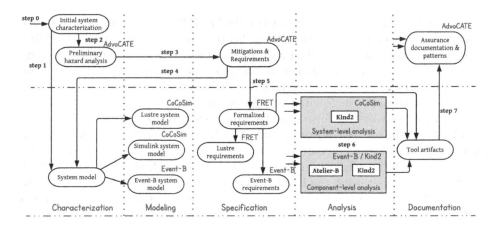

Fig. 1. Our methodology for integrating verification results via an assurance case instantiated with the selected tools for the Inspection Rover case study. The incoming arrows without a source represent all relevant artifacts from previous phases. For system-level analysis these comprise the Lustre requirements and the Simulink system model, while for component-level analysis these comprise the Lustre and Event-B system models and requirements. In the documentation phase we input all artifacts.

Figure 1 presents a detailed view of our methodology instantiated with the selected tools for the Inspection Rover case study. The upper part of Fig. 1 shows the system-level concept, design, and assurance steps that are mainly performed by the AdvoCATE tool, while the lower part shows the formal methods application steps performed by the FRET, COCOSIM, and Event-B tools. In the analysis phase (step 6) we perform two types of analysis. We use COCOSIM to perform *compositional system-level* analysis with Kind2. We also perform verification at *component-level* against the system model using the Atelier-B and Kind-2 tools. Finally, in the documentation phase, we use AdvoCATE to integrate the evidence produced by the tools within the assurance case.

Over the years, we have worked with a variety of formal approaches for the assurance of safety-critical systems. The goal of this study is to explore how such approaches can work together and be integrated within the development process of an autonomous system. With this aim, we developed a case study of a rover system. Our case study is not extracted from an actual mission. Rather, it is developed by iteratively using our expertise on various assurance approaches. The resulting Inspection Rover case study has a reasonable complexity, and demonstrates a variety of generic challenges in formal methods techniques and their integration. Most importantly, we make the details of our case study publicly available [5], since we believe that it can serve as a good basis for discussion and comparison of approaches and tools across the research community.

We target rovers for a variety of reasons. First, rovers are used in many autonomous systems, and present challenges that are typical of autonomous applications. Second, some of the authors have prior experience with autonomous

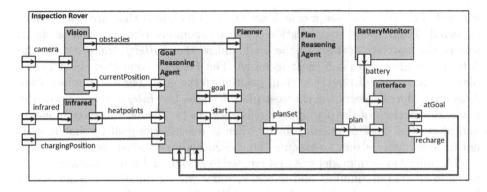

Fig. 2. Preliminary inspection rover system architecture.

robotic systems that are deployed in hazardous environments, such as the nuclear, offshore, and space domains through their involvement in projects[1]. Third, our research group at NASA Ames is in the process of building rover applications to experiment with AI technologies and their assurance techniques.

Four formal methods experts were involved: 1) a safety expert; 2) a requirements expert; 3) a Simulink and Lustre verification expert; and 4) a verification expert of robotic systems that also served as the domain expert. Step 0 was performed by the domain expert, step 1 was performed together by the Simulink and domain experts. Steps 2 and 3 were performed by the safety expert. Steps 4 and 6 were performed by the safety, domain and Simulink experts. Step 5 was performed by the requirements and domain experts, and finally step 7 was performed mainly by the safety expert with contributions from all other experts.

4   The Case Study Step-by-Step

4.1   Step 0: Characterize Initial System

We performed our case study in the context of the navigation system for an autonomous rover undertaking an inspection mission. The objective of this rover is to explore a square grid of known size and to autonomously navigate to points of interest whilst avoiding obstacles and recharging as necessary. We assumed that this system would be operated indoors to minimize environmental uncertainty.

4.2   Step 1: Create Initial System Model

In step 1, we created the initial system model, which comprises a preliminary architecture of our rover (Fig. 2). The rover must navigate to all heat positions on a 2D grid map of known size. The *Vision* system detects obstacles to be

---

[1] UKRI and EPSRC Hubs for "Robotics and AI in Hazardous Environments".

avoided. The *Infrared* component identifies grid locations that are hotter than expected. From these heat locations, the autonomous *Goal Reasoning Agent* selects the hottest location as the goal, unless the *Battery Monitor* (via the *Interface*) indicates that it must recharge. The *Planner* computes obstacle-free plans for navigating from the current position to the goal. The autonomous *Plan Reasoning Agent* selects the shortest plan. Finally, the *Interface* translates the navigation actions of the plan into the instructions for the hardware components and alerts the *Goal Reasoning Agent* when it reaches the goal or that it does not have enough battery to execute the chosen plan so it must recharge.

The initial system model was first created in AADL and can be found in [5]. It was also created in Simulink and Event-B, and it was automatically generated in Lustre via COCOSIM. In this work, we used Simulink in two different ways: 1) as an architecture description language, which allowed us to specify the architecture of the rover without providing implementations of low-level components (for compositionally verifying properties using assume-guarantee reasoning); 2) as a behavioral specification language for the implementation of some of the low-level components (for checking properties against component behavior).

4.3   Step 2: Perform Preliminary Hazard Analysis

To perform the preliminary hazard analysis in AdvoCATE as part of the safety assurance methodology [13], we first defined a functional decomposition of the Inspection Rover based on Fig. 2. Then, we performed the traditional hazard analysis (FMEA [43]) in the AdvoCATE hazard log. We identified two top-level hazards: 1) *loss of rover*, and 2) *inspection finished before visiting all of the heatpoints*. In total, we identified 25 hazards including these two. E.g., we identified the *running out of battery* and *collision with an obstacle* hazards as causes of *loss of rover*. AdvoCATE uses the information from the hazard log to automatically create a safety architecture documented via interconnected Bow Tie Diagrams (BTD) for each hazard [15]. A single BTD shown in Fig. 3 details the causes and consequences of the *running out of battery* hazard.

4.4   Step 3: Define Mitigations and Safety Requirements

After preliminary hazard analysis, we conducted a risk analysis that qualitatively analysed the severity and likelihood of the identified hazards to estimate the risk level. From this, we defined mitigations to minimize the risk of those hazards and their consequences. E.g., the *loss of rover* hazard is characterized with catastrophic severity, but its likelihood is calculated based on the events causing it. The combination of the two defines the risk associated with the hazard.

Next, we performed mitigation planning using BTDs. For example, in order to minimize the risk of *running out of battery* shown in Fig. 3: (1) we formally analysed the navigation system and battery controller, (2) we ensured that the charging station position is predefined so that we can estimate at every point whether we have enough battery to go to recharge, and (3) if the basic assumptions about battery consumption are violated, then we abort and return to the

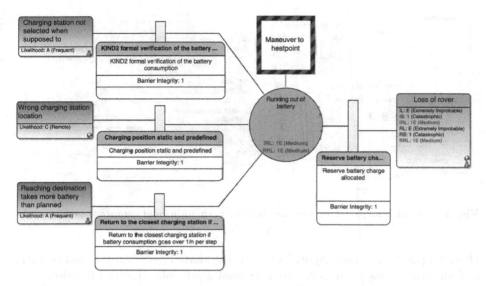

Fig. 3. Bow Tie Diagram presenting the *running out of battery* hazard (orange circle), its causes (blue rectangles to the left) and consequence (red rectangle to the right). (Color figure online)

charging station. Besides mitigating the causes to prevent the hazard from happening, we add the recovery barrier between the hazard and the consequence to reduce the severity of the consequence in case the hazard still occurs.

For each of the two top-level hazards, *loss of rover* and *inspection finished before visiting all of the heatpoints*, we define system-level requirements:

[**R1:**] The rover shall not run out of battery.
[**R2:**] The rover shall not collide with an obstacle.
[**R3:**] The rover shall visit all reachable heat points.

The requirements [**R1**] and [**R2**] correspond to the causes of *loss of rover*, while [**R3**] relates to the *inspection finished before visiting all of the heatpoints* hazard. We have decomposed these system-level requirements further into child (component-level) requirements detailing the specific mitigation mechanisms captured in the BTDs. For example, the mitigations from Fig. 3 are related to the child requirements of [**R1**], while [**R3**] scopes which heat points should be visited to those that are reachable and not visited before. The full list of child requirements for these system-level requirements is presented in [5].

4.5   Step 4: Refine System Model According to Mitigations

Some of the identified mitigations required design modifications resulting in a refined system architecture (Fig. 4), which was reassessed in terms of hazards and mitigations. For brevity, we present this as a single step but there are iterations between these steps in practice. We consider the initial rover position and the

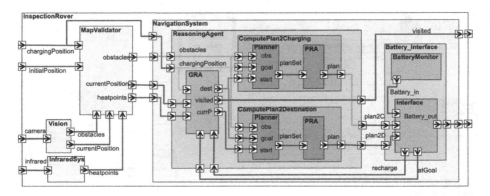

Fig. 4. Upgraded inspection rover architecture with additional components and data.

charging position as user input. Note that the charging station position is static and the rover always starts its missions from a pre-defined initial position.

We modified the original architecture by adding *MapValidator* to check that the initial position, charging position, obstacles and heat points are mutually exclusive. Furthermore, *MapValidator* checks that the initial position, as recognized by *Vision*, is equal to the pre-defined *initialPosition*.

Next, we defined the *NavigationSystem* which contains the *ReasoningAgent* and the *Battery_Interface* components. We emphasise these two components as we focus on formally verifying them. We further decompose these components.

The *ReasoningAgent* takes as input the identified and validated obstacle locations, current rover position, heat points and the charger position. It outputs: (1) a plan from the current position to the goal (*plan2D*), (2) a plan from the goal to the charger location (*plan2C*), and (3) the list of *visited* locations. Within the *ReasoningAgent*, the goal reasoning agent (*GRA*) chooses the next goal as either the hottest heat point not yet visited or as the charger, if the *recharge* flag is set to true by *Battery_Interface*. The *GRA* updates the *visited* locations.

The *ReasoningAgent* contains *ComputePlan2Charging* and *ComputePlan2Destination* which both have a *Planner* and plan reasoning agent (*PRA*). These return the shortest plan from the goal to the charger (*ComputePlan2Charging*) and the shortest plan from the current position to the goal (*ComputePlan2Destination*).

Battery_Interface contains a *BatteryMonitor* and a hardware *Interface*. The *Interface* takes the plans from *NavigationSystem* and the battery status from the *BatteryMonitor* as input, and returns two flags indicating whether the rover has reached the goal (*atGoal*) and the status of the battery charge (*recharge*). The *recharge* flag becomes true if the current battery charge is insufficient to follow the plan to the goal (*plan2D*) and return to the charging station (*plan2C*).

If the *recharge* flag is false, then the *Interface* executes the plan and returns *atGoal* as true once it reaches the goal. However, if *recharge* is true, then *atGoal* is set to false. We note that we do not need both of these outputs since we have always *recharge* $\Rightarrow$ *not atGoal*. However, we include both for simplicity. These outputs are fed back to the *ReasoningAgent* that generates the next plan, and this loop executes until all of the heat points have been visited. Note that we assume that *NavigationSystem* and *Interface* have a similar execution frequency.

4.6 Step 5: Formalize Requirements and Create Formal Specifications

We manually wrote the requirements in the restricted natural language of FRET, i.e., FRETISH, which has a precise, unambiguous meaning. FRETISH requirements contain up to six fields: scope, condition, component*, shall*, timing, and response*, with mandatory fields indicated by '*'. 'component' specifies the component that the requirement refers to and 'shall' expresses that the component's behavior must conform to the requirement. 'response' is a Boolean condition that the component's behavior must satisfy. 'scope' specifies intervals where the requirement is enforced. For example, 'scope' can specify system behavior *after* a mode ends, or when the system is *in* a mode. 'condition' defines a Boolean expression that triggers a 'response'. When triggered, the response must occur as specified by the timing, e.g., *immediately, always, for/within N time units*.

For each FRETISH requirement, FRET produces natural language and diagrammatic explanations of its exact meaning, and formalizes the requirement in temporal logic. The majority of the requirements that we formalized did not have scope or condition but they did have *always* timing, e.g.:

[**R1**]: Navigation shall always satisfy battery > 0.

Other requirements use the condition field and *immediately* timing, e.g.:

[**R1.2**]: if recharge GRA shall immediately satisfy goal = chargePosition.

Notice that if recharge is a "trigger": the requirement is only enforced when the condition becomes true from false. The use of 'immediately' states that the response must hold simultaneously with each trigger point. The natural language version of [**R1**] was shown in §4.4, while for [**R1.2**] it is: *"Charging station shall be selected as the next destination whenever the recharge flag is set to true"*.

Some requirements needed first-order temporal logic, which is not currently supported in FRET. For these, we used auxiliary variables that we instantiated with quantifiers at the Lustre level. For instance, the natural language requirement [**R3.3**] is *"The hottest heatpoint that was not visited before shall be the current goal when recharge flag is false"* and was written in FRETISH as follows:

[**R3.3**]: GRA shall always satisfy if ! recharge then (if forAll_i & i_inGrid then (if ! visited[i] then heatpoints[goal] >= heatpoints[i]))

where forAll_i represents the universal quantification over heatpoints. In total, our case study contains 28 requirements, 7 of these required first-order formulae. We were able to write all 28 requirements in FRETISH and formalize them.

FRETISH to Verification Code: FRET automatically formalizes requirements in pure future-time (fmLTL) and pure past-time (pmLTL) Linear Temporal Logic. pmLTL formulae exclusively use past-time temporal operators, i.e., Y, O, H, S, (Yesterday, Once, Historically, Since, respectively). We used the pmLTL variant since Lustre-based analysis tools only accept pmLTL specifications. The automatically generated pmLTL formulae for [**R1**] and [**R1.2**] are:

[R1]: H(battery>0);
[R1.2]: H((recharge & (Y(!recharge) | FTP))⇒(goal=chargePosition));
where FTP means First Time Point of execution (equivalent to ¬ Y TRUE). From the pmLTL formulae we automatically generated Lustre-based assume-guarantee contracts that can be directly fed into COCOSIM for verification (the full process is described in [33]). For example, below is the generated Lustre code for **[R1]**:

```
guarantee "R1" (battery > 0);
```

If requirements were based only on model inputs, e.g., **[R1.2]**, then CoCoGen generates assumptions (instead of guarantees):

```
assume "R1.2" ((recharge and ((pre (not recharge)) or FTP)) => (goal =
    chargePosition));
```

where FTP = true → false. As mentioned earlier, some requirements used first-order logic quantification such as **[R3.3]** which was generated as follows:

```
guarantee "R3.3" not recharge => (forall (i:int) (0 <= i and i < width) => (
    not visited[i] => heatpoints[goal] >= heatpoints[i] )));
```

Notice that the forAll_i placeholder was replaced by forall (i:int), and i_inGrid was replaced by (0 <= i and i < width) during generation.

We also specified the requirements in Event-B. Since Event-B does not support temporal logic, we used the FRETISH requirements to guide our modelling. FRETISH was simple enough and more useful as a starting point for formalization than the natural language requirements. E.g., the natural language requirement **[R3.4]** is *"The shortest path to the current goal shall be selected"*. The FRETISH version is: Planner shall always satisfy if (planningCompleted & returnPlan) then (if (forAll_x & x_inPlanSet) then (card(chosenPlan) <= card(x))), where the card() function computes the length of a path. The corresponding Event-B invariant was based on the FRETISH version:

$(planningCompleted = TRUE) \land (returnplan = TRUE) \Rightarrow (\forall x \cdot x \in PlanSet \Rightarrow card(chosenplan) \leq card(x))$

Similarly, **[R2.5:]** *The calculated path to destination shall not include a location with an obstacle* was defined in Event-B as follows:

$\forall p, x \cdot p \in PlanSet \land x \in p \Rightarrow x \notin Obs$, where every PlanSet element is a set of grid locations.

4.7   Step 6: Perform Verification and Simulation at System- and Component-Levels

Compositional Verification in CoCoSim: Our objective was to attach the component-level child requirements to the relevant component(s) and then, using COCOSIM, compositionally verify the system-level parent requirements. We were not able to model/verify all requirements, e.g., *The current position as recognized by the rover is its current physical position* should be physically tested.

Compositional verification in COCOSIM involves defining a top system node with associated system-level contract. During verification, the model checker attempts to show that these system-level properties can be successfully derived from the component-level contracts. Using compositional reasoning in COCOSIM, we were able to verify system-level requirements [R1] and [R3], defined in §4.4. However, we could not verify [R2] which involves the *Vision* and the *Planner* components, because there is no COCOSIM model for the *Vision* component.

Compositional verification of [R1] was achieved quite quickly ($<$ 20 secs), as the model checker only had to analyse two components: the *Interface* and *BatteryMonitor* to verify [R1]. [R3] was more complex since it involved a loop between the *Interface* and *ReasoningAgent*. Kind2 had to carry out a lot of unrolling to adequately assess this property and deal with more complex contracts including quantifiers and arrays. Thus, we were only able to prove [R3] for specific grid widths (minutes for 3×3, hours for 4×4, and larger grids timed out).

Component-Level Verification Using Kind2 and Event-B: Previously, we used compositional verification to verify that the system-level parent requirements hold based on the component-level requirements. Here, our objective was to verify that the more detailed specification/implementation of individual components obey the associated component-level requirements. Recognising that, for autonomous robotic systems, it is often necessary to use a range of verification techniques for individual components, we used two distinct formal methods here [19,30]. Specifically, we used Kind2 to verify a simple implementation of the *GRA* and, Event-B to model and verify the *ComputePlan* component.

Specification and Verification of the GRA: We constructed a simple Lustre implementation of the *GRA* that we verified using Kind2. Full details can be found in [5]. The *GRA* computes the `start`, `goal` and the `visited` cells. The `start` is initialized as the `currentPosition`, if the goal was reached during the last execution (`atGoal` is true) then the start is the previous goal (`pre_goal`), if the `recharge` flag is true then the `start` is the previous start position since the rover did not move. The `goal` is set to `chargingPosition` if the `recharge` flag is active. Otherwise we choose the hottest heat point, computed using the `hottestPoint` local array that keeps track of the hottest heat point. We used Kind2 to verify all of the properties specified in the specification. We were able to verify most properties in less than 1 second. Due to state space explosion, there were some properties, e.g., requirement [R3.3] that were only provable for specific grid sizes. E.g., we verified [R3.3] for a grid size up to 4×4.

Specification and Verification of ComputePlan using Event-B: Our Event-B model contains three contexts (modelling static aspects) and two machines (modelling dynamic aspects). Event-B supports formal refinement, so our contexts extend one another and our machines indicate refinement steps. Our most primitive context, `ctx0`, specifies basic details such as the size of the grid, valid grid locations, obstacles and heat points. We do not explicitly list the elements of these sets since this specification is for a generic planner. This is extended via `ctx1` which specifies functions that capture the behavior of the planning component.

The abstract machine, mac0, models a simple search-based planning algorithm that produces a set of plans containing the start and goal. Event-B uses sets as primitive so we ensure that these plans, encoded as sets, can be linearized using the adjacent function specified in ctx1. The refinement, mac1, incorporates a plan reasoning agent and chooses the shortest plan from PlanSet. Another context, ctx2, defines a constant to limit the number of generated plans.

We encoded [R2.1], [R2.4.1], [R2.4.3], [R2.4.4], [R2.5] and [R3.4] in our Event-B model. We could not verify [R2] compositionally but its child requirements feature in our Event-B model (e.g. [R2.5]). This ensures that the planning components do not accidentally cause the rover to collide with an obstacle. Most of the Event-B proof obligations were proven automatically by Atelier-B in Rodin. Those requiring interactive proof were relatively straightforward.

Event-B was not limited by the state space explosion that caused Kind2 to time out. We specified more complex component-level properties that would have been difficult to verify for a model-checker. The Event-B model is within [5].

4.8   Step 7: Document Verification Results and Build Safety Case

All of the verification results produced by the tools are a part of the safety case that was constructed in AdvoCATE. Some artifacts were imported automatically into AdvoCATE, while others were added manually. Since this case study did not include a full system implementation, the safety case that we report here is an interim version and contains the current safety assurance status.

The skeleton of the overall argument is generated automatically from the information defined and imported into AdvoCATE such as hazards, mitigation requirements, formalized requirements, and evidence artifacts. We have further extended the skeleton argument based on the specific application and the tools that we used. Figure 5 presents an argument fragment about mitigating the *running out of battery* hazard that causes *loss of rover*. Similar arguments exist for other causes of *loss of rover* and the other hazards. For brevity, Fig. 5 only contains a fragment of the existing argument. For example, this argument focuses on two aspects: the requirements directly related to this hazard (right branch), and the causes that lead to the hazard (left branch). Full details can be found in [5].

The goal **G14** focuses on [R1] that was verified using COCOSIM. We built a similar argument for each system-level requirement previously verified compositionally with COCOSIM. For each argument, we extended the automatically generated part with a combination of existing argumentation patterns [14,42] to support application-specific goals (base of Fig. 5): 1) the formalisation of the natural language requirement is correct (**G3-A1**); 2) the results from COCOSIM are trustworthy (**G4-A1**); 3) the different design representations are consistent (**G5-A1**); 4) the COCOSIM verification result for [R1] is valid (**G6-A1**).

To ensure that the different design representations were consistent across the tools, we performed manual reviews where automated consistency validation was not available. E.g., we used manual reviews to verify that the design as specified in AdvoCATE was consistent with the Simulink, Kind2 and Event-B models.

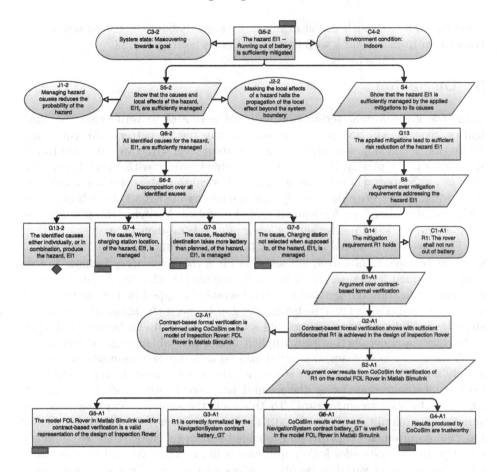

Fig. 5. The argument-fragment for the *running out of battery* hazard (rectangles represent goals, parallelograms represent strategies, ovals with a 'J' represent justifications, rounded rectangles represent context statements, green rectangles indicate arguments continues elsewhere, green diamonds represent currently undeveloped elements). (Color figure online)

The goal **G3-A1** focuses on the correct specification of [**R1**] in FRETISH and the correct functioning of FRET. While we have to verify through a manual review that the natural language requirement is correctly represented in FRETISH, the correct FRET functioning and generation of the corresponding COCOSIM contracts is supported by the automated verification framework of FRET.

The goal **G6-A1** focuses on the validity of [**R1**] through analysis with the COCOSIM tool. This part of the argument points out the dependencies to the properties of the other components, but also implicit assumptions on which these results rely. Finally, to have confidence in the results from COCOSIM, we argued the trustworthiness of COCOSIM with the goal **G4-A1**. Since COCOSIM relies on model transformations and external tools for verification, the correctness of these has to be established. For example, we argued about the correctness of the translation from Simulink to Lustre code that is used by Kind2.

5 Discussion

Using the given formal verification tools we were able to verify that the Navigation System will not cause the rover to run out of battery. We could not verify that a collision will never occur at system-level with COCOSIM due to the specification complexity. However, we were able to verify with Event-B that the Navigation System will not generate plans that contain obstacles at component-level. Finally, we were able to verify that the rover will visit all of the heat points with COCOSIM, but only for a small grid size of 4×4. Verifying the property for greater grid sizes did not terminate, even after several days of analysis.

This case study showed us that by following our methodology we were able to leverage multiple formal tools and use them in a *complementary* fashion. In this way, we applied formal methods to small, manageable chunks of the system to ease the verification burden and to avoid becoming trapped by the limitations of any single tool. Using FRET to bridge the gap between the informal and formal steps by formalizing our requirements was particularly useful because it helped us to clarify any details that were implicit in the natural language requirements.

Although in most cases, the initial natural language requirements looked relatively straightforward, a closer study revealed many questions regarding their precise meaning. Translating the natural language requirements into FRETISH was not always straightforward. To this end, the semantic explanations and simulation capabilities offered by FRET were instrumental in ensuring that the FRETISH requirements captured our intended semantics. Notice that we could not directly encode first-order logic requirements in FRETISH. We tackled this problem using auxiliary variables as placeholders for the quantifiers at requirement-level, but a FRETISH-level solution is desirable. Finally, we noticed that most of the Inspection Rover requirements follow a small number of patterns, a characteristic that we have observed in other studies within our organization.

The choice of COCOSIM and in particular Kind2 greatly influenced our design decisions. For example, in our original design, we represented cells in the grid as (x, y)-coordinates. However, we subsequently simplified this by using indices so that they were easier to represent and reason about in formal tools. Our choice of a compositional verification approach caused us to output specific variables such as the remaining battery power to verify [R1] compositionally. Furthermore, we had to adapt the hierarchical structure of the system to accommodate compositional verification. If the choice of formal verification tools is made early on in the system development process, the design of the system can be created so that it is more suitable to formal verification using the chosen method(s).

Not all of the formalized requirements were formally verifiable, some described hardware constraints and/or required physical testing. This supports the claim that the robotics domain requires both formal and informal verification processes [19]. E.g., everything depends on the accuracy of the rover's current position - a property that we could not formally verify in this case. However, by formalizing the requirements to be verified via testing, we can potentially incorporate run-time analysis. Specifically, the formalized properties can be used to generate formal run-time monitors to help with fault management during operation. These might help to create recovery barriers in the bow-tie diagrams. In this way, we could include the development of fault management at design time.

Integrating the verification results from the different formal methods in an assurance case required intensive cooperation between the assurance and formal methods experts. The effort required identifying dependencies between different tools, understanding the techniques and the tool implementations, implicit assumptions on which analyses were ran and results interpreted. The activity was greatly performed ad hoc. A more systematic approach to gathering the assurance information from formal methods applications would be beneficial.

Approaches to integrating formal methods often rely on bespoke translations between languages/tools. However, these translations can be difficult and sometimes impossible to correctly formalize/implement. Further, if used in an assurance case then the translations themselves must be assured, as for our translation from FRET to COCOSIM [5]. Although the use of tightly integrated formal methods is desirable, our approach, using an assurance case as the point of integration, incorporates tools for which such systematic translations do not exist by providing arguments demonstrating how to link models in distinct formalizms.

The case study helped us to identify limitations in the used tools (Advo-CATE, FRET, COCOSIM and Event-B) for robotics applications. In fact, it prompted an update to COCOSIM to incorporate abstract unimplemented components. Specifically, COCOSIM now generates Lustre code for these components using the `imported` keyword when no implementation is available. Other limitations include the lack of FRET support for abstract data types which caused us to manually edit the FRET-generated COCOSIM contracts. There were some difficulties when attempting to automatically import verification artifacts directly from the tools into AdvoCATE which caused us to insert some details manually.

Our methodology follows the development phases of existing development guidelines [13, 27] and builds on top of them through a set of steps (§3), which are guided by the need to devise an assurance case that integrates artifacts from different tools. Although in the presented work we used specific tools, we believe that our methodology can be followed irrespective of the choice of tools.

6   Related Work

Heterogeneous verification techniques were used to verify an autonomous Mars Curiosity rover simulation [8]. This work uses distinct verification methods for specific components but does explicitly link the verification artifacts produced. Recent work proposes first-order logic to unify heterogeneous formal methods via a compositional approach but this work currently lacks tool support [7].

Other approaches to compositional verification include AGREE [38] and OCRA [11]. We explored these as potential alternatives to COCOSIM in this work but neither offered the level of expressivity that we sought. They also did not accommodate for the use of distinct verification techniques at component-level.

Developers should choose the most appropriate formal method on a per-component basis based on the suitability of the formal method and the user's level of expertise. As such, there are many alternatives to Event-B and Kind2, including Gwendolen [17], TLA+ [44] and Dafny [29].

Isabelle/SACM [21,25] extends the Isabelle proof assistant to support assurance case development. In Isabelle/SACM, a UTP semantics must be defined for each formal verification artifact that is to be included in the assurance case.

In this paper, we have illustrated the benefits of using various formal verification techniques. Related to this, [10,28,32] demonstrate that a collaborative approach to verification, encompassing static verification and testing, is advantageous as it finds more errors and proves more properties than a single technique.

7   Conclusions and Future Work

This paper presented our methodology for integrating results from distinct formal methods via the development of an assurance case. We applied this methodology in the design of an Inspection Rover system and used the AdvoCATE, FRET COCOSIM and Event-B tools. This is the first effort to integrate the four aforementioned tools. We illustrated how the choice of verification methods can impact system design and discussed how a heterogeneous set of verification results can be linked during assurance with AdvoCATE. Further, we made our case study artifacts publicly available to fuel discussion in the research community.

This work has opened up a number of avenues for future research. In particular, we would like to support the definition of probabilistic requirements in FRET, since such requirements are increasingly used in complex robotic systems. Additionally, we intend to develop a DSL to facilitate the integration of Advo-CATE with different verification tools. Furthermore, we intend to explore the definition of a 'Taxonomy of Requirements' and classify those in this case study. This will help developers to design their system with verification in mind by demonstrating how to classify requirements based on the ways that they will be verified and argued in an assurance case early at design phase.

References

1. GSN Community Standard Version 2. Technical report, Assurance Case Working Group of The Safety-Critical Systems Club (Jan 2018)
2. Abrial, J.-R.: Modeling in Event-B: System and Software Engineering. Cambridge University Press, Cambridge (2010)
3. Abrial, J.-R., Butler, M., Hallerstede, S., Hoang, T.S., Mehta, F., Voisin, L.: Rodin: an open toolset for modelling and reasoning in Event-B. Int. J. Softw. Tools Technol. Transfer **12**(6), 447–466 (2010)
4. Banach, R.: Hemodialysis machine in hybrid event-B. In: Butler, M., Schewe, K.-D., Mashkoor, A., Biro, M. (eds.) ABZ 2016. LNCS, vol. 9675, pp. 376–393. Springer, Cham (2016). https://doi.org/10.1007/978-3-319-33600-8_32

5. Bourbouh, H., Farrell, M., Mavridou, A., Sljivo, I.: Integration and Evaluation of the Advocate, FRET, CoCoSim, and Event-B Tools on the Inspection Rover Case Study. Technical report, TM-2020-5011049, NASA (2021)
6. Bourbouh, H., Garoche, P.-L., Loquen, T.,É, Noulard, T., Pagetti, C.: CoCoSim, a code generation framework for control/command applications: an overview of CoCoSim for multi-periodic discrete simulink models. In: European Congress on Embedded Real Time Software and Systems (2020)
7. Cardoso, R.C., Dennis, L.A., Farrell, M., Fisher, M., Luckcuck, M.: Towards compositional verification for modular robotic systems. In: Workshop on Formal Methods for Autonomous Systems, pp. 15–22. Electronic Proceedings in Theoretical Computer Science (2020)
8. Cardoso, R.C., Farrell, M., Luckcuck, M., Ferrando, A., Fisher, M.: Heterogeneous verification of an autonomous curiosity rover. In: Lee, R., Jha, S., Mavridou, A., Giannakopoulou, D. (eds.) NFM 2020. LNCS, vol. 12229, pp. 353–360. Springer, Cham (2020). https://doi.org/10.1007/978-3-030-55754-6_20
9. Champion, A., Mebsout, A., Sticksel, C., Tinelli, C.: The KIND 2 model checker. In: Chaudhuri, S., Farzan, A. (eds.) CAV 2016, Part II. LNCS, vol. 9780, pp. 510–517. Springer, Cham (2016). https://doi.org/10.1007/978-3-319-41540-6_29
10. Christakis, M., Müller, P., Wüstholz, V.: Collaborative verification and testing with explicit assumptions. In: Giannakopoulou, D., Méry, D. (eds.) FM 2012. LNCS, vol. 7436, pp. 132–146. Springer, Heidelberg (2012). https://doi.org/10.1007/978-3-642-32759-9_13
11. Cimatti, A., Dorigatti, M., Tonetta, S.: OCRA: a tool for checking the refinement of temporal contracts. In: International Conference on Automated Software Engineering, pp. 702–705. IEEE (2013)
12. CoCoSim-Team. CoCoSim - Automated Analysis Framework for Simulink. https://github.com/NASA-SW-VnV/CoCoSim
13. Denney, E., Pai, G.: Automating the assembly of aviation safety cases. IEEE Trans. Reliab. 63(4), 830–849 (2014)
14. Denney, E., Pai, G.: Safety case patterns: theory and applications. NASA/TM2015218492 (2015)
15. Denney, E., Pai, G.: Architecting a safety case for UAS flight operations. In: International System Safety Conference, vol. 12 (2016)
16. Denney, E., Pai, G.: Tool support for assurance case development. Autom. Softw. Eng. 25(3), 435–499 (2017). https://doi.org/10.1007/s10515-017-0230-5
17. Dennis, L.A., Farwer, B.: Gwendolen: a BDI language for verifiable agents. In: Workshop on Logic and the Simulation of Interaction and Reasoning, pp. 16–23. AISB (2008)
18. Dezfuli, H., et al.: NASA system safety handbook. Volume 2: System Safety Concepts, Guidelines, and Implementation Examples (2015)
19. Farrell, M., Luckcuck, M., Fisher, M.: Robotics and integrated formal methods: necessity meets opportunity. In: Furia, C.A., Winter, K. (eds.) IFM 2018. LNCS, vol. 11023, pp. 161–171. Springer, Cham (2018). https://doi.org/10.1007/978-3-319-98938-9_10
20. Filliâtre, J.-C., Paskevich, A.: Why3 — where programs meet provers. In: Felleisen, M., Gardner, P. (eds.) ESOP 2013. LNCS, vol. 7792, pp. 125–128. Springer, Heidelberg (2013). https://doi.org/10.1007/978-3-642-37036-6_8
21. Foster, S.D., Nemouchi, Y., O'Halloran, C., Tudor, N., Stephenson, K.: Formal model-based assurance cases in Isabelle/SACM: an autonomous underwater vehicle case study. In: Formal Methods in Software Engineering. ACM (2020)

22. FRET-Team. FRET - Formal Requirements Elicitation Tool. https://github.com/ NASA-SW-VnV/FRET
23. Giannakopoulou, D., Mavridou, A., Pressburger, T., Rhein, J., Schumann, J., Shi, N.: Formal requirements elicitation with FRET. Foundation for software quality (Demo-Track). In: Requirements Engineering (2020)
24. Giannakopoulou, D., Pressburger, T., Mavridou, A., Schumann, J.: Generation of formal requirements from structured natural language. In: Madhavji, N., Pasquale, L., Ferrari, A., Gnesi, S. (eds.) REFSQ 2020. LNCS, vol. 12045, pp. 19–35. Springer, Cham (2020). https://doi.org/10.1007/978-3-030-44429-7_2
25. Gleirscher, M., Foster, S., Nemouchi, Y.: Evolution of formal model-based assurance cases for autonomous robots. In: Ölveczky, P.C., Salaün, G. (eds.) SEFM 2019. LNCS, vol. 11724, pp. 87–104. Springer, Cham (2019). https://doi.org/10. 1007/978-3-030-30446-1_5
26. Halbwachs, N., Caspi, P., Raymond, P., Pilaud, D.: The synchronous data flow programming language LUSTRE. Proc. IEEE **79**(9), 1305–1320 (1991)
27. Kelly, J.C.: Formal Methods Specification and Analysis Guidebook for the Verification of Software and Computer Systems Volume II: A Practitioner's Companion (1997)
28. Le, V.H., Correnson, L., Signoles, J., Wiels, V.: Verification coverage for combining test and proof. In: Dubois, C., Wolff, B. (eds.) TAP 2018. LNCS, vol. 10889, pp. 120–138. Springer, Cham (2018). https://doi.org/10.1007/978-3-319-92994-1_7
29. Leino, K.R.M.: Dafny: an automatic program verifier for functional correctness. In: Clarke, E.M., Voronkov, A. (eds.) LPAR 2010. LNCS (LNAI), vol. 6355, pp. 348–370. Springer, Heidelberg (2010). https://doi.org/10.1007/978-3-642-17511- 4_20
30. Luckcuck, M., Farrell, M., Dennis, L.A., Dixon, C., Fisher, M.: Formal specification and verification of autonomous robotic systems: a survey. ACM Comput. Surv. (CSUR) **52**(5), 1–41 (2019)
31. Mammar, A., Laleau, R.: Modeling a landing gear system in event-B. Int. J. Softw. Tools Technol. Transfer **19**(2), 167–186 (2017)
32. Maurica, F., Cok, D.R., Signoles, J.: Runtime assertion checking and static verification: collaborative partners. In: Margaria, T., Steffen, B. (eds.) ISoLA 2018, Part II. LNCS, vol. 11245, pp. 75–91. Springer, Cham (2018). https://doi.org/10. 1007/978-3-030-03421-4_6
33. Mavridou, A., Bourbouh, H., Garoche, P.-L., Giannakopoulou, D., Pressburger, T., Schumann, J.: Bridging the gap between requirements and Simulink model analysis. In: International Working Conference on Requirements Engineering: Foundation for Software Quality (REFSQ-2020, Poster) (2020)
34. Mavridou, A., Bourbouh, H., Garoche, P.-L., Hejase, M.: Evaluation of the FRET and CoCoSim tools on the ten Lockheed Martin Cyber-Physical challenge problems. Technical report, TM-2019-220374, NASA (2019)
35. Mavridou, A., et al.: The ten lockheed martin cyber-physical challenges: formalized, analyzed, and explained. In: International Requirements Engineering Conference (RE), pp. 300–310. IEEE (2020)
36. McComas, D.: NASA/GSFC's flight software core flight system. In: Flight Software Workshop, vol. 11 (2012)
37. Méry, D., Singh, N.K.: Formal development and automatic code generation: cardiac pacemaker. In: International Conference on Computers and Advanced Technology in Education (2011)

38. Murugesan, A., Whalen, M.W., Rayadurgam, S., Heimdahl, M.P.: Compositional verification of a medical device system. In: SIGAda Annual Conference on High Integrity Language Technology, pp. 51–64 (2013)

39. Quigley, M., et al.: ROS: an open-source robot operating system. In: ICRA Workshop on Open Source Software, vol. 3, p. 5 (2009)

40. Rivera, V., Cataño, N.: Translating event-B to JML-specified Java programs. In: ACM Symposium on Applied Computing, pp. 1264–1271 (2014)

41. Schneider, S., Treharne, H., Wehrheim, H.: A CSP approach to control in event-B. In: Méry, D., Merz, S. (eds.) IFM 2010. LNCS, vol. 6396, pp. 260–274. Springer, Heidelberg (2010). https://doi.org/10.1007/978-3-642-16265-7_19

42. Sljivo, I., Gallina, B., Carlson, J., Hansson, H., Puri, S.: Tool-supported safety-relevant component reuse: from specification to argumentation. In: Casimiro, A., Ferreira, P.M. (eds.) Ada-Europe 2018. LNCS, vol. 10873, pp. 19–33. Springer, Cham (2018). https://doi.org/10.1007/978-3-319-92432-8_2

43. Stamatis, D.H.: Failure Mode and Effect Analysis: FMEA from Theory to Execution. Quality Press, Milwaukee (2003)

44. Yu, Y., Manolios, P., Lamport, L.: Model checking TLA$^+$ specifications. In: Pierre, L., Kropf, T. (eds.) CHARME 1999. LNCS, vol. 1703, pp. 54–66. Springer, Heidelberg (1999). https://doi.org/10.1007/3-540-48153-2_6

Towards Verifying SHA256 in OpenSSL with the Software Analysis Workbench

Brett Decker[✉], Benjamin Winters, and Eric Mercer[ID]

Brigham Young University, Provo, UT 84601, USA
{bdecker,egm}@cs.byu.edu

Abstract. The Software Analysis Workbench (SAW) is a verification tool that has shown promise in verifying cryptographic implementations in C and Java as evidenced by the verification of Amazon's s2n HMAC. That result uses an idealized abstraction for SHA256 to simplify the proof obligations. The OpenSSL SHA256 implementation supported by s2n presents verification problems for SAW because some functions do not complete SAW's symbolic execution or verification in the backend Satisfiability Modulo Theories (SMT) solvers. Fortunately, SAW provides a compositional framework to reduce the proof complexity, replacing function calls with overrides which are nothing more than contracts stating the input to output relation of the functions. This paper illustrates the SAW compositional framework applied to the OpenSSL SHA256 implementation. It shows a refactoring of the implementation that manages symbolic variables to work with the symbolic execution engine and lends itself to overrides while preserving its connection to the original source. Early results suggest the approach effective in applying SAW to legacy cryptographic implementations that are critical to the security of almost all existing applications.

Keywords: Software Analysis Workbench · Formal verification · Symbolic execution · Cryptol · SHA · OpenSSL

1 Introduction

Cryptographic algorithms are the basis for secure software systems. As these systems become larger and more complex, the need to verify security becomes ever more important. Traditional methods of verification, such as code inspections, pose difficulties that have been well documented [1]. Formal verification decreases the need for code inspections but increases the need for verification domain expertise. In this paper, we describe our use of the *Software Analysis Workbench* (SAW) to prove correctness of OpenSSL SHA256 [6].

SAW proves functional equivalence of code in C, Java, and Cryptol [5], by creating functional models from the code. Each model is represented as a *term*, which has a value that precisely describes all possible computations of the code. Terms are created by symbolic execution of the intermediate representations for

A. Dutle et al. (Eds.): NFM 2021, LNCS 12673, pp. 72–78, 2021.
https://doi.org/10.1007/978-3-030-76384-8_5

C and Java code [4]. SAW's native support for Cryptol allows it to compile the code into a succinct term. SAW passes a proof of term equivalence to SMT solvers, with built-in support for Z3, ABC, and Yices [4]. Our SAW verification results rely on two underlying assumptions: 1) the Cryptol code is correct and 2) LLVM and JVM preserve the meaning of the original code.

Legacy cryptographic code, such as OpenSSL's SHA256, often cannot be verified in SAW as-is. Highly-optimised code must be refactored into smaller functions. Loop bounds must be made concrete, limiting the generality of the proof. SAW's compositional framework allows proofs to be built from the bottom up, replacing function calls in upper-level functions with overrides. An override is a contract stating the input to output relation for the function call. This allows a series of smaller proofs to be given to SMT solvers. We present our work in refactoring the OpenSSL SHA256 implementation into a C Reference implementation that completes verification in SAW using its compositional framework. This represents domain knowledge that is not readily apparent in the SAW documentation. The complete proof, scripts, and documentation for everything in this paper is in [8].

Related Work [3] uses SAW to prove Amazon's s2n [7] HMAC implementation correct (incorporating work from [2]). The s2n HMAC proof assumes the underlying SHA256 C implementation is correct. s2n does not implement SHA256, instead supporting existing legacy implementations, such as OpenSSL.

2   Compositional Proofs for OpenSSL SHA256

As with all tools, SAW has limitations [4]. SAW can only construct terms for a subset of C and Java programs that have fixed-size inputs, outputs, and loop iterations. One ramification for cryptographic codes is that we can only prove equivalence for a specific message size (*e.g.* a proof for SHA256 with message size of 128 bytes). Thus, we must re-run the proofs for different message sizes or construct an auxiliary proof to generalize the results to arbitrary message sizes.

The issues of applying SAW to the OpenSSL SHA256 implementation can be summarized as follows:

1. Symbolic execution reports errors when memory reads and writes are not statically guaranteed to be inside the fixed-size allocations and when there are volatile function calls.
2. Symbolic execution does not complete when memory allocations, loop initializers, and loop bounds are not constant.
3. The backend SMT solvers do not complete when symbolic execution results in a large or dissimilar – from Cryptol – term.

We chose our timeout for issues 2) and 3) to be 15 min – anything longer is not practical vis-a-vis development.

All three of the above issues are illustrated in the proofs for OpenSSL functions SHA256_Final and sha256_block_data_order. The compositional proofs

```
255  int SHA256_Final(unsigned char *md,        245  int SHA256_Final(unsigned char *md,
256                SHA256_CTX *c) {             246                SHA256_CTX *c) {
257    unsigned char *p = (unsigned char*)c->data;  247    unsigned char *p = (unsigned char*)c->data;
258    size_t n = c->num;                        248    size_t n = c->num;
259                                              249
260    p[n] = 0x80;                              250    add_one_bit(c);
261    n++;                                      251
262    if (n > (SHA256_CBLOCK - 8)) {            252    if (n > (SHA256_CBLOCK - 8)) {
263      memset(p + n, 0, SHA256_CBLOCK - n);    253      zero_fill(p, n, SHA256_CBLOCK);
264      n = 0;                                  254      n = 0;
265      sha256_block_data_order(c, p, 1);       255      sha256_block(c, p);
266    }                                         256    }
267    memset(p + n, 0, SHA256_CBLOCK - 8 - n);  257    zero_fill(p, n, SHA256_CBLOCK - 8);
268                                              258
269    p += SHA256_CBLOCK - 8;                   259    p += SHA256_CBLOCK - 8;
270    (void)HOST_l2c(c->Nh, p);                 260    (void)HOST_l2c(c->Nh, p);
271    (void)HOST_l2c(c->Nl, p);                 261    (void)HOST_l2c(c->Nl, p);
272    p -= SHA256_CBLOCK;                       262    p -= SHA256_CBLOCK;
273                                              263
274    sha256_block_data_order(c, p, 1);         264    sha256_block(c, p);
275    c->num = 0;                               265    c->num = 0;
276    OPENSSL_cleanse(p, SHA256_CBLOCK);        266    memset(p, 0, SHA256_CBLOCK);
277                                              267
278    HASH_MAKE_STRING(c, md);                  268    HASH_MAKE_STRING(c, md);
279    return 1;                                 269    return 1;
280  }                                           270  }
                   (a)                                              (b)
```

Fig. 1. Implementations for SHA256_Final. (a) OpenSSL. (b) C Reference.

require refactoring the OpenSSL code. The refactored code suitable for SAW is referred to as the C Reference implementation throughout the rest of this paper (see Fig. 1 for a side-by-side comparison of the OpenSSL and C Reference SHA256_Final functions).

First, symbolic execution reports errors because OPENSSL_Cleanse at line 276 of Fig. 1(a) calls memset that is annotated as a volatile function to prevent the call from being reordered (or removed) by the compiler. We replace the call to a static-sized and non-volatile memset call. Since removing the volatile keyword potentially changes the behavior of the compiler, this reference implementation is not intended for deployment, but only for analysis, as this transformation does not fully preserve the semantics of the initial program. Second, symbolic execution reports errors because the memory of p is written at offset n, with n being a symbolic value (line 260). In such a case, SAW cannot know if the offset is inside the allocation for p. We add a precondition in our proof script to constrain n to be less than the allocated size of p. This simple constraint enables the symbolic execution to succeed and start building a term for the function.

Symbolic execution does not complete within the allotted time bound, thus the code requires further refactoring. The calls to memset at lines 263 and 267 of Fig. 1(a) are problematic because they again use n, a symbolic variable, to determine the loop bound. We cannot override these function calls because the first parameter, p + n, cannot be modeled in SAW – there is no way in SAW to create a memory offset by a symbolic variable. Thus, we must modify the code and create a new function, zero_fill, to replace memset at lines 263 and 267. The zero_fill function must have a constant loop initialization and bound. Further decomposition is required for the SMT solvers to complete verification against the Cryptol specification. These replacement functions are not how one would normally implement memset in C (Fig. 2 compares the two).

```
206   void zero_fill(unsigned char* p,
207                  unsigned int start,
208                  unsigned int end) {
209     unsigned int i;
210     for (i = start; i < end; i++) {
211       p[i] = 0;
212     }
213   }
```

(a)

```
217   unsigned char zero_data(unsigned char value,
218                           unsigned int i,
219                           unsigned int start,
220                           unsigned int end) {
221     unsigned char result = 0;
222     if (i < start || i >= end) {
223       result = value;
224     }
225     return result;
226   }
227
228   void zero_fill(unsigned char* p,
229                  unsigned int start,
230                  unsigned int end) {
231     unsigned int i;
232     for (i = 0; i < SHA256_CBLOCK; i++) {
233       p[i] = zero_data(p[i], i, start, end);
234     }
235   }
```

(b)

```
154   zero_data : [8] -> [32] -> [32] -> [32] -> [8]
155   zero_data value i start end =
156       if (i < start) || (i >= end)
157           then value
158           else 0
159
160   type BLOCK_BYTES = 64
161   zero_fill : [BLOCK_BYTES][8]] -> [32] -> [32] ->
              [BLOCK_BYTES][8]
162   zero_fill bytes start end = out where
163       out = [zero_data value i start end | value <- bytes |
              i <- [0 .. BLOCK_BYTES]]
```

(c)

Fig. 2. Implementations for memset. (a) C default. (b) C functional. (c) Cryptol.

Manual inspection easily verifies equivalence of memset and zero_fill. With these modifications, the C Reference SHA256_Final completes symbolic execution but fails to complete in the backend SMT solvers for our specified bound.

We already identified a potential issue at line 260 of SHA256_Final where the symbolic variable n is used as an offset to memory. Cryptol cannot be implemented likewise, thus the resulting terms are very dissimilar (as shown in Table 1, row 2). We encapsulate lines 260–261 into a function, add_one_bit, to facilitate a smaller proof which we then use as an override. SHA256_Final has multiple other function calls that contribute to the large term size, since functions are symbolically executed at invocation by SAW, effectively inlining them to create a "flat" term [4]. We create overrides for zero_fill and sha256_block_data_order to use in addition to the override for add_one_bit. The overrides enable SAW to prove the C Reference equivalent to its Cryptol specification. The new overrides create additional proof obligations as the overrides must now be shown equivalent to the C code they replace. For example, SAW must prove that sha256_block_data_order is equivalent to its Cryptol override, only that proof does not complete in the backend SMT solver; thus, we must first refactor the C function to finish this secondary proof obligation.

The C Reference renames sha256_block_data_order to sha256_block. We must reduce the term size for the function, but there are no function calls in the body since all bit manipulations are encapsulated as C macros. In refactoring

```
131  void sha256_block_data_order(
132      SHA256_CTX *ctx, const void *in, size_t num) {
133      ...
134      for (i = 0; i < 16; i++) {
135          (void)HOST_c2l(data, l);
136          T1 = X[i] = l;
137          T1 += h + Sigma1(e) + Ch(e,f,g) + K256[i];
138          T2 = Sigma0(a) + Maj(a, b, c);
139          h = g;
140          g = f;
141          f = e;
142          e = d + T1;
143          d = c;
144          c = b;
145          b = a;
146          a = T1 + T2;
147      }
148
149      for (; i < 64; i++) {
150          s0 = X[(i+1) & 0x0f];
151          s0 = sigma0(s0);
152          s1 = X[(i+14) & 0x0f];
153          s1 = sigma1(s1);
154          T1 = X[i & 0xf] += s0 + s1 + X[(i+9) & 0xf];
155          T1 += h + Sigma1(e) + Ch(e,f,g) + K256[i];
156          T2 = Sigma0(a) + Maj(a,b,c);
157          h = g;
158          g = f;
159          f = e;
160          e = d + T1;
161          d = c;
162          c = b;
163          b = a;
164          a = T1 + T2;
165      }
166      ...
167  }
```

```
193  void sha256_block(
194      SHA256_CTX *c, const void* in) {
195      ...
196      for (i = 0; i < 16; i++) {
197          (void)HOST_c2l(data, l);
198          W[i] = l;
199      }
200
201      for (; i < 64; i++) {
202          W[i] = sigma1(W[i-2]) + W[i-7] +
203              sigma0(W[i-15]) + W[i-16];
204      }
205
206      for (i = 0; i < 64; i++) {
207          T1 = Sigma1(e) + Ch(e,f,g) + h +
208              K256[i] + W[i];
209          T2 = Sigma0(a) + Maj(a,b,c);
210          h = g;
211          g = f;
212          f = e;
213          e = d + T1;
214          d = c;
215          c = b;
216          b = a;
217          a = T1 + T2;
218      }
219      ...
220  }
```

(a)   (b)

Fig. 3. Loops in block hash code. (a) OpenSSL. (b) Unoptimized, naive C Reference.

the function we want to make it as similar to the Cryptol as possible as that is likely to reduce the complexity of the equivalence proof. This entails rewriting the OpenSSL speed optimization for the block hash portion with the unoptimized, simple NIST specification (see comparisons in Fig. 3). We also modify sha256_block to perform a single block, thus decreasing term size by removing the outer loop. We also had to break apart sha256_block into two functions – the split is at line 205 in Fig. 3(b). As such, the first two loops and the last loop are encapsulated into function calls. In each of these two new functions, the most complex computations inside loops W[i], T1, and T2 (lines 202–203 and 207–209) must also be refactored into functions.

We prove sha256_block_data_order and sha256_block equivalent to preserve the result of equivalence from OpenSSL to Cryptol. This proof completes in less than three seconds even though the term sizes are each over 35,000 loc. This illustrates the power of the SAW feature to compare C codes (with pointer arguments) for equivalence. SAW makes heavy use of term rewriting [4], and, as shown by our proof results, the effectiveness of the rewriting is enhanced when comparing two codes from the same programming language.

With overrides for add_one_bit, zero_fill, and sha256_block_data_order, the proof for SHA256_Final completes and succeeds. Table 1 shows the extracted term size of the overridden functions and the result of proving each function

Table 1. Term sizes and proof results without overrides.

C Reference	Term loc	Cryptol	Term loc	Proof result
zero_fill	328	zero_fill	39	Success
add_one_bit	6050	add_one_bit	26	Success
sha256_block	35501	hash_block_iterative	398	Timeout
SHA256_Final	41940	sha_finalize	1499	Timeout

Table 2. Average runtime proof results for SHA256_Final.

Overrides	Z3	ABC	Yices
sha256_block	Timeout	Timeout	Timeout
sha256_block, zero_fill	Timeout	Timeout	Timeout
sha256_block, add_one_bit	Timeout	Timeout	$\sim 5\,\mathrm{s}$
sha256_block, zero_fill, add_one_bit	Timeout	Timeout	$\sim 6\,\mathrm{s}$

equivalent to the Cryptol functions. Table 2 shows how overrides affect the completion of the proof. It is noteworthy that only Yices completes the proof. In our experience in proving SHA256, Yices handles loops with large bounds better than Z3 or ABC. Interestingly, the override for `zero_fill` does not impact proof completion because it is implemented in a functional style that causes the term to be trivially proved equivalent to the Cryptol. Thus SAW's rewriting engine is more efficient in reducing the `zero_fill` terms without an override.

3 Results and Conclusion

This paper shows how to use SAW to prove correctness of cryptographic algorithms implemented in C to Cryptol specifications. This proof is accomplished by leveraging SAW's compositional framework. The refactoring includes 1) constant memory accesses and non-volatile functions, 2) constant memory allocations and loop iterations, and 3) small functions encapsulating computationally complex code. These decompositions favor Yices. Further research could be valuable to understand why specific decompositions favor specific SMT solvers.

We have proved the C Reference is equivalent to the Cryptol code, which is equivalent to the Cryptol implementation used in the s2n HMAC proof [7]. Using the methods described in this paper, we are working to prove the entire OpenSSL SHA256 implementation with SAW. We are working to fully automate the proof of equivalence between the OpenSSL and C Reference codes, instead of partially relying on visual inspection. Finally, we plan to apply this work to modern hashes, such as SHA-3, that are much more complex in their definition and computation.

References

1. Bacchelli, A., Bird, C.: Expectations, outcomes, and challenges of modern code review. In: 2013 35th International Conference on Software Engineering (ICSE), pp. 712–721 (2013). https://doi.org/10.1109/ICSE.2013.6606617
2. Beringer, L., Petcher, A., Ye, K.Q., Appel, A.W.: Verified correctness and security of OpenSSL HMAC. In: 24th USENIX Security Symposium (USENIX Security 15), pp. 207–221. USENIX Association, Washington, D.C. (Aug 2015). https://www.usenix.org/conference/usenixsecurity15/technical-sessions/presentation/beringer
3. Chudnov, A., et al.: Continuous formal verification of Amazon s2n. In: Chockler, H., Weissenbacher, G. (eds.) CAV 2018, Part II. LNCS, vol. 10982, pp. 430–446. Springer, Cham (2018). https://doi.org/10.1007/978-3-319-96142-2_26
4. Dockins, R., Foltzer, A., Hendrix, J., Huffman, B., McNamee, D., Tomb, A.: Constructing semantic models of programs with the software analysis workbench. In: Blazy, S., Chechik, M. (eds.) VSTTE 2016. LNCS, vol. 9971, pp. 56–72. Springer, Cham (2016). https://doi.org/10.1007/978-3-319-48869-1_5
5. Erkök, L., Matthews, J.: Pragmatic equivalence and safety checking in cryptol. In: Proceedings of the 3rd Workshop on Programming Languages Meets Program Verification, pp. 73–82. PLPV 2009. Association for Computing Machinery, New York (2009). https://doi.org/10.1145/1481848.1481860
6. Galois, Inc.: The software analysis workbench. https://saw.galois.com/index.html
7. Amazon.com, Inc. s2n. https://github.com/awslabs/s2n
8. SAW verified crypto. https://bitbucket.org/byu-vv/saw-verified-crypto

Polygon Merge: A Geometric Algorithm Verified Using PVS

Ben L. Di Vito[(✉)] and Ashlie B. Hocking

Dependable Computing, Charlottesville, VA, USA
{ben.divito,ben.hocking}@dependablecomputing.com

Abstract. Geometric algorithms can present significant challenges for formal methods. We describe the formalization and verification of an algorithm posing such challenges. Given two overlapping polygons A and B, the Polygon Merge algorithm derives a new polygon whose edges are outermost, partial edges of A and B. The algorithm has been verified to satisfy correctness criteria expressed as two point-set properties. We have constructed a rigorous proof using the PVS interactive theorem prover along with support from the NASA PVS Library. While the algorithm itself is fairly compact, its proof was a moderately complicated undertaking. Owing to the complexity of reasoning about the spatial relationships of two different polygons, the proof required hundreds of supporting lemmas. Most of the definitions and lemmas introduced were needed to build a body of deductive artifacts sufficiently robust for this problem domain. Many of these artifacts will be generally useful for working with polygons, line segments and 2D vectors. Accordingly, we are distilling these products into a reusable PVS library.

Keywords: Deductive verification · Interactive theorem proving · Geometric algorithms · Polygon membership

1 Introduction

Geometry is a problem domain where human abilities in spatial reasoning and visualization are strong assets. Conducting formal proofs of geometric problems using interactive theorem provers is challenging simply because they cannot (yet) match human reasoning ability. Considerable detail must be provided during both formalization and proof to succeed in this domain. Formidable headwinds are to be expected.

Nevertheless, for problems of sufficient complexity and applications of some consequence, the return on investment of formal proofs is worthwhile. We have carried out a substantial effort to formalize and verify the Polygon Merge algorithm using PVS [10]. This effort led to the modeling of several geometric concepts found useful in reasoning about polygons. Moreover, the verification effort uncovered a latent flaw in the first version of the algorithm. This outcome confirms once again that subtle corner cases can confound human intuition and escape detection. Mechanized proof is sometimes needed to expose latent flaws.

© Springer Nature Switzerland AG 2021
A. Dutle et al. (Eds.): NFM 2021, LNCS 12673, pp. 79–94, 2021.
https://doi.org/10.1007/978-3-030-76384-8_6

A large body of lemmas has been proved and applied to the verification task. Many of these lemmas are generally useful and could be reused in other proof activities. We plan to create from this work one or more PVS libraries and make them available via the NASA PVS library collection [9].

2   Polygon Merge

Given two overlapping polygons A and B, the Polygon Merge algorithm derives a new polygon whose edges are the outermost, partial edges of A and B. Figure 1 illustrates the concept. Polygons A and B on the left of the figure are merged into polygon C on the right.

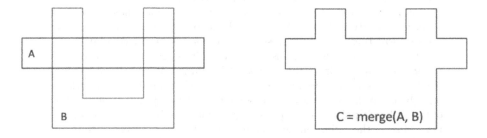

Fig. 1. Example of polygon merge operation.

Notice that crossing edges result in new vertices in C that are not present in A or B. The algorithm carries out a *vertex injection* operation on A and B, resulting in new polygons Am and Bm. A/B and Am/Bm have the same point sets for their edges and interiors. The difference is that the vertices of Am/Bm are supersets of those of A/B, and edges of A/B can be split into multiple colinear edges in Am/Bm.

Also notice from Fig. 1 that there is a region surrounded by edges of A and B whose points do not lie within either polygon. We refer to these regions as "holes." Any number of holes is possible, including zero, and all holes are included in merged polygon C. Thus, the merge operation differs from taking the union of A and B, which would not be representable as a polygon.

As a precondition for merging, we require that polygons A and B have at least one interior point in common. Polygons that share only vertices or (partial) edges are disallowed. The case of A completely containing B (or vice versa) is allowed; C would simply be the containing polygon A.

2.1   Classes of Polygons Supported

Polygon Merge is formalized as an idealized algorithm operating on simple, 2D polygons with vertices represented as x-y pairs of real numbers. Rendering the algorithm in executable form would introduce approximations inherent in floating point arithmetic, the consequences of which are not addressed in this paper.

Our definitions and lemmas are organized to work with three increasingly restrictive classes of polygons. The most general class constrains vertices to be unique (mutually distinct). Next, we add the constraints that the vertices must number at least three and edges may not cross one another (simple polygons). Finally, we add the constraint that vertices must appear in counterclockwise order. This most restrictive class is what the algorithm assumes.

2.2 Vertex Injection

Before the vertices of merged polygon C can be determined, we must first carry out a vertex injection operation to account for edge crossings in polygons A and B. Derived polygons Am and Bm represent the injected forms of A and B (Fig. 2). Wherever an edge of A crosses an edge of B (or vice versa), a new vertex appears in both Am and Bm. An injected vertex could occur at the site of an existing vertex of A or B, in which case the injection has no effect.

Injected vertices split edges of A and B into two or more colinear edges. Such edges are normally not admitted in definitions of simple polygons. This extension to conventional simple polygons is a necessary feature of our algorithm.

A special case occurs for edges of A and B that have an overlap of nonzero length. The injected vertices in this case occur at the maximum extent of the overlap. An edge of A could be overlapped by several different, colinear edges of B. In addition, a vertex of B could lie in the interior of an edge of A, which also gives rise to an injected vertex for A.

An important consequence of vertex injection is that edges of Am and Bm can intersect only at their vertices. We make heavy use of this fact in our verification. A large subset of the lemmas is concerned with characterizing line segment intersections and overlaps as well as traits of injected vertices and polygons.

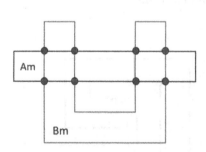

Fig. 2. Vertex injection.

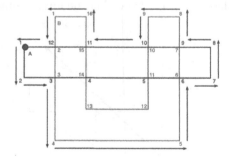

Fig. 3. Counterclockwise edge traversal.

2.3 Edge Traversal and Selection

After constructing polygons Am and Bm, the next task is to derive the vertices of the merged polygon C. The algorithm carries out a traversal of the outermost edges to collect a sequence of selected vertices. The starting point of this traversal is the *top-left vertex*, V_0. We first determine V_A and V_B, the topmost of the leftmost vertices of Am and Bm. Choosing the topmost of the leftmost of V_A and V_B yields V_0.

Proceeding from V_0, the algorithm selects one vertex at a time by examining the outgoing edges from the most recently selected vertex. If there is only one outgoing edge, the endpoint of that edge is selected. Otherwise, there is one edge from each of Am and Bm to consider. Their spatial relationship to the previous edge determines which edge is chosen. In particular, the rightmost of the edges is selected. If the edges overlap, they must be equal because they can only intersect at their endpoints. Figure 3 shows the edge traversal for our running example.

3   Correctness Requirements

Correctness requirements for the Polygon Merge algorithm focus on relating a point's membership in polygons A and B to membership in merged polygon C.

3.1   Point Membership in Polygons

A point p is on the *perimeter* of polygon G if there exists an edge e of G where p lies on e. We use a trichotomy of mutually exclusive and exhaustive conditions, namely, that a point is either inside, outside or on the perimeter of a polygon.

There are two well-known methods for identifying when a point lies within a polygon. Both have their basis as algorithms, i.e., they are computable. The first method relies on counting edge crossings [11], variously called the crossing number or ray casting algorithm. The second method is the winding number algorithm [5], also called the angle summation algorithm.

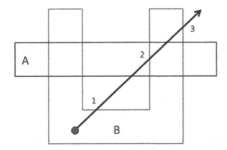

Fig. 4. Crossing-number criterion.

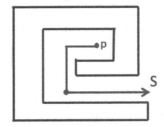

Fig. 5. Serpentine-ray criterion.

We use the crossing-number criterion in our formalization. In the basic version of the method, we begin with a point p and count all edge crossings along the ray that begins at p and emanates horizontally to the right. If the number of crossings is odd, p must be inside the polygon. We also use a variant of the method that allows the ray to point in an arbitrary direction (Fig. 4). In both variants, there are special-case rules needed when the ray passes through vertices or overlaps edges.

When formalizing properties in an expressive logic, it helps not to be confined to computable criteria for point membership. Allowing more general methods, such as those that quantify over infinite domains, can lead to simpler proofs. We have found it useful to introduce such a method, the *serpentine ray criterion*.

A serpentine ray (s-ray) is a hybrid geometric object having a tail, which is a ray pointing in an arbitrary direction, and a body, which is a finite sequence of connected line segments, the last endpoint of which forms the origin of the tail. Let S be an s-ray having starting point p at the head of S. If no part of S intersects any edge of polygon G, then point p lies outside of G. Figure 5 illustrates this criterion. Adding this existential method gives us independent criteria to determine when a point is inside, outside or on the perimeter of a polygon.

3.2 Top-Level Requirements

Formalizing correctness requirements for the merge algorithm focuses on two properties. The first requires that if a point p lies in polygon A or B or lies on their perimeters, then p must also be inside the merged polygon C or on its perimeter. The second property is the converse of the first, with a twist: if p lies in C, then p must be in or on A or B, or p must lie inside one of the holes. Figure 6 shows these properties rendered in PVS.

```
point_in_A_or_B_is_in_merge: THEOREM
  FORALL (A: (ccw_vertex_order?),
          B: (ccw_merge_pre_condition(A)), p: point_2d):
    point_in_polygon_inclusive?(p, A) OR
    point_in_polygon_inclusive?(p, B)
      IMPLIES point_in_polygon_inclusive?(p, merged_polygon(A, B))

point_in_merge_is_in_either_polygon_or_a_hole: THEOREM
  FORALL (A: (ccw_vertex_order?),
          B: (ccw_merge_pre_condition(A)), p: point_2d):
    point_in_polygon_inclusive?(p, merged_polygon(A, B)) IMPLIES
      point_in_polygon_inclusive?(p, A) OR
      point_in_polygon_inclusive?(p, B) OR
      point_in_polygon_merge_hole?(A, B)(p)
```

Fig. 6. Top-level correctness requirements.

4   Formalization and Problem Domain

We have formalized the merge algorithm using a set of PVS types and function definitions. An implementation in SPARK Ada has also been produced along with an assurance argument for its faithful rendering.

4.1   Formalization of Geometric Features

To formalize the algorithm and to express lemmas used in its verification, we have modeled several geometric concepts using PVS functions.

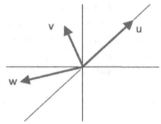   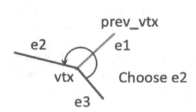

Fig. 7. Positive cross products.   **Fig. 8.** Selecting next merge vertex.

- **2D cross product.** We make extensive use of 2D vectors and their operations. While both dot products and cross products are used, we find cross products rather versatile. The 2D cross product is defined as $\mathbf{u}_x\mathbf{v}_y - \mathbf{u}_y\mathbf{v}_x$. For example, $\mathbf{u} \times \mathbf{v} > 0$ is useful for testing whether $\mathbf{v}$ is within π radians of $\mathbf{u}$ in the counterclockwise direction (Fig. 7).
- **Vector operations as sine and cosine.** We also exploit the trigonometric relationships for normalized (unit) vectors subtended by angle a: $\mathbf{u} \times \mathbf{v} = \sin a$ and $\mathbf{u} \cdot \mathbf{v} = \cos a$.
- **Minimum separation distance.** For every polygon there exists a constant D that bounds the distance between any vertex v and any point on any edge not adjacent to v. The PVS function `min_edge_sep` returns the value of D for a given polygon.
- **Angular region membership.** Given that two rays $\mathbf{x}$ and $\mathbf{y}$ both originate at point v (usually a vertex), it is helpful to determine whether a point p is "between" the rays $\mathbf{x}$ and $\mathbf{y}$. This condition holds when p can be found with a counterclockwise sweep from $\mathbf{x}$ to $\mathbf{y}$. Figure 8 depicts this notion in the context of selecting the next (rightmost) vertex for the merged polygon. Several PVS functions capture this notion, such as the one in Fig. 9.
- **Vertex wedge regions.** Every vertex v has two regions (designated *inward* and *outward*) on the inside and outside of the polygon bounded by the adjacent edges of v and a circular arc at distance `vertex_wedge_radius`, which is set to `min_edge_sep`/3.

```
point_between_rays?(s, e: segment_2d)(p: point_2d): bool =
  LET u = s'p1, v = s'p2, w = e'p2,
      vu = v - u, pu = p - u, wu = w - u IN
  IF cross(vu, wu) < 0
    THEN cross(vu, pu) > 0 OR cross(wu, pu) < 0
    ELSE cross(vu, pu) > 0 AND cross(wu, pu) < 0
  ENDIF
```

Fig. 9. Condition for a point to lie between rays aligned with line segments.

```
merge_helper(Am: simple_polygon_2d, Bm: simple_polygon_2d,
             first_vtx, vertex: (point_AB_vtx?(Am, Bm)),
             prev_vtx: point_2d,
             vtx_num: upto(Am'num_vertices + Bm'num_vertices)):
  RECURSIVE {s: (point_seq_AB_vtx?(Am, Bm)) |
                s'length <= Am'num_vertices + Bm'num_vertices - vtx_num} =
  LET next_vtx: point_2d = next_merge_vertex(Am, Bm, vertex, prev_vtx) IN
  IF next_vtx = first_vtx OR vtx_num = Am'num_vertices + Bm'num_vertices
    THEN empty_seq
    ELSE singleton_seq(next_vtx) o
            merge_helper(Am, Bm, first_vtx, next_vtx, vertex, vtx_num + 1)
  ENDIF
  MEASURE Am'num_vertices + Bm'num_vertices - vtx_num
```

Fig. 10. PVS function to find the merged polygon vertices.

```
next_merge_vertex(Am: simple_polygon_2d, Bm: simple_polygon_2d,
                  vertex: (point_AB_vtx?(Am, Bm)), prev_vtx: point_2d):
  (point_AB_vtx?(Am, Bm)) =
  LET idx_A = find_index(Am, vertex), idx_B = find_index(Bm, vertex) IN
  IF idx_A >= 0 THEN
    IF idx_B >= 0 THEN
      LET e2: segment_2d = edges_of_polygon(Am)(idx_A) IN
      LET e3: segment_2d = edges_of_polygon(Bm)(idx_B) IN
      IF prev_vtx = e3'p2 OR point_between_rays?(e3, e2)(prev_vtx)
        THEN Am'vertices(next_index(Am, idx_A))
        ELSE Bm'vertices(next_index(Bm, idx_B))
      ENDIF
      ELSE Am'vertices(next_index(Am, idx_A))
    ENDIF
    ELSE Bm'vertices(next_index(Bm, idx_B))
  ENDIF
```

Fig. 11. PVS function for selecting the next merge vertex.

4.2 Key Algorithm Functions

Two functions in the algorithm's formalization are of particular interest. First
is the recursive function for finding and collecting the merge vertices (Fig. 10).

Second is the function to select the next merge vertex at each step (Fig. 11). The recursive function carries out the edge traversal from the starting vertex (recall Fig. 3). It is unknown initially how many edges and vertices will form the merged polygon. Termination occurs when the next vertex returns to the starting vertex. The fact that the algorithm closes the loop is not shown until later in the proof development. For this reason, the function uses a secondary termination condition, namely, an upper bound on the number of possible vertices. This is necessary to convince PVS that the recursion is well-founded.

When there is a choice for the next merge edge, the algorithm selects the one further right with respect to the previous edge. (The first edge is treated as a special case.) In Fig. 11, this is done using the function point_between_rays? (from Fig. 9). Spatial relationships of the edges are illustrated in Fig. 8.

```
segment_intersect_kernel(s1, s2: segment_2d):
  [segment_intersection_type, point_2d] =
  LET p: point_2d = s1'p1 IN
  LET r: vector_2d = vector_from_point_to_point(s1'p1, s1'p2) IN
  LET q: point_2d = s2'p1 IN
  LET s: vector_2d = vector_from_point_to_point(s2'p1, s2'p2) IN
  LET r_cross_s: real = cross(r, s) IN
  LET q_minus_p_cross_r: real = cross((q - p), r) IN
  IF ((r_cross_s = 0) AND (q_minus_p_cross_r = 0)) THEN
   LET t0: real = (s2'p1 - s1'p1) * r IN
   LET t1: real = (s2'p2 - s1'p1) * r IN
   LET norm_sq: nnreal = r * r IN
   IF ((0 <= t0 AND t0 <= norm_sq) OR (0 <= t1 AND t1 <= norm_sq))
     THEN (Collinear_Overlapping, zero_point)
     ELSE (Collinear_Non_Overlapping, zero_point)
   ENDIF
  ELSIF ((r_cross_s = 0) AND (q_minus_p_cross_r /= 0)) THEN
   (Parallel, zero_point)
  ELSE
   LET q_minus_p_cross_s: real = cross((q - p), s) IN
   LET t: real = q_minus_p_cross_s / r_cross_s IN
   LET u: real = q_minus_p_cross_r / r_cross_s IN
   IF ((0 <= t AND t <= 1) AND (0 <= u AND u <= 1))
     THEN (Intersecting, mk_vect2(p'x + t * r'x, p'y + t * r'y))
     ELSE (Non_Parallel_Not_Intersecting, zero_point)
   ENDIF
  ENDIF;
```

Fig. 12. Implementable function to determine line intersection.

4.3 Implementation in SPARK Ada

The PVS algorithms for polygon merge were designed to be directly implementable. As an example of designing an algorithm for implementation, consider two ways of determining whether two line segments intersect. The first method is simple to understand, but cannot be implemented directly:

```
are_segments_intersecting_alt?(s1, s2: segment_2d): bool =
  EXISTS(p1: (is_point_on_segment?(s1))):
    is_point_on_segment?(s2)(p1);
```

The second method is harder to understand, but can be implemented directly (see Fig. 12):

```
are_segments_intersecting?(s1: segment_2d)(s2: segment_2d): bool =
  (segment_intersect_kernel(s1, s2)'1 = Intersecting or
  segment_intersect_kernel(s1, s2)'1 = Collinear_Overlapping);
```

We prove the latter definition is equal to the former definition so that an implementation of polygon merge can mirror the PVS code as closely as possible.

In general, our specification of PVS should be implementable in any common programming language, but our focus has been on making it easy to directly implement in SPARK Ada. Prior work on implementing PVS algorithms in SPARK Ada [4] derived a translation approach. This work also identified 13 issues encountered in the process. Our specification avoids these issues, with the exception of retrenchment from the ideal reals to IEEE floating point numbers.

5 Proof Decomposition

The scope and complexity of the proof effort required to conduct our verification was larger than expected. 1036 lemmas were formulated and proved. 823 TCCs (type correctness conditions) were generated by PVS. The vast majority of these were proved automatically; some were proved interactively. Replaying the proofs took 1734 s (28.9 min) of machine time (on modest hardware: MacBook Air, 1,8 GHz i5). Many of the proofs were large, requiring hundreds of proof steps. Note that not all lemmas appear in the proof chains for establishing the top-level results. Some were created out of a desire for completeness, for example, to have natural pairs (left-right, inside-outside, etc.). Compensating for the high degree of proof complexity is the side benefit of having developed many reusable definitions and lemmas.

Our verification effort introduced and proved a range of problem-specific lemmas, which can be grouped into categories to show the following:

- Points in or on polygons A and B are in or on C (forward point containment).
- Points in or on polygon C are in or on A or B or appear in one of the holes (reverse point containment).
- The selected merge vertices form a valid polygon.

– The merge algorithm is commutative.
– Equivalence of the point membership criteria.

Recall Fig. 6, which shows the top-level lemmas for the point containment. In the following sections we sketch the reasoning used to arrive at these results.

5.1 Forward Point Containment

Our first step is to reduce the point containment problem to an edge containment problem. In Fig. 13, the predicate `polygon_contained?` formalizes edge containment as the condition that any point on an edge of A must be either inside of C or on C's perimeter. The theorem in the figure establishes that edge containment implies point containment.

```
polygon_contained?(A, C: simple_polygon_2d): bool =
  FORALL (p: point_2d):
    point_on_polygon_perimeter?(A)(p)
      IMPLIES point_in_polygon?(p, C) OR
                point_on_polygon_perimeter?(C)(p)

contained_membership: THEOREM
  FORALL (p: point_2d, A, C: simple_polygon_2d):
    polygon_contained?(A, C) AND point_in_polygon?(p, A)
      IMPLIES point_in_polygon?(p, C)
```

Fig. 13. Edge containment implies point containment.

Thus, it suffices to show that all edges of Am and Bm are inside of C or part of C's perimeter. Nevertheless, this is a significant proof effort. The chain of reasoning is roughly as follows.

First, show that the wedge for the topmost, leftmost vertex is outside of C. Next, show that all outward wedges are also outside of C. To support an induction proof of this result, we introduce *wedge connector segments* that are likewise outside of the polygon. This construction enables an induction proof to propagate "outside-ness" to all outward wedges. Next, we show that the inward wedges are inside of C. This follows in a straightforward manner. Note that these are general results and are not specific to merged polygon C.

Now we establish that no edges of Am/Bm can pass through the outward wedges of C, as asserted in Fig. 14. Several intermediate lemmas are needed to carry out the proof. This implies each edge of Am/Bm either overlaps one in C or passes through an inward wedge of C, which is an interior region of C.

As stated earlier, vertex injection ensures that vertex intersections are the only kind possible for edges of Am and Bm. One additional lemma allows us to infer that Am and Bm are contained by C (Fig. 15). Given that A and B have the same point sets as Am and Bm, it follows that A and B are contained by C.

```
merge_no_edges_in_outward_wedges: LEMMA
  FORALL (A, C: (ccw_vertex_order?), B: (ccw_merge_pre_condition(A))):
    FORALL (Am: (ccw_vertex_order?), Bm: (ccw_merge_pre_condition(Am))):
      (Am, Bm) = inject_vertices_into_polygon(A, B) AND
      C = merged_polygon(A, B)
        IMPLIES no_edges_in_outward_wedges?(C, Am) AND
                no_edges_in_outward_wedges?(C, Bm)
```

Fig. 14. No edges in outward wedges.

```
contained_if_no_protruding_edges: LEMMA
  FORALL (G, H: (ccw_vertex_order?)):
    (EXISTS (q: point_2d):
      point_on_polygon_perimeter?(H)(q) AND
      (point_on_polygon_perimeter?(G)(q) OR
       point_in_polygon?(q, G))) AND
    no_edges_in_outward_wedges?(G, H) AND
    (FORALL (e: (edge_of_polygon?(H))):
      only_vertex_intersections?(G, H, e))
  IMPLIES polygon_contained?(H, G)
```

Fig. 15. Absence of protruding edges implies containment.

5.2 Reverse Point Containment

Showing point containment in the reverse direction relies on many of the lemmas already formulated. We must prove that polygon C contains both polygons A and B as well as whatever holes are created by overlaying A and B. In effect, our goal is to show that polygon C is a "tight fit" and does not admit any extraneous points. We formalize when a point lies in a hole region using the function in Fig. 16.

```
point_in_polygon_merge_hole?(A, B: simple_polygon_2d)
                            (p: point_2d): bool =
  NOT point_in_polygon_inclusive?(p, A) AND
  NOT point_in_polygon_inclusive?(p, B) AND
  FORALL (S: serpentine_ray):
    p = S'body'seq(0) IMPLIES
      EXISTS (q: point_2d):
        point_on_serp_ray?(q, S) AND
        (point_on_polygon_perimeter?(A)(q) OR
         point_on_polygon_perimeter?(B)(q))
```

Fig. 16. Predicate to determine when a point lies in a "hole" region.

This definition exploits the serpentine ray concept by asserting that for every point p and every s-ray S from p, there will necessarily be an intersection of S

with an edge of A or B. Given this definition, a proof is achieved by working through the cases and drawing from the large body of lemmas already in place.

5.3   Well-Formedness of Merged Polygon

The Polygon Merge algorithm generates a sequence of vertices pulled from the vertices of Am and Bm. It is necessary to prove that this vertex sequence V and the edges E defined by them meet the conditions we require of valid polygons: 1) length of V is at least three, 2) edges in E do not cross, 3) vertices in V are unique (mutually distinct), and 4) vertices in V appear in counterclockwise order. Three of these four conditions required moderate effort to establish, but were not particularly troublesome. The same cannot be said for condition (3). Proving the uniqueness result arguably has been the most difficult part of the entire verification effort.

```
merge_seq_has_uniq_vertex_list: LEMMA
  FORALL (A: (ccw_vertex_order?), B: (ccw_merge_pre_condition(A))):
    LET M = merge_seq(A, B) IN uniq_vertex_list?(M'length)(M'seq)
```

In large part, this difficulty stems from the need to work with a (partial) sequence of vertices rather than a complete polygon. Many previously proved lemmas about polygons cannot be applied. Instead, we need to reason about a vertex sub-sequence S and a hypothetical sub-polygon created by S when the sequence folds back on itself. Lemmas were created to describe the properties of edges and paths of edges that enter and exit polygons. In addition, we need to split out the special cases where one polygon is contained by the other.

5.4   Merge Algorithm Commutativity

Another useful result is the commutativity of the merge algorithm. Showing that merge_seq(A, B) = merge_seq(B, A) is helpful in this domain because many lemmas or cases within proofs have a dual nature. They are identical except for the substitution of B for A and vice versa. Knowing the algorithm is commutative allows many of these dual proofs to be discharged by instantiating lemmas in two different ways.

5.5   Equivalence of Point Membership Criteria

Figure 17 presents two lemmas that relate the three forms of point containment criteria used in our verification effort. Proof of the first lemma has been deferred for now given that it is a standard result from the literature on polygons.

Proving the second lemma, which relates predicates for when a point is inside or outside, is fairly benign in one direction; the other direction is more demanding. It requires a construction similar to that described in Sect. 5.1. We must exhibit a serpentine ray that is everywhere outside of the polygon. In effect, the constructed s-ray "skims" along the perimeter of the polygon until it reaches a point where the tail can point outward.

```
point_in_polygon_conds_equiv: LEMMA
  FORALL (p: point_2d, v: Normalized, G: simple_polygon_2d):
    point_in_polygon?(p, G) IFF point_in_polygon_arb?(p, v, G)

point_out_not_in: LEMMA
  FORALL (p: point_2d, G: simple_polygon_2d):
    NOT point_in_polygon?(p, G) IFF
    (point_on_polygon_perimeter?(G)(p) OR
     point_outside_polygon?(p, G))
```

Fig. 17. Equivalence properties for point membership predicates.

5.6 Supporting Lemmas

Lower-level supporting lemmas that were introduced fall into several categories. These lemmas vary in their generality and potential for reuse.

- Extensions to properties of finite sequences
- Properties of vertex injection definitions
- Facts about topmost, leftmost vertices
- Angular-region membership lemmas
- Facts about vertex wedge regions
- Supporting lemmas for polygon well-formedness

5.7 Problems Discovered

We close this discussion by noting that two changes to the algorithm were prompted by discoveries during proof development. First was a flaw in an earlier version of the algorithm that did not account for certain shared vertices. Figure 18 shows two polygons A and B sharing vertex v. This vertex is not the result of vertex injection from an edge crossing, but merely a common vertex for each.

The previous algorithm used a function segment_enters_polygon? to decide which edge to choose instead of the current approach. It allowed the anomalous behavior depicted in the figure, where erroneous and nonterminating execution was possible. Moreover, the faulty behavior would occur only for merge_seq(B, A); correct behavior would result from merge_seq(A, B). Attempts to formulate and prove a particular lemma led to this discovery. We consider it unlikely that this flaw would have been uncovered via testing. In response, we modified the algorithm so the rightmost edge is identified and selected.

The second change was not due to a flaw in the algorithm. Instead, it was a consequence of the definition of point_between_rays?, which does not hold when the point being tested lies on one of the two edges. This could lead to asymmetric behavior and an inability to discern that an edge is "doubling back" on the previously selected edge and therefore should not be selected (Fig. 19).

In reality, edge e1 in the figure would never be selected by the algorithm because it would be in the interior of the merged polygon, so this problematic

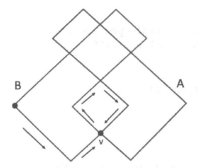

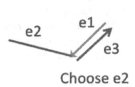

Choose e2

Fig. 18. Counterexample found in original algorithm.

Fig. 19. Overlapping edge should not be selected.

case would never arise in practice. Proving this conjecture, however, was judged to be rather difficult. As an alternative, we introduced an explicit test for this case in the `next_merge_vertex` function.

6   Related Work

Work on the PolyCARP family of algorithms [8] from NASA Langley was also focused on PVS. PolyCARP aims to compute containment, collision, resolution, and recovery information for polygons. It is intended primarily for air traffic management applications. Key differences with our work include the use of the winding number algorithm for point membership and a minimum angle between polygon edges.

Other research efforts to prove geometric algorithms focus on different formal methods tools. A method to enhance the automatability of proofs of geometric algorithms targets TLA+2 [6]. A different approach was used to apply Coq to the verification of a triangulation algorithm [1].

Algorithms intended for graphics applications that concern various polygon combinations have been developed. Computing the union, intersection and difference of two polygons is the focus of one such algorithm [7]. A second algorithm was designed to merge a set of polygons [12]. In addition, online forums for software developers often host discussions about similar algorithms.

Convex hull algorithms, e.g., the Graham scan [3], are related algorithms for computing vertices with containment properties. The computational geometry section from the book on algorithms by Cormen et al. [2] covers convex hull and similar algorithms.

7   Conclusion

We have formalized the Polygon Merge algorithm and various supporting concepts, then verified that the algorithm meets two correctness requirements.

Applications for this algorithm include the computation of keep-in and keep-out zones for autonomous vehicles. All work has been conducted using the PVS specification language and interactive theorem prover. Several portions of the NASA PVS Library were imported, including theories for 2D vectors and finite sets. More important is what was not imported: the trigonometry library. Forgoing this library reduced the formalization footprint and enhanced the prospects for tractable analyses of numeric behavior.

Notably, a latent flaw in the first version of the algorithm was discovered during the proof effort. An attempt to formulate and prove one of the conjectured properties exposed anomalous behavior. This outcome confirms, once again, the power of formal methods to illuminate dark corners of the problem space.

Concerning verification strategy, one lesson that can be drawn from our experience is to emphasize formulating lemmas on weaker structures where possible so that well-formedness requirements for stronger structures might be more easily established. For example, had we expressed some lemmas in terms of unstructured point sequences rather than polygons, we could have simplified the proof of the vertex uniqueness condition for the merged polygon.

Another lesson is not to underestimate the combinatorial impact of two polygons that can be overlaid and oriented in arbitrary ways. Complications from features such as overlapping edges are considerable. A careful strategy that can mitigate these impacts is worth pursuing, even if it requires greater effort during early project stages.

In future work, we hope to examine how to faithfully implement the algorithm's numeric features. This would include the impact of floating-point round-off errors as well as the possible use of alternative implementation techniques.

Acknowledgments. This work was funded by USAF AFRL/RQQA contract FA8650-17-F-2220. Approved for Public Release: Distribution Unlimited (Case Number: 88ABW-2020-3765).

References

1. Bertot, Y.: Formal verification of a geometry algorithm: a quest for abstract views and symmetry in Coq proofs. In: Fischer, B., Uustalu, T. (eds.) ICTAC 2018. LNCS, vol. 11187, pp. 3–10. Springer, Cham (2018). https://doi.org/10.1007/978-3-030-02508-3_1
2. Cormen, T.H., Leiserson, C.E., Rivest, R.L., Stein, C.: Introduction to Algorithms, 3rd edn. MIT Press and McGraw-Hill, Cambridge (2009)
3. Graham, R.L.: An efficient algorithm for determining the convex hull of a finite planar set. Inf. Process. Lett. **1**(4), 132–133 (1972)
4. Hocking, A.B., Rowanhill, J.C., Di Vito, B.L.: An analysis of implementing PVS in SPARK Ada. In: 2020 IEEE/AIAA 39th Digital Avionics Systems Conference (DASC). IEEE (2020)
5. Hormann, K., Agathos, A.: The point in polygon problem for arbitrary polygons. Comput. Geom. **20**(3), 131–144 (2001)
6. Kong, H., Zhang, H., Song, X., Gu, M., Sun, J.: Proving computational geometry algorithms in TLA+2. In: 5th IEEE International Conference on Theoretical Aspects of Software Engineering (TASE 2011). IEEE (2011)

7. Margalit, A., Knott, G.D.: An algorithm for computing the union, intersection or difference of two polygons. Comput. Graph. **13**(2), 167–183 (1989)
8. NASA: PolyCARP. https://github.com/nasa/PolyCARP
9. NASA Langley Research Center: PVS library collection, theories and proofs. http://shemesh.larc.nasa.gov/fm/ftp/larc/PVS-library/
10. Owre, S., Rushby, J.M., Shankar, N.: PVS: a prototype verification system. In: Kapur, D. (ed.) CADE 1992. LNCS, vol. 607, pp. 748–752. Springer, Heidelberg (1992). https://doi.org/10.1007/3-540-55602-8_217
11. Shimrat, M.: Algorithm 112: position of point relative to polygon. Comm. ACM **5**(8), 434 (1962)
12. Zalik, B.: Merging a set of polygons. Comput. Graph. **25**(1), 77–88 (2001)

Program Sketching Using Lifted Analysis for Numerical Program Families

Aleksandar S. Dimovski[1]([✉])[iD], Sven Apel[2][iD], and Axel Legay[3][iD]

[1] Mother Teresa University, St. Mirche Acev nr. 4, 1000 Skopje, North Macedonia
aleksandar.dimovski@unt.edu.mk
[2] Saarland University, Saarland Informatics Campus, E1.1,
66123 Saarbrücken, Germany
[3] Université catholique de Louvain, 1348 Ottignies-Louvain-la-Neuve, Belgium

Abstract. This work presents a novel approach for synthesizing numerical *program sketches* using *lifted (family-based) static program analysis*. In particular, our approach leverages a lifted static analysis based on abstract interpretation, which is used for analyzing program families with numerical features. It takes as input the common code base, which encodes all variants of a program family, and produces precise results for all variants in a single analysis run. The elements of the underlying lifted analysis domain are *decision trees*, in which decision nodes are labeled with linear constraints defined over numerical features and leaf nodes belong to a given single-program analysis domain.

We encode a program sketch as a program family such that holes correspond to numerical features and all possible sketch realizations correspond to variants in the program family. Then, we preform a lifted analysis of the family, so that only those variants that satisfy all assertions under all possible inputs represent correct realizations of holes in the sketch.

We have implemented an experimental program synthesizer for resolving C sketches. It is based on a lifted static analyzer for `#if`-based C program families, which uses the numerical domains from the APRON library. An evaluation yields promising results. Moreover, our approach provides speedups in some cases against the popular sketching tool `Sketch` and can solve some numerical benchmarks that `Sketch` cannot handle.

1 Introduction

Sketching [23,24] is one of the earliest and successful forms of program synthesis [1]. A *sketch* is a partial program that expresses the high-level structure of an implementation but leaves *holes* in place of low-level details. An integer hole is a placeholder that the synthesizer must replace with one of finitely many constant values. More specifically, the user provides the specification of the required program in the form of assertions, as well as a partial program with holes that needs to be completed. The goal of synthesizer is to automatically find integer values

© Springer Nature Switzerland AG 2021
A. Dutle et al. (Eds.): NFM 2021, LNCS 12673, pp. 95–112, 2021.
https://doi.org/10.1007/978-3-030-76384-8_7

for the holes so that the resulting complete program satisfies the assertions under all possible inputs. To solve the sketching problem, we need algorithms that can efficiently search to fill in holes without any user support.

In this paper, we rely on the notion of program families (a.k.a. software product lines) [2, 7] with numerical features to formalize this problem. We apply specifically designed lifted static analysis algorithms, which operate directly on program families rather than on individual programs, to solve the sketching problem. A *program family* is a set of similar, tailor-made programs, called *variants*, that is built from a common code base [21]. The variants of a program family are specified in terms of *features* (configuration options) that are statically selected for that particular variant at compile-time. In particular, we consider program families implemented using #if directives from the C preprocessor CPP [7, 17]. An #if directive specifies under which conditions parts of code should be included or excluded from a variant. At compile-time, a variant is derived by assigning concrete values to features, and only then is this variant compiled.

A key idea is that all possible program sketch realizations constitute a program family, where each integer hole is represented as a numerical feature. This way, program sketching is all about selecting correct variants (family members) from the corresponding program family. However, the automated analysis of program families for finding a correct variant is challenging since the family size (i.e., number of variants) typically grows exponentially in the number of features (i.e., holes). This is particulary apparent in the case of program families that contain numerical features with big domains, thus admitting astronomic family sizes (configuration spaces). Program sketching is also affected by this problem, since the family size corresponds to the space of sketch realizations. A naive enumerative (brute-force) solution, which analyzes each individual variant of the program family by an existing off-the-shelf single-program analyzer, has been shown to be very inefficient for large families [3, 20].

To address the program sketching problem, we use a *lifted (a.k.a. family-based or variability-aware) static program analysis* [3, 11–13, 18, 20, 28], which analyzes all variants of the family simultaneously, without generating any of them explicitly. Lifted analysis processes the common code base of a program family directly, exploiting the similarities among individual variants to reduce analysis effort. It reports analysis results for all variants that are equivalent to what a brute force approach would report. In particular, here we use an efficient, abstract interpretation-based lifted analysis of program families with numerical features [13], where *sharing* is explicitly possible between analysis elements corresponding to different variants. Inspired by the decision tree abstract domain proposed by Urban and Mine [25–27] for proving program termination, this is achieved by defining a specialized *decision tree lifted domain* [13] that provides a symbolic and compact representation of the lifted analysis elements. More precisely, the elements of the lifted domain are *decision trees*, in which decision nodes are labelled with linear constraints over numerical features, while leaf nodes belong to a given single-program analysis domain. The decision trees recursively partition the space of variants (i.e., the space of possible combinations of feature

```
void  main(unsigned int x){
①        int y;
②        y := x*??;
③        assert (y ≤ x+x); ④ }
```

Fig. 1. HELLOWORLD sketch.

```
void  main() {
①      int x := ??, y := 0;
②      while (x > ??) {
③        x := x-1;
④        y := y+1; }
⑤      assert (y > 2); ⑥ }
```

Fig. 2. LOOP sketch.

values), whereas the program properties at the leaves provide analysis information corresponding to each partition (i.e., to those variants that satisfy the constraints along the path to the given leaf node). This way, the lifted analysis partitions the given family into: "good" (correct), "bad" (incorrect), and "I don't know" (inconclusive) variants, i.e., sketch completions, with respect to a given set of assertions. Because of its special structure and possibilities for sharing of equivalent analysis results, the decision tree-based lifted analysis is able to converge to a solution very fast even for program families with astronomical search spaces. This is particularly so for sketches in which holes appear in expressions that can be exactly represented in the underlying domains for decision and leaf nodes (e.g., polyhedra). In those cases, we can design efficient lifted analysis with extended transfer functions for assignments and tests. Our approach is *sound* but *incomplete*: whatever correct sketch completions are inferred they can be trusted to hold, but we can miss some correct sketch completions.

Contributions. In summary, we make several contributions: (1) We propose a new, efficient technique for solving numerical program sketches by using lifted static analysis; (2) We implement a prototype program sketcher, called FAM-ILYSKETCHER, that uses numerical domains (e.g., polyhedra) from the APRON library as parameters; (3) We evaluate our approach on several C numerical sketches and compare its performances with the popular sketching tool Sketch and the brute-force enumeration approach.

Motivating Examples. The code snippet HELLOWORLD in Fig. 1 is regarded as the "Hello World" example of sketching [23]. This sketch contains one integer hole, denoted by ??. Note that x is an input variable that can take non-negative integer values. As observed before in the literature [5], a sketch can be represented as a program family, such that all possible realizations of holes in the sketch correspond to possible variants in the program family. The HELLOWORLD sketch can be encoded as a program family that contains one numerical feature A with domain [Min, Max] ⊆ $\mathbb{Z}$, such that the hole ?? is replaced with A[1]. There are Max−Min+1 variants that can be derived from the HELLOWORLD program family. To find a correct variant that satisfies the given assertion, we perform a lifted

---

[1] This is only high-level description of the encoding. For the precise definition, we refer to Sect. 3.3. See the HELLOWORLD program family in Fig. 5a.

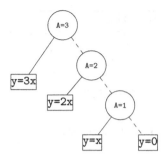

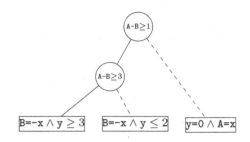

Fig. 3. Tree at loc. ③ of HEL-
LOWORLD.

Fig. 4. Tree at loc. ⑤ of LOOP.

analysis based on decision trees [13] of the corresponding HELLOWORLD program family. The decision tree (invariant) inferred at the final location ③ when A has domain [0, 3] is shown in Fig. 3. Notice that the inner nodes of the decision tree in Fig. 3 are labeled with *polyhedral* linear constraints over the numerical feature A, while the leaves are labeled with *polyhedral* linear constraints over program variables x and y. The edges of decision trees are labeled with the truth value of the decision on the parent node: we use solid edges for true (i.e., the constraint in the parent node is satisfied) and dashed edges for false (i.e., the negation of the constraint in the parent node is satisfied). As decision nodes partition the space of all possible feature's values, we implicitly assume that linear constraints in decision nodes take domains of numerical features into account. For example, the decision node $(A = 3)$ is satisfied when $(A = 3) \wedge (\text{Min} \leq A \leq \text{Max})$, whereas its negation is satisfied when $(A \neq 3) \wedge (\text{Min} \leq A \leq \text{Max})$. The final assertion is valid at leaf nodes when $(A \leq 2)$. Hence, we can replace the hole ?? in the sketch with an integer less or equal than 2, so that the assertion is always valid.

Consider the LOOP sketch in Fig. 2 taken from Syntax-Guided Synthesis Competition (https://sygus.org/) [1]. It contains two integer holes, which are replaced with two numerical features A and B in the LOOP program family. Since the domain of each numerical feature is [Min, Max], the total number of variants is $(\text{Max} - \text{Min} + 1)^2$. If we analyze the LOOP program family using a lifted analysis based on decision trees as before, we obtain the invariant shown in Fig. 4 at the location ⑤. We can see that the given assertion is valid for $(A-B \geq 3)$. Thus, the synthesizer can choose one of the variants that satisfy the above constraint (e.g., A=4, B=1) as a solution to the LOOP sketch.

2 From Sketches to Program Families

Now we introduce the languages for writing sketches and program families. Then, we define the encoding of sketches as program families and show its correctness.

2.1   Sketches

We use a simple sequential imperative language to illustrate our work. The program variables Var are statically allocated, and the only data type is the set $\mathbb{Z}$ of mathematical integers. To encode sketches, a single sketching construct is included: a basic integer hole denoted by ??. The integer hole ?? is a placeholder that the synthesizer must replace with a suitable integer constant, such that the resulting program will avoid any assertion failures. The syntax is:

$$s ::= \mathtt{skip} \mid \mathtt{x:=}e \mid s; s \mid \mathtt{if}\,(e)\,\mathtt{then}\,s\,\mathtt{else}\,s \mid \mathtt{while}\,(e)\,\mathtt{do}\,s \mid \mathtt{assert}(e)$$
$$e ::= n \mid \mathtt{x} \mid \mathtt{??} \mid e{\oplus}e$$

where n ranges over integers, $\mathtt{x}$ over program variables Var, and $\oplus$ over binary arithmetic-logic operators. Each hole occurrence is assumed to be uniquely labelled as $??_i$ and has a bounded integer domain $[n, n']$. We will sometimes write $??_i^{[n,n']}$ to make explicit the domain of a given hole. Our aim is to replace each $??_i^{[n,n']}$ with a suitable constant from $[n, n']$. By Stm and Exp we denote the set of statements s and expressions e generated by the above grammar. W.l.o.g., a program is a sequence of statements (without $\mathtt{assert}$) followed by an assertion.

Semantics. Let H be a set of holes in a program sketch. We define a *control function* $\phi : \Phi = H \to \mathbb{Z}$ to describe the value of each hole in the sketch. Thus, ϕ fully describes a candidate solution to the sketch. A *program state* $\sigma : \Sigma = Var \to \mathbb{Z}$ is a mapping from variables to values. The meaning of expressions $[\![e]\!] : \Sigma \to \Phi \to \mathbb{Z}$ is defined by induction on e:

$$[\![n]\!]\sigma\phi = n, \; [\![\mathtt{x}]\!]\sigma\phi = \sigma(\mathtt{x}), \; [\![??_i]\!]\sigma\phi = \phi(??_i), \; [\![e_0 \oplus e_1]\!]\sigma\phi = [\![e_0]\!]\sigma\phi \oplus [\![e_1]\!]\sigma\phi$$

The inference rules for a small-step operational semantics of statements are standard [20]. We write $[\![s]\!]\sigma\phi$ for the final state σ' that can be derived from $\langle s, \sigma\phi \rangle$ (if the derivation terminates successfully), that is $\langle s, \sigma\phi \rangle \to^* \sigma'$, by using the inference rules. The meaning of statements is: $[\![s]\!]^\phi = \bigcup_{\sigma \in \Sigma^{\mathrm{init}}} [\![s]\!]\sigma\phi$, where Σ^{init} denotes the set of initial input states on which s is executed.

2.2   Program Families

Let $\mathbb{F} = \{A_1, \ldots, A_k\}$ be a finite and totally ordered set of *numerical features* available in a program family. For each feature $A \in \mathbb{F}$, $\mathrm{dom}(A) \subseteq \mathbb{Z}$ denotes the set of possible values that can be assigned to A. A valid combination of feature values represents a *configuration* k, which specifies one *variant* of a program family. It is given as a *valuation function* $k : \mathbb{F} \to \mathbb{Z}$, which is a mapping that assigns a value from $\mathrm{dom}(A)$ to each feature A, that is, $k(A) \in \mathrm{dom}(A)$ for any $A \in \mathbb{F}$. We assume that only a subset $\mathbb{K}$ of all possible configurations are *valid*. An alternative representation of configurations is based upon propositional formulae. Each configuration $k \in \mathbb{K}$ can be represented by a formula: $(A_1 = k(A_1)) \wedge \ldots \wedge (A_k = k(A_k))$. The set of valid configurations $\mathbb{K}$ can be also represented as a formula: $\vee_{k \in \mathbb{K}} k$.

We define *feature expressions*, denoted $FeatExp(\mathbb{F})$, as the set of propositional logic formulas over constraints of $\mathbb{F}$ generated by the grammar:

$$\theta ::= \text{true} \mid e_{\mathbb{F}} \bowtie e_{\mathbb{F}} \mid \neg\theta \mid \theta \wedge \theta \mid \theta \vee \theta, \qquad e_{\mathbb{F}} ::= n \mid A \mid e_{\mathbb{F}} \boxplus e_{\mathbb{F}}$$

where $A \in \mathbb{F}$, $n \in \mathbb{Z}$, $\boxplus \in \{+, -, *\}$, and $\bowtie \in \{=, <\}$. When a configuration $k \in \mathbb{K}$ satisfies a feature expression $\theta \in FeatExp(\mathbb{F})$, we write $k \models \theta$, where $\models$ is the standard satisfaction relation of logic. We write $[\![\theta]\!]$ to denote the set of configurations from $\mathbb{K}$ that satisfy θ, that is, $k \in [\![\theta]\!]$ iff $k \models \theta$. For example, for the HELLOWORLD program family in Fig. 5a we have $\mathbb{F} = \{A\}$ and $\mathbb{K} = \{(A = \text{Min}), \ldots, (A = \text{Max})\}$. For the feature expression $(A > 2)$, we have $[\![(A > 2)]\!] = \{(A=3), \ldots (A=\text{Max})\}$. Thus, $(A=5) \models (A>2)$ and $(A=0) \not\models (A>2)$.

The language includes the same expression and statement productions as the language for sketches, except that the hole expression `??` is not allowed. To encode multiple variants, a new compile-time conditional statement is included. The new statement "`#if` (θ) $\overline{s}$ `#endif`" contains a feature expression $\theta \in FeatExp(\mathbb{F})$ as a *presence condition*, such that only if θ is satisfied by a configuration $k \in \mathbb{K}$ the statement $\overline{s}$ will be included in the variant corresponding to k. The syntax is:

$$\overline{s} ::= \ldots \mid \text{\#if } (\theta)\,\overline{s}\text{ \#endif}, \qquad \overline{e} ::= n \mid \text{x} \mid \overline{e} \oplus \overline{e}$$

The set of all statements $\overline{s}$ is $\overline{Stm}$; the set of all expressions $\overline{e}$ is $\overline{Exp}$. Any other preprocessor conditional constructs can be desugared and represented only by `#if` construct. For example, `#if` (θ) $\overline{s_0}$ `#elif` (θ') $\overline{s_1}$ `#endif` is translated into `#if` (θ) $\overline{s_0}$ `#endif` ; `#if` $(\neg\theta \wedge \theta')$ $\overline{s_1}$ `#endif`.

Semantics. A program family is evaluated in two stages. First, the preprocessor CPP takes a program family $\overline{s}$ and a configuration $k \in \mathbb{K}$ as inputs, and produces a variant (that is, a single program without `#if`-s) corresponding to k as the output. Second, the obtained variant is evaluated using the standard single-program semantics [20]. The first stage is specified by the projection function π_k, which is an identity for all basic statements and recursively pre-processes all sub-statements of compound statements. Hence, $\pi_k(\text{skip}) = \text{skip}$ and $\pi_k(\overline{s};\overline{s'}) = \pi_k(\overline{s});\pi_k(\overline{s'})$. For "`#if` (θ) $\overline{s}$ `#endif`", statement $\overline{s}$ is included in the variant if $k \models \theta$, otherwise, if $k \not\models \theta$ statement $\overline{s}$ is removed[2]:

$$\pi_k(\text{\#if } (\theta)\,\overline{s}\text{ \#endif}) = \begin{cases} \pi_k(\overline{s}) & \text{if } k \models \theta \\ \text{skip} & \text{if } k \not\models \theta \end{cases}.$$ For example, Fig. 5a shows the code

of the program family HELLOWORLD (only the function body) that contains one numerical feature A with domain $[\text{Min}, \text{Max}]$. Two valid variants $P_{A=0}(\text{HELLOWORLD})$ and $P_{A=1}(\text{HELLOWORLD})$ shown in Fig. 5b and Fig. 5c, respectively, can be derived from the HELLOWORLD family in Fig. 5a.

We define the semantics of variants $\pi_k(\overline{s})$, i.e. single programs without `#if`-s. A *program state* is $\sigma : \Sigma = Var \rightarrow \mathbb{Z}$. The meaning of expressions $[\![\overline{e}]\!] : \Sigma \rightarrow \mathbb{Z}$

---

[2] Since any $k \in \mathbb{K}$ is a valuation function, we have that either $k \models \theta$ holds or $k \not\models \theta$ (which is equivalent to $k \models \neg\theta$) holds, for any $\theta \in FeatExp(\mathbb{F})$.

is:

$$[\![n]\!]\sigma = n, \qquad [\![\mathbf{x}]\!]\sigma = \sigma(\mathbf{x}), \qquad [\![\overline{e_1} \oplus \overline{e_2}]\!]\sigma = [\![\overline{e_1}]\!]\sigma \oplus [\![\overline{e_2}]\!]\sigma$$

The set of statements is the same for sketches and variants, so the meaning of statements $[\![\pi_k(\overline{s})]\!]$ for variants coincides with the meaning for sketches.

`int y;`			`int x := A, y := 0;`
`#if (A=Min) y := x*Min`			`while (x > B) {`
`#elif ...`	`int y;`	`int y;`	`x := x-1;`
`#elif (A=Max-1)y :=x*(Max-1)`	`y := x*0;`	`y := x*1;`	`y := y+1;}`
`#else y := x*Max ...#endif`	`assert(y≤x+x);`	`assert(y≤x+x);`	`assert (y > 2); }`
`assert (y≤x+x);`			
(a) HelloWorld	(b) P_{A=0}(Hellow.)	(c) P_{A=1}(Hellow.)	(d) Loop

Fig. 5. The program families HelloWorld and Loop and some their variants.

2.3 Encoding of Sketches as Program Families

Our aim is to transform an input program sketch $\hat{s}$ with a set of m holes $??_1^{[n_1,n_1']}, \ldots, ??_m^{[n_m,n_m']}$ into an output program family $\overline{s}$ with a set of numerical features $A_1, \ldots, A_m$ with domains $[n_1, n_1'], \ldots, [n_m, n_m']$, respectively. The set of configurations $\mathbb{K}$ includes all possible combinations of feature values.

We now define a rewrite rule for eliminating holes $??$ from a program sketch. Let $s[??^{[n,n']}]$ be a basic (non-compound) statement in which the hole $??^{[n,n']}$ occurs. The rewrite rule is of the form:

$$s[??^{[n,n']}] \leadsto \text{#if (A=n) } s[n] \text{ #elif } \ldots \text{#elif (A=n'-1) } s[n'-1] \qquad (\text{R-1})$$
$$\text{#else } s[n'] \text{ #endif} \ldots \text{#endif}$$

The meaning of rule (R-1) is that, if the current program sketch being transformed matches the abstract syntax tree node of the shape $s[??^{[n,n']}]$, then replace $s[??^{[n,n']}]$ with the right-hand side of rule (R-1). The set of features $\mathbb{F}$ is also updated with the fresh feature A with domain $[n, n']$.

We write $\text{Rewrite}(\hat{s})$ to be the final transformed program family $\overline{s}$ obtained by repeatedly applying rule (R-1) on a program sketch $\hat{s}$ and on its transformed versions until we reach a point at which this rule can not be applied, i.e. when all occurrences of holes $??$ in $\hat{s}$ are eliminated. For example, the program sketch HelloWorld in Fig. 1 is encoded as the program family HelloWorld in Fig. 5a.

Theorem 1. *Let $\hat{s}$ be a sketch and ϕ be a control function, s.t. features $A_1, \ldots, A_n$ correspond to holes $??_1, \ldots, ??_n$. We define a configuration $k \in \mathbb{K}$, s.t. $k(A_i) = \phi(??_i)$ for $1 \le i \le n$. Let $\overline{s} = \text{Rewrite}(\hat{s})$. We have: $[\![\hat{s}]\!]^\phi = [\![\pi_k(\overline{s})]\!]$.*

3 Synthesis by Lifted Analysis

Lifted analyses are designed by *lifting* existing single-program analyses to work on program families, rather than on individual programs. Lifted analysis by abstract interpretation introduced in [13] relies on a lifted domain in the form of *decision trees* [26,27]. The leaf nodes of decision trees belong to an existing single-program analysis domain, and are separated by linear constraints over numerical features, organized in decision nodes. We first define the basic decision tree lifted domain in Sect. 3.1. Then in Sect. 3.2, we show how we can optimize the encoding of sketches as program families and extend the decision tree lifted domain to obtain more efficient program sketcher. Finally, in Sect. 3.3, we present a synthesis algorithm for resolving sketches based on lifted analysis.

3.1 Basic Lifted Analysis

Abstract Domain for Leaf Nodes. We assume that a single-program domain $\mathbb{A}$ defined over program variables *Var* is equipped with sound operators for concretization $\gamma_\mathbb{A}$, ordering $\sqsubseteq_\mathbb{A}$, join $\sqcup_\mathbb{A}$, meet $\sqcap_\mathbb{A}$, bottom $\bot_\mathbb{A}$, top $\top_\mathbb{A}$, widening $\nabla_\mathbb{A}$, and narrowing $\triangle_\mathbb{A}$, as well as sound transfer functions for tests FILTER$_\mathbb{A}$ and forward assignments ASSIGN$_\mathbb{A}$. More specifically, FILTER$_\mathbb{A}(a : \mathbb{A}, e : Exp)$ returns an abstract element from $\mathbb{A}$ obtained by restricting a to satisfy the test e, whereas ASSIGN$_\mathbb{A}(a : \mathbb{A}, \mathtt{x}\mathtt{:=}e : Stm)$ returns an updated version of a by abstractly evaluating $\mathtt{x}\mathtt{:=}e$ in it. In practice, the domain $\mathbb{A}$ will be instantiated with some of the known numerical domains $\langle \mathbb{D}, \sqsubseteq_\mathbb{D} \rangle$, such as Intervals $\langle I, \sqsubseteq_I \rangle$ [8], Octagons $\langle O, \sqsubseteq_O \rangle$ [27], and Polyhedra $\langle P, \sqsubseteq_P \rangle$ [10], defined over *Var*. For example, the elements of P are conjunctions of polyhedral constraints of the form $\alpha_1 x_1 + \ldots + \alpha_k x_k + \beta \geq 0$, where $x_1, \ldots x_k \in Var, \alpha_1, \ldots, \alpha_k, \beta \in \mathbb{Z}$.

Abstract Domain for Decision Nodes. We introduce a family of abstract domains for linear constraints $\mathbb{C}_\mathbb{D}$ defined over features $\mathbb{F}$, which are parameterized by any of the numerical property domains $\mathbb{D}$ (intervals I, octagons O, polyhedra P). For example, the set of *polyhedral constraints* is $\mathbb{C}_P = \{\alpha_1 A_1 + \ldots + \alpha_k A_k + \beta \geq 0 \mid A_1, \ldots A_k \in \mathbb{F}, \alpha_1, \ldots, \alpha_k, \beta \in \mathbb{Z}, \gcd(|\alpha_1|, \ldots, |\alpha_k|, |\beta|) = 1\}$. The set $\mathbb{C}_\mathbb{D}$ of linear constraints over features $\mathbb{F}$ is constructed by the underlying numerical property domain $\langle \mathbb{D}, \sqsubseteq_\mathbb{D} \rangle$ using the Galois connection $\langle \mathcal{P}(\mathbb{C}_\mathbb{D}), \sqsubseteq_\mathbb{D} \rangle \xleftarrow[\alpha_{\mathbb{C}_\mathbb{D}}]{\gamma_{\mathbb{C}_\mathbb{D}}} \langle \mathbb{D}, \sqsubseteq_\mathbb{D} \rangle$, where $\mathcal{P}(\mathbb{C}_\mathbb{D})$ is the power set of $\mathbb{C}_\mathbb{D}$ [13]. The concretization function $\gamma_{\mathbb{C}_\mathbb{D}} : \mathbb{D} \to \mathcal{P}(\mathbb{C}_\mathbb{D})$ maps a conjunction of constraints from $\mathbb{D}$ to a set of constraints in $\mathcal{P}(\mathbb{C}_\mathbb{D})$.

The domain of decision nodes is $\mathbb{C}_\mathbb{D}$. We assume the set of features $\mathbb{F} = \{A_1, \ldots, A_k\}$ to be totally ordered, such that the ordering is $A_1 > \ldots > A_k$. We impose a total order $<_{\mathbb{C}_\mathbb{D}}$ on $\mathbb{C}_\mathbb{D}$ to be the lexicographic order on the coefficients $\alpha_1, \ldots, \alpha_k$ and constant α_{k+1} of the linear constraints, such that:

$$(\alpha_1 \cdot A_1 + \ldots + \alpha_k \cdot A_k + \alpha_{k+1} \geq 0) \ <_{\mathbb{C}_\mathbb{D}} \ (\alpha'_1 \cdot A_1 + \ldots + \alpha'_k \cdot A_k + \alpha'_{k+1} \geq 0)$$
$$\iff \ \exists j > 0. \forall i < j.(\alpha_i = \alpha'_i) \wedge (\alpha_j < \alpha'_j)$$

The negation of linear constraints is formed as: $\neg(\alpha_1 A_1 + \ldots \alpha_k A_k + \beta \geq 0) = -\alpha_1 A_1 - \ldots - \alpha_k A_k - \beta - 1 \geq 0$. For example, the negation of $A - 3 \geq 0$ is $-A + 2 \geq 0$. To ensure canonical representation of decision trees, a linear constraint c and its negation $\neg c$ cannot both appear as decision nodes. Thus, we only keep the largest constraint with respect to $<_{\mathbb{C}_\mathbb{D}}$ between c and $\neg c$.

Abstract Domain for Decision Trees. A *decision tree* $t \in \mathbb{T}(\mathbb{C}_\mathbb{D}, \mathbb{A})$ over the sets $\mathbb{C}_\mathbb{D}$ of linear constraints defined over $\mathbb{F}$ and the leaf abstract domain $\mathbb{A}$ defined over Var is either a leaf node $\ll a \gg$ with $a \in \mathbb{A}$, or $[\![c : tl, tr]\!]$, where $c \in \mathbb{C}_\mathbb{D}$ (denoted by $t.c$) is *the smallest constraint* with respect to $<_{\mathbb{C}_\mathbb{D}}$ appearing in the tree t, tl (denoted by $t.l$) is the left subtree of t representing its *true branch*, and tr (denoted by $t.r$) is the right subtree of t representing its *false branch*. The path along a decision tree establishes the set of configurations (those that satisfy the encountered constraints), and the leaf nodes represent the analysis properties for the corresponding configurations.

Example 1. The following two decision trees t_1 and t_2 have decision and leaf nodes labelled with polyhedral linear constraints defined over numerical feature A with domain $\mathbb{Z}$ and over integer program variable y, respectively:

$$t_1 = [\![A \geq 4 : \ll[y \geq 2]\gg, \ll[y = 0]\gg]\!], \quad t_2 = [\![A \geq 2 : \ll[y \geq 0]\gg, \ll[y \leq 0]\gg]\!] \qquad \square$$

Abstract Operations. The *concretization function* $\gamma_\mathbb{T}$ of a decision tree $t \in \mathbb{T}(\mathbb{C}_\mathbb{D}, \mathbb{A})$ returns $\gamma_\mathbb{A}(a)$ for $k \in \mathbb{K}$, where k satisfies the set $C \in \mathcal{P}(\mathbb{C}_\mathbb{D})$ of constraints accumulated along the top-down path to the leaf node $a \in \mathbb{A}$. More formally, $\gamma_\mathbb{T}(t) = \overline{\gamma}_\mathbb{T}[\mathbb{K}](t)$, where $\mathbb{K} = \vee_{k \in \mathbb{K}} k$ is the set of implicit constraints over $\mathbb{F}$ taking into account the domains of features. Function $\overline{\gamma}_\mathbb{T}$ is defined as:

$$\overline{\gamma}_\mathbb{T}[C](\ll a \gg) = \prod_{k \models C} \gamma_\mathbb{A}(a), \quad \overline{\gamma}_\mathbb{T}[C]([\![c : tl, tr]\!]) = \overline{\gamma}_\mathbb{T}[C \cup \{c\}](tl) \times \overline{\gamma}_\mathbb{T}[C \cup \{\neg c\}](tr)$$

Other binary operations rely on the algorithm for *tree unification* [13, 26], which finds a common labelling of two trees t_1 and t_2. Note that the tree unification does not lose any information.

Example 2. After tree unification of t_1 and t_2 from Example 1, we obtain:

$$t_1 = [\![A \geq 4 : \ll[y \geq 2]\gg, [\![A \geq 2 : \ll[y = 0]\gg, \ll[y = 0]\gg]\!]]\!],$$
$$t_2 = [\![A \geq 4 : \ll[y \geq 0]\gg, [\![A \geq 2 : \ll[y \geq 0]\gg, \ll[y \leq 0]\gg]\!]]\!]$$

Note that the tree unification adds a decision node for $A \geq 2$ to the right subtree of t_1, whereas it adds a decision node for $A \geq 4$ to t_2 and removes the redundant constraint $A \geq 2$ from the resulting left subtree of t_2. $\qquad \square$

All binary operations are performed leaf-wise on the unified decision trees. Given two unified trees t_1 and t_2, their ordering $t_1 \sqsubseteq_\mathbb{T} t_2$ and join $t_1 \sqcup_\mathbb{T} t_2$ are:

$$\ll a_1 \gg \sqsubseteq_\mathbb{T} \ll a_2 \gg = a_1 \sqsubseteq_\mathbb{A} a_2, \quad [\![c : tl_1, tr_1]\!] \sqsubseteq_\mathbb{T} [\![c : tl_2, tr_2]\!] = (tl_1 \sqsubseteq_\mathbb{T} tl_2) \wedge (tr_1 \sqsubseteq_\mathbb{T} tr_2)$$
$$\ll a_1 \gg \sqcup_\mathbb{T} \ll a_2 \gg = \ll a_1 \sqcup_\mathbb{A} a_2 \gg, \quad [\![c : tl_1, tr_1]\!] \sqcup_\mathbb{T} [\![c : tl_2, tr_2]\!] = [\![c : tl_1 \sqcup_\mathbb{T} tl_2, tr_1 \sqcup_\mathbb{T} tr_2]\!]$$

Similarly, we compute meet $t_1 \sqcap_\mathbb{T} t_2$, widening $t_1 \nabla_\mathbb{T} t_2$, and narrowing $t_1 \triangle_\mathbb{T} t_2$ of two unified trees t_1 and t_2. The top is a tree with a single $\top_\mathbb{A}$ leaf: $\top_\mathbb{T} = \ll \top_\mathbb{A} \gg$, while the bottom is a tree with a single $\bot_\mathbb{A}$ leaf: $\bot_\mathbb{T} = \ll \bot_\mathbb{A} \gg$.

Algorithm 1: $\text{ASSIGN}_{\mathbb{T}}(t, \text{x}:=e)$

---

1 **if** isLeaf(t) **then return** $\ll\text{ASSIGN}_{\mathbb{A}}(t, \text{x}:=e)\gg$;
2 **return** $[\![t.c : \text{ASSIGN}_{\mathbb{T}}(t.l, \text{x}:=e), \text{ASSIGN}_{\mathbb{T}}(t.r, \text{x}:=e)]\!]$;

Algorithm 2: $\text{FEAT-FILTER}_{\mathbb{T}}(t, \theta)$

---

1 **switch** θ **do**
2 | **case** $(e_{\mathbb{F}} \bowtie e_{\mathbb{F}}) \mid\mid (\neg(e_{\mathbb{F}} \bowtie e_{\mathbb{F}}))$
3 | | $J = \text{FILTER}_{\mathbb{D}}(\top_{\mathbb{D}}, \theta)$; **return** $\text{RESTRICT}(t, \mathbb{K}, J)$
4 | **case** $\theta_1 \wedge \theta_2$
5 | | **return** $\text{FEAT-FILTER}_{\mathbb{T}}(t, \theta_1) \sqcap_{\mathbb{T}} \text{FEAT-FILTER}_{\mathbb{T}}(t, \theta_2)$
6 | **case** $\theta_1 \vee \theta_2$
7 | | **return** $\text{FEAT-FILTER}_{\mathbb{T}}(t, \theta_1) \sqcup_{\mathbb{T}} \text{FEAT-FILTER}_{\mathbb{T}}(t, \theta_2)$

Transfer Functions. We define lifted transfer functions for tests, forward assignments ($\text{ASSIGN}_{\mathbb{T}}$), and #if-s ($\text{IFDEF}_{\mathbb{T}}$) [13]. There are two types of tests: *expression-based tests*, denoted by $\text{FILTER}_{\mathbb{T}}$, that occur in while and if-s, and *feature-based tests*, denoted by $\text{FEAT-FILTER}_{\mathbb{T}}$, that occur in #if-s. Transfer functions $\text{ASSIGN}_{\mathbb{T}}$ and $\text{FILTER}_{\mathbb{T}}$ modify only leaf nodes, while $\text{FEAT-FILTER}_{\mathbb{T}}$ and $\text{IFDEF}_{\mathbb{T}}$ add, modify, or delete decision nodes of a decision tree. This is due to the fact that the analysis information about program variables is located in leaf nodes, while the information about features is located in decision nodes.

Transfer function $\text{ASSIGN}_{\mathbb{T}}$ for handling an assignment $\text{x}:=e$ in the input tree t is described by Algorithm 1. Note that x is a program variable, and $e \in Exp$ may contain only program variables. $\text{ASSIGN}_{\mathbb{T}}$ descends along the paths of the decision tree t up to a leaf node a, where $\text{ASSIGN}_{\mathbb{A}}$ is invoked to substitute expression e for variable x in a. Similarly, transfer function $\text{FILTER}_{\mathbb{T}}$ for handling expression-based tests $e \in Exp$ is implemented by applying $\text{FILTER}_{\mathbb{A}}$ leaf-wise, so that the test e is satisfied by all leaves.

Transfer function $\text{FEAT-FILTER}_{\mathbb{T}}$ for feature-based tests θ is described by Algorithm 2. It reasons by induction on the structure of θ (we assume negation is applied to atomic propositions). When θ is an atomic constraint over numerical features (Lines 2,3), we use $\text{FILTER}_{\mathbb{D}}$ to approximate θ, thus producing a set of constraints $J \in \mathcal{P}(\mathbb{C}_{\mathbb{D}})$ defined over $\mathbb{F}$, which are then added to the tree t, possibly discarding all paths of t that do not satisfy θ. This is done by calling function $\text{RESTRICT}(t, \mathbb{K}, J)$ that adds linear constraints from J to t in ascending order with respect to $<_{\mathbb{C}_{\mathbb{D}}}$ (see [13, Sect. 5]). Note that θ may not be representable exactly in $\mathbb{C}_{\mathbb{D}}$ (e.g., in the case of non-linear constraints over $\mathbb{F}$), so $\text{FILTER}_{\mathbb{D}}$ may produce a set of constraints approximating it. When θ is a conjunction (resp., disjunction) of two feature expressions (Lines 4,5) (resp., (Lines 6,7)), the resulting decision trees are merged by operation meet $\sqcap_{\mathbb{T}}$ (resp., join $\sqcup_{\mathbb{T}}$).

Finally, transfer function $\text{IFDEF}_\mathbb{T}$ is defined as:

$$\text{IFDEF}_\mathbb{T}(t, \texttt{\#if}\ (\theta)\ \bar{s}\ \texttt{\#end}) = [\![\bar{s}]\!]_\mathbb{T}(\text{FEAT-FILTER}_\mathbb{T}(t,\theta)) \sqcup_\mathbb{T} \text{FEAT-FILTER}_\mathbb{T}(t, \neg\theta)$$

where $[\![\bar{s}]\!]_\mathbb{T}(t)$ is transfer function for $\bar{s}$. Transfer function $\text{ASSERT}_\mathbb{T}(t, \texttt{assert}(e))$ analyzes all constraints in leaf nodes $\ll a \gg$ of a tree t and replaces a with: (1) $\top$, if test e is always valid in a (i.e., $a \sqsubseteq_\mathbb{A} \text{FILTER}_\mathbb{A}(a, e)$); (2) $\bot$ if test $\neg e$ is always valid in a (i.e., $a \sqsubseteq_\mathbb{A} \text{FILTER}_\mathbb{A}(a, \neg e)$); and (3) $\times$, otherwise.

Lifted Analysis. The abstract operations and transfer functions of $\mathbb{T}(\mathbb{C}_\mathbb{D}, \mathbb{A})$ can be used to define the lifted analysis for program families. Tree t_{in} at the initial location has only one leaf node $\top_\mathbb{A}$ and decision nodes that define the set $\mathbb{K}$. Analysis properties are propagated forward from the first program location towards the final location taking assignments, #if-s, and tests into account with widening and narrowing around while-s. We apply delayed widening [8]. The *soundness* of the lifted analysis based on $\mathbb{T}(\mathbb{C}_\mathbb{D}, \mathbb{A})$ follows immediately from the soundness of all operators and transfer functions of $\mathbb{D}$ and $\mathbb{A}$ (shown in [13]).

3.2   Extended Lifted Analysis

If holes in a program sketch occur in expressions that can be exactly represented in the underlying numerical domain $\mathbb{D}$, then we can handle those holes in a more efficient symbolic way by an extended lifted analysis. Given Polyhedra domain P, we say that a hole ?? can be *exactly represented* in P, if it occurs in an expression of the form: $\alpha_1 x_1 + \ldots \alpha_i ?? + \ldots \alpha_k x_k + \beta$, where $\alpha_1, \ldots, \alpha_k, \beta \in \mathbb{Z}$ and $x_1, \ldots x_k$ are program variables or other hole occurrences. Similarly, we define when a hole can be exactly represented in Interval and Octagon domains.

When a hole $??_i^{[n,n']}$ in a program sketch $\hat{s}$ occurs in an expression that can be represented exactly in domain $\mathbb{D}$, we eliminate ?? by using the rewrite rule:

$$s[??^{[n,n']}] \rightsquigarrow s[\text{A}] \qquad\qquad\qquad (\text{R-2})$$

where $s[??^{[n,n']}]$ is a basic statement and A is a fresh feature with domain $[n, n']$.

Example 3. The hole ?? in the HELLOWORLD sketch in Fig. 1 cannot be exactly represented in Polyhedra domain P, since it occurs in expression x*??. However, both holes in the LOOP sketch in Fig. 2 can be exactly represented in P, since they occur in expressions 1*?? and 1*x-1*?? > 0. The HELLOWORLD family is obtained using (R-1) rule as shown in Fig. 5a, while the LOOP family is given in Fig. 5d where holes are replaced with features A and B using (R-2) rule.   □

After applying (R-2) rule, features can occur in arbitrary expressions in $\text{Rewrite}(\hat{s})$, not only in presence conditions of #if-s as before. Therefore, variable assignments and tests in $\text{Rewrite}(\hat{s})$, which may contain reads of features now, might also impact some linear constraints within decision nodes as well as some invariants within leaf nodes. Thus, we define new, extended versions of

ASSIGN$_\mathbb{T}$ and FILTER$_\mathbb{T}$ that take into account possibility of features occurring in expressions. Note that ASSIGN$_\mathbb{T}$ and FILTER$_\mathbb{T}$ can now modify both leaf and decision nodes, and the analysis information about features can be located in both leaf and decision nodes. The definition of decision tree lifted domain $\mathbb{T}(\mathbb{C}_\mathbb{D}, \mathbb{A})$ is slightly refined, such that the leaf abstract domain $\mathbb{A}$ is now defined over both program and feature variables $Var \cup \mathbb{F}$, while the decision node abstract domain $\mathbb{C}_\mathbb{D}$ remains to be defined over $\mathbb{F}$.

Algorithm 3: ASSIGN$_\mathbb{T}(t, \mathrm{x} \colon= e, C)$

---

1 **if** isLeaf(t) **then**
2 | $a = $ ASSIGN$_\mathbb{A}(t, \mathrm{x} \colon= e)$;
3 | **return** $\ll$FILTER$_\mathbb{A}(a, C)\gg$
4 **if** isNode(t) **then**
5 | $l = $ ASSIGN$_\mathbb{T}(t.l, \mathrm{x} \colon= e, C \cup \{t.c\})$;
6 | $r = $ ASSIGN$_\mathbb{T}(t.r, \mathrm{x} \colon= e, C \cup \{\neg t.c\})$;
7 | **return** $[\![t.c : l, c]\!]$

Algorithm 4: FILTER$_\mathbb{T}(t, e, C)$

---

1 **if** isLeaf(t) **then**
2 | $a = $ FILTER$_\mathbb{A}(t \uplus \alpha_{\mathbb{C}_\mathbb{D}}(C), e)$;
3 | $J = \gamma_{\mathbb{C}_\mathbb{D}}(a \upharpoonright_\mathbb{F})$;
4 | **if** isRedundant(J, C) **then return** $\ll a \gg$;
5 | **else return** RESTRICT($\ll a \gg, C, J \backslash C$);
6 **if** isNode(t) **then**
7 | $l = $ FILTER$_\mathbb{T}(t.l, be, C \cup \{t.c\})$;
8 | $r = $ FILTER$_\mathbb{T}(t.r, be, C \cup \{\neg t.c\})$;
9 | **return** $[\![t.c : l, r]\!]$

Assignments. Transfer function ASSIGN$_\mathbb{T}$ calls ASSIGN$_\mathbb{T}(t, \mathrm{x} \colon= e, \mathbb{K})$ given in Algorithm 3. It accumulates into the set $C \in \mathcal{P}(\mathbb{C}_\mathbb{D})$ (initialized to $\mathbb{K}$), constraints encountered along the paths of the decision tree (Lines 5, 6), up to the leaf nodes where assignment is performed by ASSIGN$_\mathbb{A}$ (Line 2) and the obtained result is then restricted to satisfy the accumulated constraints C by using FILTER$_\mathbb{A}$ (Line 3). This is possible due to the fact that $\mathbb{A}$ is now defined over $Var \cup \mathbb{F}$.

Tests. Transfer function FILTER$_\mathbb{T}$ for handling tests e calls FILTER$_\mathbb{T}(t, e, \mathbb{K})$ described by Algorithm 4. When t is a leaf node, test e is handled using FILTER$_\mathbb{A}$ applied on an abstract element from $\mathbb{A}$, which is obtained by merging constraints from the leaf node and decision nodes along the path to that leaf (Line 2). The obtained result a is projected on feature variables using $\upharpoonright_\mathbb{F}$ to generate a new set of constraints over features $J \in \mathcal{P}(\mathbb{C}_\mathbb{D})$ (Line 3). If the constraints from J are not redundant with respect to C (this is done by checking $\alpha_{\mathbb{C}_\mathbb{D}}(C) \sqsubseteq_\mathbb{D} \alpha_{\mathbb{C}_\mathbb{D}}(J)$), they are added to the given path by calling $\mathrm{RESTRICT}(\ll a \gg, C, J \backslash C)$ (Line 5).

Example 4. Consider program families HELLOWORLD and LOOP in Fig. 5a and Fig. 5d. The HELLOWORLD family is analyzed using algorithms from the basic lifted analysis, while the LOOP family using the extended lifted analysis. Figures 3 and 4 show the inferred invariants at the locations before assertions.   □

3.3   Synthesis Algorithm

We can now frame the sketch synthesis problem as an lifted analysis problem. In particular, we delegate the effort of conducting an effective search of all possible hole realisations to an efficient lifted static analyzer. Once the lifted analysis of the corresponding program family is performed, we can see from the inferred decision trees in the final location for which variants the assertion is valid. Those variants that satisfy the encountered linear constraints along the valid top-down paths, represent the correct hole realisations that satisfy the final assertion.

The synthesis algorithm $\mathrm{SYNTHESIZE}(\hat{s} : Stm)$ for solving a sketch $\hat{s}$ consists of the following steps: (1) Program sketch $\hat{s}$ is first encoded as a program family $\overline{s} = \mathrm{Rewrite}(\hat{s})$. (2) We call function $\mathrm{LIFT\_ANALYZE}(t_{in}, \overline{s})$, which takes as input the decision tree t_{in} and the program family $\overline{s}$ and returns a decision tree t in the final location of $\overline{s}$ obtained after performing the lifted analysis of $\overline{s}$. (3) The inferred decision tree t is analyzed, and the variants $\mathbb{K}' \subseteq \mathbb{K}$ for which $\top$ ('correct') leaf nodes are found, are returned as solutions.

Theorem 2. *SYNTHESIZE($\hat{s}$) is correct and terminates.*

4   Evaluation

Implementation. We have developed a prototype program synthesizer, called FAMILYSKETCHER, which is based on the tools SPLNUM^{2}ANALYZER [13] for analyzing #if-enriched C programs with numerical features and Function [25] for proving program termination. It uses the lifted decision tree domain $\mathbb{T}(\mathbb{C}_\mathbb{D}, \mathbb{A})$, where both $\mathbb{D}$ and $\mathbb{A}$ represent numerical abstract domains (polyhedra, in our case). The abstract operations and transfer functions of the numerical polyhedra domain are provided by the APRON library [19]. The tool is written in OCAML and consists of around 7K LOC. The current front-end of the tool provides a limited support for arrays, pointers, recursion, struct and union types.

Experiment Setup and Benchmarks. All experiments are executed on a 64-bit Intel®Core^{TM} i7-8700 CPU@3.20GHz × 12, Ubuntu 18.04.5 LTS, with 8 GB memory, and we use a timeout value of 200 sec. All times are reported as average over five independent executions. We report times needed for the actual static analysis task to be performed. The implementation, benchmarks, and all

```
                                              void main(int x){        void main(unsigned int x){
                                                int y := 0;              int s := 0, y := ??1;
                          void main(unsigned int x){  while (x ≥ 0) {       int x0 := x, y0 := y;
void main(int x){          int y:=x;                x := x-1;            while (x ≥ 0) {
  int z:=??1*x+??2;          if (x+5>??) y := y+1;    if (y<??) y := y+1;     x := x-1;
  assert(z ≥ 2*x &&        else y := y-1;            else y := y-1; }       while (y ≥??2) {
          z ≤ 2*x+2);      assert (y ≤ x);          assert (y ≤ 1);          y := y-1; s := s+1; }
}                        }                        }                      } assert (s ≥ x0+y0);
                                                                        }
```

Fig. 6. LINEXP.   **Fig. 7.** CONDITIONAL.   **Fig. 8.** LOOPCOND.   **Fig. 9.** NESTEDLOOP.

obtained results are available from: https://github.com/aleksdimovski/Family_sketcher (and https://zenodo.org/record/4118540#.X7aFUWVKjIU). We compare our approach with program sketching tool **Sketch** version 1.7.6 that uses SAT-based inductive synthesis [23,24] as well as with the **Brute-Force** enumeration approach that analyzes all variants, one by one, using a single-program analysis. The evaluation is performed on several C numerical sketches collected from the **Sketch** project [23,24] and from the Syntax-Guided Synthesis Competition (https://sygus.org/) [1]. We use the following benchmarks: HELLOWORLD (Fig. 1), LOOP (Fig. 2), LINEXP (Fig. 6), CONDITIONAL (Fig. 7), LOOPCOND (Fig. 8), and NESTEDLOOP (Fig. 9).

Performance Results. Table 1 shows the results of synthesizing our benchmarks. Note that **Sketch** reports only one solution for each sketch.

The LOOP sketch is analyzed using the extended lifted analysis, so both holes are handled symbolically by (R-2) rule. Thus, our approach does not depend on sizes of hole domains. FAMILYSKETCHER terminates in (around) 0.007 sec for 5, 8, and 16-bits sizes of holes. In contrast, **Sketch** does depend on the sizes of holes. It terminates in 33.74 sec for 16-bits sizes, and times out for bigger sizes. Consider a variant of LOOP (see Fig. 2), denoted LOOP', where the assertion in location $\bigcirc{7}$ is changed to assert $(y < 8)$. The performance of our tool is the same as for LOOP. In contrast, **Sketch** cannot resolve LOOP' and fails to report a solution, since it uses only 8 unrollments of the loop by default. If the loop is unrolled 9 times, **Sketch** terminates in 0.20 sec for 5, and 2.29 sec for 16-bits sizes. FAMILYSKETCHER reports all solutions $A-B \geq 3$ for LOOP (resp., $1 \leq A-B \leq 7$ for LOOP'), while **Sketch** reports only one solution.

The LINEXP sketch contains two holes. The first one $??_1$ is handled explicitly by (R-1) rule while the second one $??_2$ symbolically by (R-2) rule. The performance of FAMILYSKETCHER depends on the size of $??_1$. The decision tree inferred in the location before the assertion contains one leaf node for each possible value of feature A $(\text{dom}(A) = [0,3]$ in this case), where features A and B represent $??_1$ and $??_2$. We obtain all solutions: $A = 2 \wedge 0 \leq B \leq 2$. **Sketch** scales better in this case reporting one solution. Similar results we obtain for HelloWorld sketch.

The Conditional sketch contains one hole that can be handled symbolically by (R-2) rule. FamilySketcher has similar running times for all domain sizes of the hole, and reports all solutions $0 \leq ?? \leq 4$. Sketch's performance declines with the size of domains, and times out for sizes greater than 19-bits.

The LoopCond sketch contains one hole that can be handled symbolically by (R-2) rule. FamilySketcher has similar running times for all domain sizes, and reports two solutions $?? \in \{0, 1\}$. In contrast, Sketch resolves this example only if the loop is unrolled as many times as is the size of the hole and inputs (e.g., 32 times for 5-bits). So, Sketch's performance declines with the growth of size of the hole, and times out for 16-bits. Consider a variant of LoopCond (see Fig. 8), denoted LoopCond', where one additional hole exists in while-guard ($x \geq ??_1$) and the assertion is changed to assert ($y \geq 1$). FamilySketcher reports all solutions: $??_1 \geq 0 \wedge ??_2 \geq 2$. Sketch performs similarly for both variants.

Finally, NestedLoop sketch contains two holes that can be handled symbolically by (R-2) rule. FamilySketcher terminates in (around) 0.05 sec for all sizes of holes. In contrast, Brute-Force takes 4.18 sec for 5-bit size of holes and times out for larger sizes, while Sketch cannot resolve this benchmark.

Discussion. In summary, we can conclude that FamilySketcher often outperforms Sketch, especially in case of numerical sketches in which holes occur in expressions that can be exactly represented in the underlying numerical domain. But in case of sketches with holes that need to be handled by (R-1) rule the performances of our tool decline. However, even in this case our tool scales better than the Brute-Force approach.

The performances of FamilySketcher can be improved in several ways. First, many abstract operations and transfer functions can be further optimized. Second, instead of APRON we can use other efficient libraries that support numerical domains, such as ELINA [22]. Finally, by using libraries that support more expressive domains, such as non-linear constraints (e.g., polynomials, exponentials [4]), our tool will benefit and more sketches will be handled by (R-2) rule.

Table 1. Performance results of FamilySketcher vs. Sketch vs. Brute-Force.

Bench.	5 bits			8 bits			16 bits		
	Family Sketcher	Sketch	Brute Force	Family Sketcher	Sketch	Brute Force	Family Sketcher	Sketch	Brute Force
Loop	0.007	0.215	0.628	0.007	0.218	67.79	0.007	33.74	timeout
Loop'	0.007	0.205	0.627	0.007	0.206	60.59	0.007	2.292	timeout
LinExp	0.165	0.222	0.479	26.99	0.238	36.80	timeout	timeout	timeout
Conditional	0.002	0.210	0.019	0.002	0.210	0.155	0.004	3.856	54.68
LoopCond	0.011	0.225	0.065	0.013	0.262	0.404	0.013	timeout	191.43
LoopCond'	0.022	0.221	1.615	0.022	0.267	199.95	0.023	timeout	timeout
NestedLoop	0.053	timeout	4.186	0.054	timeout	timeout	0.054	timeout	timeout

5   Related Work and Conclusion

The existing sketching approach Sketch [23,24], which uses SAT-based inductive synthesis, is more general than our approach although it is most successful for synthesizing bit-manipulating programs. Sketch reasons about loops by unrolling them, so is very sensitive to the degree of unrolling. Our approach does not have this constraint, as we use widening instead of fully unrolling loops, so that we can handle directly unbounded loops and an infinite number of execution paths in a sound way. This is stronger than fixing a priori a bound on the number of iterations of loops. Sketch iteratively generates a finite set of inputs and performs SAT queries to identify values for the holes. Hence, Sketch may need several iterations to converge reporting only one solution. In contrast, our approach needs only one iteration reporting several, and often all, solutions.

Decision-tree abstract domains have been used in abstract interpretation community recently [6,9,27]. Segmented decision tree abstract domains have been used [6,9] to enable path dependent static analysis, while Urban and Mine [27] use decision tree-based abstract domains to prove program termination.

Another way to speed up lifted analysis is via so-called variability abstractions [14–16], which aim tame the combinatorial explosion of the number of variants and reduce it to something more tractable. It would be interesting to apply the obtained abstract lifted analysis for resolving program sketches.

To conclude, in this work we employ techniques from abstract interpretation and product-line analysis for automatic resolving of program sketches.

References

1. Alur, R., et al.: Syntax-guided synthesis. In: Formal Methods in Computer-Aided Design, FMCAD 2013, pp. 1–8. IEEE (2013)
2. Apel, S., Batory, D.S., Kästner, C., Saake, G.: Feature-Oriented Software Product Lines - Concepts and Implementation. Springer, Heidelberg (2013). https://doi.org/10.1007/978-3-642-37521-7
3. Apel, S., von Rhein, A., Wendler, P., Größlinger, A., Beyer, D.: Strategies for product-line verification: case studies and experiments. In: 35th International Conference on Software Engineering, ICSE 2013, pp. 482–491 (2013)
4. Bradley, A.R., Manna, Z., Sipma, H.B.: The Polyranking principle. In: Caires, L., Italiano, G.F., Monteiro, L., Palamidessi, C., Yung, M. (eds.) ICALP 2005. LNCS, vol. 3580, pp. 1349–1361. Springer, Heidelberg (2005). https://doi.org/10.1007/11523468_109
5. Češka, M., Dehnert, C., Jansen, N., Junges, S., Katoen, J.-P.: Model repair revamped. In: Bartocci, E., Cleaveland, R., Grosu, R., Sokolsky, O. (eds.) From Reactive Systems to Cyber-Physical Systems. LNCS, vol. 11500, pp. 107–125. Springer, Cham (2019). https://doi.org/10.1007/978-3-030-31514-6_7
6. Chen, J., Cousot, P.: A binary decision tree abstract domain Functor. In: Blazy, S., Jensen, T. (eds.) SAS 2015. LNCS, vol. 9291, pp. 36–53. Springer, Heidelberg (2015). https://doi.org/10.1007/978-3-662-48288-9_3
7. Clements, P., Northrop, L.: Software Product Lines: Practices and Patterns. Addison-Wesley, Boston (2001)

8. Cousot, P., Cousot, R.: Abstract interpretation: a unified lattice model for static analysis of programs by construction or approximation of fixpoints. In: Conference Record of the Fourth ACM Symposium on POPL, pp. 238–252. ACM (1977)
9. Cousot, P., Cousot, R., Mauborgne, L.: A scalable segmented decision tree abstract domain. In: Manna, Z., Peled, D.A. (eds.) Time for Verification. LNCS, vol. 6200, pp. 72–95. Springer, Heidelberg (2010). https://doi.org/10.1007/978-3-642-13754-9_5
10. Cousot, P., Halbwachs, N.: Automatic discovery of linear restraints among variables of a program. In: Conference Record of the Fifth Annual ACM Symposium on POPL 1978, pp. 84–96. ACM Press (1978)
11. Dimovski, A.S.: Lifted static analysis using a binary decision diagram abstract domain. In: Proceedings of the 18th ACM SIGPLAN International Conference on GPCE 2019, pp. 102–114. ACM (2019)
12. Dimovski, A.S.: On calculating assertion probabilities for program families. Prilozi Contributions Sec. Nat. Math. Biotech. Sci, MASA **41**(1), 13–23 (2020)
13. Dimovski, A.S., Apel, S., Legay, A.: A decision tree lifted domain for analyzing program families with numerical features. In: FASE 2021. LNCS, vol. 12649, pp. 67–86. Springer, Cham (2021). https://doi.org/10.1007/978-3-030-71500-7_4
14. Dimovski, A.S., Brabrand, C., Wasowski, A.: Variability abstractions: trading precision for speed in family-based analyses. In: 29th European Conference on Object-Oriented Programming, ECOOP 2015. LIPIcs, vol. 37, pp 247–270. Schloss Dagstuhl - Leibniz-Zentrum fuer Informatik (2015)
15. Dimovski, A.S., Brabrand, C., Wąsowski, A.: Finding suitable variability abstractions for family-based analysis. In: Fitzgerald, J., Heitmeyer, C., Gnesi, S., Philippou, A. (eds.) FM 2016. LNCS, vol. 9995, pp. 217–234. Springer, Cham (2016). https://doi.org/10.1007/978-3-319-48989-6_14
16. Dimovski, A.S., Brabrand, C., Wasowski, A.: Finding suitable variability abstractions for lifted analysis. Formal Aspect Comput. **31**(2), 231–259 (2019). https://doi.org/10.1007/s00165-019-00479-y
17. Hunsen, C., et al.: Preprocessor-based variability in open-source and industrial software systems: an empirical study. Empirical Softw. Eng. **21**(2), 449–482 (2015). https://doi.org/10.1007/s10664-015-9360-1
18. Iosif-Lazar, A.F., Melo, J., Dimovski, A.S., Brabrand, C., Wasowski, A.: Effective analysis of C programs by rewriting variability. Art Sci. Eng. Program. **1**(1), 1 (2017)
19. Jeannet, B., Miné, A.: APRON: a library of numerical abstract domains for static analysis. In: Bouajjani, A., Maler, O. (eds.) CAV 2009. LNCS, vol. 5643, pp. 661–667. Springer, Heidelberg (2009). https://doi.org/10.1007/978-3-642-02658-4_52
20. Midtgaard, J., Dimovski, A.S., Brabrand, C., Wasowski, A.: Systematic derivation of correct variability-aware program analyses. Sci. Comput. Program. **105**, 145–170 (2015)
21. Parnas, D.L.: On the design and development of program families. IEEE Trans. Softw. Eng. **2**(1), 1–9 (1976)
22. Singh, G., Püschel, M., Vechev, M.T.: Making numerical program analysis fast. In: Proceedings of the 36th ACM SIGPLAN Conference on PLDI 2015, pp. 303–313. ACM (2015)
23. Solar-Lezama, A.: Program sketching. STTT **15**(5–6), 475–495 (2013)
24. Solar-Lezama, A., Rabbah, R.M., Bodík, R., Ebcioglu, K.: Programming by sketching for bit-streaming programs. In: Proceedings of the ACM SIGPLAN 2005 Conference on Programming Language Design and Implementation, pp. 281–294. ACM (2005)

25. Urban, C.: FuncTion: an abstract domain Functor for termination. In: Baier, C., Tinelli, C. (eds.) TACAS 2015. LNCS, vol. 9035, pp. 464–466. Springer, Heidelberg (2015). https://doi.org/10.1007/978-3-662-46681-0_46

26. Caterina Urban: Static analysis by abstract interpretation of functional temporal properties of programs. Ph.D. thesis, École Normale Supérieure, Paris, France (2015)

27. Urban, C., Miné, A.: A decision tree abstract domain for proving conditional termination. In: Müller-Olm, M., Seidl, H. (eds.) SAS 2014. LNCS, vol. 8723, pp. 302–318. Springer, Cham (2014). https://doi.org/10.1007/978-3-319-10936-7_19

28. von Rhein, A., Liebig, J., Janker, A., Kästner, C., Apel, S.: Variability-aware static analysis at scale: an empirical study. ACM Trans. Softw. Eng. Methodol. 27(4), 181–1833 (2018)

Specification Decomposition for Reactive Synthesis

Bernd Finkbeiner[1], Gideon Geier[2], and Noemi Passing[1(✉)]

[1] CISPA Helmholtz Center for Information Security, Saarbrücken, Germany
{finkbeiner,noemi.passing}@cispa.de
[2] Saarland University, Saarbrücken, Germany
geier@react.uni-saarland.de

Abstract. Reactive synthesis is the task of automatically deriving an implementation from a specification. It is a promising technique for the development of verified programs and hardware. Despite recent advances, reactive synthesis is still not practical when the specified systems reach a certain bound in size and complexity. In this paper, we present a modular synthesis algorithm that decomposes the specification into smaller subspecifications. For them, independent synthesis tasks are performed, and the composition of the resulting implementations is guaranteed to satisfy the full specification. Our algorithm is a preprocessing technique that can be applied to a wide range of synthesis tools. We evaluate our approach with state-of-the-art synthesis tools on established benchmarks and obtain encouraging results: The overall runtime decreases significantly when synthesizing implementations modularly.

1 Introduction

Reactive synthesis automatically derives an implementation that satisfies a given specification. Thus, it is a promising technique for the development of provably correct systems. Despite recent advances, however, reactive synthesis is still not practical when the specified systems reach a certain bound in size and complexity. In verification, breaking down the analysis of a system into several smaller subtasks has proven to be a key technique to improve scalability [4,26]. In this paper, we apply compositional concepts to reactive synthesis.

We present a modular synthesis algorithm that decomposes a specification into several subspecifications. Then, independent synthesis tasks are performed for them. The implementations obtained from the subtasks are combined into an implementation for the initial specification. Since the algorithm uses synthesis

---

An extended version of this paper is available at [12].

This work was partially supported by the German Research Foundation (DFG) as part of the Collaborative Research Center "Foundations of Perspicuous Software Systems" (TRR 248, 389792660), and by the European Research Council (ERC) Grant OSARES (No. 683300).

A. Dutle et al. (Eds.): NFM 2021, LNCS 12673, pp. 113–130, 2021.
https://doi.org/10.1007/978-3-030-76384-8_8

as a black box, it can be applied to a wide range of synthesis algorithms. In particular, the algorithm can be seen as a preprocessing step for synthesis.

Soundness and completeness of modular synthesis depends on the decomposition. We introduce a criterion, *non-contradictory independent sublanguages*, for subspecifications that ensures soundness and completeness. The key question is now how to decompose a specification such that the criterion is satisfied.

Lifting the language-based criterion to an automaton level, we propose a decomposition algorithm for specifications given as nondeterministic Büchi automata that directly implements the independent sublanguages paradigm. Thus, using subspecifications obtained with this algorithm ensures soundness and completeness of modular synthesis. A specification given in the standard temporal logic LTL can be translated into an equivalent nondeterministic Büchi automaton, and hence the decomposition algorithm can be applied as well.

However, while the algorithm is semantically precise, it involves several expensive automaton operations. Thus, for large specifications, the decomposition becomes infeasible. Therefore, we present an approximate decomposition algorithm for LTL formulas that still ensures soundness and completeness of modular synthesis but is more scalable. It is approximate in the sense that it does not necessarily find all possible decompositions. Besides, we introduce an optimization of this algorithm for formulas in a common assumption-guarantee format.

We have implemented both decomposition procedures as well as the modular synthesis algorithm and used it with the two state-of-the-art synthesis tools BoSy [9] and Strix [22]. We evaluated our algorithms on the set of established benchmarks from the synthesis competition SYNTCOMP [16]. As expected, the decomposition algorithm for nondeterministic Büchi automata becomes infeasible when the specifications grow. For the LTL decomposition algorithm, however, the experimental results are excellent: Decomposition terminates in less than 26ms on all benchmarks, and hence the overhead is negligible. Out of 39 decomposable specifications, BoSy and Strix increase their number of synthesized benchmarks by nine and five, respectively. For instance, on the generalized buffer benchmark [15,18] with three receivers, BoSy is able to synthesize a solution within 28 s using modular synthesis while neither of the non-compositional approaches terminates within one hour. For twelve and nine further benchmarks, respectively, BoSy and Strix reduce the synthesis times significantly with modular synthesis, often by an order of magnitude or more. The remaining benchmarks are too small and too simple for compositional methods to pay off. Thus, decomposing the specification into smaller subspecifications indeed increases the scalability of synthesis on larger systems.

Related Work: In model checking, compositional approaches improve the scalability of algorithms significantly [26]. The approach that is most related to our contribution is a preprocessing algorithm for model checking [6]. It analyzes dependencies between the properties to be checked to reduce the number of model checking tasks. We lift this idea from model checking to reactive synthesis. Our approach, however, differs inherently in the dependency analysis.

There exist several compositional synthesis approaches. The algorithm by Kupferman et al. is designed for incrementally adding requirements to a specification during system design [19]. Thus, it does not perform independent synthesis tasks but only reuses parts of the already existing solutions. The algorithm by Filiot et al. depends, like our LTL decomposition approach, heavily on dropping assumptions [10]. They use an heuristic that, in contrast to our criterion, is incomplete. While their approach is more scalable than a non-compositional one, one does not see as significant differences as for our algorithm. Both algorithms do not consider dependencies between the components to obtain prior knowledge about the presence or absence of conflicts in the implementations.

Assume-guarantee synthesis [2, 3, 21] takes dependencies between components into account. In this setting, specifications are not always satisfiable by one component alone. Thus, a negotiation between the components is needed. While this yields more fine-grained decompositions, it produces an enormous overhead that, as our experiments show, is often not necessary for common benchmarks. Avoiding negotiation, dependency-based compositional synthesis [13] decomposes the system based on a dependency analysis of the specification. The analysis is more fine-grained than the one presented in this paper. Moreover, a weaker winning condition for synthesis, remorsefree dominance [5], is used. While this allows for smaller synthesis tasks, it also produces a larger overhead than our approach.

The synthesis tools Strix [22], Unbeast [8], and Safety-First [27] decompose the specification. The first one does so to find suitable automaton types for internal representation and to identify isomorphic parts, while the last two identify safety parts. They do not perform independent synthesis tasks for the subspecifications. In fact, the scalability of Strix improves notably with our algorithm.

2   Preliminaries

LTL. Linear-time temporal logic (LTL) [24] is a specification language for linear-time properties. Let Σ be a finite set of atomic propositions and let $a \in \Sigma$. The syntax of LTL is given by $\varphi, \psi ::= a \mid \neg\varphi \mid \varphi \vee \psi \mid \varphi \wedge \psi \mid \bigcirc \varphi \mid \varphi \, \mathcal{U} \, \psi$. We define $true := a \vee \neg a$, $false := \neg true$, $\Diamond \varphi := true \, \mathcal{U} \, \varphi$, and $\Box \varphi := \neg \Diamond \neg \varphi$ and use standard semantics. The atomic propositions in φ are denoted by $prop(\varphi)$, where every occurrence of $true$ or $false$ in φ does not add any atomic propositions to $prop(\varphi)$. The language $\mathcal{L}(\varphi)$ of φ is the set of infinite words that satisfy φ.

Automata. For a finite alphabet Σ, a nondeterministic Büchi automaton (NBA) is a tuple $\mathcal{A} = (Q, Q_0, \delta, F)$, where Q is a finite set of states, $Q_0 \subseteq Q$ is a set of initial states, $\delta : Q \times \Sigma \times Q$ is a transition relation, and $F \subseteq Q$ is a set of accepting states. Given an infinite word $\sigma = \sigma_1\sigma_2\cdots \in \Sigma^\omega$, a run of σ on $\mathcal{A}$ is an infinite sequence $q_1q_2q_3\cdots \in Q^\omega$ of states where $q_1 \in Q_0$ and $(q_i, \sigma_i, q_{i+1}) \in \delta$ holds for all $i \geq 1$. A run is called accepting if it contains infinitely many visits to accepting states. $\mathcal{A}$ accepts a word σ if there is an accepting run of σ on $\mathcal{A}$.

The language $\mathcal{L}(\mathcal{A})$ of an NBA $\mathcal{A}$ is the set of all accepted words. Two NBAs are equivalent if their languages are equivalent. An LTL specification φ can be translated into an equivalent NBA $\mathcal{A}_\varphi$ with a single exponential blow up [20].

Implementations and Counterstrategies. An implementation of a system with inputs I, outputs O, and variables $V = I \cup O$ is a function $f : (2^V)^* \times 2^I \to 2^O$ mapping a history of variables and the current input to outputs. An infinite word $\sigma = \sigma_1 \sigma_2 \cdots \in (2^V)^\omega$ is compatible with an implementation f if for all $n \in \mathbb{N}$, $f(\sigma_1 \dots \sigma_{n-1}, \sigma_n \cap I) = \sigma_n \cap O$ holds. The set of all compatible words of f is denoted by $\mathcal{C}(f)$. An implementation f realizes a specification s if $\sigma \in \mathcal{L}(s)$ holds for all $\sigma \in \mathcal{C}(f)$. A specification is called realizable if there exists an implementation realizing it. If a specification is unrealizable, there is a counterstrategy $f^c : (2^V)^* \to 2^I$ mapping a history of variables to inputs. An infinite word $\sigma = \sigma_1 \sigma_2 \cdots \in (2^V)^\omega$ is compatible with f^c if $f^c(\sigma_1 \dots \sigma_{n-1}) = \sigma_n \cap I$ holds for all $n \in \mathbb{N}$. All compatible words of f^c violate s, i.e., $\mathcal{C}(f^c) \subseteq \overline{\mathcal{L}(s)}$.

Reactive Synthesis. Given a specification, reactive synthesis derives an implementation that realizes it. For LTL specifications, synthesis is 2EXPTIME-complete [25]. Since we use synthesis as a black box procedure in this paper, we do not go into detail here. Instead, we refer the interested reader to [11].

Notation. Overloading notation, we use union and intersection on words: For a set X and $\sigma = \sigma_1 \sigma_2 \cdots \in (2^{\Sigma_1})^\omega$, $\sigma' = \sigma'_1 \sigma'_2 \cdots \in (2^{\Sigma_2})^\omega$ with $\Sigma = \Sigma_1 \cup \Sigma_2$, $\sigma \cup \sigma' := (\sigma_1 \cup \sigma'_1)(\sigma_2 \cup \sigma'_2) \cdots \in (2^\Sigma)^\omega$ and $\sigma \cap X := (\sigma_1 \cap X)(\sigma_2 \cap X) \cdots \in (2^X)^\omega$.

3   Modular Synthesis

In this section, we introduce a modular synthesis algorithm that divides the synthesis task into independent subtasks by splitting the specification into several subspecifications. The decomposition algorithm has to ensure that the synthesis tasks for the subspecifications can be solved independently and that their results are non-contradictory, i.e., that they can be combined into an implementation satisfying the initial specification. Note that when splitting the specification, we assign a set of relevant in- and output variables to every subspecification. The corresponding synthesis subtask is then performed on these variables.

Algorithm 1 describes this modular synthesis approach. First, the specification is decomposed into a list of subspecifications using an adequate decomposition algorithm. Then, the synthesis tasks for all subspecifications are solved. If a subspecification is unrealizable, its counterstrategy is extended to a counterstrategy for the whole specification. This construction is given in the full version [12]. Otherwise, the implementations of the subspecifications are combined.

Soundness and completeness of modular synthesis depend on three requirements: Equirealizability of the initial specification and the subspecifications, non-contradictory composability of the subresults, and satisfaction of the initial specification by the parallel composition of the subresults. Intuitively, these

---

Algorithm 1: Modular Synthesis

Input: s: Specification, inp: List Variable, out: List Variable
Output: realizable: Bool, implementation: $\mathcal{T}$
1 subspecifications ← decompose(s, inp, out)
2 sub_results ← map synthesize subspecifications
3 **foreach** (real,strat) ∈ sub_results **do**
4   **if** ! real **then**
5   implementation ← extendCounterStrategy(strat, s)
6   return (⊥, implementation)

7 impls ← map second sub_results
8 **return** (⊤, compose impls)

---

requirements are met if the decomposition algorithm neither introduces nor drops parts of the system specification and if it does not produce subspecifications that allow for contradictory implementations. To obtain composability of the subresults, the implementations need to agree on shared variables. We ensure this by assigning disjoint sets of output variables to the synthesis subtasks: Since every subresult only defines the behavior of the assigned output variables, the implementations are non-contradictory. Since the language alphabets of the subspecifications differ, we define the non-contradictory composition of languages:

Definition 1 (Non-Contradictory Language Composition). *Let L_1, L_2 be languages over 2^{Σ_1} and 2^{Σ_2}, respectively. The composition of L_1 and L_2 is defined by $L_1 \parallel L_2 = \{\sigma_1 \cup \sigma_2 \mid \sigma_1 \in L_1 \wedge \sigma_2 \in L_2 \wedge \sigma_1 \cap \Sigma_2 = \sigma_2 \cap \Sigma_1\}$.*

The satisfaction of the initial specification by the composed subresults can be guaranteed by requiring the subspecifications to be independent sublanguages:

Definition 2 (Independent Sublanguages). *Let $L \subseteq (2^\Sigma)^\omega$, $L_1 \subseteq (2^{\Sigma_1})^\omega$, and $L_2 \subseteq (2^{\Sigma_2})^\omega$ be languages with $\Sigma_1, \Sigma_2 \subseteq \Sigma$ and $\Sigma_1 \cup \Sigma_2 = \Sigma$. Then, L_1 and L_2 are called* independent sublanguages *of L if $L_1 \parallel L_2 = L$ holds.*

From these two requirements, i.e., non-contradictory and independent sublanguages, equirealizability of the initial specification and the subspecifications follows. For the full proof, we refer the reader to full version [12].

Theorem 1. *Let s, s_1, s_2 be specifications with $\mathcal{L}(s) \subseteq (2^V)^\omega$, $\mathcal{L}(s_1) \subseteq (2^{V_1})^\omega$, $\mathcal{L}(s_2) \subseteq (2^{V_2})^\omega$. Recall that $I \subseteq V$ is the set of input variables. If $V_1 \cap V_2 \subseteq I$ and $V_1 \cup V_2 = V$ hold, and $\mathcal{L}(s_1)$ and $\mathcal{L}(s_2)$ are independent sublanguages of $\mathcal{L}(s)$, then s is realizable if, and only if, both s_1 and s_2 are realizable.*

Proof (Sketch). First, let s_1, s_2 be realizable and let f_1, f_2 be implementations realizing them. Let f be an implementation that acts as f_1 on $O \cap V_1$ and as f_2 on $O \cap V_2$. Since $V_1 \cap V_2 \subseteq I$ and $V_1 \cup V_2 = V$ hold, f is well-defined and defines the behavior of all outputs variables. By construction, f realizes s_1 and s_2

since f_1 and f_2 do, respectively. Since $\mathcal{L}(s_1)$ and $\mathcal{L}(s_2)$ are non-contradictory, independent sublanguages of $\mathcal{L}(s)$ by assumption, f thus realizes s.

Second, assume that s_i is unrealizable for some $i \in \{1,2\}$. Then, there is a counterstrategy f_i^c for s_i. With the construction given in the full version [12], we can construct a counterstrategy for s from f_i^c. Hence, s is unrealizable.   □

The soundness and completeness of Algorithm 1 for adequate decomposition algorithms now follows directly with Theorem 1 and the properties of such algorithms described above: They produce subspecifications that do not share output variables and that form independent sublanguages.

Theorem 2 (Soundness and Completeness). *Let s be a specification. Let $\mathcal{S} = \{s_1, \ldots, s_k\}$ be a set of subspecifications with $\mathcal{L}(s_i) \subseteq (2^{V_i})^\omega$ such that $\bigcup_{1 \le i \le k} V_i = V$, $V_i \cap V_j \subseteq I$ for $1 \le i,j \le k$ with $i \ne j$, and $\mathcal{L}(s_1), \ldots, \mathcal{L}(s_k)$ are independent sublanguages of $\mathcal{L}(s)$. If s is realizable, Algorithm 1 yields an implementation realizing s. Otherwise, Algorithm 1 yields a counterstrategy for s.*

Proof. First, let s be realizable. By applying Theorem 1 recursively, s_i is realizable for all $s_i \in \mathcal{S}$. Since $V_i \cap V_j \subseteq I$ for any $s_i, s_j \in \mathcal{S}$ with $i \ne j$, the implementations realizing the subspecifications are non-contradictory. Hence, Algorithm 1 returns their composition: Implementation f. Since $V_1 \cup \cdots \cup V_k = V$, f defines the behavior of all outputs. By construction, f realizes all $s_i \in \mathcal{S}$. Thus, since the $\mathcal{L}(s_i)$ are non-contradictory, independent sublanguages of $\mathcal{L}(s)$, f realizes s.

Next, let s be unrealizable. Then, there exists an unrealizable subspecification $s_i \in \mathcal{S}$ and Algorithm 1 returns its extension to a counterstrategy for the whole system. The correctness of this construction is proven in the full version [12]. □

4   Decomposition of Nondeterministic Büchi Automata

To ensure soundness and completeness of modular synthesis, a decomposition algorithm has to meet the language-based adequacy conditions of Theorem 1. In this section, we lift these conditions from the language level to nondeterministic Büchi automata and present a decomposition algorithm for specifications given as NBAs on this basis. Since the algorithm works directly on NBAs and not on their languages, we consider their parallel composition instead of the parallel composition of their languages: Let $\mathcal{A}_1 = (Q_1, Q_0^1, \delta_1, F_1)$ and $\mathcal{A}_2 = (Q_2, Q_0^2, \delta_2, F_2)$ be NBAs over 2^{V_1}, 2^{V_2}, respectively. The *parallel composition of $\mathcal{A}_1$ and $\mathcal{A}_2$* is defined by the NBA $\mathcal{A}_1 \parallel \mathcal{A}_2 = (Q, Q_0, \delta, F)$ over $2^{V_1 \cup V_2}$ with $Q = Q_1 \times Q_2$, $Q_0 = Q_0^1 \times Q_0^2$, $((q_1, q_2), i, (q_1', q_2')) \in \delta$ if, and only if, $(q_1, i \cap V_1, q_1') \in \delta_1$ and $(q_2, i \cap V_2, q_2') \in \delta_2$, and $F = F_1 \times F_2$. The parallel composition of NBAs reflects the parallel composition of their languages:

Lemma 1. *Let $\mathcal{A}_1$ and $\mathcal{A}_2$ be two NBAs over alphabets 2^{V_1} and 2^{V_2}, respectively. Then, $\mathcal{L}(\mathcal{A}_1 \parallel \mathcal{A}_2) = \mathcal{L}(\mathcal{A}_1) \parallel \mathcal{L}(\mathcal{A}_2)$ holds.*

Algorithm 2: Automaton Decomposition

Input: $\mathcal{A}$: NBA, inp: List Variable, out: List Variable
Output: subautomata: List (NBA, List Variable, List Variable)

1 **if** isNull checkedSubsets **then**
2 | checkedSubsets $\leftarrow \emptyset$

3 subautomata $\leftarrow [(\mathcal{A}, \text{inp}, \text{out})]$
4 **foreach** X $\subset$ out **do**
5 | Y $\leftarrow$ out\X
6 | **if** X $\notin$ checkedSubsets $\wedge$ Y $\notin$ checkedSubsets **then**
7 | | $\mathcal{A}_X \leftarrow \mathcal{A}_{\pi(X \cup \text{inp})}$
8 | | $\mathcal{A}_Y \leftarrow \mathcal{A}_{\pi(Y \cup \text{inp})}$
9 | | **if** $\mathcal{L}(\mathcal{A}_X \,\|\, \mathcal{A}_Y) \subseteq \mathcal{L}(\mathcal{A})$ **then**
10 | | | subautomata $\leftarrow$ decompose($\mathcal{A}_X$, inp, X) ++ decompose($\mathcal{A}_Y$, inp, Y)
11 | | | break

12 | checkedSubsets $\leftarrow$ checkedSubsets $\cup \{X, Y\}$

13 **return** subautomata

Proof. First, let $\sigma \in \mathcal{L}(\mathcal{A}_1 \,\|\, \mathcal{A}_2)$. Then, σ is an accepting run on $\mathcal{A}_1 \,\|\, \mathcal{A}_2$. Hence, by definition of automaton composition, for $i \in \{1, 2\}$, $\sigma \cap V_i$ is an accepting run on $\mathcal{A}_i$. Thus, $\sigma \cap V_i \in \mathcal{L}(\mathcal{A}_i)$. Since $(\sigma \cap V_1) \cap V_2 = (\sigma \cap V_2) \cap V_1$, we have $(\sigma \cap V_1) \cup (\sigma \cap V_2) \in \mathcal{L}(\mathcal{A}_1) \,\|\, \mathcal{L}(\mathcal{A}_2)$. By definition of automaton composition, $\sigma \in (2^{V_1 \cup V_2})^\omega$ and thus $\sigma = (\sigma \cap V_1) \cup (\sigma \cap V_2)$. Hence, $\sigma \in \mathcal{L}(\mathcal{A}_1) \,\|\, \mathcal{L}(\mathcal{A}_2)$.

Second, let $\sigma \in \mathcal{L}(\mathcal{A}_1) \,\|\, \mathcal{L}(\mathcal{A}_2)$. Then, there are $\sigma_1 \in (2^{V_1})^\omega$, $\sigma_2 \in (2^{V_2})^\omega$ with $\sigma = \sigma_1 \cup \sigma_2$ such that $\sigma_i \in \mathcal{L}(\mathcal{A}_i)$ for $i \in \{1, 2\}$ and $\sigma_1 \cap V_2 = \sigma_2 \cap V_1$. Hence, σ_i is an accepting run on $\mathcal{A}_i$. Thus, by definition of automaton composition and since σ_1 and σ_2 agree on shared variables, $\sigma_1 \cup \sigma_2$ is an accepting run on $\mathcal{A}_1 \,\|\, \mathcal{A}_2$. Thus, $\sigma_1 \cup \sigma_2 \in \mathcal{L}(\mathcal{A}_1 \,\|\, \mathcal{A}_2)$ and hence $\sigma \in \mathcal{L}(\mathcal{A}_1 \,\|\, \mathcal{A}_2)$ holds.   □

Using the above lemma, we can formalize the independent sublanguage criterion on NBAs directly: Two automata $\mathcal{A}_1$, $\mathcal{A}_2$ are *independent subautomata of* $\mathcal{A}$ if $\mathcal{A} = \mathcal{A}_1 \,\|\, \mathcal{A}_2$. To apply Theorem 1, the alphabets of the subautomata may not share output variables. Our decomposition algorithm achieves this by constructing the subautomata from the initial automaton by projecting to disjoint sets of outputs. Intuitively, the projection to a set X abstracts from the variables outside of X. Hence, it only captures the parts of the initial specification concerning the variables in X. Formally: Let $\mathcal{A} = (Q, Q_0, \delta, F)$ be an NBA over alphabet 2^V and let $X \subset V$. The *projection of* $\mathcal{A}$ *to* X is the NBA $\mathcal{A}_{\pi(X)} = (Q, Q_0, \pi_X(\delta), F)$ over 2^X with $\pi_X(\delta) = \{(q, a, q') \in Q \times 2^X \times Q \mid \exists\, b \in 2^{V \setminus X}.\ (q, a \cup b, q') \in \delta\}$.

The decomposition algorithm for NBAs is described in Algorithm 2. It is a recursive algorithm that, starting with the initial automaton $\mathcal{A}$, guesses a subset X of the output variables out. It abstracts from the output variables outside of X by building the projection $\mathcal{A}_X$ of $\mathcal{A}$ to X $\cup$ inp, where inp is the set of input variables. Similarly, it builds the projection $\mathcal{A}_Y$ of $\mathcal{A}$ to Y := (out \ X) $\cup$ inp. By construction of $\mathcal{A}_X$ and $\mathcal{A}_Y$ and since both X $\cap$ Y $= \emptyset$ and X $\cup$ Y $=$ out hold, we

(a) NBA $\mathcal{A}$ (b) NBA $\mathcal{A}_{\pi(V_1)}$ (c) NBA $\mathcal{A}_{\pi(V_2)}$

Fig. 1. NBA $\mathcal{A}$ for the *shift_2* specification and its projections $\mathcal{A}_{\pi(V_1)}$ and $\mathcal{A}_{\pi(V_2)}$ to $V_1 = \{i_1, i_2, o_1\}$ and $V_2 = \{i_1, i_2, o_2\}$. All states are accepting.

have $\mathcal{L}(\mathcal{A}) \subseteq \mathcal{L}(\mathcal{A}_X \parallel \mathcal{A}_Y)$. Hence, if $\mathcal{L}(\mathcal{A}_X \parallel \mathcal{A}_Y) \subseteq \mathcal{L}(\mathcal{A})$ holds, then $\mathcal{A}_X \parallel \mathcal{A}_Y$ is equivalent to $\mathcal{A}$ and therefore $\mathcal{L}(\mathcal{A}_X)$ and $\mathcal{L}(\mathcal{A}_Y)$ are independent sublanguages of $\mathcal{L}(\mathcal{A})$. Thus, since $X \cap Y = \emptyset$ holds, $\mathcal{A}_X$ and $\mathcal{A}_Y$ are a valid decomposition of $\mathcal{A}$. The subautomata are then decomposed recursively. If no further decomposition is possible, the algorithm returns the subautomata. By only considering unexplored subsets of output variables, no subset combination X, Y is checked twice.

As an example for the decomposition algorithm, consider the specification $\varphi = \square((i_1 \leftrightarrow o_2) \wedge (i_2 \leftrightarrow o_1))$ for inputs $I = \{i_1, i_2\}$ and outputs $O = \{o_1, o_2\}$. The NBA $\mathcal{A}$ that accepts $\mathcal{L}(\varphi)$ is depicted in Fig. 1a. The subautomata obtained with Algorithm 2 are shown in Figs. 1b and 1c. Clearly, $V_1 \cap V_2 \subseteq I$ holds. Moreover, their parallel composition accepts exactly those words that satisfy φ. For a slightly modified specification $\varphi' = \square((i_1 \leftrightarrow o_2) \vee (i_2 \leftrightarrow o_1))$, however, Algorithm 2 does not decompose the NBA $\mathcal{A}'$ with $\mathcal{L}(\mathcal{A}') = \mathcal{L}(\varphi')$: In fact, the only possible decomposition is $X = \{o_1\}$, $Y = \{o_2\}$ (or vice-versa), yielding NBAs $\mathcal{A}'_X$ and $\mathcal{A}'_Y$ that accept every infinite word. Clearly, $\mathcal{L}(\mathcal{A}'_X \parallel \mathcal{A}'_Y) \not\subseteq \mathcal{L}(\mathcal{A}')$ since $\mathcal{L}(\mathcal{A}'_X \parallel \mathcal{A}'_Y) = (2^{I \cup O})^\omega$ and hence $\mathcal{A}'_X$ and $\mathcal{A}'_Y$ are no valid decomposition.

Algorithm 2 ensures soundness and completeness of modular synthesis: The subspecifications do not share output variables and they are equirealizable to the initial specification. This follows directly from the construction of the subautomata, Lemma 1, and Theorem 1. The proof is given in the full version [12].

Theorem 3. *Let $\mathcal{A}$ be an NBA over alphabet 2^V. Algorithm 2 terminates on $\mathcal{A}$ with a set $\mathcal{S} = \{\mathcal{A}_1, \ldots, \mathcal{A}_k\}$ of NBAs with $\mathcal{L}(\mathcal{A}_i) \subseteq (2^{V_i})^\omega$, where $V_i \cap V_j \subseteq I$ for $1 \leq i, j \leq k$ with $i \neq j$, $V = \bigcup_{1 \leq i \leq k} V_i$, and $\mathcal{A}$ is realizable if, and only if, for all $\mathcal{A}_i \in \mathcal{S}$, $\mathcal{A}_i$ is realizable.*

Since Algorithm 2 is called recursively on every subautomaton obtained by projection, it directly follows that the nondeterministic Büchi automata contained in the returned list are not further decomposable:

Theorem 4. *Let $\mathcal{A}$ be an NBA and let $\mathcal{S}$ be the set of NBAs that Algorithm 2 returns on input $\mathcal{A}$. Then, for each $\mathcal{A}_i \in \mathcal{S}$ over alphabet 2^{V_i}, there are no NBAs $\mathcal{A}'$, $\mathcal{A}''$ over alphabets $2^{V'}$ and $2^{V''}$ with $V_i = V' \cup V''$ such that $\mathcal{A}_i = \mathcal{A}' \parallel \mathcal{A}''$.*

Hence, Algorithm 2 yields *perfect* decompositions and is semantically precise. Yet, it performs several expensive automaton operations such as projection, composition, and language containment checks. For large automata, this is infeasible. For specifications given as LTL formulas, we thus present an approximate decomposition algorithm in the next section that does not yield non-decomposable subspecifications, but that is free of the expensive automaton operations.

5 Decomposition of LTL Formulas

An LTL specification can be decomposed by translating it into an equivalent NBA and by then applying Algorithm 2. To circumvent expensive automaton operations, though, we introduce an approximate decomposition algorithm that, in contrast to Algorithm 2, does not necessarily find all possible decompositions. In the following, we assume that $V = prop(\varphi)$ holds for the initial specification φ. Note that any implementation for the variables in $prop(\varphi)$ can easily be extended to one for the variables in V if $prop(\varphi) \subset V$ by ignoring the inputs in $I \setminus prop(\varphi)$ and by choosing arbitrary valuations for the outputs in $O \setminus prop(\varphi)$.

The main idea of the decomposition algorithm is to rewrite the initial LTL formula φ into a conjunctive form $\varphi = \varphi_1 \wedge \cdots \wedge \varphi_k$ with as many top-level conjuncts as possible by applying distributivity and pushing temporal operators inwards whenever possible. Then, we build subspecifications consisting of subsets of the conjuncts. Each conjunct occurs in exactly one subspecification. We say that conjuncts are *independent* if they do not share output variables. Given an LTL formula with two independent conjuncts, the languages of the conjuncts are independent sublanguages of the language of the whole formula:

Lemma 2. *Let $\varphi = \varphi_1 \wedge \varphi_2$ be an LTL formula over Σ. Let $\mathcal{L}(\varphi_1) \in (2^{\Sigma_1})^\omega$, $\mathcal{L}(\varphi_2) \in (2^{\Sigma_2})^\omega$ be the languages of φ_1 and φ_2 over Σ_1 and Σ_2, respectively, with $\Sigma_1 \cup \Sigma_2 = V$. Then, $\mathcal{L}(\varphi_1)$ and $\mathcal{L}(\varphi_2)$ are independent sublanguages of $\mathcal{L}(\varphi)$.*

Proof. First, let $\sigma \in \mathcal{L}(\varphi)$. Then, $\sigma \in \mathcal{L}(\varphi_i)$ for all $i \in \{1, 2\}$. Since $prop(\varphi_i) \subseteq \Sigma_i$ holds by definition and since the satisfaction of an LTL formula does only depend on the valuations of the variables in $prop(\varphi_i)$, we have $\sigma \cap \Sigma_i \in \mathcal{L}(\varphi_i)$. Since clearly $(\sigma \cap \Sigma_1) \cap \Sigma_2 = (\sigma \cap \Sigma_2) \cap \Sigma_1$ holds, $(\sigma \cap \Sigma_1) \cup (\sigma \cap \Sigma_2) \in \mathcal{L}(\varphi_1) \| \mathcal{L}(\varphi_2)$. Since $\Sigma_1 \cup \Sigma_2 = \Sigma$, $\sigma = (\sigma \cap \Sigma_1) \cup (\sigma \cap \Sigma_2)$ and hence $\sigma \in \mathcal{L}(\varphi_1) \| \mathcal{L}(\varphi_2)$.

Next, let $\sigma \in \mathcal{L}(\varphi_1) \| \mathcal{L}(\varphi_2)$. Then, there are words $\sigma_1 \in \mathcal{L}(\varphi_1)$, $\sigma_2 \in \mathcal{L}(\varphi_2)$ with $\sigma_1 \cap \Sigma_2 = \sigma_2 \cap \Sigma_1$ and $\sigma = \sigma_1 \cup \sigma_2$. Since σ_1 and σ_2 agree on shared variables, $\sigma \in \mathcal{L}(\varphi_1)$ and $\sigma \in \mathcal{L}(\varphi_2)$ follows. Hence, $\sigma \in \mathcal{L}(\varphi_1 \wedge \varphi_2)$. □

Our decomposition algorithm then ensures that different subspecifications share only input variables by merging conjuncts that share output variables into the same subspecification. Then, equirealizability of the initial formula and the subformulas follows directly from Theorem 1 and Lemma 2:

Corollary 1. *Let $\varphi = \varphi_1 \wedge \varphi_2$ be an LTL formula over V with conjuncts φ_1, φ_2 over V_1, V_2, respectively, with $V_1 \cup V_2 = V$ and $V_1 \cap V_2 \subseteq I$. Then, φ is realizable if, and only if, both φ_1 and φ_2 are realizable.*

To determine conjuncts of an LTL formula $\varphi = \varphi_1 \wedge \cdots \wedge \varphi_n$ that share variables, we build the *dependency graph* $\mathcal{D}_\varphi = (V, E)$ of the output variables, where $V = O$ and $(a, b) \in E$ if, and only if, $a \in prop(\varphi_i)$ and $b \in prop(\varphi_i)$ for some $1 \leq i \leq n$. Intuitively, outputs a and b that are contained in the same connected component of $\mathcal{D}_\varphi$ depend on each other in the sense that they either occur in the same conjunct or that they occur in conjuncts that are connected by other output

---

Algorithm 3: LTL Decomposition

Input: φ: LTL, `inp`: List Variable, `out`: List Variable
Output: `specs`: List (LTL, List Variable, List Variable)

1 $\varphi \leftarrow$ rewrite(φ)
2 `formulas` $\leftarrow$ removeTopLevelConjunction(φ)
3 `graph` $\leftarrow$ buildDependencyGraph(φ, `out`)
4 `components` $\leftarrow$ `graph`.connectedComponents()
5 `specs` $\leftarrow$ new LTL[|`components`|+1] // initialized with true
6 **foreach** $\psi \in$ `formulas` **do**
7 $\quad$ `propositions` $\leftarrow$ getPropositions(ψ)
8 $\quad$ **foreach** (`spec`,`set`) $\in$ zip `specs` (`components` ++ [`inp`]) **do**
9 $\quad\quad$ **if** `propositions` $\cap$ `set` $\neq \emptyset$ **then**
10 $\quad\quad\quad$ `spec`.And(ψ)
11 $\quad\quad\quad$ break

12 **return** map ($\lambda\varphi \rightarrow (\varphi$, inputs($\varphi$), outputs($\varphi$))) `specs`

---

variables. Hence, to ensure that subspecifications do not share output variables, conjuncts containing a or b need to be assigned to the same subspecification. Output variables that are contained in different connected components, however, are not linked and therefore implementations for their requirements can be synthesized independently, i.e., with independent subspecifications.

Algorithm 3 describes how an LTL formula is decomposed into subspecifications. First, the formula is rewritten into conjunctive form. Then, the dependency graph is built and the connected components are computed. For each connected component as well as for all input variables, a subspecification is built by adding the conjuncts containing variables of the respective connected component or an input variable, respectively. Considering the input variables is necessary to assign every conjunct, including input-only ones, to at least one subspecification. By construction, no conjunct is added to the subspecifications of two different connected components. Yet, a conjunct could be added to both a subspecification of a connected component and the subspecification for the input-only conjuncts. This is circumvented by the *break* in Line 11. Hence, every conjunct is added to exactly one subspecification. To define the input and output variables for the synthesis subtasks, the algorithm assigns the inputs and outputs occurring in φ_i to the subspecification φ_i. While restricting the inputs is not necessary for correctness, it may improve the runtime of the corresponding synthesis task.

Soundness and completeness of modular synthesis with Algorithm 3 as a decomposition algorithm for LTL formulas follows directly from Corollary 1 if the subspecifications do not share any output variables:

Theorem 5. *Let φ be an LTL formula over V. Then, Algorithm 3 terminates on φ with a set $\mathcal{S} = \{\varphi_1, \ldots, \varphi_k\}$ of LTL formulas with $\mathcal{L}(\varphi_i) \in (2^{V_i})^\omega$ such that $V_i \cap V_j \subseteq I$ for $1 \leq i,j \leq k$ with $i \neq j$, $\bigcup_{1 \leq i \leq k} V_i = V$, and such that φ is realizable, if, and only if, for all $\varphi_i \in \mathcal{S}$, φ_i is realizable.*

Proof. Since an output variable is part of exactly one connected component and since all conjuncts containing an output are contained in the same subspecification, every output is part of exactly one subspecification. Therefore, $V_i \cap V_j \subseteq I$ holds for $1 \leq i, j \leq k$ with $i \neq j$. Moreover, the last component added in Line 8 contains all inputs. Hence, all variables that occur in a conjunct of φ are featured in at least one subspecification. Thus, $\bigcup_{1 \leq i \leq k} V_i = prop(\varphi)$ holds and hence, since $V = prop(\varphi)$ by assumption, $\bigcup_{1 \leq i \leq k} V_i = V$ follows. Therefore, equirealizability of φ and the formulas in $\mathcal{S}$ directly follows with Corollary 1. □

While Algorithm 3 is simple and ensures soundness and completeness of modular synthesis, it strongly depends on the structure of the formula: When rewriting formulas in assumption-guarantee format, i.e., $\varphi = \bigwedge_{i=1}^{m} \varphi_i \rightarrow \bigwedge_{j=1}^{n} \psi_j$, to a conjunctive form, the conjuncts contain both assumptions φ_i and guarantees ψ_j. Hence, if $a, b \in O$ occur in assumption φ_i and guarantee ψ_j, respectively, they are dependent. Thus, all conjuncts featuring a or b are contained in the same subspecification according to Algorithm 3. Yet, ψ_j might be realizable even without φ_i. An algorithm accounting for this might yield further decompositions.

In the following, we present a criterion for dropping assumptions in a sound and complete fashion. Intuitively, we can drop an assumption φ for a guarantee ψ if they do not share any variable. However, if φ can be violated by the system, i.e., if $\neg \varphi$ is realizable, equirealizability is not guaranteed when dropping the assumption. For instance, consider the formula $\varphi = \Diamond(i_1 \wedge o_1) \rightarrow \Box(i_2 \wedge o_2)$, where $I = \{i_1, i_2\}$ and $O = \{o_1, o_2\}$. Although assumption and guarantee do not share any variables, the assumption cannot be dropped: An implementation that never sets o_1 to *true* satisfies φ but $\Box(i_2 \wedge o_2)$ is not realizable. Furthermore, dependencies between input variables may yield unrealizability if an assumption is dropped as information about the remaining inputs might get lost. For instance, in the formula $((\Box i_1 \rightarrow i_2) \wedge (\neg \Box i_1 \rightarrow i_3) \wedge (i_2 \leftrightarrow i_4) \wedge (i_3 \leftrightarrow \neg i_4)) \rightarrow (\Box i_1 \leftrightarrow o)$, where $I = \{i_1, i_2, i_3, i_4\}$ and $O = \{o\}$, no assumption can be dropped: Otherwise the information about the global behavior of i_1, which is crucial for the existence of an implementation, is incomplete. This leads to the following criterion for dropping assumptions. For the full proof, we refer to the full version [12].

Lemma 3 (Dropping Assumptions). *Let $\varphi = (\varphi_1 \wedge \varphi_2) \rightarrow \psi$ be an LTL formula with $prop(\varphi_1) \cap prop(\varphi_2) = \emptyset$ and $prop(\varphi_2) \cap prop(\psi) = \emptyset$. Let $\neg \varphi_2$ be unrealizable. Then, $\varphi_1 \rightarrow \psi$ is realizable if, and only if, φ is realizable.*

Proof (Sketch). First, assume that $\varphi' := \varphi_1 \rightarrow \psi$ is realizable and let f be an implementation realizing it. Clearly, a strategy that ignores inputs outside of $prop(\varphi')$, behaves as f on outputs in $prop(\varphi')$, and chooses arbitrary valuations for the outputs outside of $prop(\varphi')$, realizes $(\varphi_1 \wedge \varphi_2) \rightarrow \psi$.

Next, assume that $(\varphi_1 \wedge \varphi_2) \rightarrow \psi$ is realizable and let f be an implementation realizing it. Since $\neg \varphi_2$ is unrealizable by assumption, there exists a counterstrategy f_2^c with $\mathcal{C}(f_2^c) \subseteq \mathcal{L}(\varphi_2)$. For every $\sigma \in (2^{prop(\varphi')})^\omega$, we can construct a word $\hat{\sigma} \in (2^V)^\omega$ with f_2^c that is equivalent to σ on the variables in $prop(\varphi')$ but satisfies φ_2. Let g be an implementation that for every input σ behaves as f on $\hat{\sigma}$. Since g behaves as f but ensures that φ_2 is satisfied, it realizes φ'. □

By dropping assumptions, we are able to decompose LTL formulas of the form $\varphi = \bigwedge_{i=1}^{m} \varphi_i \rightarrow \bigwedge_{j=1}^{n} \psi_j$ in further cases: Intuitively, we rewrite φ to $\bigwedge_{j=1}^{n}(\bigwedge_{i=1}^{m} \varphi_i \rightarrow \psi_j)$ and then drop assumptions for the individual guarantees. If the resulting subspecifications only share input variables, they are equirealizable to φ. For the full proof, we refer to the full version of this paper [12].

Theorem 6. *Let $\varphi = (\varphi_1 \wedge \varphi_2 \wedge \varphi_3) \rightarrow (\psi_1 \wedge \psi_2)$ be an LTL formula over V, where $prop(\varphi_3) \subseteq I$ and $prop(\psi_1) \cap prop(\psi_2) \subseteq I$. Let $prop(\varphi_1) \cap prop(\varphi_2) = \emptyset$, $prop(\varphi_1) \cap prop(\varphi_3) = \emptyset$, $prop(\varphi_2) \cap prop(\varphi_3) = \emptyset$, and $prop(\varphi_i) \cap prop(\psi_{3-i}) = \emptyset$ for $i \in \{1, 2\}$. Let $\neg(\varphi_1 \wedge \varphi_2 \wedge \varphi_3)$ be unrealizable. Then, φ is realizable if, and only if, both $\varphi' = (\varphi_1 \wedge \varphi_3) \rightarrow \psi_1$ and $\varphi'' = (\varphi_2 \wedge \varphi_3) \rightarrow \psi_2$ are realizable.*

Proof (Sketch). First, let φ be realizable and let f be an implementation realizing it. Clearly, f realizes $(\varphi_1 \wedge \varphi_2 \wedge \varphi_3) \rightarrow \psi_i$ for all $i \in \{1, 2\}$ as well. By Lemma 3, $(\varphi_1 \wedge \varphi_2 \wedge \varphi_3) \rightarrow \psi_i$ and $(\varphi_i \wedge \varphi_3) \rightarrow \psi_i$ are equirealizable since φ_1, φ_2, and φ_3 do not share any variables and φ_{3-i} and ψ_i only share input variables by assumption. Thus, there are implementations realizing φ' and φ''.

Next, let φ' and φ'' be realizable and let f_1, f_2 be implementations realizing them. Let f be an implementation that acts as f_1 on the variables in $prop(\varphi')$ and as f_2 on the variables in $prop(\varphi'')$. The formulas only share variables in $prop(\varphi_3)$ and thus only input variables. Hence, f is well-defined. By construction, f realizes both φ' and φ''. Thus, since $\varphi' \wedge \varphi''$ implies φ, f realizes φ.   □

Analyzing assumptions thus allows for decomposing LTL formulas in further cases and still ensures soundness and completeness of modular synthesis. A modified LTL decomposition algorithm needs to identify variables that cannot be shared safely among subspecifications. If an assumption contains such variables, it is *bound* to guarantees. Otherwise, it is *free*. Guarantees are decomposed as in Algorithm 3. Then, bounded assumptions are added to the subspecifications of their respective guarantees. Free assumptions can be added to all subspecifications. To obtain small subspecifications, though, further optimizations can be used. A detailed description of the algorithm is given in the full version [12].

Note that the decomposition algorithm does not check for possible violations of assumptions. Instead, we slightly modify the modular synthesis algorithm: Before decomposing, we perform synthesis on the negated assumptions. If it returns realizable, it is possible to violate an assumption. The implementation is extended to an implementation for the whole specification that violates the assumptions and thus realizes the specification. Otherwise, if the negated assumptions are unrealizable, the conditions of Theorem 6 are satisfied. Hence, we can use the decomposition algorithm and proceed as in Algorithm 1.

6   Experimental Evaluation

We implemented the modular synthesis algorithm as well as the decomposition approaches and evaluated them on the 346 publicly available SYNTCOMP [16] benchmarks. Note that only 207 of the benchmarks have more than one output

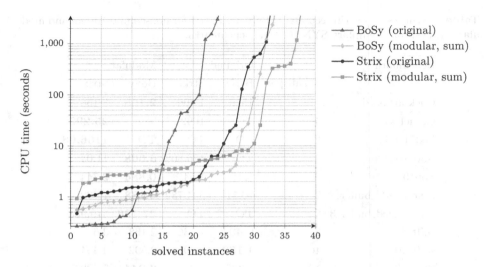

Fig. 2. Comparison of the performance of modular and non-compositional synthesis with BoSy and Strix on the decomposable SYNTCOMP benchmarks. For the modular approach, the accumulated time for all synthesis tasks is depicted.

variable and are therefore realistic candidates for decomposition. The automaton decomposition algorithm utilizes the Spot (2.9.6) automaton library [7] and the LTL decomposition relies on SyFCo (1.2.1.1) [17] for formula transformations. We first decompose the specification and then run synthesis on the resulting subspecifications. We compare the CPU Time, Gates, and Latches for the original specification to the sum of the corresponding attributes of all subspecifications. Thus, we calculate the runtime for sequential modular synthesis. Parallelization of the synthesis tasks may further reduce the runtime.

6.1   LTL Decomposition

LTL decomposition with optimized assumption handling terminates on all benchmarks in less than 26 ms. Thus, even for non-decomposable specifications, the overhead is negligible. The algorithm decomposes 39 formulas into several subspecifications, most of them yielding two or three subspecifications. Only a handful of formulas are decomposed into more than six subspecifications.

We evaluate our modular synthesis approach with two state-of-the-art synthesis tools: BoSy [9], a bounded synthesis tool, and Strix [22], a game-based synthesis tool, both in their 2019 release. We used a machine with a 3.6 GHz quad-core Intel Xeon processor and 32 GB RAM and a timeout of 60 min. In Fig. 2, the comparison of the accumulated runtimes of the synthesis of the subspecifications and the original formula is shown for the decomposable benchmarks. For both BoSy and Strix, decomposition generates a slight overhead for small specifications. For larger and more complex benchmarks, however, modular synthesis decreases the execution time significantly, often by an order of magnitude or more. Note that due to

Table 1. Synthesis time (in seconds) of BoSy and Strix for non-compositional and modular synthesis on exemplary SYNTCOMP benchmarks.

Benchmark		Original		Modular	
	# subspec.	BoSy	Strix	BoSy	Strix
Cockpitboard	8	1526.32	11.06	**2.108**	8.168
Gamelogic	4	TO	1062.27	TO	**25.292**
LedMatrix	3	TO	TO	TO	**1156.68**
Radarboard	11	TO	126.808	**3.008**	11.04
Zoo10	2	1.316	1.54	**0.884**	2.744
generalized_buffer_2	2	70.71	534.732	**4.188**	7.892
generalized_buffer_3	2	TO	TO	**27.136**	319.988
shift_8	8	**0.404**	1.336	2.168	3.6
shift_10	10	**1.172**	1.896	2.692	4.464
shift_12	12	4.336	6.232	**3.244**	5.428

the negligible runtime of specification decomposition, the plot looks similar when considering all SYNTCOMP benchmarks.

Table 1 shows the running times of BoSy and Strix for modular and non-compositional synthesis on exemplary benchmarks. On almost all of them, both tools decrease their synthesis times with modular synthesis notably compared to the original non-compositional approaches. Particularly noteworthy is the benchmark *generalized_buffer_3*. In the last synthesis competition, SYNTCOMP 2020, no tool was able to synthesize a solution for it within one hour. With modular synthesis, however, BoSy yields a result in less than 28 s.

In Table 2, the number of gates and latches of the AIGER circuits [1] corresponding to the implementations computed by BoSy and Strix for modular and non-compositional synthesis are depicted for exemplary benchmarks. For most specifications, the solutions of modular synthesis are of the same size or smaller in terms of gates than the solutions for the original specification. The size of the solutions in terms of latches, however, varies. Note that BoSy does not generate solutions with less than one latch in general. Hence, the modular solution will always have at least as many latches as subspecifications.

Table 2. Gates and latches of the solutions of BoSy and Strix for non-compositional and modular synthesis on exemplary SYNTCOMP benchmarks.

Benchmark	Gates				Latches			
	Original		Modular		Original		Modular	
	BoSy	Strix	BoSy	Strix	BoSy	Strix	BoSy	Strix
Cockpitboard	11	**7**	25	10	1	**0**	8	**0**
Gamelogic	–	26	–	**21**	–	**2**	–	**2**
LedMatrix	–	–	–	**97**	–	–	–	**5**
Radarboard	–	**6**	19	**6**	–	**0**	11	**0**
Zoo10	14	15	15	**13**	1	2	2	2
generalized_buffer_2	**3**	12	**3**	11	69	47134	**14**	557
generalized_buffer_3	–	–	**20**	3772	–	–	**3**	14
shift_8	8	**0**	8	7	1	**0**	8	**0**
shift_10	10	**0**	10	9	1	**0**	10	**0**
shift_12	12	**0**	12	11	1	**0**	12	**0**

6.2 Automata Decomposition

Besides LTL specifications, Strix also accepts specifications given as deterministic parity automata (DPAs) in extended HOA format [23], an automaton format well-suited for synthesis. Thus, our implementation performs Algorithm 2, converts the resulting automata to DPAs and synthesizes solutions with Strix.

For 235 out of the 346 SYNTCOMP benchmarks, decomposition terminated within 10 min yielding several subspecifications or proving that the specification is not decomposable. In 79 of the other cases, the tool timed out and in the remaining 32 cases it reached the memory limit of 16 GB or the internal limits of Spot. Note, however, that for 81 specifications even plain DPA generation fails. Thus, while the automaton decomposition algorithm yields more fine-grained decompositions than the approximate LTL approach, it becomes infeasible when the specifications grow. Hence, the advantage of smaller synthesis subtasks cannot pay off. However, the coarser LTL decomposition suffices to reduce the synthesis time on common benchmarks significantly. Thus, LTL decomposition is in the right balance between small subtasks and a scalable decomposition.

For 43 specifications, the automaton approach yields decompositions and many of them consist of four or more subspecifications. For 22 of these specifications, the LTL approach yields a decomposition as well. Yet, they differ in most cases, as the automaton approach yields more fine-grained decompositions.

Recall that only 207 SYNTCOMP benchmarks are realistic candidates for decomposition. The automaton approach proves that 90 of those specifications (43.6%) are not decomposable. Thus, our implementations yield decompositions for 33.33% (LTL) and 36.75% (Automaton) of the potentially decomposable specifications. We observed that decomposition works exceptionally well for specifications that stem from real system designs, for instance the Syntroids [14] case study, indicating that modular synthesis is particularly beneficial in practice.

7   Conclusions

We have presented a modular synthesis algorithm that applies compositional techniques to reactive synthesis. It reduces the complexity of synthesis by decomposing the specification in a preprocessing step and then performing independent synthesis tasks for the subspecifications. We have introduced a criterion for decomposition algorithms that ensures soundness and completeness of modular synthesis as well as two algorithms for specification decomposition satisfying the criterion: A semantically precise one for nondeterministic Büchi automata, and an approximate algorithm for LTL formulas. We have implemented the modular synthesis algorithm as well as both decomposition algorithms and we compared our approach for the state-of-the-art synthesis tools BoSy and Strix to their noncompositional forms. Our experiments clearly demonstrate the significant advantage of modular synthesis with LTL decomposition over traditional synthesis algorithms. While the overhead is negligible, both BoSy and Strix are able to synthesize solutions for more benchmarks with modular synthesis. Moreover, they improve their synthesis times on complex specifications notably. This shows that decomposing the specification is a game-changer for practical synthesis.

Building up on the presented approach, we can additionally analyze whether the subspecifications fall into fragments for which efficient synthesis algorithms exist, for instance safety specifications. Moreover, parallelizing the individual synthesis tasks may expand the advantage of modular synthesis over classical algorithms. Since the number of subspecifications computed by the LTL decomposition algorithm highly depends on the rewriting of the initial formula, a further promising next step is to develop more sophisticated rewriting algorithms.

References

1. Biere, A., Heljanko, K., Wieringa, S.: AIGER 1.9 and beyond. Technical report 11/2, Institute for Formal Models and Verification, Johannes Kepler University, Altenbergerstr. 69, 4040 Linz, Austria (2011)
2. Bloem, R., Chatterjee, K., Jacobs, S., Könighofer, R.: Assume-guarantee synthesis for concurrent reactive programs with partial information. In: Baier, C., Tinelli, C. (eds.) TACAS 2015. LNCS, vol. 9035, pp. 517–532. Springer, Heidelberg (2015). https://doi.org/10.1007/978-3-662-46681-0_50
3. Chatterjee, K., Henzinger, T.A.: Assume-guarantee synthesis. In: Grumberg, O., Huth, M. (eds.) TACAS 2007. LNCS, vol. 4424, pp. 261–275. Springer, Heidelberg (2007). https://doi.org/10.1007/978-3-540-71209-1_21
4. Clarke, E.M., Long, D.E., McMillan, K.L.: Compositional model checking. In: Proceedings of the Fourth Annual Symposium on Logic in Computer Science. LICS 1989, pp. 353–362. IEEE Computer Society (1989). https://doi.org/10.1109/LICS.1989.39190

5. Damm, W., Finkbeiner, B.: Does it pay to extend the perimeter of a world model? In: Butler, M., Schulte, W. (eds.) FM 2011. LNCS, vol. 6664, pp. 12–26. Springer, Heidelberg (2011). https://doi.org/10.1007/978-3-642-21437-0_4
6. Dureja, R., Rozier, K.Y.: More scalable LTL model checking via discovering design-space dependencies (D^3). In: Beyer, D., Huisman, M. (eds.) TACAS 2018. LNCS, vol. 10805, pp. 309–327. Springer, Cham (2018). https://doi.org/10.1007/978-3-319-89960-2_17
7. Duret-Lutz, A., Lewkowicz, A., Fauchille, A., Michaud, T., Renault, É., Xu, L.: Spot 2.0 — a framework for LTL and ω-automata manipulation. In: Artho, C., Legay, A., Peled, D. (eds.) ATVA 2016. LNCS, vol. 9938, pp. 122–129. Springer, Cham (2016). https://doi.org/10.1007/978-3-319-46520-3_8
8. Ehlers, R.: Unbeast: symbolic bounded synthesis. In: Abdulla, P.A., Leino, K.R.M. (eds.) TACAS 2011. LNCS, vol. 6605, pp. 272–275. Springer, Heidelberg (2011). https://doi.org/10.1007/978-3-642-19835-9_25
9. Faymonville, P., Finkbeiner, B., Tentrup, L.: BoSy: an experimentation framework for bounded synthesis. In: Majumdar, R., Kunčak, V. (eds.) CAV 2017. LNCS, vol. 10427, pp. 325–332. Springer, Cham (2017). https://doi.org/10.1007/978-3-319-63390-9_17
10. Filiot, E., Jin, N., Raskin, J.-F.: Compositional algorithms for LTL synthesis. In: Bouajjani, A., Chin, W.-N. (eds.) ATVA 2010. LNCS, vol. 6252, pp. 112–127. Springer, Heidelberg (2010). https://doi.org/10.1007/978-3-642-15643-4_10
11. Finkbeiner, B.: Synthesis of reactive systems. In: Esparza, J., Grumberg, O., Sickert, S. (eds.) Dependable Software Systems Engineering. NATO Science for Peace and Security Series - D: Information and Communication Security, vol. 45, pp. 72–98. IOS Press (2016). https://doi.org/10.3233/978-1-61499-627-9-72
12. Finkbeiner, B., Geier, G., Passing, N.: Specification decomposition for reactive synthesis (full version). CoRR abs/2103.08459 (2021). https://arxiv.org/abs/2103.08459
13. Finkbeiner, B., Passing, N.: Dependency-based compositional synthesis. In: Hung, D.V., Sokolsky, O. (eds.) ATVA 2020. LNCS, vol. 12302, pp. 447–463. Springer, Cham (2020). https://doi.org/10.1007/978-3-030-59152-6_25
14. Geier, G., Heim, P., Klein, F., Finkbeiner, B.: Syntroids: synthesizing a game for FPGAs using temporal logic specifications. In: Barrett, C.W., Yang, J. (eds.) 2019 Formal Methods in Computer Aided Design, FMCAD 2019, Proceedings, pp. 138–146. IEEE (2019). https://doi.org/10.23919/FMCAD.2019.8894261
15. Jacobs, S., Bloem, R.: The reactive synthesis competition: SYNTCOMP 2016 and beyond. In: Piskac, R., Dimitrova, R. (eds.) Fifth Workshop on Synthesis, SYNT@CAV 2016, Proceedings. EPTCS, vol. 229, pp. 133–148 (2016). https://doi.org/10.4204/EPTCS.229.11
16. Jacobs, S., et al.: The 5th reactive synthesis competition (SYNTCOMP 2018): benchmarks, participants & results. CoRR abs/1904.07736 (2019). http://arxiv.org/abs/1904.07736
17. Jacobs, S., Klein, F., Schirmer, S.: A high-level LTL synthesis format: TLSF v1.1. In: Piskac, R., Dimitrova, R. (eds.) Fifth Workshop on Synthesis, SYNT@CAV 2016, Proceedings. EPTCS, vol. 229, pp. 112–132 (2016). https://doi.org/10.4204/EPTCS.229.10
18. Jobstmann, B.: Applications and optimizations for LTL synthesis. Ph.D. thesis, Graz University of Technology (2007)
19. Kupferman, O., Piterman, N., Vardi, M.Y.: Safraless compositional synthesis. In: Ball, T., Jones, R.B. (eds.) CAV 2006. LNCS, vol. 4144, pp. 31–44. Springer, Heidelberg (2006). https://doi.org/10.1007/11817963_6

20. Kupferman, O., Vardi, M.Y.: Safraless decision procedures. In: 46th Annual IEEE Symposium on Foundations of Computer Science (FOCS) 2005, Proceedings, pp. 531–542. IEEE Computer Society (2005)

21. Majumdar, R., Mallik, K., Schmuck, A., Zufferey, D.: Assume-guarantee distributed synthesis. IEEE Trans. Comput. Aided Des. Integr. Circuits Syst. **39**(11), 3215–3226 (2020). https://doi.org/10.1109/TCAD.2020.3012641

22. Meyer, P.J., Sickert, S., Luttenberger, M.: Strix: explicit reactive synthesis strikes back! In: Chockler, H., Weissenbacher, G. (eds.) CAV 2018. LNCS, vol. 10981, pp. 578–586. Springer, Cham (2018). https://doi.org/10.1007/978-3-319-96145-3_31

23. Pérez, G.A.: The extended HOA format for synthesis. CoRR abs/1912.05793 (2019). http://arxiv.org/abs/1912.05793

24. Pnueli, A.: The temporal logic of programs. In: Annual Symposium on Foundations of Computer Science 1977, pp. 46–57. IEEE Computer Society (1977). https://doi.org/10.1109/SFCS.1977.32

25. Pnueli, A., Rosner, R.: On the synthesis of a reactive module. In: Conference Record of the Sixteenth Annual ACM Symposium on Principles of Programming Languages 1989, pp. 179–190. ACM Press (1989). https://doi.org/10.1145/75277.75293

26. de Roever, W.-P., Langmaack, H., Pnueli, A. (eds.): COMPOS 1997. LNCS, vol. 1536. Springer, Heidelberg (1998). https://doi.org/10.1007/3-540-49213-5

27. Sohail, S., Somenzi, F.: Safety first: a two-stage algorithm for the synthesis of reactive systems. Int. J. Softw. Tools Technol. Transf. **15**(5–6), 433–454 (2013). https://doi.org/10.1007/s10009-012-0224-3

On Symmetry and Quantification: A New Approach to Verify Distributed Protocols

Aman Goel[✉] and Karem Sakallah

University of Michigan, Ann Arbor, MI 48105, USA
{amangoel,karem}@umich.edu

Abstract. Proving that an unbounded distributed protocol satisfies a given safety property amounts to finding a quantified inductive invariant that implies the property for all possible instance sizes of the protocol. Existing methods for solving this problem can be described as search procedures for an invariant whose quantification prefix fits a particular template. We propose an alternative *constructive* approach that does not prescribe, *a priori*, a specific quantifier prefix. Instead, the required prefix is automatically inferred without any search by carefully analyzing the structural symmetries of the protocol. The key insight underlying this approach is that symmetry and quantification are closely related concepts that express protocol *invariance* under different re-arrangements of its components. We propose *symmetric incremental induction*, an extension of the finite-domain IC3/PDR algorithm, that automatically derives the required *quantified inductive invariant* by exploiting the connection between symmetry and quantification. While various attempts have been made to exploit symmetry in verification applications, to our knowledge, this is the first demonstration of a direct link between symmetry and quantification in the context of clause learning during incremental induction. We also describe a procedure to automatically find a minimal finite size, the *cutoff*, that yields a quantified invariant proving safety for any size.

Our approach is implemented in IC3PO, a new verifier for distributed protocols that significantly outperforms the state-of-the-art, scales orders of magnitude faster, and robustly derives compact inductive invariants fully automatically.

1 Introduction

Our focus in this paper is on *parameterized verification*, specifically proving *safety* properties of distributed systems, such as protocols that are often modeled above the code level (e.g., [49,63]), consisting of arbitrary numbers of *identical* components that are instances of a small set of different *sorts*. For example, a client server protocol[1] $CS(i, j)$ is a two-sort parameterized system with parameters $i \geq 1$ and $j \geq 1$ denoting, respectively, the number of clients and servers. Protocol correctness proofs are critical for establishing the correctness of actual system implementations in established methodologies such as [42,68]. Proving safety

© Springer Nature Switzerland AG 2021
A. Dutle et al. (Eds.): NFM 2021, LNCS 12673, pp. 131–150, 2021.
https://doi.org/10.1007/978-3-030-76384-8_9

properties for such systems requires the derivation of inductive invariants that are expressed as state predicates quantified over the system parameters. While, in general, this problem is undecidable [7], certain restricted forms have been shown to yield to algorithmic solutions [16]. Key to these solutions is appealing to the problem's inherent symmetry. In this paper, we exclusively focus on protocols whose sorts represent sets of indistinguishable domain constants. The behavior of this restricted class of protocols remains invariant under all possible permutations of the domain constants. We leave the exploration of other features, such as totally-ordered sorts, integer arithmetic, etc., for future work.

Our proposed symmetry-based solution is best understood by briefly reviewing earlier efforts. Initially, the pressing issue was the inevitable *state explosion* when verifying a finite, but large, parameterized system [11,28,36,60,65,67]. Thus, instead of verifying the "full" system, these approaches verified its *symmetry-reduced quotient,* mostly using BDD-based symbolic image computation [18,19,56]. The Murφ verifier [60] was a notable exception in that it a) generated a C++ program that enumerated the system's symmetry-reduced reachable states, and b) allowed for the verification of unbounded systems by taking advantage of *data saturation* which happens when the size of the symmetry-reduced reachable states become constant regardless of system size.

The idea that an unbounded *symmetric* system can, under certain data-independence assumptions, be verified by analyzing small finite instances evolved into the approach of verification by *invisible invariants* [8,9,24,64,69]. In this approach, assuming they exist, inductive invariants that are universally-quantified over the system parameters are automatically derived by analyzing instances of the system up to a *cutoff* size N_0 using a combination of symbolic reachability and symmetry-based abstraction. Noting that an invariant is an over-approximation of the reachable states, the restriction to universal quantification may fail in some cases, rendering the approach incomplete. The invisible invariant verifier IIV [9] employs some heuristics to derive invariants that use combinations of universal and existential quantifiers, but as pointed out in [58], it may still fail and is not guaranteed to be complete.

The development of SAT-based incremental induction algorithms [17,26] for verifying the safety of finite transition systems was a major advance in the field of model checking and has, for the most part, replaced BDD-based approaches. These algorithms leverage the capacity and performance of modern CDCL SAT solvers [10,27,55,57] to produce *clausal strengthening assertions* A that, conjoined with a specified safety property P, form an automatically-generated inductive invariant $Inv = A \land P$ if the property holds. The AVR hardware verifier [38–40] was adapted in [53] to produce quantifier-free inductive invariants for small instances of unbounded protocols that are subsequently generalized with universal quantification, in analogy with the invisible invariants approach, to arbitrary sizes. The resulting assertions tended, in some cases, to be quite large, and the approach was also incomplete due to the restriction to universal quantification.

In this paper we introduce IC3PO, a novel symmetry-based verifier that builds on these previous efforts while removing most of their limitations. Rather than search for an invariant with a prescribed quantifier prefix, IC3PO constructively *discovers* the required quantified assertions by performing *symmetric incremental induction* and analyzing the symmetry patterns in learned clauses to infer the corresponding quantifier prefix. Our main contributions are:

- An extension to finite incremental induction algorithms that uses protocol symmetry to boost clause learning from a *single* clause φ to a set of symmetrically-equivalent clauses, φ's *orbit*.
- A quantifier inference procedure that expresses φ's orbit by an automatically-derived *compact* quantified predicate Φ. The inference procedure is based on a simple analysis of φ's *syntactic structure* and yields a quantified form with both universal and existential quantifiers.
- A systematic *finite convergence* procedure for determining a minimal instance size sufficient for deriving a quantified inductive invariant that holds for all sizes.

We also demonstrate the effectiveness of IC3PO on a diverse set of benchmarks and show that it significantly advances the current state-of-the-art.

The paper is structured as follows: Sect. 2 presents preliminaries. Section 3 formalizes protocol symmetries. The next three sections detail our key contributions: symmetry boosting during incremental induction in Sect. 4, relating symmetry to quantification in Sect. 5, and checking for convergence in Sect. 6. Section 7 describes the IC3PO algorithm and implementation details. Section 8 presents our experimental evaluation. The paper concludes with a brief survey of related work in Sect. 9, and a discussion of future directions in Sect. 10.

2   Preliminaries

Figure 1 describes a toy consensus protocol from [5] in the TLA+ language [49].[1] The protocol has three named sorts $S = [\text{node}, \text{quorum}, \text{value}]$ introduced by the CONSTANTS declaration, and two relations $R = \{vote, decision\}$, introduced by the VARIABLES declaration, that are defined on these sorts. Each of the sorts is understood to represent an unbounded domain of distinct elements with the relations serving as the protocol's state variables. The global axiom (line 3) defines the elements of the quorum sort to be subsets of the node sort and restricts them further by requiring them to be pair-wise non-disjoint. We will refer to node (resp. quorum) as an *independent* (resp. *dependent*) sort. The protocol transitions are specified by the actions *CastVote* and *Decide* (lines 6–7) which are expressed using the current- and next-state variables as well as the definitions *didNotVote* and *chosenAt* (lines 4–5) which serve as *auxiliary non-state* variables. Lines 8–10 specify the protocol's initial states, transition relation, and safety property.

Viewed as a parameterized system, the *template* of an arbitrary n-sort distributed protocol $\mathcal{P}$ will be expressed as $\mathcal{P}(\mathbf{s_1}, \ldots, \mathbf{s_n})$ where $S = [\mathbf{s_1}, \ldots, \mathbf{s_n}]$

---

[1] The description in [5] is in the Ivy [63] language and encodes set operations in relational form with a *member* relation representing $\in$.

—————————————— MODULE *ToyConsensus* ——————————————

1   CONSTANTS **node, quorum, value**   VARIABLES *vote, decision*

2   *vote* $\in$ (**node** $\times$ **value**) $\rightarrow$ BOOLEAN   *decision* $\in$ **value** $\rightarrow$ BOOLEAN

3   ASSUME $\forall Q \in$ **quorum** : $Q \subseteq$ **node** $\wedge$ $\forall Q_1, Q_2 \in$ **quorum** : $Q_1 \cap Q_2 \neq \{\}$

4   *didNotVote*(n) $\triangleq$ $\forall V \in$ **value** : $\neg vote(n, V)$

5   *chosenAt*(q, v) $\triangleq$ $\forall N \in q : vote(N, v)$

6   *CastVote*(n, v) $\triangleq$ *didNotVote*(n) $\wedge$ *vote'* $= [vote$ EXCEPT $![n, v] =$ TRUE$]$
                                    $\wedge$ UNCHANGED *decision*

7   *Decide*(q, v) $\triangleq$ *chosenAt*(q, v) $\wedge$ *decision'* $= [decision$ EXCEPT $![v] =$ TRUE$]$
                                    $\wedge$ UNCHANGED *vote*

8   *Init* $\triangleq$ $\forall N \in$ **node**, $V \in$ **value** : $\neg vote(N, V)$ $\wedge$ $\forall V \in$ **value** : $\neg decision(V)$

9   *T* $\triangleq$ $\exists N \in$ **node**, $Q \in$ **quorum**, $V \in$ **value** : *CastVote*(N, V) $\vee$ *Decide*(Q, V)

10 *P* $\triangleq$ $\forall V_1, V_2 \in$ **value** : *decision*(V_1) $\wedge$ *decision*(V_2) $\Rightarrow$ $V_1 = V_2$

Fig. 1. Toy consensus protocol in the TLA+ language

is an ordered list of its sorts, each of which is assumed to be an unbounded uninterpreted set of distinct *constants*. As a mathematical transition system, $\mathcal{P}$ is defined by a) its state variables which are expressed as k-ary relations on its sorts, and b) its actions which capture its state transitions. We also note that non-Boolean functions/variables can be easily accommodated by encoding them in relational form, e.g., $f(x_1, x_2, \ldots) = y$. We will use *Init*, T, and P to denote, respectively, a protocol's initial states, its transition relation, and a safety property that is required to hold on all reachable states. A finite instance of $\mathcal{P}$ will be denoted as $\mathcal{P}(|s_1|, \ldots, |s_n|)$ where each named sort is replaced by its finite size in the instance. Similarly, *Init*$(|s_1|, \ldots, |s_n|)$, $T(|s_1|, \ldots, |s_n|)$ and $P(|s_1|, \ldots, |s_n|)$ will, respectively, denote the application of *Init*, T and P to this finite instance.

The template of the protocol in Fig. 1 is *ToyConsensus*(**node, quorum, value**). Its finite instance:

$$ToyConsensus(3, 3, 3) : \quad \textbf{node}_3 \triangleq \{n_1, n_2, n_3\} \qquad \textbf{value}_3 \triangleq \{v_1, v_2, v_3\} \qquad (1)$$

$$\textbf{quorum}_3 \triangleq \{q_{12} : \{n_1, n_2\}, \ q_{13} : \{n_1, n_3\}, \ q_{23} : \{n_2, n_3\}\}$$

will be used as a running example in the paper. The finite sorts of this instance are defined as sets of arbitrarily-named distinct constants. It should be noted that the constants of the **quorum**$_3$ sort are subsets of the **node**$_3$ sort that satisfy the non-empty intersection axiom and are named to reflect their symmetric dependence on the **node**$_3$ sort. This instance has 9 *vote* and 3 *decision* state variables, and a *state* of this instance corresponds to a complete Boolean assignment to these 12 state variables.

In the sequel, we will use $\hat{\mathcal{P}}$ and $\hat{T}$ as shorthand for $\mathcal{P}(|s_1|, \ldots, |s_n|)$ and $T(|s_1|, \ldots, |s_n|)$. Quantifier-free formulas will be denoted by lower-case Greek letters (e.g., φ) and quantified formulas by upper-case Greek letters (e.g., Φ). We use primes (e.g., φ') to represent a formula after a single transition step.

3 Protocol Symmetries

The symmetry group of $\hat{\mathcal{P}}$ is $G(\hat{\mathcal{P}}) = \times_{s \in S} Sym(s)$, where $Sym(s)$ is the symmetric group, i.e., the set of $|s|!$ permutations of the constants of the set s.[2] In what follows we will use G instead of $G(\hat{\mathcal{P}})$ to reduce clutter. Given a permutation $\gamma \in G$ and an arbitrary protocol relation ρ instantiated with specific sort constants, the *action* of γ on ρ, denoted ρ^γ, is the relation obtained from ρ by permuting the sort constants in ρ according to γ; it is referred to as the γ-*image* of ρ. Permutation $\gamma \in G$ can also act on any formula involving the protocol relations. In particular, the invariance of protocol behavior under permutation of sort constants implies that the action of γ on the (finite) initial state, transition relation, and property formulas causes a syntactic re-arrangement of their sub-formulas while preserving their logical equivalence:

$$\hat{Init}^\gamma \equiv \hat{Init} \qquad\qquad \hat{T}^\gamma \equiv \hat{T} \qquad\qquad \hat{P}^\gamma \equiv \hat{P} \qquad (2)$$

Consider next a clause φ which is a disjunction of literals, namely, instantiated protocol relations or their negations. The *orbit* of φ under G, denoted φ^G, is the set of its images φ^γ for all permutations $\gamma \in G$, i.e., $\varphi^G = \{\varphi^\gamma | \gamma \in G\}$. The γ-image of a clause can be viewed as a *syntactic* transformation that will either yield a new logically-distinct clause on different literals or simply re-arrange the literals in the clause without changing its logical behavior (by the commutativity and associativity of disjunction). We define the *logical action* of a permutation γ on a clause φ, denoted $\varphi^{L(\gamma)}$, as:

$$\varphi^{L(\gamma)} = \begin{cases} \varphi^\gamma & \text{if } \varphi^\gamma \not\equiv \varphi \\ \varphi & \text{if } \varphi^\gamma \equiv \varphi \end{cases}$$

and the *logical orbit* of φ as $\varphi^{L(G)} = \{\varphi^{L(\gamma)} | \gamma \in G\}$. With a slight abuse of notation, logical orbit can also be viewed as the conjunction of the logical images:

$$\varphi^{L(G)} = \bigwedge_{\gamma \in G} \varphi^{L(\gamma)}$$

To illustrate these concepts, consider $ToyConsensus(3,3,3)$ from (1). Its symmetries in cycle notation are as follows:

$$Sym(\mathbf{node_3}) = \{(), (n_1\ n_2), (n_1\ n_3), (n_2\ n_3), (n_1\ n_2\ n_3), (n_1\ n_3\ n_2)\}$$
$$Sym(\mathbf{value_3}) = \{(), (v_1\ v_2), (v_1\ v_3), (v_2\ v_3), (v_1\ v_2\ v_3), (v_1\ v_3\ v_2)\}$$
$$G = Sym(\mathbf{node_3}) \times Sym(\mathbf{value_3}) \qquad\qquad (3)$$

The symmetry group (3) of $ToyConsensus(3,3,3)$ has 36 symmetries corresponding to the 6 $\mathbf{node_3} \times$ 6 $\mathbf{value_3}$ permutations. The permutations on $\mathbf{quorum_3}$

---

[2] We assume familiarity with basic notions from *group theory* including *permutation groups, cycle notation, group action* on a set, *orbits*, etc., which can be readily found in standard textbooks on Abstract Algebra [32].

are *implicit* and based on the permutations of node_3 since quorum_3 is a dependent sort. Now, consider the example clause:

$$\varphi_1 = vote(\mathbf{n}_1, \mathbf{v}_1) \lor vote(\mathbf{n}_1, \mathbf{v}_2) \lor vote(\mathbf{n}_1, \mathbf{v}_3) \tag{4}$$

The orbit of φ_1 consists of 36 syntactically-permuted clauses. However, many of these images are logically equivalent yielding the following logical orbit of just 3 logically-distinct clauses:

$$\begin{aligned}
\varphi_1^{L(G)} = &\; [\; vote(\mathbf{n}_1, \mathbf{v}_1) \lor vote(\mathbf{n}_1, \mathbf{v}_2) \lor vote(\mathbf{n}_1, \mathbf{v}_3) \;] \land \\
&\; [\; vote(\mathbf{n}_2, \mathbf{v}_1) \lor vote(\mathbf{n}_2, \mathbf{v}_2) \lor vote(\mathbf{n}_2, \mathbf{v}_3) \;] \land \\
&\; [\; vote(\mathbf{n}_3, \mathbf{v}_1) \lor vote(\mathbf{n}_3, \mathbf{v}_2) \lor vote(\mathbf{n}_3, \mathbf{v}_3) \;]
\end{aligned} \tag{5}$$

4   *SymIC3*: Symmetric Incremental Induction

SymIC3 is an extension of the standard IC3 algorithm [17, 26] that takes advantage of the symmetries in a finite instance $\hat{\mathcal{P}}$ of an unbounded protocol $\mathcal{P}$ to *boost learning* during backward reachability. Specifically, it refines the current frame, in a *single* step, with *all* clauses in the logical orbit $\varphi^{L(G)}$ of a newly-learned quantifier-free clause φ. In other words, having determined that the backward 1-step check $F_{i-1} \land \hat{T} \land [\neg\varphi]'$ is unsatisfiable (i.e., that states in cube $\neg\varphi$ in frame F_i are unreachable from the previous frame F_{i-1}), *SymIC3* refines F_i with $\varphi^{L(G)}$, i.e., $F_i := F_i \land \varphi^{L(G)}$, rather than with just φ. Thus, at each refinement step, *SymIC3* not only blocks cube $\neg\varphi$, but also all symmetrically-equivalent cubes $[\neg\varphi]^\gamma$ for all $\gamma \in G$. This simple change to the standard incremental induction algorithm significantly improves performance since the extra clauses used to refine F_i a) are derived *without* making additional backward 1-step queries, and b) provide stronger refinement in each step of backward reachability leading to faster convergence with fewer counterexamples-to-induction (CTIs). The proof of correctness of symmetry boosting can be found in [37].

5   Quantifier Inference

The key insight underlying our overall approach is that the explicit logical orbit, in a finite protocol instance, of a learned clause φ can be exactly, and systematically, captured by a corresponding quantified predicate Φ. In retrospect, this should not be surprising since symmetry and quantification can be seen as different ways of expressing invariance under permutation of the sort constants in the clause. To motivate the connection between symmetry and quantification, consider the following quantifier-free clause from our running example and a proposed quantified predicate that *implicitly* represents its logical orbit:

$$\varphi_2 = \neg decision(\mathbf{v}_1) \lor decision(\mathbf{v}_2)$$
$$\Phi_2 = \forall X_1, X_2 \in \text{value}_3 : (\text{distinct } X_1\ X_2) \to [\; \neg decision(X_1) \lor decision(X_2) \;] \tag{6}$$

Table 1. Correlation between symmetry and quantification for Φ_2 from (6), Highlighted clauses represent the logical orbit $\varphi_2^{L(G)}$, none indicates the clause has no corresponding permutation $\gamma \in Sym(\text{value}_3)$

(X_1, X_2)	Instantiation of Φ_2	Permutation
$(\mathbf{v_1}, \mathbf{v_1})$	$(\text{distinct } \mathbf{v_1}\ \mathbf{v_1}) \rightarrow [\ \neg decision(\mathbf{v_1}) \vee decision(\mathbf{v_1})\ ]$	none
$(\mathbf{v_1}, \mathbf{v_2})$	$(\text{distinct } \mathbf{v_1}\ \mathbf{v_2}) \rightarrow [\ \neg decision(\mathbf{v_1}) \vee decision(\mathbf{v_2})\ ]$	()
$(\mathbf{v_1}, \mathbf{v_3})$	$(\text{distinct } \mathbf{v_1}\ \mathbf{v_3}) \rightarrow [\ \neg decision(\mathbf{v_1}) \vee decision(\mathbf{v_3})\ ]$	$(\mathbf{v_2}\ \mathbf{v_3})$
$(\mathbf{v_2}, \mathbf{v_1})$	$(\text{distinct } \mathbf{v_2}\ \mathbf{v_1}) \rightarrow [\ \neg decision(\mathbf{v_2}) \vee decision(\mathbf{v_1})\ ]$	$(\mathbf{v_1}\ \mathbf{v_2})$
$(\mathbf{v_2}, \mathbf{v_2})$	$(\text{distinct } \mathbf{v_2}\ \mathbf{v_2}) \rightarrow [\ \neg decision(\mathbf{v_2}) \vee decision(\mathbf{v_2})\ ]$	none
$(\mathbf{v_2}, \mathbf{v_3})$	$(\text{distinct } \mathbf{v_2}\ \mathbf{v_3}) \rightarrow [\ \neg decision(\mathbf{v_2}) \vee decision(\mathbf{v_3})\ ]$	$(\mathbf{v_1}\ \mathbf{v_2}\ \mathbf{v_3})$
$(\mathbf{v_3}, \mathbf{v_1})$	$(\text{distinct } \mathbf{v_3}\ \mathbf{v_1}) \rightarrow [\ \neg decision(\mathbf{v_3}) \vee decision(\mathbf{v_1})\ ]$	$(\mathbf{v_1}\ \mathbf{v_3}\ \mathbf{v_2})$
$(\mathbf{v_3}, \mathbf{v_2})$	$(\text{distinct } \mathbf{v_3}\ \mathbf{v_2}) \rightarrow [\ \neg decision(\mathbf{v_3}) \vee decision(\mathbf{v_2})\ ]$	$(\mathbf{v_1}\ \mathbf{v_3})$
$(\mathbf{v_3}, \mathbf{v_3})$	$(\text{distinct } \mathbf{v_3}\ \mathbf{v_3}) \rightarrow [\ \neg decision(\mathbf{v_3}) \vee decision(\mathbf{v_3})\ ]$	none

As shown in Table 1, the logical orbit $\varphi_2^{L(G)}$ consists of 6 logically-distinct clauses corresponding to the 6 permutations of the 3 constants of the value_3 sort. Evaluating Φ_2 by substituting all $3 \times 3 = 9$ assignments to the variable pair $(X_1, X_2) \in \text{value}_3 \times \text{value}_3$ yields 9 clauses, 3 of which (shown faded) are trivially true since their "distinct" antecedents are false, with the remaining 6 corresponding to each of the clauses obtained through permutations of the 3 value_3 constants. Similarly, we can show that the 3-clause logical orbit $\varphi_1^{L(G)}$ in (5) can be succinctly expressed by the quantified predicate:

$$\Phi_1 = \forall Y \in \text{node}_3,\ \exists X \in \text{value}_3 :\ vote(Y, X) \tag{7}$$

which employs universal *and* existential quantification. And, finally, φ_3 and Φ_3 below illustrate how a clause whose logical orbit is just itself can also be expressed as an existentially-quantified predicate.

$$\varphi_3 = decision(\mathbf{v_1}) \vee decision(\mathbf{v_2}) \vee decision(\mathbf{v_3})$$
$$\Phi_3 = \exists\, X \in \text{value}_3 :\ decision(X) \tag{8}$$

We will first describe basic quantifier inference for protocols with independent sorts. This is done by analyzing the syntactic structure of each quantifier-free clause learned during incremental induction to derive a quantified form that expresses the clause's logical orbit. We later discuss extensions to this approach that consider protocols with dependent sorts, such as *ToyConsensus*, for which the basic single-clause quantifier inference may be insufficient.

5.1   Basic Quantifier Inference

Given a quantifier-free clause φ, quantifier inference seeks to derive a *compact* quantified predicate that *implicitly* represents, rather than explicitly enumerates, its logical orbit. The procedure must satisfy the following conditions:

Correctness – The inferred quantified predicate Φ should be logically-equivalent to the explicit logical orbit $\varphi^{L(G)}$.

Compactness – The number of quantified variables in Φ for each sort $s \in S$ should be independent of the sort size $|s|$. Intuitively, this condition ensures that the size of the quantified predicate, measured as the number of its quantifiers, remains bounded for *any* finite protocol instance, and more importantly, for the unbounded protocol.

SymIC3 constructs the orbit's quantified representation by a) inferring the required quantifiers for each sort separately, and b) stitching together the inferred quantifiers for the different sorts to form the final result. The key to capturing the logical orbit and deriving its compact quantified representation is a simple analysis of the *structural distribution* of each sort's constants in the target clause. Let $\pi(\varphi, s)$ be a partition of the constants of sort s in φ based on whether or not they appear *identically* in the literals of φ. Two constants c_i and c_j are identically-present in φ if they occur in φ and swapping them results in a logically-equivalent clause, i.e., $\varphi^{(c_i\ c_j)} \equiv \varphi$. Let $\#(\varphi, s)$ be the number of constants of s that appear in φ, and let $|\pi(\varphi, s)|$ be the number of classes/cells in $\pi(\varphi, s)$. Consider the following scenarios for quantifier inference on sort s:

A. $\#(\varphi, s) < |s|$ (infer $\forall$)

In this case, clause φ contains a strict subset of constants from sort s, indicating that the number of literals in φ parameterized by s constants is *independent* of the sort size $|s|$. Increasing sort size simply makes the orbit *longer* by adding more symmetrically-equivalent but logically-distinct clauses. An example of this case is φ_2 and Φ_2 in (6). The quantified predicate representing such an orbit requires $\#(\varphi, s)$ universally-quantified sort variables corresponding to the $\#(\varphi, s)$ sort constants in the clause, and expresses the orbit as an implication whose antecedent is a "distinct" constraint that ensures that the variables cannot be instantiated with identical constants.

B. $\#(\varphi, s) = |s|$

When all constants of a sort s appear in a clause, the above universal quantification yields a predicate with $|s|$ quantified variables and fails the compactness requirement since the number of quantified variables becomes unbounded as the sort size increases. Correct quantification in this case must be inferred by examining the partition of the sort constants in the clause.

I. Single-cell Partition i.e., $|\pi(\varphi, \mathbf{s})| = 1$ (infer $\exists$)

When all sort constants appear *identically* in φ, $\pi(\varphi, \mathbf{s})$ is a unit partition. Applying *any* permutation $\gamma \in Sym(\mathbf{s})$ to φ yields a logically-equivalent clause, i.e., the logical orbit in this case is just a single clause. Increasing the size of sort $\mathbf{s}$ simply yields a *wider* clause and suggests that such an orbit can be encoded as a predicate with a single existentially-quantified variable that ranges over all the sort constants. For example, the partition of the $\mathbf{value_3}$ sort constants in φ_1 from (4) is $\pi(\varphi_1, \mathbf{value_3}) = \{\{\mathbf{v_1}, \mathbf{v_2}, \mathbf{v_3}\}\}$ since all three constants appear identically in φ_1. The orbit of this clause is just itself and can be encoded as:

$$\Phi_1(\mathbf{value_3}) = \exists X \in \mathbf{value_3} : vote(\mathbf{n_1}, X)$$

Also, since $\#(\varphi_1, \mathbf{node_3}) < |\mathbf{node_3}|$, universal quantification (as in Sect. 5.1.A) correctly captures the dependence of the clause's logical orbit on the $\mathbf{node_3}$ sort to get the overall quantified predicate Φ_1 in (7).

II. Multi-cell Partition i.e., $|\pi(\varphi, \mathbf{s})| > 1$ (infer $\forall\exists$)

In this case, a fixed number of the constants of sort $\mathbf{s}$ appear differently in φ with the remaining constants appearing identically, resulting in a multi-cell partition. Specifically, assume that a number $0 < k < |\mathbf{s}|$ exists that is independent of $|\mathbf{s}|$ such that $\pi(\varphi, \mathbf{s})$ has $k + 1$ cells in which one cell has $|\mathbf{s}| - k$ identically-appearing constants and each of the remaining k cells contains one of the differently-appearing constants. It can be shown that the logical orbit in this case can be expressed by a quantified predicate with k universal quantifiers and a single existential quantifier. For example, the partition of the $\mathbf{value_3}$ constants in the clause:

$$\varphi_4 = \neg decision(\mathbf{v_1}) \vee decision(\mathbf{v_2}) \vee decision(\mathbf{v_3})$$

is $\pi(\varphi_4, \mathbf{value_3}) = \{\{\mathbf{v_1}\}, \{\mathbf{v_2}, \mathbf{v_3}\}\}$ since $\mathbf{v_1}$ appears differently from $\mathbf{v_2}$ and $\mathbf{v_3}$. The logical orbit of this clause is:

$$\begin{aligned}
\varphi_4^{L(G)} = &\; [\; \neg decision(\mathbf{v_1}) \vee decision(\mathbf{v_2}) \vee decision(\mathbf{v_3}) \;] \wedge \\
&\; [\; \neg decision(\mathbf{v_2}) \vee decision(\mathbf{v_1}) \vee decision(\mathbf{v_3}) \;] \wedge \\
&\; [\; \neg decision(\mathbf{v_3}) \vee decision(\mathbf{v_2}) \vee decision(\mathbf{v_1}) \;]
\end{aligned} \qquad (9)$$

and can be compactly encoded with an outer universally-quantified variable corresponding to the sort constant in the singleton cell, and an inner existentially-quantified variable corresponding to the other $|\mathbf{value_3}| - 1$ identically-present sort constants. A "distinct" constraint must also be conjoined with the literals involving the existentially-quantified variable to exclude the constant corresponding to the universally-quantified variable from the inner quantification. $\varphi_4^{L(G)}$ can thus be shown to be logically-equivalent to:

$$\Phi_4 = \forall Y \in \mathbf{value_3}, \exists X \in \mathbf{value_3} : \neg decision(Y) \vee [(\text{distinct } Y\ X) \wedge decision(X)] \qquad (10)$$

Combining Quantifier Inference for Different Sorts— The complete quantified predicate Φ representing the logical orbit of clause φ can be obtained by applying the above inference procedure to each sort in φ separately and in any order. This is possible since the sorts are assumed to be independent: the constants of one sort do not permute with the constants of a different sort. This will yield a predicate Φ that has the quantified prenex form $\forall^*\exists^*$ < CNF expression >, where all universals for each sort are collected together and precede all the existential quantifiers.

It is interesting to note that this connection between symmetry and quantification suggests that an orbit can be visualized as a two-dimensional object whose height and width correspond, respectively, to the number of universally- and existentially-quantified variables. A proof of the correctness of this quantifier inference procedure can be found in [37].

5.2   Quantifier Inference Beyond $\forall^*\exists^*$

We observed that for some protocols, particularly those that have dependent sorts such as *ToyConsensus*, the above inference procedure violates the compactness requirement. In other words, restricting inference to a $\forall^*\exists^*$ quantifier prefix causes the number of quantifiers to become unbounded as sort sizes increase. Recalling that the $\forall^*\exists^*$ pattern is inferred from the symmetries of a *single* clause, whose literals are the protocol's state variables, suggests that inference of more complex quantification patterns may necessitate that we examine the structural distribution of sort constants across *sets of clauses*. While this is an interesting possible direction for further exploration of the connection between symmetry and quantification, an alternative approach is to take advantage of the *formula structure* of the protocol's transition relation. For example, the transition relation of *ToyConsensus* is specified in terms of two quantified sub-formulas, *didNoteVote* and *chosenAt*, that can be viewed, in analogy with a sequential hardware circuit, as internal auxiliary non-state variables that act as "combinational" functions of the state variables. By allowing such auxiliary variables to appear explicitly in clauses learned during incremental induction, the quantified predicates representing the logical orbits of these clauses (according to the basic inference procedure in Sect. 5.1) will *implicitly* incorporate the quantifiers used in the auxiliary variable definitions and automatically have a quantifier prefix that generalizes the basic $\forall^*\exists^*$ template.

Revisiting ToyConsensus— When *SymIC3* is run on the finite instance *ToyConsensus*(3,3,3), it terminates with the following two strengthening assertions:

$$A_1 = \forall\, N \in \mathsf{node}_3, V_1, V_2 \in \mathsf{value}_3 : (\text{distinct } V_1\ V_2) \rightarrow \neg vote(N, V_1) \vee \neg vote(N, V_2) \tag{11}$$

$$\begin{aligned} A_2 &= \forall\, V \in \mathsf{value}_3,\ \exists\, Q \in \mathsf{quorum}_3.\ \neg decision(V) \vee chosenAt(Q, V) \\ &= \forall\, V \in \mathsf{value}_3,\ \exists\, Q \in \mathsf{quorum}_3.\ \neg decision(V) \vee [\ \forall\, N \in Q : vote(N, V)\ ] \end{aligned} \tag{12}$$

which, together with $\hat{P}$, serve as an inductive invariant proving that $\hat{P}$ holds for this instance. Both assertions are obtained using the basic quantifier inference procedure in Sect. 5.1 that produces a $\forall^*\exists^*$ quantifier prefix in terms of the clause variables. Note, however, that A_2 is expressed in terms of the auxiliary variable *chosenAt*. Substituting the definition of *chosenAt* yields an assertion with a $\forall\exists\forall$ quantifier prefix exclusively in terms of the protocol's state variables.

6   Finite Convergence Checks

Given a safe finite instance $\hat{\mathcal{P}} \triangleq \mathcal{P}(|\mathsf{s}_1|, \ldots, |\mathsf{s}_n|)$, let $Inv_{|\mathsf{s}_1|,\ldots,|\mathsf{s}_n|}$ denote the inductive invariant derived by *SymIC3* to prove that $\hat{P}$ holds in $\hat{\mathcal{P}}$. What remains is to determine the instance size $|\mathsf{s}_1|, \ldots, |\mathsf{s}_n|$ needed so that $Inv_{|\mathsf{s}_1|,\ldots,|\mathsf{s}_n|}$ is also an inductive invariant for all sizes. If the instance size is too small, $\hat{\mathcal{P}}$ may not include all protocol behaviors and $Inv_{|\mathsf{s}_1|,\ldots,|\mathsf{s}_n|}$ will not be inductive at larger sizes. As shown in the invisible invariant approach [8,9,58,64,69], increasing the instance size becomes necessary to include new protocol behaviors missing in $\hat{\mathcal{P}}$, until protocol behaviors *saturate*. We propose an *automatic* way to update the instance size and reach saturation by starting with an initial *basesize* and iteratively increasing the size until *finite convergence* is achieved.

The initial base size can be chosen to be any non-trivial instance size and can be easily determined by a simple analysis of the protocol description. For example, any non-trivial instance of the *ToyConsensus* protocol should have $|\mathsf{node}| \geq 3$, $|\mathsf{quorum}| \geq 3$, and $|\mathsf{value}| \geq 2$.

Our finite convergence procedure can be seen as an integration of symmetry saturation and a stripped-down form of multi-dimensional mathematical induction, and has similarities with previous works on structural induction [34,47] and proof convergence [24]. To determine if $Inv_{|\mathsf{s}_1|,\ldots,|\mathsf{s}_n|}$ is inductive for any size, the procedure performs the following checks for $1 \leq i \leq \mathsf{n}$:

a) $Init(|\mathsf{s}_1|..|\mathsf{s}_i| + 1..|\mathsf{s}_n|) \rightarrow Inv_{|\mathsf{s}_1|,\ldots,|\mathsf{s}_n|}(|\mathsf{s}_1|..|\mathsf{s}_i| + 1..|\mathsf{s}_n|)$ (13)

b) $Inv_{|\mathsf{s}_1|,\ldots,|\mathsf{s}_n|}(|\mathsf{s}_1|..|\mathsf{s}_i| + 1..|\mathsf{s}_n|) \wedge T(|\mathsf{s}_1|..|\mathsf{s}_i| + 1..|\mathsf{s}_n|) \rightarrow Inv'_{|\mathsf{s}_1|,\ldots,|\mathsf{s}_n|}(|\mathsf{s}_1|..|\mathsf{s}_i| + 1..|\mathsf{s}_n|)$ (14)

where $Inv_{|\mathsf{s}_1|,\ldots,|\mathsf{s}_n|}(|\mathsf{s}_1|..|\mathsf{s}_i| + 1..|\mathsf{s}_n|)$ denotes the application of $Inv_{|\mathsf{s}_1|,\ldots,|\mathsf{s}_n|}$ to an instance in which the size of sort s_i is increased by 1 while the sizes of the other sorts are unchanged.[3]

If all of these checks pass, we can conclude that $Inv_{|\mathsf{s}_1|,\ldots,|\mathsf{s}_n|}$ is not specific to the instance size used to derive it and that we have reached *cutoff*, i.e., that $Inv_{|\mathsf{s}_1|,\ldots,|\mathsf{s}_n|}$ is an inductive invariant for *any* size. Intuitively, this suggests that adding a new protocol component (e.g., client, server, node, proposer, acceptor) does not add any unseen unique behavior, and hence proving safety till the cutoff is sufficient to prove safety for any instance size. While we believe these

---

[3] Sort dependencies, if any, should be considered when increasing a sort size.

checks are sufficient, we still do not have a formal convergence proof. In our implementation, we confirm convergence by performing the unbounded induction checks a) $Init \rightarrow Inv_{|s_1|,...,|s_n|}$, and b) $Inv_{|s_1|,...,|s_n|} \wedge T \rightarrow Inv'_{|s_1|,...,|s_n|}$ noting that they may lie outside the decidable fragment of first-order logic.

On the other hand, failure of these checks, say for sort s_i, implies that $Inv_{|s_1|...|s_n|}$ will fail for larger sizes and cannot be inductive in the unbounded case, and we need to repeat $SymIC3$ on a finite instance with an increased size for sort s_i, i.e., $\hat{P}_{new} \triangleq P(|s_1|, .., |s_i| + 1, .., |s_n|)$, to include new protocol behaviors that are missing in $\hat{P}$.

Recall from (11) and (12), running $SymIC3$ on $ToyConsensus(3,3,3)$ produces $Inv_{3,3,3} = A_1 \wedge A_2 \wedge \hat{P}$. $Inv_{3,3,3}$ passes checks (13) and (14) for instances $ToyConsensus(4,4,3)$ and $ToyConsensus(3,3,4)$, indicating finite convergence.[4] $Inv_{3,3,3}$ passes standard induction checks in the unbounded domain as well, establishing it as a proof certificate that proves the property as safe in $ToyConsensus$.

7   IC3PO: IC3 for Proving Protocol Properties

Given a protocol specification P, IC3PO iteratively invokes $SymIC3$ on finite instances of increasing size, starting with a given initial base size. Upon termination, IC3PO either a) reaches convergence on an inductive invariant $Inv_{|s_1|,...,|s_n|}$ that proves P for the unbounded protocol P, or b) produces a counterexample trace $Cex_{|s_1|,...,|s_n|}$ that serves as a finite witness to its violation in both the finite instance and the unbounded protocol. The detailed pseudo code of IC3PO is available in [37].

We also explored a number of simple enhancements to IC3PO, such as strengthening the inferred quantified predicates whenever safely possible to do during incremental induction by a) dropping the "distinct" antecedent, and b) rearranging the quantifiers if the strengthened predicate is still unreachable from the previous frame. We describe these enhancements in the extended version of the paper [37]. The results presented in this paper were obtained without these enhancements.

Implementation— Our implementation of IC3PO is publicly available at https://github.com/aman-goel/ic3po. The implementation accepts protocol descriptions in the Ivy language [63] and uses the Ivy compiler to extract a quantified, logical formulation P in a customized VMT [21] format. We use a modified version [4] of the pySMT [33] library to implement our prototype, and use the Z3 [23] solver for all SMT queries. We use the SMT-LIB [13] theory of free sorts and function symbols with datatypes and quantifiers (UFDT), which allows formulating SMT queries for both, the finite and the unbounded domains. For a safe protocol, the inductive proof is printed in the Ivy format as an *independently check-able* proof certificate, which can be further validated with the Ivy verifier.

---

[4] Since quorum is a dependent sort on node, it is increased together with the node sort.

8   Evaluation

We evaluated IC3PO on a total of 29 distributed protocols including 4 problems from [53], 13 from [46], and 12 from [2]. This evaluation set includes fairly complex models of consensus algorithms as well as protocols such as two-phase commit, chord ring, hybrid reliable broadcast, etc. Several studies [15,31,42,46,53,63] have indicated the challenges involved in verifying these protocols.

All 29 protocols are safe based on manual verification. Even though finding counterexample traces is equally important, we limit our evaluation to safe protocols where the property holds, since inferring inductive invariants is the main bottleneck of existing techniques for verifying distributed protocols [29,30,63].

We compared IC3PO against the following 3 verifiers that implement state-of-the-art IC3-style techniques for automatic verification of distributed protocols:

- I4 [53] performs finite-domain IC3 (without accounting for symmetry) using the AVR model checker [39], followed by iteratively generalizing and checking the inductive invariant produced by AVR using Ivy.
- UPDR is the implementation of the $PDR^\forall$/UPDR algorithm [44] for verifying distributed protocols, from the *mypyvy* [3] framework.
- fol-ic3 [46] is a recent technique implemented in *mypyvy* that extends IC3 with the ability to infer inductive invariants with quantifier alternations.

All experiments were performed on an Intel (R) Xeon CPU (X5670). For each run, we used a timeout of 1 h and a memory limit of 32 GB. All tools were executed in their respective default configurations. We used Z3 [23] version 4.8.9, Yices 2 [25] version 2.6.2, and CVC4 [12] version 1.7.

8.1   Results

Table 2 summarizes the experimental results. Apart from the number of problems solved, we compared the tools on 3 metrics: run time in seconds, proof size measured by the number of assertions in the inductive invariant for the unbounded protocol, and the total number of SMT queries made. Each tool uses SMT queries differently (e.g., I4 uses QF_UF for finite, UF for unbounded). Comparing the number of SMT queries still helps in understanding the run time behavior.

IC3PO solved all 29 problems, while 10 protocols were solved by all the tools. The 5 rows at the bottom of Table 2 provide a summary of the comparison. Overall, compared to the other tools IC3PO is faster, requires fewer SMT queries, and produces shorter inductive proofs even for problems requiring inductive invariants with quantifier alternations (marked with Æ in Table 2).

We did a more extensive comparison between the two finite-domain incremental induction verifiers IC3PO and I4, performed a statistical analysis using multiple runs with different solver seeds to account for the effect of randomness in

Table 2. Comparison of IC3PO against other state-of-the-art verifiers, Time: run time (seconds), Inv: # assertions in inductive proof, SMT: # SMT queries, Column "info" provides information on the strengthening assertions (i.e., A) in IC3PO's inductive proof: Æ indicates A has quantifier alternations, $\triangleq$ means A has definitions, and $\leftrightarrows$ means A adds quantifier-alternation cycles

	Human	IC3PO			I4			UPDR			fol-ic3		
Protocol (#29)	Inv	info	Time	Inv	SMT	Time	Inv	SMT	Time	Inv	SMT	Time	Inv	SMT
tla-consensus	1		**0**	1	17	4	1	7	0	1	38	1	1	29
tla-tcommit	3		**1**	2	31	unknown		71	1	3	214	2	3	162
i4-lock-server	2		**1**	2	37	2	2	35	1	2	133	1	2	66
ex-quorum-leader-election	3		**3**	5	129	32	14	15429	11	3	1007	24	8	1078
pyv-toy-consensus-forall	4		**3**	4	105	unknown		5949	10	3	590	11	5	587
tla-simple	8		**6**	3	285	4	3	1319	timeout			timeout		
ex-lockserv-automaton	2		**7**	12	594	3	15	1731	21	9	3855	10	12	1181
tla-simpleregular	9		**8**	4	346	unknown		14787	timeout			57	9	314
pyv-sharded-kv	5		10	8	590	4	15	2101	6	7	784	22	10	522
pyv-lockserv	9		11	12	702	3	15	1606	14	9	3108	8	11	1044
tla-twophase	12		14	10	984	unknown		10505	67	14	12031	9	12	1635
i4-learning-switch	8		**14**	9	589	22	11	26345	timeout			timeout		
ex-simple-decentralized-lock	5		19	15	2219	14	22	5561	4	2	677	**4**	8	291
i4-two-phase-commit	11		27	11	2541	**4**	16	4045	16	9	2799	8	9	1083
pyv-consensus-wo-decide	5		**50**	9	1886	1144	42	41137	100	4	8563	168	26	5692
pyv-consensus-forall	7		**99**	10	3445	1006	44	156838	490	6	24947	2461	27	16182
pyv-learning-switch	8		**127**	13	3388	387	49	51021	278	11	3210	timeout		
i4-chord-ring-maintenance	18		**229**	12	6418	timeout			timeout			timeout		
pyv-sharded-kv-no-lost-keys	2	Æ	**3**	2	57	unknown		1232	unknown		73	3	2	51
ex-naive-consensus	4	Æ	**6**	4	239	unknown		15141	unknown		1325	73	18	414
pyv-client-server-ae	2	Æ $\triangleq$	**2**	2	49	unknown		1483	unknown		132	877	15	700
ex-simple-election	3	Æ $\triangleq$	**7**	4	268	unknown		2747	unknown		1147	32	10	222
pyv-toy-consensus-epr	4	Æ $\triangleq$	**9**	4	370	unknown		5944	unknown		473	70	14	217
ex-toy-consensus	3	Æ $\triangleq$	**10**	3	209	unknown		2797	unknown		348	21	8	124
pyv-client-server-db-ae	5	Æ $\triangleq$	**17**	6	868	unknown		81509	unknown		422	timeout		
pyv-hybrid-reliable-broadcast	8	Æ $\triangleq$	**587**	4	1474	unknown		34764	unknown		713	1360	23	3387
pyv-firewall	2	Æ $\leftrightarrows$	**2**	3	131	unknown		344	unknown		130	7	8	116
ex-majorityset-leader-election	5	Æ $\leftrightarrows$	**72**	7	1552	error			unknown		2350	timeout		
pyv-consensus-epr	7	Æ $\triangleq$ $\leftrightarrows$	**1300**	9	29601	unknown		177189	unknown		7559	1468	30	3355
No. of problems solved (out of 29)			**29**			13			14			23		
Uniquely solved			**3**			0			0			0		
For 10 cases solved by all: $\sum$ Time			**232**			2221			667			2711		
$\sum$ Inv			85			186			**52**			114		
$\sum$ SMT			**12160**			228490			45911			27168		

SMT solving, compared the inductive proofs produced by IC3PO against human-written invariants, and performed a preliminary exploration of distributed protocols with totally-ordered domains and ring topologies. Due to space constraints, we describe these experiments in the extended version of the paper [37].

8.2   Discussion

Comparing IC3PO and I4 clearly reveals the benefits of symmetric incremental induction. For example, I4 requires 7814 SMT queries to eliminate 443 CTIs when solving $ToyConsensus(3,3,3)$, compared to 192 SMT calls and 13 CTIs for IC3PO. Even though both techniques perform finite incremental induction, symmetry-aware clause boosting in IC3PO leads to a factorial reduction in the number of SMT queries and yields compact inductive proofs.

Comparing IC3PO and UPDR reveals the benefits of finite-domain reasoning methods compared to direct unbounded verification. Even in cases where existential quantifier inference isn't necessary, symmetry-aware finite-domain reasoning gives IC3PO an edge both in terms of run time and the number of SMT queries.

Comparing IC3PO and fol-ic3, the only two verifiers that can infer invariants with a combination of universal and existential quantifiers, highlights the advantage of IC3PO's approach over the separators-based technique [46] used in fol-ic3. The significant performance edge that IC3PO has over fol-ic3 is due to the fact that a) reasoning in IC3PO is primarily in a (small) finite domain compared to fol-ic3's unbounded reasoning, and b) unlike fol-ic3 which enumeratively searches for specific quantifier patterns, IC3PO finds the required invariants without search by automatically inferring their patterns from the symmetry of the protocol.

Overall, the evaluation confirms the main hypothesis of this paper, that it is possible to use the relationship between symmetry and quantification to scale the verification of distributed protocols beyond the current state-of-the-art.

9   Related Work

Introduced by Lamport, TLA+ is a widely-used language for the specification and verification of distributed protocols [14,59]. The accompanying TLC model checker can perform automatic verification on a finite instance of a TLA+ specification, and can also be configured to employ symmetry to improve scalability. However, TLC is primarily intended as a debugging tool for small finite instances and not as a tool for inferring inductive invariants.

Several manual or semi-automatic verification techniques (e.g., using interactive theorem proving or compositional verification) have been proposed for deriving system-level proofs [20,35,42,43,62,68]. These techniques generally require a deep understanding of the protocol being verified and significant manual effort to guide proof development. The Ivy [63] system improves on these techniques by graphically displaying CTIs and interactively asking the user to provide strengthening assertions that can eliminate them.

Verification of parameterized systems using SMT solvers is further explored in MCMT [66], Cubicle [22], and paraVerifier [52]. Abdulla et al. [6] proposed *view abstraction* to compute the reachable set for finite instances using forward reachability until cutoff is reached. Our technique builds on these works with the capability to automatically infer the required quantified inductive invariant using the latest advancements in model checking, by combining symmetry-aware clause learning and quantifier inference in finite-domain incremental induction. The use of derived/ghost variables has been recognized as important in [48,58,61]. IC3PO utilizes protocol structure, namely auxiliary definitions in the protocol specification, to automatically infer inductive invariants with complex quantifier alternations.

Several recent approaches (e.g., UPDR [45], QUIC3 [41], Phase-UPDR [31], fol-ic3 [46]) extend IC3/PDR to automatically infer quantified inductive invariants. Unlike IC3PO, these techniques rely heavily on unbounded SMT solving.

Our work is closest in spirit to FORHULL-N [24] and I4 [53,54]. Similar to IC3PO, these techniques perform incremental induction over small finite instances of a parameterized system and employ a generalization procedure that transforms finite-domain proofs to quantified inductive invariants that hold for all parameter values. Dooley and Somenzi proposed FORHULL-N to verify parameterized reactive systems by running bit-level IC3 and generalizing the learnt clauses into candidate universally-quantified proofs through a process of proof saturation and convex hull computation. These candidate proofs involve modular linear arithmetic constraints as antecedents in a way such that they approximate the protocol behavior beyond the current finite instance, and their correctness is validated by checking them until the cutoff is reached. I4 uses an ad hoc generalization procedure to obtain universally-quantified proofs from the finite-domain inductive invariants generated by the AVR model checker [39].

10   Conclusions and Future Work

IC3PO is, to our knowledge, the first verification system that uses the synergistic relationship between symmetry and quantification to automatically infer the quantified inductive invariants required to prove the safety of symmetric protocols. Recognizing that symmetry and quantification are alternative ways of capturing invariance, IC3PO extends the incremental induction algorithm to learn clause orbits, and encodes these orbits with corresponding logically-equivalent and compact quantified predicates. IC3PO employs a systematic procedure to check for finite convergence, and outputs quantified inductive invariants, with both universal and existential quantifiers, that hold for all protocol parameters. Our evaluation demonstrates that IC3PO is a significant improvement over the current state-of-the-art.

Future work includes exploring methods to utilize the regularity in totally-ordered domains during reachability analysis, investigating techniques to counter undecidability in practical distributed systems verification, and exploring enhancements to further improve the scalability to complex distributed protocols and their implementations. As a long-term goal, we aim towards automatically inferring inductive invariants for complicated distributed protocols, such as Paxos [50,51], by building further on this initial work.

Data Availability Statement and Acknowledgments
The software and data sets generated and analyzed during the current study, including all experimental data, evaluation scripts, and IC3PO source code are

available at https://github.com/aman-goel/nfm2021exp. We thank the developers of pySMT [33], Z3 [23], and Ivy [63] for making their tools openly available. We thank the authors of the I4 project [53] for their help in shaping some of the ideas presented in this paper.

References

1. Client server protocol in ivy. http://microsoft.github.io/ivy/examples/client_server_example.html
2. A collection of distributed protocol verification problems. https://github.com/aman-goel/ivybench
3. mypyvy (github). https://github.com/wilcoxjay/mypyvy
4. pySMT: A library for SMT formulae manipulation and solving. https://github.com/aman-goel/pysmt
5. Toy consensus protocol. https://github.com/microsoft/ivy/blob/master/examples/ivy/toy_consensus.ivy
6. Abdulla, P., Haziza, F., Holík, L.: Parameterized verification through view abstraction. Int. J. Softw. Tools Technol. Transfer **18**(5), 495–516 (2016)
7. Apt, K.R., Kozen, D.: Limits for automatic verification of finite-state concurrent systems. Inf. Process. Lett. **22**(6), 307–309 (1986)
8. Arons, T., Pnueli, A., Ruah, S., Xu, Y., Zuck, L.: Parameterized verification with automatically computed inductive assertions? In: Berry, G., Comon, H., Finkel, A. (eds.) CAV 2001. LNCS, vol. 2102, pp. 221–234. Springer, Heidelberg (2001). https://doi.org/10.1007/3-540-44585-4_19
9. Balaban, I., Fang, Y., Pnueli, A., Zuck, L.D.: IIV: an invisible invariant verifier. In: Etessami, K., Rajamani, S.K. (eds.) CAV 2005. LNCS, vol. 3576, pp. 408–412. Springer, Heidelberg (2005). https://doi.org/10.1007/11513988_39
10. Balyo, T., Froleyks, N., Heule, M.J., Iser, M., Järvisalo, M., Suda, M.: Proceedings of SAT Competition 2020: Solver and Benchmark Descriptions (2020)
11. Barner, S., Grumberg, O.: Combining symmetry reduction and underapproximation for symbolic model checking. In: Brinksma, E., Larsen, K.G. (eds.) CAV 2002. LNCS, vol. 2404, pp. 93–106. Springer, Heidelberg (2002). https://doi.org/10.1007/3-540-45657-0_8
12. Barrett, C., et al.: CVC4. In: Gopalakrishnan, G., Qadeer, S. (eds.) CAV 2011. LNCS, vol. 6806, pp. 171–177. Springer, Heidelberg (2011). https://doi.org/10.1007/978-3-642-22110-1_14
13. Barrett, C., Fontaine, P., Tinelli, C.: The Satisfiability Modulo Theories Library (SMT-LIB). www.SMT-LIB.org (2016)
14. Beers, R.: Pre-RTL formal verification: an intel experience. In: Proceedings of the 45th Annual Design Automation Conference, pp. 806–811 (2008)
15. Berkovits, I., Lazic, M., Losa, G., Padon, O., Shoham, S.: Verification of threshold-based distributed algorithms by decomposition to decidable logics. CoRR abs/1905.07805 (2019). http://arxiv.org/abs/1905.07805
16. Bloem, R.: Decidability of parameterized verification. Synth. Lect. Distrib. Comput. Theory **6**(1), 1–170 (2015). https://doi.org/10.2200/S00658ED1V01Y201508DCT013
17. Bradley, A.R.: SAT-based model checking without unrolling. In: Jhala, R., Schmidt, D. (eds.) VMCAI 2011. LNCS, vol. 6538, pp. 70–87. Springer, Heidelberg (2011). https://doi.org/10.1007/978-3-642-18275-4_7

18. Burch, J.R., Clarke, E.M., McMillan, K.L., Dill, D.L., Hwang, L.J.: Symbolic model checking: 10^{20} states and beyond. In: Proceedings Fifth Annual IEEE Symposium on Logic in Computer Science, pp. 428–439 (1990)
19. Burch, J.R., Clarke, E.M., McMillan, K.L., Dill, D.L., Hwang, L.J.: Symbolic model checking: 10^{20} states and beyond. Inf. Comput. **98**(2), 142–170 (1992)
20. Chaudhuri, K., Doligez, D., Lamport, L., Merz, S.: Verifying safety properties with the TLA$^+$ proof system. In: Giesl, J., Hähnle, R. (eds.) IJCAR 2010. LNCS (LNAI), vol. 6173, pp. 142–148. Springer, Heidelberg (2010). https://doi.org/10.1007/978-3-642-14203-1_12
21. Cimatti, A., Roveri, M., Griggio, A., Irfan, A.: Verification Modulo Theories (2011). http://www.vmt-lib.org
22. Conchon, S., Goel, A., Krstić, S., Mebsout, A., Zaïdi, F.: Cubicle: a parallel SMT-based model checker for parameterized systems. In: Madhusudan, P., Seshia, S.A. (eds.) CAV 2012. LNCS, vol. 7358, pp. 718–724. Springer, Heidelberg (2012). https://doi.org/10.1007/978-3-642-31424-7_55
23. de Moura, L., Bjørner, N.: Z3: an efficient SMT solver. In: Ramakrishnan, C.R., Rehof, J. (eds.) TACAS 2008. LNCS, vol. 4963, pp. 337–340. Springer, Heidelberg (2008). https://doi.org/10.1007/978-3-540-78800-3_24
24. Dooley, M., Somenzi, F.: Proving parameterized systems safe by generalizing clausal proofs of small instances. In: Chaudhuri, S., Farzan, A. (eds.) CAV 2016. LNCS, vol. 9779, pp. 292–309. Springer, Cham (2016). https://doi.org/10.1007/978-3-319-41528-4_16
25. Dutertre, B.: Yices 2.2. In: Biere, A., Bloem, R. (eds.) CAV 2014. LNCS, vol. 8559, pp. 737–744. Springer, Cham (2014). https://doi.org/10.1007/978-3-319-08867-9_49
26. Een, N., Mishchenko, A., Brayton, R.: Efficient implementation of property directed reachability. In: Formal Methods in Computer Aided Design (FMCAD 2011), pp. 125–134, October 2011
27. Eén, N., Sörensson, N.: An extensible SAT-solver. In: Giunchiglia, E., Tacchella, A. (eds.) SAT 2003. LNCS, vol. 2919, pp. 502–518. Springer, Heidelberg (2004). https://doi.org/10.1007/978-3-540-24605-3_37
28. Emerson, E.A., Sistla, A.P.: Symmetry and model checking. Formal Methods Syst. Des. **9**(1–2), 105–131 (1996)
29. Feldman, Y.M.Y., Sagiv, M., Shoham, S., Wilcox, J.R.: Learning the boundary of inductive invariants. CoRR abs/2008.09909 (2020). https://arxiv.org/abs/2008.09909
30. Feldman, Y.M., Immerman, N., Sagiv, M., Shoham, S.: Complexity and information in invariant inference. In: Proceedings of the ACM on Programming Languages, vol. 4, no. POPL, pp. 1–29 (2019)
31. Feldman, Y.M.Y., Wilcox, J.R., Shoham, S., Sagiv, M.: Inferring inductive invariants from phase structures. In: Dillig, I., Tasiran, S. (eds.) CAV 2019. LNCS, vol. 11562, pp. 405–425. Springer, Cham (2019). https://doi.org/10.1007/978-3-030-25543-5_23
32. Fraleigh, J.B.: A First Course in Abstract Algebra, 6th edn. Addison Wesley Longman, Reading (2000)
33. Gario, M., Micheli, A.: PySMT: a solver-agnostic library for fast prototyping of SMT-based algorithms. In: SMT Workshop, vol. 2015 (2015)
34. German, S.M., Sistla, A.P.: Reasoning about systems with many processes. J. ACM (JACM) **39**(3), 675–735 (1992)

35. Gleissenthall, K.v., Kıcı, R.G., Bakst, A., Stefan, D., Jhala, R.: Pretend synchrony: synchronous verification of asynchronous distributed programs. In: Proceedings of the ACM on Programming Languages, vol. 3, no. POPL, pp. 1–30 (2019)
36. Godefroid, P.: Exploiting symmetry when model-checking software. In: Wu, J., Chanson, S.T., Gao, Q. (eds.) Formal Methods for Protocol Engineering and Distributed Systems. IAICT, vol. 28, pp. 257–275. Springer, Boston, MA (1999). https://doi.org/10.1007/978-0-387-35578-8_15
37. Goel, A., Sakallah, K.A.: On Symmetry and Quantification: A New Approach to Verify Distributed Protocols. CoRR. abs/2103.14831 (2021). https://arxiv.org/abs/2103.14831
38. Goel, A., Sakallah, K.: Model checking of Verilog RTL using IC3 with syntax-guided abstraction. In: Badger, J.M., Rozier, K.Y. (eds.) NFM 2019. LNCS, vol. 11460, pp. 166–185. Springer, Cham (2019). https://doi.org/10.1007/978-3-030-20652-9_11
39. Goel, A., Sakallah, K.: AVR: abstractly verifying reachability. TACAS 2020. LNCS, vol. 12078, pp. 413–422. Springer, Cham (2020). https://doi.org/10.1007/978-3-030-45190-5_23
40. Goel, A., Sakallah, K.A.: Empirical evaluation of IC3-based model checking techniques on Verilog RTL designs. In: Proceedings of the Design, Automation and Test in Europe Conference (DATE), Florence, Italy, March 2019, pp. 618–621 (2019)
41. Gurfinkel, A., Shoham, S., Vizel, Y.: Quantifiers on demand. In: Lahiri, S.K., Wang, C. (eds.) ATVA 2018. LNCS, vol. 11138, pp. 248–266. Springer, Cham (2018). https://doi.org/10.1007/978-3-030-01090-4_15
42. Hawblitzel, C., et al.: IronFleet: proving practical distributed systems correct. In: Proceedings of the 25th Symposium on Operating Systems Principles, pp. 1–17. ACM (2015)
43. Hoenicke, J., Majumdar, R., Podelski, A.: Thread modularity at many levels: a pearl in compositional verification. ACM SIGPLAN Not. 52(1), 473–485 (2017)
44. Karbyshev, A., Bjørner, N., Itzhaky, S., Rinetzky, N., Shoham, S.: Property-directed inference of universal invariants or proving their absence. J. ACM 64(1) (2017). https://doi.org/10.1145/3022187
45. Karbyshev, A., Bjørner, N., Itzhaky, S., Rinetzky, N., Shoham, S.: Property-directed inference of universal invariants or proving their absence. J. ACM (JACM) 64(1), 1–33 (2017)
46. Koenig, J.R., Padon, O., Immerman, N., Aiken, A.: First-order quantified separators. In: Proceedings of the 41st ACM SIGPLAN Conference on Programming Language Design and Implementation, PLDI 2020, pp. 703–717. Association for Computing Machinery, New York (2020). https://doi.org/10.1145/3385412.3386018
47. Kurshan, R.P., McMillan, K.: A structural induction theorem for processes. In: Proceedings of the Eighth Annual ACM Symposium on Principles of Distributed Computing, pp. 239–247 (1989)
48. Lamport, L.: Proving the correctness of multiprocess programs. IEEE Trans. Softw. Eng. 2, 125–143 (1977)
49. Lamport, L.: Specifying Systems: The TLA+ Language and Tools for Hardware and Software Engineers. Addison-Wesley Longman Publishing Co., Inc., Boston (2002)
50. Lamport, L.: The part-time parliament. In: Concurrency: The Works of Leslie Lamport, pp. 277–317 (2019)
51. Lamport, L., et al.: Paxos made simple. ACM Sigact News 32(4), 18–25 (2001)

52. Li, Y., Pang, J., Lv, Y., Fan, D., Cao, S., Duan, K.: ParaVerifier: an automatic framework for proving parameterized cache coherence protocols. In: Finkbeiner, B., Pu, G., Zhang, L. (eds.) ATVA 2015. LNCS, vol. 9364, pp. 207–213. Springer, Cham (2015). https://doi.org/10.1007/978-3-319-24953-7_15
53. Ma, H., Goel, A., Jeannin, J.B., Kapritsos, M., Kasikci, B., Sakallah, K.A.: I4: incremental inference of inductive invariants for verification of distributed protocols. In: Proceedings of the 27th Symposium on Operating Systems Principles. ACM (2019)
54. Ma, H., Goel, A., Jeannin, J.B., Kapritsos, M., Kasikci, B., Sakallah, K.A.: Towards automatic inference of inductive invariants. In: Proceedings of the Workshop on Hot Topics in Operating Systems, pp. 30–36. ACM (2019)
55. Marques-Silva, J.P., Sakallah, K.A.: GRASP: a search algorithm for propositional satisfiability. IEEE Trans. Comput. **48**(5), 506–521 (1999)
56. McMillan, K.L.: Symbolic Model Checking. Kluwer Academic Publishers, Norwell (1993)
57. Moskewicz, M.W., Madigan, C.F., Zhao, Y., Zhang, L., Malik, S.: Chaff: engineering an efficient SAT solver. In: DAC, pp. 530–535 (2001)
58. Namjoshi, K.S.: Symmetry and completeness in the analysis of parameterized systems. In: Cook, B., Podelski, A. (eds.) VMCAI 2007. LNCS, vol. 4349, pp. 299–313. Springer, Heidelberg (2007). https://doi.org/10.1007/978-3-540-69738-1_22
59. Newcombe, C., Rath, T., Zhang, F., Munteanu, B., Brooker, M., Deardeuff, M.: How amazon web services uses formal methods. Commun. ACM **58**(4), 66–73 (2015)
60. Ip, C.N., Dill, D.L.: Better verification through symmetry. Formal Methods Syst. Des. **9**(1), 41–75 (1996). https://doi.org/10.1007/BF00625968
61. Owicki, S., Gries, D.: Verifying properties of parallel programs: an axiomatic approach. Commun. ACM **19**(5), 279–285 (1976)
62. Owre, S., Rushby, J.M., Shankar, N.: PVS: a prototype verification system. In: Kapur, D. (ed.) CADE 1992. LNCS, vol. 607, pp. 748–752. Springer, Heidelberg (1992). https://doi.org/10.1007/3-540-55602-8_217
63. Padon, O., McMillan, K.L., Panda, A., Sagiv, M., Shoham, S.: Ivy: safety verification by interactive generalization. In: Proceedings of the 37th ACM SIGPLAN Conference on Programming Language Design and Implementation, PLDI 2016, pp. 614–630. ACM, New York (2016). https://doi.org/10.1145/2908080.2908118
64. Pnueli, A., Ruah, S., Zuck, L.: Automatic deductive verification with invisible invariants. In: Margaria, T., Yi, W. (eds.) TACAS 2001. LNCS, vol. 2031, pp. 82–97. Springer, Heidelberg (2001). https://doi.org/10.1007/3-540-45319-9_7
65. Pong, F., Dubois, M.: A new approach for the verification of cache coherence protocols. IEEE Trans. Parallel Distrib. Syst. **6**(8), 773–787 (1995)
66. Ranise, S., Ghilardi, S.: Backward reachability of array-based systems by SMT solving: termination and invariant synthesis. Logical Methods Comput. Sci. **6**(4) (2010). https://doi.org/10.2168/LMCS-6(4:10)2010
67. Sistla, A.P., Gyuris, V., Emerson, E.A.: SMC: a symmetry-based model checker for verification of safety and liveness properties. ACM Trans. Softw. Eng. Methodol. (TOSEM) **9**(2), 133–166 (2000)
68. Wilcox, J.R., et al.: Verdi: a framework for implementing and formally verifying distributed systems. In: Proceedings of the 36th ACM SIGPLAN Conference on Programming Language Design and Implementation, PLDI 2015, pp. 357–368. ACM, New York (2015). https://doi.org/10.1145/2737924.2737958
69. Zuck, L., Pnueli, A.: Model checking and abstraction to the aid of parameterized systems (a survey). Comput. Lang. Syst. Struct. **30**(3–4), 139–169 (2004)

Integrating Runtime Verification into a Sounding Rocket Control System

Benjamin Hertz⬥, Zachary Luppen(✉)⬥, and Kristin Yvonne Rozier⬥

Iowa State University, Ames, IA 50010, USA
zaluppen@iastate.edu

Abstract. An actuation fault in the aerobraking control system (ACS)
took down Iowa State's *Nova Somnium* rocket during the 2019 Spaceport
America Cup competition, prematurely ending the team's participation.
The ACS engaged incorrectly before motor burnout, altering the rocket's
trajectory and leading to a dangerous crash. The ability to detect this
fault in real time on-board the ACS's Arduino microcontroller would
have prevented an uncontrolled landing and rapid unscheduled disassembly, which posed a major safety threat and ended a year's worth of effort
by the 50-student team. Runtime verification (RV) specializes in efficiently catching this type of scenario; the R2U2 RV engine uniquely fits in
the project's resource constraints. We design specifications to detect ACS
faults and trigger the appropriate mitigations. We discuss specification
development, validation, coverage, and robustness against false positives.
Experimental evaluation on the real, recorded flight data demonstrates
that running R2U2 on the *Nova Somnium* ACS would have prevented
this accident from occurring. We generalize our results and outline our
plans for integrating runtime verification into future sounding rockets.

Keywords: Runtime verification · Temporal logic · System health
monitoring · Formal specification · R2U2 · Control systems · Rocket

1 Introduction

Every year, collegiate engineering teams from around the world compete in the
Spaceport America Cup in New Mexico, where each team launches an experimental sounding rocket designed and constructed by students [2]. The competition
requires teams to accurately predict their rocket's apogee altitude, which many
teams attempt by developing an onboard aerobraking control system (ACS). An
ACS must have the capacity to estimate apogee altitude during flight and alter
drag to allow a rocket to reach, but not exceed, a predefined target altitude.

Work partially supported by NSF CAREER Award CNS-1552934, NASA ECF
NNX16AR57G, and NSF PFI:BIC grant CNS-1257011. Thanks to the ISU Cyclone
Rocketry team for allowing open access to the *Nova Somnium* rocket data. Thanks to
Brian Kempa and Meaghan McCleary for help with integration testing for this project.
Reproducibility artifacts are available at http://temporallogic.org/research/NFM21/.

© Springer Nature Switzerland AG 2021
A. Dutle et al. (Eds.): NFM 2021, LNCS 12673, pp. 151–159, 2021.
https://doi.org/10.1007/978-3-030-76384-8_10

This goal poses a significant challenge to all teams, and nearly 85% of teams failed to predict their apogee altitude within 10% of their actual apogee altitude in 2019 [2]. Iowa State University's Cyclone Rocketry team developed an ACS that flew onboard their 2019 competition rocket *Nova Somnium*. During flight, *Nova Somnium*'s ACS power supply reset during liftoff and it subsequently activated earlier than intended, causing structural failure of the ACS mechanical system. This fault led to an abrupt change in trajectory and an improper parachute deployment, resulting in a dangerous crash landing.

Competition rockets follow a yearly build cycle, emphasizing learning and rapid, inexpensive development. As a result of competition parameters, time, and resource limitations, an ACS must occupy a small physical space with tight memory constraints. Sounding rockets often exceed the speed of sound, so onboard systems must make decisions efficiently in real time. The experimental nature of student projects also creates significant uncertainty, so an ACS needs to operate safely without complete knowledge of the system dynamics or operating environment. We turn to runtime verification (RV) to provide a layer of resilience to the ACS.

RV provides checks to ensure that cyber-physical systems are operating nominally in real time. RV is a popular technique for sanity checking the behaviors of other autonomous systems, like Unmanned Aircraft Systems (UAS), as they safely integrate into the national air space [3]. Sounding rocket verification, however, has not yet been investigated in literature. We present the first verification effort on sounding rockets. We must detect and mitigate unexpected faults produced by the dynamic environment in real time, on-board the resource-limited flight computer, without affecting the timing, power, weight, or other tolerances of the rocket.

Three RV engines currently exist that can fly on real systems: Copilot, LOLA and the Realizable, Responsive, Unobtrusive Unit (R2U2). Copilot is a stream-based, real-time operating system that implements embedded monitors [5,7,10,11]. This utility is incompatible with the ACS software. LOLA is a stream-based specification language that previously provided the necessary level of formalization and expressibility for this project [18], but the computational limits of *Nova Somnium*'s ACS are ill-matched for this tool and LOLA's current restriction to past-time specification presents a significant barrier to use. R2U2 was developed to monitor expressive properties of systems in real-time, with little overhead and significant resource constraints [1,6,9,17,19,20]. For this reason, R2U2 is a viable option for integrating RV onto sounding rocket systems.

We contribute (1) formal rocket specifications, (2) successful RV using R2U2 on the real ACS dataset, and (3) specification analysis for future studies. The remainder of this paper is organized as follows. Section 2 outlines the ACS on the *Nova Somnium* rocket. Section 3 illustrates our approach to integrating RV onto the ACS. Section 4 details our specification development and debugging, and outlines strategies that generalize to other projects. We demonstrate how these specifications detect multiple faults while staying robust to false positives using the real rocket dataset in Sect. 5. In Sect. 6, we conclude by exploring plans for future work.

Table 1. Output signals used during ACS operation, along with each signal's source, a description, and its units.

Signal	Source	Description	Units
Acc{X,Y,Z}	IMU	Acceleration vector of the rocket	m/s^2
AccV	IMU	Vertical acceleration of the rocket	m/s^2
Alt	BAR	Altitude above Mean Sea Level (MSL)	m
Pres	BAR	Atmospheric pressure	Pa
Temp	BAR	Ambient air temperature	$°C$
Act	CPU	Actuation status of the ACS	Boolean
Time	CPU	Computer clock-time since startup	ms
State	CPU	Current mission state of the rocket	Integer
VelV	CPU	Vertical velocity of the rocket derived from BAR	m/s

Fig. 1. Left: Rocket mission states: *Launch Pad* (0), *Boost* (1), *Coast* (2), *Descent* (3). Right Top: Model of *Nova Somnium*'s ACS, Right Bottom: the physical ACS.

2   System Description

Nova Somnium's ACS includes an Arduino-based central processing unit (CPU) and two sensors: an Inertial Measurement Unit (IMU) and a barometer (BAR). These sensors recognize four possible states of the rocket's mission: *Launch Pad* (0), *Boost* (1), *Coast* (2), and *Descent* (3). Figure 1 shows the mission states and *Nova Somnium*'s ACS. The ACS only allows brake actuation while in the *Coast* state, during which the ACS continually estimates the apogee altitude from the rocket's current altitude, vertical velocity, dynamic pressure, and geometry. The ACS compares this estimate to the target altitude, actuating the brakes whenever the estimate exceeds the target. The signals used by the ACS during runtime appear in Table 1.

3   Approach

R2U2 integrates easily with the Arduino C++ framework of the ACS and passes its verdicts to the ACS, allowing us to disable the ACS if specifications are violated [17]. Since the ACS is a reactive system with a well-defined operational timeline, we need a specification logic like Linear Temporal Logic (LTL) but with finite bounds corresponding to the mission phases. In analyzing *Nova Somnium*'s flight data, we identified deviations in the time steps between measurements. The rocket data indicated that time steps as small as ~22 ms and as large as ~86 ms occurred, despite a predefined time step of 50 ms. To account for this variable time step issue, we need to encode our requirements generically with integer-bounded time steps that can easily map to the real data. Mission-time Linear Temporal Logic (MLTL) was designed for this purpose [8,13]; it adds finite, integer-bounded intervals to each of the temporal operators in LTL. MLTL has been used in many industrial projects [1,4,6,9,13,14,19–21], and since 2018 has been an official logic of the RV Benchmark Competition [12,16].

4   Runtime Specification Development

We construct our requirements in English starting from an a priori known mission parameters. This includes constants known before launch, such as motor burn time; ideal time-varying parameters obtained from flight simulations, such as expected acceleration; and the average ACS refresh rate. We then consider the temporal nature of a nominal rocket launch. For example, the rocket should experience each mission state in order and stay in each state for a predictable time duration. From each of the English requirements, we derive a specification written in MLTL.

As we develop specifications, we track signal coverage to help capture as many sensor constraints as possible. To achieve coverage, we follow a similar methodology to [1,15], writing at least one specification involving each signal used by the ACS. We also organize our specifications into three of the categories defined in [15] and used in [1]: operating ranges (OR), rates of change (RC), and control sequences (CS). Adding specifications for the additional categories could further delineate errors to support more expansive mitigation protocols in future work.

We practice specification validation throughout the development phase, as specification creation is an iterative process [15]. We first validate the correctness of the Boolean atomics by generating atomic traces corresponding to ACS runs, checking manually that each atomic accurately represents the ACS data. We then stream the atomic traces into R2U2 and plot the specification verdict at each time step to analytically determine if the specification has correctly captured the requirement. As we test specifications, we can trace errors back to the MLTL formulation, Boolean definition, or English requirement.

Following specification validation and debugging, we must craft specifications that are robust to insignificant faults, like sensor data noise, to prevent false-positive alerts from the RV engine. We could handle this in part by tweaking

Boolean atomic definitions. However, MLTL offers powerful temporal filtering that makes such small-fault tolerance easy to alter, as demonstrated in [1]. We use this to adjust the acceptable time frame we expect something to happen within.

For example, consider CS7 (shown in Table 3): "When the rocket enters the *Boost* state, the rocket shall remain in the *Boost* state until at least 5.7 s have passed (90% of theoretical motor burntime, about 114 timesteps), but no longer than 6.5 s (about 130 timesteps)." Adjusting the bounds of the $\mathcal{U}$ operator for specification CS7 specifies the time frame in which we expect the rocket to transition from the *Boost* state to the *Coast* state, while the minimum time required before a state transition occurs is captured in the Boolean definition of *90%OfBurnTime*: timeInState1 > 113 timesteps. Flight simulation predicts boost state duration, but many environmental factors can affect the final outcome, making the fine-tunable fault tolerance provided by MLTL essential to monitoring an ACS or any real system. Table 2 summarizes our specification development results.

5   Results

We designed 19 MLTL runtime specifications for *Nova Somnium*'s ACS, shown in Table 3. The total memory for R2U2 monitoring all 19 specifications in parallel was ~400 kB of memory, which would fit on-board the ACS; we could further reduce memory by employing optimizations from [6] or down-selecting specifications to monitor. To better understand how the specifications are encoded into observation trees for R2U2, see [17, 19, 20]. To demonstrate the efficacy of our approach, we examine two specifications and the resulting R2U2 RV output from the ACS data obtained during the *Nova Somnium* launch. Figure 2 shows that the state transition from *Boost* to *Coast* occurs far too quickly, entering the *Coast* state after just 350 ms. The incorrectness of the vertical velocity measurements due to the power supply reset appears in Fig. 3. Figures 2 and 3 both demonstrate that these specifications successfully identified an error before the

Table 2. Specification development summary. Development time estimates account for the time spent debugging and validating specifications. The count of failed specifications refers to the number of specifications that flagged an error when run with R2U2 for the *Nova Somnium* ACS launch data set.

MLTL specification category	Count	Estimated development time	Count of failed specifications
All specifications	19	50 person-hours	6
OR specifications	6	14 person-hours	4
RC specifications	6	15 person-hours	0
CS specifications	7	21 person-hours	2

Table 3. MLTL runtime specifications. A detailed explanation of each specification, including the atomic definitions and temporal operator time bounds, can be found at http://temporallogic.org/research/NFM21/. An "X" in the "Err" column denotes the specification failed at least once, identifying an error. When choosing temporal operator syntax, we use the operators most similar to the English requirements; for example, though $\neg\Box_{[a,b]}\neg p \equiv \Diamond_{[a,b]}p$, we interchange these forms to improve readability.

ID	Err	MLTL specification
OR1	✓	$(altBelowMax \wedge (act \rightarrow altAboveMin))$
OR2	✗	$(actTrue \rightarrow (timeBelowMax \wedge timeAboveMin))$
OR3	✗	$(velVBelowMax)$
OR4	✗	$((inLaunchPadState \vee inBoostState \vee inCoastState) \rightarrow velVAbove0)$
OR5	✓	$(inBoostState \rightarrow accVBelowBoostMax)$
OR6	✗	$(inCoastState \rightarrow accVBelowCoastMax)$
RC1	✓	$\neg\Box_{[0,2]}\neg(absValOfTempMinusPreviousTempBelowThreshold)$
RC2	✓	$\neg\Box_{[0,2]}\neg(absValOfPresMinusPreviousPresBelowThreshold)$
RC3	✓	$(absValOfPresMinusPrevPresBelowMax)$
RC4	✓	$\neg\Box_{[0,2]}\neg(timeMinusPreviousTimeBelowThreshold)$
RC5	✓	$\neg\Box_{[0,2]}\neg(accVEqualsPreviousAccV)$
RC6	✓	$\neg\Box_{[0,2]}\neg(velVEqualsPreviousVelV)$
CS1	✓	$(inBoostState \rightarrow \Diamond_{[0,140]}inCoastState)$
CS2	✓	$(inCoastState \rightarrow \Diamond_{[0,800]}inDescentState)$
CS3	✗	$((accAngleAboveThreshold \wedge inBoostState) \rightarrow \Diamond_{[0,10]}inCoastState)$
CS4	✓	$(inBoostState \rightarrow (inBoostState\,\mathcal{U}_{[0,130]}AccVBelow0))$
CS5	✓	$(actTrue \rightarrow \Diamond_{[0,5]}accMagnitudeAboveThreshold)$
CS6	✓	$((inBoostState \wedge velVAboveThreshold) \rightarrow \Diamond_{[0,126]}accVAbove0)$
CS7	✗	$(inBoostState \rightarrow (inBoostState\,\mathcal{U}_{[0,114]}90\%OfBurnTime))$

first actuation command. Had RV been embedded into the ACS with the authority to prevent actuation, *Nova Somnium* would have stayed on course and simply overshot its target apogee altitude rather than veering abruptly and creating a serious safety hazard.

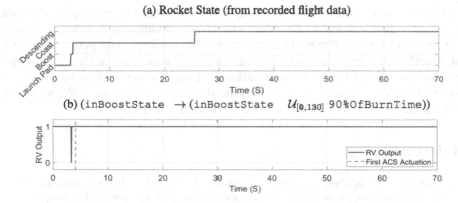

Fig. 2. R2U2 monitoring for specification CS7. (a) The state of the rocket versus time throughout the flight. (b) RV output from the R2U2 tool, correctly identifying a fault when the ACS enters the *Coast* state before 90% of motor burnout, which for *Nova Somnium* takes approximately 5.7 s after ignition, or about 114 time steps. The $\mathcal{U}$ upper bound is set to 130 time steps (∼6.5 s) to allow for minor deviations in motor performance. A dashed red line indicates when the ACS was actuated. (Color figure online)

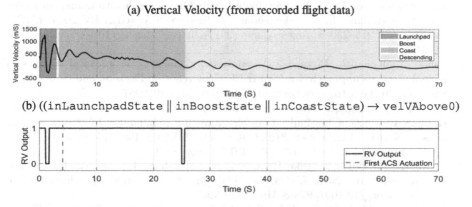

Fig. 3. R2U2 monitoring for specification OR4. (a) The rocket's vertical velocity versus time throughout the flight. (b) RV output from the R2U2 tool, correctly identifying multiple faults indicating vertical velocity measurements are negative before the *descent* state. A dashed red line indicates when the ACS was actuated. (Color figure online)

6   Conclusion

Our MLTL specifications with R2U2's RV engine successfully identified the faults that *Nova Somnium*'s ACS experienced during the 2019 Spaceport America Cup competition. Detection of these faults in real time through embedded RV would have triggered a predetermined mitigation action, such as disabling the ACS prior to the dangerous premature actuation. The ability to monitor a rocket's on-board systems autonomously during flight to prevent failures applies to other sounding rockets, owing to the wide variety of autonomous systems on-board. In future work, the R2U2 tool can be embedded into a new competition rocket's ACS with our specifications to provide real-time reasoning of the system and monitor for critical faults. We will author additional specifications to more precisely identify errors and allow for advanced mitigation protocols. We also look to map R2U2 outputs to a wider range of mitigation strategies.

References

1. Cauwels, M., Hammer, A., Hertz, B., Jones, P.H., Rozier, K.Y.: Integrating runtime verification into an automated UAS traffic management system. In: Muccini, H., et al. (eds.) ECSA 2020. CCIS, vol. 1269, pp. 340–357. Springer, Cham (2020). https://doi.org/10.1007/978-3-030-59155-7_26
2. ESRA Board of Directors: 2019 spaceport America cup (2019). http://www.soundingrocket.org/2019-sa-cup.html
3. Federal Aviation Administration (FAA): FAA Aerospace Forecast - Fiscal Years 2019–2039 (2019). https://www.faa.gov/data_research/aviation/aerospace_forecasts/media/FY2019-39_FAA_Aerospace_Forecast.pdf
4. Geist, J., Rozier, K.Y., Schumann, J.: Runtime observer pairs and Bayesian network reasoners on-board FPGAs: flight-certifiable system health management for embedded systems. In: Bonakdarpour, B., Smolka, S.A. (eds.) RV 2014. LNCS, vol. 8734, pp. 215–230. Springer, Cham (2014). https://doi.org/10.1007/978-3-319-11164-3_18
5. Jones, A., Kong, Z., Belta, C.: Anomaly detection in cyber-physical systems: a formal methods approach. In: 53rd IEEE Conference on Decision and Control, pp. 848–853 (2014). https://doi.org/10.1109/CDC.2014.7039487
6. Kempa, B., Zhang, P., Jones, P.H., Zambreno, J., Rozier, K.Y.: Embedding online runtime verification for fault disambiguation on Robonaut2. In: Bertrand, N., Jansen, N. (eds.) FORMATS 2020. LNCS, vol. 12288, pp. 196–214. Springer, Cham (2020). https://doi.org/10.1007/978-3-030-57628-8_12
7. Laurent, J., Goodloe, A., Pike, L.: Assuring the guardians. In: Bartocci, E., Majumdar, R. (eds.) RV 2015. LNCS, vol. 9333, pp. 87–101. Springer, Cham (2015). https://doi.org/10.1007/978-3-319-23820-3_6
8. Li, J., Vardi, M.Y., Rozier, K.Y.: Satisfiability checking for mission-time LTL. In: Dillig, I., Tasiran, S. (eds.) CAV 2019. LNCS, vol. 11562, pp. 3–22. Springer, Cham (2019). https://doi.org/10.1007/978-3-030-25543-5_1
9. Moosbrugger, P., Rozier, K.Y., Schumann, J.: R2U2: monitoring and diagnosis of security threats for unmanned aerial systems. Formal Methods Syst. Des. 1–31 (2017). https://doi.org/10.1007/s10703-017-0275-x
10. Perez, I., Dedden, F., Goodloe, A.: Copilot 3. NASA Langley Research Center (2020). https://ntrs.nasa.gov/citations/20200003164
11. Pike, L., Wegmann, N., Niller, S., Goodloe, A.: Experience report: a do-it-yourself high-assurance compiler. In: Proceedings of the ACM SIGPLAN International Conference on Functional Programming, ICFP 47, September 2012. https://doi.org/10.1145/2364527.2364553
12. Reger, G., Rozier, K.Y., Stolz, V.: Runtime verification benchmark challenge (RVBC) (2018)

13. Reinbacher, T., Rozier, K.Y., Schumann, J.: Temporal-logic based runtime observer pairs for system health management of real-time systems. In: Ábrahám, E., Havelund, K. (eds.) TACAS 2014. LNCS, vol. 8413, pp. 357–372. Springer, Heidelberg (2014). https://doi.org/10.1007/978-3-642-54862-8_24

14. Rozier, K.Y., Schumann, J., Ippolito, C.: Intelligent hardware-enabled sensor and software safety and health management for autonomous UAS. Technical Memorandum NASA/TM-2015-218817, NASA, NASA Ames Research Center, Moffett Field, CA 94035, USA, May 2015

15. Rozier, K.Y.: Specification: the biggest bottleneck in formal methods and autonomy. In: Blazy, S., Chechik, M. (eds.) VSTTE 2016. LNCS, vol. 9971, pp. 8–26. Springer, Cham (2016). https://doi.org/10.1007/978-3-319-48869-1_2

16. Rozier, K.Y.: On the evaluation and comparison of runtime verification tools for hardware and cyber-physical systems. In: Proceedings of International Workshop on Competitions, Usability, Benchmarks, Evaluation, and Standardisation for Runtime Verification Tools (RV-CUBES), vol. 3, pp. 123–137. Kalpa Publications, Seattle, September 2017. TBD, https://easychair.org/publications/paper/877G

17. Rozier, K.Y., Schumann, J.: R2U2: tool overview. In: Proceedings of International Workshop on Competitions, Usability, Benchmarks, Evaluation, and Standardisation for Runtime Verification Tools (RV-CUBES), vol. 3, pp. 138–156. Kalpa Publications, Seattle, September 2017. TBD, https://easychair.org/publications/paper/Vncw

18. Schirmer, S.: Runtime monitoring with LOLA. Master's thesis, Saarland University, November 2016. https://elib.dlr.de/113126/

19. Schumann, J., Moosbrugger, P., Rozier, K.Y.: R2U2: monitoring and diagnosis of security threats for unmanned aerial systems. In: Bartocci, E., Majumdar, R. (eds.) RV 2015. LNCS, vol. 9333, pp. 233–249. Springer, Cham (2015). https://doi.org/10.1007/978-3-319-23820-3_15

20. Schumann, J., Moosbrugger, P., Rozier, K.Y.: Runtime analysis with R2U2: a tool exhibition report. In: Falcone, Y., Sánchez, C. (eds.) RV 2016. LNCS, vol. 10012, pp. 504–509. Springer, Cham (2016). https://doi.org/10.1007/978-3-319-46982-9_35

21. Schumann, J., Rozier, K.Y., Reinbacher, T., Mengshoel, O.J., Mbaya, T., Ippolito, C.: Towards real-time, on-board, hardware-supported sensor and software health management for unmanned aerial systems. Int. J. Prognostics Health Manag. (IJPHM) 6(1), 1–27 (2015)

Verification of Functional Correctness of Code Diversification Techniques

Jae-Won Jang[1(✉)], Freek Verbeek[1,2], and Binoy Ravindran[1]

[1] Virginia Tech, Blacksburg, VA, USA
{jjang3,freek,binoy}@vt.edu
[2] Open University of The Netherlands, Heerlen, The Netherlands

Abstract. Code diversification techniques are popular code-reuse attacks defense. The majority of code diversification research focuses on analyzing non-functional properties, such as whether the technique improves security. This paper provides a methodology to verify functional equivalence between the original and a diversified binary. We present a formal notion of binary equivalence resilient to diversification. Moreover, an algorithm is presented that checks whether two binaries – one original and one diversified – satisfy that notion of equivalence. The purpose of our work is to allow untrusted diversification techniques in a safety-critical context. We apply the methodology to three state-of-the-art diversification techniques used on the GNU Coreutils package. Overall, results show that our method can prove functional equivalence for 85,315 functions in the analyzed binaries.

Keywords: Code diversification · Functional equivalence · Verification

1 Introduction

Generally, a binary is a result of compiling source code into machine code. Binary compilation is a deterministic process where if the source code is unchanged, the resulting binary will remain the same. Due to this deterministic nature, if a binary contains a critical error that adversaries can attack, this issue propagates to all instances of binaries. Code diversification is a software technique used to defend such attacks (e.g., code-reuse [11] or return-oriented programming (ROP) [6,41]). The technique consists – broadly described – of modifying the compilation process so that the same source code produces different binaries that offer the same functionality. Code diversification ensures that when an attacker has compromised a binary, the knowledge gained cannot easily be reused on the other binaries (of the same type).

There have been a plethora of proposed code diversification techniques presented in the literature [21,28]. Many of these techniques are based on either recompilation from source-code or rewriting at the machine-code level. Examples include **nop** insertion [20,24], stack layout randomization [15], and relocation of basic blocks, functions, and instructions [27]. Without exception, these

© Springer Nature Switzerland AG 2021
A. Dutle et al. (Eds.): NFM 2021, LNCS 12673, pp. 160–179, 2021.
https://doi.org/10.1007/978-3-030-76384-8_11

Table 1. Covered code diversification techniques

Diversification technique	Reference
Instruction reordering	$[15, 19, 23, 25, 36]$
Basic block reordering	$[9, 15, 27]$
Stack layout randomization	$[2, 15, 17, 31]$
nop insertion	$[9, 20-22, 24, 28, 46]$
Function reordering	$[3, 17, 23, 27]$
Static binary rewriting	$[10, 18, 19, 27, 47]$

diversification techniques are evaluated on non-functional properties, such as whether the entropy is increased, performance overhead, etc. Without exception, these diversification techniques are evaluated on non-functional properties (e.g., increased entropy). None of the existing techniques are evaluated on whether the diversification preserves functional equivalence, which reduces trust in deploying such techniques in production settings. Upon diversification, no proof or theorem shows that the diversified binary is functionally equivalent to the vanilla (i.e., original) binary. A key challenge is that strictly speaking, they are *not* functionally equivalent. Various registers and memory locations may contain different values in both worlds. However, the binaries should be *similar* for *relevant* state parts, such as the registers storing in- and output.

In this paper, we propose a definition of functional equivalence between vanilla and diversified binary. The definition is based on stuttering bisimulation [1], thereby showing that the binaries share a large class of temporal properties. Moreover, we propose a methodology that takes an input of a disassembled vanilla and diversified binary and establishes whether that definition holds or provides a counterexample. We fold our methodology in a tool and evaluate with several different code diversification techniques listed in Table 1. The purpose of our work is to allow untrusted diversification techniques to be used in safety-critical context. As a benchmark, we diversify GNU Coreutils with these diversification techniques and show functional equivalence for many functions. The main limitation is that we are not able to deal with indirect branching. Moreover, we assume the a binaries can be successfully disassembled.

The state-of-the-art provides various techniques to compare two binaries [7, 12, 33, 35, 39, 42, 50]. A broad class of the comparison techniques is statistical or learning-based [13, 48, 50]. They give a *probability* instead of a *guarantee* that the two binaries are related. Luo et al. [35] provide a binary similarity comparison technique that is resilient to code diversification. Another class of comparison techniques focuses on strong equivalence (e.g., requiring that the same registers are used for the same variables) [7, 39]. They thus cannot deal with code diversification since this produces two binaries that are not strongly equivalent. In Sect. 6, we provide a further discussion of the state-of-the-art. A verified diversifier is out of reach of the current state-of-the-art: a diversifier typically is based on gcc or clang with specific compiler options. Thus verifying the

```
1 | void *foo();
2 | void *bar();

3 | int main(int argc,
        char** argv)
4 | {
5 |   int a = 0;
6 |   if (a == 0)
7 |   {
8 |       foo();
9 |   }
10 |  else
11 |  {
12 |      bar();
13 |  }
14 |  return 0;
15 | }

16 | void *foo()
17 | {
18 |   printf("Foo\n");
19 | }

20 | void *bar()
21 | {
22 |   int c = 17;
23 | }
```

(a) Source code

```
1 | main:
2 |   push rbp
3 |   mov rbp, rsp
4 |   sub rsp, 0x30
5 |   mov dword ptr [rbp-0x4], 0
6 |   mov dword ptr [rbp-0x8], edi
7 |   jne .label_8
8 |   call foo
9 |   mov qword ptr [rbp-0x20], rax
10 |  jmp .label_9
11 | .label_8:
12 |   call bar
13 |   mov qword ptr [rbp-0x28], rax
14 | .label_9:
15 |   xor eax, eax
   ...
19 | foo:
   ...
24 |   mov dword ptr [rbp-0xc], eax
25 | bar:
26 |   push rbp
27 |   mov rbp, rsp
28 |   mov dword ptr [rbp-0xc], 0x11
29 |   mov rax, qword ptr [rbp-0x8]
```

(b) Disassembled Code

```
19 | foo:
   ...
24 |   mov dword ptr [rbp-0x4], eax
   ...
11 | .label_11:
        nop
12 |   call bar
13 |   mov qword ptr [rbp-0x28], rax
14 | .label_5:
15 |   xor eax, eax
   ...
1 | main:
2 |   push rbp
3 |   mov rbp, rsp
        mov rbp, rbp
4 |   sub rsp, 0x30
5 |   mov dword ptr [rbp-0x14], 0
5 |   mov dword ptr [rbp-0x04], edi
7 |   jne .label_11
        lea rdi, [rdi]
8 |   call foo
9 |   mov qword ptr [rbp-0x20], rax
10 |  jmp .label_5
25 | bar:
26 |   push rbp
27 |   mov rbp, rsp
28 |   mov dword ptr [rbp-4], 0x11
        mov rbp, rbp
29 |   mov rax, qword ptr [rbp-0x10]
```

(c) Disassembled div. code

(d) Vanilla code CFG   (e) Div. code CFG   (f) Framework output

Label relationship :
label_8 ↔ label_11
label_9 ↔ label_5

Local variable relationship (Symbolic):
$[rsp_0 - 28, 4] \leftrightarrow \{[rsp_0 - 32, 4], [rsp_0 - 28, 4]\}$
$[rsp_0 - 16, 4] \leftrightarrow \{[rsp_0 - 12, 4]\}$
$[rsp_0 - 12, 4] \leftrightarrow \{[rsp_0 - 32, 4], [rsp_0 - 28, 4]\}$

Successful check!
Relevant vanilla text sections: 3
Success: 3 text sections

Fig. 1. Example

diversifier implies verifying one of those compilers. Moreover, such an approach would limit the applicability of the methodology to that specific diversifier. For these reasons, we consider the *output* of some *black-box* and *untrusted* diversifiers and verify whether the diversified binary is functionally similar to its vanilla version.

The main contributions of our work are:

1. A formal definition of functional equivalence resilient to code diversification
2. A scalable methodology for establishing that equivalence between a vanilla and a diversified binary
3. The application of this methodology to different diversification techniques on GNU Coreutils binaries

To the best of our knowledge, this paper is the first to present a formal definition of functional equivalence for diversified binaries and to verify that equivalence.

This paper is organized in the following structure. Section 2 presents an overview of our method. In Sect. 3, we formally define the equivalence relation, followed by the algorithm for equivalence checking in Sect. 4. The evaluation and limitations of our work are presented in Sect. 5. Section 6 presents related work and compares them with our work. Lastly, we conclude in Sect. 7.

2   System Overview

This section provides an overview of the input, intermediate steps and the output of our method, using Fig. 1 as a running example. Note that the C code in Fig. 1a is shown for the sake of presentation only: it is not required as input to our method; we use this example to demonstrate how a diversification technique affects the original binary.

2.1   Disassembly

The methodology takes as input a vanilla and a diversified (div.) binary. The first step for our methodology is disassembly (see Figs. 1b and 1c). An example of diversification is shown in Fig. 1c, where text sections (e.g., `main`, `foo`, `bar`) are reordered due to function reordering. A key feature of disassembly that we require is *symbolization*. Symbolization replaces concrete addresses with symbolic values, i.e., labels. Binaries are usually compiled (or translated into machine-readable code) from high-level source code. After compilation, it goes through the assembler to generate an object file (architecture-dependent), which is linked with different libraries to create a binary executable. During this process, a large portion of useful high-level information disappears. Specifically, relocation information disappears, which a linker uses to maintain the coherence between multiple libraries that the binary calls. Symbolization aims at recovering relocation-related information.

An example of symbolization is shown in Lines 11 and 14 of Figs. 1b and 1c. The text section names of `main`, `foo` and `bar` are preserved by compilation from the source code. The labels (`.label_8` and `.label_9`), however, are not present in the original binary. They are the result of symbolizing concrete addresses.

We use `Ramblr` for disassembly and symbolization [45]. `Ramblr` is a subset of an open-source disassembler framework `angr`. `angr` reliably disassembles the binary, and this was demonstrated on a set of binaries from the DARPA cyber grand challenge (a computer security competition dealing with malicious binaries) [43].

2.2   Control-Flow Graph Construction

The second step is the CFG construction. We extract CFGs from the binary using an off-the-shelf algorithm similar to `angr`'s CFGFast [43]. A CFG consists of nodes and edges. A node consists of a basic block, (i.e., a list of instructions). Edges are labeled with flags. We construct one CFG per text section (for both vanilla and diversified binaries). The reason for this is because our methodology proves functional equivalence per text section rather than iterating through the complete CFG of an entire binary.

The vanilla and diversified binaries are supposed to be functionally equivalent, but as Figs. 1d and 1e show, the diversified CFG is different. The process of nop insertion [20] actually inserted a lea instruction just before the call foo statement (between Lines 7–8 in Fig. 1c). This causes the difference in CFGs, and it complicates the functional equivalence verification process, as we cannot only check whether the two CFGs are equal. Instead, we must check whether they are stuttering bisimilar.

2.3   Local Variable Normalization

Variables are storage locations that the program can manipulate. Local variables are referenced by an offset from special-purpose registers (the frame pointer rbp or the stack pointer rsp). Register rbp points to the top of the current stack frame, and rsp points to the bottom.

After constructing CFGs, we normalize local variables to prepare for our comparison algorithm. Normalizing in this context means that local variable offsets become relative to the *initial* value of the stack (rsp_0) pointer. For example, in Fig. 1b, the memory address rbp − 0x4 is accessed at Line 5. Since the frame pointer is a copy of the stack pointer (Line 3), which has been decremented with 8, this memory address becomes rsp_0 − 0x12 after normalization. Normalization allows us to compare memory locations that are shuffled.

2.4   CFG Comparison

Bisimulation is a relation between two transition systems, where one can simulate the others' (transitions) and vice versa. In particular, we use *divergence-sensitive stuttering bisimulation* [1,4] for our work. To check whether two CFGs are stuttering bisimilar, we treat them as transition systems and check whether they are stuttering bisimulation-equivalent. In other words, we check if there exists a stuttering bisimulation between both transition systems.

The intuition behind a stuttering bisimulation is that it deals with internal steps, steps that perform no visible behavior. Stuttering bisimulation allows two transition systems to be equivalent regardless of how many internal steps it takes to get to the next state, and mainly deals with basic blocks consisting solely of instructions that perform no state change, such as a basic block [main_18, main_19] in Fig. 1e. Divergence-sensitivity prevents a situation where one of the transition systems permanently executes internal steps, whereas the other does not.

A divergence-sensitive stuttering bisimulation is a strong notion of equivalence, as it preserves a large set of properties. This set of properties includes safety, liveness, and reachability properties. Formally, the set of properties preserved is computation tree logic (CTL) except the next operator, i.e., $CTL^*\backslash\mathbf{X}$ [1]. In words, this means that any CTL^* property is preserved as long as it does not concern specifically the current branching decision.

2.5   Output

If our methodology finds no counterexample, it provides an output stating that the binaries are functionally equivalent (see Fig. 1f). In addition, our work offers evidence for that claim, which is a mapping between vanilla and diversified parts of the binaries. If we find any potential issues (e.g., limitations or problems), our work can provide the output stating the basic block causing the discrepancy. A third possible output is "Unsupported" (see Sect. 5.2).

When a program becomes diversified by a technique such as reordering of instruction or basic blocks, relocation information of such a program gets affected. For example, `.label_8` and `.label_11` from Figs. 1b and 1c are semantically equivalent (Line 11 for both), but different in label names. The CFG comparison algorithm thus keeps track of a map relating labels in the vanilla world to labels in the diversified world. Similarly, stack shuffling may cause local variables to be put into different memory regions. A mapping is maintained that relates diversified memory regions to vanilla ones. For example, the 4-byte vanilla memory region $[\text{rsp}_0 - 16, 4]$ (accessed at Line 6 in Fig. 1b) is mapped to the diversified memory region $[\text{rsp}_0 - 12, 4]$ (accessed at Line 6 in Fig. 1c).

3   Soundness of Code Diversification

This section defines an equivalence relation over binaries. We will call a code diversification effort *sound* if the vanilla binary and the produced diversified binary are equivalent under that relation.

The key idea is to establish a *divergence-sensitive stuttering bisimulation* over the transition systems modeling the two binaries [1]. Formally, a transition system TS is defined by a tuple $\langle S, \rightsquigarrow, I \rangle$. Here S is a set of states, $\rightsquigarrow$ of type $S \times S \mapsto \mathbb{B}$ is a transition relation, and I is a set of initial states.

Note that this definition omits either a labeling function or actions on edges. Typically, definitions of stuttering bisimulation are based on one of these two. However, due to stack-frame shuffling, neither of these is convenient. For example, let both the vanilla and diversified binaries have two labeling functions L_0 and L_1. Both translate concrete states to atomic propositions. Stuttering bisimulation then considers two states s and s' to be equal only if $L_0(s) = L_1(s')$. Consider again function `main` in Figs. 1b and 1c. The labeling functions should translate states to atomic propositions in such a way that the value stored at the vanilla memory region $[\text{rsp}_0 - 16, 4]$ and the value stored at the diversified memory region $[\text{rsp}_0 - 12, 4]$ map to the same atomic proposition. The labeling function is thus hard to define, as it is dependent on the relation established between the two binaries. Instead, we will formalize a *state comparison function* $\doteq$ of type $S_0 \times S_1 \mapsto \mathbb{B}$, and define stuttering bisimilarity relative to the given state comparison function.

Definition 1. *Let TS_0 and TS_1 be two transition systems, and let $\doteq$ of type $S_0 \times S_1 \mapsto \mathbb{B}$ be a state comparison function. Binary relation $\mathcal{B}$ of type $S_0 \times S_1 \mapsto \mathbb{B}$ is a* divergence-sensitive stuttering bisimulation *wrt. $\doteq$, if and only if, for any states $s_0 \in S_0$ and $s_1 \in S_1$, such that $\mathcal{B}(s_0, s_1)$:*

1. $s_0 \doteq s_1$
2. if $s_0 \leadsto_0 s_0'$ and $\neg\mathcal{B}(s_0', s_1)$, then there exists a finite path fragment $[s_1, t_0 \ldots t_n, s_1']$ such that $\mathcal{B}(s_0, t_i)$ for all i and $\mathcal{B}(s_0', s_1')$
3. if $s_1 \leadsto_1 s_1'$ and $\neg\mathcal{B}(s_0, s_1')$, then there exists a finite path fragment $[s_0, t_0 \ldots t_n, s_0']$ such that $\mathcal{B}(t_i, s_1)$ for all i and $\mathcal{B}(s_0', s_1')$
4. there exists an infinite path fragment $[s_0, t_0, t_1 \ldots]$ such that $\mathcal{B}(t_i, s_1)$ for all i, if and only if, there exists an infinite path fragment $[s_1, u_0, u_1 \ldots]$ such that $\mathcal{B}(s_0, u_j)$ for all j.

Two transition systems are divergence-sensitive stuttering bisimilar wrt. $\doteq$, notation $TS_0 \approx TS_1$, if and only if there exists a divergence-sensitive stuttering bisimulation $\mathcal{B}$ that relates all initial states, i.e., for all $s_0 \in I_0$, there exists some $s_1 \in I_1$ such that $R(s_0, s_1)$, and the other way around.

Soundness of diversification is expressed as a property over CFGs. We assume the existence of a function cfg that takes as input a binary and produces a CFG. Formally, a CFG consists of a tuple $\langle B, \rightarrow, e \rangle$, where B denotes a set of basic blocks, $\rightarrow$ of type $B \times B \mapsto \mathbb{B}$ denotes a transition relation, and e of type B denotes the entry point. The start address of a basic block b can be accessed via $b.\texttt{addr}$, the list of instructions via $b.\texttt{instrs}$.

We consider the transition system corresponding to a given CFG. The transition system consists of concrete states that map registers, 64-bit byte-addressable memory, and flags to values. We use S_C to denote the set of concrete states, R to denote the set of registers, and A to denote the address space. Given a concrete state s, we use $s.\texttt{rip}$ to denote the value stored in register $\texttt{rip}$, and similar for other registers and flags. Notation $s.\texttt{mem}(a)$ returns given a 64-bit address a the byte-value stored in the memory at that address. Function run of type $B \times S_C \mapsto \{S_C\}$ takes as input a basic block and the current concrete state, and runs the list of instructions in the basic block. It returns the set of possible next concrete states. Since a basic block does not have loops, this function terminates.

Definition 2. Let $g = \langle B, \rightarrow, e \rangle$ be a CFG. The transition system of g, notation $\overline{g}$, is defined by $\langle S_C, \leadsto, I \rangle$. Here set of initial concrete states I is defined as follows:

$$I \stackrel{def}{=} \{s \mid s.\texttt{rip} = e.\texttt{addr}\}$$

and transition relation $\leadsto$ is constructed as follows:

$$\frac{s' \in run(b, s) \wedge b \rightarrow b' \wedge s.\texttt{rip} = b.\texttt{addr} \wedge s'.\texttt{rip} = b'.\texttt{addr}}{s \leadsto s'}$$

In words, the transition system $\overline{g}$ starts at states whose instruction pointer $\texttt{rip}$ is equal to that of the first instruction of the basic block that is the CFGs' entry point. It then moves from state to state by executing entire basic blocks. The transition system is thus at the same granularity as the CFG.

Definition 1 depends on a state comparison function. The stronger this comparison function, the stronger the equivalence. As illustrated, if $s_0 \doteq s_1$ is true for any state, then any two transition systems are bisimilar. We thus define a comparison function for concrete states that is as strong as possible. Ideally, we want to compare all state parts, i.e., all registers, memory, and flags. In practice, we consider only the set of *relevant* registers. For instance, the instruction pointer (`rip`) is irrelevant: in the two worlds, it will differ since the executed instructions have different addresses due to, e.g., `nop` insertion. The frame-and stack-pointers are irrelevant since stack frame shuffling can enlarge the stack frame. Which registers are relevant may depend on the current state. This is modeled with a function $\mathcal{R}$ that returns relevant registers (e.g., all registers except the irrelevant ones) given the current state. In practice, we ignore flags: their impact on execution is covered by proving that the same branching decisions are made. Finally, we need to map diversified memory addresses to their vanilla counterparts. This is modeled with a mapping $\mathcal{M}$.

Definition 3. *Let $\mathcal{R}$ of type $S_C \mapsto \{R\}$ be a function that returns a set of relevant registers given a concrete state. Let $\mathcal{M}$ of type $A \mapsto A$ be a mapping from diversified memory addresses to vanilla memory addresses. The* concrete state comparison function *of M, notation $\stackrel{c}{=}_{\langle \mathcal{R},\mathcal{M} \rangle}$, is defined as follows:*

$$
s_0 \stackrel{c}{=}_{\langle \mathcal{R},\mathcal{M} \rangle} s_1 \stackrel{def}{=} \begin{cases} \forall \mathbf{r} \in \mathcal{R}(s_0) \cdot s_0.\mathbf{r} = s_1.\mathbf{r} \\ \wedge \; \forall a \in A \cdot s_0.\mathrm{mem}(a) = s_1.\mathrm{mem}(\mathcal{M}(a)) \end{cases}
$$

In words, two concrete states are considered equal if all relevant registers are equal and all memory in both worlds is the same after mapping diversified addresses to vanilla addresses. For example, in Fig. 1, the values stored at vanilla address $\mathrm{rsp}_0 - 16$ and diversified address $\mathrm{rsp}_0 - 12$ will be compared.

```
1  | main:
2  |   push rbp
3  |   mov rbp, rsp
4  |   sub rsp, 0x30
5  |   lea rdi, [rdi]
6  |   xor eax, eax
7  |   mov dword ptr [rbp - 0x14], eax
8  |   mov dword ptr [rbp - 0x4], edi
9  |   cmp dword ptr [rbp - 0x4], esi
10 |   jne .label_22
```

rsp   := rsp − 0x38
rbp   := rsp − 0x8
rax   := 0
[rsp − 0x8, 8] := rbp
[rsp − 0x1c, 4] := 0
[rsp − 0xc, 4] := ⟨31, 0⟩(rdi)
ZF   := ⟨31, 0⟩(rdi) = ⟨31, 0⟩(rsi)
CF   := ⟨31, 0⟩(rdi) < ⟨31, 0⟩(rsi)
SF   := ⟨31, 0⟩(rdi) <$_s$ ⟨31, 0⟩(rsi)

(a) Diversified **main** Basic Block   (b) **Symbolic Execution Output**

Fig. 2. Symbolic execution example

Definition 4. *Let B be a binary and let D be a diversification function that takes as input a binary and produces a diversified binary. Diversification D is* sound *for binary B, if and only if, there exists a function $\mathcal{R}$ and mapping $\mathcal{M}$ such that the transition systems of the CFGs are divergence-sensitive stuttering bisimilar wrt. the concrete state comparison function of $\mathcal{R}$ and $\mathcal{M}$.*

$$
\mathrm{sound}(D, B) \stackrel{def}{=} \exists \mathcal{R}, \mathcal{M} \cdot \overline{\mathrm{cfg}(B)} \approx \overline{\mathrm{cfg}(D(B))} \; wrt. \; \stackrel{c}{=}_{\langle \mathcal{R},\mathcal{M} \rangle}
$$

4   Algorithm

In order to check soundness (see Definition 4), a witness must be found for function $\mathcal{R}$ and mapping $\mathcal{M}$. This section presents an algorithm to find these witnesses. It consists of four steps:

1. Produce the function $\mathcal{R}$ and mapping $\mathcal{M}$ by running symbolic execution on each basic block in the two CFGs; for each symbolic block, keep track of the relevant registers.
2. Express all local variables in terms of the initial value of the stack pointer rsp_0.
3. Check for stuttering bisimulation on the symbolized CFGs, while keeping track of memory mapping $\mathcal{M}$.

Step 1 (Symbolic Execution). The purpose of symbolic execution is to express the semantics of each basic block in a way that is independent of the actual instructions. Figure 2 depicts an example of symbolic execution where we show a basic block and its symbolic output. The symbolic output consists of assignments of symbolic expressions to state parts (registers, memory flags). Symbolic expressions consist of, among others, immediate values, reading from state parts, and common bit-vector operations. These operations include taking bit subsets, concatenation, logical operators, casting operators, floating-point operators, and signed and unsigned arithmetic. For example, after the execution of the basic block in Fig. 2, register rax (eax is the lower 32 bits of rax) has become 0, and the sign flag is set by a signed integer comparison of the lower 32 bits of the rdi and rsi registers. All values are relative to the initial state of the basic block. For example, the instruction at Line 8 uses the frame pointer rbp, but since that value at that line is equal to the initial stack pointer minus 8, the instruction results in a write to the symbolic memory region $[rsp - 0xc, 4]$.

In Fig. 2b, it can be seen that symbolic execution produces a result largely agnostic of diversification. For the sake of presentation, the basic block has been manually modified with two features found in typical diversification tools. At Line 5 in Fig. 2a, a lea instruction has been inserted that performs no state change: it is effectively a nop. Instead of directly writing 0 to memory with one instruction, we use two instructions (Lines 6 and 7). First, xor is used to write zero to register eax (which denotes the lower 32 bits of register rax), and then mov is used to do the memory write. Symbolization does not reflect these modifications since they do not influence the semantics of the basic block. The basic block without the manual modifications would have produced the same symbolic output. Finally, the example shows that to compare a vanilla and a diversified basic block, only the register modified in the vanilla world is to be considered relevant. Register rax would not have been part of the symbolic output for the non-modified basic block. However, all state parts that are modified in the vanilla world are similarly modified in the diversified world.

Formally, a symbolic state σ consists of registers, memory and flags (we use s and σ for resp. concrete and symbolic states). For each modified register r, notation $\sigma.r$ returns a symbolic expression. The set of modified registers is returned by σ.regs. The memory is modeled by assigning symbolic expressions to symbolic memory regions. Consider again example in Fig. 2b. The notation $\sigma.[\text{rsp} - \text{0x8}, 8]$ returns the symbolic expression rbp. The set of modified memory regions is denoted by σ.mems.

The algorithm will compare symbolic states instead of concrete ones. This requires us to formulate a *symbolic* state comparison function, which is the symbolic counterpart to its concrete version (see Definition 3).

Definition 5. *Let $\mathcal{N}$ be a mapping from diversified symbolic memory regions to vanilla symbolic memory regions. The symbolic state comparison function of $\mathcal{N}$, notation $\stackrel{s}{=}_{\mathcal{N}}$, is defined as follows:*

$$\sigma_0 \stackrel{s}{=}_{\mathcal{N}} \sigma_1 \stackrel{def}{=} \begin{cases} \forall \text{r} \in \sigma_0.\text{regs} \cdot \sigma_0.\text{r} = \sigma_1.\text{r} \\ \land \forall \text{r} \in \sigma_0.\text{mems} \cdot \sigma_0.\text{r} = \sigma_1.\mathcal{N}(\text{r}) \end{cases}$$

Mapping $\mathcal{N}$ is defined over symbolic memory regions and symbolic expressions. Given a concrete state, the memory regions, all symbolic values can be concretized. Function γ takes as input a symbolic mapping $\mathcal{N}$, and produces a concrete mapping $\mathcal{M} = \gamma(\mathcal{N})$. For example, if diversified memory region $[\text{rsp} - 8, 8]$ is mapped by $\mathcal{N}$ to vanilla region $[\text{rsp} - 16, 8]$, then $\mathcal{M}$ will relate 8 individual concrete addresses based on the values of the concrete stack pointers.

Definition 6. *Symbolic execution is sound, if and only if, for any basic blocks b_0 and b_1, assumption*

$$\text{se}(b_0) \stackrel{s}{=}_{\mathcal{N}} \text{se}(b_1)$$

implies:

$$\forall s_0, s_1 \in S_C \cdot s_0.\text{rip} = b_0.\text{addr} \land s_1.\text{rip} = b_1.\text{addr} \implies run(b_0, s_0) \stackrel{c}{=}_{\langle \mathcal{R}, \mathcal{M} \rangle} run(b_1, s_1)$$

where

$$\mathcal{R}(s_0) = \text{se}(b_0).\text{regs}$$
$$\mathcal{M} \quad = \gamma(\mathcal{N})$$

In words, comparing two symbolic states should suffice to show successful comparison of all the concrete states they represent. The set of relevant registers $\mathcal{R}$ is the set of all modified registers in the vanilla world. The concrete memory map $\mathcal{M}$ is obtained by concretizing the symbolic memory region map.

Step 2 (Substitute for rsp_0). Local variables are addressed relative to either the stack pointer rsp or the frame pointer rbp. The values in these registers are not static, i.e., they change during the execution of the function. This change complicates formulating a static address mapping $\mathcal{M}$. Consider, Lines 5 and 9 of Fig. 1b, which deal with addresses $[\text{rbp} - \text{0x4}]$ and $[\text{rbp} - \text{0x20}]$. In between these lines, the value of register rbp may have changed in such a way that these addresses are actually equal. To formulate a static mapping $\mathcal{M}$, we thus make all local variables relative to the initial value of the stack pointer rsp_0. This is achieved by propagating two substitutions through the symbolized CFG. Initially, these two substitutions are $\text{rsp} := \text{rsp}_0$ and $\text{rbp} := \text{rbp}_0$. Thus, for the entry block, any occurrence of the stack pointer is simply replaced by rsp_0. The substitutions are updated if the current basic block updates either the stack- or frame pointer. In the example, after the first basic block, the current substitution is $\text{rsp} := \text{rsp}_0 - \text{0x38}$ and $\text{rbp} := \text{rsp}_0 - \text{0x8}$.

In this fashion, substitutions are propagated through the CFG. In case of an encountering a visited node (i.e., a loop or paths in the CFG converging), it is verified that the current substitution is equal to the substitution already applied to the visited node. If this holds any time a visited node is encountered, then the current substitutions constitute an invariant.

Step 3 (Checking for Stuttering Bisimulation). Algorithm 1 presents a procedure CHECK that compares two CFGs. It takes as input the current basic blocks – initially starting with the entry points – and traverses the CFGs simultaneously. It provides as output a Boolean indicating the existence of a stuttering bisimulation (Line 19). Before we explain the algorithm in more detail, we introduce some definitions.

Definition 7. *Let b_0 and b_1, be two basic blocks (vanilla and diversified respectively). Branching for basic blocks is equivalent, if and only if:*

$$\text{eq\_branching}(b_0, b_1) \overset{def}{=} \forall f \cdot (\exists b_0' \cdot b_0 \overset{f}{\to} b_0') \Leftrightarrow (\exists b_1' \cdot b_1 \overset{f}{\to} b_1')$$

In words, equal branching returns true if both blocks have the same number of children with the same flags.

Definition 8. *Let b_0 and b_1, be two basic blocks (vanilla and diversified respectively). The set of children of b_0 and b_1 is defined as follows:*

$$\text{get\_children}(b_0, b_1) \overset{def}{=} \{(b_0', b_1') \cdot \exists f \cdot b_0 \overset{f}{\to} b_0' \wedge b_1 \overset{f}{\to} b_1'\}$$

In words, *get_children* returns the set of children that is to be explored from current basic blocks b_0 and b_1.

Definition 9. *Basic block b is a* skip *if and only if:*

$$\text{is\_skip}(b) \overset{def}{=} \sigma.\text{regs} \subseteq \{\text{rip}\} \wedge \sigma.\text{mems} = \emptyset$$

In words, a basic block is a skip if it does not modify memory and the only register that is modified (if any) is the instruction pointer rip.

Algorithm 1 essentially is a simultaneous depth-first exploration. If both basic blocks are flagged as visited, a stuttering bisimulation for the current basic blocks b_0 and b_1 has been established. If not, both basic blocks are flagged as visited, and the comparison continues. Each block is first symbolically executed, producing symbolic states σ_0 and σ_1. The currently established stuttering bisimulation relation is updated (Line 6). This update stores that from now on, $\mathcal{R}(s_0)$ returns the set of registers modified by basic block b_0, i.e., $\mathcal{R}(s_0) = \sigma_0.\text{regs}$ for all states s_0 such that $s_0.\text{rip} = \sigma_0.\text{rip}$. Moreover, memory mapping $\mathcal{N}$ is updated.

Algorithm 1. Check Between Vanilla and Diversified CFGs

```
1: function CHECK(b₀, b₁)
2:     if b₀ and b₁ are unvisited then
3:         mark b₀ and b₁ as visited
4:         σ₀ = se(b₀)
5:         σ₁ = se(b₁)
6:         UPDATE (N, σ₀, σ₁)
7:         if σ₀ ≐_N σ₁ ∧ eq_branching(b₀, b₁) then
8:             for each (b₀', b₁') ∈ get_children(b₀, b₁) do
9:                 CHECK (b₀', b₁')
10:            end for
11:        else if is_skip(b₁) then
12:            mark b₁ as visited
13:            CHECK (b₀, b₁') with b₁ ↠ b₁'
14:        else
15:            mark current b₁ text section as counterexample
16:            return False
17:        end if
18:    else
19:        return True
20:    end if
21: end function
```

If the two basic blocks are semantically equivalent and they have equal branching (Line 7) the check proceeds by exploring all children. If not, then the current diversified basic block may be a skip. In that case, the check proceeds by comparing the current vanilla basic block b_0 to the child of the skip b_1'. If diversified basic block b_1 was not a skip, then a discrepancy has been found and the algorithm returns false (Line 16).

Theorem 1. *Let $g_0 = \langle B_0, \rightarrow_0, e_0 \rangle$ and $g_1 = \langle B_1, \rightarrow_1, e_1 \rangle$ be the control flow graphs of the vanilla and diversified binaries respectively. Let $\mathcal{R}$ and $\mathcal{M} = \gamma(\mathcal{N})$ be the mappings produced by the algorithm. The algorithm decides a divergence-blind stuttering bisimulation:*

$$\text{CHECK}(e_0, e_1) \longleftrightarrow g_0 \approx g_1 \; wrt. \; \stackrel{c}{=}_{\langle \mathcal{R}, \mathcal{M} \rangle}$$

Proof. Soundness of the algorithm is based on the work of Fernandez et al. [14]. In that paper, it is shown that a bisimulation can be decided by a depth-first search that explores two transition systems simultaneously. Proposition 3.2 of that paper states that two deterministic transition systems are bisimilar, if and only if, a simultaneous depth-first search is not able to find a path to a pair of states with a different number of children. That is exactly what is verified by our algorithm. A key difference is that the work of Fernandez et al. is formulated for an algorithm checking strong bisimulation. Line 11 of Algorithm 1 adds an additional case for dealing with stuttering steps: the diversified world can do an arbitrary number of skips before a bisimilar node is encountered. Divergence-sensitivity is guaranteed by checking whether the number of children is always equivalent for all encountered bisimilar nodes (Line 7).

5 Evaluation

The methodology is applied to all 93 binaries of GNU coreutils 8.31. The source code is compiled on Linux Ubuntu 16.04 × 86-64 using the clang with a variety of optimization levels (-O0 to -O3) (depending on the diversification tool). All experiments are run on a machine with an AMD FX-8350 CPU and 8 GB RAM. GNU Coreutils is a suitable benchmark as it contains realistic and sufficiently complex binaries, ranging from small (10,692 assembly LOCs) to large (133,065 assembly LOCs).

We cover three off-the-shelf diversification tools which, combined, cover all techniques listed in Table 1: 1) nop insertion [20], 2) Compiler-assisted Code Randomization (CCR) [27], and 3) stack shuffling [15]. nop insertion inserts nop in front of targeted instruction [20]. CCR [27] leverages a compiler-rewriter process to transform inserted metadata into security primitive. The stack shuffling technique [15] diversifies the stack layout per binary.

5.1 Results

Table 2 presents the results. Consider the data for the CCR tool on binaries compiled with -O1. Out of 93 binaries, 87 binaries were analyzed. The remainder is split into one binary that could not be diversified by CCR (column Not Div.) and five binaries that could not be disassembled by Ramblr (column Not Dis.). Of the 11769 text sections of the 87 analyzed binaries, 10808 text sections were analyzed and proven to be soundly diversified. Zero text sections were shown to be unsoundly diversified, and 961 text sections contained behavior unsupported by our tool (see Sect. 5.2).

The table shows we did not find a diversification issue in any of the binaries. However, for each of the listed techniques in Table 1, we manually introduced bugs indicative of that technique. For example, we manually inserted one nop too

Table 2. The evaluation of our methodology on GNU Coreutils v8.31

Diversification tools		Analyzed	Not Div.	Not Dis.	Sound	Counterexample	Unsupported
		Binaries			Text Sections		
nop ins. [20]	-O0	93	0	0	12966	0	546
	-O1	91	0	2	7427	0	831
	-O2	88	0	5	7519	0	930
	-O3	88	0	5	7694	0	1079
CCR [27]	-O0	93	0	0	12805	0	697
	-O1	87	1	5	10808	0	961
	-O2	83	2	8	6681	0	868
	-O3	79	8	6	6619	0	836
S. shuf. [15]	-O0	93	0	0	12796	0	706

Binaries = result with respect to the number of binaries
Text Sections = result with respect to the number of text sections from analyzed binaries

many in the diversified version of the wc program and reran our tool. For each inserted bug, our methodology reports a counterexample. This report provides information on which text section that the bug is in. Moreover, it also gives the line number of parsed disassembled code for both vanilla and diversified binaries for in-depth debugging purposes.

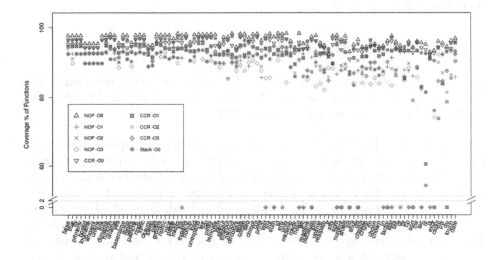

Fig. 3. The coverage rate per diversification techniques over all GNU `Coreutils`

Figure 3 shows, per binary, the percentage of text sections proven to be soundly diversified. The binaries are sorted from the least number of assembly LOCs (`false`, 10,692 LOCs) to the largest number of LOCs (`date`, 133,065 LOCs). The zero-outliers are the 31 cases where a binary could either not be diversified or be disassembled for the given diversification technique and the given optimization level. For the remaining binaries the average coverage is 91.26% with a minimum of 87.7% for `nop` insertion with optimization O3 and a maximum of 95.95% for `nop` insertion without optimizations.

5.2 Limitations

Our work's main limitation is that we cannot deal with indirect branching (e.g., indirect jumps). Indirect branching occurs when jump- or call-addresses are computed dynamically, and solving indirect branching requires assembly-level invariants on the values involved in that computation. Second, we cannot reason about shuffled local arrays, e.g., due to an `alloca` statement. The key problem here is that the array-size is not known at the assembly-level. Third, as the optimization level increases, a compiler performs expensive analyses and applies more aggressive transformations (e.g., perform a scalar replacement or loop transformations) to improve the binary. Therefore, as Fig. 3 shows, as the optimization level increases, proving functional equivalence becomes harder, due to optimized instructions (e.g., packed instructions such as `puncpkhbw`). Lastly, if a disassembler is unable to disassemble the binary, then our tool cannot do any verification. Currently, our methodology only supports *diversification* techniques. Proving the functional equivalence between *code obfuscated* binaries to the vanilla binaries is more difficult due to the convoluted modifications that obfuscation techniques do to camouflage the code.

6   Past and Related Work

Our work is closely related to the topic of software similarity detection, which has been widely studied in the context of code plagiarism, clone detection, bug finding, and identifying zero-day vulnerability.

Static and Dynamic Analysis. There are static and dynamic approaches to analyze software similarity. Static approach analyzes the code without executing it [40], while dynamic approach run functions of the target binaries with the same input and dynamically measure similarity [13]. Among many static approaches, our work is closely related to the graph-based method. [5,26,32,34,48]. Graph-based methods parse code into CFGs whose subtrees are searched using different graph matching techniques to obtain matching pairs. Lim and Nagarakatte [32] checked for equivalence using a graph-based methodology and symbolic execution. However, this work focused specifically on cryptographic algorithms and does not deal with diversified binaries.

Equivalence Checking Using Symbolic Execution. Various research projects use symbolic execution to prove equivalence, such as BinHunt [16], KLEE [39], and many others [33,38,44]. KLEE checks, among others, code equivalence. However, this work is source-code based. The most similar work to ours is BinHunt, where the authors propose a technique based on backtracking to find semantical differences in binaries that have different register allocation and basic block reordering. However, they do not deal with instruction reordering and stack-frame shuffling. Moreover, they do not provide a formal definition of their soundness criterion and therefore do not show what class of properties is preserved between the vanilla and the diversified binaries. The other papers are similar in that their focus lies on different subjects such as finding bugs or equivalence checking between cross-architecture. Lastly, CoP [35] is a code-obfuscation resilient work that searches for the semantical difference of the original and the suspicious binary. However, CoP approximates the similarity between the binaries and reports a score indicating the likelihood that the original binary's components will be reused. This is different from our work as we check and prove the functional equivalence between the binaries.

Learning-Based Analysis. In recent years, there has been significant research on applying learning-based techniques such as machine learning [30,37,42], deep neural networks [33,48], and natural language processing [50] for similarity detection. Although learning-based methods are efficient and show promising results, they require extraneous training of an available dataset. Moreover, pre-processing necessary information for different diversification techniques is difficult due to the uncertainty of target modification. Hence, learning-based binary similarity detection is not yet resilient concerning code diversification techniques.

Low-Level Formal Verification. Formal verification of low-level code (e.g., assembly Language) has been an active research field for decades [8,49]. CompCert [29] is a formally verified compiler which provides the guarantee that safety properties proved on the source code hold for executable. However, to the best of our knowledge, CompCert cannot be used for binary diversification.

Address Space Layout Randomization. Address Space Layout Randomization (ASLR) is a widely deployed code diversification technique. ASLR randomly arranges the addresses of various parts of a process without major modifications to the actual binary; instead, the operating system ensures diversification at execution time. In other words, it executes the *same* binary in different ways. Our methodology thus does not apply to ASLR, as our methodology is targeted towards establishing equivalence between two *different* binaries.

7   Conclusion

Code diversification is a security technique that produces multiple binaries that are different but semantically equal. This paper presents the first scalable and automated technique to establish the soundness of a diversification tool. Soundness is expressed by establishing an equivalence relation between vanilla and diversified binary. The technique is based on disassembly, symbolic execution, establishing stack-pointer related invariants, and establishing mappings between memory regions in both the vanilla and the diversified world. Overall, our work provides proof of semantical equivalence between roughly 87% and 96% of the text sections in the binaries. Our work's main limitation is indirect branching (e.g., indirect jumps) due to dynamically computed addresses. We aim to resolve these limitations for future work.

Acknowledgement. Project information can be found at: https://llrm-project.org/. All source codes and scripts are available at: https://github.com/jjang3/NFM_2021. This work is supported in part by the US Office of Naval Research (ONR) under grant N00014-17-1-2297 and NSWCDD/NEEC under grant N00174-20-1-0009.

References

1. Baier, C., Katoen, J.P.: Principles of Model Checking. Representation and Mind Series. The MIT Press, Cambridge (2008)

2. Bhatkar, S., DuVarney, D.C., Sekar, R.: Address obfuscation: an efficient approach to combat a board range of memory error exploits. In: Proceedings of the 12th Conference on USENIX Security Symposium - Volume 12, SSYM 2003, p. 8. USENIX Association, USA (2003)

3. Bhatkar, S., Sekar, R., DuVarney, D.C.: Efficient techniques for comprehensive protection from memory error exploits. In: Proceedings of the 14th Conference on USENIX Security Symposium - Volume 14, SSYM 2005, p. 17. USENIX Association, USA (2005)

4. Browne, M., Clarke, E., Grümberg, O.: Characterizing finite Kripke structures in propositional temporal logic. Theor. Comput. Sci. **59**(1), 115–131 (1988). https://doi.org/10.1016/0304-3975(88)90098-9

5. Chae, D.K., Ha, J., Kim, S.W., Kang, B., Im, E.G.: Software plagiarism detection: a graph-based approach. In: Proceedings of the 22nd ACM International Conference on Information & Knowledge Management, CIKM 2013, pp. 1577–1580. ACM, New York (2013). https://doi.org/10.1145/2505515.2507848

6. Checkoway, S., Davi, L., Dmitrienko, A., Sadeghi, A.R., Shacham, H., Winandy, M.: Return-oriented programming without returns. In: Proceedings of the 17th ACM Conference on Computer and Communications Security, CCS 2010, pp. 559–572. ACM, New York (2010). https://doi.org/10.1145/1866307.1866370

7. Churchill, B., Padon, O., Sharma, R., Aiken, A.: Semantic program alignment for equivalence checking. In: Proceedings of the 40th ACM SIGPLAN Conference on Programming Language Design and Implementation, PLDI 2019, pp. 1027–1040. ACM, New York (2019). https://doi.org/10.1145/3314221.3314596

8. Clutterbuck, D.L., Carré, B.A.: The verification of low-level code. Softw. Eng. J. **3**(3), 97–111 (1988). https://doi.org/10.1049/sej.1988.0012

9. Cohen, F.B.: Operating System Protection Through Program Evolution, vol. 12, pp. 565–584. Elsevier Advanced Technology Publications, GBR (1993). https://doi.org/10.1016/0167-4048(93)90054-9

10. Crane, S., Homescu, A., Larsen, P.: Code randomization: haven't we solved this problem yet? In: 2016 IEEE Cybersecurity Development (SecDev), pp. 124–129 (2016)

11. Crane, S., et al.: Readactor: practical code randomization resilient to memory disclosure. In: Proceedings of the 2015 IEEE Symposium on Security and Privacy, SP 2015, pp. 763–780. IEEE Computer Society, Washington, DC (2015). https://doi.org/10.1109/SP.2015.52

12. David, Y., Partush, N., Yahav, E.: Statistical similarity of binaries. In: Proceedings of the 37th ACM SIGPLAN Conference on Programming Language Design and Implementation, PLDI 2016, pp. 266–280. ACM, New York (2016) https://doi.org/10.1145/2908080.2908126

13. Egele, M., Woo, M., Chapman, P., Brumley, D.: Blanket execution: dynamic similarity testing for program binaries and components. In: 23rd USENIX Security Symposium (USENIX Security 2014), San Diego, CA, pp. 303–317. USENIX Association, August 2014

14. Fernandez, J.C., Mounier, L.: Verifying bisimulations "on the fly". FORTE. **90**, 95–110 (1990)

15. Forrest, S., Somayaji, A., Ackley, D.: Building diverse computer systems. In: Proceedings of the 6th Workshop on Hot Topics in Operating Systems (HotOS-VI), HOTOS 1997, p. 67. IEEE Computer Society, Washington, DC (1997). https://doi.org/10.1109/hotos.1997.595185

16. Gao, D., Reiter, M.K., Song, D.: BinHunt: automatically finding semantic differences in binary programs. In: Chen, L., Ryan, M.D., Wang, G. (eds.) ICICS 2008. LNCS, vol. 5308, pp. 238–255. Springer, Heidelberg (2008). https://doi.org/10.1007/978-3-540-88625-9_16

17. Giuffrida, C., Kuijsten, A., Tanenbaum, A.S.: Enhanced operating system security through efficient and fine-grained address space randomization. In: Proceedings of the 21st USENIX Conference on Security Symposium, Security 2012, p. 40. USENIX Association, USA (2012)

18. Hiser, J., Nguyen-Tuong, A., Co, M., Hall, M., Davidson, J.W.: ILR: where'd my gadgets go? In: 2012 IEEE Symposium on Security and Privacy, pp. 571–585 (2012)

19. Hiser, J., Nguyen-Tuong, A., Hawkins, W., McGill, M., Co, M., Davidson, J.: Zipr++: exceptional binary rewriting. In: Proceedings of the 2017 Workshop on Forming an Ecosystem Around Software Transformation, FEAST 2017, pp. 9–15. Association for Computing Machinery, New York (2017). https://doi.org/10.1145/3141235.3141240

20. Homescu, A., Neisius, S., Larsen, P., Brunthaler, S., Franz, M.: Profile-guided automated software diversity. In: Proceedings of the 2013 IEEE/ACM International Symposium on Code Generation and Optimization (CGO), CGO 2013, pp. 1–11. IEEE Computer Society, Washington, DC (2013). https://doi.org/10.1109/CGO.2013.6494997

21. Hosseinzadeh, S., et al.: Diversification and obfuscation techniques for software security: a systematic literature review. Inf. Softw. Technol. **104**, 72–93 (2018)

22. Jackson, T., Homescu, A., Crane, S., Larsen, P., Brunthaler, S., Franz, M.: Diversifying the software stack using randomized NOP insertion. In: Jajodia, S., Ghosh, A.K., Subrahmanian, V.S., Swarup, V., Wang, C., Wang, X.S. (eds.) Moving Target Defense. Advances in Information Security, vol. 100, pp. 151–173. Springer, New York (2013). https://doi.org/10.1007/978-1-4614-5416-8_8

23. Jackson, T., et al.: Compiler-Generated Software Diversity. In: Jajodia, S., Ghosh, A., Swarup, V., Wang, C., Wang, X. (eds.) Moving Target Defense. Advances in Information Security, vol. 54, pp. 77–98. Springer, New York (2011). https://doi.org/10.1007/978-1-4614-0977-9_4

24. Junod, P., Rinaldini, J., Wehrli, J., Michielin, J.: Obfuscator-LLVM - software protection for the masses. In: Wyseur, B. (ed.) Proceedings of the IEEE/ACM 1st International Workshop on Software Protection, SPRO 2015, Firenze, Italy, 19th May 2015, pp. 3–9. IEEE (2015). https://doi.org/10.1109/SPRO.2015.10

25. Kil, C., Jun, J., Bookholt, C., Xu, J., Ning, P.: Address space layout permutation (ASLP): towards fine-grained randomization of commodity software. In: 2006 22nd Annual Computer Security Applications Conference (ACSAC 2006), pp. 339–348 (2006)

26. Komondoor, R., Horwitz, S.: Using slicing to identify duplication in source code. In: Cousot, P. (ed.) SAS 2001. LNCS, vol. 2126, pp. 40–56. Springer, Heidelberg (2001). https://doi.org/10.1007/3-540-47764-0_3

27. Koo, H., Chen, Y., Lu, L., Kemerlis, V.P., Polychronakis, M.: Compiler-assisted code randomization. In: 2018 IEEE Symposium on Security and Privacy (SP), pp. 461–477, May 2018. https://doi.org/10.1109/SP.2018.00029

28. Larsen, P., Homescu, A., Brunthaler, S., Franz, M.: SoK: automated software diversity. In: 2014 IEEE Symposium on Security and Privacy, pp. 276–291, May 2014. https://doi.org/10.1109/SP.2014.25

29. Leroy, X.: Formal verification of a realistic compiler. Commun. ACM **52**(7), 107–115 (2009). https://doi.org/10.1145/1538788.1538814

30. Li, L., Feng, H., Zhuang, W., Meng, N., Ryder, B.: CCLearner: a deep learning-based clone detection approach. In: 2017 IEEE International Conference on Software Maintenance and Evolution (ICSME), pp. 249–260, September 2017. https://doi.org/10.1109/ICSME.2017.46

31. Liang, Yu., et al.: Stack layout randomization with minimal rewriting of Android binaries. In: Kwon, S., Yun, A. (eds.) ICISC 2015. LNCS, vol. 9558, pp. 229–245. Springer, Cham (2016). https://doi.org/10.1007/978-3-319-30840-1_15

32. Lim, J.P., Nagarakatte, S.: Automatic equivalence checking for assembly implementations of cryptography libraries, pp. 37–49 (2019). https://doi.org/10.1109/cgo.2019.8661180

33. Liu, B., et al.: αdiff: cross-version binary code similarity detection with DNN. In: Proceedings of the 33rd ACM/IEEE International Conference on Automated Software Engineering, ASE 2018, pp. 667–678. ACM, New York (2018). https://doi.org/10.1145/3238147.3238199

34. Liu, C., Chen, C., Han, J., Yu, P.S.: GPLAG: detection of software plagiarism by program dependence graph analysis. In: Proceedings of the 12th ACM SIGKDD International Conference on Knowledge Discovery and Data Mining, KDD 2006, pp. 872–881. ACM, New York (2006). https://doi.org/10.1145/1150402.1150522

35. Luo, L., Ming, J., Wu, D., Liu, P., Zhu, S.: Semantics-based obfuscation-resilient binary code similarity comparison with applications to software plagiarism detection. In: Proceedings of the 22Nd ACM SIGSOFT International Symposium on Foundations of Software Engineering, FSE 2014, pp. 389–400. ACM, New York (2014). https://doi.org/10.1145/2635868.2635900

36. Pappas, V., Polychronakis, M., Keromytis, A.D.: Practical software diversification using in-place code randomization. In: Jajodia, S., Ghosh, A., Subrahmanian, V., Swarup, V., Wang, C., Wang, X. (eds.) Moving Target Defense II. Advances in Information Security, vol. 100. Springer, New York (2013). https://doi.org/10.1007/978-1-4614-5416-8_9

37. Peng, H., Mou, L., Li, G., Liu, Y., Zhang, L., Jin, Z.: Building program vector representations for deep learning. In: Zhang, S., Wirsing, M., Zhang, Z. (eds.) KSEM 2015. LNCS (LNAI), vol. 9403, pp. 547–553. Springer, Cham (2015). https://doi.org/10.1007/978-3-319-25159-2_49

38. Pewny, J., Garmany, B., Gawlik, R., Rossow, C., Holz, T.: Cross-architecture bug search in binary executables. In: 2015 IEEE Symposium on Security and Privacy, pp. 709–724, May 2015. https://doi.org/10.1109/SP.2015.49

39. Ramos, D.A., Engler, D.R.: Practical, low-effort equivalence verification of real code. In: Gopalakrishnan, G., Qadeer, S. (eds.) CAV 2011. LNCS, vol. 6806, pp. 669–685. Springer, Heidelberg (2011). https://doi.org/10.1007/978-3-642-22110-1_55

40. Roy, C.K., Cordy, J.R., Koschke, R.: Comparison and evaluation of code clone detection techniques and tools: a qualitative approach. Sci. Comput. Program. **74**(7), 470–495 (2009). https://doi.org/10.1016/j.scico.2009.02.007

41. Shacham, H.: The geometry of innocent flesh on the bone: return-into-libc without function calls (on the x86). In: Proceedings of the 14th ACM Conference on Computer and Communications Security, CCS 2007, pp. 552–561. ACM, New York (2007). https://doi.org/10.1145/1315245.1315313

42. Shalev, N., Partush, N.: Binary similarity detection using machine learning. In: Proceedings of the 13th Workshop on Programming Languages and Analysis for Security, PLAS 2018, pp. 42–47. ACM, New York (2018). https://doi.org/10.1145/3264820.3264821

43. Shoshitaishvili, Y., et al.: SOK: (state of) the art of war: offensive techniques in binary analysis. In: 2016 IEEE Symposium on Security and Privacy (SP), pp. 138–157 (2016)
44. Siegel, S.F., Mironova, A., Avrunin, G.S., Clarke, L.A.: Using model checking with symbolic execution to verify parallel numerical programs. In: Proceedings of the 2006 International Symposium on Software Testing and Analysis, ISSTA 2006, pp. 157–168. ACM, New York (2006). https://doi.org/10.1145/1146238.1146256
45. Wang, R., et al.: Ramblr: making reassembly great again. In: The Network and Distributed System Security Symposium, NDSS 2017 (2017). https://doi.org/10.14722/ndss.2017.23225
46. Wang, S., Wang, P., Wu, D.: Composite software diversification. In: 2017 IEEE International Conference on Software Maintenance and Evolution (ICSME), pp. 284–294 (2017)
47. Wartell, R., Mohan, V., Hamlen, K.W., Lin, Z.: Binary stirring: self-randomizing instruction addresses of legacy x86 binary code. In: Proceedings of the 2012 ACM Conference on Computer and Communications Security, CCS 2012, pp. 157–168. Association for Computing Machinery, New York (2012). https://doi.org/10.1145/2382196.2382216
48. Xu, X., Liu, C., Feng, Q., Yin, H., Song, L., Song, D.: Neural network-based graph embedding for cross-platform binary code similarity detection. In: Proceedings of the 2017 ACM SIGSAC Conference on Computer and Communications Security, CCS 2017, pp. 363–376. ACM, New York (2017). https://doi.org/10.1145/3133956.3134018
49. Xu, Z., Miller, B.P., Reps, T.: Safety checking of machine code. In: Proceedings of the ACM SIGPLAN 2000 Conference on Programming Language Design and Implementation, PLDI 2000, pp. 70–82. ACM, New York (2000). https://doi.org/10.1145/349299.349313
50. Zuo, F., Li, X., Zhang, Z., Young, P., Luo, L., Zeng, Q.: Neural machine translation inspired binary code similarity comparison beyond function pairs. CoRR abs/1808.04706 (2018). https://arxiv.org/abs/1808.04706

Scalable Reliability Analysis by Lazy Verification

Shahid Khan[1]([✉])[iD], Joost-Pieter Katoen[1][iD], Matthias Volk[1][iD],
and Marc Bouissou[2][iD]

[1] RWTH Aachen University, Aachen, Germany
{shahid.khan,katoen,matthias.volk}@cs.rwth-aachen.de
[2] Électricité de France, Palaiseau, France
marc.bouissou@edf.fr

Abstract. This paper presents an iterative method to analyse system reliability models. The key idea is to analyse a partial state space of a reliability model in a conservative and an optimistic manner. By considering unexplored states as being always operational or, dually, already failed, our analysis yields sound upper- and lower-bounds on the system's reliability. This approach is applied in an iterative manner until the desired precision is obtained. We present details of our approach for Boolean-logic driven Markov processes (BDMPs), an expressive fault tree variant intensively used in analysing energy systems. Based on a prototypical implementation on top of the probabilistic model checker STORM, we experimentally compare our technique to two alternative BDMP analysis techniques: discrete-event simulation obtaining statistical bounds, and a recent closed-form technique for obtaining pessimistic system lifetimes. Our experiments show that mostly only a fragment of the state space needs to be investigated enabling the reliability analysis of models that could not be handled before.

1 Introduction

Reliability Analysis of Safety-Critical Systems. Reliability analysis is concerned with analysing system models to determine measures-of-interest such as the mean-time-to-failure (MTTF) and the system's reliability, i.e., the probability that the system is continuously operational up to a given mission time? Model-based analysis such as the numerical evaluation of Markov chains suffer from the state-space explosion problem. A possible remedy is discrete-event simulation. Simulation is applicable to a large class of reliability models, e.g., it supports general failure and repair rates, and has a low memory footprint as only the current model state needs to be kept in memory. Simulation results though come with statistical bounds only[1] and excessively many simulation runs are needed for rare events, events that happen with very low probability. Failures in safety-critical

---

S. Khan—supported by a HEC-DAAD scholarship.
[1] Known as confidence intervals.

© Springer Nature Switzerland AG 2021
A. Dutle et al. (Eds.): NFM 2021, LNCS 12673, pp. 180–197, 2021.
https://doi.org/10.1007/978-3-030-76384-8_12

systems such as autonomous cars, nuclear power plants, satellites, launchers, etc., are (supposed to be) rare events, and standards such as ISO 26262 require hard guarantees—safe lower- and upper-bounds.

Lazy Verification. The challenge is to come up with a reliability analysis technique that provides hard guarantees, can deal with rare events, and preferably provides results with numerical accuracy.

This paper proposes to use *lazy verification* for reliability analysis. The idea is conceptually simple: generate a *partial* state space of a reliability model description and carry out a fast analysis that takes a conservative and an optimistic perspective. By considering unexplored states as being always operational or, dually, already failed, the analysis yields a sound upper- and lower-bound (*ub* and *lb*) on the system's reliability, see Fig. 1. Fast analysis is done using the state-of-the-art probabilistic

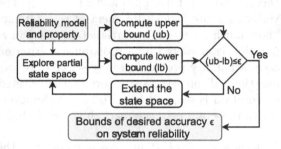

Fig. 1. Lazy verification for reliability

model-checking techniques [2,4,25] for continuous-time Markov models. If the gap between the lower and upper-bound is below an a priori user-defined tolerance ε, i.e., $ub\text{-}lb \leq \varepsilon$, the analysis halts: the system reliability is certainly between these bounds. In case the results are not tight enough, $ub\text{-}lb > \varepsilon$, the partial state space is extended with some unexplored states. This iterative approach thus has a *lazy* character: only a state-space fragment required to obtain the system's reliability (or measures such as MTTF) with a given accuracy is generated and explored.

Lazy Verification of BDMPs. Our lazy approach is applicable to a wide range of *dynamic* reliability models, in particular those containing *state-dependent* failure mechanisms such as temporal orderings, spare management, and failure dependencies. This includes, e.g., dynamic fault trees [17], state-event fault trees [24], dynamic reliability block diagrams [16], and Pandora temporal fault trees [31]. Our lazy verification approach is also applicable to the *static* (non-state-dependent) reliability models such as static fault trees and reliability block diagrams. However, our approach will not be competitive to the binary decision diagram-based analysis of these models. We present details of our lazy verification approach for *Boolean logic-driven Markov processes* (BDMPs), an expressive dynamic fault tree variant extensively used by engineers at Électricité de France (EDF) [9]. EDF is one of the world's largest producers of electricity and is active in technologies such as nuclear power, hydropower, wind power, solar and geothermal energy. BDMPs contain VOTing gates (generalisation of AND and OR gates), priority AND-gates, basic events that model system components whose lifetime is exponentially distributed, instantaneous events, and two forms of triggers. While the general definition of BDMPs in [9] allows the use of arbitrary Markov processes for defining basic events, we restrict ourselves to the commonly used exponential distributions. The semantics of BDMPs has been translated into Markov automaton in [26], and generalised stochastic Petri nets in [27]. The underlying stochastic process of a BDMP is a continuous-time Markov chain (CTMC). Polynomial-time model-checking algorithms for computing lifetimes on CTMCs have been given [4] and are part of probabilistic model checkers such as PRISM [28] and STORM [22]. The main questions for lazy BDMP verification are "which fragment of the state space needs to be explored?" and "how much to extend a partial state space in an iteration of Fig. 1?" The first question is answered by a probabilistic criterion, i.e., the states with the highest reachability probabilities are selected for exploration. Regarding the second question, all one-step-successors of the selected state(s) are explored and the exploration is stopped based on an exploration threshold, e.g., if all remaining states in iteration i have reachability probability $< 2^{-i}$.

Experimental Evaluation. We implemented the BDMP lazy verification approach on top of the probabilistic model checker STORM [22] whose performance is among the best as witnessed in recent tool competitions (see qcomp.org). Distinguishing features of STORM are its modular set-up enabling the rapid exchange of solvers, its facility to generate counterexamples, and its support for multiple modelling languages such as the reliability models dynamic fault trees and BDMPs. To validate our results, we compare to a free discrete-event simulation tool [7]. To indicate the "goodness" of the obtained bounds, we compare to initiator and all barriers (I&AB), a recent closed-form technique for obtaining pessimistic system reliability of BDMPs [11][2]. We distinguish between *non-repairable* and *repairable* reliability models, as some analysis techniques perform better for a particular class. The main findings of the experimental evaluation:

- Exploring small state-space fragments mostly suffices, in particular for repairable models. This extends the findings of lazy verification of dynamic fault trees that do not include repairs, as in [29].
- Reliability model sizes that could not be handled before come within range.
- In contrast to I&AB, lazy verification is generally applicable (non-repairable and repairable models, arbitrary mission times, acyclic models, and models with loops), and provides sound *lower-* and *upper-bounds* within a given accuracy ε.

Note that solving reliability models is much more difficult when the model includes repairs, for several reasons:

- Merging failure states into a single state is not correct for repairs any more, because these states are usually associated with different repair rates.

---

[2] https://www.lr.org/en/riskspectrum/support-and-downloads/#accordion-rsat3.4.5 released(riskspectrumpsa1.4.0/rsat3.4.5)(15june2020).

- The existence of repairs can create new states that cannot be reached from the initial state by a path containing only failures. This is exemplified by the case of the PAND-gate given in Sect. 2.
- The failure and repair rates usually differ by several orders of magnitude creating stiffness problems for solvers based on matrix calculations.

2 Boolean Logic-Driven Markov Processes

This section briefly explains the main principles of BDMPs; for more details we refer to [9]. BDMPs extend static fault trees with triggers and associate a pair of CTMCs with leaves to model various failure modes. Triggers model activation mechanisms that are useful to model dynamic failure dependencies, e.g., failure on-demand, mutual exclusion, and causal failure dependencies. Semantically, BDMPs augment the *failure* predicate of static fault trees with *activation* and *trimming* predicates. While activation predicates govern the activation status (active or dormant) of BDMP elements, the trimming predicates curtail the BDMP's state space, e.g., by inhibiting the failure of non-failed inputs of OR-gates once the gate fails. (If such input is shared with other parts of the BDMP, then it is not pruned.) Fig. 2 depicts the main BDMP elements.

Gates (the first row of Fig. 2). A VOT-gate has two parameters: the number N of inputs and the number $1 \leq K \leq N$ of inputs that need to fail for the VOT gate to fail. The gate is repaired once the number of input failures is below K. The AND-and OR-gates are special cases of VOT with $K = N$ and $K = 1$, respectively. The priority-AND (PAND) gate fails once both its inputs fail in a left-to-right order. Simultaneous input failures of PAND do not lead to a gate failure. (Other fault tree variants use inclusive PAND [23].) Four repair strategies for PAND exist in BDMPs: (1) on

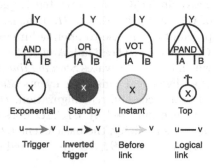

Fig. 2. BDMP elements

the repair of the first input (*repair-first*), (2) on the repair of the second input (*repair-last*), (3) on the repair of both inputs (*repair-all*), or (4) on the repair of any input (*repair-any*).

Basic events (the second row of Fig. 2). The EXP-type basic events fail and are repaired following an exponential distribution. They can fail only in active mode; their repair is independent of their activation status. The STDBY-type basic events can switch between active and passive failure rates depending on their activation status. The INST-type basic events fail upon activation with probability γ. The repair behavior of both STDBY and INST is the same as for EXP. The failure of the top event TOP represents the system's failure.

Triggers and links (the third row of Fig. 2). The trigger TRIG activates its target when its source fails and if at least one parent of TRIG's target is active.

The inverted trigger InvTRIG achieves the inverse behavior, i.e., it activates the target node when at least one parent of the target node is active and the origin of InvTRIG is not failed. The BeforeLINK forces an order on simultaneously enabled INST leaves to reduce the number of combinations to be examined thanks to the trimming mechanism. The LogicLINK propagates the failure and activation status among BDMP elements.

Example 1. As a running example we consider a reconfiguration strategy adopted from [11]. The system, see Fig. 3 (left), has two power sources for the *Main_line*: (1) a *Grid*, and (2) a diesel generator *Dies_gen*. The red dotted line indicates the reconfiguration strategy. Initially, the *Normal_line* is active and powers the *Main_line*. On its failure, the load is switched to the *Standby_line*. A repair will switch back the load to the *Normal_line*. Reconfigurations are realised by circuit breakers; they can fail due to: (1) inadvertent failure during normal operation, (2) a refuse-to-open failure, or (3) a refuse-to-close failure. The latter two modes are failure on-demand as they happen while switching the load from the *Normal_line* to *Standby_line* and vice versa. *Dies_gen* has two failure modes: failure in-operation, and failure on-demand. Whereas, *Grid* can only fail in-operation.

A BDMP model is shown in Fig. 3 (right). The red (blue) arrow represents TRIG (InvTRIG). The inverted trigger models mutually exclusive failure modes of the circuit breaker *CB1*. That is, the inadvertent opening of *CB1* (*CB1_IO*) preempts its refuse-to-open failure mode *CB1_RO*. In the BDMP, initially either *Grid* or *CB1_IO* can fail. Any of these failures causes a failure of *Normal_line_fail*, which in turn activates *Standby_line_fail*. This also activates its children. A failure of an INST leaf causes the events *Standby_line_fail* and the *Main_line_fail* to fail. After a successful reconfiguration, *Dies_gen* can fail. We point out that a failing sequence initiated by *CB1_IO* does not lead to *CB1_RO* being tested. For the sake of simplicity, the basic event *CB2_IO* is omitted from the model. Moreover, *CB2_RO* and *CB1_RC* are omitted due to their negligible failure probability.

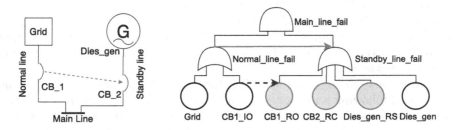

Fig. 3. Running example of a system (left) and a BDMP modeling it (right) (Color figure online)

3 Lazy Probabilistic Verification

This section introduces the partial state-space exploration for continuous-time Markov chains (CTMCs), the underlying model of BDMPs. CTMCs are finite transition systems with a designated initial state, whose transitions are labelled with rates (positive reals) of exponential distributions. For state s with transition rates $R(s, u) = \lambda$ and $R(s, v) = \mu$, say, the probability to move from s to u is $\lambda/\lambda+\mu$, and the state residence time is random: the probability to stay for t time units in s equals $1-e^{-(\lambda+\mu)\cdot t}$. To enable CTMC analysis by model checking [4], states are labelled with sets of atomic propositions.

3.1 State-Space Generation

The (compositional) semantics of BDMPs in terms of CTMCs is fully explained in [26, 27]. We present the general idea by an example.

Example 2 (CTMC for BDMP). Consider again the BDMP in Fig. 3 (right). Figure 5 depicts a fragment of its corresponding CTMC. Initially, the BDMP elements *Grid* and *CB1_IO* can fail. The initial state thus has two outgoing transitions labelled with the failure rates of *Grid* and *CB1_IO*. The failure of *Grid* causes the testing of three independent Bernoulli trials through the trigger. Thus, the failure of *Grid* is succeeded by $2^3 = 8$ probabilistic transitions. The failure of *CB1_IO* causes two independent Bernoulli trials, as testing of *CB1_RO* is inhibited by the inverted trigger. We combine these probabilistic transitions to the preceding exponential transitions. This gives rise to 12 outgoing transitions in the initial state, e.g., s_1 represents the scenario where *CB1_IO* fails, but both instantaneous events *CB1_RO* and *CB2_RC* have not failed. The failure rate of *CB1_IO* is 0.0001 and the failure probabilities of the two instantaneous events are 0.0001. We have a transition rate of $0.0001 \cdot (1-0.0001)^2 = 9.998e^{-5}$. We indicate the failure of component *CB1_IO* by adding the corresponding label $\{CB1\_IO\}$ to state s_1. The other transition rates are obtained similarly. For state s_1, there are two possibilities: either *CB1_IO* is repaired, or *Dies_gen* fails. The transitions have rates 0.1 and 0.0001, respectively.

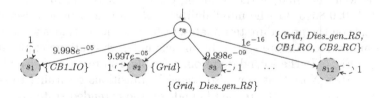

Fig. 4. State space after the first iteration

On completing the state-space generation process, the resulting CTMC is amenable to standard CTMC analysis techniques such as model checking [3].

This is supported by state-of-the-art model checkers such as STORM [22]. Time-bounded properties are important for reliability analysis. The *unreliability* is the probability of system failure within T time units. Expressed in a timed probabilistic temporal logic such as CSL [4]:

$$\mathbb{P}\left(\Diamond^{[0,\,T]} \text{ "failed"}\right),$$

where "failed" represents the failure of the top-level event in the BDMP. The *unavailability* is the probability that the system is failed at a given time point t:

$$\mathbb{P}\left(\Diamond^{[t,\,t]} \text{ "failed"}\right).$$

3.2 Lazy Verification

While efficient probabilistic model-checking algorithms exist [21], the state-space explosion remains a limiting factor. This issue can partially be mitigated by using bisimulation minimization [5], but this requires the entire state space to be generated first. We resort to partial state-space generation. This is supported by STORM to analyse *non-repairable* dynamic fault trees [29] and yields safe upper- and lower-bounds of unreliability (and other measures). In this work, we generalise this to *repairable* models described by BDMPs.

The idea is to perform *iterative* state-space exploration. Let us explain this using Fig. 4. In each iteration, we explore a certain number of unexplored states—prioritized according to some heuristic. In our example of Fig. 4, we start by first exploring the initial state s_0 which yields successor states $s_1, \ldots, s_{12}$. State s_0 is now explored (white), and all other states are discovered (gray). All discovered states are equipped with a self-loop in order to distinguish them from deadlock states. Deadlocks are attributed to modelling errors. The resulting partial state space is used to obtain safe lower and upper bounds. As both unreliability and unavailability use the label "failed" we pursue as follows. To obtain a *lower bound* lb, we mark all *explored* states that correspond to a system failure with the label "failed" and analyse the unreliability (or unavailability) of the resulting CTMC. For the *upper bound* ub, we additionally label all *discovered* states with label "failed" as well and analyse the resulting CTMC. For our example, we obtain the interval $[0, 0.8646]$ for the unreliability. If $ub - lb$ is less than a user-defined accuracy ϵ, then the procedure terminates. Otherwise, it continues with the next iteration and explores more states. In our example, we continue exploration as indicated in Fig. 5. In the second iteration, we explore states s_1 and s_2 and obtain three new states. Note that now also "repair" transitions returning to state s_0 are inserted. Computing the refined bounds on the extended state space yields $[0, 0.0044]$. (The nominal unreliability of this example is 0.0024).

"Failed" Labels for Discovered States. Note that we could have already added "failed" labels to many discovered states of the first iteration as they already represent system-level failure, e.g., state s_{12}. While this will help to significantly

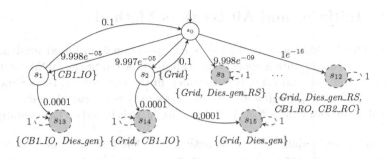

Fig. 5. State space after the second iteration

tighten the bounds for the unreliability computation, it can give non-monotonic behavior for the unavailability. A discovered state which is marked as failed can never be left due to the self-loop. However, further exploration might introduce repair transitions such that non-failed states can be reached now. In such scenarios, the lower bound for the unavailability would decrease between iterations, which could yield unsound bounds. We, thus, keep our bound differences strictly non-increasing by applying a more conservative approach for discovered states.

Exploration Heuristics. The order in which states are explored and the threshold when to stop exploration for an iteration are determined by *exploration heuristics*. We use two types of heuristics in STORM: *depth-based* and *probability-based*. The *depth-based* heuristic explores the state space up to a predefined depth, i.e., distance to the initial state. This method is beneficial if one wants to analyse a system for a certain number of consecutive failures. The *probability-based* heuristic orders the states by their probability to eventually reach the state from the initial state. That way, we give priority to states which are more likely to occur and disregard unlikely events.

In the second iteration of our example in Fig. 5, we explored states s_1 and s_2, because they have the highest incoming transition probabilities. We set the exploration threshold to 10^{-5} for iteration 2. That means, the other states are not explored in this iteration, because their probabilities are below the threshold.

Proposition 1. *The lazy verification technique provides* sound *lower and upper bounds, i.e., the exact unreliability (or unavailability) lies within* $[lb, ub]$.

This can be seen as follows. The approximation accounts for both extremes. Either all of the discovered states lead to the failure (upper bound) or none of the discovered states lead to a failure (lower bound). Moreover, the difference between the upper and the lower bounds is strictly non-increasing for increasing iterations. The algorithm terminates at the latest when the complete state space is explored. The lower and upper bound then equal the exact result (up to the machine precision) as no discovered states are present anymore.

4   The Initiator and All Barriers Method

Context. The I&AB method [10,11] is an approximation-based analysis app-roach. It aims to compute a conservative approximation of the BDMP's unrelia-bility for a given mission time. It is included in the commercial RISKSPECTRUM *PSA 1.4.0/RSAT 3.4.5* software tool to assess repairs in real-life nuclear proba-bilistic safety assessments (PSAs) (cf. footnote [4]). It is based on two assumptions:

- all standby redundancies become active upon the failure of an initiator, and
- the repair of initiator i inhibits the system failure (due to the sequence initi-ated by i).

As the I&AB method relies on the repair of initiators, it is applicable to repairable systems only. It requires the repair rates to be at least ten times higher than the failure rates. We describe the four steps of the I&AB method and demonstrate each step on the sample BDMP in Fig. 3 (right):

Step-1: Marking initiators and barriers. The I&AB method starts by partition-ing the set of basic events into *initiators* and *barriers*. Initiators are the basic events that can take the system out of its perfect state (aka: initial state). Bar-riers are basic events that get activated upon the failure of an initiator. Once an initiator fails, all non-failed initiators are—as barriers—activated.

Example 3. As *Grid* and *CB1_IO* are the only basic events that can be active at the start, we mark them as initiators. All other basic events are barriers.

Step-2: Generating minimal contents of sequences. After declaring the initiators, the I&AB method computes the *set of minimal contents of sequences* (MCSS). This set contains sequences of failures—initiated by an initiator—that cause the top event to fail. Such sequence m is minimal in the sense that none of its proper prefixes causes a top event failure. To compute the MCSS, an SFT with NOT-gates is derived from the BDMP while respecting the triggers and precedence links. A PAND-gate is replaced by an AND-gate. The minimal cut sets[3] of the SFT computed using SCRAM[4] correspond to MCSS of the BDMP.

Example 4. Applying the proprietary EDF-tool KB3[5] to our running example yields the SFT of Fig. 6. The black circles above basic events represent negated literals. The two top layers of the SFT are as in the BDMP. The top event AND *Main_line_fail* has two inputs: *Normal_line_fail*, and *Standby_line_fail*. Consider the boxed fragment of the SFT. *Normal_line_fail* occurs when either *CB1_IO* or *Grid* fails. Since they are initiators, their failures as initiators are mutually exclusive. This is captured by the negated literals, e.g., the left input of *CB1_IO* fails if *CB1_IO_init* fails and *Grid_init* does not. As *CB1_IO* is an initiator and

---

[3] A cut set of an SFT is a set of basic events that cause the top event to fail.
[4] https://github.com/rakhimov/scram.
[5] https://www.edf.fr/en/the-edf-group/who-we-are/activities/research-and-develop ment/design-codes/design-code-kb3.

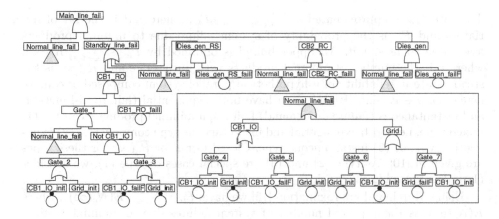

Fig. 6. SFT generated for the running example

its mode of failure switches from *init* to *failF* (failure in-function) when *Grid_init* fails, the right input of *CB1_IO* has *Grid_init* and *CB1_IO_failF* as inputs.

Now consider the right input of *Main_line_fail*, i.e., *Standby_line_fail*. The *Standby_line_fail* of Fig. 3 (right) has four components, and it is the target of a trigger. Correspondingly, four AND gates in the SFT capture the failure of each component. *Dies_gen_RS*, *CB2_RC*, and *Dies_gen* fail once the trigger source *Normal_line_fail* fails. The failure conditions of *CB1_RO* are more involved, as it is a target of an inverted trigger. The right input of *CB1_RO* depicts that *CB1_RO_failI* (*failI* is a failure on-demand) must fail for *CB1_RO* to fail. Whereas the left input of *CB1_RO* ensures that the trigger source, i.e., *Normal_line_fail* has failed and this failure is caused by *Grid*. The SFT's minimal cut sets are:

{CB1_IO_init, Dies_gen_failF}, {CB1_IO_init, Dies_gen_RS_failI},
{CB1_IO_init,
CB2_RC_failI}, {Grid_init, CB1_RO_failI}, {Grid_init, CB2_RC_failI},
{Grid_init, Dies_gen_RS_failI}, and {Grid_init, Dies_gen_failF}.

Step-3: Computing minimal products. The MCSS are arranged as *minimal products*, partial minimal sequences associated to initiators. It amounts to stripping initiator *ie* from sequence $m \in MCSS$ and designating $m \setminus ie$ as minimal product associated to *ie*. The minimal products are arranged as dictionary structure. The minimal products for MCSS are:

CB1_IO_init: {{Dies_gen_failF}, {Dies_gen_RS_failI}, {CB2_RC_failI}} and
Grid_init: {{CB1_RO_failI}, {CB2_RC_failI}, {Dies_gen_RS_failI},
{Dies_gen_failF}}.

Step-4: Computing unreliability. Based on minimal products, a closed-form formula approximates the BDMP's unreliability. To that end, the system failure distribution is assumed to be exponential, and the key is to approximate its failure rate λ_{eq}. For mission time t, the unreliability is approximated by $1 - e^{-\lambda_{eq} \cdot t}$.

The rate λ_{eq} is approximated as $\sum_{ie \in init} \lambda_{ie} \cdot P_{ie}$, where $init$ is the set of initiators and P_{ie} is the probability of system failure due to minimal products associated to $ie \in init$. An upper bound is obtained by $P_{ie} \leq \sum_{c=1}^{k} \overline{R}_c(\infty)$, where k is the number of minimal products with initiator ie and $\overline{R}_c(\infty)$ is the steady-state unreliability of a hypothetical parallel system composed of components $comp \in c$. Since BDMPs can have both exponential (failure in-function) and instantaneous (failure on-demand) failures, a minimal product c can be: (1) mixed type, i.e., both exponential and instantaneous type components, (2) exponential type, or (3) instantaneous type. Closed-forms for $\overline{R}_c(\infty)$ for these types are given in [10]. As type (2) and (3) are special cases of type (1), we consider (1) in the following.

Using Murchland approximation [15] we have: $P_{ie} \leq \sum_{c=1}^{k} E(N_c(\infty))$, where $E(N_c(\infty))$ is the expected number of system failures due to minimal product c within time interval $(0, \infty)$. Consider a minimal product c involving ℓ instantaneous and m exponential components. Let $\lambda_{c,i}$ denote the failure rate of the ith exponential component, $\gamma_{c,i}$ denote the failure probability of the ith instantaneous component and $\mu_{c,i}$ denote the repair rate of the ith component. Using $r_{c,i} = \lambda_{c,i} + \mu_{c,i}$ and $\mu_c = \mu_{c,ie} + \sum_{j=1}^{\ell} \mu_{c,j}$, where $\mu_{c,ie}$ is the repair rate of initiator ie, $E(N_c(\infty))$ equals:

$$
\overbrace{\prod_{i=1}^{\ell} \gamma_{c,i}}^{(INST)} \sum_{i=1}^{m} \lambda_{c,i} \underbrace{\left(\prod_{\substack{j=1 \\ j \neq i}}^{m} \frac{\lambda_{c,j}}{r_{c,j}} \int_{0}^{\infty} \overbrace{e^{-\sum_{k=1}^{\ell} \mu_{c,k} \cdot x}}^{INST} \sum_{\substack{j=1 \\ j \neq i}}^{m} (1 - e^{-r_{c,j}x}) dx - \prod_{j=1}^{m} \frac{\lambda_{c,j}}{r_{c,j}} \int_{0}^{\infty} \overbrace{e^{-\sum_{k=1}^{\ell} \mu_{c,k} \cdot x}}^{INST} \sum_{j=1}^{m} (1 - e^{-r_{c,j}x}) dx \right)}_{expr_1} }_{}
$$

Intuitively, $expr_1$ represents the probability that all components of c except component i failed. The term $expr_2$ represents the probability that all components of c failed. Their difference is the contribution of component i to c's failure probability. The repair of instantaneous components also contributes to these probabilities (these parts are identified by overbraces). Solving $expr_2$ yields:

$$
\frac{1}{\mu_c} - \sum_{i=1}^{m} \frac{1}{\mu_c + r_{c,i}} + \sum_{i=1}^{m} \sum_{j>i}^{m} \frac{1}{\mu_c + r_{c,i} + r_{c,j}} - \sum_{i=1}^{m} \sum_{j>i}^{m} \sum_{k>j}^{m} \frac{1}{\mu_c + r_{c,i} + r_{c,j} + r_{c,k}} + \cdots + (-1)^m \frac{1}{\mu_c + \sum_{i=1}^{m} r_{c,i}}
$$

The formula for $expr_1$ is similar except that index i is ignored.

Example 5. In our running example, let the failure rate (probability) of all exponential (instantaneous) events be 0.0001, and the repair rate be 0.1. We have that $c_1 = \{\text{Grid\_init} : \{\text{CB2\_RC\_failI}\}\}$ is instantaneous, and $c_2 = \{\text{CB1\_IO\_init}: \{\text{Dies\_gen\_failF}\}\}$ is exponential. For c_1 and c_2 we obtain:

$$
P_{Grid\_init}(c_1) = \lambda_{Grid} \cdot \gamma_{CB2\_RC\_failI} = 1 \cdot 10^{-8}, \text{ and}
$$
$$
P_{CB1\_IO\_init}(c_2) = \lambda_{CB1\_IO} \cdot E(N_{c_2}(\infty)) = 9.995 \cdot 10^{-8},
$$

where for $\lambda_1 = \lambda_{Dies\_gen\_failF}$, $\mu_1 = \mu_{Dies\_gen\_failF}$, $\mu = \mu_{CB1\_IO}$, $r_1 = \lambda_1 + \mu_1$:

$$
E(N_{c_2}(\infty)) = \lambda_1 \cdot ((1/\mu) - (\lambda_1/\mu_1 \cdot (1/\mu - 1/\mu_1 + r_1))).
$$

As there are two exponential and five instantaneous components, all of the same cardinality and equal reliability parameters:

$$\lambda_{eq} = 5 \cdot (1 \cdot 10^{-8}) + 2 \cdot (9.995 \cdot 10^{-8}) = 2.499 \cdot 10^{-7}.$$

The system unreliability for mission time $t = 10,000$ thus is: $1 - e^{-t \cdot \lambda_{eq}} = 0.0025$. (The nominal unreliability of this example is 0.0024, see Sect. 3.2.)

5   Case Studies

We first tested our implementation on 24 BDMP test cases available online[6]. Though useful as a sanity check for our implementation, the test cases are too small to meet our objective: investigating scalable analysis on real-world case studies. There is only one larger test case in the literature: a power supply of a nuclear power plant [8], so other test cases were obtained by a semi-automatic translation from DFTs to BDMPs using the approach outlined in [6]. We selected DFTs from the online DFT repository[7], and added repairs. This yields:

Dual Processor Reactor Regulation System. This DFT models a power regulator in a nuclear reactor [18]. The model available on the benchmark website is non-repairable and we adopted the repair rates from the original paper [18].

Emergency Power Supply of Nuclear Power Plant. This BDMP is given by EDF as a challenge for BDMP analysis tools [8]. The repairable model captures most of the scenarios encountered while analysing complex dynamic systems.

Railway Crossing. This DFT models a railway level crossing [20]. We consider variant $RC\_5\_5\_sc$ in this paper. It consists of 5 barriers with independent motors, 5 groups of sensors, and the controller is modeled as a single basic event.

Vehicle Guidance Case Study. These DFTs stem from an industrial case study on safety concepts from the automotive domain [19]. We extended the original (non-repairable) DFTs by adding repair rates of 0.1 to all basic events. We consider all eight variants of this test case.

Railway Station. These DFTs model the influence of infrastructure failures in German railway station areas on the routability of trains [30]. We consider all six variants and made them repairable by adding repair rates of 0.1 to all basic events. Note that this model is not yet available on the benchmark website.

Sensor Filter. This DFT is automatically synthesized from an AADL description using the Compass tool-chain [13]. We use variant sf_3_2 modelling a network consisting of three sensors and two filters.

---

[6] https://sourceforge.net/projects/visualfigaro/files/Doc_and_examples/.
[7] https://dftbenchmarks.utwente.nl/.

6   Results and Discussion

We implemented the incremental verification (Sect. 3.2) in the probabilistic
model checker STORM [22], called STORM-APPROX. We also implemented the
I&AB method (Sect. 4). We validated the outcomes of our open-source prototypical implementation with the commercial RISKSPECTRUM tool[8]. While the
results coincide for both implementations, our implementation is not competitive
in terms of computation time and scalability. (We calibrated our implementation
using [8] as the RISKSPECTRUM results were online for this test case [12].) We
compare both approaches with the Monte Carlo simulator YAMS [7] and evaluate
both repairable and non-repairable BDMPs. We use the trimming feature [9]—
which reduces the state space—to be able to treat large BDMPs. All the results
discussed in this Section are available online[9].

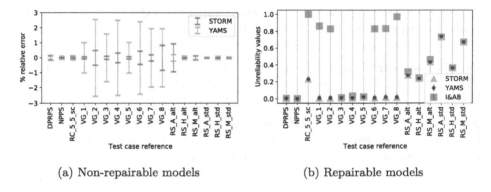

(a) Non-repairable models   (b) Repairable models

Fig. 7. Accuracy of results computed by STORM, YAMS and I&AB

6.1   Accuracy

Non-repairable Models. As the I&AB method is not applicable to non-repairable
systems, we only compare YAMS and STORM-APPROX and give the results in
Fig. 7a. Since the absolute deviations between both tools are negligible, we
plot the % deviations relative to the respective mean value. YAMS provides a
mean value and a confidence interval $[\ell, u]$. In Fig. 7a, the extremities of seg-
ments correspond to $\frac{\ell - u}{2 \cdot mean\_value} \cdot 100$ and $\frac{u - \ell}{2 \cdot mean\_value} \cdot 100$ STORM-APPROX
gives an *upper_bound* and a *lower_bound*. We compute % error bounds by using
$\frac{upper\_bound - mean\_value}{mean\_value} \cdot 100$ and $\frac{lower\_bound - mean\_value}{mean\_value} \cdot 100$ where *mean_value* is
the middle of the obtained bounds. Since we used 10^7 simulations for each test
case with YAMS, the width of the confidence interval depends on the probability

---

[8] https://www.lr.org/en/riskspectrum/.
[9] https://github.com/moves-rwth/dft-bdmp.

Table 1. Computation time and state spaces statistics

Test case	BDMP			Non-repairable				Repairable				
				State space		Comp. time		State space		Comp. Time		
	#BE	#Gates	#Trig.	#States	#Trans.	STORM	YAMS	#States	#Trans.	STORM	YAMS	I& AB*
DPRPS	40	14	1	2.7 K	5.9 K	0.54 s	30 m	2.7 K	11.5 K	1.25 s	3.28 h	1.79 s
	(Non-trimmed version)			23.6 M	50 M	4.33 h	42.2 m	67.6 K	0.22 M	59 s	3.16 h	–
NPPS	81	54	12	10.3 M	21 M	9.5 h	3.8 h	45.5 M	96.6 M	11 m	3.76 h	11.3 m
RC_5_5_sc	41	28	25	12.3 M	35.9 M	3.6 h	2.4 h	5.3 M	18.2 M	1.7 h	4.7 h	0.52 s
VG_1	73	65	35	0.68 M	1.7 M	18 m	17 m	99.8 K	0.20 M	1.8 m	1.2 h	2.75 s
VG_2	67	63	31	0.30 M	75 M	5.6 m	7 m	39.5 K	82.6 K	33.4 s	41.8 m	11.14 s
VG_3	54	50	24	0.14 M	0.38 M	2.5 m	8.2 m	26.9 K	55.9 K	19.2 s	37.3 m	1.2 s
VG_4	54	52	25	37.2 K	86 K	30.8 s	5 m	4.9 K	10.1 K	3.2 s	10.7 m	1.2 s
VG_5	55	53	27	12.3 K	32.3 K	12.9 s	5.5 m	3.1 K	6.3 K	2.4 s	14 m	0 s
VG_6	61	58	21	0.11 M	0.29 M	2.1 m	6.5 m	37.3 K	78.2 K	30.6 s	38.5 m	0.52 s
VG_7	87	80	38	4.5 M	11.3 M	1.6 h	10.3 m	0.16 M	0.32 M	2.7 m	50.3 m	0 s
VG_8	99	95	44	18.9 M	45.8 M	8.8 h	13 m	0.87 M	1.8 M	18.5 m	3.45 h	0.31 s
RS_A_alt	556	531	111	15.6 M	20.6 M	18.2 h	8.5 h	7.0 M	19 M	11.2 h	8.45 h	2 h
RS_H_alt	194	161	38	18.6 K	39.2 K	25.6 s	2 h	3.8 K	8.9 K	6.8 s	7.5 h	4.18 s
RS_M_alt	520	492	104	8.5 M	11 M	8.6 h	8.8 h	0.87 M	2.18 M	1.4 h	8.8 h	1.2 h
RS_A_std	544	466	108	113	224	0.93 s	5.3 h	1134	224	1.03 s	5.3 h	3.8 m
RS_H_std	184	142	41	41	80	0.1 s	1.1 h	41	80	0.116 s	6.8 h	1.82 s
RS_M_std	450	338	90	91	180	0.56 s	3.93 h	91	180	0.705 s	8.8 h	468 s

* I&AB computation time includes cut set computation and quantification times.

to be estimated. Figure 7a indicates that the magnitude of the unreliability values of both tools coincides. However, *the STORM bounds are significantly tighter than the simulation bounds of* YAMS with the notable exception of test case *RS_A_alt*. For this test case, STORM-APPROX took 18 h and explored 15.6 M states with 20.6 M transitions, cf. Table 1. This means that the number of states required to compute tighter bounds is too big to explore within the time-limit of 24 h.

Repairable Models. Figure 7b presents the (absolute) unreliability values obtained by STORM, YAMS and I&AB. The results of YAMS and STORM coincide. However, the results of the I&AB method are very pessimistic for six benchmarks. This is mostly due to the fact that I&AB does not work if there are looped interactions of structure functions through triggers, i.e., cyclic dependencies. Such loops inhibit the generation of SFTs for MCSS computation. One must manually break the loops by modifying the activation conditions of some instantaneous type basic events. The BDMPs of *VG*-variants contain such loops making them inappropriate for processing with I&AB. This yields trivial bounds.

6.2   Computation Time

Table 1 gives a detailed account of the model statistics and tool performances. For each test case, we list the number of BDMP elements. For both repairable and non-repairable variants, we give the explored state space sizes of STORM and the computation times required by the three tools. The error bound of STORM-APPROX is set to 10^{-3} and the number of simulations for YAMS is 10^7.

The state-space sizes might seem small at first glance, but they are the result of enabling trimming for the BDMP and partial exploration of these trimmed

state spaces. The effect of trimming can be seen for the DPRPS test case, where
the state space without trimming is several orders of magnitudes larger.

The computation times of STORM and I&AB are within a few minutes for
most of the repairable test cases whereas YAMS requires significantly more computation time. Note that some of these times could be considerably reduced by
adapting the number of simulations to the probability to be calculated. The performance of STORM and I&AB is comparable for the test cases where I&AB
returns accurate results. For *RS_M_alt*, I&AB is 5 times faster than STORM,
whereas STORM is faster on *RS_A_std*. Note that the timings for STORM are not
directly correlated to the state space sizes, compare, e.g., *NPPS* and *RC_5_5_sc*.
As failure and repair rates typically differ by at least one order of magnitude,
computing unreliability becomes expensive due to the *stiffness* of the CTMC.

The I&AB method requires more than one hour for *RS_A_alt* and *RS_M_alt*.
For both BDMPs, a high number of cut sets needs to be computed. We address
this issue using SCRAM by limiting the cardinality of a cut set. But by doing so
we introduce an error that cannot be mastered. The implementation of I&AB
in RISKSPECTRUM would be much faster and yet more precise, as it is able to
eliminate cut sets with probabilities lower than a given threshold during their
generation.

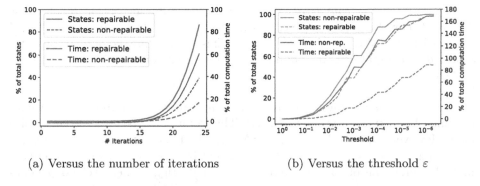

(a) Versus the number of iterations   (b) Versus the threshold ε

Fig. 8. Percentage of explored state space and computation time

6.3   Gained Insights on Lazy Verification

We provide insights into the lazy verification technique using the sensor filter
sf_3_2 test case. The observed trends for this benchmark are representative for
the other benchmarks as well. The exhaustive non-trimmed state-space of the
non-repairable (repairable) version consists of 5.19 M (5.19 M) states and 14 M
(66 M) transitions and was verified in 10 m (56 m). The (approximate) trimmed
state-space for non-repairable (repairable) case consists of the same number of
states and 14 M (50 M) transitions and verified in 18 m (50 m).

State Space Coverage Versus Number of Iterations. The first trend we studied is the percentage of the total state space explored in each iteration and the total computation time up to this iteration. The trends for both repairable and non-repairable models are shown in Fig. 8a. Both graphs are plotted for an accuracy of 10^{-3}. Interestingly, the repairable model converges faster as compared to the non-repairable version and explores fewer states. One reason is the fact that while exploring the state space, we enter the region which does not lead to system failure but both our lazy verification and BDMP trimming are agnostic of this. Such region can exist due to, e.g., fail-safe behavior of a PAND-gate.

State Space Coverage Versus Accuracy. The next trend we studied is the dependency of the state space coverage on the accuracy. Figure 8b shows that a larger percentage of the state-space is explored for increasing accuracy. After the threshold of 10^{-3}, the time for approximating the non-repairable model exceeds the verification time of the exact approach, i.e., 10 m. However, for the repairable case, the computation time is less than that required to fully explore the state space. This implies that our approximation technique, combined with the trimming feature, is more efficient for analyzing repairable systems.

Convergence of Approximate Results. Figure 9 plots the % relative errors of upper and lower bound to the exact value. We see that the bounds converge faster for increasing number of iterations and the error is negligible after 20 iterations.

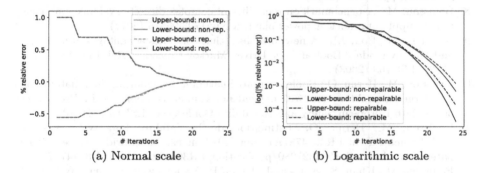

(a) Normal scale   (b) Logarithmic scale

Fig. 9. Iteration versus bound convergence

7   Conclusion

We presented an iterative verification procedure for BDMPs based on partial state-space exploration. Our evaluation shows that this approach allows scalable analysis of BDMPs while providing sound upper and lower bounds of the exact result. Our technique is applicable to other dynamic reliability models too. Lazy verification is a promising approach and we plan to further improve it by developing better exploration heuristics, e.g., using learning techniques [1,14].

References

1. Ashok, P., Butkova, Y., Hermanns, H., Křetínský, J.: Continuous-time Markov decisions based on partial exploration. In: Lahiri, S.K., Wang, C. (eds.) ATVA 2018. LNCS, vol. 11138, pp. 317–334. Springer, Cham (2018). https://doi.org/10.1007/978-3-030-01090-4_19
2. Baier, C., de Alfaro, L., Forejt, V., Kwiatkowska, M.: Model checking probabilistic systems. In: Clarke, E., Henzinger, T., Veith, H., Bloem, R. (eds.) Handbook of Model Checking, pp. 963–999. Springer, Cham (2018). https://doi.org/10.1007/978-3-319-10575-8_28
3. Baier, C., Hahn, E.M., Haverkort, B.R., Hermanns, H., Katoen, J.P.: Model checking for performability. Math. Struct. Comput. Sci. **23**(4), 751–795 (2013)
4. Baier, C., Haverkort, B.R., Hermanns, H., Katoen, J.P.: Model-checking algorithms for continuous-time Markov Chains. IEEE Trans. Softw. Eng. **29**(6), 524–541 (2003)
5. Baier, C., Katoen, J.P.: Principles of Model Checking. MIT Press, Cambridge (2008)
6. Bouissou, M.: A generalization of dynamic fault trees through Boolean logic driven markov processes (BDMP). In: Proceedings of the 16th European Safety and Reliability Conference (ESREL) (2007)
7. Bouissou, M.: A simple yet efficient acceleration technique for Monte Carlo simulation. In: Proceedings of the 22nd European Safety and Reliability Conference (ESREL), pp. 27–36 (2013)
8. Bouissou, M.: A benchmark on reliability of complex discrete systems: emergency power supply of a nuclear power plant. arXiv:1703.06575 (2017)
9. Bouissou, M., Bon, J.L.: A new formalism that combines advantages of fault-trees and Markov models: Boolean logic Driven Markov Processes. Rel. Eng. Sys. Safety **82**(2), 149–163 (2003)
10. Bouissou, M., Hernu, O.: Boolean approximation for calculating the reliability of a very large repairable system with dependencies among components. In: Proceedings of the 25th European Safety and Reliability Conference (ESREL) (2016)
11. Bouissou, M., Hernu, O.: Estimation de la fiabilite d'un systeme industriel. French Patent FR3044787A1, June 2017. https://worldwide.espacenet.com/patent/search/family/056321980/publication/FR3044787A1?q=FR3044787
12. Bouissou, M., Khan, S., Katoen, J., Krcál, P.: Various ways to quantify BDMPs. In: MARS@ETAPS. EPTCS, vol. 316, pp. 1–14 (2020)
13. Bozzano, M., Cimatti, A., Katoen, J.P., Nguyen, V.Y., Noll, T., Roveri, M.: Safety, dependability and performance analysis of extended AADL models. Comput. J. **54**(5), 754–775 (2011)
14. Brázdil, T., et al.: Verification of Markov decision processes using learning algorithms. In: Cassez, F., Raskin, J.-F. (eds.) ATVA 2014. LNCS, vol. 8837, pp. 98–114. Springer, Cham (2014). https://doi.org/10.1007/978-3-319-11936-6_8
15. Collet, J., Bruyère, F.: An efficient tool for taking repairs into account in Boolean Models. In: Probabilistic Safety Assessment and Management, vol. 4 (1998)
16. Distefano, S., Puliafito, A.: Dynamic reliability block diagrams vs dynamic fault trees. In: Annual Reliability and Maintainability Symposium (RAMS), pp. 71–76. IEEE (2007)
17. Dugan, J.B., Bavuso, S.J., Boyd, M.A.: Dynamic fault-tree models for fault-tolerant computer systems. IEEE Trans. Rel. **41**(3), 363–377 (1992)

18. Durga Rao, K., Gopika, V., Sanyasi Rao, V., Kushwaha, H., Verma, A., Srividya, A.: Dynamic fault tree analysis using Monte Carlo simulation in probabilistic safety assessment. Reliab. Eng. Syst. Saf. **94**(4), 872–883 (2009)
19. Ghadhab, M., Junges, S., Katoen, J.P., Kuntz, M., Volk, M.: Safety analysis for vehicle guidance systems with dynamic fault trees. Reliab. Eng. Syst. Saf. **186**, 37–50 (2019)
20. Guck, D., Katoen, J.P., Stoelinga, M.I., Luiten, T., Romijn, J.: Smart railroad maintenance engineering with stochastic model checking. In: Proceedings of Railways, pp. 950–953. Saxe-Coburg Publications (2014)
21. Hahn, E.M., et al.: The 2019 comparison of tools for the analysis of quantitative formal models. In: Beyer, D., Huisman, M., Kordon, F., Steffen, B. (eds.) TACAS 2019. LNCS, vol. 11429, pp. 69–92. Springer, Cham (2019). https://doi.org/10.1007/978-3-030-17502-3_5
22. Hensel, C., Junges, S., Katoen, J.P., Quatmann, T., Volk, M.: The probabilistic model checker storm. CoRR abs/2002.07080 (2020). https://arxiv.org/abs/2002.07080
23. Junges, S., Guck, D., Katoen, J.P., Stoelinga, M.: Uncovering dynamic fault trees. In: DSN, pp. 299–310. IEEE Computer Society (2016)
24. Kaiser, B., Gramlich, C., Förster, M.: State/event fault trees - a safety analysis model for software-controlled systems. Reliab. Eng. Syst. Saf. **92**(11), 1521–1537 (2007)
25. Katoen, J.P.: The probabilistic model checking landscape. In: LICS, pp. 31–45. ACM (2016). https://doi.org/10.1145/2933575.2934574
26. Khan, S., Katoen, J.-P., Bouissou, M.: A compositional semantics for repairable BDMPs. In: Casimiro, A., Ortmeier, F., Bitsch, F., Ferreira, P. (eds.) SAFECOMP 2020. LNCS, vol. 12234, pp. 82–98. Springer, Cham (2020). https://doi.org/10.1007/978-3-030-54549-9_6
27. Khan, S., Katoen, J.P., Bouissou, M.: Explaining Boolean-logic driven Markov processes using GSPNs. In: EDCC, pp. 119–126. IEEE (2020)
28. Kwiatkowska, M., Norman, G., Parker, D.: PRISM 4.0: verification of probabilistic real-time systems. In: Gopalakrishnan, G., Qadeer, S. (eds.) CAV 2011. LNCS, vol. 6806, pp. 585–591. Springer, Heidelberg (2011). https://doi.org/10.1007/978-3-642-22110-1_47
29. Volk, M., Junges, S., Katoen, J.P.: Fast dynamic fault tree analysis by model checking techniques. IEEE Trans. Ind. Inf. **14**(1), 370–379 (2018)
30. Volk, M., Weik, N., Katoen, J.-P., Nießen, N.: A DFT modeling approach for infrastructure reliability analysis of railway station areas. In: Larsen, K.G., Willemse, T. (eds.) FMICS 2019. LNCS, vol. 11687, pp. 40–58. Springer, Cham (2019). https://doi.org/10.1007/978-3-030-27008-7_3
31. Walker, M.D.: Pandora: a logic for the qualitative analysis of temporal fault trees. Ph.D. dissertation, University of Hull, Kingston upon Hull, UK (2009)

Robustifying Controller Specifications of Cyber-Physical Systems Against Perceptual Uncertainty

Tsutomu Kobayashi[1,2(✉)], Rick Salay[3], Ichiro Hasuo[2], Krzysztof Czarnecki[3], Fuyuki Ishikawa[2], and Shin-ya Katsumata[2]

[1] Japan Science and Technology Agency, Saitama, Japan
[2] National Institute of Informatics, Tokyo, Japan
{t-kobayashi,hasuo,f-ishikawa,s-katsumata}@nii.ac.jp
[3] University of Waterloo, Waterloo, Canada
{rsalay,kczarnec}@gsd.uwaterloo.ca

Abstract. Formal reasoning on the safety of controller systems interacting with plants is complex because developers need to specify behavior while taking into account perceptual uncertainty. To address this, we propose an automated workflow that takes an Event-B model of an uncertainty-unaware controller and a specification of uncertainty as input. First, our workflow automatically injects the uncertainty into the original model to obtain an uncertainty-aware but potentially unsafe controller. Then, it automatically robustifies the controller so that it satisfies safety even under the uncertainty. The case study shows how our workflow helps developers to explore multiple levels of perceptual uncertainty. We conclude that our workflow makes design and analysis of uncertainty-aware controller systems easier and more systematic.

Keywords: Controller systems · Perceptual uncertainty · Robustness · Event-B

1 Introduction

The core function of controller systems is perceiving the state of the plant and taking appropriate actions to satisfy desirable properties of the plant. In reality, however, such interactions have uncertainty. Particularly, *perceptual uncertainty*, namely the gap between the *true value* of the plant and a *perceived value* is significant, because basing a controller's action on an incorrect state can cause safety risk. For example, misperceiving the position of a car ahead may make the difference between a collision and safely following it [12]. Therefore, for safety,

The work is supported by JST ERATO HASUO Metamathematics for Systems Design Project (No. JPMJER1603) and JSPS KAKENHI grant number 19K20249. TK is supported by JST ACT-I (No. JPMJPR17UA). RS and KC are partly supported by NSERC Discovery and DND Supplement Grants.

© Springer Nature Switzerland AG 2021
A. Dutle et al. (Eds.): NFM 2021, LNCS 12673, pp. 198–213, 2021.
https://doi.org/10.1007/978-3-030-76384-8_13

developers need to account for perceptual uncertainty when constructing controllers.

However, designing a controller to address its core requirements at the same time as addressing perceptual uncertainty can be complex. In addition, the details of perceptual uncertainty may be unclear at the design phase since they can depend on the environment where the controller system is deployed. An alternative is to add support for perceptual uncertainty to an existing controller in such a way that it provides formal safety guarantees.

In this paper, we propose a workflow for robustifying a model of an uncertainty-unaware controller against perceptual uncertainty. Specifically, the whole workflow (Fig. 1) is composed of three methods. The first method (*uncertainty injection*, Sect. 3) takes an uncertainty-unaware model of the controller and plant (*original model* $\mathcal{M}$, Sect. 2) and a specification of perceptual uncertainty (*uncertainty specification* ε) as the input, and injects ε into $\mathcal{M}$ to obtain an uncertainty-aware version, $\mathcal{M}^\varepsilon$. The model $\mathcal{M}^\varepsilon$ may be unsafe and the next two methods attempt to *robustify* it to return it to safety. The more conservative *action-preserving robustification* method is attempted first producing model $\mathcal{M}^{\varepsilon,\mathsf{pR}}$. If this model is not feasible, the more aggressive *action-repurposing robustification* method is applied to $\mathcal{M}^\varepsilon$ to obtain model $\mathcal{M}^{\varepsilon,\mathsf{rR}}$. When the level of uncertainty is too large, $\mathcal{M}^{\varepsilon,\mathsf{rR}}$ will too fail to be feasible. In this case, the developer may take other manual actions such as upgrading sensor devices to decrease the level of uncertainty or relax the safety invariant.

Our workflow assumes Event-B [1] as the modeling formalism and we have implemented the workflow as a plug-in of the IDE for Event-B (Sect. 5).

With our workflow, developers can start with constructing and analyzing controllers without considering perceptual uncertainty, and then handle the uncertainty as a second step. Moreover, the generated model of a robustified controller is suitable for analysis because it defines a set of constraints the controller should satisfy. For instance, if we use an uncertainty specification parameterized with the level of uncertainty, then the generated model is also parameterized with the level, and therefore it facilitates the exploration of different levels such as finding the maximum allowed uncertainty. We demonstrate this in Sect. 6.

Contributions and paper structure. In Sect. 2, we introduce a special sort of Event-B model of controller systems, assumed as input. In Sect. 3 and 6, we describe the following contributions, before discussing related work and concluding in Sect. 7 and 8.

- A method for injecting given perceptual uncertainty into a given model (Sect. 3).
- Two methods for automated robustification of a controller (Sect. 4).
- An implementation of the whole workflow (Sect. 5).
- A case study of analyzing the maximum allowed level of uncertainty (Sect. 6).

2   Controller-Plant Models in Event-B

We require a specific format for an input Event-B model to our workflow.

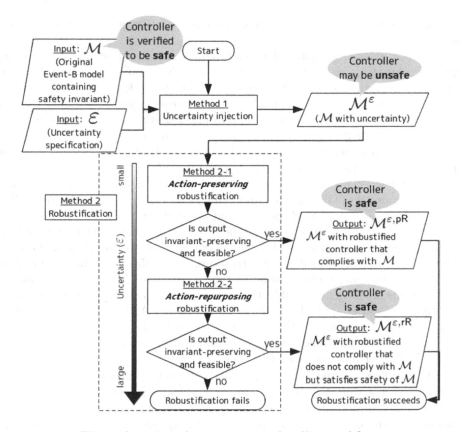

Fig. 1. Overview of our uncertainty handling workflow

```
1    Machine M
2        State space S
3        Invariants
4            Safety invariant Iˢ ⊆ S
5        Initial states A₀ ⊆ S
6        Transition function π : S → P(S), given by
7            π(s) = ⋃{ Aᵢᵖ(s,p) | i ∈ [1, Nₚ], s ∈ S, p ∈ Pᵢᵖ, Gᵢᵖ(s,p) }    where
                    ∪⋃{ Aᵢᶜ(s,p) | i ∈ [1, Nᶜ], s ∈ S, p ∈ Pᵢᶜ, Gᵢᶜ(s,p) },
8            Plant event Eᵢᵖ (where i ∈ [1, Nₚ])
9                Parameter set Pᵢᵖ
10               Guard Gᵢᵖ ⊆ S × Pᵢᵖ
11               Action Aᵢᵖ : S × Pᵢᵖ → P(S)
12           Controller event Eᵢᶜ (where i ∈ [1, Nᶜ])
13               Parameter set Pᵢᶜ
14               Guard Gᵢᶜ ⊆ S × Pᵢᶜ
15               Action Aᵢᶜ : S × Pᵢᶜ → P(S)
16       Subject to partitioning: ∀s ∈ S. ∃!i ∈ [1, Nᶜ]. ∃p ∈ Pᵢᶜ. Gᵢᶜ(s,p)
```

Fig. 2. A controller-plant model $\mathcal{M}$

Definition 1 (A controller-plant model). A *controller-plant model* $\mathcal{M}$ is an Event-B model that follows the format shown in Fig. 2.

In essence, an Event-B model is a transition system $(\mathcal{S}, \pi \colon \mathcal{S} \to \mathcal{P}(\mathcal{S}))$ with a designated set A_0 of initial states, equipped with *invariants* $I \subseteq \mathcal{S}$ that are meant to be transition-preserved (i.e., $s \in I \implies \pi(s) \subseteq I$). (In an Event-B model, "invariants" are something stated as invariants and checked if they are indeed transition-preserved—see Definition 2.) In Event-B, transitions are specified by *events* E_i, each coming with a parameter set P_i, a guard G_i (the transition is enabled if the guard is true), and a function $A_i \colon \mathcal{S} \times P_i \to \mathcal{P}(\mathcal{S})$ called an *action*.

Definition 1 imposes the following additional key assumptions on Event-B models.

- Events are classified into *plant events* and *controller events*, since our target systems are closed-loop control systems with controllers and plants. N_p and N_c denote the numbers of plant and controller events, respectively.
- A *partitioning* requirement is imposed in Line 16—it is the responsibility of the modeler to ensure that $\mathcal{M}$ satisfies this property. The requirement says that, from each state s, only one controller event E_i^c is enabled.

The following "correctness" notions are standard in Event-B [1]. The presentation here is adapted to controller-plant models.

Definition 2 (Invariant preservation, feasibility). Let $\mathcal{M}$ be a controller-plant model presented as in Definition 1.

- $\mathcal{M}$ is *invariant-preserving* if 1) the safety invariant I^S is indeed transition-preserved (i.e., $s \in I^\mathrm{S} \implies \pi(s) \subseteq I^\mathrm{S}$), and 2) $A_0 \subseteq I^\mathrm{S}$.
- $\mathcal{M}$'s controller is *feasible* if controller events have feasible actions, that is precisely, $\forall s \in I^\mathrm{S}. \forall i \in [1, N_\mathrm{c}]. \left(\forall p. G_i^\mathrm{c}(s, p) \implies A_i^\mathrm{c}(s, p) \neq \emptyset \right)$

When using a controller-plant model $\mathcal{M}$ as the input to the workflow in Fig. 1, we assume that $\mathcal{M}$ is invariant-preserving and feasible.

Example 1 (The heater model $\mathcal{M}_{\mathrm{ht0}}$). The Event-B model $\mathcal{M}_{\mathrm{ht0}}$ in Fig. 3 models a heater(-cooler) system in a pool.[1] Due to an unstable water source, the pool temperature can randomly change (the plant event E_1^p). The system heats or cools the pool so that the temperature becomes between $30\,^\circ\mathrm{C}$ and $40\,^\circ\mathrm{C}$.

To state that the safety invariant should be checked only after the behavior of the controller (the heater system), the "turn" variable tn indicates if the current state is after plant's (p) or controller's (c) behavior. There are three controller events (events ctrl_*). If the temperature is too cold (Lines 10–13), the controller uses the heater to increase the temperature by an appropriate amount dh. If the temperature is already appropriate (Lines 14–17), the controller changes the temperature within the safety region $[30, 40]$. If the temperature is too hot (Lines 18–21), the controller cools the water appropriately.

---

[1] For clarity, we use a different notation than Event-B's standard syntax [1].

```
1   Machine M_ht0
2      State space S = {p,c} × Z          /* variables tn and temp */
3      Invariants
4         Safety invariant I^S = {⟨tn, temp⟩ | tn = c ⟹ 30 ≤ temp ≤ 40}
5      Initial states A_0
6      Plant event E_1^p                    /* plant_change_temp */
7         Parameter set P_1^p = Z           /* parameter dt */
8         Guard G_1^p⟨⟨tn, temp⟩, dt⟩ ⟺ ⊤
9         Action A_1^p⟨⟨tn, temp⟩, dt⟩ = {⟨tn', temp'⟩ | tn' = p ∧ temp' = temp + dt}
10     Controller event E_1^c               /* ctrl_heat */
11        Parameter set P_1^c = Z           /* parameter dh */
12        Guard G_1^c⟨⟨tn, temp⟩, dh⟩ ⟺ temp < 30 ∧ 30 ≤ temp + dh ≤ 40
13        Action A_1^c⟨⟨tn, temp⟩, dh⟩ = {⟨tn', temp'⟩ | tn' = c ∧ temp' = temp + dh}
14     Controller event E_2^c               /* ctrl_keep_safe */
15        Parameter set P_2^c = Z           /* parameter dt */
16        Guard G_2^c⟨⟨tn, temp⟩, dt⟩ ⟺ 30 ≤ temp ≤ 40 ∧ 30 ≤ temp + dt ≤ 40
17        Action A_2^c⟨⟨tn, temp⟩, dt⟩ = {⟨tn', temp'⟩ | tn' = c ∧ temp' = temp + dt}
18     Controller event E_3^c               /* ctrl_cool */
19        Parameter set P_3^c = Z           /* parameter dc */
20        Guard G_3^c⟨⟨tn, temp⟩, dc⟩ ⟺ 40 < temp ∧ 30 ≤ temp − dc ≤ 40
21        Action A_3^c⟨⟨tn, temp⟩, dc⟩ = {⟨tn', temp'⟩ | tn' = c ∧ temp' = temp − dc}
```

Fig. 3. The heater model $\mathcal{M}_{ht0}$

3   Uncertainty Injection

The first step of our workflow (Fig. 1) is to inject specification of potential perceptual uncertainty to an input model $\mathcal{M}$—a controller-plant model that does not include perceptual uncertainty. In the following definition, the function $\varepsilon \colon \mathcal{S} \to \mathcal{P}(\mathcal{S})$ specifies the kind of uncertainty to be taken into account.

Definition 3 (Uncertainty injection $(\_)^\varepsilon$). Let $\mathcal{M}$ be a controller-plant model (Definition 1, Fig. 2), and $\varepsilon \colon \mathcal{S} \to \mathcal{P}(\mathcal{S})$ be a function such that $s \in \varepsilon(s)$. We call ε uncertainty specification. *Uncertainty injection* is a construction that returns the Event-B model $\mathcal{M}^\varepsilon$ shown in Fig. 4.

The key difference of $\mathcal{M}^\varepsilon$ from $\mathcal{M}$ (Fig. 2) is that the state space $\mathcal{S}$ is duplicated—i.e., $\mathcal{S} \times \mathcal{S}$ is the state space of $\mathcal{M}^\varepsilon$. In $\langle s, \hat{s} \rangle \in \mathcal{S} \times \mathcal{S}$, s is a *true* state and $\hat{s}$ is a *perceived* state. The rest of the model $\mathcal{M}^\varepsilon$ closely follows $\mathcal{M}$, but whether a plant event $E_i^{p,\varepsilon}$ is enabled or not is decided based on the true state s (Line 10); while, the guard of a controller event $E_i^{c,\varepsilon}$ looks at the perceived state $\hat{s}$ (Line 14). Note, however, that, all actions $A_i^{p,\varepsilon}$ and $A_i^{c,\varepsilon}$ act on true states (s and s'). In particular, controller actions are assumed to operate on the plant (i.e., the physical reality) via actuators. In Line 4, the safety invariant $I^{S,\varepsilon}$ checks if the *true* state s is safe.

The uncertainty specification ε occurs in Lines 5, 6, 11, 15. Lines 11 & 15 model the assumption that perception is made after each action with respect to the current true state ($s' \in \varepsilon(\hat{s}')$)—this means in particular that perception errors do not accumulate over time. The uncertainty invariant is added in $\mathcal{M}^\varepsilon$ (Line 5); this is maintained by the definition of actions (Lines 11 & 15). We also note that the partitioning requirement (Line 16) for $\mathcal{M}^\varepsilon$ remains satisfied.

Although the original model $\mathcal{M}$ is "safe" (in the Event-B sense of *invariant preservation*, see Sect. 2), the uncertainty-injected model $\mathcal{M}^\varepsilon$ may not be

```
1   Machine M^ε
2   State space S × S
3   Invariants (I^ε ⊆ S × S such that ⟨s, ŝ⟩ ∈ I^ε ⟹ π^ε(⟨s, ŝ⟩) ⊆ I^ε)
4      Safety invariant I^{S,ε}(⟨s, ŝ⟩) = I^S(s) /* events may violate this */
5      Uncertainty invariant I^{U,ε}(⟨s, ŝ⟩) = (s ∈ ε(ŝ))
6   Initial states A_0^ε = {⟨s, ŝ⟩ | s ∈ A_0 ∧ s ∈ ε(ŝ)}
7   Transition function π^ε : S × S → P(S × S), given by
        π^ε(⟨s, ŝ⟩) = ⋃{ A_i^{p,ε}(⟨s, ŝ⟩, p) | i ∈ [1, N_p], p ∈ P_i^{p,ε}, G_i^{p,ε}(⟨s, ŝ⟩, p) }
                  ∪ ⋃{ A_i^{c,ε}(⟨s, ŝ⟩, p) | i ∈ [1, N_c], p ∈ P_i^{c,ε}, G_i^{c,ε}(⟨s, ŝ⟩, p) },   where
8      Plant event E_i^{p,ε}   (where i ∈ [1, N_p])
9         Parameter set P_i^{p,ε} = P_i^p
10        Guard G_i^{p,ε}(⟨s, ŝ⟩, p) ⟺ G_i^p(s, p)
11        Action A_i^{p,ε}(⟨s, ŝ⟩, p) = {⟨s', ŝ'⟩ | s' ∈ A_i^p(s, p) ∧ s' ∈ ε(ŝ')}
12     Controller event E_i^{c,ε}   (where i ∈ [1, N_c])
13        Parameter set P_i^{c,ε} = P_i^c
14        Guard G_i^{c,ε}(⟨s, ŝ⟩, p) ⟺ G_i^c(ŝ, p)
15        Action A_i^{c,ε}(⟨s, ŝ⟩, p) = {⟨s', ŝ'⟩ | s' ∈ A_i^c(s, p) ∧ s' ∈ ε(ŝ')}
16  Subject to partitioning: ∀⟨s, ŝ⟩ ∈ S × S. ∃! i ∈ [1, N_c]. ∃p ∈ P_i^{c,ε}. G_i^{c,ε}(⟨s, ŝ⟩, p)
```

Fig. 4. The controller-plant model $\mathcal{M}^\varepsilon$ given by uncertainty injection from $\mathcal{M}$ (Fig. 2) and $\varepsilon \colon \mathcal{S} \to \mathcal{P}(\mathcal{S})$. Here s, s' are *true* states while $\hat{s}, \hat{s}'$ are *perceived* states. Note that $\mathcal{M}^\varepsilon$ may not preserve $I^{S,\varepsilon}$ due to the uncertainty.

invariant-preserving. In Sect. 4, we present syntactic model transformations to make it safe.

Example 2 (The heater model $\mathcal{M}_{\mathrm{ht0}}^{\varepsilon_0}$). Figure 5 is the model given by injecting the uncertainty to $\mathcal{M}_{\mathrm{ht0}}$ (Fig. 3). Here the uncertainty specification ε_0 is

$$\varepsilon_0 \colon \mathcal{S} \to \mathcal{P}(\mathcal{S}), \quad \langle \widehat{tn}, \widehat{temp} \rangle \mapsto \{\langle tn, temp \rangle \mid tn = \widehat{tn} \wedge temp \in [\widehat{temp} - 3, \widehat{temp} + 3]\}.$$

This specifies that sensed values of temperature can have errors up to $3\,^\circ\mathrm{C}$.

The controller does not preserve the safety invariant I^{S,ε_0} (Line 4). For example, when $temp = 32$ and $\widehat{temp} = 29$, the event ctrl_heat (Line 7) can fire with parameter $dh = 11$—i.e., with perceived $\widehat{temp} = 29$ and maximum safe temperature 40, the controller thinks that it can raise the temperature by 11. This leads $temp$ to 43, violating the safety invariant $30 \leq temp \leq 40$.

4 Robustification

We propose two syntactic transformations that modify the uncertainty-injected controller for the purpose of regaining safety. They are called *action-preserving robustification* (_)^{pR} and *action-repurposing robustification* (_)^{rR}, respectively.

4.1 Types of Robustified Events

The basic idea is as follows, common to the two robustification transformations.

Assume the situation on the left in Fig. 6. If the controller was sure that the true state s belonged to the region of $G_1^{c,\varepsilon}$,[2] then the controller could take

---

[2] This is the same as G_1^c, see Fig. 4, Line 14.

```
1   Machine M_{ht0}^{ε0}
2       ...
3     Invariants
4       Safety invariant  I^{S,ε0} = {⟨⟨tn, temp⟩, ⟨t̂n, t̂ê̂mp⟩⟩ | tn = c ⟹ 30 ≤ temp ≤ 40}
5       Uncertainty invariant  I^{U,ε0} = {⟨⟨tn, temp⟩, ⟨t̂n, t̂ê̂mp⟩⟩ | ⟨tn, temp⟩ ∈ ε_0(⟨t̂n, t̂ê̂mp⟩)}
6       ...
7     Controller event  E_1^{c,ε0}              /* ctrl_heat */
8       Parameter set  P_1^{c,ε0} = ℤ           /* parameter dh */
9       Guard  G_1^{c,ε0}⟨⟨⟨tn, temp⟩, ⟨t̂n, t̂ê̂mp⟩⟩, dh⟩ ⟺ t̂ê̂mp < 30 ∧ 30 ≤ t̂ê̂mp + dh ≤ 40
10      Action  A_1^{c,ε0}⟨⟨⟨tn, temp⟩, ⟨t̂n, t̂ê̂mp⟩⟩, dh⟩ = {⟨⟨tn', temp'⟩, ⟨t̂n', t̂ê̂mp'⟩⟩ |
           tn' = c ∧ temp' = temp + dh ∧ ⟨tn', temp'⟩ ∈ ε_0(⟨t̂n', t̂ê̂mp'⟩)}
11      ...
```

Fig. 5. The heater model $\mathcal{M}_{ht0}^{\varepsilon_0}$ produced by uncertainty injection

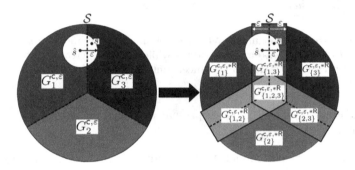

Fig. 6. Uncertainty robustification

the action $A_1^{c,\varepsilon}$. This way the controller can achieve the system's safety, since the original model $\mathcal{M}$ is safe. (Note that we implicitly rely on the *partitioning* requirement of $\mathcal{M}$, Fig. 2, Line 16). Unfortunately, the controller cannot be sure that the true state s belongs to the region of $G_1^{c,\varepsilon}$ because, due to uncertainty, the set $\varepsilon(\hat{s})$ of potential true states overlaps with the region of another guard $G_3^{c,\varepsilon}$. Therefore, it is not clear from just looking at the perceived state $\hat{s}$ whether the controller should take the controller action $A_1^{c,\varepsilon}$ or $A_3^{c,\varepsilon}$.

To overcome the challenge, we first refine the partitioning of the state space—so that each compartment stands for the set of controller actions that are potentially enabled. For example, on the right in Fig. 6, we have seven compartments, such as $\{1, 3\}$ for "the true state s must be either in $G_1^{c,\varepsilon}$ or in $G_3^{c,\varepsilon}$."

We create new events for the new compartments that arise this way (i.e., for those states that potentially enable multiple controller actions). These new events are called *heterogeneous events*. For example, on the right in Fig. 6, we have four heterogeneous events $E_{\{1,2\}}^{c,\varepsilon}, E_{\{1,3\}}^{c,\varepsilon}, E_{\{2,3\}}^{c,\varepsilon}, E_{\{1,2,3\}}^{c,\varepsilon}$, in addition to the *homogeneous events* $E_{\{1\}}^{c,\varepsilon}, E_{\{2\}}^{c,\varepsilon}, E_{\{3\}}^{c,\varepsilon}$, which are for cases where the controller is sure that it can use a particular action.

There are different ways that the actions of these heterogeneous events can be defined, leading to the two robustification methods presented in Sect. 4.2 and 4.3.

- In *action-preserving* robustification (_)^{pR}, the set of states reachable with a heterogeneous event $E^{\text{c},\varepsilon,\text{pR}}_{\{i_1,\dots,i_k\}}$ is the *intersection* of those reachable with $E^{\text{c},\varepsilon}_{i_1},\dots,E^{\text{c},\varepsilon}_{i_k}$. Therefore, the action of a heterogeneous event $E^{\text{c},\varepsilon,\text{pR}}_{\{i_1,\dots,i_k\}}$ satisfies all requirements satisfied by $A^{\text{c},\varepsilon}_{i_1},\dots,A^{\text{c},\varepsilon}_{i_k}$. This way, the system generated with this method $\mathcal{M}^{\varepsilon,\text{pR}}$ can be forward-simulated[3] by the original system $\mathcal{M}$, that is, any execution trace of $\mathcal{M}^{\varepsilon,\text{pR}}$ is an execution trace of $\mathcal{M}$ $(s \in \epsilon(\hat{s}) \wedge \langle s',\hat{s}'\rangle \in \pi^{\varepsilon,\text{pR}}(\langle s,\hat{s}\rangle) \implies s' \in \pi(s))$. In particular, $\mathcal{M}^{\varepsilon,\text{pR}}$ is safe since so is $\mathcal{M}$.
- In *action-repurposing* robustification (_)^{rR}, the action of a heterogenerous event $E^{\text{c},\varepsilon,\text{rR}}_{\{i_1,\dots,i_k\}}$ does not consider satisfying all requirements satisfied by $A^{\text{c},\varepsilon}_{i_1},\dots,A^{\text{c},\varepsilon}_{i_k}$. The event $E^{\text{c},\varepsilon,\text{rR}}_{\{i_1,\dots,i_k\}}$ uses at least *one* (but not necessarily all) of $A^{\text{c},\varepsilon}_{i_1},\dots,A^{\text{c},\varepsilon}_{i_k}$ with parameters that are *guaranteed to preserve the safety invariant* $I^{\text{S},\varepsilon}$ regardless of which guard can be satisfied by the true state. Therefore, an action originally from $E^{\text{c},\varepsilon}_i$ may be invoked from the region of the guard of $E^{\text{c},\varepsilon}_j$ with $i \neq j$, making the behavior of the resulting model different from that of $\mathcal{M}$. In this way, actions from one event may be "repurposed" for another event, hence the name of the method.

In our workflow (Fig. 1), we prefer the action-preserving robustification since it yields a controller that can be forward-simulated by the original one. In case it is not feasible (i.e., when no action is shared by the events $E^{\text{c},\varepsilon}_{i_1},\dots,E^{\text{c},\varepsilon}_{i_k}$), we try the action-repurposing robustification.

4.2   Action-Preserving Robustification

Definition 4 (Action-preserving robustification (_)^{pR}). *Action-preserving robustification is a construction that takes an Event-B model* $\mathcal{M}^\varepsilon$ *as shown in Fig. 4 as input, and returns the Event-B model* $\mathcal{M}^{\varepsilon,\text{pR}}$ *in Fig. 7. In Fig. 7 (and elsewhere below), we use the following functions.*

- The function $\text{idx}^{\text{c}}: \mathcal{S} \to [1,N_{\text{c}}]$ returns, for each state $s \in \mathcal{S}$ (in the original system $\mathcal{M}$), the index of the unique controller event enabled at s in the original model $\mathcal{M}$. That is, $\exists p \in P^{\text{c}}_{\text{idx}^{\text{c}}(s)} \cdot G^{\text{c}}_{\text{idx}^{\text{c}}(s)}(s,p)$ holds.
- The function par^{c} takes a state $s \in \mathcal{S}$ and returns the set of parameter values that are compatible, that is, $\text{par}^{\text{c}}(s) = \{p \in P^{\text{c}}_{\text{idx}^{\text{c}}(s)} \mid G^{\text{c}}_{\text{idx}^{\text{c}}(s)}(s,p)\}$.
- The function $\text{par}^{\text{c},\varepsilon}_i$ takes a state $\hat{s} \in \mathcal{S}$ and returns $\text{par}^{\text{c},\varepsilon}_i(\hat{s}) = \bigcap\{\text{par}^{\text{c}}(\tilde{s}) \mid \text{idx}^{\text{c}}(\tilde{s}) = i, \tilde{s} \in \varepsilon(\hat{s})\}$, i.e., the set of parameter values compatible with any state $\tilde{s}$ that is in the ε-neighborhood of $\hat{s}$ and enables E^{c}_i.

The parameter value for the index $i \in u$ may be $\perp_i$ (Line 7) such that $\forall s \in \mathcal{S}.A^{\text{c}}_i(s,\perp_i) = \emptyset$. $P^{\text{c}}_i = \perp_i$ means that there is no i-th parameter that satisfies constraints on parameters for safety and feasibility (Lines 10–11).

---

[3] This does not mean the refinement in Event-B, which requires every concrete event to have guards stronger than guards of abstract events.

```
1   Machine 𝓜^{ε,pR}
2   (State space, invariant, and initial states are the same as 𝓜^ε)
3     Transition function π^{ε,pR} : S × S → 𝓟(S × S), given by
        π^{ε,pR}(⟨s, ŝ⟩) =
4         ∪{ A_i^{p,ε}(⟨s, ŝ⟩, p^p) | i ∈ [1, N_p], p^p ∈ P_i^{p,ε}, G_i^{p,ε}(⟨s, ŝ⟩, p^p) }
          ∪∪{ A_u^{c,ε,pR}(⟨s, ŝ⟩, p^c) | u ∈ 𝓟([1, N_c]) \ ∅, p^c ∈ P_u^{c,ε,pR}, G_u^{c,ε,pR}(⟨s, ŝ⟩, p^c) },
5       Plant event E_i^{p,ε,pR} = E_i^{p,ε}
6       Controller event E_u^{c,ε,pR}   (where u ∈ 𝓟([1, N_c]) \ ∅)
7       Parameter set P_u^{c,ε,pR} = ∏_{i∈u}(P_i^c ∪ {⊥_i})
8       Guard G_u^{c,ε,pR}(⟨s, ŝ⟩, p^c) ⟺
9         u = {idx^c(s̃) | s̃ ∈ ε(ŝ)}  /* s̃: a potential true state */
10        ∧ ∀i ∈ u. ((par_i^{c,ε}(ŝ) ≠ ∅ ⟹ p_i^c ∈ par_i^{c,ε}(ŝ)) ∧ (par_i^{c,ε}(ŝ) = ∅ ⟹ p_i^c = ⊥_i))
11        ∧ ∀s̃ ∈ ε(ŝ). (∩_{i∈u} A_i^c(s̃, p_i^c) ≠ ∅)
12      Action A_u^{c,ε,pR} : (S × S) × P_u^{c,ε,pR} → 𝓟(S × S)
13      A_u^{c,ε,pR}(⟨s, ŝ⟩, p^c) = {⟨s', ŝ'⟩ | s' ∈ ∩_{i∈u} A_i^c(s, p_i^c) ∧ ŝ' ∈ ε(ŝ')}
14    Subject to partitioning: ∀⟨s, ŝ⟩ ∈ S × S. ∃!u ∈ 𝓟([1, N_c]). ∃p^c ∈ P_u^{c,ε,pR}. G_u^{c,ε,pR}(⟨s, ŝ⟩, p^c)
```

Fig. 7. A controller-plant model $\mathcal{M}^{\varepsilon,\mathrm{pR}}$ produced by action-preserving robustification from $\mathcal{M}^\varepsilon$ from Fig. 4

Theorem 1. *Regarding the model* $\mathcal{M}^{\varepsilon,\mathrm{pR}}$ *in Definition 4 (Fig. 7), assume the following condition (i.e., for all events, there exist parameter values such that they are compatible with all possible states under the ε-uncertainty and there exist actions common in all original actions) is satisfied.*

$$\forall u \in \mathcal{P}([1, N_c]). \forall \langle s, \hat{s} \rangle \in S \times S. (s \in \varepsilon(\hat{s}) \wedge u = \{\mathrm{idx}^c(\tilde{s}) | \tilde{s} \in \varepsilon(\hat{s})\} \Longrightarrow$$
$$\exists p^c = \langle p_{i_1}^c, \ldots, p_{i_k}^c \rangle \in P_u^{c,\varepsilon,\mathrm{pR}}.$$
$$((\forall \tilde{s} \in \varepsilon(\hat{s}). p_{\mathrm{idx}^c(\tilde{s})}^c \in \mathrm{par}^c(\tilde{s})) \wedge (\exists s' \in S. \forall i \in u. s' \in A_i^c(s, p_i^c))).$$

Then $\mathcal{M}^{\varepsilon,\mathrm{pR}}$ *satisfies the partitioning requirement (Fig. 7, Line 14), and is invariant-preserving and feasible (Definition 2).*

We judge the success of the action-preserving robustification by the condition in Theorem 1. If it fails, then we try the action-repurposing robustification (Fig. 1).

Example 3 (The heater model $\mathcal{M}_{\mathrm{ht0}}^{\varepsilon_0,\mathrm{pR}}$). Figure 8 is an excerpt from the model obtained by applying the action-preserving robustification to $\mathcal{M}_{\mathrm{ht0}}^{\varepsilon_0}$ (Fig. 5) showing the heterogeneous event $E_{\{1,2\}}^{\varepsilon,\mathrm{c},\mathrm{pR}}$ generated from the event ctrl_heat and the event ctrl_keep_safe from $\mathcal{M}_{\mathrm{ht0}}$. Constraints on the perceived temperature (Lines 6–8) mean that $u = \{1, 2\}$ in this event (Line 9 of Fig. 7). Constraints on parameters (Lines 9–10) mean that dh and dt are compatible with every state $\widetilde{temp}$ around $\widehat{temp}$ (Line 10 of Fig. 7). Line 11 means that there are common actions in ctrl_heat and ctrl_keep_safe (Line 11 of Fig. 7).

The event $E_{\{1,2\}}^{\varepsilon,\mathrm{c},\mathrm{pR}}$ is indeed feasible and it preserves the safety invariant I^S as all other events of $\mathcal{M}_{\mathrm{ht0}}^{\varepsilon_0,\mathrm{pR}}$ do. Lines 6–8 mean that $27 \leq \widehat{temp} < 33$. Also, Lines 9–10 mean that $33 - \widehat{temp} \leq dh \leq 10$ and $0 \leq dt \leq 37 - \widehat{temp}$. In addition, line 11 requests that $dh = dt$, thus $33 - \widehat{temp} \leq dh = dt \leq 37 - \widehat{temp}$. Since $temp \in [\widehat{temp} - 3, \widehat{temp} + 3]$, we can guarantee that I^S is preserved, namely $30 \leq temp + dh = temp + dt \leq 40$. For example, if $\widehat{temp} = 29$, then

```
1    Machine  M_hto^{ε0,pR}
2      ...
3        Controller event  E_{1,2}^{c,ε0,pR}      /* ctrl_heat_keep_safe_hetero */
4          Parameter set  P_{1,2}^{c,ε0,pR} = ℤ × ℤ    /* parameter dh and dt */
5          Guard  G_{1,2}^{c,ε0,pR}⟨⟨⟨tn, temp⟩, ⟨t̃n, t̃ẽmp⟩⟩, ⟨dh, dt⟩⟩ ⟺
6              ∀t̃ẽmp ∈ [t̃ẽmp − 3, t̃ẽmp + 3]. (t̃ẽmp < 30 ∨ 30 ≤ t̃ẽmp ≤ 40)
7            ∧ ∃t̃ẽmp ∈ [t̃ẽmp − 3, t̃ẽmp + 3]. (t̃ẽmp < 30)
8            ∧ ∃t̃ẽmp ∈ [t̃ẽmp − 3, t̃ẽmp + 3]. (30 ≤ t̃ẽmp ≤ 40)
9            ∧ ∀t̃ẽmp ∈ [t̃ẽmp − 3, t̃ẽmp + 3]. (t̃ẽmp < 30 ⟹ 30 ≤ t̃ẽmp + dh ≤ 40)
10           ∧ ∀t̃ẽmp ∈ [t̃ẽmp − 3, t̃ẽmp + 3]. (30 ≤ t̃ẽmp ≤ 40 ⟹ 30 ≤ t̃ẽmp + dt ≤ 40)
11           ∧ ∀t̃ẽmp ∈ [t̃ẽmp − 3, t̃ẽmp + 3].
                 ({t̃ẽmp′|t̃ẽmp′ = t̃ẽmp + dh} ∩ {t̃ẽmp′|t̃ẽmp′ = t̃ẽmp + dt}) ≠ ∅
12       Action  A_{1,2}^{c,ε0,pR}⟨⟨⟨tn, temp⟩, ⟨t̃n, t̃ẽmp⟩⟩, ⟨dh, dt⟩⟩ = {⟨⟨tn′, temp′⟩, ⟨t̃n′, t̃ẽmp′⟩⟩ |
                 tn′ = c ∧ temp′ = temp + dh ∧ temp′ = temp + dt ∧ ⟨tn′, temp′⟩ ∈ ε_0(⟨t̃n′, t̃ẽmp′⟩)}
13     ...
```

Fig. 8. The heater model $\mathcal{M}_{hto}^{ε0,pR}$ produced by action-preserving robustification

$26 ≤ \widetilde{temp} ≤ 32$. In case of $26 ≤ \widetilde{temp} < 30$, the event ctrl_heat would heat to increase the temperature by dh where $4 ≤ dh ≤ 10$ (Line 9). Otherwise (i.e., $30 ≤ \widetilde{temp} ≤ 32$), the event ctrl_keep_safe would change the temperature for dt where $0 ≤ dt ≤ 8$ (Line 10). The common actions here are changing temperature by $dh = dt ∈ [4, 8]$, which is safe for all $\widetilde{temp} ∈ [26, 32]$.

4.3   Action-Repurposing Robustification

Definition 5 (Action-repurposing robustification (_)^{rR}). *Action-repurposing robustification is a construction that takes an Event-B model $\mathcal{M}^ε$ as shown in Fig. 4 as input, and returns the Event-B model $\mathcal{M}^{ε,rR}$ (Fig. 9). In Fig. 9 (and elsewhere below), we use the following function.*

- The function $\mathsf{safpar}_i^{c,ε}$ takes a state $\hat{s} ∈ \mathcal{S}$ and a safety invariant I and returns $\bigcap_{\tilde{s}∈ε(\hat{s})}\{p|\emptyset ⊂ A_i^c(\tilde{s}, p) ⊆ I\}$, i.e., the set of parameter values that preserve the safety invariant I when used with the action of the i-th event of $\mathcal{M}$ (A_i^c) at any state $\tilde{s}$ that is in the $ε$-neighborhood of $\hat{s}$ and enables E_i^c.

The model $\mathcal{M}^{ε,rR}$ is the same as $\mathcal{M}^{ε,pR}$ (Fig. 7) except lines 10, 11, and 13. For each original controller event E_i^c, the parameter of the event is restricted so that it satisfies the safety invariant I^S for all possible states under the $ε$-uncertainty (Line 10). The robustified controller uses *one of* the events that have such parameter values (Line 13). This guarantees that the safety invariant I^S is satisfied for every possible true state (i.e., those in $ε(\hat{s})$).

Theorem 2. *Regarding the model $\mathcal{M}^{ε,rR}$ in Definition 5, assume the following condition (i.e., there exist original controller events and their parameter values that satisfy the safety at all possible states under the $ε$-uncertainty) is satisfied.*

$$∀u ∈ \mathcal{P}([1, N_c]). ∀⟨s, \hat{s}⟩ ∈ \mathcal{S} × \mathcal{S}. (s ∈ ε(\hat{s}) ∧ \{\mathsf{idx}^c(\tilde{s})|\tilde{s} ∈ ε(\hat{s})\} ⟹$$
$$∃i ∈ u, p_i^c ∈ P_i^c. (∀\tilde{s} ∈ ε(\hat{s}). A_i^c(\tilde{s}, p_i^c) ⊆ I^S)).$$

```
1  │ Machine 𝓜^{ε,rR}
2  │ (State space, invariant, and initial states are same as 𝓜^ε)
3  │ Transition function π^{ε,rR} : S × S → 𝒫(S × S), given by
   │     π^{ε,rR}(⟨s, ŝ⟩) =
4  │       ∪{ A_i^{p,ε}(⟨s, ŝ⟩, p^p) | i ∈ [1, N_p], p^p ∈ P_i^{p,ε}, G_i^{p,ε}(⟨s, ŝ⟩, p^p) }
   │       ∪∪{ A_u^{c,ε,rR}(⟨s, ŝ⟩, p^c) | u ∈ 𝒫([1, N_c]) \ ∅, p^c ∈ P_u^{c,ε,rR}, G_u^{c,ε,rR}(⟨s, ŝ⟩, p^c) },
5  │    Plant event E_i^{p,ε,rR} = E_i^{p,ε}
6  │    Controller event E_u^{c,ε,rR}    (where u ∈ 𝒫([1, N_c]) \ ∅)
7  │      Parameter set P_u^{c,ε,rR} = ∏_{i∈u}(P_i^c ∪ {⊥_i})
8  │      Guard G_u^{c,ε,rR}(⟨s, ŝ⟩, p^c) ⟺
9  │        u = {idx^c(s̃) | s̃ ∈ ε(ŝ)}   /* s̃: a potential true state */
10 │        ∧ ∀i ∈ u. ((safpar_i^{c,ε}(ŝ, I^S) ≠ ∅ ⇒ p_i^c ∈ safpar_i^{c,ε}(ŝ, I^S)) ∧ (safpar_i^{c,ε}(ŝ, I^S) = ∅ ⇒ p_i^c = ⊥_i))
11 │        ∧ ∃i ∈ u. p_i^c ≠ ⊥_i
12 │      Action A_u^{c,ε,rR} : (S × S) × P_u^{c,ε,rR} → 𝒫(S × S)
13 │        A_u^{c,ε,rR}(⟨s, ŝ⟩, p^c) = {⟨s', ŝ'⟩ | i ∈ u ∧ p_i^c ≠ ⊥_i ∧ s' ∈ A_i^c(s, p_i^c) ∧ s' ∈ ε(ŝ')}
14 │ Subject to partitioning: ∀⟨s, ŝ⟩ ∈ S × S. ∃!u ∈ 𝒫([1, N_c]). ∃p^c ∈ P_u^{c,ε,rR}. G_u^{c,ε,rR}(⟨s, ŝ⟩, p^c)
```

Fig. 9. A controller-plant model $\mathcal{M}^{ε,rR}$ produced by action-repurposing robustification from $\mathcal{M}_ε$ from Fig. 4

Then $\mathcal{M}^{ε,rR}$ satisfies the partition requirement (Fig. 9, line 14), and is invariant-preserving and feasible (Definition 2).

Example 4 (The heater model $\mathcal{M}_{ht0}^{ε_0,rR}$). Figure 10 is an excerpt from the model obtained by applying the action-repurposing robustification to $\mathcal{M}_{ht0}^{ε_0}$ (Fig. 5), showing the heterogeneous event $E_{\{1,2\}}^{ε,c,rR}$ constructed from ctrl_heat and ctrl_keep_safe. The action of ctrl_heat is adopted as the action of the event $E_{\{1,2\}}^{c,ε_0,rR}$ (Line 10). The parameter dh is restricted so that the safety invariant is preserved by the event even under the uncertainty (Line 9). Thus, this event safely deals with the case where the controller is unsure if $temp < 30$ or $30 \leq temp \leq 40$ by *repurposing* the action for the $temp < 30$ case.

4.4 Checking Vacuity of Heterogeneous Events

A controller event of a robustified model corresponds to a non-empty subset of original controller events. Therefore, if the original model has n controller events, then the robustified model can have $2^n - 1$ controller events.

However, there may be heterogeneous events of *vacuous* cases. For instance, in the robustified heater model (Fig. 8), the heterogeneous event $E_{\{1,2,3\}}^{c,ε_0,pR}$ (an event for when the controller is not sure if it should heat, keep safe, or cool) is vacuous because $\widehat{temp}$ should satisfy $(\exists \tau \in ε_\tau(\widehat{temp}). \tau < 30) \wedge (\exists \tau \in ε_\tau(\widehat{temp}). 30 \leq \tau \leq 40) \wedge (\exists \tau \in ε_\tau(\widehat{temp}). 40 < \tau)$, where $ε_\tau = (\lambda\tau. [\tau - 3, \tau + 3])$; but, this is not satisfiable. The vacuity of heterogeneous events depends on the uncertainty; for example, $E_{\{1,2,3\}}^{c,ε',pR}$ is not vacuous when $ε'$ defines errors up to 7 because if $\widehat{temp} = 35$ then $temp$ can be in the range $[35 - 7, 35 + 7]$.

Detecting and removing vacuous heterogeneous events is important because developers want meaningful descriptive models for reasoning. In addition, it improves reasoning efficiency because it reduces the number of events.

```
1  │ Machine  M_ht0^{ε0,rR}
2  │ ...
3  │     Controller event  E_{1,2}^{c,ε0,rR}        /* ctrl_heat_keep_safe_hetero */
4  │        Parameter set  P_{1,2}^{c,ε0,rR} = Z × Z     /* parameter dh and dt */
5  │        Guard  G_{1,2}^{c,ε0,rR}⟨⟨⟨tn, temp⟩, ⟨t̃n, t̃emp⟩⟩, ⟨dh, dt⟩⟩ ⟺
6  │           ∀t̃emp ∈ [t̃emp − 3, t̃emp + 3]. (t̃emp < 30 ∨ 30 ≤ t̃emp ≤ 40)
7  │           ∧ ∃t̃emp ∈ [t̃emp − 3, t̃emp + 3]. t̃emp < 30
8  │           ∧ ∃t̃emp ∈ [t̃emp − 3, t̃emp + 3]. 30 ≤ t̃emp ≤ 40
9  │           ∧ ∀t̃emp ∈ [t̃emp − 3, t̃emp + 3]. 30 ≤ t̃emp + dh ≤ 40
10 │        Action  A_{1,2}^{c,ε0,rR}⟨⟨⟨tn, temp⟩, ⟨t̃n, t̃emp⟩⟩, ⟨dh, dt⟩⟩ = {⟨⟨tn′, temp′⟩, ⟨t̃n′, t̃emp′⟩⟩ |
    │           tn′ = c ∧ temp′ = temp + dh ∧ ⟨tn′, temp′⟩ ∈ ε0(⟨t̃n′, t̃emp′⟩)}
11 │ ...
```

Fig. 10. A heater model $\mathcal{M}_{ht0}^{ε0,rR}$ produced by action-repurposing robustification

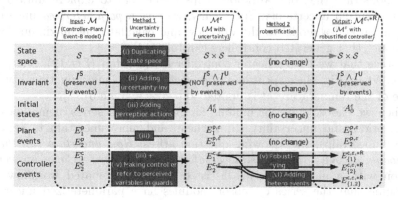

Fig. 11. Overview of manipulations performed by our tool

5 Implementation

Figure 11 is an overview of the model transformations used in the workflow of Fig. 1. Note that each transformation step is syntactic and thus can be automated. We implemented the workflow[4] as a plug-in of the Rodin Platform [2,5], which is the modeling environment of Event-B. In the robustification process, it calculates (assisted by the Z3 SMT solver [11]) if robustification methods can generate invariant-preserving and feasible models. It also checks if each generated heterogeneous event is vacuous and thus should be removed (Sect. 4.4).

---

[4] Available at http://research.nii.ac.jp/robustifier/.

```
1    Machine 𝓜ₕₜ₁
2        ...
3        Controller event E₂ᶜ                    /* ctrl_keep_safe_eco */
4            Parameter set P₂ᶜ = ℤ               /* parameter dt */
5            Guard G₂ᶜ⟨⟨tn, temp⟩, dt⟩ ⟺ 30 ≤ temp ≤ 40
6                ∧ 30 ≤ temp + dt ≤ 40 ∧ −4 ≤ dt ≤ 4  /* Only small changes */
7            Action A₂ᶜ⟨⟨tn, temp⟩, dt⟩ = {⟨tn′, temp′⟩ | tn′ = c ∧ temp′ = temp + dt}
8        ...
```

Fig. 12. Model $\mathcal{M}_{\mathrm{ht1}}$: a variant of $\mathcal{M}_{\mathrm{ht0}}$ (Fig. 3)

6   Case Study

We demonstrate that our workflow helps developers to explore multiple levels of perceptual uncertainty. Specifically, we give a *parameterized* uncertainty specification and a model to the workflow and calculate the maximum level of uncertainty that generated controllers can tolerate.

Assume that we have a heater controller model $\mathcal{M}_{\mathrm{ht1}}$ (Fig. 12). $\mathcal{M}_{\mathrm{ht1}}$ is the same as $\mathcal{M}_{\mathrm{ht0}}$ (Fig. 3) except it has an *ecological* "keep_safe" functionality— the change of the temperature dt is limited to $[-4, +4]$ (Line 6).

When we choose a sensor module for $\mathcal{M}_{\mathrm{ht1}}$ from a series of modules with various prices and uncertainty (from cheap and more uncertain to expensive and less uncertain), the following question arises: *How uncertain can the sensor module of $\mathcal{M}_{\mathrm{ht1}}$ be and still be safe?* We show how we can answer this question with a manual analysis assisted by our automated workflow. Here we assume that the series of sensor modules have parameterized uncertainty $\varepsilon_{\Delta t} = \lambda temp. [temp - \Delta t, temp + \Delta t]$, where $0 \leq \Delta t$.

Action-preserving robustification. The action-preserving robustification generates the model $\mathcal{M}_{\mathrm{ht1}}^{\varepsilon_{\Delta t}, \mathrm{pR}}$ (Fig. 13) from $\mathcal{M}_{\mathrm{ht1}}$. We examine the event $E_{\{1,2\}}^{\mathsf{c}, \varepsilon_{\Delta t}, \mathrm{pR}}$, which is for the case where $\widehat{temp}$ satisfies $\phi_{\{1,2\}}^{\mathsf{c}, \varepsilon_{\Delta t}}(\widehat{temp}) = (\Delta t \leq 5 \Longrightarrow \widehat{temp} \in [30 - \Delta t, 30 + \Delta t)) \wedge (5 < \Delta t \Longrightarrow \widehat{temp} \in [30 - \Delta t, 40 - \Delta t])$ (Lines 6–8).

Lines 6–9 mean $dh \in [30 - (\widehat{temp} - \Delta t), 11]$. Lines 6–8 & 10 mean $dt \in [30 - \max(30, \widehat{temp} - \Delta t), 40 - \min(40, \widehat{temp} + \Delta t)] \cap [-4, 4]$. Moreover, since the intersection of actions should be nonempty for the feasibility of $E_{\{1,2\}}^{\mathsf{c}, \varepsilon_{\Delta t}, \mathrm{pR}}$ (Lines 11), dh should be equal to dt. The existence of such dh and dt is equivalent to $\Delta t \leq 2$. Therefore, an expensive sensor module with $\Delta t \leq 2$ will make the event $E_{\{1,2\}}^{\mathsf{c}, \varepsilon_{\Delta t}, \mathrm{pR}}$ invariant-preserving and feasible.

Action-repurposing robustification. The model $\mathcal{M}_{\mathrm{ht1}}^{\varepsilon_{\Delta t}, \mathrm{rR}}$ (Fig. 14) is generated by the action-repurposing robustification from $\mathcal{M}_{\mathrm{ht1}}$ using the action of ctrl_heat event. We examine the event $E_{\{1,2\}}^{\mathsf{c}, \varepsilon_{\Delta t}, \mathrm{rR}}$ for the $\phi_{\{1,2\}}^{\mathsf{c}, \varepsilon_{\Delta t}}(\widehat{temp})$ case again.

Line 9 means $dh \in [30 + \Delta t - \widehat{temp}, 40 - \Delta t - \widehat{temp}]$. The existence of such dh is equivalent to $30 + \Delta t - \widehat{temp} \leq 40 - \Delta t - \widehat{temp}$, which is also equivalent to $\Delta t \leq 5$. Thus, we find that we should use a sensor module with $\Delta t = 5$ at

```
1   Machine  M_{ht1}^{εΔt,pR}
2       ...
3       Controller event  E_{{1,2}}^{c,εΔt,pR}      /* ctrl_heat_keep_safe_eco_hetero */
4           Parameter set  P_{{1,2}}^{c,εΔt,pR} = ℤ × ℤ    /* parameter dh and dt */
5           Guard  G_{{1,2}}^{c,εΔt,pR}⟨⟨⟨tn, temp⟩, ⟨t͠n, t͠emp⟩⟩, ⟨dh, dt⟩⟩  ⟺
6               ∀t͠emp ∈ [t͠emp − Δt, t͠emp + Δt]. (t͠emp < 30 ∨ 30 ≤ t͠emp ≤ 40)
7               ∧ ∃t͠emp ∈ [t͠emp − Δt, t͠emp + Δt]. (t͠emp < 30)
8               ∧ ∃t͠emp ∈ [t͠emp − Δt, t͠emp + Δt]. (30 ≤ t͠emp ≤ 40)
9               ∧ ∀t͠emp ∈ [t͠emp − Δt, t͠emp + Δt]. (t͠emp < 30 ⟹ 30 ≤ t͠emp + dh ≤ 40)
10              ∧ ∀t͠emp ∈ [t͠emp − Δt, t͠emp + Δt].
                    (30 ≤ t͠emp ≤ 40 ⟹ 30 ≤ t͠emp + dt ≤ 40 ∧ −4 ≤ dt ≤ 4)
11              ∧ ∀t͠emp ∈ [t͠emp − Δt, t͠emp + Δt].
                    ({t͠emp'|t͠emp' = t͠emp + dh} ∩ {t͠emp'|t͠emp' = t͠emp + dt}) ≠ ∅
12          Action  A_{{1,2}}^{c,εΔt,pR}⟨⟨⟨tn, temp⟩, ⟨t͠n, t͠emp⟩⟩, ⟨dh, dt⟩⟩ = {⟨⟨tn', temp'⟩, ⟨t͠n', t͠emp'⟩⟩ |
                tn' = c ∧ temp' = temp + dh ∧ t͠emp' = t͠emp + dt ∧ ⟨tn', temp'⟩ ∈ ε_{Δt}(⟨t͠n', t͠emp'⟩)}
13      ...
```

Fig. 13. The heater model $\mathcal{M}_{ht1}^{εΔt,pR}$ produced by action-preserving robustification

```
1   Machine  M_{ht1}^{εΔt,rR}
2       ...
3       Controller event  E_{{1,2}}^{c,εΔt,rR}      /* ctrl_heat_keep_safe_eco_hetero */
4           Parameter set  P_{{1,2}}^{c,εΔt,rR} = ℤ × ℤ    /* parameter dh and dt */
5           Guard  G_{{1,2}}^{c,εΔt,rR}⟨⟨⟨tn, temp⟩, ⟨t͠n, t͠emp⟩⟩, ⟨dh, dt⟩⟩  ⟺
6               ∀t͠emp ∈ [t͠emp − Δt, t͠emp + Δt]. (t͠emp < 30 ∨ 30 ≤ t͠emp ≤ 40)
7               ∧ ∃t͠emp ∈ [t͠emp − Δt, t͠emp + Δt]. (t͠emp < 30)
8               ∧ ∃t͠emp ∈ [t͠emp − Δt, t͠emp + Δt]. (30 ≤ t͠emp ≤ 40)
9               ∧ ∀t͠emp ∈ [t͠emp − Δt, t͠emp + Δt]. (30 ≤ t͠emp + dh ≤ 40)
10          Action  A_{{1,2}}^{c,εΔt,rR}⟨⟨⟨tn, temp⟩, ⟨t͠n, t͠emp⟩⟩, ⟨dh, dt⟩⟩ = {⟨⟨tn', temp'⟩, ⟨t͠n', t͠emp'⟩⟩ |
                tn' = c ∧ temp' = temp + dh ∧ ⟨tn', temp'⟩ ∈ ε_{Δt}(⟨t͠n', t͠emp'⟩)}
11      ...
```

Fig. 14. The heater model $\mathcal{M}_{ht1}^{εΔt,rR}$ produced by action-repurposing robustification

least to obtain an invariant-preserving and feasible robustified $E_{{1,2}}^{c,εΔt,rR}$. In this way, the action-repurposing robustification generates a controller that tolerates larger uncertainty at the sacrifice of the compliance with some of original actions (e.g., $\mathcal{M}_{ht1}^{εΔt,rR}$ lacks the ecological "keep_safe" functionality).

7   Related Work

The topic of controller robustness to observation noise is a traditional topic in control theory. In this context, the majority of work focuses on robustness with respect to controller stability (e.g., [8]), rather than arbitrary safety properties. Recent work shows how perceptual uncertainty from visual sensors can be incorporated into the design of a stable controller [7].

In the area of controller synthesis from temporal logic specifications, there are approaches for robustifying synthesized controllers by using special interpretations of temporal logic formulas [6,9,10]. The basic idea is to contract the regions that must be visited, and inflating those that must be avoided, by δ.

These works synthesise hybrid controller implementations with the desired safety property under observation uncertainty; in contrast, in our approach we focus on transforming controller specifications to satisfy the property under observation uncertainty. On the other hand, our current approach is limited to discrete-event and discrete-time systems.

In the context of software systems, Zhang et al. [13] define robustness as the scope of environmental misbehavior that the system can tolerate without violating its safety property. They find this scope by computing the weakest assumption about the environment that will keep the property, expressed in LTL, satisfied. In contrast, we consider robustness to perceptual uncertainty, and support not only analysis but also automated redesign.

The area of software modeling has a variety of studies on uncertainty, such as combining business rules models and probabilistic relational models for answering probabilistic queries [3], augmenting UML/OCL with new datatypes and operations for modeling and propagation analysis of uncertainty [4], and transforming fuzzy UML models into fuzzy description logic knowledge bases for verification [14]. However, to the best of our knowledge, robustifying software models is not proposed.

8   Conclusion

This work provides a workflow to robustify a controller specification against perceptual uncertainty. Since safety properties and action safety are normally specified with respect to the true state of the world, our approach allows designers to first consider the idealized case, and then introduce the perceptual uncertainty as a subsequent step. Our case study demonstrated that our workflow supports the design exploration of the perceptual uncertainty levels that the controller could tolerate. Our methods operate on system specifications expressed in Event-B; however, the ideas of uncertainty injection, and action-preserving and action-repurposing robustification are more general. Specifically, our injection method shows how to introduce perceptual uncertainty into a state machine-based model of an uncertainty-unaware controller. Our robustification methods take the intersection of applicable actions or calculate parameters that guarantee safety for cases where the controller cannot determine which given actions should be taken due to uncertainty.

In future work, we will extend our methods to improve generality. For instance, taking probability into account can be promising for extending the application area. Moreover, we plan to propose a method for systematically relaxing requirements to gain more robustness.

References

1. Abrial, J.R.: Modeling in Event-B: System and software engineering. Cambridge University Press (2010)

2. Abrial, J.R., Butler, M., Hallerstede, S., Hoang, T.S., Mehta, F., Voisin, L.: Rodin: an open toolset for modelling and reasoning in event-B. Int. J. Softw. Tools Technol. Transf. **12**(6), 447–466 (2010). https://doi.org/10.1007/s10009-010-0145-y

3. Agli, Hamza., Bonnard, Philippe., Gonzales, Christophe, Wuillemin, Pierre-Henri: Business rules uncertainty management with probabilistic relational models. In: Alferes, Jose Julio Julio, Bertossi, Leopoldo, Governatori, Guido, Fodor, Paul, Roman, Dumitru (eds.) RuleML 2016. LNCS, vol. 9718, pp. 53–67. Springer, Cham (2016). https://doi.org/10.1007/978-3-319-42019-6_4

4. Bertoa, Manuel F., Burgueño, Loli., Moreno, Nathalie, Vallecillo, Antonio: Incorporating measurement uncertainty into OCL/UML primitive datatypes. Softw. Syst. Model. **19**(5), 1163–1189 (2019). https://doi.org/10.1007/s10270-019-00741-0

5. Event-B.org: Event-B.org. http://www.event-b.org/

6. Fainekos, G.E., Girard, A., Kress-Gazit, H., Pappas, G.J.: Temporal logic motion planning for dynamic robots. Automatica **45**(2), 343–352 (2009). https://doi.org/10.1016/j.automatica.2008.08.008

7. Jarin-Lipschitz, L., Li, R., Nguyen, T., Kumar, V., Matni, N.: Robust, perception based control with quadrotors. In: Proceedings of the 2020 IEEE/RSJ International Conference on Intelligent Robots and Systems (IROS), pp. 7737–7743 (2020). https://doi.org/10.1109/IROS45743.2020.9341507

8. Le Gorrec, Y., Chiappa, C.: Controller parametric robustification using observer-based formulation and multimodel design technique. IEEE Trans. Autom. Control **50**(4), 526–531 (2005). https://doi.org/10.1109/TAC.2005.844895

9. Liu, J., Topcu, U., Ozay, N., Murray, R.M.: Reactive controllers for differentially flat systems with temporal logic constraints. In: Proceedings of the 51st IEEE Conference on Decision and Control (CDC), pp. 7664–7670 (2012). https://doi.org/10.1109/CDC.2012.6425981

10. Liu, J., Ozay, N.: Abstraction, discretization, and robustness in temporal logic control of dynamical systems. In: Proceedings of the 17th International Conference on Hybrid Systems: Computation and Control (HSCC), HSCC 2014, pp. 293–302. ACM (2014). https://doi.org/10.1145/2562059.2562137

11. de Moura, Leonardo, Bjørner, Nikolaj: Z3: an efficient SMT solver. In: Ramakrishnan, C.R., Rehof, Jakob (eds.) TACAS 2008. LNCS, vol. 4963, pp. 337–340. Springer, Heidelberg (2008). https://doi.org/10.1007/978-3-540-78800-3_24

12. Salay, R., Czarnecki, K., Elli, M.S., Alvarez, I.J., Sedwards, S., Weast, J.: PURSS: towards perceptual uncertainty aware responsibility sensitive safety with ML. In: Proceedings of the Artificial Intelligence Safety (SafeAI) Workshop, collocated with AAAI, pp. 91–95 (2020)

13. Zhang, C., Garlan, D., Kang, E.: A behavioral notion of robustness for software systems. In: Proceedings of the 28th ACM Joint Meeting on European Software Engineering Conference and Symposium on the Foundations of Software Engineering (ESEC/FSE), pp. 1–12. ACM (2020). https://doi.org/10.1145/3368089.3409753

14. Zhang, F., Cheng, J.: Verification of fuzzy UML models with fuzzy description logic. Appl. Soft Comput. **73**, 134–152 (2018). https://doi.org/10.1016/j.asoc.2018.08.025

Good Fences Make Good Neighbors

Using Formally Verified Safe Trajectories to Design a Predictive Geofence Algorithm

Yanni Kouskoulas[1], Rosa Wu[1,2], Joshua Brulé[1], Daniel Genin[1],
Aurora Schmidt[1(✉)], and T. J. Machado[1,3]

[1] Johns Hopkins University Applied Physics Laboratory, Laurel, USA
`aurora.schmidt@jhuapl.edu`
[2] Defense Nuclear Facilities Safety Board, Washington, D.C., USA
[3] Department of Mathematics, New Mexico State University, Las Cruces, USA

Abstract. For AI-controlled mobile platforms, avoiding collisions with walls and boundaries is an important safety requirement. This is a problem especially for fast-moving aerial vehicles, such as fixed-wing aircraft, that cannot be brought to a stop in an emergency. To enable geographic confinement of such AI-controlled vehicles, we present a formally verified algorithm for predicting geofence violations and selecting a safe maneuver that will keep the vehicle within the designated operations area. The algorithm is based on a higher-order dynamics model that generalizes circular turns using linearly changing centripetal acceleration and allows handling of uncertainty in model parameters. The proposed algorithm was implemented along with extensions to handle non-determinism, and flight-tested on an autonomous aircraft.

1 Introduction

There are a host of mobile autonomous and semi-autonomous vehicles being developed today. Examples of these systems include: aerial vehicles used for surveillance and situational awareness, underwater vehicles used for mapping and research of lakes and oceans, surface vehicles used for commercial transport and inspection of bridges, ground vehicles such as autonomous cars and mobile robots. All such systems require a fail-safe confinement mechanism that will prevent them from leaving operations area in case of AI misbehavior.

Geofences are location-defined keep-in/keep-out regions[1]. Geofencing algorithms provide the logic to select actions that limit a system's motion within a geofence. These are especially useful with large and fast moving mobile

---

[1] For our purposes, we will focus on geofencing for keep-in regions only.

Defense Nuclear Facilities Safety Board—The views expressed herein are solely those of the authors, and no official support or endorsement by the Defense Nuclear Facilities Safety Board or the U.S. Government is intended or should be inferred.

© Springer Nature Switzerland AG 2021
A. Dutle et al. (Eds.): NFM 2021, LNCS 12673, pp. 214–230, 2021.
https://doi.org/10.1007/978-3-030-76384-8_14

autonomous systems such as jet propelled aircraft, for which physical confinement devices such as barriers and nets are not practical. Most geofencing algorithms in use today are reactive [15,16], i.e. a safety remediation maneuver is triggered when the vehicle crosses a geofence boundary. This means that a geofence cannot be set at the true boundary of a keep-in area since a certain amount of space must be allocated to allow for the remediation maneuver. In order to prevent excursions outside the keep-in area, the interior buffer must be large enough to encompass the safety remediation maneuver, no matter the speed and direction of the motion of the vehicle. In practice, this often means that the resulting geofenced area—allowing unimpeded operation of the vehicle—is significantly smaller than the actual keep-in area, unduly restricting the operational area.

To address this shortcoming of the reactive approach we develop a predictive geofencing algorithm. Rather than waiting for a geofence violation to begin a safety remediation maneuver, our approach is to continuously compute the envelope of possible future positions of the vehicle during a remediation maneuver that is initiated one time step in the future, given its current state. We account for uncertainty in the state estimation, dynamics model and environment, and activate remediation maneuvers only when the future prediction violates the geofence boundary.

Many approaches model vehicle motion using Dubins paths, which are composed of straight lines and circular arcs. However, based on private conversations with experts [13], existing evidence [1], and our own analysis of flight test and simulation data, it is clear that Dubins trajectories deviate from what is actually observed in the fast autonomous aircraft that are the focus of our work. It has also been observed in [2] that differential-drive mobile ground robots have similar deviations from Dubins.

One factor that creates a deviation between modeled and observed trajectories is the change in centripetal acceleration during a turn transition. The dynamics for some vehicles lead to gradual changes in centripetal acceleration during a turn, which doesn't match the step function assumed by the Dubins model. As an improvement, we model a turn transition with a linear ramp in centripetal acceleration. This is a more accurate model – one order higher than Dubins – that more closely matches gradual turn transition dynamics. For vehicles that cannot change their turn rate rapidly, this can make a significant difference in the overall trajectory, as shown in Fig. 1. The kinematics that are produced from such a ramp create a path that follows an Euler spiral [17] (sometimes called Cornu spirals or clothoids).

We develop a mathematically rigorous analysis of the Euler-spiral-augmented Dubins paths that allows us to predict *when* and *which* safety remediation maneuver should be used to keep the vehicle within the geofenced area. The core calculations for analyzing Euler-spiral kinematics are formally verified to guarantee safety, conferring a much higher level of assurance and reliability than is available from other approaches. The analysis is easily converted into a computationally efficient algorithm. By extending the analysis to accommodate uncertainty in state estimation, dynamic model parameters and random environmental factors we make the algorithm robust to errors and noise inevitable in any

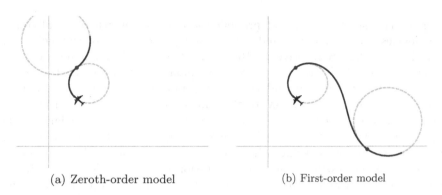

(a) Zeroth-order model   (b) First-order model

Fig. 1. Comparing a path with zeroth- and first-order models for centripetal accelera-tion changes. The first-order model has an extra curve between the end points of circle arcs created by the linear (vs. discontinuous step) change in centripetal acceleration.

real-world cyber-physical system. Our formal proofs also provide a foundation – a necessary first step – for formally verifying the extensions to the algorithm that are used in the overall approach for even higher levels of reliability.

Finally, we briefly sketch how the algorithm can be used to develop a verified safety fallback controller following ideas developed in [8].

The rest of the paper is structured as follows: in Sect. 3 we develop the anal-ysis of the Euler spiral-augmented Dubins paths.[2] The analysis is subsequently extended to accommodate uncertainty in vehicle state estimation and dynam-ics model parameters, and random environmental factors (e.g., wind gusts) in Sects. 4. In Sect. 5 we present flight test results of a prototype implementation of the proposed algorithm. We summarize our work and outline directions for future research in Sect. 6.

2   Prior Work

There are a variety of challenges associated with enforcing motion boundaries. For example, [15] concentrates on the problem of identifying geofence violations; unlike the present work, it handles combinations of keep-in and keep-out bound-aries but provides no predictive dynamics for the vehicle's trajectory and no formal guarantees. Work in [12] combines wavefront-path planning with a vec-tor field describing target orientation to maintain a Dubins path and recover from violations in the presence of fixed obstacles; unlike the present work, the algorithm is grid-based and can handle arbitrary shaped geofences, but is not applicable to vehicles that do not follow Dubins paths and also does not offer

---

[2] All theorems have been formalized and verified in Coq theorem prover, and are available at https://bitbucket.org/ykouskoulas/egeof-proofs. These proofs rely on the property – admitted as an axiom – that the shortest distance between two points is a straight line.

any formal guarantees. A range of solutions require the creation of inner and outer boundaries to ensure geofence enforcement [4,5]; however, the predictive geofencing algorithm in this work accounts for the aircraft state and future maneuver viability to allow maximum use of space within the geofenced region. This can be a key consideration for ensuring safety on limited sized test-ranges. Predictive geofence violation detection algorithm proposed in [19] uses an innovative approach combining probabilistic aircraft motion model and a viability theory-based approach to predicting violations with high probability. The aircraft motion model, however, is constrained to a linear model, while the approach in the present paper handles nonlinear Euler spiral and Dubins dynamics. In addition, the authors of [19] focus on linear model parameter estimation and cannot guarantee that the obtained model is a strict overapproximation of the aircraft's path, which leads to undetected geofence violations. Our approach seeks to better approximate the path that a fixed wing aircraft follows when performing banked angle turns and seeks to capture the range of future possible positions with non-deterministic envelopes. Finally, to make the approach tractable the authors of [19] had to assume that only one geofence edge would be violated at a time, i.e., violations occur away from corners, while the presented approach handles any number of linear fence constraints simultaneously.

Implementation of motion that respects virtual fixtures in [7] is similar to the geofence problem, but applied to surgical systems. Unlike the present work, the virtual boundaries are planar surfaces oriented in three dimensions and dynamics is for cooperative control with uncertainty; abrupt adversarial acceleration changes are usefully conservative so Euler spirals are not used.

A number of efforts have used Euler spirals to model turning vehicles, but are not formally verified and do not accommodate for envelopes of uncertainty. Euler spirals are used in [2] to create turn transitions; unlike the present work, they are used to smooth existing paths constructed from straight-line segments to allow ground robots to follow them more accurately – obstacle avoidance must be treated separately. In [14], Euler spirals are used to transitions between Dubins turns for path planning; unlike the present work, obstacles are both mobile and cooperative and timing and obstacle avoidance is evaluated by numerical simulation of the path evolution.

Many approaches to horizontal collision avoidance and obstacle avoidance are based on Dubins turns and do not address variations in centripetal acceleration during the turn. For example, [10] searches through a branching set of possibilities to generate 3D Dubins paths for path planning that avoid constant-velocity or stationary obstacles; [18] uses a similar branching search in 2D using a "tentacle" algorithm to find paths that optimize a cost function accounting for turn radii and occupant comfort; and [6] modifies waypoint-based paths by directly calculating additional waypoints based on Dubins-style maneuvers to keep clear of ground obstacles. Unlike the present work, these efforts are not designed to avoid a set of stationary, linear boundaries, and are not formally verified or associated with any guarantees.

The approach we take to developing a controller that uses our proofs to enforce safety in a realistic system is derived from [8], adapted for horizontal motion using a dictionary limited to left/right circling maneuvers; we do not concern ourselves with vertical motion.

Each remediation maneuver in our dictionary ends in a circling trajectory, so the safety computation is similar to [11]. However, this work models gradual changes in centripetal acceleration, so the final circling trajectory is placed differently, and we analyze fixed rather than cooperatively moving obstacles.

3   Provably Safe Remediation Maneuvers

In this section we develop the mathematical machinery necessary to determine availability of a safe (with respect to the geofence) turning maneuver with an unlimited time horizon given the current vehicle state. The unlimited time horizon is guaranteed by completing the safe turning maneuver with a provably safe circling pattern that can be maintained until the system is ready to proceed.

The bulk of the work in the current section is devoted to developing properties of Euler spiral turns, since analyzing boundary collisions for the circular path that follows the turn transition is straightforward. The core approach has been formally verified using the Coq proof assistant; each theorem has a corresponding machine-checked proof. We begin by laying down basic assumptions and definitions.

We assume that the vehicle motion is constrained to the horizontal plane, i.e., horizontal motion can be decoupled from vertical motion. This assumption is trivially true for surface vehicles. UAVs (and UUVs) generally maneuver in three dimensions but typically have a control mode that maintains altitude (depth) and allows horizontal control to be effectively decoupled from vertical.

3.1   Geofence Representation

We will use geofence to mean a (virtual) boundary made of a non-intersecting curve that divides horizontal plane into a *safe* and *unsafe* regions. We can approximate a geofence boundary with any type of curvature as accurately as necessary with a series of inscribed line segments. We restrict our attention to convex keep-in safe regions, each of which thus approximated can be decomposed into a set of linear boundaries whose union provides a safe approximation.

In practice, geofences are usually specified by providing an ordered list of latitude-longitude pairs corresponding to the vertices of the safe region. We will assume that the safe region is sufficiently small that the curvature of the Earth can be safely ignored. In reality, our computations only require a much weaker assumption, that the safety remediation maneuver path in the flat east-north coordinate system has a negligible error, which is true in all practical situations. The stronger assumption allows us to represent all linear boundaries approximating the safe region as lines in a single Cartesian-coordinate system, which simplifies the presentation.

In our computations, linear geofence segments will be represented as pairs of two dimensional Cartesian points and vectors. A single line passing through point $\mathbf{p} = (p_x, p_y)$ with angular direction ϕ, measured counterclockwise from the x-axis (east) has equation $m_x(y - p_y) = m_y(x - p_x)$, where $m_y = \sin\phi$ and $m_x = \cos\phi$. The corresponding geofence segment will be represented by the pair $(\mathbf{p}, \mathbf{m})$, where $\mathbf{m} = (m_x, m_y)$. In addition, we use the convention that the safe region is always to the left of the line when looking in the direction of ϕ, or more formally safe region is the set $\{\mathbf{q} | \langle \mathbf{q} - \mathbf{p}, \mathbf{m}^\perp \rangle > 0\}$, where $\perp$ is the counterclockwise rotation operator defined by $(x, y)^\perp \equiv (-y, x)$.

We also define a safety metric that evaluates the safety of a point $\mathbf{q}$ with respect to a geofence $F = (\mathbf{p}, \mathbf{m})$

$$\text{safe}(\mathbf{q}, F) \equiv \langle (\mathbf{q} - \mathbf{p}), \mathbf{m}^\perp \rangle \tag{1}$$

Simply put, $\text{safe}(\mathbf{q}, F)$ is the signed perpendicular distance from q to the line defining F, positive for points left of F and negative for points on the right. Note that safe is defined by exactly the same expression as the safe region. Thus, we have

Property 1. $\mathbf{q}$ is in the safe region defined by F, or simply safe, if and only if $\text{safe}(\mathbf{q}, F) > 0$.

Property 2. The magnitude of $\text{safe}(\mathbf{q})$ is the distance between $\mathbf{q}$ and the closest (via straight-line perpendicular distance) point on the line defined by F. Lower valued points are "less safe" than higher valued points.

$$|\text{safe}(\mathbf{q})| = \|\mathbf{m}\| \min_{\langle \mathbf{u} - \mathbf{p}, \mathbf{m}^\perp \rangle = 0} \|\mathbf{q} - \mathbf{u}\| \tag{2}$$

For brevity, $\text{safe}(\mathbf{q})$ will be used when F is clear from context.

A geofence-avoiding safety remediation maneuver is safe if it is entirely contained within the safe geofence region. Since we are restricting our attention to convex geofence regions which are approximated by the intersection of safe half-plane regions, it is enough to check the safety of a maneuver for each linear geofence boundary separately. A maneuver is safe if it is safe for all linear geofence pieces. Thus, it is enough to develop maneuver safety analysis for a single linear geofence. This does not restrict us to solely linear boundaries, as it can ensure safety for curved boundaries and even those with sharp (acute) cusps in the keep-in region.

We next proceed to develop an algorithm for safety analysis of an Euler spiral turn terminating in a circling holding pattern with respect to a single linear geofence. Figure 2(b), shows a turn transition path that is an Euler spiral in which the centripetal acceleration changes linearly based on a finite, constant jerk assumption. To evaluate whether such a maneuver remains on the safe side of a linear boundary, we need to evaluate the safety of the initial turn and the safety of the final circling maneuver. We evaluate safety by finding the least safe (according to the safety metric) point for each of the trajectory segments. Without loss of generality we assume that at the beginning of the maneuver the vehicle is located at the origin and heading east (along the positive x-axis).

3.2 Euler Spiral Turns

Creating accurate paths for dynamics with linearly changing centripetal acceleration require curved transitions whose shape is that of an Euler spiral. The Euler spiral is a two-sided, two-dimensional spiral (see Fig. 2(a)) that has applications in areas as diverse as cartography, optics and railroad track construction [9]. It is defined to have a linearly varying curvature, which is the reciprocal of the radius of curvature, and which means that a mass moving with constant speed along an Euler spiral experiences linearly increasing centripetal acceleration, proportional to the distance traveled on the curve. This observation makes it easy to construct Euler spiral turns given initial and final desired centripetal accelerations, e.g., as in when transitioning to a circling pattern. By selecting a subset of the Euler spiral, we can work with a finite-length curve that we can use to model position during a gradual turn. It can represent a smoothly increasing turn, or a transition curve between two different circular arcs. In Cartesian coordinates, the parameterized Euler spiral is given by

$$\xi(k) \equiv \big(\xi_x(k), \xi_y(k)\big) \equiv (\ell C(k/\ell), \ell S(k/\ell)) \tag{3}$$

where $\ell \equiv \sqrt{\pi/\alpha}$, and α is the rate of change of centripetal acceleration in units of $distance/time^3$, and $C(z) \equiv \int_0^z \cos\left(\frac{1}{2}\pi v^2\right) dv$ and $S(z) \equiv \int_0^z \sin\left(\frac{1}{2}\pi v^2\right) dv$ are Fresnel integrals. We use k (standard notation for curvature) to emphasize the relationship between distance and curvature.

These equations give a very convenient arc-length parameterization of the Euler spiral. It follows that the magnitude of parameter k is equal to distance along the curve from the origin, and the sign of k determines the direction of motion – positive to the right and negative to the left. We summarize this in

Theorem 1 (Euler spiral turn rate). *After traveling a distance k on the Euler spiral, the radius of curvature at that point is given by $r = 1/(\alpha k)$, corresponding to turn rate $\theta' = \|v\|\alpha k$ (in rad/s) (assuming constant speed $\|v\|$).*

In summary, a transition from straight-line motion to a leftward turn of θ' rad/s can be represented by a segment of the spiral starting at $k_i = 0$ (the origin) and ending at $k_f = \frac{\theta'}{\|v\|\alpha}$. At the end of the transition, we assume the trajectory follows a circular path shown by the dashed, osculating circle in Fig. 2(b).

Our proofs begin by showing that the Euler spiral is indeed a spiral – something that may or may not have been obvious to Bernoulli when he first started working with these curves – i.e. that further segments of the curve are in some sense contained by the earlier segments of the curve.

Theorem 2 (Euler spiral is spiral). *The osculating circle at each point on the right half of the curve $\xi(\cdot)$ contains all the rest of the points in the curve that follow, so that*

$$\forall p, q,\ 0 < p < q \rightarrow \left\| \xi(q) - \left(\xi(p) + \frac{\xi'(p)^\perp}{\alpha p} \right) \right\|^2 < \frac{1}{(\alpha p)^2} \tag{4}$$

We approached this by defining an osculating circle, formalizing properties of the Frenet-Serret equations for 2D paths, instantiating those properties for Eq. 3, and then using them to formalize a variant of Kneser's nesting theorem.

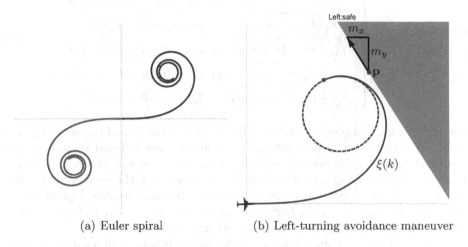

(a) Euler spiral   (b) Left-turning avoidance maneuver

Fig. 2. (a) A full Euler spiral, realized as parametric equation of two Fresnel integrals. We analyze the blue portion of the spiral for a left turn avoidance maneuver. (b) The shaded region represents the area outside the geofence boundary. Initial state starts at the origin traveling straight towards the positive x-axis. The path transitions (solid curve, following $\xi(k)$ from $k \in [k_i, k_f]$) from initial state to circle counterclockwise (dashed curve with radius $r = 1/(\alpha k_f)$). (Color figure online)

3.3 Determining Euler Spiral Turn Safety

The Euler spiral has a monotonically changing curvature, with an inflection point at the origin where the turn direction changes from right to left. These properties can be exploited to rigorously evaluate safety of a turn transition by looking at four points along the spiral.

We will define a set of *candidate safety minima* that will include the worst-case dominant point closest to violating the geofence or, if the turn is unsafe, the point deepest into the unsafe region. This set is made up of the points that could be maximally unsafe positions during the maneuver, i.e. the potential minima of the safety metric along the Euler spiral segment. The minimum of a function on a closed interval is either a critical point with positive second derivative or one of the endpoints. The critical points of the safety function can be explicitly computed by setting its derivative to zero

$$\frac{d}{ds} \, \text{safe}\, (\xi(s)) = -\cos\left(\frac{\pi}{2}\left(\frac{s}{\ell}\right)^2\right) m_y + \sin\left(\frac{\pi}{2}\left(\frac{s}{\ell}\right)^2\right) m_x = 0 \qquad (5)$$

Solving for s_n, the nth critical point is given by

$$
s_n = \begin{cases}
\ell\sqrt{\frac{2}{\pi}(\gamma + n\pi)} & \text{for } m_x \neq 0 \wedge n \geq 0 \wedge \gamma \geq 0 \\
\ell\sqrt{\frac{2}{\pi}(\gamma + (n+1)\pi)} & \text{for } m_x \neq 0 \wedge n \geq 0 \wedge \gamma < 0 \\
\ell\sqrt{\frac{2}{\pi}\left(\frac{\pi}{2} + n\pi\right)} & \text{for } m_x = 0 \wedge n \geq 0 \\
-\ell\sqrt{\frac{2}{\pi}(\gamma - (n+1)\pi)} & \text{for } m_x \neq 0 \wedge n < 0 \wedge \gamma \geq 0 \\
-\ell\sqrt{\frac{2}{\pi}(\gamma - n\pi)} & \text{for } m_x \neq 0 \wedge n < 0 \wedge \gamma < 0 \\
-\ell\sqrt{\frac{2}{\pi}\left(\frac{\pi}{2} - (n+1)\pi\right)} & \text{for } m_x = 0 \wedge n < 0
\end{cases}
\tag{6}
$$

where $\gamma = \tan^{-1}(m_y/m_x)$, which is only sensitive to the sign of the ratio m_y/m_x, so s_n enumerates all local extrema. The solutions are indexed so that $n \geq 0$ represent critical points on the right-hand side of the spiral, and $n < 0$ critical points on the left-hand side of the spiral. Note that when the geofence is parallel to the x-axis, the inflection point at the origin becomes a critical point of the safety metric and has a double representation as $s_0 = s_{-1}$. Otherwise, each critical point is uniquely determined by its integer index.

The local maxima and minima of the safety function alternate along the spiral as indicated in Fig. 3(a). Key observations that follow from this pattern can be formalized as follows

Theorem 3 (Critical point safety ordering). *If N is a positive even integer and $m_y \leq 0$ or N is a positive odd integer and $m_y \geq 0$ then*

$$\text{safe}(s_N) < \text{safe}(s_{N+2})$$

Moreover, for any two points $s_a < s_b$ in $[s_N, s_{N+1}]$ we have $\text{safe}(s_a) < \text{safe}(s_b)$ and for any $s_a < s_b$ in $[s_{N+1}, s_{N+2}]$, $\text{safe}(s_b) < \text{safe}(s_a)$.

A symmetric result with opposite inequalities holds if the constraints on m_y are reversed (refer to proofs at the provided link for more details). Additional results and detailed reasoning about the $m_y = 0$ case is included in the formal proofs. The corresponding result for $N < 0$ can be deduced from the central symmetry of the Euler spiral about the origin.

Thus, the set of candidate safety minima is the set of positions along the spiral consisting of the endpoints $k_i = 0$ and $k_f = \frac{\theta'}{\|v\|\alpha}$ of the spiral segment (corresponding to the Euler spiral turn), and the set containing at most two critical points with the lowest valued indices contained within the segment $[k_i, k_f]$

$$\mathcal{M} \equiv \{k_i, k_f, \mu_{even}, \mu_{odd}\} \cap \mathbb{R} \tag{7}$$

where

$$\mu_{even} \equiv \inf\{s_{2n} | k_i < s_{2n} < k_f, n \in \mathbb{Z}\}$$
$$\mu_{odd} \equiv \inf\{s_{2n+1} | k_i < s_{2n+1} < k_f, n \in \mathbb{Z}\}$$

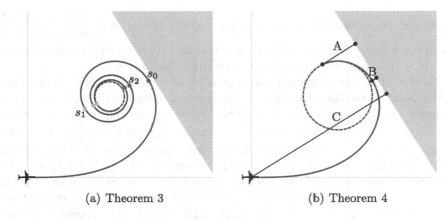

(a) Theorem 3   (b) Theorem 4

Fig. 3. Theorem visualizations. (a) The critical points of the safety metric, s_n, on the Euler spiral alternate between minima and maxima. The points shown in green and red are the local maxima and minima, respectively, of the safety metric. (b) A, B, and C are shortest distances from the critical points of the Euler spiral to the geofence. By Property 2, these distances are proportional to the safety metric; $B < A < C$ so B is the closest approach point by Theorem 4

The intersection with $\mathbb{R}$ is necessary to eliminate potential infinities resulting from the standard convention that $\inf(\varnothing) = \infty$.

Finally, we have the following criterion for determining the safety of an Euler spiral turn:

Theorem 4 (Euler spiral turn safety). *An Euler spiral turn, defined by a section of the Euler spiral on parameter interval $[k_i, k_f]$, is safe if and only if* safe$(\mathcal{M}) > 0$, *where* safe$(\mathcal{M}) = \min_{s \in \mathcal{M}}$ safe(s). *Moreover, if positive,* safe$(\mathcal{M})$ *is the distance of the point of closest approach from the geofence, and, if negative, it is the point of the farthest excursion beyond the geofence.*

This follows directly from definitions of safe and $\mathcal{M}$ (Eqs. 1 and 7, respectively), and Theorem 3.

After determining the safety of the Euler spiral turn, analysis of the safety of the final circling pattern is straightforward. Given the center of the terminal circle $\xi(k_f) + (\alpha k_f)^{-1} \xi'(k_f)^{\perp}$, we can determine whether the circumference crosses the geofence.

3.4 Arbitrary Initial Conditions

It is straightforward to compute the safety of a turn for a vehicle with arbitrary initial position $\mathbf{q}_0$, θ_0 and θ_0'. We simply need to apply a pair of affine transformations that translate and rotate this initial position and the geofence so that the Euler spiral turn segment of the remediation maneuver lines up with the standard Euler spiral given by $\xi(k)$. To achieve this, we first map the initial position and velocity so that they match up with the origin and the positive x-axis respectively. This transformation is defined by $T(\mathbf{q}) \equiv R_{-\theta_0}(\mathbf{q} - \mathbf{q}_0)$, where

R_θ is the counter-clockwise rotation by θ given by $R_\theta \equiv \begin{bmatrix} \cos(\theta) & -\sin(\theta) \\ \sin(\theta) & \cos(\theta) \end{bmatrix}$.
This transforms a geofence defined by $\mathbf{p}$ and $\mathbf{m} = (\cos(\phi), \sin(\phi))$ into F' with $\mathbf{p}' = R_{-\theta_0}(\mathbf{p} - \mathbf{q_0})$, $m_x' = \cos(\phi - \theta_0)$, and $m_y' = \sin(\phi - \theta_0)$.

Next we map this standard initial position of the vehicle and the geofence to the point along the Euler spiral with the matching turn rate. It is easy to compute the correct point because of the linear relationship between distance and curvature for $\xi(k)$. If the initial turn rate is θ_0' then $k_i = \frac{\theta_0'}{\|v\|\alpha}$. The affine transformation that aligns vehicle in standard position with the corresponding Euler spiral point is $S(\mathbf{q}) = R_\gamma \mathbf{q} + \xi(k_i)$, where $\gamma = \text{atan}_2(\xi_x'(k_i), \xi_y'(k_i))$. So, the composition $S \circ T$, will map the given initial conditions to the corresponding point on the Euler spiral and transform geofence accordingly. The transformed geofence F' has the form: $\mathbf{p}' = R_{\gamma-\theta_0}(\mathbf{p} - \mathbf{q_0}) + \xi(k_i)$, $m_x' = \cos(\phi + \gamma - \theta_0)$, and $m_y' = \sin(\phi + \gamma - \theta_0)$.

The safety of a turn starting with initial conditions $\mathbf{q_0}$, θ_0, θ_0' with respect to F is equivalent to the safety of the same Euler spiral segment in standard position with respect to F'.

Depending on the relationship between the initial and final turn rates, and the direction of the turn, the Euler spiral may need to be traversed in the reverse direction, and one may also need to consider the symmetric Euler spiral $\hat{\xi}(k) = (-\xi_x(k), \xi_y(k))$. It is easy to derive the equivalent of Theorem 3 for $\hat{\xi}(k)$ and the corresponding Theorem 4.

3.5   Computational Efficiency

The Euler spiral turn model generalizes the Dubins path model, but remains nearly as computationally efficient for this application. For each safety calculation that evaluates a turning trajectory and a linear boundary, we need to compute, at most, four points – the beginning and end of the Euler spiral segment, and the first two critical points s_n, if they fall within the spiral segment of interest. For example, in Fig. 3(b) three critical points will need to checked for safety, the two segment endpoints and the spiral minimum.

Calculating the critical points and evaluating the safety metric at each point involves (a fixed number of) elementary operations, square roots, the `atan2` function, and evaluation of the Fresnel integral, which can be efficiently numerically approximated [3].

In summary, evaluating safety requires linear (in the number of linear segments used to create the geofence boundary) time and no dynamic memory allocations. Safety can be computed for every state update that a controller receives and is practical for real-time applications.

4   Extensions to Nondeterministic Trajectories

Until now, we have treated the safety of a specific trajectory. This section describes – without formal proof – extensions to ensure safety for a range of possible trajectories and a set of boundaries. Each of these extensions may be combined with the others to allow an assessment of safety that includes realistic variations in future possibilities. Whatever procedure we can use to establish safety for a single, linear boundary can be used to establish safety for a set of linear boundaries that we use to safely approximate an arbitrarily curved, convex keep-in area.

Position Uncertainty. We can use our analysis to compute safety when knowledge of position in the environment is uncertain. Positional uncertainty may represent sensor noise related to measurement of our absolute position, (x_0, y_0), as well as uncertainty in the exact positioning of the linear boundary (p_x, p_y), or perturbations due to wind during the maneuver. Each of these types of positional uncertainty create an envelope around the aircraft or fence, encompassing a range of possibilities for relative positions for the fence and vehicle.

We add an additional buffer, made by combining these factors into a offset d, which quantifies the maximum amount by which our uncertainty can unexpectedly push us closer to the fence during the maneuver. If we choose our reference frame to be fixed on the aircraft these uncertainties shift the fence by d in a direction perpendicular to its orientation, so the linear boundary defined by $\mathbf{p} = (p_x, p_y)$, $m_x = \cos\phi$, and $m_y = \sin\phi$ becomes a linear boundary defined by $\mathbf{p} + d(-m_y, m_x)$. When there is more than one linear boundary that makes up the geofence, each linear boundary must shift the point that defines its position according to its individual m_x and m_y slope components. This shifting of boundaries moves the geofence "inward," giving us a margin of error to safely handle position uncertainty.

Circling Radius Uncertainty. The turn radius we use is an upper bound for a safe turn radius. All else equal, smaller turn radii are also safely contained on the safe side of the linear boundary, because the osculating circle at any given point in the Euler spiral contains the rest of the spiral, and also contains any osculating circle that is further along the spiral, as shown in Theorem 2. Any final turn radius we determine to be safe also ensures that any smaller turn radius is also safe.

Orientation Uncertainty. We can use our analysis to compute safety when knowledge of our orientation in the environment is uncertain, which may be due to noise related to estimation of our absolute orientation $\theta \in [\theta_l, \theta_h]$ defined by the direction of motion.

We must check the safety of positions within a convex region created by the union of convex hulls associated with the range of spirals possible for the uncertainty in orientation. This union is made from the convex hull for a single orientation θ, rotated around its starting position (x_0, y_0), through the range of possible direction angles $[\theta_l, \theta_h]$. The union is shown for two different turns by the shaded areas in Fig. 4(c). Checking the safety may be done in two steps: first, we check the safety of the convex hulls associated with limiting orientations θ_l and θ_h; second, check the safety of points within a pie slice shape whose vertex

(x_0, y_0) is connected with line segments to points the furthest points in the limiting hulls connected to each other by a circular arc.

We can find the distance to the furthest point on the curve ρ_s from (x_0, y_0), our present position, by solving for the minimum value of k in $D_s(k) \cdot \frac{d}{dk} \xi(k) = 0$ where $D_s(k) = \xi(k) - \xi(k_i)$ is the vector from the start of the turn to each future position in the trajectory identified by k. Recall k_i is the parameter identifying the start point of the spiral segment that models our turn transition. If no such solution exists, then $\rho_s = k_f$. Similarly, we can solve for the furthest point on the turning circle ρ_c from (x_0, y_0) and the distance associated with this point $D_c(\rho_c)$.

We then find the furthest point for the convex hull at that angle by taking the point associated with the maximum of the two possibilities,

$$f_\theta = \begin{cases} \rho_c \text{ for } \|D_c(\rho_c)\| \geq \|D_s(\rho_s)\| \\ \rho_s \qquad \text{otherwise} \end{cases} \tag{8}$$

5   Application

This project included testing the formally verified predictive geofencing algorithm in a US Air Force flight test. We have implemented our analysis of the Euler spiral turning model as a fallback safety controller which was integrated into an on-board watchdog controller. The predictive geofence violation detection logic was synthesized directly from the technique described in [8]. To ensure that an autonomous vehicle's motion respects a geofence, we created a dictionary of predictive models of its future trajectory, sampling both left and right turns. A remediation maneuver is chosen to be a transition to a circular holding pattern. This ensures that if we remediate, we can continue to safely follow the remediation maneuver for as long as necessary, abandoning it and transitioning to a safe alternative trajectory when one becomes available.

At each time-step, the watchdog evaluates whether we can: allow the present motion (within uncertainty bounds) to continue until the next control time-step and then, at that future time, initiate and follow a remediation maneuver that keeps us within the geofence boundary. While propagating the current state of the plane to a future state at which the remediation might be applied, we incorporate future state uncertainty by allowing a range of possible positions and orientations. If we can ensure at each control time-step that we can initiate remediation at the next control action, then we can allow the autonomy to operate without interference. If we find that the present trajectory cannot be made safe by future remediation, then we immediately initiate remediation in the current control time-step. It is guaranteed safe under our assumptions by the analysis we made during the previous control interval. Figure 4 illustrates the evaluation of the safety of initiating left and right turns in the future for a single trajectory. Our approach can safely handle a range of future possibilities using the extensions in Sect. 4 to check the convex hulls that represent positional uncertainty, uncertainty in final turn radius, and uncertainty in the direction of travel.

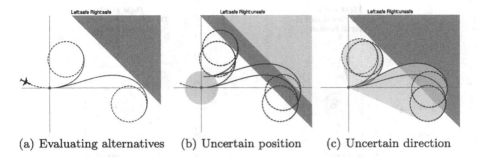

(a) Evaluating alternatives   (b) Uncertain position   (c) Uncertain direction

Fig. 4. Practical extensions described in Sect. 4 allow us to safely evaluate turns initiated in the future that simultaneously have uncertainty in position and direction of travel. The modeled uncertainty can ensure that safety assessments are relevant despite wind, sensor error, and other deviations from the modeled kinematics.

This safety controller was integrated on a fixed-wing Swift Radioplanes Lynx aircraft (cruise speed 17 m/s) with an additional Raspberry Pi board. The controller operates as part of a larger message-passing system and subscribes to aircraft state messages published by the aircraft's autopilot (ArduPilot running on Pixhawk hardware). During normal operation, the aircraft is controlled by a primary controller. The fallback controller only intervenes when a predicted violation of the geofence is imminent. Upon a predicted violation of the geofence, the fallback controller issues a request to the ArduPilot autopilot to return to and then loiter around a known, safe waypoint. The parameters of the fallback controller were set according to our prior knowledge of the aircraft's roll rate and maximum (safe) turning rate used by the autopilot. We included one additional parameter not present in our theoretical model: the maximum round-trip time between receiving state information from the aircraft and executing the remediation. For our initial tests, we set this conservatively at 1 s.

Figure 5 plots the trajectories of the flight tests, showing rectangular geofence boundaries and a set of waypoints that the aircraft was asked to fly to sequentially. As the aircraft approached each waypoint, the safety controller would predict a future violation, take over, and override the autonomy by commanding a return to and loiter around the known safe waypoint in the interior. This implementation did not incorporate wind estimates, since they were unavailable at the time. Instead, we used a conservative estimate of worst-case wind effects to set model position uncertainty. We see that the wind, which blew primarily from the northeast that day, pushed the aircraft closer to the leftmost boundary, using up the margin of safety for the approach to the lower left waypoint in Flight Test 1.

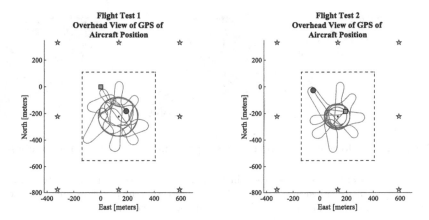

Fig. 5. Results of flight tests: Aircraft trajectories (in blue), from the start (green box) to the end (red circle), as the autonomy flies to each of the 8 commanded points (yellow stars) outside of the geofence. (Color figure online)

6   Conclusions and Future Work

We have extended predictive geofencing to turning models that increase the realism of predicted aircraft flight. The core of our approach has several desirable properties: the proofs of safety are formally verified and the computation of safety admits an efficient algorithm. We demonstrated the use of the predictive geofence safety theorem as a fallback controller, which was successfully flight-tested.

Future work regarding the formal proofs includes proofs of the extensions outlined in Sect. 4 to model uncertain parameter ranges and symmetry arguments that are currently associated with paper-only proofs.

Future work in integration and testing of these approaches includes further testing and calibration of the flight parameter ranges that serve as input to our algorithm. Initial testing of the predictive geofencing function was successful and further testing would enable wider adoption of this approach to verifying real-time safety controllers. In the long term, automatic extraction of the geofencing algorithm from the proofs would yield even higher assurances of correctness.

Acknowledgements. This work was supported by the US Air Force Research Laboratory's Strategic Development Planning and Experimentation Office under contract number HQ0034-19-D-0006. The authors would also like to thank Dr.'s Christopher Eaton, Edward White, and Reed Young for their leadership and fostering of this work. Additionally, we thank the entire team, especially Dorothy Kirlew and Andrea Jensenius, for their dedication in making the flight-testing of this approach possible.

References

1. Brandse, J., Mulder, M., Van Paassen, M.M.: Clothoid-augmented trajectories for perspective flight-path displays. Int. J. Aviat. Psychol. **17**, 1–29 (2007)

2. Brezak, M., Petrović, I.: Path smoothing using clothoids for differential-drive mobile robots. In: Proceedings of the 18th World Congress the International Federation of Automatic Control, IFAC 2011, Milano, Italy, 28 August – 2 September 2011, vol. 18, pp. 1133–1138 (January 2011)
3. Cody, W.: Chebyshev approximations for the Fresnel integrals. Math. Comput. **22**(102), 450–453 (1968)
4. Dill, E.T., Young, S.D., Hayhurst, K.J.: SAFEGUARD: an assured safety net technology for UAS. In: 2016 IEEE/AIAA 35th Digital Avionics Systems Conference (DASC), pp. 1–10 (2016). https://doi.org/10.1109/DASC.2016.7778009
5. Gilabert, R.V., Dill, E.T., Hayhurst, K.J., Young, S.D.: SAFEGUARD: progress and test results for a reliable independent on-board safety net for UAS. In: 2017 IEEE/AIAA 36th Digital Avionics Systems Conference (DASC), pp. 1–9 (2017). https://doi.org/10.1109/DASC.2017.8102087
6. Kikutis, R., Stankūnas, J., Rudinskas, D., Masiulionis, T.: Adaptation of Dubins paths for UAV ground obstacle avoidance when using a low cost on-board GNSS sensor. Sensors **17**, 2223 (2017)
7. Kouskoulas, Y., Renshaw, D., Platzer, A., Kazanzides, P.: Certifying the safe design of a virtual fixture control algorithm for a surgical robot. In: Belta, C., Ivancic, F. (eds.) Proceedings of the 16th International Conference on Hybrid Systems: Computation and Control, HSCC 2013, Philadelphia, PA, USA, 8–11 April 2013, pp. 263–272. ACM (2013). https://doi.org/10.1145/2461328.2461369
8. Kouskoulas, Y., Schmidt, A., Jeannin, J.B., Genin, D., Lopez, J.: Provably safe controller synthesis using safety proofs as building blocks. In: IEEE 7th International Conference on Software Engineering Research and Innovation, CONISOFT 2019, Mexico City, Mexico, 23–25 October 2019, pp. 26–35 (2019)
9. Levien, R.: The Euler spiral: a mathematical history. Technical report, UCB/EECS-2008-111, EECS Department, University of California, Berkeley (September 2008). http://www2.eecs.berkeley.edu/Pubs/TechRpts/2008/EECS-2008-111.html
10. Lin, Y., Saripalli, S.: Path planning using 3d Dubins curve for unmanned aerial vehicles. In: 2014 International Conference on Unmanned Aircraft Systems (ICUAS), Orlando, FL, USA, pp. 296–304 (2014)
11. Loos, S.M., Renshaw, D.W., Platzer, A.: Formal verification of distributed aircraft controllers. In: Proceedings of the 16th International Conference on Hybrid Systems: Computation and Control, HSCC 2013, Philadelphia, PA, USA, 8–11 April 2013, pp. 125–130 (2013). https://doi.org/10.1145/2461328.2461350
12. Miraglia, G., Hook, L.: Dynamic geo-fence assurance and recovery for nonholonomic autonomous aerial vehicles. In: 2017 IEEE/AIAA 36th Digital Avionics Systems Conference (DASC), St. Petersburg, FL, USA, pp. 1–7 (2017)
13. Monk, W.: Personal communication
14. Shanmugavel, M., Tsourdos, A., White, B., Żbikowski, R.: Co-operative path planning of multiple UAVs using Dubins paths with clothoid arcs. Control Eng. Pract. **18**(9), 1084–1092 (2010). https://doi.org/10.1016/j.conengprac.2009.02.010
15. Stevens, M.N., Rastgoftar, H., Atkins, E.M.: Specification and evaluation of geofence boundary violation detection algorithms. In: 2017 International Conference on Unmanned Aircraft Systems (ICUAS), Miami, FL, USA, pp. 1588–1596 (2017)
16. Team, P.: Px4 user guide: Geofence (2012). https://docs.px4.io/v1.10/en/flying/geofence.html. Accessed 7 Jan 2020
17. West, M.: Track transition curves (2012). http://dynref.engr.illinois.edu/avt.html. Accessed 7 Jan 2020

18. Wu, L., Zha, H., Xiu, C., He, Q.: Local path planning for intelligent vehicle obstacle avoidance based on Dubins curve and tentacle algorithm. In: SAE Technical Paper. SAE International (September 2017). https://doi.org/10.4271/2017-01-1951
19. Yoon, H., Chou, Y., Chen, X., Frew, E., Sankaranarayanan, S.: Predictive runtime monitoring for linear stochastic systems and applications to geofence enforcement for UAVs. In: Finkbeiner, B., Mariani, L. (eds.) RV 2019. LNCS, vol. 11757, pp. 349–367. Springer, Cham (2019). https://doi.org/10.1007/978-3-030-32079-9_20

Online Shielding for Stochastic Systems

Bettina Könighofer[1,3]([✉]), Julian Rudolf[1], Alexander Palmisano[1],
Martin Tappler[2,3,4], and Roderick Bloem[1]

[1] Institute IAIK, Graz University of Technology, Graz, Austria
bettina.konighofer@iaik.tugraz.at
[2] Institute IST, Graz University of Technology, Graz, Austria
[3] Silicon Austria Labs, TU-Graz SAL DES Lab, Graz, Austria
[4] Schaffhausen Institute of Technology, Schaffhausen, Switzerland

Abstract. We propose a method to develop trustworthy reinforcement learning systems. To ensure safety especially during exploration, we automatically synthesize a correct-by-construction runtime enforcer, called a shield, that blocks all actions of the agent that are unsafe with respect to a temporal logic specification. Our main contribution is a new synthesis algorithm for computing the shield online. Existing offline shielding approaches compute exhaustively the safety of all states-action combinations ahead-of-time, resulting in huge computation times, large memory consumption, and significant delays at runtime due to the look-ups in huge databases. The intuition behind online shielding is to compute at runtime the set of all states that could be reached in the near future. For each of these states, the safety of all available actions is analysed and used for shielding as soon as one of the considered states is reached. Our proposed method is general and can be applied to a wide range of planning problems with stochastic behaviour. For our evaluation, we selected a 2-player version of the classical computer game SNAKE. The game requires fast decisions and the multiplayer setting induces a large state space, computationally expensive to analyze exhaustively. The safety objective of collision avoidance is easily transferable to a variety of planning tasks.

1 Introduction

Reinforcement Learning (RL) proved successful in solving complex tasks that are difficult to solve using classic controller design, including applications in computer games [33], multi-agent planning [40], and robotics [37]. RL learns high-performance controllers by optimizing objectives expressed via rewards in unknown, stochastic environments. Although learning-enabled controllers (LECs) have the potential to outperform classical controllers, safety concerns prevent LECs from being widely used in real-world tasks [3]. In RL, optimal strategies are obtained without prior knowledge about the environment. Therefore, the safety of actions is not known before their executions. Even after training, there is no guarantee that no unsafe actions are part of the final policy. Having no safety guarantees is unacceptable for safety-critical areas, such as

A. Dutle et al. (Eds.): NFM 2021, LNCS 12673, pp. 231–248, 2021.
https://doi.org/10.1007/978-3-030-76384-8_15

autonomous driving. Safety guarantees take different forms. Especially safety-critical operations require the absence of all unsafe behaviour, while achieving absolute safety for all operations may be impossible due to uncertain, stochastic behaviour. In these cases, safety guarantees may limit the probability of unsafe events.

Shielding [7] is a runtime enforcement technique to ensure safe decision making. By augmenting an RL-agent with a shield unsafe actions are blocked by the shield and the learning agent can only pick a safe action to be sent to the environment. Shields are automatically constructed via correct-by-construction formal synthesis methods from a model of the environment dynamics and a safety specification. Consequently, an agent augmented with a shield is guaranteed to satisfy the safety objective as long as the shield is used. We model the environment via Markov decision processes (MDPs), a popular modelling formalism for decision-making under uncertainty [36,38]. We assess safety by means of probabilistic *temporal logic constraints* [5], which can express different forms of safety guarantees. In this paper, we generally limit the probability to reach critical states in the MDP. For each state and action, exact probabilities are computed on how likely it is that executing this action results in a safety violation from the current state. The shield then blocks all actions whose probability of leading to safety violations exceeds a threshold with respect to an optimally safe action.

The problem with offline shielding. The computation of an offline shield for discrete-event systems requires an exhaustive, ahead-of-time safety analysis for all possible state-action combinations. Therefore, the complexity of offline shield synthesis grows exponentially in the state and action dimension, which limits the application of offline shielding to small environments. Previous work that applied shields in complex, high-dimensional environments relied on over-approximations of the reachable states and domain-oriented abstractions [2,4]. However, this may result in imprecise safety computations of the shield. This way, the shield may become over-restrictive, hindering the learning agent in properly exploring the environment and finding its optimal policy [19].

Our Solution – Online Shielding. Our approach is based on the idea of computing the safety of actions on-the-fly during run time. In many applications, the learning agent does not have to take a decision at every time step. Instead, the learning agent only has to make a decision when reaching a *decision state*. As an example consider a service robot traversing a corridor. The agent has time until the service robot reaches the end of the corridor, i.e., the next decision state, to decide where the service robot should go next. Online shielding uses the time between two decision states to compute the safety of all possible actions in the next decision state. When reaching the next decision state, this information is used to block unsafe actions of the agent. While the online safety analysis incurs a runtime overhead, every single computation of the safety of an action is efficient and parallelisable. Thus, in many settings, expensive offline pre-computation and huge shielding databases with costly lookups are not necessary. Since the safety analysis is performed only for decision states that are actually reached, online shielding is applicable to large, changing, or unknown environments.

In this paper, we solve the problem of shielding a controllable RL-agent in an environment shared with other autonomous agents that perform tasks concurrently. Some combinations of agent positions are safety-critical, as they e.g., correspond to collisions. A safety property may describe the probability of reaching such positions (or other safety properties expressible in temporal logic). The task of the shield is to block actions with a too high risk of leading to such a state. In online shielding, the computation of the safety for any action in the next decision state starts as soon as the controllable agent leaves the current decision state. The tricky part of online shielding in the multi-agent setting is that during the time the RL agent has between two consecutive decisions, the other agents also change their positions. Therefore, online shielding needs to compute the safety of actions with respect to all possible movements of the other agents.

Technically, we use MDPs to formalize the dynamics of the agents operating within the environment. At runtime, we create a small MDP for each decision. These MDPs model the immediate future from the viewpoint of the RL. Via model checking, we determine for the next actions the minimal probability of violating safety. An action is blocked by the shield, if the action violates safety with a probability higher than a threshold relative to the minimal probability.

Contributions. The contributions of this paper comprise (1) the formalisation of online shielding, (2) its implementation via probabilistic model-checking including a demonstrator that is available online[1], and (3) an evaluation of online shielding. The implementation and the evaluation apply shielding to a two-player version of the classic computer game SNAKE. The evaluation demonstrates that shields can be efficiently computed at runtime, guarantee safety, and have the potential to positively influence learning performance.

Outline. The rest of the paper is structured as follows. Section 1.1 discusses related work. We discuss the relevant foundations in Sect. 2. In Sect. 3, we present the setting and formulate the problem that we address. We present online shielding in Sect. 4, by defining semantics for autonomous agents in the considered setting and defining online shield computations based on these semantics. In Sect. 5, we report on the evaluation of online shielding for the classic computer game SNAKE. Section 6 concludes the paper with a summary and an outlook on future work.

1.1 Related Work

Runtime enforcement (RE) [12,30,41] covers a wide range of techniques to enforce the correctness of a controller at run-time. The concept of a correct-by-construction *safety-shield* to enforce such correctness with respect to a temporal logic specification was first proposed in [7]. Shields are usually constructed offline by computing a maximally permissive policy containing all actions that will not violate the safety specification. Several extensions exist [4,6,29,39]. The shielding approach has been shown to be successful in combination with RL [2,21].

---

[1] http://www.onlineshielding.at, accessed: 2020-11-27.

Jansen et al. [19] introduced offline shielding with respect to probabilistic safety. Our work on online shielding directly extends their notion of shielding to the online setting. The offline approach was limited as every action for every state has to be analyzed ahead of time, making the offline approach infeasible for complex environments. Our proposed extension to perform the safety analysis online allows the application of shielding in large, high-dimensional environments.

Pranger et al. [29] proposed *adaptive shields* to enforce quantitative objectives at run-time. While the computation of their shields is performed offline, the authors deal with the consequences of an incorrect or incomplete model that is used for the computation of the shield. During runtime, the authors use abstraction refinement and online probability estimation to update the model and synthesize new shields from the updated models periodically.

Li et al. [24] proposed model predictive shielding (MPS). Given an optimal policy and a safe policy, MPS checks online for each visited state, whether safety will be maintained using the optimal policy. If not, MPS switches to the safe policy. In online shielding, we compute the safety of actions before a decision state is visited, thereby preventing delays at runtime. Furthermore, in online shielding, we do not switch between policies but evaluate all possible decisions to be maximally permissive to the shielded agent.

Safe RL [13,15,27] is concerned with providing safety guarantees for learned agents. Our work focusses on the safe exploration [26], we refer to [15] for other types of safe RL. Using their taxonomy, shielding is an instance of "teacher provides advice" [9], where a teacher with additional information about the system guides the RL agent to pick the right actions. Apprenticeship learning [1] is a closely related variant where the teacher gives (positive) examples and has been used in the context of verification [42]. UPPAAL STRATEGO synthesizes safe, permissive policies that are optimized via learning to create controllers for real-time systems [10]. Some of the work does not assume a model for the environment, making the problem intrinsically harder—and often limiting safety during exploration. We refer to [8,14,16–18] for some interesting approaches.

2   Preliminaries

Sequence and Tuple Notation. We denote sequences of elements by $t = e_0 \cdots e_n$ with ϵ denoting the empty sequence. The length of t is denoted $|t| = n + 1$. We use $t[i] = e_i$ for 0-based indexed access on tuples and sequences. The notation $t[i \leftarrow e_i']$ represents overwriting of the ith element of t by e_i', that is, $t[j] = t[i \leftarrow e_i'][j]$ for all $j \neq i$ and $t[i \leftarrow e_i'][i] = e_i'$.

A *probability distribution* over a countable set X is a function $\mu \colon X \to [0,1]$ with $\sum_{x \in X} \mu(x) = 1$. $Distr(X)$ denotes all distributions on X. The support of $\mu \in Distr(X)$ is $supp(\mu) = \{x \in X \mid \mu(x) > 0\}$.

A *Markov decision process* (MDP) $\mathcal{M} = (\mathcal{S}, s_0, \mathcal{A}, \mathcal{P})$ is a tuple with a finite set $\mathcal{S}$ of states, a unique initial state $s_0 \in \mathcal{S}$, a finite set $\mathcal{A} = \{a_1 \ldots, a_n\}$ of actions, and a (partial) *probabilistic transition function* $\mathcal{P} : \mathcal{S} \times \mathcal{A} \to Distr(\mathcal{S})$, where $\mathcal{P}(s, a) = \bot$ denotes undefined behaviour. For all $s \in \mathcal{S}$ the available actions are $\mathcal{A}(s) = \{a \in \mathcal{A}|\mathcal{P}(s,a) \neq \perp\}$ and we assume $|\mathcal{A}(s)| \geq 1$. A *path* in an MDP $\mathcal{M}$ is a finite (or infinite) sequence $\rho = s_0 a_0 s_1 a_1 \ldots$ with $\mathcal{P}(s_i, a_i)(s_{i+1}) > 0$ for all $i \geq 0$ unless otherwise noted.

Non-deterministic choices in an MDP are resolved by a so-called *policy*. For the properties considered in this paper, memoryless deterministic policies are sufficient [5]. These are functions $\pi : \mathcal{S} \to \mathcal{A}$ with $\pi(s) \in \mathcal{A}(s)$. We denote the set of all memoryless deterministic policies of an MDP by Π. Applying a policy π to an MDP yields an induced *Markov chain* $\mathcal{D} = (\mathcal{S}, s_I, P)$ with $\mathcal{P} : \mathcal{S} \to Distr(\mathcal{S})$ where all nondeterminism is resolved. A *reward function* $r : \mathcal{S} \times \mathcal{A} \to \mathbb{R}_{\geq 0}$ for an MDP adds a reward to every state s and action a enabled in s.

In formal methods, safety properties are often specified as *linear temporal logic* (LTL) properties [28]. For an MDP $\mathcal{M}$, probabilistic model checking [20,22] employs value iteration or linear programming to compute the probabilities of *all states and actions of the MDP* to satisfy a safety property φ.

Specifically, we compute $\eta_{\varphi,\mathcal{M}}^{\max} : \mathcal{S} \to [0,1]$ or $\eta_{\varphi,\mathcal{M}}^{\min} : \mathcal{S} \to [0,1]$, which yields for all states the maximal (or minimal) probability over all possible policies to satisfy φ. For instance, for φ encoding to reach a set of states T, $\eta_{\varphi,\mathcal{M}}^{\max}(s)$ is the maximal probability to "eventually" reach a state in T from state $s \in \mathcal{S}$.

3   Setting and Problem Statement

Setting. We consider a setting similar to [19], where one controllable agent, called the *avatar*, and multiple uncontrollable agents, called *adversaries* operate within an *arena*. The arena is a compact, high-level description of the underlying model and captures the dynamic of the agents. Any information on rewards is neglected within the arena since it is not needed for safety computations.

From this arena, potential agent locations may be inferred. Within the arena, the agents perform *tasks* that are sequences of *activities* performed consecutively.

Formally, an *arena* is a pair $G = (V, E)$, where V is a set of nodes and E is a finite set of $E \subseteq V \times V$. An agent's *location* is defined via the current node $v \in V$. An edge $(v, v') \in E$ represents an *activity* of an agent. By executing an activity, the agent moves to its next location v'. A *task* is defined as a non-empty sequence $(v_1, v_2) \cdot (v_2, v_3) \cdot (v_3, v_4) \cdots (v_{n-1}, v_n) \in E^*$ of connected edges. To ease representation, we denote tasks also as sequences of locations $v_1 \cdot v_2 \cdots v_n$.

The set of tasks available in a location $v \in V$ is given by the function $Task(v)$. The set of all tasks of an arena G is denoted by $Task(G)$. The avatar is only able to select a next task at a *decision location* in $V_D \subseteq V$. To avoid deadlocks, we require for any decision location $v \in V_D$ that $Task(v) \neq \emptyset$ and for all $v \cdots v' \in Task(v)$ that $v' \in V_D$, i.e., any task ends in another decision location from which the agent is able to decide on a new task. A safety property may describe that some combinations of agent positions are safety-critical and should not be reached (or any other safety property from the safety fragment of LTL).

Example 1 (Gridworld). Figure 1 shows a simple gridworld with corridors represented by white tiles and walls represented by black tiles. A tile is defined via its (x, y) position. We model this gridworld with an arena $G = (V, E)$ by

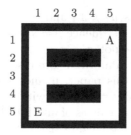

Fig. 1. Gridworld with avatar A (top right) and an adversary E (bottom left).

associating each white tile with a location in V and creating an edge in E for each pair of adjacent white tiles. Corners and crossings are decision locations, i.e., $V_d = \{(1,1),(1,3),(1,5),(5,1),(5,3),(5,5)\}$. At each decision location, tasks define sequences of activities needed to traverse adjoining corridors, e.g., $Task((1,3)) = \{(1,3) \cdot (2,3) \cdot (3,3) \cdot (4,3) \cdot (5,3), (1,3) \cdot (1,2) \cdot (1,1), (1,3) \cdot (1,4) \cdot (1,5)\}$.

Problem. Consider an environment described by an arena as above and a safety specification. We assume stochastic behaviours for the adversaries, e.g., obtained using RL [31,32]. In fact, this stochastic behaviour determines all actions of the adversaries via probabilities. The underlying model is then an MDP: the avatar executes an action, and upon this execution, the next exact positions (the state of the system) are determined stochastically.

Our aim is to *shield* the decision procedure of the avatar to avoid unsafe behaviour regarding the stochastic movements of the adversaries. *The problem is to compute a shield that prevents the avatar to violate the given safety specification by more than a threshold δ with respect to the optimal safety probability.* The safety analysis of actions is performed on-the-fly allowing the avatar to operate within large arenas.

Example 2 (Gridworld). In Fig. 1, the tile labelled A denotes the location of the avatar and the tile labelled E denotes the position of an adversary. Let (x_A, y_A) and (x_E, y_E) be the positions of the avatar and the adversary, respectively. A safety property in this scenario is $\neg\mathbf{F}(x_A = x_E \wedge y_A = y_E)$. The negated "eventually" operator $\mathbf{F}$ states that we must not eventually reach a state where the agents collide. Thus, the property specifies safety by requiring that unsafe states must not be reached. We give more details in Sect. 4.3 on how to construct a shield for this setting.

4   Online Shielding for MDPs

In this section, we outline the workflow of online shielding in Fig. 2 and describe it below. Given an arena and behaviour models for adversaries, we define an MDP $\mathcal{M}$ that captures all safety-relevant information. At runtime, we use current

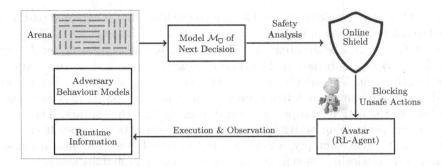

Fig. 2. Workflow of the shield construction.

runtime information to create sub-MDPs $\mathcal{M}_\Box$ of $\mathcal{M}$ that model the immediate future of the agents up to some finite horizon. Given such a sub-MDP $\mathcal{M}_\Box$ and a safety property φ, we compute via model checking the probability to violate φ within the finite horizon for each task available. The shield then blocks tasks involving a too large risk from the avatar.

4.1 Behaviour Models for Adversaries

The adversaries and the avatar operate within a shared environment, which is represented by an arena $G = (V, E)$, and perform tasks independently. We assume that we are given a stochastic behaviour model of each adversary that determines all task choices of the respective adversary via probabilities. The behaviour of an adversary is formally defined as follows.

Definition 1 (Adversary Behaviour). *For an arena $G = (V, E)$, we define the behaviour B_i of an adversary i as a function $B_i \colon V_D \to Distr(Task(G))$ from decision locations to distributions over tasks, with $supp(B_i(v)) \subseteq Task(v)$.*

Behaviour models of adversaries may be derived using domain knowledge or generalised from observations using machine learning or automata learning [25,35]. A potential approach is to observe adversaries in smaller arenas and transfer knowledge gained in this way to larger arenas [19]. Cooperative and truly adverse behaviour of adversaries may require considering additional aspects in the adversary behaviour, such as the arena state at a specific point in time. Such considerations are beyond the scope of this paper, since complex adversary behaviour generally makes the creation of behaviour models more difficult, whereas the online shield computations are hardly affected.

4.2 Safety-Relevant MDP $\mathcal{M}$

In the following, we describe the safety-relevant MDP $\mathcal{M}$ underlying the agents operating within an arena. This MDP includes non-deterministic choices of the avatar and stochastic behaviour of the adversaries. Note that the safety-relevant

MDP $\mathcal{M}$ is never explicitly created for online shielding, but is explored on-the-fly for the safety analysis of tasks.

Let $G = (V, E)$ be an arena, let *Task* be a task function for G, let B_i with $i \in \{1 \dots m\}$ be the behaviour functions of m adversaries, and let the avatar be the zeroth agent. The safety-relevant MDP $\mathcal{M} = (\mathcal{S}, s_0, \mathcal{A}, \mathcal{P})$ models the arena and agents' dynamics as follows. Each agent has a *position* and a *task queue* containing the activities to be performed from the last chosen task. The agents take turns performing activities from their respective task queue. If the task queue of an agent is empty, a new task has to be selected. The avatar chooses non-deterministically, whereas the adversaries choose probabilistically.

Hence, $\mathcal{M}$ has three types of states: (1) states where the avatar's task queue is empty and the avatar makes a *non-deterministic* decision on its next task, (2) states where an adversary's task queue is empty and the adversary selects its next task *probabilistically*, and (3) states where the currently active agent has a non-empty task queue and the agent processes its task queue *deterministically*.

Formally, the *states* $\mathcal{S} = V^{m+1} \times (E^*)^{m+1} \times \{0, \dots, m\}$ are triples $s = (v, q, t)$ where v encodes the agent positions, q encodes the task queue states of all agents, and t encodes whose turn it is. To enhance readability, we use $pos(s) = s[0] = v$, $task(s) = s[1] = q$, and $turn(s) = s[2] = t$ to access the elements of a state s. We additionally define $ava = 0$, thus $pos(s)[ava]$ and $task(s)[ava]$ are the position and task of the avatar, whereas $turn(s) = ava$ specifies that it is the turn of the avatar. There is a unique action α_{adv} representing adversary decisions, there is a unique action α_{e} representing individual activities (movement along edges), and there are actions for each task available to the avatar, thus $\mathcal{A} = \{\alpha_{\mathrm{adv}}, \alpha_{\mathrm{e}}\} \cup Task(G)$.

Definition 2 (Decision State). *Given a safety-relevant MDP $\mathcal{M}$. We define the set of* decision states $\mathcal{S}_D \subseteq \mathcal{S}$ *via* $\mathcal{S}_D = \{s_D \in \mathcal{S} \mid task(s_D)[ava] = \epsilon \wedge turn(s_D) = ava\}$, *i.e., it is the turn of the avatar and its task queue is empty.*

This implies that if $s_D \in \mathcal{S}_D$, then $pos(s_D)[ava]$ is a decision location in V_D. A policy for $\mathcal{M}$ needs to define actions only for states in $\mathcal{S}_D$, thereby defining the decisions for the avatar. All other task decisions in states s, where $turn(s) \neq ava$, are performed stochastically by adversaries and cannot be controlled.

At run-time, in each turn each agent performs two steps:

(1) If its task queue is empty, the agent has to select its next task.
(2) The agent performs the next activity of its current task queue.

Selecting a new task. A new task has to be selected in all states s with $turn(s) = i$ and $task(s)[i] = \epsilon$, i.e., it is the turn of agent i and agent i's task queue is empty.

If $i = ava$, the avatar is in a decision state $s \in \mathcal{S}_D$, with actions $\mathcal{A}(s) = Task(pos(s)[ava])$. For each task $t \in \mathcal{A}(s)$, there is a successor state s' with $task(s') = task(s)[ava \leftarrow t]$, $pos(s') = pos(s)$, $turn(s') = turn(s)$, and $\mathcal{P}(s, t, s') = 1$. Thus, there is a transition that updates the avatar's task queue with the edges of task t with probability one. Other than that, there are no changes.

If $i \neq ava$, an adversary makes a decision, thus $\mathcal{A}(s) = \alpha_{\mathrm{adv}}$. For each $t \in Task(pos(s)[i])$, there is a state s' with $task(s') = task(s)[i \leftarrow t]$, $pos(s') = pos(s)$,

$turn(s') = turn(s)$, and $\mathcal{P}(s, \alpha_{\mathrm{adv}}, s') = B_i(pos(s)[i])(t)$. There is a single action with a stochastic outcome determined according to the adversary behaviour B_i.

Performing Activities. After potentially selecting a new task, the task queue of agent i is non-empty. We are in a state s', where $task(s')[i] = t = (v_i, v_i') \cdot t'$ with $pos(s')[i] = v_i$. Agent i moves along the edge (v_i, v_i') deterministically and we increment the turn counter modulo $m+1$, i.e., $\mathcal{A}(s') = \{\alpha_e\}$ and $\mathcal{P}(s', \alpha_e, s'') = 1$ with $s''[0] = pos(s')[i \leftarrow v_i']$, $task(s'') = task(s')[i \leftarrow t']$, and $turn(s'') = turn(s') + 1 \mod m + 1$.

4.3   Sub-MDP $\mathcal{M}_\square$ for Next Decision

The idea of online shielding is to compute the safety value of actions in the decision states on the fly and block actions that are too risky. For infinite horizon properties, the probability to violate safety, in the long run, is often one and errors stemming from modelling uncertainties may sum up over time [19]. Therefore, we consider safety relative to a *finite horizon* such that the action values (and consequently, a policy for the avatar) carry guarantees for the next steps. Explicitly constructing an MDP $\mathcal{M}$ as outlined above yields a very large number of decision states that may be infeasible to check. The finite horizon assumption allows us to prune the safety-relevant MDP and construct small sub-MDPs $\mathcal{M}_\square$ capturing the immediate future of individual decision states.

More concretely, we consider runtime situations of being in a state s_t, the state visited immediately after the avatar decided to perform a task t. In such situations, we can use the time required to perform t for shield computations for the next decision. We create a sub-MDP $\mathcal{M}_\square$ by determining all states reachable within a finite horizon and use $\mathcal{M}_\square$ to check the safety probability of each action (task) available in the next decision and block unsafe actions.

Construction of $\mathcal{M}_\square$. Online shielding relies on the insight that after deciding on a task t, the time required to complete t can be used to compute a shield for the next decision. Thus, we start the construction of the sub-MDP $\mathcal{M}_\square$ for the next decision location v_D' from the state s_t that immediately follows a decision state s_D, where the avatar has chosen a task $t \in \mathcal{A}(s_D)$. The MDP $\mathcal{M}_\square$ is computed with respect to a finite horizon h for v_D'.

By construction, the task is of the form $t = v_D \cdots v_D'$, where v_D is the avatar's current location and v_D' is the next decision location. While the avatar performs t to reach v_D', the adversaries perform arbitrary tasks and traverse $|t|$ edges, i.e., until v_D' is reached only adversaries take decisions. This leads to a set of possible next decision states. We call these states the *first decision states* $S_{FD} \subseteq \mathcal{S}_\mathcal{D}$. After reaching v_D', both avatar and adversaries decide on arbitrary tasks and all agents traverse h edges. This behaviour defines the structure of $\mathcal{M}_\square$.

Given a safety-relevant MDP $\mathcal{M} = (\mathcal{S}, s_0, \mathcal{A}, \mathcal{P})$, a decision state s_D and its successor s_t with $task(s_t)[ava] = t$, and a finite horizon $h \in \mathbb{N}$ representing a number of turns taken by all agents following the next decision. These turns and the (stochastic) agent behaviour leading to the next decision are modelled by the sub-MDP $\mathcal{M}_\square$. $\mathcal{M}_\square = (\mathcal{S}_\square, s_{0\,\square}, \mathcal{A}_\square, \mathcal{P}_\square)$ is formally constructed as follows. The actions are the same as for $\mathcal{M}$, i.e., $\mathcal{A}_\square = \mathcal{A}$. The initial state is given by $s_{0\,\square} = (s_t, 0)$. The states of $\mathcal{M}_\square$ are a subset of $\mathcal{M}$'s states augmented with the distance from $s_{0\,\square}$, i.e., $\mathcal{S}_\square \subseteq \mathcal{S} \times \mathbb{N}_0$. The distance is measured in terms of the number of turns taken by all agents.

We define transitions and states inductively by:

(1) *Decision Actions.* If $(s, d) \in \mathcal{S}_\square$, $d < |t| + h$, and there is an $s' \in \mathcal{S}$ such that $\mathcal{P}(s, \alpha, s') > 0$ and $\alpha \in \{\alpha_{\mathrm{adv}}\} \cup Task(G)$ then $(s', d) \in \mathcal{S}_\square$ and $\mathcal{P}_\square((s, d), \alpha, (s', d)) = \mathcal{P}(s, \alpha, s')$.

(2) *Movement Actions.* If $(s, d) \in \mathcal{S}_\square$, $d < |t| + h$, and there is an $s' \in \mathcal{S}$ such that $\mathcal{P}(s, \alpha_e, s') > 0$, then $(s', d') \in \mathcal{S}_\square$ and $\mathcal{P}_\square((s, d), \alpha_e, (s', d')) = \mathcal{P}(s, \alpha_e, s')$, where $d' = d + 1$ if $turn(s) = m$ and $d' = d$ otherwise.

Movements of the last of $m + 1$ agents increase the distance from the initial state. Combined with the fact that every movement action increases the agent index and every decision changes a task queue, we can infer that the structure of $\mathcal{M}_\square$ is a directed acyclic graph. This enables an efficient probabilistic analysis.

By construction, it holds for every state $(s, d) \in \mathcal{S}_\square$ with $d < |t|$, s is not a decision state of $\mathcal{M}$. The set of first decision states S_{FD} consists of all states $s_{FD} = (s, |t|)$ such that $s_{FD} \in \mathcal{S}_\square$ with $task(s)[ava] = \epsilon$ and $turn(s) = ava$, i.e., all first decision states reachable from the initial state of $\mathcal{M}_\square$. We use $Task(S_{FD}) = \{t \mid s \in S_{FD}, t \in \mathcal{A}(s)\}$ to denote the tasks available in these states. $\mathcal{M}_\square$ does not define actions and transitions from states $(s, |t| + h) \in \mathcal{S}_\square$, as their successor states are beyond the considered horizon h. We have $\mathcal{A}((s, d)) \neq \emptyset$ for all states at distance $d < |t| + h$ from the initial state.

4.4 Shield Construction

The probability of reaching a set of unsafe states $T \in \mathcal{S}$ from any state in the safety-relevant MDP should be low. In the finite horizon setting, we are interested in bounded reachability from decision states $s_D \in \mathcal{S}_D$ within the finite horizon h. We concretely evaluate reachability on sub-MDPs $\mathcal{M}_\square$ and use $T_\square = \{(s, d) \in \mathcal{S}_\square \mid s \in T\}$ to denote the unsafe states that may be reached within the horizon covered by $\mathcal{M}_\square$. The property $\varphi = \lozenge T_\square$ encodes the **violation** of the safety constraint, i.e., eventually reaching $T_\square$ within $\mathcal{M}_\square$. The shield needs to limit the probability to *satisfy* φ.

Given a sub-MDP $\mathcal{M}_\square$ and a set of first decision states S_{FD}. For each task $t \in Task(S_{FD})$, we evaluate t with respect to the minimal probability to satisfy φ from the initial state $s_{0\,\square}$ when executing t by computing $\eta_{\varphi, \mathcal{M}_\square}^{\min}(s_{0\,\square})$. This is formalised with the notion of task-valuations below.

Definition 3 (Task-valuation). *A task-valuation for a task t in a sub-MDP $\mathcal{M}_\square$ with initial state $s_{0\,\square}$ and first decision states S_{FD} is given by*

$$val_{\mathcal{M}_\square} : Task(S_{FD}) \to [0, 1], \text{ with } val_{\mathcal{M}_\square}(t) = \eta_{\varphi, \mathcal{M}_\square}^{\min}(s_{0\,\square}),$$

$$\text{and } \mathcal{A}(s_{FD}) = \{t\} \text{ for each } s_{FD} \in S_{FD}.$$

The optimal task-value *for* $\mathcal{M}_{\square}$ *is* $optval_{\mathcal{M}_{\square}} = \min_{t' \in Task(S_{FD})} val_{\mathcal{M}_{\square}}(t')$.

A task-valuation is the minimal probability to reach an unsafe state in T from each immediately reachable decision state $s_{FD} \in S_{FD}$ weighted by the probability to reach s_{FD}. When the avatar chooses an optimal task t (with $val_{\mathcal{M}_{\square}}(t) = optval_{\mathcal{M}_{\square}}$) as next task in a state s_{FD}, $optval_{\mathcal{M}_{\square}}$ can be achieved if all subsequent decisions are optimal as well.

We now define a shield for the decision states S_{FD} in a sub-MDP $\mathcal{M}_{\square}$ using the task-valuations. Specifically, a *shield* for a threshold $\delta \in [0,1]$ determines a set of tasks available in S_{FD} that are δ-optimal for the specification φ. All other tasks are "shielded" or "blocked".

Definition 4 (Shield). *For task-valuation* $val_{\mathcal{M}_{\square}}$ *and a threshold* $\delta \in [0,1]$*, a shield for* S_{FD} *in* $\mathcal{M}_{\square}$ *is given by*

$$shield_{\delta}^{\mathcal{M}_{\square}} \in 2^{Task(S_{FD})} \ with$$

$$shield_{\delta}^{\mathcal{M}_{\square}} = \{t \in Task(S_{FD}) \mid \delta \cdot val_{\mathcal{M}_{\square}}(t) \leq optval_{\mathcal{M}_{\square}}\}.$$

Intuitively, δ enforces a constraint on tasks that are acceptable w.r.t. the optimal probability. The shield is *adaptive* with respect to δ, as a high value for δ yields a stricter shield, a smaller value a more permissive shield. In particularly critical situations, the shield can enforce the decision maker to resort to (only) the optimal actions w.r.t. the safety objective. This can be achieved by temporarily setting $\delta = 1$. Online shielding creates shields on-the-fly by constructing sub-MDPs $\mathcal{M}_{\square}$ and computing task-valuations for all available tasks.

Through online shielding, we transform the safety-relevant MDP $\mathcal{M}$ into a *shielded MDP* with which the avatar interacts (which is never explicitly created) that is obtained from the composition of all sub-MDP $\mathcal{M}_{\square}$. Due to the assumption on the task functions that requires a non-empty set of available tasks in all decision locations and due to the fact that every decision for shielding is defined w.r.t. an optimal task, the shielded MDP is deadlock-free. Hence, our notion of online shielding guarantees deadlock-freedom and optimality w.r.t. safety. By using the minimal probability as task valuation $val_{\mathcal{M}_{\square}}(t)$, we assume that the avatar performs optimally with respect to safety in upcoming decisions. Alternatively, we could use the maximal probability in combination with a fixed threshold $\lambda \in [0,1]$ such that only tasks t with $val_{\mathcal{M}_{\square}}(t) \leq \lambda$ are allowed. This would place weaker assumptions on the avatar behaviour, but it may induce deadlocks in case there are no sufficiently safe actions.

4.5   Optimisation – Updating Shields After Adversary Decisions

After the avatar decides on a task, we use the time to complete the task to compute shields based on task-valuations (see Definition 3 and Definition 4). Such shield computations are inherently affected by uncertainties stemming from stochastic adversary behaviour. These uncertainties consequently decrease

Fig. 3. A screenshot of the SNAKE game with colour-coded shield display. (Color figure online)

whenever we observe a concrete decision from an adversary that we considered stochastic in the initial shield computation.

An optimisation of the online shielding approach is to compute a new shield after any decision of an adversary, if there is enough remaining time until the next decision location. Suppose that after visiting a decision state, we computed a shield based on $\mathcal{M}_{\square}$. While moving to the next decision state, an adversary decides on a new task and we observe the concrete state s. We can now construct a new sub-MDP $\mathcal{M}'_{\square}$ using $s'_{0\,\square} = s$ as initial state, thereby resolving a stochastic decision between the original initial state $s_{0\,\square}$ and $s'_{0\,\square}$. Using $\mathcal{M}'_{\square}$, we compute a new shield for the next decision location.

The facts that the probabilistic transition function of $\mathcal{M}_{\square}$ does not change during updates and that we consider safety properties enable a very efficient implementation of updates. For instance, if value iteration is used to compute task-valuations, we can simply change the initial state and reuse computations from the initial shield computation. Note that if a task is completely safe, i.e., tasks with a valuation of zero, the value of this task will not change under a re-computation, since the task is safe under any sequence of adversary decisions.

5   Implementation and Experiments

2-Player SNAKE. We implemented online shielding for a two-player version of the classic computer game SNAKE. We picked the game because it requires fast decision making during runtime, and provides in an intuitive and fun setting to show the potential of shielding such that it can potentially be used for teaching formal methods. Figure 3 shows a screenshot of the 2-Player SNAKE game on the map that was used for the experiments. In the game, each player controls a snake of a different colour. Here, the green snake is controlled by the avatar (the RL-agent) and the purple snake by the adversary. The goal for each player is to eat five randomly positioned apples of their own colour. The score for the

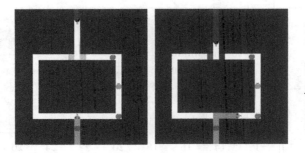

Fig. 4. Screenshots from the SNAKE game to demonstrate recalculation.

green snake (the avatar) is positively affected (+10) by collecting a green apple and by wins of the avatar (+50), i.e., if it collects all green apples before the adversary snake collects all purple apples. If a snake has a collision, the snake loses. In case that the heads of both snakes collide, the avatar loses.

We implemented a shield to protect the avatar snake from collisions with the adversary snake. The shield computes online the minimal probability that taking the next corridor will lead to a collision. The game, as shown in Fig. 3, indicates the risk of taking a corridor from low to high by the colours green, yellow, orange, red.

We also implemented the optimisation to recalculate the shield after a decision of the adversary snake. Figure 4 contains two screenshots of the game on a simple map to demonstrate the effect of a shield update. In the left figure, the available tasks of the green snake are picking the corridor to the left or the corridor to the right. Both choices induce a risk of a collision with the purple snake. After the decision of the purple snake to take the corridor to its right-hand-side, the shield is updated and the safety values of the corridors change.

Experimental Set-up. The Python-based implementation can be found at http:// onlineshielding.at along with videos, evaluation data and a Docker image that enables easy experimentation. For shield computations, we use the probabilistic model checker `Storm` [11] and its Python interface. We use the `PRISM` [23] language to represent MDPs and domain-specific optimisations to efficiently encode agents and tasks, that is, snakes and their movements. Reinforcement learning is implemented via approximate Q-learning [34] with the feature vector denoting the distance to the next apple. The Q-learning uses the learning rate $\alpha = 0.1$ and the discount factor $\gamma = 0.5$ for the Q-update and an ϵ-greedy exploration policy with $\epsilon = 0.6$. The pygame[2] library is used to implement the game's interface and logic. All experiments have been performed on a computer with an Intel®Core™ i7-4700MQ CPU with 2.4 GHz, 8 cores and 16 GB RAM.

---

[2] https://www.pygame.org/, accessed 2020-11-27.

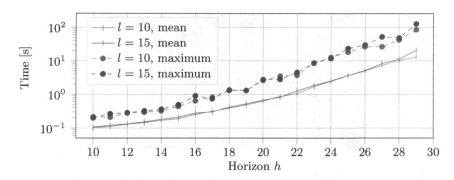

Fig. 5. Shield computation time for varying horizon values and snake lengths.

Evaluation Criteria. We report on two types of experiments: (1) the time required to compute shields relative to the computation horizon and (2) the performance of shielded reinforcement learning compared to unshielded reinforcement learning measured in terms of gained reward. The experiments on computation time indicate how many steps shielding can look ahead within some given time. The experiments on learning performance demonstrate the effect of shielding.

Computation Time Measurements. When playing the game on the map illustrated in Fig. 3, we measured the time to compute shields, i.e., the time to construct sub-MDPs $\mathcal{M}_\Box$ and to compute the safety values. We measured the time of 200 such shield computations and report the maximum computation times and the mean computation times. Figure 5 presents the results for two different snake lengths $l \in \{10, 15\}$ and different computation horizons $h \in \{10, 11, \ldots, 29\}$. The x-axis displays the computation horizon h and the y-axis displays the computation time in seconds in logarithmic scale.

We can observe that up to a horizon h of 17, all computations take less than one second, even in the worst case. Assuming that every task takes at least one second, we can plan ahead by taking into account safety hazards within the next 17 steps. A computation horizon of 20 still requires less than one second on average and about 3 seconds in the worst case. Horizons in this range are often sufficient, as we demonstrate in the next experiment by using $h = 15$.

We compare our timing results with a similar case study presented by Jansen et al. [19]. In a similar multi-agent setting on a comparably large map, the decisions of the avatar were shielded using an offline shield with a finite horizon of 10. The computation time to compute the offline shield was about 6 h on a standard notebook. Note, that although the setting has four adversaries, the offline computation was performed for one adversary and the results were combined for several adversaries online.

Furthermore, Fig. 5 shows that the snake length affects the computation time only slightly. This observation supports our claim that online shielding scales

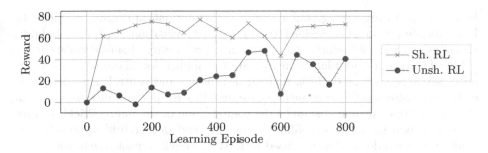

Fig. 6. Reward gained throughout learning for shielded and unshielded RL.

well to large arenas, i.e., scenarios where the safety-relevant MDP $\mathcal{M}$ is large. Note that the number of game configurations grows exponentially with the snake length (assuming a sufficiently large map), as the snake's tail may bend in different directions at each crossing.

The experiments further show that the computation time grows exponentially with the horizon. Horizons close to 30 may be advantageous in especially safety-critical settings, such as factories with industrial robots acting as agents. Since individual tasks in a factory may take minutes, online shielding would be feasible, as worst-case computation times are in the range of minutes. However, offline shielding would be infeasible due to the average computation time of more than 10 s that would be required for all decision states.

RL with Online Shielding. Figure 6 shows plots of the reward gained during learning in the shielded and the unshielded case. The online shield uses a horizon of $h = 15$. The y-axis displays the reward and the x-axis displays the learning episodes, where one episode corresponds to one play of the SNAKE game. The reward has been averaged over 50 episodes for each data point.

The plot demonstrates that shielding improves the gained reward significantly. By blocking unsafe actions, the avatar did not encounter a single loss due to a collision. For this reason, we see a consistently high reward right from the start of the learning phase. In the execution phase, shielded RL manages to win about 96% of all plays, whereas unshielded RL wins only about 54%.

6   Conclusion and Future Work

Online shielding is an efficient approach to enforce safe behaviour of autonomous agents operating within a stochastic environment. The approach exploits the time required to complete tasks to model and analyse the immediate future w.r.t. a safety property. For every decision at runtime, we create MDPs to model the current state of the environment and the behaviour of the agents. Given these MDP models, we employ probabilistic model-checking to evaluate every action possible in the next decision. In particular, we determine the probability of unsafe behaviour following every possible choice. This information is used by shields to block unsafe actions, i.e., actions leading to safety violations with a probability exceeding a threshold relative to the minimal probability of safety violations.

For future work, we plan to investigate the application of online shielding in other settings, such as decision making in robotics and control. Another interesting extension would be to incorporate quantitative performance measures in the form of rewards and costs into the computation of the online shield, as previously demonstrated in an offline manner [4] and in a hybrid approach [29], where runtime information was used to learn the environment dynamics.

Acknowledgments. This work has been supported by the "University SAL Labs" initiative of Silicon Austria Labs (SAL) and its Austrian partner universities for applied fundamental research for electronic based systems.

References

1. Abbeel, P., Ng, A.Y.: Exploration and apprenticeship learning in reinforcement learning. In: ICML. ACM International Conference Proceeding Series, vol. 119, pp. 1–8. ACM (2005)
2. Alshiekh, M., Bloem, R., Ehlers, R., Könighofer, B., Niekum, S., Topcu, U.: Safe reinforcement learning via shielding. In: AAAI. AAAI Press (2018)
3. Amodei, D., Olah, C., Steinhardt, J., Christiano, P., Schulman, J., Mané, D.: Concrete problems in AI safety. CoRR, abs/1606.06565 (2016)
4. Avni, G., Bloem, R., Chatterjee, K., Henzinger, T.A., Könighofer, B., Pranger, S.: Run-time optimization for learned controllers through quantitative games. In: Dillig, I., Tasiran, S. (eds.) CAV 2019. LNCS, vol. 11561, pp. 630–649. Springer, Cham (2019). https://doi.org/10.1007/978-3-030-25540-4_36
5. Baier, C., Katoen, J.: Principles of Model Checking. MIT Press, Cambridge (2008)
6. Bharadwaj, S., Bloem, R., Dimitrova, R., Könighofer, B., Topcu, U.: Synthesis of minimum-cost shields for multi-agent systems. In: ACC, pp. 1048–1055. IEEE (2019)
7. Bloem, R., Könighofer, B., Könighofer, R., Wang, C.: Shield synthesis: runtime enforcement for reactive systems. In: Baier, C., Tinelli, C. (eds.) TACAS 2015. LNCS, vol. 9035, pp. 533–548. Springer, Heidelberg (2015). https://doi.org/10.1007/978-3-662-46681-0_51
8. Cheng, R., Orosz, G., Murray, R.M., Burdick, J.W.: End-to-end safe reinforcement learning through barrier functions for safety-critical continuous control tasks. In: AAAI (2019)
9. Clouse, J.A., Utgoff, P.E.: A teaching method for reinforcement learning. In: ML, pp. 92–110. Morgan Kaufmann (1992)
10. David, A., Jensen, P.G., Larsen, K.G., Mikučionis, M., Taankvist, J.H.: UPPAAL STRATEGO. In: Baier, C., Tinelli, C. (eds.) TACAS 2015. LNCS, vol. 9035, pp. 206–211. Springer, Heidelberg (2015). https://doi.org/10.1007/978-3-662-46681-0_16
11. Dehnert, C., Junges, S., Katoen, J.-P., Volk, M.: A STORM is coming: a modern probabilistic model checker. In: Majumdar, R., Kunčak, V. (eds.) CAV 2017. LNCS, vol. 10427, pp. 592–600. Springer, Cham (2017). https://doi.org/10.1007/978-3-319-63390-9_31

12. Falcone, Y., Pinisetty, S.: On the runtime enforcement of timed properties. In: Finkbeiner, B., Mariani, L. (eds.) RV 2019. LNCS, vol. 11757, pp. 48–69. Springer, Cham (2019). https://doi.org/10.1007/978-3-030-32079-9_4

13. Fulton, N., Platzer, A.: Verifiably safe off-model reinforcement learning. In: TACAS, pp. 413–430 (2019)

14. Fulton, N., Platzer, A.: Verifiably safe off-model reinforcement learning. In: Vojnar, T., Zhang, L. (eds.) TACAS 2019. LNCS, vol. 11427, pp. 413–430. Springer, Cham (2019). https://doi.org/10.1007/978-3-030-17462-0_28

15. Garcıa, J., Fernández, F.: A comprehensive survey on safe reinforcement learning. J. Mach. Learn. Res. **16**(1), 1437–1480 (2015)

16. Hahn, E.M., Perez, M., Schewe, S., Somenzi, F., Trivedi, A., Wojtczak, D.: Omega-regular objectives in model-free reinforcement learning. In: Vojnar, T., Zhang, L. (eds.) TACAS 2019. LNCS, vol. 11427, pp. 395–412. Springer, Cham (2019). https://doi.org/10.1007/978-3-030-17462-0_27

17. Hasanbeig, M., Abate, A., Kroening, D.: Logically-correct reinforcement learning. CoRR, abs/1801.08099 (2018)

18. Hasanbeig, M., Kantaros, Y., Abate, A., Kroening, D., Pappas, G.J., Lee, I.: Reinforcement learning for temporal logic control synthesis with probabilistic satisfaction guarantees. In: CDC, pp. 5338–5343. IEEE (2019)

19. Jansen, N., Könighofer, B., Junges, S., Serban, A., Bloem, R.: Safe reinforcement learning using probabilistic shields (invited paper). In: Konnov, I., Kovács, L. (eds.) CONCUR, volume 171 of LIPIcs, pp. 3:1–3:16. Schloss Dagstuhl - Leibniz-Zentrum für Informatik (2020)

20. Katoen, J.-P.: The probabilistic model checking landscape. In: LICS, pp. 31–45. ACM (2016)

21. Könighofer, B., Lorber, F., Jansen, N., Bloem, R.: Shield synthesis for reinforcement learning. In: Margaria, T., Steffen, B. (eds.) ISoLA 2020. LNCS, vol. 12476, pp. 290–306. Springer, Cham (2020). https://doi.org/10.1007/978-3-030-61362-4_16

22. Kwiatkowska, M.Z.: Model checking for probability and time: from theory to practice. In: LICS, pp. 351. IEEE CS (2003)

23. Kwiatkowska, M., Norman, G., Parker, D.: PRISM 4.0: verification of probabilistic real-time systems. In: Gopalakrishnan, G., Qadeer, S. (eds.) CAV 2011. LNCS, vol. 6806, pp. 585–591. Springer, Heidelberg (2011). https://doi.org/10.1007/978-3-642-22110-1_47

24. Li, S., Bastani, O.: Robust model predictive shielding for safe reinforcement learning with stochastic dynamics. In: ICRA, pp. 7166–7172. IEEE (2020)

25. Mao, H., Chen, Y., Jaeger, M., Nielsen, T.D., Larsen, K.G., Nielsen, B.: Learning deterministic probabilistic automata from a model checking perspective. Mach. Learn. **105**(2), 255–299 (2016). https://doi.org/10.1007/s10994-016-5565-9

26. Moldovan, T.M., Abbeel, P.: Safe exploration in Markov decision processes. In: ICML. icml.cc/Omnipress (2012)

27. Pecka, M., Svoboda, T.: Safe exploration techniques for reinforcement learning - an overview. In: Hodicky, J. (ed.) MESAS 2014. LNCS, vol. 8906. Springer, Cham (2014). https://doi.org/10.1007/978-3-319-13823-7_31

28. Pnueli, A.: The temporal logic of programs. In: Foundations of Computer Science, pp. 46–57. IEEE (1977)

29. Pranger, S., Könighofer, B., Tappler, M., Deixelberger, M., Jansen, N., Bloem, R.: Adaptive shielding under uncertainty. CoRR, abs/2010.03842 (2020)

30. Renard, M., Falcone, Y., Rollet, A., Jéron, T., Marchand, H.: Optimal enforcement of (timed) properties with uncontrollable events. Math. Struct. Comput. Sci. **29**(1), 169–214 (2019)
31. Sadigh, D., Landolfi, N., Sastry, S.S., Seshia, S.A., Dragan, A.D.: Planning for cars that coordinate with people: leveraging effects on human actions for planning and active information gathering over human internal state. Auton. Robot. **42**(7), 1405–1426 (2018). https://doi.org/10.1007/s10514-018-9746-1
32. Sadigh, D., Sastry, S., Seshia, S.A., Dragan, A.D.: Planning for autonomous cars that leverage effects on human actions. Science and Systems. In: Robotics (2016)
33. Silver, D., et al.: Mastering the game of Go with deep neural networks and tree search. Nature **529**(7587), 484 (2016)
34. Sutton, R.S., Barto, A.G.: Reinforcement Learning: An Introduction. MIT Press, Cambridge (1998)
35. Tappler, M., Aichernig, B.K., Bacci, G., Eichlseder, M., Larsen, K.G.: L^*-based learning of Markov decision processes. In: ter Beek, M.H., McIver, A., Oliveira, J.N. (eds.) FM 2019. LNCS, vol. 11800, pp. 651–669. Springer, Cham (2019). https://doi.org/10.1007/978-3-030-30942-8_38
36. Thrun, S., Burgard, W., Fox, D.: Probabilistic Robotics. The MIT Press, Cambridge (2005)
37. Wang, A., Kurutach, T., Liu, K., Abbeel, P., Tamar, A.: Learning robotic manipulation through visual planning and acting. arXiv preprint arXiv:1905.04411 (2019)
38. White, D.J.: Real applications of Markov decision processes. Interfaces **15**(6), 73–83 (1985)
39. Wu, M., Wang, J., Deshmukh, J., Wang, C.: Shield synthesis for real: enforcing safety in cyber-physical systems. In: FMCAD, pp. 129–137. IEEE (2019)
40. Zhang, W., Bastani, O.: MAMPS: safe multi-agent reinforcement learning via model predictive shielding. CoRR, abs/1910.12639 (2019)
41. Zhou, W., Gao, R., Kim, B., Kang, E., Li, W.: Runtime-safety-guided policy repair. In: RV, pp. 131–150 (2020)
42. Zhou, W., Li, W.: Safety-aware apprenticeship learning. In: Chockler, H., Weissenbacher, G. (eds.) CAV 2018. LNCS, vol. 10981, pp. 662–680. Springer, Cham (2018). https://doi.org/10.1007/978-3-319-96145-3_38

Verification of Eventual Consensus in Synod Using a Failure-Aware Actor Model

Saswata Paul[1]([✉]), Gul A. Agha[2], Stacy Patterson[1], and Carlos A. Varela[1]

[1] Rensselaer Polytechnic Institute, Troy, NY 12180, USA
pauls4@rpi.edu, {sep,cvarela}@cs.rpi.edu
[2] University of Illinois at Urbana-Champaign, Champaign, IL 61820, USA
agha@illinois.edu

Abstract. Successfully attaining consensus in the absence of a centralized coordinator is a fundamental problem in distributed multi-agent systems. We analyze progress in the Synod consensus protocol—which does not assume a unique leader—under the assumptions of asynchronous communication and potential agent failures. We identify a set of sufficient conditions under which it is possible to guarantee that a set of agents will eventually attain consensus. First, a subset of the agents must behave correctly and not permanently fail until consensus is reached, and second, at least one proposal must be eventually uninterrupted by higher-numbered proposals. To formally reason about agent failures, we introduce a failure-aware actor model (FAM). Using FAM, we model the identified conditions and provide a formal proof of eventual progress in Synod. Our proof has been mechanically verified using the Athena proof assistant and, to the best of our knowledge, it is the first machine-checked proof of eventual progress in Synod.

1 Introduction

Consensus, which requires a set of processes to reach an agreement on some value, is a fundamental problem in distributed systems. Under *asynchronous* communication settings, where message transmission and processing delays are unbounded, it is impossible to guarantee consensus [18] since message delays cannot be differentiated from process failures. Nevertheless, in distributed *multi-agent* systems, where there is no centralized *coordinator* to manage safe operation, it is necessary for the agents to use *distributed consensus protocols* [58] for coordination. An important application of such systems is decentralized *air-traffic control* (ATC) for *Urban Air Mobility* (UAM) [63].

The integration of *uncrewed aircraft systems* (UAS) and *micro-aircraft* in the *National Airspace System* (NAS) for package delivery, scientific data collection, and urban transportation will significantly increase the density of urban air traffic [44], elevating the possibilities of hazards such as *near mid-air collisions* (NMAC) [35] and *wake-vortex induced rolls* [37]. Since centralized, human-operated ATC is not scalable to high densities and is prone to human errors [22],

© Springer Nature Switzerland AG 2021
A. Dutle et al. (Eds.): NFM 2021, LNCS 12673, pp. 249–267, 2021.
https://doi.org/10.1007/978-3-030-76384-8_16

UAS operating in UAM scenarios must be capable of autonomous *UAS traffic management* (UTM) [9]. To ensure safety in UTM, they must coordinate with each other by using distributed consensus protocols[1] (*e.g.* – [10,54]).

In [51], we have proposed an *Internet of Planes* (IoP), consisting of an asynchronous *vehicle-to-vehicle* (V2V) [41] network of aircraft, to facilitate autonomous capabilities such as *decentralized admission control* (DAC) [53]. In DAC, a *candidate* aircraft generates a *conflict-aware flight plan* that avoids NMACs with a set of *owner* aircraft of a *controlled airspace* [52]. The candidate then requests admission into the airspace by proposing this flight plan to the owners. As there may be multiple candidates concurrently competing for admission into an airspace, the owners may only admit candidates sequentially. This is because candidates do not consider each other in their proposals: in fact, a candidate may not even be aware of other candidates. Thus, admitting one candidate potentially invalidates the proposals of all other candidates. Since UAM applications are *time-critical*, any consensus protocol used for DAC must guarantee that a proposal will be eventually chosen. In this paper, we present an analysis of consensus that is primarily motivated by the requirements of DAC.

In [29], Lamport describes three variants of a consensus protocol that strongly guarantees the *safety* property that only one value will be chosen:

- *The Basic Synod protocol* or *Synod* guarantees safety if one or more agents are allowed to initiate new proposals for consensus.
- *The Complete Synod protocol* or *Paxos* is a variant of Synod in which only a distinguished agent (*leader*) is allowed to initiate proposals [30]. Other agents may only introduce values through the leader. This is done to guarantee the *progress* property that consensus will eventually be achieved.
- *The Multi-Decree protocol* or *Multi-Paxos* allows multiple values to be chosen using a separate instance of Paxos for each value, but using the same leader for each of those instances.

Both Paxos and Multi-Paxos use Synod as the underlying consensus protocol.

A progress guarantee contingent upon a unique leader has several drawbacks from the perspective of DAC. First, *leader election* itself is a consensus problem. Therefore, a progress guarantee that relies on successful leader election as a precondition would be circular, and therefore fallacious. Second, the Fischer, Lynch, and Paterson *impossibility result* (FLP) [18] implies that unique leadership cannot be guaranteed in asynchronous systems where agents may unpredictably fail. In some cases, network partitioning may also erroneously cause multiple leaders to be elected [4]. Third, V2V networks like the IoP are expected to be highly dynamic where membership frequently changes. Consensus is used in DAC for agreeing on only a single candidate, after which the set of owners changes by design. Hence, the benefits of electing a stable leader that apply for *state machine replication* (*e.g.* – [27]), where reconfiguration is expected to be infrequent [34], are not applicable to DAC. Finally, channeling proposals through a unique leader

---

[1] An approach for *implicit coordination* between two aircraft has been proposed in [43], but that is only applicable for the purpose of *pairwise tactical conflict avoidance*.

creates a communication bottleneck and introduces the leader as a single point of failure: there can be no progress if the specified leader fails. In the absence of a unique leader, a system implementing Paxos falls back to the more general Synod protocol. Therefore, in this paper, we focus on identifying sufficient conditions under which the fundamental Synod protocol can make eventual progress.

The failure of *safety-critical* aerospace systems can lead to the loss of human life [24,61] and property [25]. Hence, formal methods must be used for the rigorous verification of any algorithm used in such systems. The *actor model* [1,21] is a theoretical model of concurrent computation that can be used for formal reasoning about distributed algorithms [42]. It assumes asynchronous communication as the most primitive form of interaction and it also assumes *fairness*, which is useful for reasoning about the progress of actor systems [62]. In the context of DAC, aircraft may experience temporary or permanent communication failures where they are unable to send or receive any messages [46]. Our verification of Synod must model the possibility of such failures. To support explicit reasoning about such failures in actors, we introduce a *(predicate-fair) failure-aware actor model* (FAM) that assumes *predicate fairness* [55] in addition to the standard actor model's fairness properties. Predicate fairness states that if a predicate is *enabled infinitely often* in a given path, then it must be eventually satisfied. We use Varela's dialect [62] of Agha, Mason, Smith, and Talcott's actor language (AMST) [3] and modify its semantics to model failures.

In order to ensure that our formalization of Synod and its eventual progress property are correct, we machine-check our proof using the *Athena proof assistant* [5,7]. Along with a language for expressing proofs, Athena also provides an interactive proof development environment. Athena's theorem proving capabilities are based on *many-sorted first-order logic* [39] and it uses a *natural deduction* [6] style of proofs. All terms have an associated *sort* and Athena can automatically detect and report *ill-sorted* terms and expressions in proofs. Athena is *sound*: all methods that successfully execute produce a theorem that is guaranteed to be a logical consequence of its *assumption base*. It also allows the use of *automated theorem provers* like Vampire [59] and SPASS [64].

The main contributions of this work are:

- We identify a set of conditions under which progress in Synod can be guaranteed in purely asynchronous settings, without assuming a unique leader.
- We introduce a failure-aware actor model to support formal reasoning about temporary or permanent actor failures.
- We show that progress can be guaranteed in Synod under the identified conditions and mechanically verify our proof using Athena. To our knowledge, this is the first machine-checked proof of eventual progress in Synod.

It is important to note here that a guarantee of eventual progress *alone* is insufficient for time-critical UAM applications, but it is a necessary precondition for providing *timely progress* guarantees that can be directly applicable for UAM.

The paper is structured as follows – Sect. 2 informally describes Synod and discusses the conditions required for progress; Sect. 3 introduces FAM; Sect. 4 presents the formal verification of progress in Synod; Sect. 5 relates our work to prior research on formal verification of consensus protocols; and Sect. 6 concludes the paper including potential future directions of work.

· 2   The Synod Protocol

Synod assumes an asynchronous, non-Byzantine system model in which agents operate at arbitrary speed, may fail and restart, and have stable storage. Messages can be duplicated, lost, and have arbitrary transmission time, but cannot be corrupted[30]. It consists of two logically separate sets of agents:

- *Proposers* - The set of agents that can propose values to be chosen.
- *Acceptors* - The set of agents that can vote on which value should be chosen.

Synod requires a subset of acceptors, which satisfy a *quorum*, to proceed. To ensure that if there is a consensus in one quorum, there cannot also be another quorum with a consensus, any two quorums must intersect. A subset of acceptors which constitutes a simple majority is an example of a quorum. Other methods of determining quorums can be found in [23].

There are four types of messages in Synod:

- *prepare (1a)* messages include a *proposal number*.
- *accept (2a)* messages include a proposal number and a *value*.
- *promise (1b)* messages include a proposal number and a value.
- *voted (2b)* messages include a proposal number and a value.

For each proposer, the algorithm proceeds in two distinct *phases*[30]:

- **Phase 1**
  (a) A proposer P selects a *unique proposal number* b and sends a *prepare* request with b to a subset Q of acceptors, where Q constitutes a quorum.
  (b) When an acceptor A receives a *prepare* request with the proposal number b, it checks if b is greater than the proposal numbers of all *prepare* requests to which A has already responded. If this condition is satisfied, then A responds to P with a *promise* message. The *promise* message implies that A will not accept any other proposal with a proposal number less than b. The promise includes (i) the highest-numbered proposal b' that A has previously accepted and (ii) the value corresponding to b'. If A has not accepted any proposals, it simply sends a default value.
- **Phase 2**
  (a) If P receives a *promise* message in response to its *prepare* requests from all members of Q, then P sends an *accept* request to all members of Q. These *accept* messages contain the proposal number b and a value v, where v is the value of the highest-numbered proposal among the responses or an arbitrary value if all responses reported the default value.
  (b) If an acceptor A receives an *accept* request with a proposal number b and a value v from P, it accepts the proposal unless it has already responded to a *prepare* request having a number greater than b. If A accepts the proposal, it sends P a *voted* message which includes b and v[29].

A proposer *determines* that a proposal was successfully *chosen* if and only if it receives *voted* messages from a quorum for that proposal.

Synod allows multiple proposals to be chosen. Safety is ensured by the invariant - *"If a proposal with value v is chosen, then every higher numbered-proposal that is chosen has value v"* [30]. Therefore, there may be situations where a proposer P proposes a proposal number after one or more lower-numbered proposals have already been chosen, resulting in some value v being chosen. By design, Synod will ensure that P proposes the same value v in its Phase 2. Since proposers can initiate proposals in any order and communication is asynchronous, the only fact that can be guaranteed about any chosen value is that it must have been proposed by the first proposal to have been chosen by any quorum. From the context of admission control, it implies that if a candidate P_2 successfully completes both phases after another candidate P_1 has completed both phases, then P_2 will simply learn that P_1 has been granted admission. So P_2 will update its set of owners to include P_1, create a new conflict-aware flight plan, and request admission by starting the Synod protocol again.

2.1 Progress in Synod

Some obvious scenarios in which progress may be affected in Synod are:

- Two proposers P_1 and P_2 may complete Phase 1 with proposal numbers b_1 and b_2 such that $b_2 > b_1$. This will cause P_1 to fail Phase 2. P_1 may then propose a fresh proposal number $b_3 > b_2$ and complete Phase 1 before P_2 completes its Phase 2. This will cause P_2 to fail Phase 2 and propose a fresh proposal number $b_4 > b_3$. This process may repeat infinitely [30] (*livelock*).
- Progress may be affected even if one random agent fails unpredictably [18].

Paxos assumes that a distinguished proposer (leader) is elected as the only proposer that can initiate proposals [29]. Lamport states *"If the distinguished proposer can communicate successfully with a majority of acceptors, and if it uses a proposal with number greater than any already used, then it will succeed in issuing a proposal that is accepted."* [30]. The FLP impossibility result [18] implies that in purely asynchronous systems, where agent failures cannot be differentiated from message delays, leader election cannot be guaranteed. Moreover, it is possible that due to network partitioning, multiple proposers are elected as leaders [4]. In the absence of a unique leader, a system implementing Paxos falls back to Synod. Therefore, it is important to identify the conditions under which progress can be formally guaranteed in Synod in the absence of a unique leader.

To guarantee progress, it suffices to show that *some* proposal number b will be chosen. This will happen if b satisfies the following conditions:

P1 When an acceptor A receives a *prepare* message with b, b should be greater than all other proposal numbers that A has previously seen.

P2 When an acceptor A receives an *accept* message with b, b should be greater than or equal to all other proposal numbers that A has previously seen.

P1 and *P2* simply suggest that for *b*, there will be a long enough period without *prepare* or *accept* messages with a proposal number greater than *b*, allowing messages corresponding to *b* to get successfully processed without being interrupted by messages corresponding to a higher-numbered proposal. The non-interruption condition follows from two assumptions. First, we assume that a proposer *P* will keep retrying until it successfully receives votes from a quorum. Second, we assume that the system has a form of fairness called *predicate fairness* [55]. With predicate fairness, if a predicate is enabled infinitely often in a given path, then the predicate must be satisfied (this is a recursive definition in that the path could begin from any state along the path). Conditions *P1* and *P2* are infinitely often enabled in any path corresponding to livelock. Therefore, by predicate fairness, these conditions must eventually happen, allowing consensus to be reached[2].

Since progress cannot be guaranteed if too many agents permanently fail or if too many messages are lost, Lamport [33] presents some conditions for informally proving progress in Paxos. A *nonfaulty* agent is defined as *"an agent that eventually performs the actions that it should"*, and a *good* set is defined as a set of nonfaulty agents, such that, if an agent repeatedly sends a message to another agent in the set, it is eventually received by the recipient. It is then assumed that the unique leader and a quorum of acceptors form a good set and that they infinitely repeat all messages that they have sent. These conditions are quite strong since they depend on the future behavior of a subset of agents and may not always be true of an implementation. However, since they have been deemed reasonable for informally proving progress even in the presence of a unique leader, we partially incorporate them in our conditions under which progress in Synod can be formally guaranteed in the absence of a unique leader. Our complete set of conditions for guaranteeing progress in Synod, therefore, informally states that *eventually, a nonfaulty proposer must propose a proposal number, that will satisfy P1 and P2, to a quorum of nonfaulty acceptors, and the Synod-specific messages between these agents must be eventually received*.

We can see that the conditions for progress in Paxos constitute a special case of our conditions for progress in Synod where *P1* and *P2* are satisfied by a proposal proposed by the unique leader. If the unique leader permanently fails, then the corresponding guarantee is only useful if leader re-election is successful. However, if leader election is assumed to have already succeeded, there will be no need for further consensus, rendering the guarantee moot. Synod's progress guarantee remains useful as long as at least one random proposer is available to possibly propose at least one successful proposal, thereby remaining pertinent even if multiple (not all) proposers arbitrarily fail. Moreover, the conditions do not assume that consensus (leader election) will have already succeeded.

---

[2] We do not use the predicate fairness assumption in the formal proof associated with this paper. Instead, we use a system-specific derived property: that eventually, at least one proposal must be uninterrupted by higher-numbered proposals.

3   A Failure-Aware Actor Model

We use the actor model to formally reason about progress in Synod since it assumes asynchronous communication and fairness, which is helpful for reasoning about progress [3]. Fairness in the standard actor model has the following consequences [62]:

- guaranteed message delivery[3], and
- an actor infinitely often ready to process a message will eventually process the message.

The IoP is an open network in which aircraft communicate asynchronously and may experience permanent or temporary communication failures that render them unable to send or receive any messages. All messages to and from an aircraft may get delayed because of transmission problems or internal processing delays (or processing failures) in the aircraft. In asynchronous communication, since message transmission times are unbounded, it is not possible to distinguish transmission delays from processing delays or failures. However, it is important to take into account if an actor has failed at any given time, *i.e.*, if it is incapable of sending or receiving messages. For this reason, we introduce a (predicate-fair) failure-aware actor model (FAM) that allows reasoning about such actor failures.

FAM models two states for an actor at any given time—*available* or *failed*. Actors can switch states as *transitions* between *configurations*. From the perspective of message transmission and reception, a failed actor cannot send or receive *any* messages, but an available actor can. The failure model of FAM also assumes that every actor has a stable storage that is persistent across failures. In addition to the standard actor model's fairness assumptions, FAM assumes predicate fairness [55], which states that a predicate that is infinitely often enabled in a given path will eventually be satisfied.

Varela [62] presents a dialect of AMST's *lambda-calculus* based actor language [3] whose operational semantics are a set of *labeled transitions* from *actor configurations* to actor configurations[4]. An actor configuration κ is a temporal snapshot of actor system components, namely the individual actors and the messages "en route". It is denoted by $\langle\!\langle \alpha \parallel \mu \rangle\!\rangle$, where α is a map from actor names to *actor expressions*, and μ is a multi-set of messages. An actor expression e is either a value v or a *reduction context* R filled with a *redex* r, denoted as $e = \mathsf{R} \blacktriangleright \mathsf{r} \blacktriangleleft$. $\kappa_1 \xrightarrow{l} \kappa_2$ denotes a *transition rule* where κ_1, κ_2, and l are the initial configuration, the final configuration, and the transition label respectively. There are four possible transitions – **fun, new, snd**, and **rcv**. To model failures, we modify Varela's dialect of AMST and categorize its original transitions (**fun, new, snd**, and **rcv**) as *base-level* transitions.

For a base-level transition in FAM to be enabled to occur for an *actor in focus* at any time, the actor needs to be available at that time. To denote available and

---

[3] "Delivery" here implies that the message will be available to the recipient. The recipient may or may not eventually receive and process the message.
[4] Interested readers can refer to Section 4.5 of [62] for more details.

failed actors at a given time, we redefine an actor configuration as $\langle\!\langle \alpha \parallel \bar{\alpha} \parallel \mu \rangle\!\rangle$, where α is a map from actor names to actor expressions for available actors, $\bar{\alpha}$ is a map from actor names to actor expressions for failed actors, and μ is a multi-set of messages "en route".

To model actor failure and restart, we define two *meta-level* transitions **stp** (*stop*) and **bgn** (*begin*) that can stop an available actor or start a failed actor in its persistent state before failure. The **stp** transition is only enabled for an actor in the available state and the **bgn** transition is only enabled for an actor in the failed state. Figure 1 and Fig. 2 show the operational semantics of our actor language as labelled transition rules[5,6].

$$\frac{e \rightarrow_\lambda e'}{\langle\!\langle \alpha, [\mathsf{R} \blacktriangleright e \blacktriangleleft]_a \parallel \bar{\alpha} \parallel \mu \rangle\!\rangle \overset{[\mathbf{fun}:a]}{\longrightarrow} \langle\!\langle \alpha, [\mathsf{R} \blacktriangleright e' \blacktriangleleft]_a \parallel \bar{\alpha} \parallel \mu \rangle\!\rangle}$$

$$\langle\!\langle \alpha, [\mathsf{R} \blacktriangleright \mathtt{new}(b) \blacktriangleleft]_a \parallel \bar{\alpha} \parallel \mu \rangle\!\rangle \overset{[\mathbf{new}:a,a']}{\longrightarrow} \langle\!\langle \alpha, [\mathsf{R} \blacktriangleright a' \blacktriangleleft]_a, [\mathtt{ready}(b)]_{a'} \parallel \bar{\alpha} \parallel \mu \rangle\!\rangle \quad a' \ fresh$$

$$\langle\!\langle \alpha, [\mathsf{R} \blacktriangleright \mathtt{send}(a',v) \blacktriangleleft]_a \parallel \bar{\alpha} \parallel \mu \rangle\!\rangle \overset{[\mathbf{snd}:a]}{\longrightarrow} \langle\!\langle \alpha, [\mathsf{R} \blacktriangleright \mathtt{nil} \blacktriangleleft]_a \parallel \bar{\alpha} \parallel \mu \uplus \{\langle a' \Leftarrow v \rangle\} \rangle\!\rangle$$

$$\langle\!\langle \alpha, [\mathsf{R} \blacktriangleright \mathtt{ready}(b) \blacktriangleleft]_a \parallel \bar{\alpha} \parallel \{\langle a \Leftarrow v \rangle\} \uplus \mu \rangle\!\rangle \overset{[\mathbf{rcv}:a,v]}{\longrightarrow} \langle\!\langle \alpha, [b(v)]_a \parallel \bar{\alpha} \parallel \mu \rangle\!\rangle$$

Fig. 1. Operational semantics for the base-level transition rules.

$$\langle\!\langle \alpha, [e]_a \parallel \bar{\alpha} \parallel \mu \rangle\!\rangle \overset{[\mathbf{stp}:a]}{\longrightarrow} \langle\!\langle \alpha|_{dom(\alpha)-\{a\}} \parallel \bar{\alpha}, [e]_a \parallel \mu \rangle\!\rangle$$

$$\langle\!\langle \alpha \parallel \bar{\alpha}, [e]_a \parallel \mu \rangle\!\rangle \overset{[\mathbf{bgn}:a]}{\longrightarrow} \langle\!\langle \alpha, [e]_a \parallel \bar{\alpha}|_{dom(\bar{\alpha})-\{a\}} \parallel \mu \rangle\!\rangle$$

Fig. 2. Operational semantics for the meta-level transition rules.

For an actor configuration $\kappa = \langle\!\langle \alpha \parallel \bar{\alpha} \parallel \mu \rangle\!\rangle$ to be syntactically well-formed in our actor language, it must conform to the following[7]:

1. $\forall a,\ a \in dom(\alpha) \cup dom(\bar{\alpha}),\ fv(\alpha(a)) \subseteq dom(\alpha) \cup dom(\bar{\alpha})$
2. $\forall m,\ m \in \mu,\ m = \langle a \Leftarrow v \rangle,\ fv(a) \cup fv(v) \subseteq dom(\alpha) \cup dom(\bar{\alpha})$
3. $dom(\alpha) \cap dom(\bar{\alpha}) = \emptyset$

The standard actor model's fairness assumptions apply only to the base-level transitions in our language and not to the meta-level transitions.

---

[5] $\rightarrow_\lambda$ denotes lambda calculus semantics, essentially beta-reduction. **new**, **send**, and **ready** are actor redexes. $\langle a \Leftarrow v \rangle$ denotes a message for actor a with value v. $\alpha, [e]_a$ denotes the extended map α', which is the same as α except that it maps a to e. $\uplus$ denotes multiset union. $\alpha|_S$ denotes restriction of mapping α to elements in set S. $dom(\alpha)$ is the domain of α.

[6] More details about actor language semantics can be found in [2,3], and [62].

[7] $fv(e)$ is the set of free variables in the expression e.

4   Formal Verification of Eventual Progress in Synod

This section presents our proof of eventual progress in the Synod protocol. The notations used in this section have been introduced in Table 1 and Table 2.

Table 1. Set symbols for our formal specification.

Symbol	Description	Symbol	Description
$\mathcal{A}$	Set of all actors	$\mathcal{M}$	Set of all messages
$\mathbb{P}$	Set of all proposer actors	$\mathbb{A}$	Set of all acceptor actors
$\mathcal{V}$	Set of all values	$\mathcal{Q}$	Set of all quorums
$\mathcal{B}$	Set of all proposal numbers	$\mathbb{M}$	Set of all sets of messages
$\mathcal{C}$	Set of all actor configurations	$\mathcal{S}$	Set of all transition steps
$\mathcal{T}$	Set of all fair transition paths	$\mathbb{N}$	Set of all natural numbers

Table 2. Relation symbols for our formal specification.

Symbol	Description	Input	Output
ς	Get last configuration	$\mathcal{T}$	$\mathcal{C}$
ρ	Get transition path up to index	$\mathcal{T} \times \mathbb{N}$	$\mathcal{T}$
τ	Transition path constructor	$\mathcal{T} \times \mathcal{S}$	$\mathcal{T}$
σ	Choose a value to propose based on configuration	$\mathcal{C} \times \mathcal{A}$	$\mathcal{V}$
$\mathfrak{s}$	Construct a snd transition step	$\mathcal{A} \times \mathcal{M}$	$\mathcal{S}$
$\mathfrak{r}$	Construct a rcv transition step	$\mathcal{A} \times \mathcal{M}$	$\mathcal{S}$
$\mathfrak{m}$	Get set of messages "en route"	$\mathcal{C}$	$\mathbb{M}$
$\mathfrak{a}$	Actor is in α	$\mathcal{C} \times \mathcal{A}$	Bool
$\Re$	Actor is ready for a step	$\mathcal{T} \times \mathcal{A} \times \mathcal{S}$	Bool
ϕ	Proposer has promises from a quorum	$\mathcal{A} \times \mathcal{B} \times \mathcal{Q} \times \mathcal{C}$	Bool
Φ	Proposer has votes from a quorum	$\mathcal{A} \times \mathcal{B} \times \mathcal{Q} \times \mathcal{C}$	Bool
$\mathfrak{d}$	Actor is nonfaulty	$\mathcal{A}$	Bool
$\mathfrak{p}$	Proposal number satisfies $P1$ and $P2$	$\mathcal{B}$	Bool
$\mathfrak{L}$	Proposer has learned of successful consensus	$\mathcal{A} \times \mathcal{B} \times \mathcal{C}$	Bool

A message is a tuple $\langle \mathbf{s} \in \mathcal{A}, \mathbf{r} \in \mathcal{A}, \mathbf{k} \in \xi, \mathbf{b} \in \mathcal{B}, \mathbf{v} \in \mathcal{V} \rangle$ where $\xi = \{1a, 1b, 2a, 2b\}$, s is the sender, r is the receiver, k is the type of message, b is a proposal number, and v is a value. $\bar{v} \in \mathcal{V}$ is a null value constant used in $1a$ (*prepare*) messages.

The local state of an actor x can be extracted from a configuration κ as a tuple $\langle \eta_\kappa^x \in \mathbb{M}, \beta_\kappa^x \in \mathcal{B}, v_\kappa^x \in \mathcal{V} \rangle$ where η_κ^x is the set of messages received but not yet responded to, β_κ^x is the highest proposal number seen, and v_κ^x is the value corresponding to the highest proposal number accepted.

Transition paths represent the dynamic changes to actor configurations as a result of transition steps [42]. *Indexed positions* in transition paths correspond to logical steps in time and are used to express eventuality.

$\mathbb{P} \subset \mathcal{A}$ and $\mathbb{A} \subset \mathcal{A}$ are the sets of proposers and acceptors respectively and a quorum is a possibly equal non-empty subset of $\mathbb{A}$, *i.e.*, $\forall Q \in \mathcal{Q} : Q \subseteq \mathbb{A} \wedge Q \neq \emptyset$.

4.1 Fairness Assumptions for Transitions

We assume two fairness axioms for the **snd** and **rcv** transitions that follow from the fairness assumptions of FAM. The **F-Snd-axm** and the **F-Rcv-axm** state that if a **snd** or **rcv** transition is enabled at some time, it must either eventually happen or eventually, it must become permanently disabled.

$$
\begin{aligned}
&\texttt{F-Snd-Axm} \equiv \\
&\forall x \in \mathcal{A}, m \in \mathcal{M}, T \in \mathcal{T}, i \in \mathbb{N} : (\Re(\rho(T,i), x, \mathfrak{s}(x,m)) \implies \\
&\qquad\qquad ((\exists j \in \mathbb{N} : (j \ge i) \\
&\qquad\qquad\qquad \wedge\ \rho(T, j+1) = \tau(\rho(T,j), \mathfrak{s}(x,m))) \\
&\qquad\qquad \vee\ (\exists k \in \mathbb{N} : (k > i) \\
&\qquad\qquad\qquad \wedge\ (\forall j \in \mathbb{N} : (j \ge k) \implies \neg\Re(\rho(T,j), x, \mathfrak{s}(x,m)))))))
\end{aligned}
$$

$$
\begin{aligned}
&\texttt{F-Rcv-Axm} \equiv \\
&\forall x \in \mathcal{A}, m \in \mathcal{M}, T \in \mathcal{T}, i \in \mathbb{N} : ((m \in \mathfrak{m}(\varsigma(\rho(T,i))) \ \wedge\ \Re(\rho(T,i), x, \mathfrak{r}(x,m))) \implies \\
&\qquad\qquad ((\exists j \in \mathbb{N} : (j \ge i) \\
&\qquad\qquad\qquad \wedge\ \rho(T, j+1) = \tau(\rho(T,j), \mathfrak{r}(x,m))) \\
&\qquad\qquad \vee\ (\exists k \in \mathbb{N} : (k > i) \\
&\qquad\qquad\qquad \wedge\ (\forall j \in \mathbb{N} : (j \ge k) \implies \\
&\qquad\qquad\qquad\qquad \neg(m \in \mathfrak{m}(\varsigma(\rho(T,j))) \ \wedge\ \Re(\rho(T,j), x, \mathfrak{r}(x,m)))))))))
\end{aligned}
$$

4.2 Rules Specifying the Actions of Synod Actors

The Synod protocol is presented in [29] as a high-level abstraction of the behavior of the agents, while leaving out the implementation details to the discretion of the system developers [47]. We specify rules over actor local states that dictate if an available Synod actor should become ready to send a message. Since Synod does not specify *when* a proposer should send a *prepare* message, we leave that behavior unspecified. For proving progress, we will assume that eventually, a proposer will be ready to send *prepare* messages to a quorum.

$$
\begin{aligned}
&\texttt{Snd-1b-Rul} \equiv \\
&\forall a : \mathbb{A}, p \in \mathbb{P}, T \in \mathcal{T}, i \in \mathbb{N}, b \in \mathcal{B} : \\
&(\langle p, a, 1a, b, \bar{v} \rangle \in \eta^a_{\varsigma(\rho(T,i))} \ \wedge\ \beta^a_{\varsigma(\rho(T,i))} < b \ \wedge\ \mathfrak{a}(\varsigma(\rho(T,i)), a)) \implies \\
&\qquad\qquad \Re(\rho(T,i), a, \mathfrak{s}(a, \langle a, p, 1b, b, v^a_{\varsigma(\rho(T,i))} \rangle)))
\end{aligned}
$$

$$
\begin{aligned}
&\texttt{Snd-2a-Rul} \equiv \\
&\forall p \in \mathbb{P}, T \in \mathcal{T}, i \in \mathbb{N}, b \in \mathcal{B}, Q \in \mathcal{Q} : \\
&(\phi(p, b, Q, \varsigma(\rho(T,i))) \ \wedge\ \mathfrak{a}(\varsigma(\rho(T,i)), p)) \implies \\
&\qquad\qquad (\forall a \in Q : \Re(\rho(T,i), p, \mathfrak{s}(p, \langle p, a, 2a, b, \sigma(\varsigma(\rho(T,i))), p \rangle))))
\end{aligned}
$$

$$
\begin{aligned}
&\texttt{Snd-2b-Rul} \equiv \\
&\forall a : \mathbb{A}, p \in \mathbb{P}, T \in \mathcal{T}, i \in \mathbb{N}, b \in \mathcal{B}, v \in \mathcal{V} : \\
&(\langle p, a, 2a, b, v \rangle \in \eta^a_{\varsigma(\rho(T,i))} \ \wedge\ \beta^a_{\varsigma(\rho(T,i))} \le b \ \wedge\ \mathfrak{a}(\varsigma(\rho(T,i)), a))) \implies \\
&\qquad\qquad \Re(\rho(T,i), a, \mathfrak{s}(a, \langle a, p, 2b, b, v \rangle))
\end{aligned}
$$

Since the response to a message in Synod is a finite set of actions, if there is a message in the multi-set for a Synod actor and the actor is also available, then a receive transition is enabled.

Rcv-Rul $\equiv$
$\forall s, r \in \mathcal{A}, T \in \mathcal{T}, i \in \mathbb{N}, k \in \xi, b \in \mathcal{B}, v \in \mathcal{V} :$
$(\langle s, r, k, b, v \rangle \in \mathsf{m}(\varsigma(\rho(T,i))) \;\wedge\; \mathsf{a}(\varsigma(\rho(T,i)), r))) \implies \Re(\rho(T,i), r, \mathfrak{r}(r, \langle s, r, k, b, v \rangle))$

4.3   Assumptions About the Future Behavior of Agents

To prove progress in Synod, we borrow some assumptions about the future behavior of nonfaulty agents used by Lamport for informally proving progress in Paxos [33]. It is worth noting that being nonfaulty does not prohibit an agent from temporarily failing. It simply means that for every action that needs to be performed by the agent, eventually the agent is available to perform the action and the action happens. In FAM, a nonfaulty actor can be modelled by asserting that an enabled **snd** or **rcv** transition for the actor will eventually happen. However, given the **F-Snd-Axm** and **F-Rcv-Axm** axioms, it suffices to assume that for a nonfaulty actor, if a **snd** or **rcv** transition is enabled, then it will either eventually occur or it will be infinitely often enabled. As FAM does not model message loss, any message in the multi-set will persist until it is received.

We introduce a predicate đ to specify an actor as nonfaulty, such that:

- đ(x) implies that the actor x will be eventually available if there is a message "en route" that x needs to receive.
- đ(x) implies that the actor x will be eventually available if x's local state dictates that it needs to send a message.
- đ(x) implies that if a **snd** or **rcv** transition is enabled for the actor x, it will either eventually occur or it will be infinitely often enabled.

Prp-NF-Axm $\equiv$
$\forall p \in \mathbb{P} : \mathsf{d}(p) \implies$
$\quad (\forall b \in \mathcal{B}, k \in \xi, v \in \mathcal{V}, T \in \mathcal{T}, i \in \mathbb{N}, a \in \mathbb{A}, Q \in \mathcal{Q} :$
$\qquad (\phi(p, b, Q, \varsigma(\rho(T,i)))$
$\qquad \vee \; \langle a, p, k, b, v \rangle \in \mathsf{m}(\varsigma(\rho(T,i)))) \implies$
$\qquad\qquad (\mathsf{a}(\varsigma(\rho(T,i)), p)$
$\qquad\qquad \vee \; (\exists j \in \mathbb{N} : (j > i) \;\wedge\; \mathsf{a}(\varsigma(\rho(T,j)), p))))$

Acc-NF-Axm $\equiv$
$\forall a \in \mathbb{A} : \mathsf{d}(a) \implies$
$\quad (\forall p \in \mathbb{P}, k \in \xi, v \in \mathcal{V}, T \in \mathcal{T}, i \in \mathbb{N}, b \in \mathcal{B} :$
$\qquad (((\langle p, a, 1a, b, \bar{v} \rangle \in \eta^a_{\varsigma(\rho(T,i))} \;\wedge\; (\beta^a_{\varsigma(\rho(T,i))} < b))$
$\qquad \vee \; (\langle p, a, 2a, b, v \rangle \in \eta^a_{\varsigma(\rho(T,i))} \;\wedge\; (\beta^a_{\varsigma(\rho(T,i))} \leq b))$
$\qquad \vee \; (\langle p, a, k, b, v \rangle \in \mathsf{m}(\varsigma(\rho(T,i))))) \implies$
$\qquad\qquad (\mathsf{a}(\varsigma(\rho(T,i)), a)$
$\qquad\qquad \vee \; (\exists j \in \mathbb{N} : (j > i) \;\wedge\; \mathsf{a}(\varsigma(\rho(T,j)), a))))$

```
NF-IOE-Axm ≡
```
$\forall x \in \mathcal{A} : \mathrm{d}(x) \implies$
$\quad (\forall T \in \mathcal{T}, i \in \mathbb{N}, m \in \mathcal{M} :$
$\quad\quad ((m \in \mathrm{m}(\varsigma(\rho(T,i)))) \ \wedge \ \Re(\rho(T,i), x, \mathfrak{r}(x,m))) \implies$
$\quad\quad ((\exists j \in \mathbb{N} : (j \geq i)$
$\quad\quad\quad\quad \wedge \ \rho(T, j+1) = \tau(\rho(T,j), \mathfrak{r}(x,m)))$
$\quad\quad\quad \vee \ (\forall k \in \mathbb{N} : (k > i)$
$\quad\quad\quad\quad\quad \implies \quad (\exists j \in \mathbb{N} : (j \geq k)$
$\quad\quad\quad\quad\quad\quad\quad \wedge \ (m \in \mathrm{m}(\varsigma(\rho(T,j))) \ \wedge \ \Re(\rho(T,j), x, \mathfrak{r}(x,m))))))))$
$\quad \wedge \ (\Re(\rho(T,i), x, \mathfrak{s}(x,m)) \implies$
$\quad\quad ((\exists j \in \mathbb{N} : (j \geq i)$
$\quad\quad\quad\quad \wedge \ \rho(T, j+1) = \tau(\rho(T,j), \mathfrak{s}(x,m)))$
$\quad\quad\quad \vee \ (\forall k \in \mathbb{N} : (k > i)$
$\quad\quad\quad\quad\quad \implies \quad (\exists j \in \mathbb{N} : (j \geq k) \ \wedge \ \Re(\rho(T,j), x, \mathfrak{s}(x,m)))))))$

We then introduce a predicate þ that is true of a proposal number if and only if it satisfies the conditions P1 and P2 described informally in Sect. 2.1.

```
P1-P2-Def ≡
```
$\forall b \in \mathcal{B} : \text{þ}(b) \iff$
$\quad (\forall p \in \mathbb{P}, T \in \mathcal{T}, i \in \mathbb{N}, v \in \mathcal{V}, a \in \mathbb{A} :$
$\quad\quad\quad\quad (((\langle p, a, 1a, b, \bar{v} \rangle \in \eta^a_{\varsigma(\rho(T,i))} \implies \beta^a_{\varsigma(\rho(T,i))} < b)$
$\quad\quad\quad\quad \wedge \ (\langle p, a, 2a, b, v \rangle \in \eta^a_{\varsigma(\rho(T,i))} \implies \beta^a_{\varsigma(\rho(T,i))} \leq b)))$

Finally, the conditions for formally guaranteeing progress state that – *in all fair transition paths, some nonfaulty proposer p will be eventually ready to propose some proposal number b, that will satisfy P1 and P2, to some quorum Q whose members are all nonfaulty.*

```
CND ≡
```
$\forall T \in \mathcal{T} :$
$\quad (\exists i \in \mathbb{N}, p \in \mathbb{P}, b \in \mathcal{B}, Q \in \mathcal{Q} :$
$\quad\quad (\mathrm{d}(p) \ \wedge \ \text{þ}(b) \ \wedge \ (\forall a \in Q : (\mathrm{d}(a) \ \wedge \ \Re(\rho(T,i), p, \mathfrak{s}(p, \langle p, a, 1a, b, \bar{v} \rangle)))))))$

4.4   The Proof of Progress

To prove progress in Synod, it suffices to prove that eventually, at least one proposal number will be chosen by some quorum (Sect. 2). In our set of conditions CND, we have assumed that some proposer p will eventually propose a proposal number b, that will satisfy *P1* and *P2*, to a quorum Q. Our proof strategy is to show that eventually, p will learn that b has been chosen by all members of Q. Theorem 1 formally states our main progress guarantee while Lemma 1 and Lemma 2 state progress in Phase 1 and Phase 2 respectively.

Theorem 1. *Given* CND, *in all fair transition paths, eventually some proposer p will learn that some proposal number b has been chosen.*

```
Theorem-1 ≡
```
$\text{CND} \implies (\forall T \in \mathcal{T} : (\exists i \in \mathbb{N}, p \in \mathbb{P}, b \in \mathcal{B} : \text{Ł}(p, b, \varsigma(\rho(T,i)))))$

Lemma 1. *In a fair transition path, if eventually a nonfaulty proposer p becomes ready to propose a proposal number b, that satisfies P1 and P2, to a quorum Q whose members are all nonfaulty, then eventually p will receive promises from all members of Q for b.*

Lemma-1 $\equiv$
$\forall T \in \mathcal{T}, i \in \mathbb{N}, p \in \mathbb{P}, b \in \mathcal{B}, Q \in \mathcal{Q}:$
$\quad (\mathrm{d}(p) \;\wedge\; \mathrm{p}(b) \;\wedge\; (\forall a \in Q : (\mathrm{d}(a) \;\wedge\; \Re(\rho(T,i), p, \mathrm{s}(p, \langle p, a, 1a, b, \bar{v}\rangle)))))$
$\qquad\qquad\qquad \implies (\exists j \in \mathbb{N} : (j \geq i) \;\wedge\; \phi(p, b, Q, \varsigma(\rho(T,j))))$

Lemma 2. *In a fair transition path, if eventually a nonfaulty proposer p receives promises for a proposal number b, that satisfies P1 and P2, from a quorum Q whose members are all nonfaulty, then eventually p will receive votes from all members of Q for b.*

Lemma-2 $\equiv$
$\forall T \in \mathcal{T}, i \in \mathbb{N}, p \in \mathbb{P}, b \in \mathcal{B}, Q \in \mathcal{Q}:$
$\quad (\mathrm{d}(p) \;\wedge\; \mathrm{p}(b) \;\wedge\; \phi(p, Q, \varsigma(\rho(T,i))) \;\wedge\; (\forall a \in Q : \mathrm{d}(a)))$
$\qquad\qquad\qquad \implies (\exists j \in \mathbb{N} : (j \geq i) \;\wedge\; \Phi(p, b, Q, \varsigma(\rho(T,j))))$

Given below are the proof sketches of Theorem 1, Lemma 1, and Lemma 2:
Theorem 1 *Proof Sketch* -

(1) By Lemma 1 and CND, some nonfaulty proposer p will eventually receive promises from some quorum Q, whose members are all nonfaulty, for some proposal number b that satisfies *P1* and *P2*.
(2) By Lemma 2, p will eventually receive votes from Q for b and learn that b has been chosen.
$\qquad\qquad\qquad\qquad\qquad\qquad\qquad\qquad\qquad\qquad\qquad\qquad\qquad$ $\square$

Lemma 1 *Proof Sketch* -

(1) By Prp-NF-Axm, NF-IOE-Axm, and F-Snd-Axm *prepare* messages from p will eventually be sent to all members of Q.
(2) By Acc-NF-Axm, NF-IOE-Axm, F-Rcv-Axm all members of Q will eventually receive the *prepare* messages.
(3) By P1-P2-Def, Snd-1b-Rul, and Acc-NF-Axm, each member of Q will eventually be ready to send *promise* messages to p.
(4) By Acc-NF-Axm, NF-IOE-Axm, and F-Snd-Axm the *promise* messages from each member of Q will eventually be sent.
(5) By Prp-NF-Axm, F-Rcv-Axm, and NF-IOE-Axm p will eventually receive the *promise* messages from all members of Q.
$\qquad\qquad\qquad\qquad\qquad\qquad\qquad\qquad\qquad\qquad\qquad\qquad\qquad$ $\square$

Lemma 2 *Proof Sketch* -

(1) By Snd-2a-Rul, and Prp-NF-Axm, p will eventually be ready to send *accept* messages to all members of Q with proposal number b.

(2) By `Prp-NF-Axm`, `NF-IOE-Axm`, and `F-Snd-Axm`, *accept* messages from p will eventually be sent to all members of Q.

(3) By `Acc-NF-Axm`, `NF-IOE-Axm`, `F-Rcv-Axm` all members of Q will eventually receive the *accept* messages.

(4) By `P1-P2-Def`, `Snd-2b-Rul`, and `Acc-NF-Axm`, each member of Q will eventually be ready to send *voted* messages to p.

(5) By `Acc-NF-Axm`, `NF-IOE-Axm`, and `F-Snd-Axm` the *voted* messages from each member of Q will eventually be sent

(6) By `Prp-NF-Axm`, `F-Rcv-Axm`, and `NF-IOE-Axm` p will eventually receive the *voted* messages from all members of Q.

□

We have formalized all the theory and proof sketches presented in this section using Athena. The proofs of Theorem 1, Lemma 1, and Lemma 2 have been mechanically verified for correctness. The high-level structures of the proofs were developed in a hierarchical manner consisting of well-connected steps. The SPASS [64] automatic theorem prover was then guided with appropriate premises for mechanically verifying each step (more details can be found in the companion technical report [50]). We have made extensive use of Athena's existing library of natural number theory for reasoning about indexed points in transition paths. The complete proof consists of about 6000 lines of Athena code[8].

5   Related Work

Prior work on verification of Synod-related protocols exists in the literature. Prisco *et al.* [15] present a rigorous hand-written proof of safety for Paxos along with an analysis of time performance and fault tolerance. Chand *et al.* [12] provide a specification of Multi-Paxos in TLA$^+$ [31] and use TLAPS [14] to prove its safety. Padon *et al.* [48] have verified the safety property for Paxos, *Vertical Paxos* [34], *Fast Paxos* [33], and *Stoppable Paxos* [38] using deductive verification. Küfner *et al.* [28] provide a methodology to develop machine-checkable proofs of fault-tolerant round-based distributed systems and verify the safety property for Paxos. Schiper *et al.* [60] have formally verified the safety property of a Paxos-based totally ordered broadcast protocol using EventML [11] and the Nuprl [45] proof assistant. Howard *et al.* [23] have presented *Flexible Paxos* by introducing flexible quorums for Paxos and have model checked its safety property using the TLC model checker [32]. Rahli *et al.* [56,57] have used EventML and Nuprl to formally verify the safety of an implementation of Multi-Paxos. Attiya *et al.* [8] provide bounds on the time to reach progress in consensus by assuming a synchronous model with known bounds on message delivery and processing time of non-faulty processes. Keidar *et al.* [26] consider a partial synchrony model with known bounds on processing times and message delays and use it to guarantee progress in a consensus algorithm when the bounds hold. Malkhi *et al.* [38] introduce Stoppable Paxos, a variant of Paxos for implementing a stoppable

---

[8] Complete Athena code available at http://wcl.cs.rpi.edu/pilots/fvcafp.

state machine and provide an informal proof of safety and progress for Stoppable Paxos with a unique leader. McMillan et al. [40] machine-check and verify the proofs of safety and progress properties of Stoppable Paxos [38] using Ivy [49]. Dragoi et al. [17] introduce PSync, a language that allows writing, execution, and verification of high-level implementations of fault-tolerant systems, and use it to verify the safety and progress properties of LastVoting [13]. LastVoting is an adaptation of Paxos in the Heard-Of model [13] that guarantees progress under the assumption of a single leader. A machine-checked proof of safety and progress of LastVoting also appeared in [16]. Hawblitzel et al. [19,20] introduce a framework for designing provably correct distributed algorithms called Iron-Fleet and use it to prove the safety and progress properties for a Multi-Paxos implementation called IronRSL by embedding TLA^{+} specifications in Dafny [36]. Their proof of progress relies on the assumption that eventually, all messages will arrive within a maximum network delay and leader election will succeed.

All of the aforementioned work has either analyzed the safety property or both the safety and progress properties of Synod-related protocols. Where progress has been verified, the authors have either assumed a unique leader, synchrony, or both. Our work improves upon existing work by identifying a set of asynchronous conditions under which the fundamental Synod consensus protocol can make eventual progress in the absence of a unique leader, and providing the first mechanically verified proof of eventual progress in Synod.

6   Conclusion

We have identified a set of sufficient conditions under which the Synod protocol can make progress, in asynchronous communication settings and in the absence of a unique leader. Leader election itself being a consensus problem, our conditions generalize Paxos' progress conditions by eliminating their cyclic reliance on consensus. Consequently, our weaker assumptions do not impose a communication bottleneck or proposal restrictions. We have introduced a failure-aware actor model (FAM) to reason about communication failures in actors. Using this reasoning framework we have formally demonstrated that eventual progress can be guaranteed in Synod under the identified conditions. Finally, we have used Athena to develop the first machine-checked proof of progress in Synod.

It is important to note that a guarantee of eventual progress only states that consensus will be achieved, but does not provide any bound on the amount of time that may be required for the same. Since air traffic data usually has a short useful lifetime and aircraft have limited time to remain airborne, a guarantee of eventual progress alone is insufficient for UAM applications. To be useful, a progress guarantee should have some associated time bounds that the aircraft can use to make important decisions, e.g., if there is a guarantee that consensus will take at least 5 s, then a candidate can decide to only compute flight plans that start after 5 s. Nevertheless, we see this work as a valuable exercise in perceiving the nuances involved in guaranteeing eventual consensus in the presence of multiple unrestricted proposers. This is important because a guarantee of eventual progress is a necessary precondition for providing a guarantee of timely progress that can be directly applicable for UAM.

A potential direction of future work would be to investigate formal proofs of probabilistic guarantees of timely progress by using data-driven statistical results. Such properties may be provided by using statistical observations about message transmission and processing delays, which cannot be deterministically predicted in asynchronous conditions but can be observed at run-time. Another potential direction of work would be to model message loss in FAM by introducing additional meta-level transitions. This would allow us to weaken the conditions further by requiring the guaranteed delivery of only a subset of messages, thereby weakening the current fairness assumptions of FAM. To avoid livelocks, it may also suffice to replace predicate fairness with a weaker assumption that *infinitely often enabled finite transition sequences must eventually occur.*

Acknowledgment. This research was partially supported by the National Science Foundation (NSF), Grant No. – CNS-1816307 and the Air Force Office of Scientific Research (AFOSR), DDDAS Grant No. – FA9550-19-1-0054. The authors would like to express their gratitude to Elkin Cruz-Camacho, Dan Plyukhin, and the anonymous reviewers of NFM 2021 for their helpful comments on improving the manuscript.

References

1. Agha, G.: Actors: A Model of Concurrent Computation in Distributed Systems. The MIT Press, Cambridge (1986)
2. Agha, G., Mason, I.A., Smith, S., Talcott, C.: Towards a theory of actor computation. In: Cleaveland, W.R. (ed.) CONCUR 1992. LNCS, vol. 630, pp. 565–579. Springer, Heidelberg (1992). https://doi.org/10.1007/BFb0084816
3. Agha, G.A., Mason, I.A., Smith, S.F., Talcott, C.L.: A foundation for actor computation. J. Funct. Program. **7**(1), 1–72 (1997)
4. Alquraan, A., Takruri, H., Alfatafta, M., Al-Kiswany, S.: An analysis of network-partitioning failures in cloud systems. In: 13th USENIX Symposium on Operating Systems Design and Implementation, pp. 51–68 (2018)
5. Arkoudas, K.: Athena. http://proofcentral.org/athena
6. Arkoudas, K.: Simplifying proofs in fitch-style natural deduction systems. J. Autom. Reasoning **34**(3), 239–294 (2005)
7. Arkoudas, K., Musser, D.: Fundamental Proof Methods in Computer Science: A Computer-Based Approach. MIT Press, Cambridge (2017)
8. Attiya, H., Dwork, C., Lynch, N., Stockmeyer, L.: Bounds on the time to reach agreement in the presence of timing uncertainty. J. ACM (JACM) **41**(1), 122–152 (1994)
9. Aweiss, A.S., Owens, B.D., Rios, J., Homola, J.R., Mohlenbrink, C.P.: Unmanned aircraft systems (UAS) traffic management (UTM) National Campaign II. In: 2018 AIAA Information Systems-AIAA Infotech@ Aerospace, p. 1727 (2018)
10. Balachandran, S., Muñoz, C., Consiglio, M.: Distributed consensus to enable merging and spacing of UAS in an urban environment. In: 2018 International Conference on Unmanned Aircraft Systems (ICUAS), pp. 670–675. IEEE (2018)
11. Bickford, M., Constable, R.L., Rahli, V.: Logic of events, a framework to reason about distributed systems. In: Languages for Distributed Algorithms Workshop (2012)

12. Chand, S., Liu, Y.A., Stoller, S.D.: Formal verification of multi-paxos for distributed consensus. In: Fitzgerald, J., Heitmeyer, C., Gnesi, S., Philippou, A. (eds.) FM 2016. LNCS, vol. 9995, pp. 119–136. Springer, Cham (2016). https://doi.org/10.1007/978-3-319-48989-6_8

13. Charron-Bost, B., Schiper, A.: The heard-of model: computing in distributed systems with benign faults. Distrib. Comput. **22**(1), 49–71 (2009)

14. Chaudhuri, K., Doligez, D., Lamport, L., Merz, S.: Verifying safety properties with the TLA$^+$ proof system. In: Giesl, J., Hähnle, R. (eds.) IJCAR 2010. LNCS (LNAI), vol. 6173, pp. 142–148. Springer, Heidelberg (2010). https://doi.org/10.1007/978-3-642-14203-1_12

15. De Prisco, R., Lampson, B., Lynch, N.: Revisiting the PAXOS algorithm. Theor. Comput. Sci. **243**(1–2), 35–91 (2000)

16. Debrat, H., Merz, S.: Verifying fault-tolerant distributed algorithms in the heard-of model. Arch. Formal Proofs **2012**, 1–166 (2012)

17. Drăgoi, C., Henzinger, T.A., Zufferey, D.: PSync: a partially synchronous language for fault-tolerant distributed algorithms. In: ACM SIGPLAN Notices, vol. 51, pp. 400–415. ACM (2016)

18. Fischer, M.J., Lynch, N.A., Paterson, M.S.: Impossibility of distributed consensus with one faulty process. J. ACM (JACM) **32**(2), 374–382 (1985)

19. Hawblitzel, C., et al.: IronFleet: proving practical distributed systems correct. In: Proceedings of the 25th Symposium on Operating Systems Principles, pp. 1–17. ACM (2015)

20. Hawblitzel, C., et al.: IronFleet: proving safety and liveness of practical distributed systems. Commun. ACM **60**(7), 83–92 (2017)

21. Hewitt, C.: Viewing control structures as patterns of passing messages. Artif. Intell **8**(3), 323–364 (1977)

22. Hopkin, V.D.: Human Factors in Air Traffic Control. CRC Press, Boca Raton (2017)

23. Howard, H., Malkhi, D., Spiegelman, A.: Flexible Paxos: Quorum Intersection Revisited. arXiv preprint arXiv:1608.06696 (2016)

24. Imai, S., Varela, C.A.: A programming model for spatio-temporal data streaming applications. In: Dynamic Data-Driven Applications Systems, Omaha, NE, USA, pp. 1139–1148 (2012)

25. Imai, S., Blasch, E., Galli, A., Zhu, W., Lee, F., Varela, C.A.: Airplane flight safety using error-tolerant data stream processing.IEEE Aerosp. Electron. Syst. Mag. **32**(4), 4–17 (2017)

26. Keidar, I., Rajsbaum, S.: Open questions on consensus performance in well-behaved runs. In: Schiper, A., Shvartsman, A.A., Weatherspoon, H., Zhao, B.Y. (eds.) Future Directions in Distributed Computing. LNCS, vol. 2584, pp. 35–39. Springer, Heidelberg (2003). https://doi.org/10.1007/3-540-37795-6_7

27. Kirsch, J., Amir, Y.: Paxos for system builders: an overview. In: Proceedings of the 2nd Workshop on Large-Scale Distributed Systems and Middleware, pp. 1–6 (2008)

28. Küfner, P., Nestmann, U., Rickmann, C.: Formal verification of distributed algorithms. In: Baeten, J.C.M., Ball, T., de Boer, F.S. (eds.) TCS 2012. LNCS, vol. 7604, pp. 209–224. Springer, Heidelberg (2012). https://doi.org/10.1007/978-3-642-33475-7_15

29. Lamport, L.: The part-time parliament. ACM Trans. Comput. Syst. (TOCS) **16**(2), 133–169 (1998)

30. Lamport, L.: Paxos made simple. ACM Sigact News **32**(4), 18–25 (2001)

31. Lamport, L.: Specifying Systems: The TLA+ Language and Tools for Hardware and Software Engineers. Addison-Wesley Longman Publishing Co., Inc., Boston (2002)
32. Lamport, L.: Real-time model checking is really simple. In: Borrione, D., Paul, W. (eds.) CHARME 2005. LNCS, vol. 3725, pp. 162–175. Springer, Heidelberg (2005). https://doi.org/10.1007/11560548_14
33. Lamport, L.: Fast Paxos. Distrib. Comput **19**(2), 79–103 (2006)
34. Lamport, L., Malkhi, D., Zhou, L.: Vertical paxos and primary-backup replication. In: Proceedings of the 28th ACM Symposium on Principles of Distributed Computing, pp. 312–313 (2009)
35. Lee, S.M., Park, C., Johnson, M.A., Mueller, E.R.: Investigating effects of well clear definitions on UAS sense-and-avoid operations in enroute and transition airspace. In: 2013 Aviation Technology, Integration, and Operations Conference, p. 4308 (2013)
36. Leino, K.R.M.: Dafny: an automatic program verifier for functional correctness. In: Clarke, E.M., Voronkov, A. (eds.) LPAR 2010. LNCS (LNAI), vol. 6355, pp. 348–370. Springer, Heidelberg (2010). https://doi.org/10.1007/978-3-642-17511-4_20
37. Luckner, R., Höhne, G., Fuhrmann, M.: Hazard criteria for wake vortex encounters during approach. Aerosp. Sci. Technol. **8**(8), 673–687 (2004)
38. Malkhi, D., Lamport, L., Zhou, L.: Stoppable Paxos. Technival report, Microsoft Research (2008)
39. Manzano, M., Manzano, T.D.L.M.: Extensions of First-Order Logic, vol. 19. Cambridge University Press, Cambridge (1996)
40. McMillan, K.L., Padon, O.: Deductive verification in decidable fragments with ivy. In: Podelski, A. (ed.) SAS 2018. LNCS, vol. 11002, pp. 43–55. Springer, Cham (2018). https://doi.org/10.1007/978-3-319-99725-4_4
41. Molisch, A.F., Tufvesson, F., Karedal, J., Mecklenbrauker, C.F.: A survey on vehicle-to-vehicle propagation channels. IEEE Wirel. Commun. **16**(6), 12–22 (2009)
42. Musser, D.R., Varela, C.A.: Structured reasoning about actor systems. In: Proceedings of the 2013 Workshop on Programming Based on Actors, Agents, and Decentralized Control, Agere! 2013, pp. 37–48. ACM, New York (2013)
43. Narkawicz, A., Muñoz, C., Dutle, A.: Coordination logic for repulsive resolution maneuvers. In: 16th AIAA Aviation Technology, Integration, and Operations Conference, p. 3156 (2016)
44. National Academies of Sciences: Engineering, and Medicine: Assessing the Risks of Integrating Unmanned Aircraft Systems (UAS) into the National Airspace System. The National Academies Press, Washington (2018)
45. Naumov, P., Stehr, M.-O., Meseguer, J.: The HOL/NuPRL proof translator. In: Boulton, R.J., Jackson, P.B. (eds.) TPHOLs 2001. LNCS, vol. 2152, pp. 329–345. Springer, Heidelberg (2001). https://doi.org/10.1007/3-540-44755-5_23
46. Okcu, H.: Operational requirements of unmanned aircraft systems data link and communication systems. J. Adv. Comput. Netw. **4**(1), 28–32 (2016)
47. Ongaro, D., Ousterhout, J.: In search of an understandable consensus algorithm. In: 2014 USENIX Annual Technical Conference (USENIX ATC 14), pp. 305–319 (2014)
48. Padon, O., Losa, G., Sagiv, M., Shoham, S.: Paxos made EPR: decidable reasoning about distributed protocols. In: Proceedings of the ACM on Programming Languages 1(OOPSLA), pp. 1–31 (2017)

49. Padon, O., McMillan, K.L., Panda, A., Sagiv, M., Shoham, S.: Ivy: safety verification by interactive generalization. ACM SIGPLAN Notices **51**(6), 614–630 (2016)
50. Paul, S., Agha, G.A., Patterson, S., Varela, C.A.: Verification of Eventual Consensus in Synod using a Failure-Aware Actor Model. Technical report, Rensselaer Polytechnic Institute, Department of Computer Science (2021)
51. Paul, S., Kopsaftopoulos, F., Patterson, S., Varela, C.A.: Dynamic data-driven formal progress envelopes for distributed algorithms. In: Dynamic Data-Driven Application Systems (InfoSymbiotics/DDDAS 2020), pp. 245–252 (2020)
52. Paul, S., Patterson, S., Varela, C.A.: Conflict-aware flight planning for avoiding near mid-air collisions. In: The 38th IEEE/AIAA Digital Avionics Systems Conference, San Diego, CA, pp. 1–10 (2019)
53. Paul, S., Patterson, S., Varela, C.A.: Collaborative situational awareness for conflict-aware flight planning. In: The 39th IEEE/AIAA Digital Avionics Systems Conference, pp. 1–10 (2020)
54. Peters, A., Balachandran, S., Duffy, B., Smalling, K., Consiglio, M., Muñoz, C.: Flight test results of a distributed merging algorithm for autonomous UAS operations. In: The 39th IEEE/AIAA Digital Avionics Systems Conference, pp. 1–7 (2020)
55. Queille, J.P., Sifakis, J.: Fairness and related properties in transition systems – a temporal logic to deal with fairness. Acta Informatica **19**(3), 195–220 (1983)
56. Rahli, V., Guaspari, D., Bickford, M., Constable, R.L.: Formal specification, verification, and implementation of fault-tolerant systems using EventML. Electron. Commun. EASST **72**, 1–15 (2015)
57. Rahli, V., Guaspari, D., Bickford, M., Constable, R.L.: EventML: specification, verification, and implementation of crash-tolerant state machine replication systems. Sci. Comput. Program. **148**, 26–48 (2017)
58. Ren, W., Beard, R.W.: Distributed Consensus in Multi-Vehicle Cooperative Control. Springer, Heidelberg (2008). https://doi.org/10.1007/978-1-84800-015-5
59. Riazanov, A., Voronkov, A.: The design and implementation of VAMPIRE. AI Commun. **15**(23), 91–110 (2002)
60. Schiper, N., Rahli, V., Van Renesse, R., Bickford, M., Constable, R.L.: Developing correctly replicated databases using formal tools. In: 2014 44th Annual IEEE/IFIP International Conference on Dependable Systems and Networks, pp. 395–406. IEEE (2014)
61. Sommerville, I.: Software Engineering. Addison-Wesley/Pearson, Boston (2011)
62. Varela, C.A.: Programming Distributed Computing Systems. The MIT Press, Cambridge (2013)
63. Vascik, P.D., Hansman, R.J., Dunn, N.S.: Analysis of urban air mobility operational constraints. J. Air Transp. **26**(4), 133–146 (2018)
64. Weidenbach, C., Dimova, D., Fietzke, A., Kumar, R., Suda, M., Wischnewski, P.: SPASS version 3.5. In: Schmidt, R.A. (ed.) CADE 2009. LNCS (LNAI), vol. 5663, pp. 140–145. Springer, Heidelberg (2009). https://doi.org/10.1007/978-3-642-02959-2_10

An Infrastructure for Faithful Execution of Remote Attestation Protocols

Adam Petz$^{(\boxtimes)}$ and Perry Alexander

Information and Telecommunication Technology Center, The University of Kansas,
Lawrence, KS 66045, USA
{ampetz,palexand}@ku.edu

Abstract. Remote attestation is a technology for establishing trust in a remote computing system. Copland is a domain-specific language for specifying attestation protocols that operate in diverse, layered measurement topologies. An accompanying reference semantics characterizes attestation-relevant system events and bundling of cryptographic evidence. In this work we formally define and verify the Copland Compiler and Copland Virtual Machine for executing Copland protocols. The compiler and vm are implemented as monadic, functional programs in the Coq proof assistant and verified with respect to the Copland reference semantics. In addition we introduce the Attestation Manager Monad as an environment for managing attestation freshness, binding results of Copland protocols to variables, and appraising evidence results. These components lay the foundation for a verified attestation stack.

Keywords: Remote attestation · Verification · Domain specific languages

1 Introduction

Semantic Remote Attestation is a technique for establishing trust in a remote system by requesting *evidence* of its behavior, *meta-evidence* describing evidence properties, and locally *appraising* the result. Remote attestation by virtual machine introspection was introduced by Haldar and Franz [18] and subsequently refined [5,7,8,19,40,41] to become an important technology for security and trust establishment.

In its simplest form remote attestation involves an *attester* (or *target*) and an *appraiser*. The appraiser requests evidence from an attester that executes an *attestation protocol* sequencing *measurements* to gather evidence and meta-evidence. Upon receiving evidence from the attester, the appraiser performs an *appraisal* to determine if it can trust the attester.

This work is funded by the NSA Science of Security initiative contract #H98230-18-D-0009 and Defense Advanced Research Project Agency contract #HR0011-18-9-0001. The views and conclusions contained in this document are those of the authors and should not be interpreted as representing the official policies, either expressed or implied, of the U.S. Government.

© Springer Nature Switzerland AG 2021
A. Dutle et al. (Eds.): NFM 2021, LNCS 12673, pp. 268–286, 2021.
https://doi.org/10.1007/978-3-030-76384-8_17

As system complexity increases so increases attestation and appraisal complexity. Federations of targets, systems-of-systems, privacy and security, and layering all introduce a need for complex, multi-party attestations. To address this need the authors and their colleagues developed Copland [39], a language for defining and executing attestation protocols. Copland has a formal semantics defining measurement, where measurement is performed, measurement ordering, and evidence bundling.

Our aspirational goal is developing a formally verified execution environment for Copland protocols. This work centers on a formal model for compiling and executing Copland in an operational environment. We define a compiler, virtual machine, and run-time environment as functional programs in Coq, then prove them compliant with the Copland formal semantics. As such it informs our development of an attestation manager in CakeML by providing a detailed formal definition of Copland protocol execution.

2 Virus Checking as Attestation

A simple motivating example for Copland is treating virus checking as attestation. Suppose that an appraiser would like to establish if a target system is virus free. The obvious approach is for the appraiser to request virus checking results as an attestation of the remote machine and appraise the result to determine the remote machine's state. The Copland phrase for this attestation is:

$$@_p \, [(\mathsf{ASP} \; vc \; \bar{a} \; p \; t)]$$

asking platform p to invoke virus checker vc as an attestation service provider targeting applications t running on p.

Simply doing a remote procedure call places full trust in vc and its operational environment. The target could lie about its results or an adversary could tamper with the virus checking system by compromising the checker or its signature file. An adversary could also compromise the operational environment running the checker or execute a man-in-the-middle replay attack.

A stronger attestation would make a request of the target that includes an encrypted nonce to ensure measurement freshness. The target would decrypt the nonce, gather evidence from the checker, and return the evidence and nonce signed using its private key. The appraiser would check the signature and nonce as well as checking the virus checker results. While the virus checker produces evidence of system state, the signature and nonce produce *meta-evidence* describing how evidence is handled. The Copland phrase for this attestation is:

$$@_p \, \{n\} [(\mathsf{ASP} \; vc \; \bar{a} \; p \; t) \rightarrow \mathsf{SIG}]$$

adding an input nonce, n, and asking p to sign the measurement result.

Evidence from the virus checker may still be compromised if the virus checker executable or signature file were compromised by an adversary. The attestation protocol can be improved to return a measurement of the checker's operational environment in addition to virus checking results. The Copland phrase for this stronger attestation is:

$$@_p \{n\}[@_{ma} \{n\}[(\text{ASP } h \; \bar{b} \; p \; v) \to \text{SIG}] \to (\text{ASP } vc \; \bar{a} \; p \; t) \to \text{SIG}]$$

where ma is a trusted and isolated measurement and attestation domain with read access to p's execution environment. h is a composite measurement of v, the virus checking infrastructure–p's operating system along with the virus checking executable and signature file. These all occur before virus checking with the result included in a signed evidence bundle.

Measurement order is critical. An active adversary may compromise a component, engage in malice, and cover its tracks while avoiding detection. Ordering constrains the adversary by making this process more difficult [40]. If the virus checker is run before its executable or signature file are hashed the adversary has much longer to compromise the checker than if they are hashed immediately before invoking the checker. Ensuring measurement order is thus critical when verifying attestation protocols and critical to any execution or transformation of protocol representations.

The attestation becomes yet stronger by extending to include the signature file *server* used to update application signatures. This server operates on a different system that is remote to the system being appraised. However, its state impacts the overall state of the virus checking infrastructure. The target system can include information about the server by performing a *layered attestation* where evidence describing the remote signature server is included in the target's evidence. The target p sends an attestation request to the server q that responds in the same manner as p:

$$@_p \{n\}[@_q \{n\}[(\text{ASP } m \; \bar{c} \; q \; ss) \to \text{SIG}] \to @_{ma} \{n\}[(\text{ASP } h \; \bar{b} \; p \; v) \to \text{SIG}] \to (\text{ASP } vc \; \bar{a} \; p \; t) \to \text{SIG}]$$

While the virus checking-as-attestation example is trivial, it exposes critical characteristics of attestation protocols that motivate and impact verification:

- Flexible mechanism—There is no single way for performing attestation or appraisal. A language-based approach for specifying attestation protocols is warranted [7].
- Order is important—Confidence in measurement ordering is critical to trusting an appraisal result. Preserving measurement ordering from protocol specification to execution is a critical correctness property [39–41].
- Trust is relative—Different attestations and appraisals result in different levels of trust. Formally specifying the semantics of attestation and appraisal is necessary for choosing the best protocol [7,8].

3   Copland Language and Reference Semantics

Copland is a domain specific language and formal semantics for specifying remote attestation protocols [39]. A *Copland phrase* is a term that specifies the order and place where an attestation manager invokes attestation services. Such services include basic measurement, cryptographic bundling, and remote attestation requests. Copland is designed with expressivity and generality as foremost goals. As such Copland parameterizes attestation scenarios over work leaving specifics of measurement, cryptographic functions, and communication capabilities to protocol negotiation and instantiation.

3.1 Copland Phrases

The Copland grammar appears in Fig. 1. The non-terminal A represents primitive attestation actions including measurements and evidence operations. The constructor ASP defines an *Attestation Service Provider* and represents an atomic measurement. ASP has four static parameters, m, $\bar{a}$, p, and r that identify the measurement, measurement parameters, the place where the measurement runs, and the measurement target. A *place* parameter identifies an attestation manager environment, and supports cross-domain measurements that chain trust across attestation boundaries. Parameters to an ASP are static and must be bound during protocol selection. Protocol participants must ensure they are properly supported by the platforms involved.

$$t \leftarrow A \mid @_p\, t \mid (t \rightarrow t) \mid (t \overset{\pi}{\prec} t) \mid (t \overset{\pi}{\sim} t)$$
$$A \leftarrow \mathsf{ASP}\; m\; \bar{a}\; p\; r \mid \mathsf{CPY} \mid \mathsf{SIG} \mid \mathsf{HSH} \mid \cdots$$

Fig. 1. Copland Phrase Grammar where: $m = asp\_id \in \mathbb{N}$; $p = place\_id \in \mathbb{N}$; $r = target\_id \in \mathbb{N}$; $\bar{a}$ is a list of string arguments; and $\pi = (\pi_1, \pi_2)$ is a pair of evidence splitting functions.

Remaining primitive terms specify cryptographic operations over evidence already collected in a protocol run. CPY, SIG, and HSH copy, sign and hash evidence, respectively. The cryptographic implementations underlying SIG and HSH are negotiated among appraiser and target when a protocol is selected.

The key to supporting attestation of layered architectures is the remote request operator, @, that allows attestation managers to request attestations on behalf of each other. The subscript p specifies the place to send the attestation request and the subterm t specifies the Copland phrase to send. As an example, the phrase $@_1(@_2(\mathsf{t}))$ specifies that the attestation manager at place 1 should send a request to the attestation manager at place 2 to execute the phrase t. Nesting of @ terms is arbitrary within a phrase allowing expressive layered specifications parameterized over the attestation environment where they execute.

The three structural Copland terms specify the order of execution and the routing of evidence among their subterms. The phrase $t1 \rightarrow t2$ specifies that $t1$ should finish executing strictly before $t2$ begins with evidence from $t1$ consumed by $t2$. The phrase $t1 \overset{\pi}{\prec} t2$ specifies that $t1$ and $t2$ run in sequence with π specifying how input evidence is routed to the subterms. Conversely, $t1 \overset{\pi}{\sim} t2$ places no restriction on the order of execution for its subterms allowing parallel execution. Both branching operators ($\prec$ and $\sim$) produce the product of executing their subterms.

3.2   Concrete Evidence

Copland evidence is structured data representing the result of executing a Copland phrase. Evidence and meta-evidence allow an appraiser to make a trust decision about the attesting platform. The concrete evidence definition appears in Fig. 2 and its structure corresponds closely to that of Copland phrases. Of note are the mt and N constructors that do not correspond to a Copland phrase. The former stands for "empty", or absence of evidence, and the latter for nonce evidence. Concrete measurement results are raw binary data and could be anything from a hash of software–the bs in U bs e–to a digital signature over evidene e– the bs in G bs e. The inductive e parameter accumulates sequential evidence via the $\rightarrow$ phrase, where deeper nesting implies earlier collection. Ultimately, the *guarantee* of measurement ordering comes from the Copland Virtual Machine semantics rather than the evidence structure.

$$e \leftarrow \text{mt} \mid \text{U bs } e \mid \text{G bs } e \mid \text{H bs} \mid \text{N n bs } e \mid \text{SS } e \ e \mid \text{PP } e \ e \mid \cdots$$

Fig. 2. Concrete Evidence grammar where bs is raw binary data and n = *nonce_id* $\in \mathbb{N}$

3.3   Copland LTS Semantics

The Copland framework provides an abstract specification of Copland phrase execution in the form of a small-step operational Labeled Transition System (LTS) semantics. States of the LTS correspond to protocol execution states, and its inference rules transform a Copland phrase from a protocol description to an evidence shape.

A single step is specified as $s_1 \overset{\ell}{\leadsto} s_2$ where s_1 and s_2 are states and ℓ is a label that records attestation-relevant system events. The reflexive, transitive closure of such steps, $s_1 \overset{c}{\leadsto}{}^* s_2$, collects a trace, c, of event labels representing observable attestation activity. $\mathcal{C}(t, p, e)$ represents an initial configuration with Copland phrase t, starting place p, and initial evidence e. $\mathcal{D}(p, e')$ represents the end of execution at place p with final evidence e'. Therefore, $\mathcal{C}(t, p, e) \overset{c}{\leadsto}{}^* \mathcal{D}(p, e')$ captures the complete execution of Copland phrase t that exhibits event trace c.

In addition to the operational LTS semantics, the Copland specification defines a strict partial order on attestation events called an Event System. Event Systems are constructed inductively where: (i) Leaf nodes represent base cases and hold a single event instance; and (ii) Before nodes ($t1 \triangleright t2$) and Merge nodes ($t1 \bowtie t2$) are defined inductively over terms. Before nodes impose ordering while Merge nodes capture parallel event interleaving where orderings within each sub-term are maintained. The Event System denotation function, $\mathcal{V}$, maps an

$$\mathcal{V}([\mathsf{SIG}]^i_{i+1}, p, e) = \mathsf{SIG}_{\mathsf{event}}(i, p, \llbracket e \rrbracket_p)$$
$$\mathcal{V}([\mathsf{ASP}\ m\ \bar{a}\ q\ r]^i_{i+1}, p, e) = \mathsf{ASP}_{\mathsf{event}}(i, p, q, r, m, \bar{a}, \mathsf{U}_{p,q,m}(e))$$
$$\mathcal{V}([@_q\ t]^i_j, p, e) = \mathsf{REQ}(i, p, q, t, e) \triangleright \mathcal{V}(t, q, e) \triangleright \mathsf{RPY}(j-1, p, q, \mathcal{E}(t, q, e))$$
$$\mathcal{V}([t_1 \overset{(\pi_1, \pi_2)}{\sim} t_2]^i_j, p, e) = \mathsf{SPLIT}(i, (\pi_1, \pi_2), ...) \triangleright$$
$$(\mathcal{V}(t_1, p, \pi_1(e)) \bowtie \mathcal{V}(t_2, p, \pi_2(e))) \triangleright$$
$$\mathsf{JOIN}(j-1, ..)$$

Fig. 3. Event system semantics (a representative subset of rules)

annotated Copland term, place, and initial evidence to a corresponding Event System. A representative subset of this semantics [39] appears in Fig. 3.

Each event instance is labeled by a unique natural number and an identifier for the place where it occurred. Measurement and cryptographic events correspond exactly to primitive Copland terms, while communication events REQ and RPY model a request and reply interaction to a remote place. The SPLIT event captures functions π_1 and π_2 that filter evidence passed to subterms, and JOIN captures the gathering of evidence from each subterm post-execution when they are combined as a composite evidence structure. Taken together, these rules are useful as a reference semantics to characterize attestation manager execution and denote evidence structure. Any valid implementation of Copland execution will obey this semantics.

4 Copland Compiler and Virtual Machine

Copland execution is implemented as a compiler targeting a monadic, virtual machine run-time. The Copland Compiler translates a Copland phrase into a sequence of commands to be executed in the Copland Virtual Machine (CVM). copland_compile (Fig. 7) takes as input an Annotated Copland term and returns a computation in the Copland Virtual Machine Monad. Annotated Copland terms extend Copland phrases with a pair of natural numbers that represent a range of identifiers. The compiler uses these ranges to assign a unique label to every system event that will occur during execution. The LTS semantics does this similarly. Event identifiers play a key role in the proof that links the LTS and CVM semantics.

The Copland Virtual Machine (CVM) Monad is a state and exception monad in Coq adapted from the Verdi framework for formally verifying distributed systems [38,47]. The CVM Monad implements the standard state monad primitives bind, return, put, and get in the cannonical way. It also provides the standard functions for executing state monad computations (runState, evalState, execState), the always-failing computation (failm), and getters/putters specialized to the CVM internal state fields. Accompanying these definitions are proofs that the CVM Monad obeys the cannonical state monad laws [15].

A general monadic computation St takes a state parameter of type S as input, and returns a pair of an optional return value of type A and an updated state. The Coq signature for St is:

```
Definition St(S A : Type) : Type := S -> (option A) * S
```

The CVM Monad is a specialization of St with the CVM_st type as its state structure. CVM_st is a record datatype with fields that hold configuration data for the CVM as it executes.

Measurement primitives build computations in the CVM Monad that perform two primary functions: simulate invocation of measurement services and explicitly bundle the evidence results. To simulate measurement, invoke_ASP (Fig. 4) appends a measurement event to the st_trace field of CVM_st, tagging it with the parameters of the service invoked along with the unique identifier x derived from annotations on the originating ASP term. Because x is guaranteed unique per-protocol due to the way Copland terms are annotated, it can also serve as an abstract representation of the binary string measurement result. This approach accounts for multiple, independent invocations of the same ASP during a protocol and captures changes in a target's state over time. To finish, invoke_ASP bundles the result in a Copland Evidence constructor for ASPs. A single function do_prim compiles all primitive Copland terms using a similar strategy. A concrete instantiation of the CVM will require additional plumbing to map ASP_IDs and digital signature invocations to concrete measurement and cryptographic services independently validated for robustness.

```
Definition invoke_ASP (x:nat) (i:ASP_ID) (l:list Arg) : CVM EvidenceC :=
    p <- get_pl ;;
    e <- get_ev ;;
    add_tracem [Term.umeas x p i l];;
    ret (uuc i x e).
```

Fig. 4. Example monadic measurement primitive

When interpreting a remote request term $@_p t$ or a parallel branch $t1 \overset{\pi}{\sim} t2$ CVM execution relies on an external attestation manager that is also running instances of the CVM. To pass evidence to and from these external components we use the shared memory st_store component of the CVM_st, relying on glue code to manage external interaction with st_store. sendReq in Fig. 5 is responsible for placing initial evidence into the shared store at index $reqi$ and initiating a request to the appropriate platform, modeled by a REQ system event. It then returns, relying on receiveResp to retrieve the evidence result after the remote place has finished execution. Uniqueness of event ids like $reqi$ ensures that CVM threads will not interfere with one another when interacting with st_store.

Figure 6 shows two uninterpreted functions that simulate the execution of external CVM instances. remote_evidence represents evidence collected by running the term t at place p with initial evidence e. Similarly, remote_trace represents the list of events generated by running term t at place p. There is no evidence parameter to remote_trace because the system events generated for a term are independent of initial evidence. We provide specializations of these

```
Definition sendReq (t:AnnoTerm) (q:Plc) (reqi:nat) : CVM unit :=
  p <- get_pl ;;
  e <- get_ev ;;
  put_store_at reqi e ;;
  add_tracem [REQ reqi p q (unanno t)].
```

Fig. 5. Example monadic communication primitive

```
Definition remote_evidence (t:AnnoTerm) (p:Plc) (e:EvidenceC) : EvidenceC.

Definition remote_trace (t:AnnoTerm) (p:Plc) : list Ev.
```

Fig. 6. Primitive IO Axioms

functions for both remote and local parallel CVM instances. Because the core CVM semantics should be identical for these specializations, we also provide rewrite rules to equate them. However, their decomposition enables a smoother translation to a concrete implementation where differences in their glue code may be significant.

Each case of the Copland Compiler in Fig. 7 uses the monadic sequence operation to translate a Copland phrase into an instance of the CVM Monad over unit. The individual operations are not executed by the compiler, but returned as a computation to be executed later. This approach is inspired by work that uses a monadic shallow embedding in HOL to synthesize CakeML [20]. The shallow embedding style [16] allows the protocol writer to leverage the sequential, imperative nature of monadic notation while also having access to a rigorous formal environment to analyze chunks of code written in the monad. It also leverages Coq's built-in name binding metatheory, avoiding this notoriously difficult problem in formal verification of deeply embedded languages [1].

The first three compiler cases are trivial. The ASP term case invokes the do_prim function discussed previously that generates actions for each primitive Copland operation. The @ term case invokes sendReq, doRemote, receiveResp in sequence. sendReq was described previously and receiveResp is defined similarly. doRemote models execution of a remote CVM instance by retrieving initial evidence from the store, adding a simulated trace of remote events to st_trace, then placing the remotely-computed evidence back in the shared store. Finally, the linear sequence term $(t_1 \rightarrow t_2)$ case invokes copland_compile recursively on the subterms t_1 and t_2 and appends the results in sequence.

The branch sequence case $(t_1 \overset{(sp1,sp2)}{\prec} t_2)$ filters the initial evidence into evidence for the two subterms using the split_evm helper function. The commands for the t_1 and t_2 subterms are then compiled in sequence, placing initial evidence for the respective subterm in the CVM_st before executing each, and extracting evidence results after each. A sequential evidence constructor combines evidence to indicate sequential execution and emits a join event.

In the branch parallel case ($t_1 \overset{(sp1,sp2)}{\sim} t_2$) the commands for each subterm will execute in a parallel CVM thread. The helper function startParThreads starts threads for the two subterms then appends the trace (shuffled_events el_1 el_2) to st_trace, where el_1 and el_2 are event traces for the two subterms derived from uninterpreted functions that mimic CVM execution. shuffled_events is itself an uninterpreted function that models an interleaving of the two event traces. Event shuffling is modeled explicitly in the LTS semantics, thus we add an axiom stating that shuffled_events behaves similarly. Similar to the @ term case, we use the shared store to pass evidence to and from the parallel CVM thread for each subterm. After running both threads, we retrieve the final evidence from the result indices, combine evidence for the two subterms with a parallel evidence constructor, and emit a join event. We leave the thread model abstract in the CVM semantics so that attestation managers can run in diverse environments that may or may not provide native support for concurrency.

```
Fixpoint copland_compile (t:AnnoTerm): CVM unit :=
  match t with
  | aasp (n,_) a =>
      e <- do_prim n a ;;
      put_ev e
  | aatt (reqi,rpyi) q t' =>
      sendReq t' q reqi ;;
      doRemote t' q reqi rpyi ;;
      e' <- receiveResp rpyi q ;;
      put_ev e'
  | alseq r t1 t2 =>
      copland_compile t1 ;;
      copland_compile t2
  | abseq (x,y) (sp1,sp2) t1 t2 =>
      e <- get_ev ;;
      p <- get_pl ;;
      (e1,e2) <- split_evm x sp1 sp2 e p ;;
      put_ev e1 ;;  copland_compile t1 ;;
      e1r <- get_ev ;;
      put_ev e2 ;; copland_compile t2 ;;
      e2r <- get_ev ;;
      join_seq (Nat.pred y) p e1r e2r
  | abpar (x,y) (sp1,sp2) t1 t2 =>
      e <- get_ev ;;
      p <- get_pl ;;
      (e1,e2) <- split_evm x sp1 sp2 e p ;;
      let (loc_e1, loc_e1') := range t1 in
      let (loc_e2, loc_e2') := range t2 in
      put_store_at loc_e1 e1 ;;
      put_store_at loc_e2 e2 ;;
      startParThreads t1 t2 p (loc_e1, loc_e1') (loc_e2, loc_e2') ;;
      (e1r, e2r) <- get_store_at_2 (loc_e1', loc_e2') ;;
      join_par (Nat.pred y) p e1r e2r
  end.

Definition run_cvm (t:AnnoTerm) (st:cvm_st) : cvm_st :=
  execSt (copland_compile t) st.
```

Fig. 7. The Copland Compiler–builds computations as sequenced CVM commands

Monadic values represent computations waiting to run. run_cvm t st (bottom of Fig. 7) interprets the monadic computation (copland_compile t) with initial state st, producing an updated state. This updated state contains the collected evidence and event trace corresponding to execution of the input term and initial evidence in st. The evidence and event trace are sufficient to verify correctness of run_cvm with respect to the LTS semantics.

5 Verification

Verifying the Copland Compiler and Copland Virtual Machine is proving that running compiled Copland terms results in evidence and event sequences that respect the Copland reference semantics. In earlier work [39] we proved for any event v that precedes an event v' in an Event System generated by Copland phrase t ($\mathcal{V}(t, p, e) : v \prec v'$), that event also precedes v' in the trace c exhibited by the LTS semantics $\leadsto^*$. This fact is repeated here as Theorem 1, where the notation $v \ll_c v'$ means that v precedes v' in event sequence c.

Theorem 1 (LTS_Respects_Event_System). *If* $\mathcal{C}(t, p, e) \overset{c}{\leadsto^*} \mathcal{D}(p, e')$ *and* $\mathcal{V}(t, p, e) : v \prec v'$, *then* $v \ll_c v'$.

To verify the compiler and virtual machine we replace the LTS evaluation relation with executing the compiler and virtual machine and show execution respects the same Event System. Theorem 2 defines this goal:

Theorem 2 (CVM_Respects_Event_System)

> *If* run_cvm *(*copland_compile t*)*
> { st_ev := e, st_pl := p, st_trace := [ ] } $\Downarrow$
> { st_ev := e', st_pl := p, st_trace := c } *and*
> $\mathcal{V}(t, p, e) : v \prec v'$, *then* $v \ll_c v'$.

The $\Downarrow$ notation emphasises that run_cvm is literally a functional program written in Coq. This differentiates it from the $\overset{c}{\leadsto^*}$ notation used to represent steps taken in the relational LTS semantics. run_cvm takes as input parameters a sequence of commands in the CVM Monad and a CVM_st structure that includes fields for initial evidence (st_ev), starting place (st_pl), initial event trace (st_trace), and a shared store (st_store, omitted in this theorem). It outputs final evidence, ending place, and a final trace. The first assumption of Theorem 2 states that running the CVM on a list of commands compiled from the Copland phrase t, initial evidence e, starting place p, and an empty starting trace produces evidence e' and trace c at place p. The remainder is identical to the conclusion of Theorem 1.

5.1 Lemmas

To prove Theorem 2, it is enough to prove intermediate Lemma 3 that relates event traces in the CVM semantics to those in the LTS semantics. Lemma 3 is the heart of our verification and proves that any trace c produced by the CVM semantics is also exhibited by the LTS semantics. Lemma 3 also critically proves that the CVM transforms Copland Evidence consistently with the LTS

(e_t denotes the shape of evidence e and $\mathcal{E}$ the evidence reference semantics). This allows an appraiser to rely on precise cryptographic bundling and the shape of evidence produced by a valid CVM. We can combine Lemma 3 transitively with Theorem 1 to prove the main correctness result, Theorem 2.

Lemma 3 (CVM_Refines_LTS_Event_Ordering)

> If run_cvm (copland_compile t)
> { st_ev := e, st_pl := p, st_trace := [ ] } $\Downarrow$
> { st_ev := e′, st_pl := p, st_trace := c } then
> $\mathcal{C}(t, p, e_t) \overset{c}{\leadsto}{}^* \mathcal{D}(p, e_t′)$ and $\mathcal{E}(t, p, e_t) = e_t′$

Lemma 3 rules out any "extra" CVM event traces not captured by the LTS semantics. It is worth pointing out that we could extend the CVM semantics with additional, perhaps non-attestation-relevant, system events and still prove Theorem 2 directly. This is because Theorem 2 only mentions the *ordering* of *attestation-relevant* system events captured by Event Systems. However, the indirection through the LTS semantics was a convenient refinement because of its closer compatibility with fine-grained CVM execution. The proof of Lemma 3 proceeds by induction on the Copland phrase t that is to be compiled and run through the CVM. Each case corresponds to a constructor of the Copland phrase grammar and begins by careful simplification and unfolding of run_cvm. Each case ends with applying a semantic rule of the LTS semantics.

Because we cannot perform IO explicitly within Coq, we use st_trace to accumulate a trace of calls to components external to the CVM. This trace records every IO invocation occurring during execution and their relative ordering. Lemma 4 says that st_trace is irrelevant to the remaining fields that handle evidence explicitly during CVM execution. This verifies that erasing the st_trace field from CVM_st is safe after analysis.

Lemma 4 (st_trace_irrel)

> If run_cvm (copland_compile t)
> { st_ev := e, st_store := o, st_pl := p, st_trace := tr$_1$ } $\Downarrow$
> { st_ev := e′, st_store := o′, st_pl := p′, st_trace := _ } and
>
> run_cvm (copland_compile t)
> { st_ev := e, st_store := o, st_pl := p, st_trace := tr$_2$ } $\Downarrow$
> { st_ev := e″, st_store := o″, st_pl := p″, st_trace := _ } then
> $e′ = e″$ and $o′ = o″$ and $p′ = p″$

Another key property upheld by the CVM semantics is that event traces are *cumulative*. This means that existing event traces in st_trace remain unmodified as CVM execution proceeds. Lemma 5 encodes this, saying: If a CVM state with initial trace $m + + k$ interprets a compiled Copland term t and transforms the state to some new state $st′$, and similarly t transforms a starting state with initial trace k (the suffix of the other initial trace) to another state $st″$, then the st_trace field of $st′$ is the same as m appended to the st_trace field of $st″$. We proved this vital "distributive property" over traces and leveraged it in several other Lemmas to simplify event insertion and trace composition.

Lemma 5 (st_trace_cumul)

If run_cvm *(copland_compile t)*
{ st_ev := e, st_store := o, st_pl := p, st_trace := m ++ k *}* ⇓ *st' and*

run_cvm *(copland_compile t)*
{ st_ev := e, st_store := o, st_pl := p, st_trace := k *}* ⇓ *st'' then*
*(*st_trace *st')* = *m* ++ *(*st_trace *st'')*

5.2 Automation

There are many built-in ways to simplify and expand expressions in Coq. Unfortunately, it is easy to expand either too far or not enough. The Coq cbv (call-by-value) tactic unfolds and expands as much as it can, often blowing up recursive expressions making them unintelligible. The milder cbn (call-by-name) tactic often avoids this, but fails to unfold user-defined wrapper functions. To reach a middle-ground, we define custom automation in Ltac. First we define a custom "unfolder" that carefully expands primitive monadic operations like bind and return, along with CVM-specific helper functions like invoke_ASP.

Next we define a larger simplifier that repeatedly invokes the targeted unfolder followed by cbn and other conservative simplifications. This custom simplification is the first step in most proofs and is repeated throughout as helper Lemmas transform the proof state to expose more reducible expressions. We also leveraged the StructTact [48] library, a collection of general-purpose automation primitives for common Coq structures like match and if statements, originally developed for use in the Verdi [38,47] framework. Combined with our custom automation this made our proofs robust against small changes to the CVM implementation (i.e. re-naming/re-ordering monadic helper functions), and greatly simplified proof maintenance after more significant refactoring.

Lemma 6 (abpar_store_non_overlap)

If well_formed *(abpar _ _ t_1 t_2) and range t_1 = (a,b) and range t_2 = (c,d)*
then a ≠ c and b ≠ c and b ≠ d

A final custom piece of automation involves Lemmas that ensure accesses to the shared store do not overlap when interpreting Copland terms that interact with external components. When compiling the branch parallel term we derive indices from term annotations and use them to insert initial evidence and retrieve final evidence from the store. We must prove arithmetic properties like Lemma 6 to show that store accesses do not overlap. The proof follows from the definition of the well_formed predicate and the annotation strategy. We provide Ltac scripts to recognize proof states that are blocked by store accesses and discharge them using Lemma 6.

6   Attestation Manager(AM) Monad

While the CVM Monad supports faithful execution of an individual Copland phrase, many actions before and after execution are more naturally expressed at a layer above Copland. Actions preceding execution prepare initial evidence, collect evidence results from earlier runs, and generate fresh nonces. Actions following CVM execution include appraisal and preparing additional Copland phrases for execution. These pre- and post-actions are encoded as statements in the Attestation Manager (AM) Monad.

An early prototype of the AM Moand in Haskell [37] uses monad transformers to provide a sufficient computational context for attestation and appraisal. An example pseudo-code sequence of AM Monad commands appears in Fig. 8. The run_cvm(t, n) command runs an entire Copland phrase t with initial evidence n inside the CVM Monad, lifting its evidence result into the AM Monad. Rather than performing measurements directly, the AM Monad relies on run_cvm as a well-defined interface to the CVM. This allows an AM to abstract away details of Copland phrase execution and compose facts about the CVM like those verified in Sect. 5 about events and evidence shapes. An initial formal definition of the AM Monad in Coq, including nonce management and Copland phrase invocation, is complete. The design of appraisal and its verification are ongoing.

```
let t = @₄₂ (ASP 1 ā p r  →  SIG)
     n ← generate_nonce
     e ← run_cvm(t,n)
     b ← appraise(t,e)
     trust_decision(b)
```

Fig. 8. Example sequence of commands in the AM Monad.

Using nonces is a common mechanism for preventing a man-in-the-middle adversary from re-transmitting stale measurements that do not reflect current system state. Nonces are critical to attestation and appear in Copland as primitive evidence. Since evidence collection is cumulative in the CVM semantics, nonces are generated and stored in the AM Monad state, embedded as initial evidence alongside Copland attestation requests, then retrieved during appraisal.

Appraisal is the final step in a remote attestation protocol where an indirect observer of a target platform must analyze evidence in order to determine the target's trustworthiness. Regardless of its level of scrutiny, an appraiser must have a precise understanding of the structure of evidence it examines. The Copland framework provides such a shared evidence structure, and Copland phrases executed by the CVM produce evidence with a predictable shape. The AM Monad provides an ideal context to perform appraisal because it can access golden measurement and nonce values, cryptographic keys, and also link evidence to the Copland phrase that generated it. This combination of capabilities enables automatic synthesis of appraisal routines left for future work.

7   Related Work

Integrity measurement tools include both static [29,42] and dynamic [10,17,21, 22,43,49] approaches that support both baseline and recurring measurements of target systems. More general frameworks [27,31,35] support higher-level attestation goals by combining primitive attestation services. Of note is the Maat framework [31] that introduced the term *Attestation Service Provider* and motivated the design of the Copland language. Other tools provide more specialized measurement capabilities like userspace monitoring [14,32], VMM [13,46] and kernel-level [28,33,34] introspection, and attestation of embedded/IoT platforms [3,6,25,44,45].

The framework presented in the current work is designed as a complimentary operational environment for the above tools. For more general frameworks like Maat, we envision invoking sequences of ASPs within their environment as a service (and vice-versa). For the more specialized measurement tools, we can plug them in as primitive ASPs and compose their results as Copland Evidence.

Prior work in analysis of remote attestation systems involves virtualized environments [2,7,27], comparing protocol alternatives [40,41], and semantics of attestation [9,12]. These analyses articulate the complexities in the attestation design space and lay a foundation for future frameworks. Coker et al. [7] is of particular influence, as the design principle of Trustworthy Mechanism was a primary motivation of this work.

HYDRA [11] (Hybrid Design for Remote Attestation) was the first hardware/software hybrid RA architecture to build upon formally-verified components, and that achieved design goals laid out in their prior work [12]. ERASMUS [4] levereged HYDRA as a base security architecture, but added real-time assurances for resource-critical embedded platforms. VRASED (Verifiable Remote Attestation for Simple Embedded Devices) extended these ideas to a concrete RA design, becoming the first formal verification "of a HW/SW co-design implementation of any security service" [30]. They verify end-to-end security and attestation soundness properties in LTL by automatically extracting hardware properties from Verilog specifications and manually incorporating independently-verified cryptographic software properties. While their end-to-end security guarantees are convincing for a specific embedded platform, our attestation managers support a wider range of attestation scenarios.

8   Future Work and Conclusion

In this work we have verified the Coq implementation of a Copland compiler and monadic virtual machine. Specifically, we proved that the output of compilation and virtual machine execution respects the small-step LTS Copland semantics. Artifacts associated with this verification are publicly available on github [36]. All proofs are fully automated and the only admitted theorems are axioms that model interaction with IO components external to the core virtual machine.

Verification of the compiler and vm are part of our larger effort to construct a formally verified attestation system. Figure 9 shows this work in context with

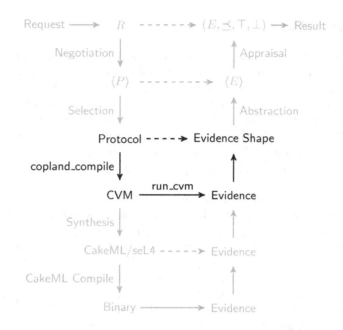

Fig. 9. Verification stack showing verification dependencies and execution path. Solid lines represent implementations while dashed lines represent mathematical definitions.

gray elements representing supporting work or work in progress. Above protocol execution is a negotiation process that selects a protocol suitable to both appraiser and target. Ongoing work will formally define a "best" protocol and verify the negotiated protocol is sufficient and respects privacy policy of all parties.

Below protocol execution is an implementation of the Copland Compiler and Copland Virtual Machine in CakeML [26] running on the verified seL4 microkernal [23,24]. CakeML provides a verified compilation path from an ML subset to various run-time architectures while seL4 provides separation guarantees necessary for trusted measurement. We are embedding the semantics of CakeML in Coq that will in turn be used to verify the compiler and vm implementations. Unverified implementations of both components have been implemented and demonstrated as a part of a hardened UAV flight control system.

When completed our environment will provide a fully verified tool stack that accepts an attestation request, returns evidence associated with that request, and supports sound appraisal of that evidence. Analysis tools that compare protocol alternatives will benefit from implementations that are faithful to formal artifacts, ultimately enabling more robust trust decisions. This work is an important first step creating a verified operational environment for attestation.

References

1. Aydemir, B., Charguéraud, A., Pierce, B.C., Pollack, R., Weirich, S.: Engineering formal metatheory. In: Proceedings of the 35th annual ACM SIGPLAN-SIGACT Symposium on Principles of Programming Languages, POPL 2008, pp. 3–15. ACM, New York (2008). https://doi.org/10.1145/1328438.1328443
2. Berger, S., Caceres, R., Goldman, K., Perez, R., Sailer, R., van Doorn, L.: vTPM: Virtualizing the Trusted Platform Module. iBM T. J. Watson Research Center, Hawthorne (2006). http://www.kiskeya.net/ramon/work/pubs/security06.pdf
3. Brasser, F., El Mahjoub, B., Sadeghi, A.R., Wachsmann, C., Koeberl, P.: Tytan: tiny trust anchor for tiny devices. In: Proceedings of the 52nd Annual Design Automation Conference. DAC 2015. Association for Computing Machinery, New York (2015). https://doi.org/10.1145/2744769.2744922
4. Carpent, X., Rattanavipanon, N., Tsudik, G.: ERASMUS: efficient remote attestation via self- measurement for unattended settings. CoRR abs/1707.09043 (2017). http://arxiv.org/abs/1707.09043
5. Challener, D., Yoder, K., Catherman, R.: A Practical Guide to Trusted Computing. IBM Press, Indianapolis (2008)
6. Clemens, J., Pal, R., Sherrell, B.: Runtime state verification on resource-constrained platforms. In: MILCOM 2018–2018 IEEE Military Communications Conference (MILCOM), pp. 1–6 (2018)
7. Coker, G., et al.: Principles of remote attestation. Int. J. Inf. Secur. 10(2), 63–81 (2011)
8. Coker, G.S., Guttman, J.D., Loscocco, P.A., Sheehy, J., Sniffen, B.T.: Attestation: evidence and trust. In: Proceedings of the International Conference on Information and Communications Security, vol. LNCS 5308 (2008)
9. Datta, A., Franklin, J., Garg, D., Kaynar, D.: A logic of secure systems and its application to trusted computing. In: 2009 30th IEEE Symposium on Security and Privacy, pp. 221–236. IEEE (2009)
10. Davi, L., Sadeghi, A.R., Winandy, M.: Dynamic integrity measurement and attestation: Towards defense against return-oriented programming attacks. In: Proceedings of the 2009 ACM Workshop on Scalable Trusted Computing, STC 2009, pp. 49–54. Association for Computing Machinery, New York (2009). https://doi.org/10.1145/1655108.1655117
11. Eldefrawy, K., Rattanavipanon, N., Tsudik, G.: Hydra: hybrid design for remote attestation (using a formally verified microkernel). In: Proceedings of the 10th ACM Conference on Security and Privacy in Wireless and Mobile Networks, WiSec 2017, pp. 99–110. Association for Computing Machinery, New York (2017). https://doi.org/10.1145/3098243.3098261
12. Francillon, A., Nguyen, Q., Rasmussen, K.B., Tsudik, G.: A minimalist approach to remote attestation. In: 2014 Design, Automation Test in Europe Conference Exhibition (DATE), pp. 1–6 (2014)
13. Garfinkel, T., Rosenblum, M.: A virtual machine introspection based architecture for intrusion detection. In: NDSS (2003)
14. Gevargizian, J., Kulkarni, P.: Msrr: measurement framework for remote attestation. In: 2018 IEEE 16th Intl Conf on Dependable, Autonomic and Secure Computing, 16th Intl Conf on Pervasive Intelligence and Computing, 4th Intl Conf on Big Data Intelligence and Computing and Cyber Science and Technology Congress (DASC/PiCom/DataCom/CyberSciTech), Dependable, Autonomic and Secure Computing (DASC 2018), pp. 748–753 (2018)

15. Gibbons, J.: Unifying theories of programming with monads. In: Wolff, B., Gaudel, M.-C., Feliachi, A. (eds.) UTP 2012. LNCS, vol. 7681, pp. 23–67. Springer, Heidelberg (2013). https://doi.org/10.1007/978-3-642-35705-3_2

16. Gill, A.: Domain-specific languages and code synthesis using Haskell. Commun. ACM **57**(6), 42–49 (2014). https://doi.org/10.1145/2605205, also appeared in ACM Queue **12**(4) (2014)

17. Gopalan, A., Gowadia, V., Scalavino, E., Lupu, E.: Policy driven remote attestation. In: Prasad, R., Farkas, K., Schmidt, A.U., Lioy, A., Russello, G., Luccio, F.L. (eds.) MobiSec 2011. LNICST, vol. 94, pp. 148–159. Springer, Heidelberg (2012). https://doi.org/10.1007/978-3-642-30244-2_13

18. Haldar, V., Chandra, D., Franz, M.: Semantic remote attestation - a virtual machine directed approach to trusted computing. In: Proceedings of the Third Virtual Machine Research and Technology Symposium. San Jose, CA (2004)

19. Halling, B., Alexander, P.: Verifying a privacy CA remote attestation protocol. In: Brat, G., Rungta, N., Venet, A. (eds.) NFM 2013. LNCS, vol. 7871, pp. 398–412. Springer, Heidelberg (2013). https://doi.org/10.1007/978-3-642-38088-4_27

20. Ho, S., Abrahamsson, O., Kumar, R., Myreen, M.O., Tan, Y.K., Norrish, M.: Proof-producing synthesis of cakeml with I/O and local state from monadic HOL functions. In: Galmiche, D., Schulz, S., Sebastiani, R. (eds.) Automated Reasoning - 9th International Joint Conference (IJCAR). Lecture Notes in Computer Science, vol. 10900, pp. 646–662. Springer, Heidelberg (2018). https://doi.org/10.1007/978-3-319-94205-6_42, https://cakeml.org/ijcar18.pdf

21. Jaeger, T., Sailer, R., Shankar, U.: Prima: Policy-reduced integrity measurement architecture. In: Proceedings of the Eleventh ACM Symposium on Access Control Models and Technologies, SACMAT 2006, pp. 19–28. Association for Computing Machinery, New York (2006). https://doi.org/10.1145/1133058.1133063

22. Kil, C., Sezer, E.C., Azab, A.M., Ning, P., Zhang, X.: Remote attestation to dynamic system properties: Towards providing complete system integrity evidence. In: 2009 IEEE/IFIP International Conference on Dependable Systems Networks, pp. 115–124 (2009). https://doi.org/10.1109/DSN.2009.5270348

23. Klein, G., et al.: sel4: formal verification of an operating-system kernel. Commun. ACM **53**(6), 107–115 (2010). https://doi.org/10.1145/1743546.1743574

24. Klein, G., et al.: sel4: formal verification of an os kernel. In: SOSP 2009: Proceedings of the ACM SIGOPS 22nd Symposium on Operating Systems Principles, pp. 207–220. ACM, New York (2009). https://doi.org/10.1145/1629575.1629596

25. Koeberl, P., Schulz, S., Sadeghi, A.R., Varadharajan, V.: Trustlite: a security architecture for tiny embedded devices. In: Proceedings of the Ninth European Conference on Computer Systems, EuroSys 2014. Association for Computing Machinery, New York (2014). https://doi.org/10.1145/2592798.2592824

26. Kumar, R., Myreen, M.O., Norrish, M., Owens, S.: Cakeml: a verified implementation of ml. In: Proceedings of the 41st ACM SIGPLAN-SIGACT Symposium on Principles of Programming Languages,POPL 2014, pp. 179–191. ACM, New York (2014). , https://doi.org/10.1145/2535838.2535841

27. Lauer, H., Salehi, S.A., Rudolph, C., Nepal, S.: User-centered attestation for layered and decentralised systems. Workshop on Decentralized IoT Security and Standards (DISS) (2018)

28. Loscocco, P.A., Wilson, P.W., Pendergrass, J.A., McDonell, C.D.: Linux kernel integrity measurement using contextual inspection. In: Proceedings of the 2007 ACM workshop on Scalable trusted computing, STC 2007, pp. 21–29. ACM, New York (2007). https://doi.org/10.1145/1314354.1314362

29. Maliszewski, R., Sun, N., Wang, S., Wei, J., Qiaowei, R.: Trusted boot (tboot) (2). http://sourceforge.net/p/tboot/wiki/Home/

30. Nunes, I.D.O., Eldefrawy, K., Rattanavipanon, N., Steiner, M., Tsudik, G.: Vrased: a verified hardware/software co-design for remote attestation. In: Proceedings of the 28th USENIX Conference on Security Symposium, SEC 2019, pp. 1429–1446. USENIX Association, USA (2019)

31. Pendergrass, J.A., Helble, S., Clemens, J., Loscocco, P.: A platform service for remote integrity measurement and attestation. In: MILCOM 2018–2018 IEEE Military Communications Conference (MILCOM), pp. 1–6 (2018). https://doi.org/10.1109/MILCOM.2018.8599735

32. Pendergrass, J.A., et al.: Runtime detection of userspace implants. In: MILCOM 2019–2019 IEEE Military Communications Conference (MILCOM), pp. 1–6 (2019). https://doi.org/10.1109/MILCOM47813.2019.9020783

33. Petroni, N.L., Hicks, M.: Automated detection of persistent kernel control-flow attacks. In: Proceedings of the 14th ACM Conference on Computer and Communications Security, CCS 2007, pp. 103–115. Association for Computing Machinery, New York (2007). https://doi.org/10.1145/1315245.1315260

34. Petroni Jr, N., Fraser, T., Walters, A., Arbaugh, W.: An architecture for specification-based detection of semantic integrity violations in kernel dynamic data. In: Proceedings of the 15th USENIX Security Symposium, pp. 289–304 (2006)

35. Petz, A., Alexander, P.: A copland attestation manager. In: Hot Topics in Science of Security (HoTSoS 2019), Nashville, TN (2019)

36. Petz, A.: copland-avm, nfm21 release (2020). https://github.com/ku-sldg/copland-avm/releases/tag/v1.0

37. Petz, A., Komp, E.: haskell-am (2020). https://github.com/ku-sldg/haskell-am

38. Plse, U.: Verdi (2016). https://github.com/uwplse/verdi

39. Ramsdell, J., et al.: Orchestrating layered attestations. In: Principles of Security and Trust (POST 2019), Prague, Czech Republic (2019)

40. Rowe, P.D.: Confining adversary actions via measurement. In: Third International Workshop on Graphical Models for Security, pp. 150–166 (2016)

41. Rowe, P.D.: Bundling evidence for layered attestation. In: Franz, M., Papadimitratos, P. (eds.) Trust 2016. LNCS, vol. 9824, pp. 119–139. Springer, Cham (2016). https://doi.org/10.1007/978-3-319-45572-3_7

42. Sailer, R., Zhang, X., Jaeger, T., van Doorn, L.: Design and implementatation of a TCG-based integrity measurement architecture. In: Proceedings of the 13th USENIX Security Symposium. USENIX Association, Berkeley (2004)

43. Shi, E., Perrig, A., Van Doorn, L.: Bind: A fine-grained attestation service for secure distributed systems. In: 2005 IEEE Symposium on Security and Privacy, pp. 154–168. IEEE (2005)

44. Tan, H., Tsudik, G., Jha, S.: Mtra: multiple-tier remote attestation in IoT networks. In: 2017 IEEE Conference on Communications and Network Security (CNS), pp. 1–9 (2017). https://doi.org/10.1109/CNS.2017.8228638

45. Wedaj, S., Paul, K., Ribeiro, V.J.: Dads: decentralized attestation for device swarms. ACM Trans. Priv. Secur. **22**(3), 19:1–19:29 (2019). https://doi.org/10.1145/3325822

46. Wei, J., Pu, C., Rozas, C.V., Rajan, A., Zhu, F.: Modeling the runtime integrity of cloud servers: a scoped invariant perspective. In: 2010 IEEE Second International Conference on Cloud Computing Technology and Science, pp. 651–658 (2010). https://doi.org/10.1109/CloudCom.2010.29

47. Wilcox, J.R., et al.: Verdi: a framework for implementing and formally verifying distributed systems. In: Proceedings of the 36th ACM SIGPLAN Conference on Programming Language Design and Implementation, PLDI 2015, pp. 357–368. Association for Computing Machinery, New York (2015). https://doi.org/10.1145/2737924.2737958

48. Woos, D., Wilcox, J.R., Simmons, K., Palmskog, K., Doenges, R.: Structtact coq library (2020). https://github.com/uwplse/StructTact

49. Xu, W., Ahn, G.-J., Hu, H., Zhang, X., Seifert, J.-P.: DR@FT: efficient remote attestation framework for dynamic systems. In: Gritzalis, D., Preneel, B., Theoharidou, M. (eds.) ESORICS 2010. LNCS, vol. 6345, pp. 182–198. Springer, Heidelberg (2010). https://doi.org/10.1007/978-3-642-15497-3_12

Verifying Min-Plus Computations
with Coq

Lucien Rakotomalala[✉], Pierre Roux, and Marc Boyer

ONERA/DTIS, Université de Toulouse, Toulouse, France
lucien.rakotomalala@onera.fr

Abstract. *Network-calculus* is a theory that bounds delays in embedded networks such as AFDX networks used in modern airplanes. Effective computations rely on operators from the *min-plus* algebra on real functions. Algorithms on specific subsets can be found in the literature. Such algorithms and related implementations are however complicated. Instead of redeveloping a provably correct implementation, we take an existing implementation as an oracle and propose a *Coq* based verifier.

Keywords: Network-calculus · Min-plus computations · Coq · Functions on real numbers

1 Problem Statement

Network Calculus is a static analysis method used to bound worst case traversal times of networks. It has noticeably been used since a few decades to certify embedded networks, called Avionics Full DupleX (AFDX), on modern civil aircrafts [9]. Basically, given bounds on emission rates of each end node of the network and hypotheses on the scheduling policy implemented in each switch, *Network Calculus* computes sound bounds on the time taken by any packet to travel between any two nodes.

Network Calculus is based on tropical algebra, more precisely the min-plus dioid of functions on real numbers (used to represent both time and amounts of data). Thus, as an intermediate step in the analysis, the method produces algebraic formulas in this dioid, whose computation eventually gives actual numerical bounds. Soundness of the bounds then crucially relies on both the soundness of the *Network Calculus* theory and of those computations. The soundness of *Network Calculus* theory is outside the scope of this paper [17], we will focus here on verification of computations of algebraic operators in the min-plus dioid of functions.

Efficient algorithms are known for these computations and a few effective implementations do exist [6–8]. However, these algorithms are rather tricky, hence the interest in formal proofs to greatly increase the level of confidence in their results. We use the proof assistant Coq [13] to provide formal proofs

Supported by the ANR/DFG Project RT-proofs (ANR-17-CE25-0016).

A. Dutle et al. (Eds.): NFM 2021, LNCS 12673, pp. 287–303, 2021.
https://doi.org/10.1007/978-3-030-76384-8_18

of correctness of such results. To avoid a costly entire reimplementation of the algorithms, we adopt a skeptical approach, using existing implementations as untrusted oracles and only providing verified implementations of verifiers for each algebraic operation.

Sections 2 and 3 introduce a few notations and give an overview of the objects and operations manipulated throughout the paper. Then, Sect. 4 recalls the state of the art. Sections 5 and 6 detail the formalization of these objects, while Sects. 7 and 8 prove some of their fundamental properties. Finally Sect. 9 prove the core soundness arguments of the expected verifiers, Sect. 10 discuss the implementation and Sect. 11 concludes. Pen and paper proofs are in appendix[1]

2   Notations

Let $\mathbb{R}$ denote real numbers, $\mathbb{R}_+ \triangleq \mathbb{R} \cap [0; +\infty[$ and $\overline{\mathbb{R}} \triangleq \mathbb{R} \cup \{-\infty, +\infty\}$. Let $\mathbb{Q}$ denote rational numbers, $\mathbb{Q}_+ \triangleq \mathbb{Q} \cap [0; +\infty[$ and $\mathbb{Q}_+^\star \triangleq \mathbb{Q}_+ \setminus \{0\}$. Let $\mathbb{N}$ denote rational numbers, $\mathbb{N}^\star \triangleq \mathbb{N} \setminus \{0\}$ and $\mathcal{F}$ denote functions from $\mathbb{R}_+$ to $\overline{\mathbb{R}}$. Let $\vee$ denote the logical *or* and $\wedge$ the logical *and*. For any finite set S, let $\#S \in \mathbb{N}$ denote its cardinal and for any sequence s, $last(s)$ denote its last element.

In Coq code appearing in this paper, `nat` will stand for $\mathbb{N}$, `R` for $\mathbb{R}$, `Rbar` for $\overline{\mathbb{R}}$, `R+` for $\mathbb{R}_+$, `Q` for $\mathbb{Q}$, `Q+` for $\mathbb{Q}_+$, `Q+*` for $\mathbb{Q}_+^\star$ and `&&` for logical conjunction $\wedge$.

We also use some list manipulating functions of Coq: `nth`, `head` and `last`. `nth x0 l i` returns the element of index `i` (starting at 0) of the list `l` or `x0` if `l` contains less than `i` elements. `n.+1` and `n.-1` are the successor and the predecessor of any natural number `n` (the predecessor of 0 is 0). The notation `%/` is used for euclidean division. To ease readability of the Coq code, we omit scope annotations in the paper. For each result, we give the name of its Coq implementation: for instance `F_UPP` for Definition 1 below. The code is available at https://www.onera.fr/sites/default/files/447/NCCoq.tar.

3   *(min, plus)* Operators on Functions

Network Calculus handles functions in $\mathcal{F}$ and uses *(min, plus)* operations over this set: addition, minimum, convolution and deconvolution. We assume that $+\infty + -\infty = +\infty$. We first present these operators. Then, we introduce subclasses of $\mathcal{F}$ stable for these operators and amenable for effective computations.

3.1   *(min, plus)* Operators

The addition $f + g$ and the minimum $\min(f, g)$ of two functions f and g of $\mathcal{F}$ are pointwise extensions of the corresponding operators on $\overline{\mathbb{R}}$, that is $f + g \triangleq t \mapsto f(t) + g(t)$ and $\min(f, g) \triangleq t \mapsto \min(f(t), g(t))$. We also use two operators, the

---

[1] https://hal.archives-ouvertes.fr/hal-03176024/document.

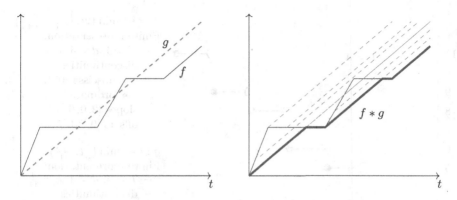

Fig. 1. Two functions f, g (on the left) and their convolution $f * g$ (on the right). Intuitively, the convolution of two functions can be obtained by sliding one function along the other and taking the minimum hull.

convolution $f * g$ and the deconvolution $f \oslash g$ that are not pointwise operators, defined as:

$$f * g \triangleq t \mapsto \inf_{\substack{u,v \geqslant 0 \\ u+v=t}} (f(u) + g(v)), \qquad f \oslash g \triangleq \inf \{h | f \leqslant h * g\}. \qquad (1)$$

where inf on a set $S \subseteq \mathcal{F}$ is $\inf\{S\} \triangleq t \mapsto \inf \{f(t) | f \in S\}$. On Fig. 1, we plot an example of convolution. Details can be found in Chap. 2 of [5], dedicated to *(min, plus)* theory.

3.2 Sub-classes of Functions for Effective Computation

Network Calculus tools do not manipulates the complete F class but only sub-classes with good stability properties and effective computations [7].

In *Network Calculus*, it is quite common to have periodic behaviors. To describe them, we use functions that are ultimately pseudo-periodic (UPP), denoted $\mathcal{F}_{\text{UPP}}$. A function f belongs to the set $\mathcal{F}_{\text{UPP}}$ if, given a point T (an initial segment), a period d and an increasing element c, it holds, for all t greater than T that $f(t + d) = f(t) + c$. To have a description of these functions, it is sufficient to have the values of T, d and c and the description of the function on the initial segment plus one period.

We consider the sub-class of $\mathcal{F}$ made of the Piecewise Affine (PA) functions, denoted $\mathcal{F}_{\text{PA}}$. For these functions, it is sufficient to give, for each piece, the point of discontinuity, the slope and the offset. These parameters can be recorded in a list although this list can be infinite.

We define $\mathcal{F}_{\text{UPP-PA}} \triangleq \mathcal{F}_{\text{UPP}} \cap \mathcal{F}_{\text{PA}}$. Its elements can be finitely represented by giving T, d and c from $\mathcal{F}_{\text{UPP}}$ and the initial segment of the list from $\mathcal{F}_{\text{PA}}$ representing the function on $[0; T + d)$.

The contributions of this paper are:

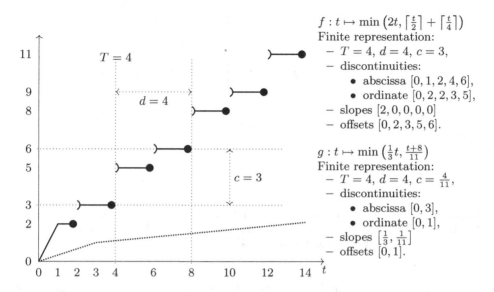

Fig. 2. f (solid) and g (dotted) are UPP-PA functions. Given a UPP-PA function h with compatible parameters, to prove the equality $f + g = h$, it is enough to check $f(t_i) + g(t_i) = h(t_i)$ for a list of t_i: [0; 0.1; 0.9; 1; 1.1; 1.9; 2; 2.1; 2.9; 3; 3.1; 3.9; 4; 4.1; 5.9; 6; 6.1; 7.9].

- a formalization in Coq of $\mathcal{F}_{\text{UPP-PA}}$ in Sects. 5 and 6 and stability properties under *(min, plus)* operations in Sects. 7 and 8.
- a check for correctness of addition, minimum and convolution in Sect. 9.

Intuitively, with the addition, if some tool provides three functions f, g and h and claims that $f + g = h$, we want to check this relation with a finite number of tests. To this end, we will prove that checking the equality $f(t_i) + g(t_i) = h(t_i)$ on a set of points $t_1, ..., t_n$, plus some compatibility tests on initial segments, periods and increments, is enough to ensure the equality on $\mathbb{R}_+$. We illustrate this on Fig. 2.

The minimum and convolution can be checked using similar arguments. Regarding the deconvolution, in practice *Network Calculus* only requires, given two functions f and g, a function h such that $h \geqslant f \oslash g$. It is then enough to check that $h * g \geqslant f$, that is $\min(f, h * g) = f$ which only involve checking a minimum and a convolution.

4   State of the Art

There exist two main classes of curves used in network calculus: the set of concave or convex piecewise linear functions, C[x]PL [19], and the, strictly larger, set of ultimately pseudo-periodic piecewise linear functions UPP-PA, commonly known as UPP [7].

The class of the CPL linear functions has nice mathematical properties: it is stable under the addition and the minimum, and moreover, the convolution can be implemented as a minimum plus a constant. The data structure and related algorithms are so simple that they, to our knowledge, have never been published. The class of convex piecewise linear functions has very similar properties, replacing minimum by maximum, and its (min,plus) convolution can also be implemented very efficiently [5, Sect. 4.2]. Nevertheless, they cannot accurately model packetized traffic, whereas the UPP-PA class gives better results at the expense of higher computation times [8].

An open implementation of the operators on the C[x]PL class can be found in the DISCO network calculus tool [4].

The algorithms of the operators on the UPP-PA class are given in [7]. An open implementation has been developed but is no longer maintained [6] to our knowledge. An industrial implementation exists, which is the core of the network calculus tool PEGASE [10]. The UPP-PA implementation can be accessed through an on-line console [1].

The Real-Time Calculus toolbox (RTC) does performance analysis of distributed real-time systems [22,23]. Its kernel implements minimum, sum, and convolution on Variability Characterization Curves (VCC's), a class very close to UPP-PA, but no explicit comparison of those two classes has been done up to now.

None of these implementations were formally proved correct.

The first works on the formal verification of network calculus computation were presented in [15]. The aim was to verify that a tool was correctly using the network calculus theory. An Isabelle/HOL library was developed, providing the main objects of network calculus (flows and servers, arrival and service curves) and the statement of the main theorems, but not their proofs. They were assumed to be correct, since they have been established in the literature for long. Then, the tool was extended to provide not only a result, but also a proof on how that network calculus has been used to produce this result. Then, Isabelle/HOL was in charge of checking the correctness of this proof.

Another piece of work, presented in [17], consists in proving, in Coq, the network calculus results themselves: building the min-plus dioid of functions, the main objects of network calculus and the main theorems (statements and proofs).

The PROSA library also provides proofs of correctness for the response time of real-time systems, but focuses on scheduling tasks for processors [11].

5   Ultimately Pseudo Periodic Functions

We now present the formal definition of the set of UPP functions.

Definition 1 (Ultimately Pseudo Periodic Functions, F_UPP). $\mathcal{F}_{UPP}$ is the set of functions $f \in \mathcal{F}$ such that there exists $T \in \mathbb{Q}_+$, $d \in \mathbb{Q}_+^\star$ and $c \in \mathbb{Q}$ for which

$$\forall t \in \mathbb{R}_+, t \geqslant T \implies f(t+d) = f(t) + c. \tag{2}$$

Remark 1. The values of T, d and c could have been in $\mathbb{R}$. However, we know from [7] that $\mathcal{F}_{\text{UPP}}$ is stable over more operators if T, d and c are rationals. It is not a practical restriction since $\mathbb{Q}$ is the set used in computation.

We represent $\mathcal{F}_{\text{UPP}}$ in Coq as follows.

```
1   Record F_UPP := {
2     F_UPP_val :> R+ → Rbar;
3     F_UPP_T : Q+; F_UPP_d : Q+*; F_UPP_c : Q;
4     _ : ∀ t : R+, F_UPP_T ≤ t →
5         F_UPP_val (t + F_UPP_d) = F_UPP_val t + toR F_UPP_c }.
```

This code means that a value of type F_UPP is:

line 2 a function F_UPP_val from nnR to Rbar. The notation :> is a Coq notation for coercion: Coq introduces automatically F_UPP_val whenever we give a value of type F_UPP when a function from R+ to Rbar is expected.

line 3 F_UPP_T, F_UPP_d and F_UPP_c, the three parameters T, d and c of (2).

lines 4 and 5 the property (2). We use toR to cast a rational as a real.

The command Record creates a constructor of F_UPP named Build_F_UPP. To declare a value in F_UPP, Coq will require a function, three parameters and a proof of (2).

6   UPP and Piecewise Affine Functions

We briefly presented in Sect. 3 the set $\mathcal{F}_{\text{UPP-PA}}$ of functions that are both UPP and *PA*. We give in this section a formal definition.

In [7], this set was introduced as the intersection of two sets of functions: $\mathcal{F}_{\text{UPP}}$ and $\mathcal{F}_{\text{PA}}$, the set of PA functions. In this paper, we rather choose to formalize the subset of functions in $\mathcal{F}_{\text{UPP}}$ that are PA, as this greatly simplifies the formalization.

To define PA functions, we need to record points of discontinuities and change of slopes: *jump sequences*.

Definition 2 (Jump Sequence, JS). *For any $n \in \mathbb{N}^*$, we call* Jump Sequence *(JS) a tuple $a \in \mathbb{Q}_+^n$ such that $a_0 = 0$ and: $\forall i \in \{0, \ldots, n-2\}, a_i < a_{i+1}$. We call n the* size *of the JS and the set of JS of size n is denoted JS_n.*

We represent jump sequences in Coq as follows.

```
Record JS := {
  JS_list :> seq Q+;
  _ : (JS_list != [::]) && (head 0 JS_list == 0) && sorted < JS_list }.
```

A JS is a list: JS_list of $\mathbb{Q}_+$ that is not an empty list (denoted by [::]), whose initial element is 0 and which is sorted by the usual strict order <. The function head is a total function: it returns the first element of a list or a default value when empty, here 0.

Each piece is linear on an interval with a slope and an offset.

Definition 3 ((ρ, σ)-affine on, r_s_affine_on). *Given* $\rho, \sigma \in \mathbb{Q}$ *and* $x, y \in \mathbb{Q}_+$, *a function* $f \in \mathcal{F}$ *is called* (ρ, σ)-affine on $]x; y[$ *when, for all* $t \in]x; y[$:

$$f(t) = \rho(t - x) + \sigma. \tag{3}$$

We state this definition in Coq as follows.

```
Definition r_s_affine_on (f : F) (rho sigma : Q) (x y : Q+) :=
   ∀ t : R+, x < t < y → f t = toR rho * (t − x) + toR sigma.
```

We want to define a subset of $\mathcal{F} = \mathbb{R}_+ \to \overline{\mathbb{R}}$. So, our functions can return infinite values. The next definition formalizes this point.

Definition 4 (Affine on, affine_on). *A function* $f \in \mathcal{F}$ *is affine on* $]x; y[$ *if*

$$(\forall t \in]x; y[, f(t) = +\infty) \tag{4}$$
$$\vee (\forall t \in]x; y[, f(t) = -\infty) \tag{5}$$
$$\vee (\exists \rho, \sigma \in \mathbb{Q}, f \text{ is } (\rho, \sigma) - \text{affine} \text{ on }]x; y[). \tag{6}$$

We state this definition in Coq as follows.

```
Variant affine_on (f : F) (x y : Q+) :=
  | affine_on_p_infty of ∀ t : R+, x < t < y → f t = +∞
  | affine_on_m_infty of ∀ t : R+, x < t < y → f t = −∞
  | affine_on_finite rho sigma of r_s_affine_on f rho sigma x y.
```

We use `Variant` that is a disjunctive version of `Record`.

PA are then functions that are *affine on* all intervals of a JS.

Definition 5 (JS of a Function, JS_of). *Let* $n \in \mathbb{N}^{\star}$, $a \in JS_n$ *and* $f \in \mathcal{F}$. *We say that* a *is a JS of* f, *denoted* $a \in JS(f)$, *when for all* $i < n - 1$, f *is affine on* $]a_i; a_{i+1}[$.

We state this definition in Coq as follows.

```
Definition JS_of a (f : F) :=
   ∀ i, (i.+1 < size a) → r_s_affine_on f (nth 0 a i) (nth 0 a i.+1).
```

So, according to the previous definition, each PA function is associated to a JS but it is not unique. We illustrate this in Fig. 3. Also notice that a function $f \in \mathcal{F}$ with $a \in JS(f)$ is a PA function at least up to the last point of a.

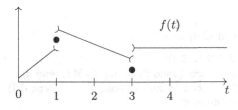

Fig. 3. The function f is piecewise affine. $a \triangleq \{0, 1, 3\}$ and $b \triangleq \{0, 1, 2, 3\}$ are JS of this function: $a \in JS(f)$ and $b \in JS(f)$. We notice that $c \triangleq \{0, 2, 4\} \in JS$ but $c \notin JS(f)$.

Definition 6 (UPP-PA Functions, F_UPP_PA). *The set $\mathcal{F}_{UPP\text{-}PA}$ of UPP-PA functions is the set of functions $f \in \mathcal{F}_{UPP}$ with T for initial segment and d for period, such that there exists $a \in JS(f)$ and $last(a) = T + d$.*

We represent $\mathcal{F}_{UPP\text{-}PA}$ in Coq as follows.

```
Record F_UPP_PA := {
  F_UPP_PA_UPP :> F_UPP;
  F_UPP_PA_JS : JS;
  _ : JS_of F_UPP_PA_JS F_UPP_PA_UPP;
  _ : last 0 F_UPP_PA_JS = F_UPP_T F_UPP_PA_UPP + F_UPP_d F_UPP_PA_UPP }.
```

The functions presented in Fig. 2 belong to $\mathcal{F}_{UPP\text{-}PA}$. The list of abscissas of discontinuities given in the caption are jump sequences of the functions.

A UPP-PA function with initial segment T and period d is PA in $[0; T + d[$ by construction, and also PA after $T + d$ by periodicity. This point is developed in the following property.

Lemma 1 (F_UPP_PA_JS_upto_spec in Coq). *Let $f \in \mathcal{F}_{UPP\text{-}PA}$ with $a \in JS(f)$. For any $l \in \mathbb{Q}_+$ such that $last(a) \leqslant l$, there exists $a' \in JS$ such that $a' \in JS(f)$ and $last(a') = l$.*

7 Stability of UPP Functions by *(min, plus)* Operators

We now want to prove stability of $\mathcal{F}_{UPP}$ over *(min, plus)* operators: addition, minimum and convolution. These operators have been presented in Sect. 3. We need another operator on rational numbers: a notion of least common integer multiple such that, for any $d, d' \in \mathbb{Q}$, there exists $k, k' \in \mathbb{N}$ satisfying $kd = k'd' = lcm_{\mathbb{Q}}(d, d')$.

Definition 7 ($lcm_{\mathbb{Q}_+^*}$). *For all $d, d' \in \mathbb{Q}_+^*$, for all $a, a' \in \mathbb{Z}$ and $b, b' \in \mathbb{N}^*$ such that $d = \frac{a}{b}$ and $d' = \frac{a'}{b'}$, we define*

$$lcm_{\mathbb{Q}_+^*}(d, d') \triangleq \frac{lcm\left(a\frac{lcm(b,b')}{b}, a'\frac{lcm(b,b')}{b'}\right)}{lcm(b, b')} \quad (7)$$

where lcm *is the least common multiple on $\mathbb{Z}$.*

Lemma 2 (dvdq_lcml in Coq). *For $d, d' \in \mathbb{Q}_+$, there is $k \in \mathbb{N}$ s.t. $lcm_{\mathbb{Q}_+^*}(d, d') = k\, d$.*

We state this lemma in Coq as follows.

```
Definition lcm_Q (d d' : Q) : Q :=
  fracq (lcmz (numq d * (lcmz (denq d) (denq d') %/ denq d))
              (numq d' * (lcmz (denq d) (denq d') %/ denq d')),
         lcmz (denq d) (denq d')).
Program Definition lcm_posQ (d d' : Q+*) : Q+* := mk_posQ (lcm_Q d d') _.
Lemma dvdq_lcml d d' : ∃ k : nat, lcm_posQ d d' = k * d.
```

We first define lcm_Q: the definition of $lcm_{\mathbb{Q}_+^*}$ on $\mathbb{Q}$. The functions fracq, numq and denq are respectively the constructor and destructors of Q. The command Program Definition is similar to Definition except that it accepts holes _ and automatically generates the corresponding proof obligations.

To ease notations, we want to transform this binary operator, into a set operator such as $\sum_{i=1}^{3} i = (1+2) + 3$. There exists a library in Coq designed with this objective: the bigop theory of *Mathcomp* [2]. To fully use this library, we need to prove that $lcm_{\mathbb{Q}_+^*}$ satisfies the monoid laws. In other words, we need to prove that $lcm_{\mathbb{Q}_+^*}$ is associative and has a neutral element. However, $lcm_{\mathbb{Q}_+^*}$ does not have a neutral element. The lcm on $\mathbb{N}$ has a neutral element 1. It is not the case for $lcm_{\mathbb{Q}_+^*}$: for instance $lcm_{\mathbb{Q}_+^*}\left(1, \frac{2}{3}\right) = 2$. To get out of it, we need to extend the definition of $lcm_{\mathbb{Q}_+^*}$:

Definition olcm_posQ (x y : option Q+*) : option Q+* := match x, y with
 | None, _ ⇒ y | _, None ⇒ x | Some x, Some y ⇒ Some (lcm_posQ x y)
 end.

The option type is used to extend the type of Q+* with a None element. Then, this element is the neutral element for this optional definition of $lcm_{\mathbb{Q}_+^*}$. We add then a Notation for the big operator.

Notation "\biglcm_posQ_ (i < n) F" :=
 (odflt one_posQ (\big[olcm_posQ/None]_(i < n) some F)) : ring_scope.

\big[oclm_posQ\None]_(i < n) some F is the iterated application of oclm_posQ for all i such that i < n on some F. The function odflt removes the option when it is Some and returns a default value otherwise.

The following lemmas prove stability of $\mathcal{F}_{UPP}$ by addition, minimum and convolution.

Lemma 3 (F_UPP_n_add in Coq). *Let* $n \in \mathbb{N}^*$, $f \in \mathcal{F}_{UPP}^n$ *with initial segments* $T \in \mathbb{Q}_+^n$, *periods* $d \in (\mathbb{Q}_+^*)^n$ *and increments* $c \in \mathbb{Q}^n$ *respectively. The sum* $\sum_i f_i$ *is a UPP function with an initial segment* $\max_i\{T_i\}$, *a period* $lcm_{\mathbb{Q}_+^*}(d_i)$ *and an*

increment $lcm_{\mathbb{Q}_+^*}(d_i) \left(\sum_i \frac{c_i}{d_i}\right)$.

Lemma 4 (F_UPP_n_min in Coq). *Let* $n \in \mathbb{N}^*$ *and* $f \in \mathcal{F}_{UPP}^n$ *with initial segments* $T \in \mathbb{Q}_+^n$, *periods* $d \in (\mathbb{Q}_+^*)^n$ *and increments* $c \in \mathbb{Q}^n$ *respectively. Defining:*

$$s \triangleq \min_{i \in [0;n-1]} \left(\frac{c_i}{d_i}\right) \qquad I \triangleq \left\{i \in [0;n-1] \middle| \frac{c_i}{d_i} = s\right\} \qquad (8)$$

and assuming there exists $M \in \mathbb{Q}$ *and* $m \in \mathbb{Q}^n$ *such that:*

$$\exists i \in I, \forall t \in [T_i; T_i + d_i [, f_i(t) \leqslant M + st \qquad (9)$$

$$\forall i \notin I, \forall t \in [T_i; T_i + d_i \left[, m_i + \frac{c_i}{d_i}t \leqslant f_i(t) \qquad (10)$$

the function $\min_{i=1}^{n}\{f_i\}$ *is UPP with an initial segment* $\tilde{T}$, *a period* $\tilde{d}$ *and an increment* $\tilde{c}$ *with* $\tilde{d} \triangleq lcm_{\mathbb{Q}_+^\star}(d_i)$, $\tilde{c} \triangleq \tilde{d}s$ *and*

$$\tilde{T} = \max\left(\max_{i\notin I}\left(\frac{M-m_i}{\frac{c_i}{d_i}-s}\right), \max_{j\in[0;n-1]}\{T_j\}\right).$$

These lemmas are a straightforward generalization of Proposition 6 in [7] where it is proved for binary addition and minimum. This generalization is useful for the next lemma on convolution of two UPP functions.

Remark 2. In the case of PA functions, it is easy to find values for M and m_i satisfying (9) and (10) by computing the bounds $\sup_{t\in[T_i;T_i+d_i[}\{f_i(t)-st\}$ and $\inf_{t\in[T_i;T_i+d_i[}\left\{f_i(t)-\frac{c_i}{d_i}t\right\}$.

Lemma 5 (F_UPP_conv in Coq). *Let* $f, f' \in \mathcal{F}_{UPP}$ *with initial segments* $T, T' \in \mathbb{Q}_+$, *periods* $d, d' \in \mathbb{Q}_+^\star$ *and increments* $c, c' \in \mathbb{Q}$ *respectively. For all* $M, M', m, m' \in \mathbb{Q}$ *such that*

$$M \geqslant \sup_{t\in[T,T+d[}\left\{f(t)-\frac{c}{d}(t+T')\right\} + f'(T') \tag{11}$$

$$m' \leqslant \inf_{t\in[0,T[}\left\{f(t)-\frac{c'}{d'}t\right\} + \inf_{t\in[T',T'+d'[}\left\{f'(t)-\frac{c'}{d'}t\right\} \tag{12}$$

and similarly for M' *and* m, *by permuting the primed and non-primed variables, the convolution* $f * f'$ *is a UPP function with a period* $\tilde{d} \triangleq lcm_{\mathbb{Q}_+^\star}(d,d')$, *an increment* $\tilde{c} \triangleq \tilde{d}\min\left(\frac{c}{d},\frac{c'}{d'}\right)$ *and an initial segment:*

$$\tilde{T} = \begin{cases} T+T'+lcm_{\mathbb{Q}_+^\star}(d,d') & \text{if } \frac{c}{d}=\frac{c'}{d'} \\ \max\left(\frac{M-m'}{\frac{c'}{d'}-\frac{c}{d}}, T+T'+lcm_{\mathbb{Q}_+^\star}(d,d')\right) & \text{if } \frac{c}{d}<\frac{c'}{d'} \\ \max\left(\frac{M'-m}{\frac{c}{d}-\frac{c'}{d'}}, T+T'+lcm_{\mathbb{Q}_+^\star}(d,d')\right) & \text{if } \frac{c'}{d'}<\frac{c}{d} \end{cases} \tag{13}$$

This lemma is proved into Coq as **F_UPP_conv**. It generalizes Proposition 6 of [7] by expliciting the initial value giving a value for $\tilde{T}$. Remark 2 also applies here.

8   Stability of UPP-PA Functions by *(min, plus)* Operators

We are now focusing on stability of $\mathcal{F}_{UPP\text{-}PA}$ by *(min, plus)* operators. Let us first define the union of two jump sequences.

Definition 8 (Union of two JS, union). *For any $n, m \in \mathbb{N}^*, a \in JS_n, b \in JS_m$, the tuple of size $\#(\{a_i \mid 0 \leqslant i < n\} \cup \{b_j \mid 0 \leqslant j < m\})$ containing the elements of $\{a_i \mid 0 \leqslant i < n\} \cup \{b_j \mid 0 \leqslant j < m\}$ sorted by increasing order, is called union of the jump sequences a and b. This union is denoted $a \cup b$.*

If jump sequences are implemented by lists, the union can be implemented by the merge part of a merge sort, followed by a removal of duplicates. We state this definition in Coq as follows.

```
Program Definition union (a b : JS) := @Build_JS (undup (merge ≤ a b)) _.
```

The following Lemma gives a jump sequence for the sum of PA functions.

Lemma 6 (JS of n-ary Addition, JS_of_n_add). *For $n \in \mathbb{N}^*$, for $f \in \mathcal{F}^n$ and for $a \in JS^n$, if for all i, $a_i \in JS(f_i)$ and all the last points of a are equal $(\forall i, j, last(a_i) = last(a_j))$, then $\bigcup_i a_i \in JS\left(\sum_i f_i\right)$.*

We state this lemma in Coq as follows.

```
Lemma JS_of_n_add n (f : 'I_n.+1 → F) (a : 'I_n.+1 → JS) :
  (∀ i, JS_of (a i) (f i)) → (∀ i j, last 0 (a i) = last 0 (a j)) →
  JS_of (\bigcup_i a i) (\sum_i f i).
```

The term `bigcup_i` is the notation for $\bigcup_i$. Thanks to Lemma 1, the equality of last points can always be satisfied. Stability of $\mathcal{F}_{\text{UPP-PA}}$ by n-ary addition can then be derived from this Lemma and Lemmas 1 and 3.

Whereas the jump sequence of a sum is the union of the jump sequences, the minimum can introduce new points as shown in Fig. 4. The following definition gives such a jump sequence.

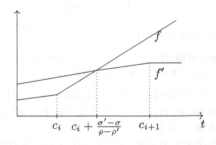

Fig. 4. Example of point added by the min operator in a JS. f and f' are respectively (ρ, σ)-affine and (ρ', σ')-affine on $]c_i; c_{i+1}[$ with different slopes ρ and ρ'. Since we have $c_i + \frac{\sigma' - \sigma}{\rho - \rho'} \in]c_i; c_{i+1}[$, this point must be added to the jump sequence.

Definition 9 (Union min, union_min). *Let f and $f' \in \mathcal{F}$ with $a \in JS(f)$ and $a' \in JS(f')$ such that $last(a) = last(a')$. Set $c \triangleq a \cup a'$. We define the $\cup_{\min}$ operator as*

$$\cup_{\min}(f, f', a, a') \triangleq c \cup \left\{ c_i + \frac{\sigma' - \sigma}{\rho - \rho'} \middle| \begin{array}{l} \exists i, i < \#c - 1 \\ \wedge\ f\ is\ (\rho, \sigma) - affine\ on\ ]c_i, c_{i+1}[\\ \wedge\ f'\ is\ (\rho', \sigma') - affine\ on\ ]c_i, c_{i+1}[\\ \wedge\ \rho \neq \rho' \wedge\ c_i < c_i + \frac{\sigma' - \sigma}{\rho - \rho'} < c_{i+1}. \end{array} \right\}$$

(14)

Using this $\cup_{\min}$ operator, we can establish a JS for n-ary minimum.

Lemma 7 (JS_of_n_min in Coq). *For all $n \in \mathbb{N}^*$ and $f \in \mathcal{F}^n$, if for all i, $a_i \in JS(f_i)$ and all the last points of a are equal then*

$$\left(\bigcup_{i,j \in [0, n-1]} \cup_{\min}(f_i, f_j, a_i, a_j) \right) \in JS\left(\min_i \{f_i\} \right).$$

(15)

Just as we mentioned for the addition, this Lemma and Lemmas 1 and 4 are sufficient to prove stability of $\mathcal{F}_{\text{UPP-PA}}$ by n-ary minimum under mild conditions[2].

We are now interested in the convolution of two UPP-PA functions. Like in [7], we rely on the property that: $\forall f, g, h \in \mathcal{F}, \min(f, g) * h = \min(f * h, g * h)$. Then, any UPP-PA function can be decomposed as the minimum of elementary functions whose convolution is easy to compute.

In the following, we give such a decomposition.

Definition 10 (Cutting Operator, cutting_operator). *Given $f \in \mathcal{F}$, $a \in JS(f)$ and $i \in \mathbb{N}$ such that $i < \#a - 1$, we define the cutting operator:*

$$(f \downarrow a)_i \triangleq t \mapsto \begin{cases} f(t) & if\ t \in [a_i; a_{i+1}[\\ +\infty & otherwise\ . \end{cases}$$

(16)

We state this definition in Coq as follows.

```
Definition cutting_operator (f : F) a i : F := fun t ⇒
  if i.+1 < size a && (nth 0 a i ⩽ t < nth 0 a i.+1) then f t else +∞ .
```

The convolution of two functions $(f \downarrow a)_i$ and $(f' \downarrow a')_j$ can be computed by case disjunction in the same way as in Fig. 5 but considering possible discontinuities lead to more than two sub-cases.

We need a last definition to specify the previous *cutting operator*.

Definition 11 (Cutting Below, cutting_below). *Let $f \in \mathcal{F}$ and $l \in \mathbb{R}_+$, we denote $f_{<l}$ the function that is equal to f up to l and $+\infty$ afterwards.*

Lemma 8 (cutting_operator_spec in Coq). *Given $f \in \mathcal{F}$ and $a \in JS(f)$, we have $f_{<last(a)} = \min_{i < \#a - 1} (f \downarrow a)_i$.*

We can now give the decomposition of the convolution using these operators.

---

[2] Existence of m and M for Lemma 4.

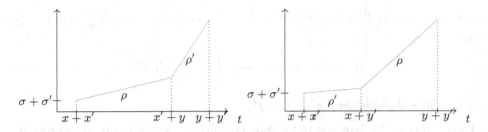

Fig. 5. Convolution of two segments. Let f and f' be two functions that are respectively (ρ, σ)-affine on $[x; y[$ and (ρ', σ')-affine on $[x'; y'[$ and $+\infty$ elsewhere. We plot the two cases of $f * f'$ on $[x + x', y + y'[$: left is for $\rho < \rho'$ and right is $\rho' < \rho$.

Lemma 9 (Piecewise Affine Convolution, PA_conv). *Let $f, f' \in \mathcal{F}$ with $a \in JS(f)$ and $a' \in JS(f')$ and let l such that $l = last(a) = last(a')$. We have*

$$(f * f')_{<l} = \left(\min_{i,j} \left((f \downarrow a)_i * (f' \downarrow a')_j \right) \right)_{<l}. \tag{17}$$

9 Finite Equality Criteria on UPP-PA

In Sects. 5 to 8, we proved in Coq slight variations of results from the literature. Here are the main results: the finite equality tests briefly introduced in Fig. 2.

Definition 12 (Equality on a Segment, eq_segment). *For all $a \in JS, i \in \mathbb{N}$ and $f, g \in \mathcal{F}$, we define eq_segment(a, i, f, g), the following property:*

$$f(a_i) = g(a_i) \wedge \exists x, y \in \,]a_i; a_{i+1}[, x \neq y \wedge f(x) = g(x) \wedge f(y) = g(y). \tag{18}$$

We state this definition in Coq as follows.

```
Definition eq_segment (a : JS) i (f g : F) := f (a i) = g (a i)
  ∧ ∃ x y : R+, a i < x < a i.+1
  ∧ a i < y < a i.+1 ∧ x ≠ y ∧ f x = g x ∧ f y = g y.
```

This definition is useful to check equality on an interval. Given two functions f, g both *affine* on $]a_i; a_{i+1}[$, eq_segment(a, i, f, g) ensures that $f = g$ on $[a_i; a_{i+1}[$.

Combined with previous results, we get an equality criteria for the addition.

Proposition 1 (UPP_PA_n_add in Coq). *For all $n \in \mathbb{N}^\star$, $f \in \mathcal{F}^n_{UPP\text{-}PA}$, $f' \in \mathcal{F}_{UPP\text{-}PA}$ with initial segments $T \in \mathbb{Q}^n_+$ and $T' \in \mathbb{Q}_+$, periods $d \in (\mathbb{Q}^\star_+)^n$ and $d' \in \mathbb{Q}^\star_+$, increments $c \in \mathbb{Q}^n$ and $c' \in \mathbb{Q}$ respectively, we define $l \triangleq$*

$$\max\{\max_i\{T_i\}, T'\} + lcm_{\mathbb{Q}^\star_+} \left(lcm_{\mathbb{Q}^\star_+}(d_i), d' \right), \text{ and } u \triangleq \left(\bigcup_i a_i \right) \cup a', \text{ where for all}$$

i, $a_i \in JS(f_i)$ and $last(a_i) = l$, $a' \in JS(f')$ and $last(a') = l$. If $\sum_i \left(\frac{c_i}{d_i}\right) = \frac{c'}{d'}$ then

$$\forall i < \#u - 1, \; eq\_segment\left(u, i, \sum_j f_j, f'\right) \tag{19}$$

is a sufficient condition for $\sum_i f_i = f'$.

The condition (19) happens to be also necessary but we do not need to prove it.

Remark 3. This criteria can be computed in finite time. a_i and a' can be obtained using Lemma 1. To check $eq\_segment(a, i, f, f')$, one can take $x = \frac{a_i + a_{i+1}}{2}$ and $y = \frac{a_i + x}{2}$.

We get similar criteria for the minimum and the convolution.

Proposition 2 (UPP_PA_n_min in Coq). *Let $n \in \mathbb{N}^*$ and $f \in \mathcal{F}^n_{UPP\text{-}PA}$. For all $f' \in \mathcal{F}_{UPP\text{-}PA}$ with initial segment $T' \in \mathbb{Q}_+$, periods $d' \in \mathbb{Q}_+^*$ and increment $c' \in \mathbb{Q}$, assume M and m satisfying the hypotheses of Lemma 4 and define $\tilde{T}, \tilde{d}$ and $\tilde{c}$ as in Lemma 4. We define $l \triangleq \max(\tilde{T}, T') + lcm_{\mathbb{Q}_+^*}(\tilde{d}, d')$ and $u \triangleq \left(\bigcup_{i,j} \cup_{\min}(f_{<l_i}, f_{<l_j}, a_i, a_j)\right) \cup a'$, where for all i, $a_i \in JS(f_i)$ and $last(a_i) = l$, $a' \in JS(f')$ and $last(a') = l$. If $\frac{\tilde{c}}{\tilde{d}} = \frac{c'}{d'}$, then:*

$$\forall i < \#u - 1, \; eq\_segment\left(u, i, \min_j(f_j), f'\right) \tag{20}$$

is a sufficient condition for $\min_i(f_i) = f'$.

Proposition 3 (F_UPP_conv in Coq). *Let $f, f' \in \mathcal{F}_{UPP\text{-}PA}$. For all $f'' \in \mathcal{F}_{UPP\text{-}PA}$ with initial segment $T'' \in \mathbb{Q}_+$, period $d'' \in \mathbb{Q}_+$ and increment $c'' \in \mathbb{Q}$, assume M, M', m and $m' \in \mathbb{Q}$ satisfying hypotheses of Lemma 5 and define $\tilde{T}, \tilde{d}, \tilde{c}$ as in Lemma 5. We define $l \triangleq \max(\tilde{T}, T'') + lcm_{\mathbb{Q}_+^*}(\tilde{d}, d'')$. Assume $a \in JS(f)$ and $last(a) = l$, $a' \in JS(f')$ and $last(a') = l$, $a'' \in JS(f'')$ and $last(a'') = l$ and define $k \triangleq \#a - 1$ and $k' \triangleq \#a' - 1$. Assuming $\tilde{a} \in JS^{\{0,\dots,k-1\} \times \{0,\dots,k'-1\}}$ such that for all i, i', $\tilde{a}_{i,i'} \in JS((f \downarrow a)_i * (f' \downarrow a')_{i'})$ and $last(\tilde{a}_{i,i'}) = l$, define*

$$u \triangleq \left(\bigcup_{(i,i'),(j,j')} \cup_{\min}\left((f \downarrow a)_i * (f' \downarrow a')_{i'}, (f \downarrow a)_j * (f' \downarrow a')_{j'}, \tilde{a}_{i,i'}, \tilde{a}_{j,j'}\right)\right) \cup a'', \tag{21}$$

if $\frac{\tilde{c}}{\tilde{d}} = \frac{c''}{d''}$ then

$$\forall j < \#u - 1, \; eq\_segment\left(u, i, \min_{i,j}\left((f \downarrow a)_i * (f' \downarrow a')_j\right), f''\right) \tag{22}$$

is a sufficient condition for $f * f' = f''$.

Just as for Proposition 1, these sufficient criteria can be checked in finite time.

10   Implementation

The implementation consists of 6.3k lines of Coq code. It uses the rational numbers defined in the MathComp library [16] and the real numbers from Coq's standard library [21]. These real numbers are linked to the algebraic structures from MathComp thanks to the Rstruct.v file of the MathComp Analysis library [18]. This enables in particular the use of the big operators from MathComp [2]. The extended real numbers $\overline{\mathbb{R}}$ and a few other definitions on real numbers are based on the Coquelicot library [3]. The real numbers from the standard library and Coquelicot could probably now be fully replaced by the MathComp Analysis library, which was in an early development stage when we started this work but now looks much more usable. This would avoid many painful translations back and forth between the two different formalizations.

To obtain executable Coq programs, some adjustments were required, such as making the ρ and σ of Definition 5 explicit in the jump sequences. The final executable version consist of 9k lines of Coq (including the previous formalization) and uses the refinement of MathComp's rational numbers by the one in the bignums library [14] provided by the CoqEAL library [12].

Here is an example proof on the sum of the two functions f and g from Fig. 2. We first declare f and g: (mk_sequpp is a mapping function)

```
Let f := F_of_sequpp (mk_sequpp 4 (* T *) 4 (* d *) 3 (* c *) [:: (0, (0, (2, 0)));
    (1, (2, (0, 2))); (2, ( 2, (0, 3)));   (4, ( 3, (0, 5))); (6, ( 5, (0, 6)))]).
Let g := F_of_sequpp (mk_sequpp 4 4 (4/11) [:: (0, (0, (1/3, 0)));
                            (3, (1, (1/11, 1)))]).
```

Then a function h that we want to prove equal to $f + g$ (this function could be obtained from an external oracle):

```
Let h := F_of_sequpp (mk_sequpp 4 4 (37/11) [:: (0, ( 0, (7/3, 0)));
    (1, (7/3, (1/3, 7/3))); (2, (8/3, (1/3, 11/3))); (3, (4, (1/11, 4)));
    (4, (45/11, (1/11, 67/11))); (6, (69/11, (1/11, 80/11)))]).
```

We can then use our new tactic nccoq to automatically prove the equality:

```
Goal f + g = h. Proof. nccoq. Qed.
```

This tactic performs proofs by reflection: it reduces the goal to prove down to a computation which is then performed by Coq and whose success concludes the proof. This reduction is done with the help of the machinery provided by the CoqEAL library [12].

11   Conclusion

Confidence in latency bounds computed by *Network Calculus* tools [8,20] relies, among other parts, on the correctness of the evaluation of algebraic expressions on *(min, plus)* operators [1,6]. Instead of developing another toolbox, we developed, formalized and proved equality criteria that can be checked in finite time for each algebraic operation involved in actual computation of *Network Calculus* bounds.

The expected usage of this library is to delegate the evaluation of arbitrary algebraic expressions to an external tool [1] before checking the final result with our Coq contribution. This external tool would then act as an untrusted oracle.

References

1. RealTime-at-Work online Min-Plus interpreter for Network Calculus. https://www.realtimeatwork.com/minplus-playground, Accessed 18 Nov 2020
2. Bertot, Y., Gonthier, G., Ould Biha, S., Pasca, I.: Canonical big operators. In: Mohamed, O.A., Muñoz, C., Tahar, S. (eds.) TPHOLs 2008. LNCS, vol. 5170, pp. 86–101. Springer, Heidelberg (2008). https://doi.org/10.1007/978-3-540-71067-7_11
3. Boldo, S., Lelay, C., Melquiond, G.: Coquelicot: a user-friendly library of real analysis for coq. Math. Comput. Sci. **9**(1), 41–62 (2015)
4. Bondorf, S., Schmitt, J.B.: The DiscoDNC v2 - a comprehensive tool for deterministic network calculus. In: Proceedings of the International Conference on Performance Evaluation Methodologies and Tools, ValueTools 2014, pp. 44–49 (2014)
5. Bouillard, A., Boyer, M., Le Corronc, E.: Deterministic Network Calculus: From Theory to Practical Implementation (2018)
6. Bouillard, A., Cottenceau, B., Gaujal, B., Hardouin, L., Lagrange, S., Lhommeau, M., Thierry, E.: COINC library: a toolbox for the network calculus. In: Proceedings of the 4th International Conference on Performance Evaluation Methodologies and Tools, ValueTools, vol. 9 (2009)
7. Bouillard, A., Thierry, E.: An algorithmic toolbox for network calculus. Disc. Event Dyn. Syst. Theory Appl. **18**, 03 (2008)
8. Boyer, M., Migge, J., Fumey, M.: PEGASE, a robust and efficient tool for worst case network traversal time. In: Proceedings of the SAE 2011 AeroTech Congress & Exhibition, Toulouse, France. SAE International (2011)
9. Boyer, M., Navet, N., Fumey, M.: Experimental assessment of timing verification techniques for AFDX. In: 6th European Congress on Embedded Real Time Software and Systems, Toulouse, France (2012)
10. Boyer, M., Navet, N., Olive, X., Thierry, E.: The PEGASE project: precise and scalable temporal analysis for aerospace communication systems with network calculus. In: Margaria, T., Steffen, B. (eds.) ISoLA 2010. LNCS, vol. 6415, pp. 122–136. Springer, Heidelberg (2010). https://doi.org/10.1007/978-3-642-16558-0_13
11. Cerqueira, F., Stutz, F., Brandenburg, B.B.: PROSA: a case for readable mechanized schedulability analysis. In: 2016 28th Euromicro Conference on Real-Time Systems (ECRTS), pp. 273–284. IEEE (2016)
12. Cohen, C., Dénès, M., Mörtberg, A.: Refinements for free!. In: Gonthier, G., Norrish, M. (eds.) CPP 2013. LNCS, vol. 8307, pp. 147–162. Springer, Cham (2013). https://doi.org/10.1007/978-3-319-03545-1_10
13. The Coq development team. The Coq proof assistant reference manual, 2020. Version 8.12
14. Grégoire, B., Théry, L.: A purely functional library for modular arithmetic and its application to certifying large prime numbers. In: Furbach, U., Shankar, N. (eds.) IJCAR 2006. LNCS (LNAI), vol. 4130, pp. 423–437. Springer, Heidelberg (2006). https://doi.org/10.1007/11814771_36

15. Mabille, E., Boyer, M., Fejoz, L., Merz, S.: Towards certifying network calculus. In: Proceedings of the 4th Conference on Interactive Theorem Proving (ITP 2013), Rennes, France (2013)
16. Mahboubi, A., Tassi, E.: Mathematical Components (2018)
17. Rakotomalala, L., Boyer, M., Roux, P.: Verification, formal, of real-time networks. In: JRWRTC: Junior Workshop RTNS 2019, Toulouse, France, p. 2019 (2019)
18. Rouhling, D.: Formalisation Tools for Classical Analysis - A Case Study in Control Theory. (Outils pour la Formalisation en Analyse Classique - Une Étude de Cas en Théorie du Contrôle). PhD thesis, University of Côte d'Azur, Nice, France (2019)
19. Sariowan, H., Cruz, R.L., Polyzos, G.C.: SCED: a generalized scheduling policy for guaranteeing quality-of-service. IEEE/ACM Trans. Netw. 7(5), 669–684 (1999)
20. Schmitt, J., Zdarsky, F.: The DISCO network calculator: a toolbox for worst case analysis, p. 8 (2006)
21. Semeria, V.: Nombres réels dans Coq. In: JFLA, pp. 104–111 (2020)
22. Wandeler, E.: Modular performance analysis and interface based design for embedded real time systems (2006)
23. Wandeler, E., Thiele, L.: Real-Time Calculus (RTC) Toolbox (2006)

Efficient Verification of Optimized Code
Correct High-Speed X25519

Marc Schoolderman[1,2]([✉]), Jonathan Moerman[1], Sjaak Smetsers[1],
and Marko van Eekelen[1,2]

[1] Radboud University, Nijmegen, The Netherlands
{m.schoolderman,jmoerman,s.smetsers,marko}@science.ru.nl
[2] Open University of the Netherlands, Heerlen, The Netherlands
{marc.schoolderman,marko.vaneekelen}@ou.nl

Abstract. Code that is highly optimized poses a problem for program-level verification: programmers can employ various clever tricks that are non-trivial to reason about. For cryptography on low-power devices, it is nonetheless crucial that implementations be functionally correct, secure, and efficient. These are usually crafted in hand-optimized machine code that eschew conventional control flow as much as possible.

We have formally verified such code: a library which implements elliptic curve cryptography on 8-bit AVR microcontrollers. The chosen implementation is the most efficient currently known for this microarchitecture. It consists of over 3000 lines of assembly instructions.

Building on earlier work, we use the Why3 platform to model the code and prove verification conditions, using automated provers.

We expect the approach to be re-usable and adaptable, and it allows for validation. Furthermore, an error in the original implementation was found and corrected, at the same time reducing its memory footprint.

This shows that practical verification of cutting-edge code is not only possible, but can in fact add to its efficiency—and is clearly necessary.

1   Introduction

Although formal verification is considered to give the highest level of assurance in security-critical software [21], it is seldom applied. Even if a verification technique is expressive enough to reason about a given problem domain, for its use to make economic sense, it must be usable by programmers proficient in that domain, and not require an excessive amount of time. These criteria are hard to meet.

Cryptographic implementations are always security-critical: subtle bugs can have disastrous consequences [9], and the security of a system is only as strong as its weakest link. As Chen et al. [10] note, the desire to avoid risk in cryptographic implementations can hamper adoption of new and more efficient crypto libraries, simply because the correctness of these implementations cannot be properly demonstrated. As they also note, a full audit in addition to testing can be extremely expensive, and impractical for high-performance implementations

© Springer Nature Switzerland AG 2021
A. Dutle et al. (Eds.): NFM 2021, LNCS 12673, pp. 304–321, 2021.
https://doi.org/10.1007/978-3-030-76384-8_19

due to extensive use of clever optimizations. In this context the case of applying formal verification looks very reasonable, and indeed this is actively pursued [7,10].

However, this poses many important challenges. First, at what level should verification occur? Compilers have been known to be a source of concern, as they can cause subtle problems [22]. Second, understanding the formal verification process used can be a daunting task: powerful tools such as the Verification Software Toolchain [1] have a substantial learning curve. If instead an ad-hoc method is used, the correctness of the method itself needs to be clearly established for it to be trustworthy. Lastly, cryptography by its nature involves the exploitation of carefully engineered mathematics, which a formal method must be able to state and work with, which adds to the effort required in showing correctness of implementations.

To rely on the verification of any code—cryptographic or otherwise—its specification must be validated as well. This demands a formal specification that is succinct, and comprehensible by a domain expert. Furthermore, we do not want to decide between efficiency and correctness: both are important, and in fact verification ideally assists in making implementations more efficient. Finally, for a verification technique to be practical, it should be re-usable for other verification tasks in the future, and not simply a one-shot operation.

In this paper, we present such a technique, by applying the existing Why3 verification platform [17] to prove the functional correctness of a highly optimized library used for X25519 elliptic curve cryptography on 8-bit microcontrollers [14]. We arrive at a succinct specification, and we expect our technique to be capable of verifying similar code for more powerful processors with less effort.

1.1 Contributions

We provide a corrected version of an X25519 implementation optimized for the 8-bit AVR architecture. Our modifications, described in Sect. 6, improve upon the fastest implementation currently known for this challenging architecture [14].

We demonstrate functional correctness and memory safety of this implementation by providing a machine-checked proof using the Why3 verification platform [17]. Concretely, we prove that the code calculates a scalar multiplication on Curve25519 by applying a double-and-add scheme—the *Montgomery ladder*—using Montgomery's x-coordinate-only formulas [27].

We also provide a formal Why3 model of a subset of the AVR instruction set, that has been carefully constructed for easy validation with respect to the official specification [2]. This model can be re-used for other purposes, or modified to fit a different verification purpose without loss of its validity.

We describe our approach in using Why3 for this verification task; this is an extension of earlier work [30], and has been demonstrated to have a low barrier to understanding [31]. This approach should work similarly well for other architectures such as ARM or RISC-V. The overall methodology is not specific to the domain of cryptographic implementations.

1.2 Availability of Results

The code belonging to this paper is available online in an open repository.[1] To check the proofs, Why3 version 0.88.3 is required.[2] For discharging the verification conditions the provers CVC3 (2.4.1), CVC4 (1.4 and 1.6), Z3 (4.6.0), and E-prover (2.0) were used.

2 Elliptic Curve Cryptography on Small Devices

X25519 is a public key cryptography scheme built around a Diffie-Hellman key exchange [5,24]. 'Original' Diffie-Hellman obtains its security through the observation that, given a primitive root g for a prime p, it is (in general) hard to compute g^{xy} from g^x and g^y (mod p) without knowing the integers x or y [12]. For proper security, a sufficiently large prime modulus p is needed—2048 bits is a recommended minimum [33]. Performing the required exponentiation and modular reduction steps on such large integers is hard to do efficiently on restricted devices [20]. Also, the viability of side-channel attacks prescribes various precautions on all code that computes using secret data, to ensure that an implementation does not inadvertently leak information [18].

2.1 Curve25519

Using elliptic curves eases some of these issues [5]. Given a field $\mathbb{F}$, and coefficients $A, B \in \mathbb{F}$, a *Montgomery curve over* $\mathbb{F}$ is defined as all the points $x, y \in \mathbb{F}$ that satisfy the formula:

$$By^2 = x^3 + Ax^2 + x$$

To this set of points is added a 'point at infinity' denoted $\mathcal{O}$ to form an additive group. When P, Q are *distinct* points on the curve, $P + Q$ is defined as the third point on the curve that intersects the straight line passing through P and Q, reflected around the x-axis. For $P + P$, the tangent of the curve at point P is used to find this point. The point at infinity $\mathcal{O}$ acts as the neutral element.

The separate cases of point *adding* and *doubling*, can be used to compute a *scalar multiple* $n \cdot P$, or P added to itself n times, using a double-and-add scheme. Again a *Diffie-Hellman assumption* [23] applies: if $\mathbb{F}$ is a finite field of prime order, it is assumed to be hard to compute $nm \cdot P$ from $n \cdot P$ and $m \cdot P$.

X25519 performs a scalar multiplication on Curve25519: a Montgomery curve over the finite field $\mathbb{F}_p$ where $p = 2^{255} - 19$, and coefficients $A = 486662, B = 1$. The choice of p facilitates efficient modular reductions. Furthermore, Montgomery [27] gives efficient formulas for both *doubling* and *differential addition* of points, which only requires the x-coordinates of points. These formulas derive their efficiency by representing an x-coordinate by the ratio $X : Z$, with $x \equiv X \cdot Z^{-1} \bmod p$.

---

[1] https://doi.org/10.5281/zenodo.4640377.
[2] Later versions do not yet support our approach—see Sect. 8.

The scalar multiple $n \cdot P$, finally, is computed using the *Montgomery ladder*. This can be mathematically described by the following formula:

$$\text{LADDER } n \ P = \begin{cases} (\mathcal{O},\ P) & \text{if } n = 0 \\ (2R_0,\ R_1 + R_0) & \text{if } n > 0 \text{ and even} \\ (R_1 + R_0,\ 2R_1) & \text{if } n > 0 \text{ and odd} \end{cases}$$

where in the last two cases $(R_0,\ R_1) = \text{LADDER } \lfloor n/2 \rfloor\ P$

It can be shown that for every $n \geq 0$, LADDER $n\ P = (n \cdot P,\ (n+1)P)$, but instead of computing $n \cdot P$ using a naive double-and-add scheme, this definition performs the same arithmetic operations in both recursive cases—the only difference between the recursive cases is a swap of the arguments. This enables a constant-time implementation [6].

2.2 X25519 on AVR

The AVR microarchitecture is an 8-bit RISC architecture [2], and so we can only represent an element $x \in \mathbb{F}_p$ by splitting it into 32 bytes. Since the AVR only has 32 registers (of which some are needed as index registers), no single element $x \in \mathbb{F}_p$ can be loaded from memory entirely. Therefore, judicious register allocation is of prime concern for an efficient implementation. Therefore, all of the primitives operations in $\mathbb{F}_p$ are rendered in assembly code in [14]. These comprise the following:

- A $256 \rightarrow 256$-bit routine subtracting $2^{255} - 19$ from its input (with borrow).
- A $256 \times 256 \rightarrow 512$-bit multiplication routine, constructed by recursive application of Karatsuba's algorithm out of smaller $32 \times 32 \rightarrow 64$-bit multiplication routines.
- A $256 \rightarrow 512$-bit dedicated squaring routine of similar construction
- A $512 \rightarrow 256$-bit modular reduction function, which given a $m \in \mathbb{F}_p$ computes $\hat{m}$ so that $\hat{m} \equiv m \pmod{p}$ and $\hat{m} < 2^{256}$, used to reduce the results of the previous two functions.
- $256 \times 256 \rightarrow 256$-bit modular addition/subtraction routines which perform a multi-precision addition/subtraction with a built-in modular reduction.
- A specialized $256 \rightarrow 256$-bit routine for efficient modular multiplication with the constant 121666.

Other operations are rendered in C code: these are either very simple, or consist mostly of function calls to these primitive operations. Examples of such functions would be a $256 \times 256 \rightarrow 256$-bit modular multiplication, a function that canonicalizes an element $x \in \mathbb{F}_p$ by repeated subtraction of p, and a function that computes $x^{-1} \pmod{p}$ using Fermat's little theorem.

The Montgomery ladder is implemented in C iteratively as illustrated by Algorithm 1. Essentially this computes the scalar multiple using the same double-and-add scheme as the LADDER function defined above, starting at the most significant bit of its input, and swapping the roles of $(X_1 : Z_1)$ and $(X_2 : Z_2)$

as needed. We will show in Sect. 5.1 that the informal specification given here is *not* entirely correct. The LADDERSTEP procedure shown in Algorithm 1 is an optimized implementation of Montgomery's formulas [27] for doubling and adding points. Note that the literature usually only presents the Montgomery ladder in this iterated version, often—confusingly—with minor variations to the LADDERSTEP procedure [5, 24]. We find this optimized form of the Montgomery ladder hard to understand, making its full formal verification desirable.

Algorithm 1. Montgomery ladder for scalar multiplication

Require: A 255-bit scalar n, and a x-coordinate x_P of a point P
Ensure: Result $(X:Z)$ satisfies $x_{n \cdot P} \equiv X \cdot Z^{-1}$
    $(X_1:Z_1) \leftarrow (1:0)$; $(X_2:Z_2) \leftarrow (x_P:1)$; $prev \leftarrow 0$; $j \leftarrow 6$
    for $i \leftarrow 31$ **downto** 0 **do**
        while $j \geq 0$ **do**
            $bit \leftarrow$ **bit** $8i + j$ **of** n
            $swap \leftarrow bit \oplus prev$; $prev \leftarrow bit$
            if swap **then** $(X_1:Z_1, X_2:Z_2) \leftarrow (X_2:Z_2, X_1:Z_1)$ ▷ by conditional moves
            LADDERSTEP$(x_P, X_1 : Z_1, X_2:Z_2)$
            $j \leftarrow j - 1$
        end while
        $j \leftarrow 7$
    end for
    return $(X_1:Z_1)$

procedure LADDERSTEP	$Z_1 \leftarrow T_2 \cdot 121666$
$T_1 \leftarrow X_2 + Z_2$	$Z_1 \leftarrow Z_1 + X_1$
$X_2 \leftarrow X_2 - Z_2$	$Z_1 \leftarrow T_2 \cdot Z_1$
$Z_2 \leftarrow X_1 + Z_1$	$X_1 \leftarrow Z_2 \cdot X_1$
$X_1 \leftarrow X_1 - Z_1$	$Z_2 \leftarrow T_1 - X_2$
$T_1 \leftarrow T_1 \cdot X_1$	$Z_2 \leftarrow (Z_2)^2$
$X_2 \leftarrow X_2 \cdot Z_2$	$Z_2 \leftarrow Z_2 \cdot x_P$
$Z_2 \leftarrow (Z_2)^2$	$X_2 \leftarrow T_1 + X_2$
$X_1 \leftarrow (X_1)^2$	$X_2 \leftarrow (X_2)^2$
$T_2 \leftarrow Z_2 - X_1$	**end procedure**

---

3   Why3 Verification Platform

Why3 [17] is a verification platform for deductive program verification. It comprises the typed programming language WhyML (which can be annotated with functional contracts and assertions), as well as libraries for reasoning about specific types of objects (such as arrays, bit-vectors, bounded and unbounded integers), which the user can also extend. A weakest-precondition calculus generates the correctness condition for an annotated program, which Why3 then transforms into the input language for various automated or interactive provers. Besides assertions and contracts, WhyML also provides other means of instrumenting programs to aid verification. We highlight two:

Ghost code is guaranteed by the type system to not have any effect on the actual execution on the code, but can be used to compute witnesses for use in verification goals.

Abstract blocks can be used to summarize multiple operations with a single functional contract.

An advantage of Why3's reliance on automatic provers is that verification does not need to be the last step in a waterfall-like process. When a program (or specification) is changed, most of the verification conditions that held previously can usually be solved again at the press of a button, even when the change affects them. Similarly, if a prover can solve one instance of a problem, it can usually— given enough time—handle similar or larger instances, allowing for proofs to be transplanted. For instance, we recycled parts of the proofs of [30]. Since Why3 uses multiple provers in concert, we are not restricted by the limitations of one particular (version of) a prover. In this sense, proofs seem robust.

On the other hand, too much irrelevant information can hinder automatic provers. Sometimes an assertion frustrates a proof that is completely unrelated to it. In this sense, proofs can also be brittle. Thus, for large verification tasks keeping the proof context small is vitally important. We used Why3's module system, *ghost code* and *abstract blocks* to keep the proof context manageable.

4   Correctness of Low-Level Code

In the implementation we are considering, all primitives for implementing the field arithmetic needed for computing in $\mathbb{F}_p$ are implemented in assembly code. With the exception of the multiplication routine, this code is free of conditional branches. In the multiplication routine, branches are used, but in every case, both branches take the same amount of clock cycles and perform the same sequence of memory accesses. This should prevent a side-channel attack such as described by Genkin et al. [18], which exploits observed timing differences. Our formal verification effort therefore only focuses on the functional correctness and memory-safety of these routines.

Since 256-bit operations are not natively supported on any CPU, an X25519 implementation usually chooses a representation where an element $x \in \mathbb{F}_p$ is represented in n *limbs* in radix 2^w; that is, $x = \sum_{i=0}^{n} 2^{iw} x_{[i]}$ for the limbs $x_{[0]}, x_{[1]}, \ldots x_{[n-1]}$. If these limbs can contain more than w bits of information, this representation is called *unpacked*, and any carry that occurs during computation does not need to be propagated to the next limb immediately. An *unpacked* representation with few limbs is more efficient, and is thought to be more convenient for verification [10,35]. On the implementation for the AVR a *packed* representation of 32 limbs in radix 2^8 is used, and every part of the code is forced to handle carry-propagation.

Globally, our approach follows that of [30]; we specify the representation of a 256-bit multi-precision integer in terms of an 8-bit memory model, model every AVR mnemonic that is needed as a WhyML function, and mechanically translate the assembly code to this model for verification with Why3.

4.1 A Re-Usable Validated AVR Machine Model

For modeling the processor state, we use the concept of an *8-bit address space*, which is a Why3 `map` of addresses to integers, suitably restricted:

```
type address_space = { mutable data: map int int }
  invariant { forall i. 0 <= self.data[i] < 256 }
```

The AVR register file, data segment, and stack are all modeled as separate address spaces. This of course means that our model is an underspecification, but most assembly code conforms to this simplified model. Memory size restrictions are not part of the definition of an *address space*, as it is more convenient to express them as pre-conditions for the AVR instructions that manipulate memory. To model the carry and 'bit transfer' CPU flags, we use the equivalent of a `ref bool`; the value of all other flags are unspecified. We also use *ghost registers* [30] to track register updates inside abstract blocks using Why3's type system.

Since we needed to model many AVR instructions, we first implemented (in WhyML) a *primitive instruction set* of common operations on these *address spaces*, such as reading and writing 8-bit and 16-bit values represented either by their integer value, or as bit-vectors. These operations are verified for consistency with the *8-bit address space*. This instruction set is then used to *implement* all required AVR instructions following the official specification [2].

For example, for the `SUBI` instruction, the AVR specification tells us that a constant K will be subtracted from its destination register, and the carry flag will be set to $\overline{r_7} \cdot K_7 + K_7 \cdot r'_7 + r'_7 \cdot \overline{r_7}$ (in boolean arithmetic), where x_7 denotes the most significant bit of an 8-bit value x, and r, r' are the previous and updated values of the destination register, respectively. In terms of our primitives, we can state this as:

```
let subi (rd: register) (k: int)
  requires { 0 <= k <= 255 }
= let rdv = read_byte reg rd in
  let res = clip (rdv - k) in
  set_byte reg rd res;
  cf.value <- (not ar_nth rdv 7 && ar_nth k 7 ||
              ar_nth k 7 && ar_nth res 7 ||
              ar_nth res 7 && not ar_nth rdv 7)
```

While this follows the official specification closely, it is not very useful for verifying programs. Capturing the common notion that the carry flag gets set if and only if $r < K$ can be done by adding a Why3 contract for `subi`:

```
ensures { reg = old reg[rd <- mod (old (reg[rd] - k)) 256] }
ensures { ?cf = -div (old (reg[rd] - k)) 256 }
```

That is, the register file gets updated with the destination register receiving $(r - K)$ mod 256, and the numeric value of the carry flag will be $-\lfloor \frac{r-K}{256} \rfloor$.

Why3 allows us to verify that this contract is satisfied by the AVR specification.[3] Also, if a different contract were discovered to be more useful, it could easily be replaced while maintaining validity of the model.

Extensions to the Model. Some of the code verified featured a limited form of branching. We modeled this using a WhyML function that throws an exception if the branch is taken; this exception is then handled at the appropriate location.

In two locations, data on the stack was allocated for use with memory operations, which our simplified model did not support. We resolved this by adding the requirement that the stack pointer does not alias with any of the ordinary data inputs, and checking manually whether the code conforms to the conventions for accessing memory on the stack. As we will explain in Sect. 6.2, this turned out not to be the case, necessitating modifications.

4.2 Proving the Correctness of AVR Assembly Code

For all of the assembly routines, we of course want to show *functional correctness*. However, since these routines must interface with C code, we also have to verify that they are well-behaved. This means proving that they only modify the memory that they are allowed to (i.e. temporary data on the stack or that passed by the caller as a pointer), that they leave the stack in a consistent state, and that they adhere to the C calling convention for the AVR [19].

Note that there are two versions of the 256-bit multiplication routines in [14]: one which uses function calls to the respective 128-bit operation, and one which inlines everything for a very minor increase in speed. We consider the former to be the more relevant one, and so have chosen that as our verification target.

Quantitative verification results are shown in Table 1. The vast majority of the goals were discharged by CVC3 and CVC4. The number of annotations required gives a *rough* measure of the manual effort. This is a subjective number since not every annotation represents the same amount of effort. As a point of reference, verifying fe25519_mul121666 was measured to take 16 h of work.

Verification by Partitioning into Blocks. The 256 × 256-bit multiplication is constructed by using calls to a 128 × 128-bit multiplication routine using Karatsuba's method. The 128 × 128-bit multiplication routine itself, is comprised of three in-line applications of a 64 × 64-bit Karatsuba multiplication, the basic version of which was verified earlier in [30]. Some parts of this earlier proof could in fact simply be re-used.

---

[3] For SUBI, this also revealed a mistake in online documentation.

Table 1. Results of verifying the X25519 field arithmetic in AVR assembly

Function	Instructions	User annotations	Generated goals	CPU time
bigint_mul256:mul128	1078	122	300	1504.6 s
bigint_mul256	693	85	506	2000.1 s
bigint_square256:sqr128	672	26	135	363.8 s
bigint_square256	493	38	359	1796.6 s
bigint_subp	103	12	84	184.0 s
fe25519_red	305	41	182	155.3 s
fe25519_add	242	52	209	156.4 s
fe25519_sub	242	53	212	119.6 s
fe25519_mul121666	138	56	149	393.0 s

For the 128-bit and 256-bit larger versions, the proofs followed a similar approach, with one notable change. For the smaller Karatsuba routines, it sufficed to identify 7 'blocks' of code, and state their operations in *contextual terms*—i.e., specifying which part of Karatsuba's algorithm each block performed. For more than one level of Karatsuba, this becomes unwieldy. While we kept the identified blocks the same, we found it much more useful—even for routines verified in [30]—to specify their effects in purely *local* terms—i.e., only specifying what its effect is in terms of its immediately preceding state. For some blocks, this simplifies the specification, and actually makes the work for automatic provers slightly easier. In cases where this contextual information *is* required, it can always be re-asserted later. The only drawback we have found to this method was that on assembly code of this size, it is easy to lose sight of what one is trying to achieve without reliable contextual information.

The 256-bit squaring routine is similarly constructed out of calls to a 128-bit squaring routine; both compute the square of $A = 2^w A_h + A_l$ as $A^2 = (2^w + 1)(2^w A_h^2 + A_l^2) - 2^w (A_l - A_h)^2$, which we are able to verify by partitioning these routines into 5 blocks.

Instrumenting Programs with Ghost Code. The routines that perform modular arithmetic are very different in style from the multiplication routines. In the latter, we can apply a decomposition into a small number of large blocks, which allows SMT solvers to do most of the work. The reduction, addition and subtraction routines, by contrast, are highly repetitive—essentially the same read-modify-write sequence repeated several times.

In this case, it was more logical to use a bottom-up approach, summarizing the effects of these short sequences using a WhyML function (essentially the same idea as using an assembly *macro*), which is then iterated. We discovered, however, that after a few macro applications, SMT solvers were unable to prove memory safety or absence of aliasing. The culprit here seemed to be that the macros accessed memory via LD+/ST+ instructions (which perform a load/store, followed by a pointer increment). Perhaps unsurprisingly, it becomes increasingly hard for SMT solvers to reason about out what address an index register is referring to after many modifications have been applied to it.

In our routines (and we suspect, commonly in similar cases) such addresses are however perfectly obvious, and can be statically deduced. We therefore instrumented the code with *ghost arguments*, which supply this missing information. As a simple example of this technique (which was also used in the 256×256-bit multiplication routine), we can make the AVR LD+ instruction (modeled as the WhyML function AVRint.ld_inc) more amenable to verification by instrumenting it with ghost arguments:

```
let ld_inc' (dst src: register) (ghost addr: int)
  ... (* the specification of AVRint.ld_inc *)
  requires { uint 2 reg src = addr }
= AVRint.ld_inc dst src
```

On the surface, this just appears to add a needless pre-condition; however, once this correlation between addr and uint 2 reg src is established, SMT solvers can use this information to easily deduce what address the index register used is referring to.

5   Correctness of the C Code

The X25519 implementation we verify also consists of around 300 lines of C code, which interfaces directly with the assembly routines verified in Sect. 4. Many routines are short and simple, and verification for them is a straight-forward application of Why3.

To ensure that the C code and the assembly code are both verified with respect to the same logical foundations, we translate C by hand into the WhyML primitives from Sect. 4.1, that underpin the AVR instruction set model. However, since a C compiler handles allocation of global and local variables, using one address_space to model memory would be impractical and incorrect, as it would force the model to make assumptions about the memory layout. So instead, every array object is modeled as residing in its own address_space. An added benefit of this is that Why3's type system will enforce that arguments do not alias. The minor drawback is that some functions can be called to perform in-place updates, which does requires aliasing. These functions have to be modeled and verified for both cases separately.

For the assembly routines that interface with the C code, abstract specifications are added by duplicating the contracts of the verified assembly routines, and removing the pre- and post-conditions related to the C calling conventions.

The verification results are listed in Table 2. Among the field operations, it is notable that fe25519_unpack and fe25519_invert generate more goals. The former is due to its (RFC-required) bit-masking of its input, which we specify as a reduction mod 2^{255}. We suspect our proof of this function can be further optimized, but decided against spending time on this. Note that the field arithmetic code actually operates on a *packed* representation, so unpack and pack functions are otherwise simply copy-operations.

The `fe25519_invert` function computes $x^{2^{255}-21}$ (mod p) using sequences of modular square-and-multiply steps. This makes it very similar to repetitive assembly code, and it is treated the same way: we instrument the code with *ghost arguments* in a highly regular fashion which specify the actual value of intermediate results—which interestingly was more or less a formalization of the *inline comments* provided by the original authors. Also, *abstract blocks* helped keep the number of verification conditions small.

For the verification of the last three routines in Table 2, verification was 'simply' an effort of finding the correct invariants and assertions that guided the automatic provers to the desired conclusion within an acceptable amount of CPU time. To achieve the final conclusion presented in Sect. 5.2, it is required to know that $2^{255}-19$ is a prime number; we took the pragmatic route and stated this as an axiom in Why3. To see that $x^{2^{255}-21}$ is the multiplicative inverse of x also requires Fermat's little theorem, which we instead proved inside Why3 using *ghost code* that traces a direct proof using modular arithmetic—showing that for any integer a not divisible by a prime p, it is the case that $a^{p-1} \prod_{i=1}^{p-1} i \equiv \prod_{i=1}^{p-1} a \cdot i \equiv \prod_{i=1}^{p-1} i$, and therefore $a^{p-1} \equiv 1$.

Table 2. Results of verifying the X25519 C routines

Function	Lines	User annotations	Generated goals	CPU time
fe25519_setzero	3	2	7	0.4 s
fe25519_setone	4	2	7	0.4 s
fe25519_neg	3	0	3	0.2 s
fe25519_cmov	5	3	10	36.5 s
fe25519_freeze	4	2	9	4.7 s
fe25519_unpack	4	8	30	41.0 s
fe25519_pack	5	2	11	1.6 s
fe25519_mul	3	0	1	0.2 s
fe25519_square	3	0	1	0.1 s
fe25519_invert	51	49	306	557.3 s
work_cswap	8	0	13	3.8 s
ladderstep	26	22	80	202.8 s
mladder	26	22	140	345.1 s
crypto_scalar_mult_curve25519	13	27	57	74.2 s

5.1   Verifying the Montgomery Ladder

Montgomery [27] provides formulas for doubling and differential addition of points on an elliptic curve, where only the x-coordinates of these points on the curve are used. As mentioned in Sect. 2.1, these x-coordinates are represented as *ratios* $(X : Z)$, where $x \equiv X \cdot Z^{-1} \bmod p$. The point at infinity $\mathcal{O}$, which is not on the curve, is represented by $(X : Z)$ with $X \neq 0, Z = 0$. The degenerate case $(0 : 0)$ does not represent anything.

For Curve25519, Montgomery's formulas are proven correct for all cases by Bernstein [5], and look as follows:

$$X_{2n} = (X_n^2 - Z_n^2)^2 \qquad\qquad X_{m+n} = 4Z_{m-n}(X_m X_n - Z_m Z_n)^2$$
$$Z_{2n} = 4X_n Z_n(X_n^2 + 486662 X_n Z_n + Z_n^2) \quad Z_{m+n} = 4X_{m-n}(X_m Z_n - Z_m X_n)^2$$

If the x-coordinate of the point nP is the ratio $(X_n : Z_n)$, then $(X_{2n} : Z_{2n})$ is the ratio for the point $(2n)P$. Likewise, from x_{nP} and x_{mP}, we can compute $x_{(m+n)P}$ provided we also know $x_{(m-n)P}$.

We have proven that the `ladderstep` procedure (see Algorithm 1), given values $(x, X_n : Z_n, X_m : Z_m)$, computes $(X_{2n} : Z_{2n}, X_{m+n} : Z_{m+n})$ as specified by these point doubling and addition formulas, with $X_{m-n} = x$, and $Z_{m-n} = 1$.

To verify the function `mladder` (Algorithm 1), we define a formal specification in Why3 of the Montgomery ladder as presented in Sect. 2.1, but using the above formulas for doubling and addition. We verify that `mladder` adheres to this specification: if for some 255-bit integer s and x-coordinate x_P, LADDER s $(x_P : 1)$ returns $(X : Z)$ as the first component of its result, `mladder` computes $(\tilde{X} : \tilde{Z})$ such that $\tilde{X} \equiv X$ and $\tilde{Z} \equiv Z \pmod{p}$.

Importantly, for this result to hold, we found it necessary to require that s is even, and has its most significant bit set. The former is necessary, as an odd s would leave the results of Algorithm 1 in a state where a final swap is still needed. Having bit 254 in s set is necessary, as it prevents Algorithm 1 from performing the doubling formula on the 'point at infinity', which would make it impossible to demonstrate the strict correspondence.

These requirements on s are however taken care of by the existence of the 'clamping' operation in X25519, which requires $s \in \{2^{254} + 8k : 0 \leq k < 2^{251}\}$. Having s a multiple of 8 is crucial for the mathematical security of X25519 [24]. Setting the high bit is done for entirely different reasons: to prevent programmers from applying a non-constant-time optimization that reveals information about the scalar s [23]. Our formal proof was greatly helped by this choice, perhaps providing more justification for it.

5.2   A Succinct Specification of X25519

The function `crypto_scalar_mult` is our ultimate verification goal. We show the most important part of the specification proven in Why3 here:

```
val crypto_scalarmult_curve25519 (r s p: address_space)
  ensures { uint 32 r = mod (uint 32 r) p25519 }
  ensures { let xp   = mod (uint 32 p) (pow2 255) in
            let mult = scale (clamp (uint 32 s)) xp in
            if mult ~ infty then
              uint 32 r === 0
            else
              uint 32 r ==~ mult }
```

Informally, the first post-condition states that the result is in canonical form, i.e. fully reduced. The second post-condition states that, after the high bit of the x-coordinate of P is masked (as per RFC7748 [24]), a ratio $(X:Z)$ representing the x-coordinate of $[s] \cdot P$ is computed using repeated application of Montgomery's formulas (where $[s]$ is the clamped value of s). If $[s] \cdot P$ happens to be $\mathcal{O}$, the function writes a zero result; otherwise the result will be equivalent to $x_{[s] \cdot P}$.

Note that is not possible to distinguish the result $[s] \cdot P = \mathcal{O}$ and $x_{[s]P} = 0$. However, for every point P whose y-coordinate is not-zero, X25519 also does not distinguish P and $-P$; this specification elucidates that $\mathcal{O}$ and the point at the origin $(x = 0, y = 0)$ are similarly unified.

6   Improved X25519 for AVR

Several small improvements were observed, which we confirmed by a formal proof. Two instructions in the 128×128-bit multiplication assembly routine could be removed with no impact on the formal proof, confirming they were unnecessary. In `fe25519_freeze`, the routine `bigint_subp` is called twice to fully reduce an integer mod $2^{255} - 19$. We were able to verify that one call suffices, since in the current implementation it is always applied to a result that is already partially reduced.

6.1   Memory Safety

In [30], several version of the Karatsuba implementations could compute incorrect results if the memory locations used for storing input and output were aliased, so we were naturally curious about aliasing in the X25519 implementation. We found that the prohibition on aliasing also applies to the 128-bit and 256-bit multiplication/squaring routines,[4] and the `fe25519_red` modular reduction function. The modular addition/subtraction routines and `fe25519_mul121666` were verified to be safe when used for in-place update operations.

The C code calls all these functions accordingly, so aliasing never becomes an issue. We did add a `restrict` keyword to the function prototypes for which argument aliasing results in undefined behavior.

---

[4] As a peculiar exception: the 128-bit squaring routine will function properly when reading from address i and writing to address $i + 8$.

6.2 Interrupt Safety

The 256-bit multiplication and squaring routines use function calls to the 128-bit versions to compute their results, which expect their arguments to be in memory. One of these calls multiplies an intermediate result and so has to write this back to memory using the stack.

However, the original code did this by writing the data below the stack pointer. This means that if the microcontroller is interrupted importunely (e.g. due to a timer or I/O event), and an associated interrupt service routine needs this stack space for local variables, this data is clobbered. The problem can be demonstrated by forcing an interrupt.

This problem was discovered during the modeling phase of verification, as our initial AVR model needed an extension to support direct access to the stack pointer, forcing us to consider the conditions under which this is allowed. We replaced the faulty code with code that moves the stack pointer using an idiomatic sequence [3], which we added to our model. Due to our formal proof, we were also able to see that in the 256×256-bit multiplication some of the memory reserved for the final output was available for use as a temporary, reducing the amount of total stack space required by 32 bytes.

7 Related Work

Verified cryptography has gained much interest. In [35], a verified library of elliptic curves written in F* is presented. These provide the foundation for the C implementation of X25519 in the HACL* library [34]: an implementation is created in a intermediate language Low*, verified against the F* specifications, and then mechanically translated into C. EverCrypt [29] includes a similar C implementation, as well as an efficient implementation in x86-64 assembly code, which is similarly generated, but using the Vale [8] tool. Vale is essentially a high-level assembly language with support for deductive reasoning, with a focus on cryptographic applications. A similar X25519 implementation, now included in BoringSSL [15], uses Coq [11] to generate efficient C code. All these approaches involve *generation* of *new* implementations.

Efforts to verify *existing* full implementations also exist. In [13], an ECDSA implementation in Java is proven equivalent with a Cryptol [16] specification. This is also a partially automated proof, requiring 1500 lines of annotation guiding the proof (in the form of SAWScript). Compared to our approach, the Cryptol specification is less succinct—it actually is a complete, low-level implementation in its own right, written in a functional language.

Recently, the X25519 implementation in TweetNaCl has been verified [32] using Coq and VST [1]. This implementation was, however, designed with verification in mind. The proof states that TweetNaCl (when compiled with CompCert [25]) correctly implements a scalar multiplication. Like [35], the authors show this with respect to a formal *mathematical* specification of elliptic curves.

Two efficient X25519 implementations written in 64-bit qhasm were partially verified by Chen et al. [10]. Their approach is comparable to ours, in that they generate verification conditions which they solve using Boolector. However, where we use Why3 for this, they uses a custom approach, and report lengthier verification times. Their verification is partial, in the sense that they show that their Montgomery ladderstep implementation matches that of Algorithm 1, but don't verify the ladder itself. Similarly, Liu et al. [26] have verified several C routines of OpenSSL by compiling them to the LLVM intermediate representation, and translating that to the dedicated verification language CRYPTOLINE.

8 Conclusion

To our knowledge, our result is the first to fully verify an existing high-speed implementation of X25519 scalar multiplication, and the first to present a verified implementation optimized for low-power devices. We show correctness with respect to short formulas that are themselves proven correct in the literature [5, 27].

Like [32], only general purpose, well-understood verification methods were used. Why3 in particular has an easy learning curve [31]. Our method for translating C and assembly code into WhyML is straight-forward, and the AVR model of Sect. 4.1 can be validated, so trust in our results mainly resides with trusting the verification condition generation of Why3, the soundness of the automated provers, and the compilation-toolchain (C compiler, assembler and linker) used for producing AVR binaries. The weakest link in this chain is definitely the use of automated provers: during our work we discovered a soundness error in Alt-Ergo 2.0, forcing us to preclude its use. We eagerly await the ability to perform proof reconstruction in Why3 using verified SMT solvers [4, 28].

We used a version of Why3 compatible with [30]. Newer versions are available, which in principle allow for an improved AVR model and specification. However, due to a change in the meaning of *type invariants*, the versions available to us generated inefficient SMT output for the verified multiplication routines of [30]. Since our use of type invariants can be avoided, we explored several alternatives, but in the end chose to use the older version for time-efficiency reasons.

Our verification was performed in an amount of time that seems commensurate with the time it took the original implementers to engineer the code. Most time was spent on the multiplication routines in assembly code. For the C code, the most time-consuming part was, in fact, finding the right abstraction level for a simple specification of the Montgomery ladder.

Due to our general purpose approach, our findings are encouraging for other low-level language applications. In particular, due to the limitations of AVR, the code we encountered was quite long, and performed arithmetic on many *limbs* (32 instead of the more usual four or five). We expect our approach to work well for verifying the 32-bit ARM code in [14], requiring less time and with the possibility of some proof re-use. We would also like to verify the compiler-generated assembly code of routines verified at a higher level (such as in Sect. 5), by translating high-level specifications to the assembly level. This would strengthen our result by removing the C compiler from the trusted code base.

Acknowledgments. The authors thank Benoît Viguier and Peter Schwabe for their advice, as well as the anonymous reviewers for their comments. This material is based upon work supported by the Defense Advanced Research Projects Agency (DARPA) under Agreement No. HR.00112090028. This work is part of the research programme 'Sovereign' with project number 14319 which is (partly) financed by the Netherlands Organisation for Scientific Research (NWO).

References

1. Appel, A.W.: Verified software toolchain. In: Goodloe, A.E., Person, S. (eds.) NFM 2012. LNCS, vol. 7226, pp. 2–2. Springer, Heidelberg (2012). https://doi.org/10.1007/978-3-642-28891-3_2
2. Atmel Corporation: AVR Instruction Set Manual, revision 0856L (2016)
3. AVR Libc Project: avr-libc User Manual. https://www.nongnu.org/avr-libc/user-manual/FAQ.html
4. Barbosa, H., Blanchette, J.C., Fleury, M., Fontaine, P., Schurr, H.J.: Better SMT proofs for easier reconstruction. In: AITP 2019–4th Conference on Artificial Intelligence and Theorem Proving. Obergurgl, Austria, April 2019
5. Bernstein, D.J.: Curve25519: new Diffie-Hellman speed records. In: Yung, M., Dodis, Y., Kiayias, A., Malkin, T. (eds.) PKC 2006. LNCS, vol. 3958, pp. 207–228. Springer, Heidelberg (2006). https://doi.org/10.1007/11745853_14
6. Bernstein, D., Lange, T.: Montgomery curves and the Montgomery ladder. Cryptology ePrint Archive, IACR (2017)
7. Bhargavan, K., et al.: Everest: towards a verified, drop-in replacement of HTTPS. In: Lerner, B.S., Bodík, R., Krishnamurthi, S. (eds.) 2nd Summit on Advances in Programming Languages (SNAPL 2017). Leibniz International Proceedings in Informatics (LIPIcs), vol. 71, pp. 1:1–1:12. Schloss Dagstuhl-Leibniz-Zentrum fuer Informatik, Dagstuhl, Germany (2017)
8. Bond, B., et al.: Vale: verifying high-performance cryptographic assembly code. In: Proceedings of the 26th USENIX Conference on Security Symposium, pp. 917–934 (2017)
9. Brumley, B.B., Barbosa, M., Page, D., Vercauteren, F.: Practical realisation and elimination of an ECC-related software bug attack. In: Dunkelman, O. (ed.) CT-RSA 2012. LNCS, vol. 7178, pp. 171–186. Springer, Heidelberg (2012). https://doi.org/10.1007/978-3-642-27954-6_11
10. Chen, Y.F., et al.: Verifying Curve25519 software. In: Proceedings of the 2014 ACM SIGSAC Conference on Computer and Communications Security, pp. 299–309. CCS '14, Association for Computing Machinery, New York, NY, USA (2014)
11. The Coq proof assistant reference manual (2015). https://coq.inria.fr/documentation
12. Diffie, W., Hellman, M.: New directions in cryptography. IEEE Trans. Inf. Theor. **22**(6), 644–654 (1976)
13. Dockins, R., Foltzer, A., Hendrix, J., Huffman, B., McNamee, D., Tomb, A.: Constructing semantic models of programs with the software analysis workbench. In: Blazy, S., Chechik, M. (eds.) VSTTE 2016. LNCS, vol. 9971, pp. 56–72. Springer, Cham (2016). https://doi.org/10.1007/978-3-319-48869-1_5
14. Düll, M., et al.: High-speed Curve25519 on 8-bit, 16-bit, and 32-bit microcontrollers. Des. Codes Crypt. **77**(2–3), 493–514 (2015)

15. Erbsen, A., Philipoom, J., Gross, J., Sloan, R., Chlipala, A.: Simple high-level code for cryptographic arithmetic - with proofs, without compromises. In: 2019 IEEE Symposium on Security and Privacy (SP), pp. 1202–1219 (2019)
16. Erkök, L., Carlsson, M., Wick, A.: Hardware/software co-verification of cryptographic algorithms using Cryptol. In: 2009 Formal Methods in Computer-Aided Design, pp. 188–191 (2009). https://doi.org/10.1109/FMCAD.2009.5351121
17. Filliâtre, J.-C., Paskevich, A.: Why3 — where programs meet provers. In: Felleisen, M., Gardner, P. (eds.) ESOP 2013. LNCS, vol. 7792, pp. 125–128. Springer, Heidelberg (2013). https://doi.org/10.1007/978-3-642-37036-6_8
18. Genkin, D., Valenta, L., Yarom, Y.: May the fourth be with you: a microarchitectural side channel attack on several real-world applications of Curve25519. In: Proceedings of the 2017 ACM SIGSAC Conference on Computer and Communications Security, pp. 845–858. CCS '17, Association for Computing Machinery, New York, NY, USA (2017)
19. GNU Project: avr-gcc ABI. https://gcc.gnu.org/wiki/avr-gcc
20. Gura, N., Patel, A., Wander, A., Eberle, H., Shantz, S.C.: Comparing elliptic curve cryptography and RSA on 8-bit CPUs. In: Joye, M., Quisquater, J.-J. (eds.) CHES 2004. LNCS, vol. 3156, pp. 119–132. Springer, Heidelberg (2004). https://doi.org/10.1007/978-3-540-28632-5_9
21. ISO: ISO/IEC 15408–1:2009 Information technology–Security techniques–Evaluation criteria for IT security–Part 1: Introduction and general model (2009)
22. Kaufmann, T., Pelletier, H., Vaudenay, S., Villegas, K.: When constant-time source yields variable-time binary: exploiting Curve25519-donna built with MSVC 2015. In: Foresti, S., Persiano, G. (eds.) CANS 2016. LNCS, vol. 10052, pp. 573–582. Springer, Cham (2016). https://doi.org/10.1007/978-3-319-48965-0_36
23. Kleppmann, M.: Implementing Curve25519/X25519: A tutorial on elliptic curve cryptography. University of Cambridge, Department of Computer Science and Technology, Technical report (2020)
24. Langley, A., Hamburg, M., Turner, S.: Elliptic Curves for Security. RFC 7748, January 2016. https://rfc-editor.org/rfc/rfc7748.txt
25. Leroy, X.: Formal certification of a compiler back-end, or: programming a compiler with a proof assistant. In: 33rd ACM Symposium on Principles of Programming Languages, pp. 42–54. ACM Press (2006)
26. Liu, J., Shi, X., Tsai, M.H., Wang, B.Y., Yang, B.Y.: Verifying arithmetic in cryptographic c programs. In: 2019 34th IEEE/ACM International Conference on Automated Software Engineering (ASE), pp. 552–564. IEEE (2019)
27. Montgomery, P.L.: Speeding the Pollard and elliptic curve methods of factorization. Math. Comput. 48, 243–264 (1987)
28. de Moura, L.M., Bjørner, N.: Proofs and refutations, and Z3. In: LPAR Workshops, vol. 418, pp. 123–132. Doha, Qatar (2008)
29. Protzenko, J., et al.: Evercrypt: a fast, verified, cross-platform cryptographic provider. In: 2020 IEEE Symposium on Security and Privacy (SP), pp. 983–1002. IEEE (2020)
30. Schoolderman, M.: Verifying branch-free assembly code in Why3. In: Paskevich, A., Wies, T. (eds.) VSTTE 2017. LNCS, vol. 10712, pp. 66–83. Springer, Cham (2017). https://doi.org/10.1007/978-3-319-72308-2_5
31. Schoolderman, M., Smetsers, S., van Eekelen, M.: Is deductive program verification mature enough to be taught to software engineers? In: Proceedings of the 8th Computer Science Education Research Conference, pp. 50–57. CSERC '19, Association for Computing Machinery, New York, NY, USA (2019)

32. Schwabe, P., Viguer, B., Weerweg, T., Wiedijk, F.: A Coq proof of the correctness of x25519 in TweetNaCl. In: 2021 IEEE 31th Computer Security Foundations Symposium (CSF). (to appear) (2021)
33. Velvindron, L., Baushke, M.D.: Increase the Secure Shell Minimum Recommended Diffie-Hellman Modulus Size to 2048 Bits. RFC 8270, December 2017. https://rfc-editor.org/rfc/rfc8270.txt
34. Zinzindohoué, J.K., Bhargavan, K., Protzenko, J., Beurdouche, B.: HACL*: a verified modern cryptographic library. In: ACM Conference on Computer and Communications Security (CCS). Dallas, United States, October 2017
35. Zinzindohoué, J.K., Bartzia, E., Bhargavan, K.: A verified extensible library of elliptic curves. In: 2016 IEEE 29th Computer Security Foundations Symposium (CSF), pp. 296–309 (2016)

A Formal Proof of the Lax Equivalence Theorem for Finite Difference Schemes

Mohit Tekriwal$^{(\boxtimes)}$, Karthik Duraisamy, and Jean-Baptiste Jeannin

University of Michigan, Ann Arbor, MI 48109, USA
{tmohit,kdur,jeannin}@umich.edu

Abstract. The behavior of physical systems is typically modeled using differential equations which are too complex to solve analytically. In practical problems, these equations are discretized on a computational domain, and numerical solutions are computed. A numerical scheme is called convergent, if in the limit of infinitesimal discretization, the bounds on the discretization error is also infinitesimally small. The approximate solution converges to the "true solution" in this limit. The Lax equivalence theorem enables a proof of convergence given consistency and stability of the method.

In this work, we formally prove the Lax equivalence theorem using the Coq Proof Assistant. We assume a continuous linear differential operator between complete normed spaces, and define an equivalent mapping in the discretized space. Given that the numerical method is consistent (i.e., the discretization error tends to zero as the discretization step tends to zero), and the method is stable (i.e., the error is uniformly bounded), we formally prove that the approximate solution converges to the true solution. We then demonstrate convergence of the difference scheme on an example problem by proving both its consistency and stability, and then applying the Lax equivalence theorem. In order to prove consistency, we use the Taylor–Lagrange theorem by formally showing that the discretization error is bounded above by the nth power of the discretization step, where n is the order of the truncated Taylor polynomial.

Keywords: Lax equivalence theorem · Finite difference scheme · Convergence · Taylor–lagrange theorem

1 Introduction

Physical systems are typically modeled by differential equations. For instance, the aerodynamics of an airplane can be represented by the Navier–Stokes equations [1], which are too complex to solve analytically.

Since analytical solutions are intractable for most practical problems of interest, numerical solutions are sought in a discretized domain. The process of discretization in space and time results in approximate solutions to the governing equations. A numerical scheme is called *convergent*, if in the limit of infinitesimal discretization, the bound on the discretization error is also infinitesimally

© Springer Nature Switzerland AG 2021
A. Dutle et al. (Eds.): NFM 2021, LNCS 12673, pp. 322–339, 2021.
https://doi.org/10.1007/978-3-030-76384-8_20

small. Under these conditions, the numerical solution converges or approaches the analytic solution. This idea is formally articulated by the Lax equivalence theorem [25], which states that if a numerical method is *consistent* and *stable*, then it is *convergent*.

Proofs of consistency, stability, and convergence are typically performed by hand, making them prone to possible errors. Formal verification of mathematical proofs provides a much higher level of confidence of the correctness of manual proofs. Further, formal verification offers a pathway to leverage mathematical constructs therein, and to extend these proofs to more complex scenarios.

Recently, much effort has been dedicated to the definition of mathematical structures such as metric spaces, normed spaces, derivatives, limits etc. in a formal setting using proof assistants such as Coq [8,16,27,30]. Using automatic provers and proof assistants, a number of works have emerged in the formalization of numerical analysis [5]. Pasca has formalized the properties of the Newton method [31]. Mayero et al. [28] presented a formal proof, developed in the Coq system, of the correctness of an automatic differentiation algorithm. Besides Coq, numerical analysis of ordinary differential equations has also been done in Isabelle/HOL [20]. Immler et al. [19,21,22], present a formalization of ordinary differential equations and the verification of rigorous (with guaranteed error bounds) numerical algorithms in the interactive theorem prover Isabelle/HOL. The formalization comprises flow and Poincaré map of dynamical systems. Immler [18] implements a functional algorithm that computes enclosures of solutions of ODEs in the interactive theorem prover Isabelle/HOL. In [9], Brehard et al. present a library to verify rigorous approximations of univariate functions on real numbers, with the Coq proof assistant. Brehard [11], worked on rigorous numerics that aims at providing certified representations for solutions of various problems, notably in functional analysis. Work has also been done in formalizing real analysis for polynomials [12]. Boldo and co-workers [4-6] have made important contributions to formal verification of finite difference schemes. They proved consistency, stability and convergence of a second-order centered scheme for the wave equation. However, the Lax equivalence theorem – sometimes referred to as the fundamental theorem of numerical analysis – which is central to finite difference schemes, has not been formally proven in the general case.

In this paper, we present a formal proof of the Lax equivalence theorem for a general family of finite difference schemes. We use the definitions of consistency and stability and prove convergence. To prove the consistency of a second-order centered scheme for the wave equation, Boldo et al. [6] made assumptions on the regularity of the exact solution. This regularity is expressed as the existence of Taylor approximations of the exact solution up to some appropriate order. Our formalization instead takes the Taylor–Lagrange theorem of [27], to prove the consistency of a finite difference scheme of any order. It should be noted that the order of accuracy of an explicit finite difference scheme depends on the number of points in the discretized domain (called *stencils*) appearing in the numerical derivative. Our approach is to carry the Taylor series expansion for each of those stencils using the Taylor–Lagrange theorem, and appropriately instantiate the order of the truncated polynomial, to achieve the desired order of accuracy. By incorporating the discretization error into the Lagrange remainder and proving an upper bound for the Lagrange remainder, we propose a rigorous method of proving consistency of a finite difference scheme.

Since the Lax equivalence theorem is an essential tool in the analysis of numerical schemes using finite differences, its formalization in the general case opens the door to the formalization and certification of finite difference-based numerical software. The present work will enable the formalization of convergence properties for a large class of finite difference numerical schemes, thereby providing formal proofs of convergence properties usually proved by hand, making explicit the underlying assumptions, and increasing the level of confidence in these proofs.

Overall this paper makes the following contributions:

- We provide a formalization in the Coq proof assistant of a general form of the Lax equivalence theorem.
- We prove consistency and stability of a second order accurate finite difference scheme for the example differential equation $\frac{d^2u}{dx^2} = 1$.
- We formally apply the Lax equivalence theorem on this finite difference scheme for the example differential equation, thereby formally proving convergence for this scheme.
- We also provide a generalized framework for a symmetric tri-diagonal (sparse) matrix in Coq. We define its eigen system and provide an explicit formulation of its inverse in Coq. We show that since the symmteric tri-diagonal matrix is normal, one can perform the stability analysis by just uniformly bounding the eigen values of the inverse. This is important because discretizations of mathematical model of physical systems are usually sparse [23].

This paper is structured as follows. In Sect. 2, we review the definitions of consistency, stability and convergence, state the Lax equivalence theorem [25, 32], and discuss its formalization in the Coq proof assistant. In Sect. 3, we discuss the consistency of a finite difference scheme. In particular, we consider the central difference approximation of the second derivative and formally prove the order of accuracy using the Taylor–Lagrange theorem in the Coq proof assistant. We also relate the pointwise consistency of the finite difference scheme with the Lax equivalence theorem, by instantiating it with an example. In Sect. 4, we discuss the generalized formalization of a symmetric tri-diagonal matrix and later instantiate it with the scheme to prove stability of the scheme. In Sect. 5, we apply the Lax equivalence theorem to the concrete finite difference scheme that we are considering. In Sect. 6, we conclude by summarizing key takeaways from the paper, and discussing future work.

2   Lax Equivalence Theorem

In this section, we review the definitions of consistency, stability and convergence, discuss the problem set up and state the Lax equivalence theorem [25]. In this paper and for the formalization, we choose to follow the presentation of Sanz-Serna and Palencia [32]. We also discuss the proof of the Lax equivalence theorem which is then formalized in the Coq proof assistant.

2.1 Consistency, Stability and Convergence

Definition 1 (The Continuous Problem [32]). *Let X (the space of solutions) and Y (the space of data) be normed spaces, both real or both complex. We consider a linear operator A with domain $D \subset X$ and range $R \subset Y$. The problem to be solved is of the form*

$$Au = f, \qquad f \in Y \qquad (1)$$

Here A is not assumed to be bounded, so that unbounded differential operators are included. The problem (1) is assumed to be well-posed, i.e., there exists a *bounded, linear operator*, $E \in B(Y, X)$, such that $EA = I$ in D, and that for $f \in Y$, Eq. (1) has a unique solution, $u = Ef$. Furthermore, the solution u depends continuously on the data.

Definition 2 (The Approximate Problem [32]). *Let H be a set of positive numbers such that 0 is the unique limit point of H. For each $h \in H$, let X_h, Y_h be normed spaces and consider the approximate or discretized problem*

$$A_h u_h = f_h, \qquad f_h \in Y_h \qquad (2)$$

where A_h is a linear operator $A_h : X_h \longrightarrow Y_h$.

We assume that for each $h \in H$, problem (2) is well-posed and there exists a solution operator, $E_h = A_h^{-1}$, i.e. $u_h = E_h f_h$. The true solution u and the approximate solution u_h can be related with each other by defining a *bounded, linear operator*, $r_h : X \to X_h$ for each $h \in H$. Similarly, data $f \in Y$ can be related to data in a discrete space, $f_h \in Y_h$ by defining a restriction operator s_h. For each $h \in H$, $s_h : Y \to Y_h$ is also a *bounded, linear operator*. We assume that the operator norms can be uniformly bounded:

$$||r_h|| \leq C_1, \qquad ||s_h|| \leq C_2, \qquad (3)$$

where the constants C_1, C_2 are independent of h. The true solution $u = Ef$ is compared with the discrete solution $u_h = E_h s_h f$ corresponding to the discretized datum f. The family $(X_h, Y_h, A_h, r_h, s_h)$ defines a *method* for the solution of (1) [32].

Definition 3 (Convergence [32]). *Let f be a given element in Y. The method $(X_h, Y_h, A_h, r_h, s_h)$ is convergent for the problem (1) if*

$$\lim_{h \to 0} ||r_h Ef - E_h s_h f||_{X_h} = 0 \qquad (4)$$

We say that the method is convergent if it is convergent for each problem (1) for any f in Y.

Intuitively, this means that in the limit of the discretization step, h, tending to zero, the numerical solution $E_h s_h f$ approaches the analytical solution $r_h E f$. The analytical solution $r_h E f$ is the restriction of the true (analytical) solution, $u = Ef$, onto the grid of size $N = 1/h$, and $E_h s_h f$ is the discrete solution, $u_h = E_h f_h$ computed on the grid of size N.

Definition 4 (Consistency [32]). *Let u be a given element in D. The method is consistent at u if*

$$\lim_{h \to 0} ||A_h r_h u - s_h A u||_{Y_h} = 0 \tag{5}$$

A method is consistent if it is consistent at each u in a set D_o such that the image $A(D_o)$ is dense in Y.

Intuitively, this means that in the limit of the discretization step, h, tending to zero, the finite difference scheme $A_h u_h = f_h$ approaches the differential equation $Au = f$, i.e., we are discretizing the right differential equation.

Definition 5 (Stability [32]). *The method is stable if there exists a constant K such that*

$$||E_h||_{B(Y_h, X_h)} \le K \tag{6}$$

Intuitively, stability of the numerical scheme means that a small numerical perturbation does not allow the solution to blow up. Uniform boundedness of the inverse $E_h = A_h^{-1}$ is a check on the conditioning of matrices (sensitivity to small perturbations), i.e., it ensures that the matrix A_h is not ill-conditioned. Thus, if the numerical problem (2) were unstable, even though we were trying to solve the right differential equation, we would never converge to the true solution. Hence, both stability and consistency are sufficient for proving convergence of the numerical scheme.

The quantities within the norms (4) and (5) are, respectively, the *global* and *local* discretization errors.

Theorem 1 (Lax Equivalence Theorem [32]). *Let $(X, Y, A, X_h, Y_h, A_h, r_h, s_h)$ be as above. If the method is consistent and stable, then it is convergent.*

Proof. We start with the definition of *convergence* in (4),

$$\lim_{h \to 0} ||r_h E f - E_h s_h f||_{X_h}$$

$$= \lim_{h \to 0} ||r_h u - E_h s_h f||_{X_h} \quad (u \stackrel{\Delta}{=} Ef)$$

$$= \lim_{h \to 0} ||r_h u - E_h s_h A u||_{X_h} \quad (f \stackrel{\Delta}{=} Au)$$

$$= \lim_{h \to 0} ||I r_h u - E_h s_h A u||_{X_h} \quad (r_h u = I r_h u)$$

$$= \lim_{h \to 0} ||E_h A_h r_h u - E_h s_h A u||_{X_h} \quad (E_h A_h \stackrel{\Delta}{=} I)$$

$$\le \lim_{h \to 0} ||E_h||_{B(Y_h, X_h)} ||(A_h r_h u - s_h A u)||_{Y_h}$$

$$\le K \lim_{h \to 0} ||(A_h r_h u - s_h A u)||_{Y_h} \quad \text{(From stability: (6))}$$

$$= 0 \quad \text{(From Consistency: (5))}$$

2.2 Formalization in the Coq Proof Assistant

In this Section we show how we formalized the proof of the Lax equivalence theorem [32] in the Coq proof assistant. All of the Coq formal proofs mentioned in this paper, containing the proofs of consistency, stability and convergence of finite difference schemes, and of the Lax equivalence theorem, are available at http://www-personal.umich.edu/~jeannin/papers/NFM21.zip.

The `Coquelicot` library [7,8] defines mathematical structures required for implementing the proof. Since we use the Coquelicot and standard reals libraries which are based on classical axiomatization of reals [8], our proofs are also non-constructive. We define the *Banach spaces* (complete normed spaces, complete in the metric defined by the norm [24]) (X, Y, X_h, Y_h) using a canonical structure, `CompleteNormedModule`, in Coq [16].

The definitions of the true problem (1) and the approximate problem (2) require that the mappings $A : X \to Y$ and $A_h : X_h \to Y_h$ be linear, and the solution operators $E : Y \to X$ and $E_h : Y_h \to X_h$ be linear and bounded. The linear mappings A_h and E_h are defined as functions of $h \in \mathbb{R}$. Boldo et al. [3] have defined linear mapping in the context of a `ModuleSpace` and bounded linear mapping in the context of a `NormedModule` in their formalization of the *Lax Milgram Theorem* in Coq [2,15]. We extended these definitions in the context of `CompleteNormedModule`.

The definition of *consistency* (5) and *convergence* (4) hold in the limit of h tending to zero. Thus, an important step in the proof is to express these limits in Coq. Formally, the notion of f tending to l at the limit point x requires, for any $\epsilon > 0$, to find a neighborhood V of x such that any point u of V satisfies $|f(u) - l| < \epsilon$ [8]. This notion has been formalized in `Coquelicot` [7] using the concept of *filters*. In topology, a filter is a set of sets, which is nonempty, upward closed, and closed under intersection [13]. It is commonly used to express the notion of convergence in topology. We have used a filter, `locally` x [26] to denote an open neighborhood of x, and predicate `filterlim` [26] to formalize the notion of convergence (in the context of limits) of f towards l at limit point x, i.e. $\lim_{x \to a} f(x) = l$. Therefore, the definition of consistency (5) is expressed as:

```
(is_lim (fun h:R => norm (minus (Ah h (rh h u)) (sh h (A u)))) 0 0
```

where the limits of functions is expressed using `is_lim` [8].

We next discuss the formalization of the statement of convergence of a finite difference scheme in Coq. We note that from Theorem 1, *consistency* and *stability* imply *convergence*. This notion is expressed in Coq as follows:

```
(is_lim (fun h:R => norm (minus (Ah h (rh h u)) (sh h (A u)))) 0 0
     (*Consistency*) /\
(exists K:R , forall (h:R), operator_norm(Eh h)<=K ) (* Stability*) ->
is_lim(fun h:R=>norm (minus (rh h (E(f))) (Eh h (sh h (f)))))) 0 0)
     (*Convergence*).
```

where the *operator norm* is defined as $\|f\|_\phi = sup_{u \neq 0_E \wedge \phi(u)} \frac{\|f(u)\|_F}{\|u\|_E}$ and has been formally defined in [3].

The basic idea is that we bound the *global discretization error* ($||r_h Ef -$ $E_h s_h f||$) above using the stability criterion, i.e. $||r_h Ef - E_h s_h f|| \leq K||A_h r_h u - s_h Au||$, and then prove that as the *local discretization error* ($||A_h r_h u - s_h Au||$) tends to zero in the limit of h tending to zero, the upper bound on the global discretization error tends to zero (using the property of limits). Using the property of norm , i.e. $0 \leq ||r_h Ef - E_h s_h f||$, we arrive at the inequality

$$0 \leq ||r_h Ef - E_h s_h f|| \leq K||A_h r_h u - s_h Au||$$

In Coq, we define the lower bound of the inequality as a constant function with value 0 as: `fun _ => 0`. Since the limit of a constant function is the constant itself, i.e. $\lim_{h \to 0} 0 = 0$, and $\lim_{h \to 0} ||A_h r_h u - s_h Au|| = 0$ (Consistency), using the *sandwich theorem* for limits, $\lim_{h \to 0} ||r_h Ef - E_h s_h f|| = 0$. The *sandwich theorem* states that if we have functions obeying the inequality: $f(x) \leq g(x) \leq h(x)$ and $\lim_{x \to a} f(x) = L \quad \wedge \quad \lim_{x \to a} h(x) = L$ on some open neighborhood of $x = a$, then $\lim_{x \to a} g(x) = L$. This proves the convergence of Definition 4 and completes the proof of the Lax equivalence theorem.

3   Proof of Consistency of a Sample Finite Difference Scheme

A finite difference scheme (FD) approximates a differential equation with a difference equation. The derivatives are expressed in terms of function values at finite number of points in the dicretized domain. For instance, consider a simple differential equation, $\frac{d^2 u}{dx^2} = 1$ on a domain $x \in (0, L)$ with boundary conditions $u(0) = 0$ and $u(L) = 0$, where L is the length of the domain. A second order accurate finite difference approximation would be $\frac{u(x+\Delta x) - 2u(x) + u(x - \Delta x)}{\Delta x^2} = 1$, where Δx is the discretization step and x is the point at which the difference equation is evaluated. We will refer to this as numerical scheme $\mathcal{N}_h$. Since we are computing a numerical approximation to the actual derivatives, we are interested in knowing the order of the discretization error.

Definition 6 (Discretization Error). *Let $D(u)$ denote the true derivative of a function $u : \mathbb{R} \to \mathbb{R}$ and $N(u)$ denote the finite difference approximation of the true derivative. The discretization error (commonly referred to as the truncation error) (τ) is then defined as:*

$$\tau \stackrel{\Delta}{=} D(u) - N(u) \tag{7}$$

If the function u is *analytic*, it can be expressed as a *Taylor series expansion* at the point of evaluation. The truncation error is then evaluated by expressing the numerical derivatives in terms of a truncated Taylor polynomial and then taking a difference of the true derivative and the numerical derivative. This gives us an upper bound on the discretization error. If a numerical method is consistent, the truncation error can be expressed as:

$$\tau = \mathcal{O}(\Delta x^n)$$

when Δx tends to zero, and where n is the order of the truncated Taylor polynomial. We use this idea to formalize the proof of consistency of a finite difference scheme. This requires the use of an important theorem from calculus, the Taylor–Lagrange theorem.

Theorem 2 (Taylor–Lagrange Theorem). *Suppose that f is $n + 1$ times differentiable on some interval containing the center of convergence c and x, and let $P_n(x) = f(c) + \frac{f^{(1)}(c)}{1!}(x - c) + \frac{f^2(c)}{2!}(x - c)^2 + .. + \frac{f^{(n)}(c)}{n!}(x - c)^n$ be the nth order Taylor polynomial of f at $x = c$. Then $f(x) = P_n(x) + E_n(x)$ where $E_n(x)$ is the error term of $P_n(x)$ from $f(x)$. i.e. $E_n = f(x) - P_n(x)$, and for ξ between c and x, the Lagrange remainder form of the error E_n is given by the formula $E_n(x) = \frac{f^{n+1}(\xi)}{(n+1)!}(x - c)^{(n+1)}$.*

Martin-Dorel et al. [27] proved the Taylor–Lagrange theorem formally in Coq, and it is available in the `Coq.Interval` library [10,29]. We used this formalization of the Taylor–Lagrange theorem to prove the consistency of a finite difference scheme.

We will specifically prove that for a central difference approximation of the second derivative, $\frac{d^2u}{dx^2}$, expressed as: $\frac{u(x+\Delta x)-2u(x)+u(x-\Delta x)}{(\Delta x)^2}$, the truncation error τ is quadratic in Δx:

$$\tau = \left| \frac{d^2u}{dx^2} - \frac{u(x + \Delta x) - 2u(x) + u(x - \Delta x)}{(\Delta x)^2} \right| = \mathcal{O}(\Delta x^2)$$

3.1 Proof of Consistency for the Finite Difference Scheme

We want to prove that for a central difference approximation of the second derivative in the numerical scheme $\mathcal{N}_h$, the truncation error, $\tau = \mathcal{O}(\Delta x^2)$. By invoking the definition of Big-O notation, the theorem statement can be stated as:

$$\exists \gamma > 0, \Gamma > 0, \left| \frac{d^2u}{dx^2} - \frac{u(x + \Delta x) - 2u(x) + u(x - \Delta x)}{(\Delta x)^2} \right| \le \Gamma(\Delta x^2), \ 0 < |\Delta x| < \gamma. \quad (8)$$

The Eq. (8) is stated formally in Coq as:

```
Theorem taylor_FD (x:R): Oab x ->exists gamma:R, gamma >0 /\ exists G:R,
G>0/\ forall dx:R, dx>0 -> Oab (x+dx) -> Oab (x-dx)->(dx< gamma ->
Rabs((D 0 (x+dx)- 2*(D 0 x) + D 0 (x-dx))*/(dx * dx)- D 2 x)<= G*(dx^2)).
```

where `Oab x` mean $a < x < b$ and `D k x` denotes k^{th} derivative of u with respect to x.

We start by introducing the following lemmas required to complete the proof.

Lemma 1 ($|F(x)| \sim \mathcal{O}(\Delta x)^4$). $\forall x \in (a, b), \exists \eta \in \mathbb{R}, \eta > 0 \wedge \exists M \in \mathbb{R}, M > 0 \wedge \forall \Delta x \in \mathbb{R}, \Delta x > 0 \to (x + \Delta x) \in (a, b) \to \Delta x < \eta \to |F(x)| \le M(\Delta x)^4$.

Here, $F(x)$ is the Lagrange remainder in the expansion of $u(x + \Delta x)$ up to degree 3 and is defined as:

$$F(x) \triangleq u(x + \Delta x) - u(x) - \Delta x \frac{du}{dx}\Big|_x - \frac{1}{2!}(\Delta x)^2 \frac{d^2 u}{dx^2}\Big|_x - \frac{1}{3!}(\Delta x)^3 \frac{d^3 u}{dx^3}\Big|_x \quad (9)$$

Thus, Lemma 1 states that the Lagrange remainder $F(x) = \frac{1}{4!}(\Delta x)^4 \frac{d^4 u(\xi)}{dx^4}$ is of order $(\Delta x)^4$ for all $\xi \in (x, x + \Delta x)$.

Lemma 2 $(|G(x)| \sim \mathcal{O}(\Delta x)^4)$. $\forall x \in (a, b), \exists \delta \in \mathbb{R}, \delta > 0 \wedge \exists K \in \mathbb{R}, K > 0 \wedge \forall \Delta x \in \mathbb{R}, \Delta x > 0 \rightarrow (x - \Delta x) \in (a, b) \rightarrow \Delta x < \delta \rightarrow |G(x)| \leq K(\Delta x)^4$.

Here, $G(x)$ is the Lagrange remainder in the expansion of $u(x - \Delta x)$ up to degree 3 and is defined as:

$$G(x) \triangleq u(x - \Delta x) - u(x) + \Delta x \frac{du}{dx}\Big|_x - \frac{1}{2!}(\Delta x)^2 \frac{d^2 u}{dx^2}\Big|_x + \frac{1}{3!}(\Delta x)^3 \frac{d^3 u}{dx^3}\Big|_x \quad (10)$$

Thus, Lemma 2 states that the Lagrange remainder $G(x) = \frac{1}{4!}(\Delta x)^4 \frac{d^4 u(\xi)}{dx^4}$ is of order $(\Delta x)^4$ for all $\xi \in (x - \Delta x, x)$.

Both the lemmas are a straightforward application of the Taylor–Lagrange theorem (Theorem 2), and are crucial to the formalization of the proof of the consistency of the finite difference scheme.

Next, we present an informal proof of the theorem followed by a discussion on the formal proof of the consistency theorem.

Proof.

$$|F(x)| \leq M(\Delta x)^4 \quad \text{[From Lemma 1]} \quad (11)$$

$$|G(x)| \leq K(\Delta x)^4 \quad \text{[From Lemma 2]} \quad (12)$$

Adding Eqs. (11) and (12), we get:

$$|F(x)| + |G(x)| \leq (M + K)(\Delta x)^4$$
$$\implies |F(x) + G(x)| \leq (M + K)(\Delta x)^4$$
$$\text{[Using the triangle inequality, } (|F(x) + G(x)| \leq |F(x)| + |G(x)|) \text{]}$$
$$\implies |F(x) + G(x)| \leq \Gamma(\Delta x)^4 \quad (\text{Instantiating}\, \Gamma := M + K) \quad (13)$$

Unfolding the definitions $F(x)$ and $G(x)$, and doing the algebra we get:

$$\left| u(x + \Delta x) - 2u(x) + u(x - \Delta x) - (\Delta x)^2 \frac{d^2 u}{dx^2} \right| \leq \Gamma(\Delta x^4)$$

$$\implies \left| \frac{u(x + \Delta x) - 2u(x) + u(x - \Delta x)}{(\Delta x)^2} - \frac{d^2 u}{dx^2} \right| \leq \Gamma(\Delta x^2) \quad \text{[QED]} \quad (14)$$

An important point to note is that the condition $|F(x)| + |G(x)| \leq M(\Delta x)^4 + K(\Delta x)^4$ holds when $0 < |\Delta x| < \gamma$, where γ is as defined in (8). We therefore choose, $\gamma = min(\eta, \delta)$, where η is such that, $|F(x)| \leq M(\Delta x)^4$ holds when $0 < |\Delta x| < \eta$, and δ is such that, $|G(x)| \leq K(\Delta x)^4$ holds when $0 < |\Delta x| < \delta$.

3.2 Formalization in the Coq Proof Assistant

We followed the proof above and formalized it in the Coq proof assistant. To apply the Taylor–Lagrange theorem [27] to the consistency analysis of a central difference approximation, we broke down the theorem statement into two lemmas as discussed in the previous section. Therefore, in this section, we will discuss the proof of Lemma 1 and 2.

Proof of Lemma 1: Formally Lemma 1 is stated in Coq as:

```
Lemma taylor_uupper (x:R): Oab x-> exists eta: R, eta>0 /\
    exists M :R, M>0  /\ forall dx:R, dx>0 -> Oab (x+dx) ->
    (dx<eta -> Rabs(D 0 (x+dx)- Tsum 3 x (x+dx))<=M*(dx^4)).
```

In the proof of the Lemma, existential quantification associated with η and M has to be addressed. We chose η as $b - x$, since the interval in which we are studying Taylor–Lagrange for $u(x + \Delta x)$ is $[x, b]$. Since $\Delta x \in (x, b)$ and $\Delta x < \eta$, it seems logical to chose $\eta = b - x$. For the choice of M, we obtained extreme bounds in the interval. Since the function u and its derivatives are continuous in a compact set $[x, b]$, we are guaranteed to get maximum and minimum values. In Coq, we applied the lemma `continuity_ab_max` to obtain a maximum value, $\left(\frac{d^4 u}{dx^4}\right)_{max} = \frac{d^4 u(F)}{dx^4}$ such that $\frac{d^4 u(\xi)}{dx^4} \leq \frac{d^4 u(F)}{dx^4}, \forall \xi \in [x, b]$. Similarly, we apply the lemma `continuity_ab_min` to obtain a minimum value, $\left(\frac{d^4 u}{dx^4}\right)_{min} = \frac{d^4 u(G)}{dx^4}$ such that $\frac{d^4 u(G)}{dx^4} \leq \frac{d^4 u(\xi)}{dx^4}, \forall \xi \in [x, b]$.

Thus, M is chosen as $M = max\left(\left|\frac{d^4 u(G)}{dx^4}\right|, \left|\frac{d^4 u(F)}{dx^4}\right|\right)$. With this choice of M, we can bound the Lagrange remainder or the trunction error from above and thus prove Lemma 1.

Proof of Lemma 2: Formally Lemma 2 is stated in Coq as:

```
Lemma taylor_ulower (x:R): Oab x -> exists delta: R, delta>0 /\
    exists K :R, K>0 /\ forall dx:R, dx>0 ->Oab (x-dx) ->
    (dx<delta -> Rabs(D 0 (x-dx)-Tsum 3 x (x-dx))<=K*(dx^4)).
```

The proof of Lemma 2 follows the same approach as that of Lemma 1. Here, we chose δ as $x - a$, since the interval in which we are studying Taylor–Lagrange theorem for $u(x - \Delta x)$, $\Delta x \in (a, x)$, and $\Delta x < \delta$. We chose K in the same way as we chose M in Lemma 1 except that the interval in which we obtain maximum and minimum values for $\frac{d^4 u}{dx^4}$ is $[a, x]$ in this case. Thus, $\left(\frac{d^4 u}{dx^4}\right)_{min} = \frac{d^4 u(G)}{dx^4}$, $\left(\frac{d^4 u}{dx^4}\right)_{max} = \frac{d^4 u(F)}{dx^4}$, and $K = max\left(\left|\frac{d^4 u(G)}{dx^4}\right|, \left|\frac{d^4 u(F)}{dx^4}\right|\right), \forall c \in [a, x]$.

To prove the main theorem statement on consistency, we break the statement into Lemma 1 and 2, by instantiating $\Gamma = M + K$, and $\gamma = \min(\eta, \delta)$, where (M, η) and (K, δ) have been defined as in Lemma 1 and 2 respectively, in the manner shown in Sect. (3.1). To implement this instantiation, we have to carefully *destruct* the lemmas introduced in the theorem statement. Then, we simply apply lemma 1 and 2, to complete the main proof.

3.3 Relating Pointwise Consistency to the Lax Equivalence Theorem

In this section, we relate the proof of consistency from Sect. 3.1 with the Lax equivalence Theorem 1. The numerical discretization of the differential equation can be expressed in the discrete domain as:

$$
\frac{1}{h^2}
\underbrace{
\begin{bmatrix}
1 & 0 & 0 & 0 & \dots & 0 \\
1 & -2 & 1 & 0 & \dots & 0 \\
\vdots & \ddots & \ddots & \ddots & & \vdots \\
0 & \dots & 1 & -2 & 1 & 0 \\
0 & \dots & 0 & 1 & -2 & 1 \\
0 & \dots & 0 & 0 & 0 & 1
\end{bmatrix}
}_{A_h}
\underbrace{
\begin{bmatrix}
u_o \\ u_1 \\ \vdots \\ u_{N-2} \\ u_{N-1} \\ u_N
\end{bmatrix}
}_{r_h u}
=
\underbrace{
\begin{bmatrix}
0 \\ 1 \\ \vdots \\ 1 \\ 1 \\ 0
\end{bmatrix}
}_{s_h A u}
\tag{15}
$$

Comparing with the statement of consistency (5), we have

$$
\lim_{h \to 0}
\left\|
\frac{1}{h^2}
\begin{bmatrix}
1 & 0 & 0 & 0 & \dots & 0 \\
1 & -2 & 1 & 0 & \dots & 0 \\
\vdots & \ddots & \ddots & \ddots & & \vdots \\
0 & \dots & 1 & -2 & 1 & 0 \\
0 & \dots & 0 & 1 & -2 & 1 \\
0 & \dots & 0 & 0 & 0 & 1
\end{bmatrix}
\begin{bmatrix}
u_o \\ u_1 \\ \vdots \\ u_{N-2} \\ u_{N-1} \\ u_N
\end{bmatrix}
-
\begin{bmatrix}
0 \\ 1 \\ \vdots \\ 1 \\ 1 \\ 0
\end{bmatrix}
\right\|
=
\lim_{h \to 0}
\left\|
\begin{bmatrix}
\frac{u_o}{h^2} \\
\frac{u_o - 2u_1 + u_2}{h^2} - 1 \\
\frac{u_1 - 2u_2 + u_3}{h^2} - 1 \\
\vdots \\
\frac{u_{N-2} - 2u_{N-1} + u_N}{h^2} - 1 \\
\frac{u_N}{h^2}
\end{bmatrix}
\right\|
= 0
\tag{16}
$$

Taking the vector norm in the L_1 sense, $||.||_1$, Eq. (16) can be written as:

$$
\lim_{h \to 0}
\left[
\left| \frac{u_o}{h^2} \right|
+ \left| \frac{u_o - 2u_1 + u_2}{h^2} - 1 \right|
+ .. +
\left| \frac{u_{N-2} - 2u_{N-1} + u_N}{h^2} - 1 \right|
+ \left| \frac{u_N}{h^2} \right|
\right] = 0
\tag{17}
$$

$\lim_{h \to 0} \frac{u_o}{h^2} = 0$ and $\lim_{h \to 0} \frac{u_N}{h^2} = 0$, trivially because of the boundary conditions we imposed, i.e. $u_o = 0$ and $u_N = 0$. The norm used in (16) are in the space Y_h, i.e., $||.||_{Y_h}$.

This reduces to proving:

$$
\sum_{i=1}^{N-1} \lim_{h \to 0} \left| \frac{u_{i-1} - 2u_i + u_{i+1}}{h^2} - 1 \right| = 0
\tag{18}
$$

But from the Taylor–Lagrange analysis discussed in Sect. (3.1), we have

$$
\left| \frac{u_{i-1} - 2u_i + u_{i+1}}{h^2} - \frac{d^2 u}{dx^2} \Big|_{x_i} \right| \le Ch^2
\tag{19}
$$

where C is a constant, and $u_i = u(x_i), u_{i-1} = u(x_i - h), u_{i+1} = u(x_i + h)$. Substituting $\frac{d^2 u}{dx^2}\Big|_{x_i} = 1$, and using the inequality (19) and Eq. (18), we get

$$
\sum_{i=1}^{N-1} 0 \le \sum_{i=1}^{N-1} \lim_{h \to 0} \left| \frac{u_{i-1} - 2u_i + u_{i+1}}{h^2} - 1 \right| \le \sum_{i=1}^{N-1} \lim_{h \to 0} |Ch^2|
\tag{20}
$$

But, $\sum_{i=1}^{N-1} \lim_{h\to 0} |Ch^2| = 0$. Hence, using the sandwich theorem, we prove that

$$\sum_{i=1}^{N-1} \lim_{h\to 0} \left| \frac{u_{i-1} - 2u_i + u_{i+1}}{h^2} - 1 \right| = 0 \quad [\textbf{QED}]$$

3.4 Formalization in Coq

In order to represent, x_i, $i = 0..N$, we define x of type: nat → R. The boundary conditions are imposed as hypothesis statements:

```
Hypothesis u_0 :  (D 0 (x 0))= 0.
Hypothesis u_N: (D 0 (x N)) =0.
```

The differential equation is defined as:

```
Hypothesis u_2x: forall i:nat, (D 2 (x i)) =1.
```

Equation (18) is formalized as a lemma statement:

```
Lemma lim_sum:is_lim (fun h:R =>
  sum_n_m (fun i:nat =>Rabs (( D 0 (x i -h) -2* (D 0 (x i))
  + D 0 (x i +h))*/(h^2) -1)) 1%nat (pred N)) 0 0.
```

This is where we integrate the proof of pointwise consistency of the FD scheme from Sect. (3).

The main theorem statement which is an application of the statement of consistency required in the proof of Lax equivalence theorem from Sect. (2) is as follows:

```
Theorem consistency_inst: forall (U:X) (f:Y) (h:R) (uh: Xh h)
  (rh: forall (h:R), X -> (Xh h)) (sh: forall (h:R), Y->(Yh h))
  (E: Y->X) (Eh:forall (h:R),(Yh h)->(Xh h)),
  is_lim (fun h:R => norm (minus (Ah h (rh h U)) (sh h (A U)))) 0 0.
```

We note here that the above-mentioned formalization is not unique to the second order scheme that we discussed. The approach we discuss can easily be generalized to verify consistency of any finite difference scheme. The crucial step in such a generalization is the appropriate instantiation of the A_h matrix and the vectors $r_h u$ and $s_h Au$.

4 Stability of the Scheme

In this section we discuss the stability of the scheme $\mathcal{N}_h$. From Sect. 2, stability of a numerical scheme requires the solution operator $E_h = A_h^{-1}$ to be uniformly bounded. We prove this by bounding the eigenvalues of E_h uniformly. Eigenvalues of E_h are just inverse of the eigenvalues of A_h. A formal proof of this can be referred to in the companion technical report [33].

We will first discuss a generalized framework for the formalization of stability for a symmetric tri-diagonal matrix in Coq. We denote this matrix with

$A_h(a, b, c)$ with $c = a$ for symmetry. This notation means that b is on the diagonal, c is on the upper diagonal and a is on the lower diagonal. All the other entries are zero. Since we are treating stability from a spectral viewpoint, we next discuss the formalization of the Eigen system for $A_h(a, b, a)$.

4.1 Lemma to Verify that the Eigenvalues and Eigenvectors Belong to the Spectrum of $A_h(a, b, a)$

Analytical expressions for the eigenvalues and eigenvectors of $A_h(a, b, c)$ are given by:

$$\lambda_m = b + 2\sqrt{ac}\cos\left[\frac{m\pi}{N+1}\right]; \quad s_m = (s_j)_m = \left[\frac{a}{c}\right]^{j-1/2}\sqrt{\frac{2}{N+1}}\sin\left[j\frac{m\pi}{N+1}\right]$$

$\forall m, j = 1..N$. In Coq, we defined λ_m and s_m as follows:

```
Definition Eigen_vec (m N:nat) (a b c:R):= mk_matrix N 1%nat (fun i j =>
    sqrt ( 2 / INR (N+1))*(Rpower (a */c) (INR i +1 -1*/2))*
        sin(((INR i +1)*INR(m+1)*PI)*/INR (N+1))).

Definition Lambda (m N:nat) (a b c:R):= mk_matrix 1%nat 1%nat (fun i j =>
    b + 2* sqrt(a*c)* cos ( (INR (m+1) * PI)*/INR(N+1))).
```

Since naturals in Coq start with 0, we write INR (m+1) and INR i+1.

We then formally verify that the analytical expressions for the pair (λ_m, s_m) indeed belong to the spectrum of A_h. From now on, we will refer to $A_h(a, b, a)$ as A_h for the sake of brevity. In Coq, we state this formally as:

```
Lemma eigen_belongs (a b c:R): forall (m N:nat), (2 < N)%nat ->
    (0 <= m < N)%nat -> a=c /\ 0<c-> (LHS m N a b c) = (RHS m N a b c).
```

where, $LHS \triangleq A_h s_m$ and $RHS \triangleq s_m \lambda_m$. Here we used the definition of eigenvalue-eigenvector, i.e., $A_h s_m \triangleq \lambda_m s_m$. Formalizing the proof of the lemma eigen_belongs was challenging due to the structure of the matrix A_h. A_h is a tri-diagonal matrix with non-zero entries on the diagonal, sub-diagonal and super-diagonal. The other entries are zero and hence the matrix is sparse.

$$\therefore \underbrace{\sum_{j=0}^{N-1} A_h(i, j)s_m(i)}_{A_h(i,j)\neq 0} + \underbrace{\sum_{j=0}^{N-1} A_h(i, j)s_m(i)}_{A_h(i,j)=0} = \lambda_m s_m(i); \quad 0 \leq i \leq N - 1 \quad (21)$$

In Coq, we have to carefully destruct the matrix A_h to separate the non-zero and zero sums in the LHS of Eq. (21). The idea is to do a case analysis on the row-index i. Details on the formal proof of the zero and non-zero cases are presented in the companion technical report [33].

Next, we discuss formalization of the boundedness of the matrix norm of $E_h = A_h^{-1}$. We have used an explicit formulation of A_h^{-1} [17] in our formalization and we verify this formally using the definition: $A_h^{-1}A_h = I \land A_h A_h^{-1} = I$. Details on the proof can also be found in the in the companion technical report [33].

4.2   Lemma on the Boundedness of the Matrix Norm for Scheme $\mathcal{N}_h$

Here, we have used the definition of the spectral (2-norm): $||A||_2 = \rho(A)$, where $\rho(A)$ is the spectral radius of A and is defined as the maximum eigen-value of A, i.e. $\rho(A) = max_m |\lambda_m(A)|$. For the symmetric tri-diagonal matrix A_h, $A = E_h$ and $\lambda_m(E_h) = 1/\lambda_m(A_h)$. Since $\lambda_m(A_h) < 0$, $max_m |\lambda_m(E_h)| = 1/|\lambda_{min}(A_h)|$. Hence, we define the matrix norm in Coq as follows:

```
Definition matrix_norm (N:nat):= 1/ Rabs (Lambda_min N).
```

To show that the matrix norm is uniformly bounded, we need to show that $1/|\lambda_{min}(A_h)|$ is uniformly bounded. This is where we instantiate the tri-diagonal matrix A_h with the scheme $\mathcal{N}_h$. Thus, we prove the following lemma in Coq:

```
Lemma spectral: forall(N:nat),(2<N)%nat -> 1/Rabs(Lambda_min N) <= L^2/4.
```

where L is the length of the domain, independent of h, and is constant throughout. Lambda_min is the minimum eigenvalue for the instantiated matrix, $A'_h = A_h(\frac{1}{h^2}, \frac{-2}{h^2}, \frac{1}{h^2})$. We provide a paper proof of this bound in the companion technical report [33].

To show that all the eigenvalues have the same bound, we prove that $\frac{1}{\lambda_{min}(A'_h)}$ is the maximum eigenvalue of E'_h. The lemma statement is as follows:

```
Lemma eigen_relation: forall (i N:nat), (2<N)%nat ->(0<=i<N)%nat ->
    Rabs (lam i N) <= 1/ Rabs( Lambda_min N).
```

This completes the proof on the boundedness of the eigenvalues of E'_h. The lemma, eigen_relation also shows that the spectral radius of E'_h is $\frac{1}{|\lambda_{min}(A'_h)|}$, and justifies the defintion of matrix_norm.

We note that the definition of the matrix norm of A_h^{-1} is valid only if A_h^{-1} is a normal matrix. We therefore verify that A_h^{-1} is normal. We also provide the proof that A_h is diagonalizable. This helps us to formally establish that the eigen vectors are orthogonal and hence the eigen space is complete. Both the proofs can be found in the companion technical report [33].

4.3   Main Stability Theorem

In this section, we integrate all of the previous lemmas to prove the main stability theorem (6).

```
Theorem stability: forall (u:X) (f:Y) (h:R) (uh: Xh h)
    (rh: forall (h:R), X -> (Xh h))(sh: forall (h:R), Y->(Yh h))
    (E: Y->X) (Eh:forall (h:R), (Yh h)->(Xh h)),
    exists K:R , forall (h:R), operator_norm(Eh h)<=K.
```

where the operator norm is instantiated with the matrix norm using the following hypothesis:

```
Hypothesis mat_op_norm: forall (u:X) (f:Y) (h:R) (uh: Xh h)
    (rh: forall (h:R), X -> (Xh h))(sh: forall (h:R), Y->(Yh h))
    (E: Y->X) (Eh:forall (h:R),(Yh h)->(Xh h)),
    operator_norm (Eh h) = matrix_norm m.
```

5   Application of the Lax Equivalence Theorem to the Example Problem

In this section, we apply the Lax equivalence theorem that we proved in Sect. 2 to a concrete differential equation $\frac{d^2u}{dx^2} = 1$ and the numerical scheme $\mathcal{N}_h$ given by $\frac{u_{i+1} - 2u_i + u_{i-1}}{\Delta x^2} = 1$. We recall that the proof of convergence using the Lax equivalence theorem requires that the difference scheme is consistent with respect to the differential equation and is stable. We discussed the proof of consistency of the scheme in Sect. 3 and the stability in Sect. 4. Thus, we apply these proofs to complete the proof of convergence for the scheme. We provide the theorem statement to verify convergence of the scheme in the companion technical report [33].

6   Conclusion and Future Work

This work investigated the formalization of convergence, stability and consistency of a finite difference scheme in the Coq proof assistant. Any continuously differentiable function can be approximated by a Taylor polynomial. The Lagrange remainder of a Taylor series provides an estimate of the truncation error and we formally proved that this error can be bound by n^{th} power of the discretization step, Δx, where $n - 1$ is the order of the Taylor polynomial. We implemented the proof of the consistency of a finite difference scheme by breaking down the theorem statement into lemmas, each corresponding to function values at points neighboring the point of evaluation. These lemmas were proved individually by applying the Taylor–Lagrange theorem, the proof of which is already formalized in the `Coq.Interval` library [27]. Consistency and stability guarantees convergence as stated by the Lax equivalence theorem. Following the proof of the Lax equivalence theorem, we formally proved convergence of a specific finite difference scheme. Specifically, we proved that the global discretization error could be bounded above by a constant times the local discretization error. Then, by applying the sandwich theorem for limits, we proved that the convergence condition is satisfied in the limit $\Delta x \to 0$. In the process of formalizing the proof of stability for the numerical scheme, we also developed tools for linear algebra and spectral theory, for the `Coquelicot` definition of matrices in Coq, which can be reused. As noted earlier, the approach we follow is not specific to the sample numerical scheme, but can be easily extended to other numerical schemes with appropriate instantiation of the matrix A_h, and vectors, $r_h u$, $s_h A u$. Formalization of the proof of orthogonality of the eigenvectors helped us report the missing constant $\sqrt{\frac{2}{N+1}}$ in s_m that occurs in most textbooks/literature on numerical analysis.

This work considered the impact of the discretization error on the convergence of a numerical method to the exact solution. In a practical setting, floating point errors have to be also accounted for, as an accumulation of such errors can lead to deviations from the true solution. In future work, we will extend our results to incorporate floating point errors and their impact on the convergence of finite difference numerical schemes. We also plan on working with iterative solvers, which would be an extension of our current work on direct solvers (explicit inversion of the matrix A_h). We also plan on working with the Frama-C toolkit [14] for verification of existing programs and be able to discharge the generated verification conditions using the Coq proofs we present in this paper.

6.1 Effort and Challenges

The total length of the Coq code and proofs is about 14,000 lines, of which about 1,200 lines are specific to the scheme. The rest of the formalization can be reused for a generic symmetric tridiagonal matrix. It took us about 15 months for the entire formalization. Much of the effort was spent on destructing the matrices and developing required linear algebra tools to handle the matrix manipulation. Since we are treating stability from a spectral point of view, lack of spectral theory for numerical analysis for the `Coquelicot` definition of matrices has been challenging for us. For the proof of consistency, the primary challenge was the right placement of the quantifiers to bound the Lagrange remainder using the definition of big-O notation. To instantiate $\Gamma = M + K$, we had to carefully destruct the lemmas into the main theorem. We believe that a generic library with an automated implementation of the big-O definitions would save considerable effort here. We also encountered issues in selecting appropriate instantiations for other existential parameters. In the proof of convergence, we had to carefully construct the application of properties of limit with filters of neighborhoods.

References

1. Navier-stokes equations. https://www.grc.nasa.gov/WWW/k-12/airplane/nseqs. html. Accessed 20 Sep 2020
2. Boldo, S., Clément, F., Faissole, F., Martin, V., Mayero, M.: Elfic Coq library for formalization of Lax-Milgram theorem. https://www.lri.fr/sboldo/elfic/index. html. Accessed 20 Sep 2020
3. Boldo, S., Clément, F., Faissole, F., Martin, V., Mayero, M.: A Coq formal proof of the Lax-Milgram theorem. In: Proceedings of the 6th ACM SIGPLAN Conference on Certified Programs and Proofs, pp. 79–89. ACM (2017)
4. Boldo, S., Clément, F., Filliâtre, J.-C., Mayero, M., Melquiond, G., Weis, P.: Formal proof of a wave equation resolution scheme: the method error. In: Kaufmann, M., Paulson, L.C. (eds.) ITP 2010. LNCS, vol. 6172, pp. 147–162. Springer, Heidelberg (2010). https://doi.org/10.1007/978-3-642-14052-5_12
5. Boldo, S., Clément, F., Filliâtre, J.C., Mayero, M., Melquiond, G., Weis, P.: Wave equation numerical resolution: a comprehensive mechanized proof of a c program. J. Autom. Reasoning **50**(4), 423–456 (2013)
6. Boldo, S., Clément, F., Filliâtre, J.C., Mayero, M., Melquiond, G., Weis, P.: Trusting computations: a mechanized proof from partial differential equations to actual program. Comput. Math. Appl. **68**(3), 325–352 (2014)
7. Boldo, S., Lelay, C., Melquiond, G.: Hierarchy Coq library. http://coquelicot. saclay.inria.fr/html/Coquelicot.Hierarchy.html. Accessed 20 Sep 2020

8. Boldo, S., Lelay, C., Melquiond, G.: Coquelicot: a user-friendly library of real analysis for Coq. Math. Comput. Sci. **9**(1), 41–62 (2015)
9. Bréhard, F., Mahboubi, A., Pous, D.: A certificate-based approach to formally verified approximations. In: ITP 2019-Tenth International Conference on Interactive Theorem Proving, pp. 1–19 (2019)
10. Brisebarre, N., et al.: Rigorous polynomial approximation using taylor models in Coq. In: Goodloe, A.E., Person, S. (eds.) NFM 2012. LNCS, vol. 7226, pp. 85–99. Springer, Heidelberg (2012). https://doi.org/10.1007/978-3-642-28891-3_9
11. Bréhard, F.: Numerical computation certified in functional spaces: A trilogue between rigorous polynomial approximations, symbolic computation and formal proof. Ph.D. thesis (2019)
12. Cohen, C.: Formalizing real analysis for polynomials (2010)
13. Cohen, C., Rouhling, D.: A formal proof in Coq of lasalle's invariance principle. In: Ayala-Rincón, M., Muñoz, C.A. (eds.) ITP 2017. LNCS, vol. 10499, pp. 148–163. Springer, Cham (2017). https://doi.org/10.1007/978-3-319-66107-0_10
14. Eleftherakis, G., Hinchey, M., Holcombe, M. (eds.): SEFM 2012. LNCS, vol. 7504. Springer, Heidelberg (2012). https://doi.org/10.1007/978-3-642-33826-7
15. Faissole, F.: Library on lax-milgram theorem (coqlm). https://www.lri.fr/faissole/these_coq.html. Accessed 30 Dec 2019
16. Garillot, F., Gonthier, G., Mahboubi, A., Rideau, L.: Packaging mathematical structures. In: Berghofer, S., Nipkow, T., Urban, C., Wenzel, M. (eds.) TPHOLs 2009. LNCS, vol. 5674, pp. 327–342. Springer, Heidelberg (2009). https://doi.org/10.1007/978-3-642-03359-9_23
17. Hu, G., O'Connell, R.F.: Analytical inversion of symmetric tridiagonal matrices. J. Phys. A Math. Gen. **29**(7), 1511 (1996)
18. Immler, F.: Formally verified computation of enclosures of solutions of ordinary differential equations. In: Badger, J.M., Rozier, K.Y. (eds.) NFM 2014. LNCS, vol. 8430, pp. 113–127. Springer, Cham (2014). https://doi.org/10.1007/978-3-319-06200-6_9
19. Immler, F.: A Verified ODE Solver and Smale's 14th Problem. Dissertation, Technische Universität München, München (2018)
20. Immler, F., Hölzl, J.: Numerical analysis of ordinary differential equations in isabelle/HOL. In: Beringer, L., Felty, A. (eds.) ITP 2012. LNCS, vol. 7406, pp. 377–392. Springer, Heidelberg (2012). https://doi.org/10.1007/978-3-642-32347-8_26
21. Immler, F., Traut, C.: The flow of ODEs. In: Blanchette, J.C., Merz, S. (eds.) ITP 2016. LNCS, vol. 9807, pp. 184–199. Springer, Cham (2016). https://doi.org/10.1007/978-3-319-43144-4_12
22. Immler, F., Traut, C.: The flow of odes: formalization of variational equation and poincaré map. J. Autom. Reasoning **62**(2), 215–236 (2019)
23. Kirk, D.B., Mei, W., Hwu, W.: Chapter 10 - parallel patterns: sparse matrix-vector multiplication: an introduction to compaction and regularization in parallel algorithms. In: Kirk, D.B., Mei, W., Hwu, W. (eds.) Programming Massively Parallel Processors (Second Edition), pp. 217–234. Morgan Kaufmann, Boston, second edition edn. (2013). https://doi.org/10.1016/B978-0-12-415992-1.00010-9, http://www.sciencedirect.com/science/article/pii/B9780124159921000109
24. Kreyszig, E.: Introductory Functional Analysis with Applications, vol. 1. Wiley, New York (1978)
25. Lax, P.D., Richtmyer, R.D.: Survey of the stability of linear finite difference equations. Commun. Pure Appl. Math. **9**(2), 267–293 (1956)

26. Lelay, C.: How to express convergence for analysis in coq (2015)
27. Martin-Dorel, É., Rideau, L., Théry, L., Mayero, M., Pasca, I.: Certified, efficient and sharp univariate taylor models in coq. In: 2013 15th International Symposium on Symbolic and Numeric Algorithms for Scientific Computing, pp. 193–200. IEEE (2013)
28. Mayero, M.: Using theorem proving for numerical analysis correctness proof of an automatic differentiation algorithm. In: Carreño, V.A., Muñoz, C.A., Tahar, S. (eds.) TPHOLs 2002. LNCS, vol. 2410, pp. 246–262. Springer, Heidelberg (2002). https://doi.org/10.1007/3-540-45685-6_17
29. Melquiond, G., Érik Martin-Dorel, M.M., Pasca, I., Rideau, L., Théry, L.: Interval Coq Library. http://coq-interval.gforge.inria.fr/. Accessed 20 Sep 2020
30. O'Connor, R.: Certified exact transcendental real number computation in Coq. In: Mohamed, O.A., Muñoz, C., Tahar, S. (eds.) TPHOLs 2008. LNCS, vol. 5170, pp. 246–261. Springer, Heidelberg (2008). https://doi.org/10.1007/978-3-540-71067-7_21
31. Pasca, I.: Formal Verification for Numerical Methods. Ph.D. thesis, Université Nice Sophia Antipolis (2010)
32. Sanz-Serna, J., Palencia, C.: A general equivalence theorem in the theory of discretization methods. Math. Comput. **45**(171), 143–152 (1985)
33. Tekriwal, M., Duraisamy, K., Jeannin, J.B.: A formal proof of the Lax equivalence theorem for finite difference schemes. arXiv preprint arXiv:2103.13534, https://arxiv.org/abs/2103.13534 (2021)

Recursive Variable-Length State Compression for Multi-core Software Model Checking

Freark I. van der Berg[(✉)]

Formal Methods and Tools, University of Twente, Enschede, The Netherlands
f.i.vanderberg@utwente.nl

Abstract. High-performance software typically uses dynamic memory allocations and multi-threading to leverage multi-core CPUs. Model checking such software not only has to deal with state space explosion, but also with variable-length states due to dynamic allocations. Moreover, changes between states are typically small, calling for incremental updates. Many model checkers, although efficiently dealing with the latter, only support fixed-length state vectors. In this paper, we introduce DTREE, a concurrent compression tree data structure that compactly stores variable-length states while allowing partial state reconstruction and incremental updates without reconstructing states. We implemented DTREE in the DMC multi-core model checker. We show that, for models with states of varying length, DTREE is up to 2.9 times faster and uses on average 29% less memory than state-of-the-art tools.

1 Introduction

High-performance concurrent software is complex to write and even harder to reason about. The more threads run in parallel, the more different interleavings are possible, easily causing billions (or trillions) of reachable program states. Programmers want to make sure that they are valid, i.e. none represent an error due to stack overflows, race conditions, buffer overruns, null pointer dereferences, or other erroneous operations. One way to verify such properties is to *model check* [1] the program, during which the entire state space is explored. We can remember the visited states to avoid visiting them multiple times and thus avoid doing the same work redundantly. A complication when model checking software is dealing with variable-length states, due to dynamic memory allocations, e.g. heap memory. However, changes between states are typically small. Model checkers can take advantage of this for efficiency. Thus, model checking software has four major requirements: **R1)** efficiently store billions or trillions of states; **R2)** efficiently calculate successor states; **R3)** efficiently

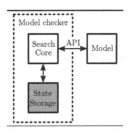

© Springer Nature Switzerland AG 2021
A. Dutle et al. (Eds.): NFM 2021, LNCS 12673, pp. 340–357, 2021.
https://doi.org/10.1007/978-3-030-76384-8_21

determine whether or not a state has been visited; **R4**) support states of varying length, due to dynamic memory. These requirements have implications on
how states are stored, but also on how next states are determined and communicated between model, model checker and state storage, in a modularized
implementation as shown on the right.

1.1 Related Work

LTSmin [2], together with its compression trees TreeDBS [3] and Compact
Tree [4] is one example on how to approach these requirements in a modular implementation. LTSmin is a model checker with multi-core [5] (up to 64
threads), distributed [6] and symbolic implementations [7]. These implementations share a common interface: PINS, the Partitioned Next-State Interface, their
API between search core and model. PINS does not lend itself well for software,
because it only support fixed-length states. Moreover, it requires the complete
state to be available when the model is asked for successor states. Because these
states are stored in TreeDBS or Compact Tree, these states need to be recon-
structed first, which comes at a price. Communicating a next state is also done
using a complete state. LTSmin can use a projection [2] to detect the changed
parts to minimize copying. However, this projection requires static information
on which parts of the state are touched, which is not guaranteed available in
software due to the dynamic nature of heap memory and spawning threads
dynamically. LTSmin does have a software front-end [8], but since LTSmin only
supports fixed-length states, that front-end uses a sub-optimal uncompressed
chunk table to model heap memory, which also lacks projection.

TreeDBS [3] is a thread-safe state storage for fixed-length states. It uses a
binary compression tree, based on work by Blom et al. [9], in order to identify
common sub-vectors. Laarman et al. show it to be efficient (R1, R2 and R3),
but it does not support states of varying length (R4). Compact Tree [4] is an
evolution of TreeDBS, where a Cleary table [10] is used for its root set. We will
explain TreeDBS and Compact Tree in more detail in Sect. 2.1.

SPIN version 6 [11] is an explicit-state model checker for PROMELA models. It
supports a dynamic number of PROMELA processes by having a variable length
root state. Moreover, it has a state compression method COLLAPSE [12]: instead
of fully storing all combinations of PROMELA process states in the root state,
the states of the processes themselves are stored and mapped to a unique ID,
and those IDs are stored in the root state instead. Thus, a state is a two-level
tree of states: a root state and the process states. This is similar to using the
chunk table of LTSmin. SPIN supports a number of search algorithms, among
which is parallel BFS up to 63 threads.

DIVINE version 4 [13] is an explicit-state model checker for LLVM IR assembly
code [14]. It uses a graph to model the stack and heap. Each node in this graph
represents an allocated section of memory, for example space allocated for a
struct. Edges on this graph represent reachability, e.g. a pointer in a struct
to another struct.

Other, more remote approaches to state compression, are Binary Decision Diagrams [15,16] and PTries [17]. BDDs compress by sharing prefixes and suffixes of (Boolean) state vectors, and are used in symbolic model checking; in their standard form, they are restricted to static vector lengths. PTries compress by only sharing prefixes of subvectors; they do support dynamic state lengths natively. Laarman compares the compression and performance of BDDs and PTries to Compact Tree [4].

1.2   Contributions

In this paper we introduce DTREE, a state storage data structure that satisfies R1–R4: it is concurrent, compresses states, can handle variable-length states and provides partial reconstruction of a stored state and incremental updates to states *without the need for reconstructing the entire state*. We implemented DTREE as part of the DMC MODEL CHECKER.

To showcase the potential of DTREE, we compare it to other state storage components using models with variable-length states. In the case of TreeDBS, we *pad* all vectors to the length of the largest vector (manually determined). Here, DTREE is able to perform up to 2.9 times faster than TreeDBS using 29% less memory on average, without the a priori need to manually determine the largest vector. The advantage of DTREE increases as the difference in length between states increases. To evaluate how much efficiency is lost to gain variable-length support, we compare DMC using DTREE to LTSmin and SPIN using models from the BEEM database [18] with fixed-length states. In this setting, DTREE is actually marginally faster than TreeDBS, but uses 30% more memory. Compact Tree compresses fixed-length states 2.3x more than DTREE. Compared to SPIN using COLLAPSE, DTREE is 8.1x faster and uses 6.1x less memory.

2   Tree Compression

We now explain TreeDBS and Compact Tree, which inspired DTREE. States are vectors of *state slots*; a variable in a model occupies one or more state slots. For the sake of simplicity, let us assume these state slots are 32-bit. The principle behind the compression is to insert pairs of state slots, thus 64-bit values, into an *indexed hash set* with a 32-bit index. In an indexed hash set, the index is determined by *hashing* the value. A pair of 32-bit indices forms another 64-bit

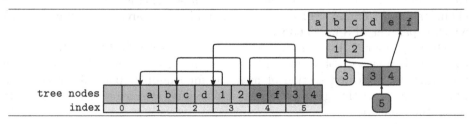

Fig. 1. The layout of the indexed hash set after inserting abcd and abcdef.

value, which in turn can be put into the set. This process continues, creating an ordered tree of *nodes*. This is illustrated in Fig. 1: the vectors `abcd` and `abcdef` share a common sub-vector `abcd` and index `3` maps to this sub-vector. This also illustrates the compression: common nodes are only inserted once. The higher up the common node is in the tree, the larger the common sub-vector it maps to, the more memory is saved. Which common sub-vectors can be identified and reused, depends on the structure of the binary tree: while `abcd` can be identified, `cdef` cannot. If we were to add the vector `cdef`, we would add the node `24`. Similarly, we would add the node `42` for `efcd` and the node `33` for `abcdabcd`.

Note that the rounded boxes ③ and ⑤ are the indices to the root nodes of the trees mapping to the states. However, an index is not enough to identify a state, as index ③ could map to `12` as well. Indeed, if we would have added the state `12` (with index ③), this would be completely correct, thus we need more information other than ③ to distinguish ③ from ③. This gives rise to two issues: uniquely identifying a state and determining whether or not a state has already been added.

2.1   TreeDBS and Its Implementation

TreeDBS solves the first issue by only supporting fixed-length states and having the length of the state dictate the shape of the tree. Thus, all trees are isomorphic and an index uniquely identifies a state. However, the implementation [19] of how the length dictates the shape of the tree differs from the how it was originally presented [3]. We show both versions in Fig. 2, ignoring ■ (top) and only focusing

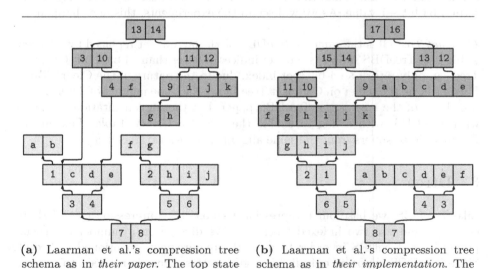

(a) Laarman et al.'s compression tree schema as in *their paper*. The top state adds 7 nodes, bringing the total to 16.

(b) Laarman et al.'s compression tree schema as in *their implementation*. The top state adds 10 nodes; 19 nodes in total.

Fig. 2. An illustration of the difference between the *paper* and *implementation* of the compression tree of Laarman et al. Given a 40 byte state `abcdefghij` (bottom tree), the next state `abcdefghijk` (top tree) appends `k`, 4 bytes.

on ▢ (bottom) for now. The paper version recursively divides the vector in two, associating one half with the left child of a node and the other half with the right child (Fig. 2a). For efficiency, the implementation version represents the tree as an array, where a node at index n has its children at indices $2n$ and $2n + 1$ (Fig. 2b). Inserting the nodes of a vector then becomes a simple for-loop since children are always adjacent. Both versions produce a balanced tree, but their balancing is different, influencing locality. For example, the paper version has a single pair of adjacent state slots (`ef`) that requires traversing both the left and right side of the tree, whereas the implementation version has two (`bc` and `fg`). The importance of this will become apparent in Sect. 3.2.

To determine whether a state has been added already, the paper version of TreeDBS uses a single indexed hash set and a root-bit in the nodes to indicate whether a node is a root node or a tree node. This distinction is needed because otherwise a leaf node could be mistaken for a root node and it could be erroneously concluded a state was already added. The current implementation removes the root-bit in favour of using two hash sets: a root hash set that stores the root nodes and a hash set that stores all other nodes. Not needing the root-bit, 32-bit indices can be used instead of just 31-bit indices and this lifts the 31-bit restriction on the data in state slots as well. In addition, it allows the root set to be larger than 2^{32}, since its indices need not fit in 32 bits. The data set is still limited to 32-bit indices, because paired they are limited to 64 bits. However, one specific 64-bit value in the hash map is still reserved to indicate the *empty value*. This value is needed to distinguish between an empty bucket and a used bucket. In the case of TreeDBS, this is the value -1, which means a model cannot pair two state slots that have a -1 value, because together they would form a 64-bit -1 value. As we will see in the experiments, this does happen.

Compact Tree [4] is the same as TreeDBS, with the root set replaced by a Cleary Table [10]. TreeDBS supports root set indices of fewer than 64 bits, but Compact Tree can only return a 64-bit root index, due to the nature of the Cleary Table. Furthermore, the paper on Compact Tree shows the same manner of determining the shape of the tree as the TreeDBS paper, but the implementation is shared with TreeDBS, with a flag to enable the use of a Cleary Table. This means Compact Tree suffers from the same alignment issues as TreeDBS.

3   Dtree

Like TreeDBS, we base our compression tree on the compression tree of Blom et al. [9] and use two indexed hash sets. We diverge on a number of crucial points from TreeDBS in order to meet the requirements mentioned in Sect. 1. Since TreeDBS supports only fixed-length vectors, there is no need to remember the length of each individual vector, but we do (R4). We also introduce a different compression tree structure that benefits dynamic memory allocation (R4). Furthermore, we extend the capabilities of the compression tree to store and reconstruct only parts of states in order to improve calculating next states

(R2). Lastly, our approach supports any data, including −1 values in adjacent state slots.

First, we show why we need a different tree structure. Let us consider the scenario where a model has allocated 40 bytes (10 state slots) and in the next state the model wishes to allocate 4 more bytes. The model does this by growing the state by one state slot. Figure 2 shows how this scenario is supported by the two versions of TreeDBS. The implementation version starts forming 64-bit sections starting at the end, so a change of 4 bytes (32 bits) to the size of the state will unalign the tree nodes compared to the previous state. This results in storing the same information twice. This effect is not limited to the last level of the tree: a change of 8 bytes in the size of the state results in the second to last level of the tree to become unaligned. A change of 16 bytes would unalign the third to last level, etc. Figure 3 shows two improvements to these structures. Figure 3a describes the structure of the implementation version of TreeDBS, but backwards in an attempt to limit the alignment issue. This works for the leaves, but one level higher in the tree we face the same issue: instead of `12`, `34` we get `23`, `45`. Moreover, this approach still has two pairs of adjacent state slots that require traversing both the left and right side of the tree (`de` and `hi`).

3.1   A Chain of Perfectly Balanced Binary Trees

Figure 3b shows our approach, named *the chain of perfectly balanced binary trees*. This approach does not suffer from the issues of the other tree shapes as Fig. 3b clearly demonstrates. In a chain, the length of the sub-vector the left child of a node leads to is always lpst(len(V)), where lpst(x) is the largest **power-of-two** smaller than x, len(V) is the length of the vector V and V is the vector that the node itself leads to. Thus, a left child is always perfectly balanced. The right part maps to the remainder of the vector. For example, the state `abcdefghijk` of length 11 in Fig. 3b, is shaped by perfectly balanced trees mapping to 8, 2

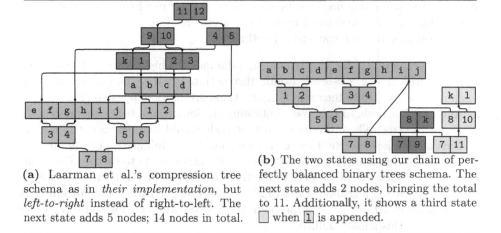

(a) Laarman et al.'s compression tree schema as in *their implementation*, but *left-to-right* instead of right-to-left. The next state adds 5 nodes; 14 nodes in total.

(b) The two states using our chain of perfectly balanced binary trees schema. The next state adds 2 nodes, bringing the total to 11. Additionally, it shows a third state ▢ when `1` is appended.

Fig. 3. Like Fig. 2, given a 40 byte state ▢, the next state ▢ appends `k`, 4 bytes.

and 1 state slots; the state `abcdefghijkl` is shaped by trees mapping to 8 and 4 state slots. This can result in a less balanced tree than TreeDBS. For example, for the state `abcdefghij`, TreeDBS (Fig. 2b) has 2 nodes on the lowest level (`gh`, `ij`) and 3 on the second-to-lowest level (`ab`, `cd`, `ef`). DTREE (Fig. 3b) on the other hand has 4 on the lowest level (`ab`, `cd`, `ef`, `gh`) and one on the second-to-highest level (`ij`). This means changes to `ab`, `cd` or `ef` require DTREE an *extra* node and changes to `ij` require two *fewer* nodes, compared to TreeDBS. We will investigate the impact of the difference in Sect. 5. Figure 3b illustrates that this approach does lend itself to appending to states. This targets a combination of R1 and R4 from Sect. 1: to more efficiently handle dynamic memory allocation. It also has a single pair of adjacent state slots requiring traversing both sides of the tree (`hi`).

3.2   Incremental Updates

The importance of minimizing such adjacent pairs becomes apparent when adding support for incremental updates. With this, a model conveys to the model checker only what *changed* compared to a previous state, in lieu of a complete state. TreeDBS supports incremental updates by *detecting* unchanged parts, when inserting a complete state, but it does not support simply applying an incremental update to a state. We describe the difference with an example. Considering the state `abcdef`, the model determines that in the next state `cd` changes to `gh`. We have two options of communicating this to the model checker:

1. the model can communicate the entire new state `abghef`; or
2. the model can communicate only the change of `gh` at offset 2, denoted `gh`@2.

For small states the difference in performance is likely negligible. However, since we want to model check software, our states can be quite large and thus this could save a significant amount of copying.

When communicating only changes, the model checker also needs to know which state the change needs to be applied to. `34` (as per Fig. 1) alone does not identify `abcdef`: we need the length of the vector as well.

We considered three ways to solve this:

1. Always remember the length alongside the index. This has the downside that high-performance low-level atomic instructions such as `compare-and-swap` cannot be used. 128-bit atomic instructions are more expensive [20].
2. Add another node to the tree, containing the length and index to the remainder of the tree. Thus, the index to that node would uniquely identify a state. This adds a level to the tree, which can negatively influence performance.
3. Remember index and length, but limit their combination to 64 bits. For example, 40 bits for the index and 24 for the length. This has the disadvantage of only supporting a trillion states of $2^{24} - 1$ state slots each. At the current technological age, both seem upperbounds on what we need for the foreseeable future, so this should suffice.

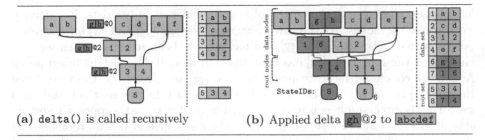

(a) delta() is called recursively   **(b)** Applied delta gh@2 to abcdef

Fig. 4. The delta-vector gh is applied at offset 2 to abcdef from Fig. 1.

We chose the third alternative. We call this combination the StateID and we write this for example as 5_6, which uniquely identifies abcdef: 5 is the index, 6 is the length of the state. Applying a delta (incremental update) such as gh@2 to 5_6 is described in Fig. 4. First, in Fig. 4a, we recursively traverse the tree to find the leaves that need change. At each node that leads to vector V, we check which of the children are affected. From Sect. 3.1 follows that the left child is affected iff the offset is smaller than lpst(len(V)). The right child is affected iff the offset plus the length of the delta is greater than lpst(len(V)). Thus, the tree is traversed as follows:

gh@2 to 5_6 only affects the left child, since $2 <$ lpst(6) and $2 + 2 \not> $ lpst(6)

gh@2 to 3_4 only affects the left child, since $2 \not< $ lpst(4) and $2+2 > $ lpst(4)

gh@0 to 2_2 completely replaces the leaf node.

At this point we can traverse back, inserting new nodes along the path. First we insert the new node gh at index 6 in the data set, then we use that index to create a new node 16, where we copy the index of the left child from 12. Finally, we insert the root node 74, providing StateID 8_6 (Fig. 4b). A delta beyond the length of a state is also supported. For example, we could have applied gh@5 to 5_6, resulting in abcdegh. When applying gh@8 to 5_6 it would yield abcdef00gh.

3.3   Partial Reconstruction of States

In a similar fashion to incremental updates, we can reconstruct (parts of) states. We recursively traverse the tree of nodes until we reach the correct leaf nodes. Then, we copy the contents of these leaf nodes into a buffer, yielding (a part of) a state.

3.4   Determining a State Is New

When creating a new state, either by inserting a complete new one or by incremental update, the model checker needs to know if the state has already been visited or not. This is accomplished by use of the root set. A state has already been inserted into DTREE iff there is a corresponding root node. As an example, let us insert `abcdef` into the DTREE of Fig. 4b, which already exists. Recursively, we traverse the nodes. At the leaves, we conclude `ab`, `cd` and `ef` have already been inserted. The tree node `12` also has already been inserted. Then we conclude that the root node `34` has been inserted as well. Now let us insert `abcd`. Again, we conclude the leave nodes `ab` and `cd` are already in the tree. Even though `12` is already in the data set, it is not yet in the root set and thus we correctly conclude it is a new state. Additionally, DTREE supports inserting states/vectors that are inserted purely in the data set and not its root node in the root set. This can be useful to compress data that is not a state in the model as we will see later in Sect. 4.1. Thus, DTREE provides the following API:

```
StateID insert(Slot[] V, bool root)
StateID delta(StateID s, int offset, Slot[] D, bool root)
Slot[]  get(StateID s, bool root)
Slot[]  get(StateID s, int offset, int length, bool root)
```

Here, `root` indicates if the root node should indeed be placed in the root set. Note that this is also needed for `get()` because we need to look for the root node in the right set. The interfaces `insert()` and `delta()` insert a new state (Sect. 3.2). The two `get()` interfaces allow to obtain (parts of) the state (Sect. 3.3).

4 DMC Model Checker

We now expand on the concept of a modular model checker as described in Sect. 1. A model M implements the NEXTSTATE (NS) API:

```
void initialState()
void nextStates(StateID s)
```

Here, `initialState()` sets up the initial state and `nextStates()` computes the next states of the specified state s. Communicating ("uploading") states to the model checker is done using the DTREE API, which is exposed to the model via the search core. This flow is illustrated in Fig. 5. The NEXTSTATE API is called by a search core, which defines the search strategy. For example, in Listing 1a we define

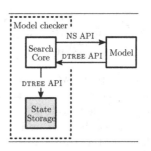

Fig. 5. The modular DMC model checker

a search core that simply pops a `StateID` from a queue Q and requests the next states of the model M until the queue is empty. An example of such a model M is shown in Listing 1b, modeling four counters, going from 0 to 9, looping back to 0. With each invocation of `nextStates()`, four next states are generated. For each Slot 0–3 in the state (line 5), the current value is obtained (line 6), it is incremented modulo 10 (line 7) and this delta is communicated to the model checker (line 8) using the `delta()` interface. Thus, the initial state is `0000` and for example `0974` generates the next states `1974`, `0074`, `0984` and `0975`. The search core wraps the DTREE interface to add new states to the queue Q. An example of this is shown in Listing 2. Line 2 inserts the potentially new state in DTREE and is returned a `StateID` and an indicator if the state was new. If the state s is new and a root state (we will see a use case for non-root states in

Listing 1. A search core and a simple model with a state space size of 10^4.

```
1 Q = {};
2 M.initialState();
3 while(!Q.isEmpty())
4    StateID s = Q.pop();
5    M.nextStates(s);
```

(a) A basic search core that simply requests next states from a model M until all have been visited. For brevity, the on-the-fly checking of properties is left out.

```
1 void initialState()
2    MC.insert({0,0,0,0}, true);
3    # ^ implicitly pushes to Q
4 void nextStates(StateID s)
5    for i in {0,1,2,3}
6       Slot v = MC.get(s, i, 1);
7       v = (v + 1) % 10;
8       MC.delta(s, i, {v}, true);
```

(b) A model with four counters.

Listing 2. An implementation of the `delta()` interface of the DMC API.

```
1 StateID delta(StateID s, int offset, Slot[] D, bool root)
2    {StateID s, bool isNew} = DTREE.delta(s, offset, D, root);
3    if(isNew and root) Q.push(s);
4    return s;
```

Sect. 4.1), it is added to the queue Q in line 3. The `insert()` interface is implemented similarly, updating Q if needed. The `get()` interfaces are simply passed on.

4.1 An Example Using a Tree of States

We can use the basic building blocks of uploading and downloading states for a more interesting concept: *tree-structured states*. The basic idea is that a state can contain a `StateID` that is associated with a non-root state, a sub-state. These are called sub-states because they could well be states of processes of which the combined state is the root state.

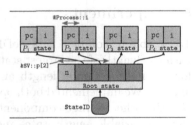

Fig. 6. A tree of states

To illustrate this, we constructed a small model using processes in Listing 3, which conceptually does the same as the model in Listing 1b. Figure 6 illustrates what a complete state looks like. The important lines are 10–12, where we obtain the value of i of the current process (10), change it (11) and create a new sub-state with the changed value (12). Note that the `get()` in line 8 has `root=true`, indicating that the specified `StateID` is a root state, while the `get()` in line 10 does not. This matches with the corresponding `insert()`s and `delta()`s.

This is much like the COLLAPSE method of SPIN [12] as briefly touched on in Sect. 1.1. SPIN supports a varying number of processes by having exactly this kind of structure: a root state with indices to indicate the state of individual

Listing 3. Four processes counting from 0 to 9 and wrapping.

```
1   struct Process
2     int pc;        # program counter
3     int i;         # some variable
4   struct SV
5     int n;         # number of processes
6     StateID p[];
7   void nextStates(StateID rootID)
8     SV sv = MC.get(rootID, true)                        # root state
9     for(p in [0..sv.n])
10      int pi = MC.get(sv.p[p], &Process::i, 1, false)
11      pi = (pi + 1) % 10;
12      int newP = MC.delta(sv.p[p], &Process::i, {pi}, false);
13      int offset = &SV::p[p]              # offset to p[p] within SV
14      MC.delta(rootID, offset, {newP}, true);          # root state
15    void initialState(StateID rootID)
16      Process p = {1,0}                    # pc is 1, i is 0
17      StateID initP = MC.insert(p, false)
18      SV rootState = {4, initP, initP, initP, initP}
19      MC.insert(rootState, true)                        # root state
```

processes. Just as COLLAPSE, this allows to leverage the fact that duplicate processes share states. Since these states are inserted separately instead of a single, large vector, their data aligns, which helps in identifying common sub-vectors. However, DTREE supports arbitrary deep hierarchies of nested states.

5   Experiments

To be able to compare to TreeDBS, we have two options: 1) initialise TreeDBS with the length of the largest state and pad others with 0's; 2) initialise TreeDBS for the most common length and use a different storage component for other lengths. We implemented both options we call $\text{TreeDBS}_{\text{pad}}$ and TreeDBS_S, where S is the other storage component. Without these measures, TreeDBS would not support variable-length states and could not run the variable-length experiments.

While we compared to std::unordered_map of the STL library surrounded by an std::mutex, and a concurrent chaining hash map (cchm) [21], we omit the results for them as in all cases they perform roughly an order of magnitude worse. This is not unexpected, since they store an order of magnitude more memory because they do not compress the inserted states. The hash map std::unordered_map specifically has a global mutex around it, causing high contention. We could not make Compact Tree into a DMC storage component because it needs a 64-bit index and the DMC API reserves only 40 bits for that purpose.

In addition to comparing these storages to each other, we compare DMC to the multicore implementation of LTSmin 3.0.2 with both TreeDBS and Compact

Tree, both parallel DFS and BFS, using 64 threads. We also compare to SPIN 6.5.1 using COLLAPSE and parallel BFS with 63 threads, as that is SPIN's maximum. This gives us a baseline of where the performance of our model checker DMC as a whole is.

We ran DMC at 64 threads for a fair comparison, but it can use any number of threads. We tried both the DFS and BFS strategy for LTSmin, but these showed only minor difference. We will show the results for BFS, as we run SPIN using BFS as well and DMC currently only has a BFS search core.

The hardware that we ran our experiments on is "caserta", a Dell R930 with 2TiB of RAM and four E7-8890-v4 CPUs. Each CPU has 24 cores, 60MiB of L3 cache and 512GiB of RAM, offering 96 physical cores in total. We ran our experiments on Linux 4.4.0 and all tools were compiled using GCC 9.3.0.

5.1 Variable-Length State Models

The design of DTREE is meant for software that uses dynamic memory. To test this we implemented three models: 1) a model that implements a concurrent hash map with a number of inserts [21]; 2) a model of the concurrent Michael Scott queue [22] with various enqueue (E) and dequeue (D) operations; 3) a model of a sorted linked list (SSL). All these data structures are modeled by creating a model that inserts a number of elements into them. The initial state is constructed by creating a number of processes, like in the example in Sect. 4.1. These processes then run, with every interleaving explored, akin to how every interleaving of incrementing one of the four counters in the example of Sect. 4.1 is explored. For the Michael-Scott queue, we made a model that runs 3 enqueue operations and 3 dequeue operations in parallel. The Sorted Linked List model models a number of processes (6) that each insert a single element of 48 bytes (12 slots), dynamically allocated. The hash map model similarly inserts 9 pointers to elements of 16 slots in parallel. Dynamic memory is modeled using a `StateID` at the beginning of the root state to a memory slab sub-state that can expand.

The effect these dynamic allocations and parallel insertions have on the distribution of the length of states is shown in Fig. 7. For example, the hash map model is most pronounced: starting with an initial global memory of 130 slots (some string data), the first process dynamically allocates 16 slots and inserts the element, yielding a number of states of length 146. If we add a second process and all the interleavings, we get many more states of length 162, etc.

The results for variable-length state models are shown in Table 1. Overall, DTREE is clearly the faster of the three storages. It is up to 44 times faster than TreeDBS$_{cchm}$ and 1.2–2.9 times faster than TreeDBS$_{pad}$. The slow times of TreeDBS$_{cchm}$ are largely caused by the slower, uncompressed cchm that is used for states of lengths other than the root state so the results have to be interpreted as such. For TreeDBS$_{pad}$, we see the downside of padding with zeroes: with increased state-length variance, the overhead increases and performance drops.

Regarding compression, we notice TreeDBS$_{cchm}$ is actually better for the MSQ and Sorted Linked List models. This can be explained by looking at the variance of the distribution of state lengths: the root state length (18) dominates

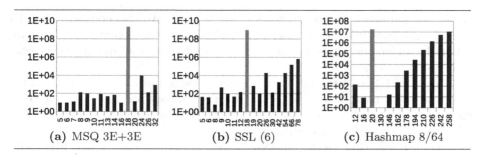

Fig. 7. The number of states (y-axis) inserted of a certain length in `ints` (x-axis). The length of the root state is highlighted.

Table 1. Experiments that use the DMC API. Set scale X-Y(-Z) means 2^X root set nodes, 2^Y data set nodes, 2^Z entries for the sub-storage. TreeDBS$_{cchm}$ (L) and TreeDBS$_{pad}$ (L) mean they are initialized for states of length L (in `ints`).

Model	Storage	Set Scale	Time	B/state
MSQ 3E+3D	TreeDBS$_{cchm}$ (18)	32-30-24	4917.33 s	8.03
	TreeDBS$_{pad}$ (32)	32-30	469.86 s	9.16
	DTREE	32-30	392.45 s	9.16
SLL (6 inserts)	TreeDBS$_{cchm}$ (20)	34-32-24	2497.33 s	8.97
	TreeDBS$_{pad}$ (78)	34-32	777.18 s	24.86
	DTREE	34-32	416.22 s	12.89
Hashmap (8 inserts)	TreeDBS$_{cchm}$ (18)	28-28-28	187.01 s	1072.95
	TreeDBS$_{pad}$ (258)	28-28	65.18 s	75.62
	DTREE	28-28	24.01 s	55.00
Hashmap (9 inserts)	TreeDBS$_{cchm}$ (18)	34-32-30	21171.64 s	1137.57
	TreeDBS$_{pad}$ (274)	34-32	1391.79 s	75.62
	DTREE	34-32	477.25 s	54.30

all other lengths. The shape of the tree of nodes of TreeDBS has 2 nodes on the lowest level and 7 on the second-to-lowest. DTREE on the other hand, has 8 nodes on the deepest level and 1 on the second-to-highest, because it uses a chain of balanced trees, in this case leading to 16 state slots (left) and 2 (right). As theorised in Sect. 3.1, this difference causes that DTREE often needs *one more node* for even a small change. Since often the memory is changed, which is modeled by a `StateID` at the beginning of the root state, this is precisely what happens. Thus, the root state length is so dominant that the overhead of uncompressed cchm entries is less than the overhead of the less balanced tree that DTREE uses.

When we look at the Hashmap model, which has a significantly higher variance, we see that TreeDBS$_{cchm}$ requires an order of magnitude more space. Here,

TreeDBS stores only states of length 20 and all others are stored in the sub-storage cchm, which does not compress states.

In general these results show that dedicated support for variable-length outperforms padding zeroes (TreeDBS$_{pad}$) and offloading other-sized vectors (TreeDBS$_{cchm}$). The results also show that an increase of variance in state-length increases the advantage of DTREE.

5.2 Fixed-Length State Models

To evaluate the cost of adding variable-length support, we also run experiments using models with fixed-length states. We modified SpinS [23] to emit models that implement the API of DMC for models from the BEEM database [18]. For SPIN, these states could be of varying length, but SpinS emits fixed-length states models since its primary target is PINS for LTSmin. Thus, these tests do not use the delta() interface, but only insert and get complete states. Of these models, we include the results for 118 models. Other models could not be compared because either they have two adjacent state slots with -1 values (TreeDBS and Compact Tree do not support that, e.g. GEAR.1, in which case LTSmin aborts), the PROMELA could not be translated (e.g. TRAIN-GATE.1) or they are too large for all tools to finish (e.g. PUBLIC_SUBSCRIBE.5).

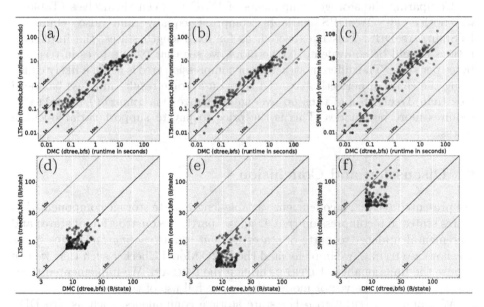

Fig. 8. DMC/dtree compared to LTSmin/TreeDBS (a,d), LTSmin/compact (b,e) and SPIN (c,f) on runtime (a,b,c) and bytes per state (d,e,f).

The results for the comparison to LTSmin and SPIN using models from the BEEM database are shown in Fig. 8 and Table 2. When looking at Fig. 8a, we can see that the combination of DMC with DTREE is nearing the performance of LTSmin with TreeDBS time-wise. There are a number of outliers in both directions, but in the more time-consuming models one can see that LTSmin with TreeDBS has the edge over

Table 2. Totals for 118 models from the BEEM database.

Tool	Total time (s)	Average B/state
SPIN (collapse)	6081	71.8
SPIN (bfspar)	1050	146
DMC/TreeDBS$_{cchm}$	780	8.98
DMC/TreeDBS$_{pad}$	773	8.98
DMC/TreeDBS$_{stdmap}$	749	8.98
DMC/dtree	748	11.7
LTSmin/treedbs	598	8.98
LTSmin/compact	428	4.98

DMC, still. In terms of bytes per state (Fig. 8d) we see a similar result. This shows in the total runtime and B/states as well: LTSmin/TreeDBS takes 20% less time and 23% less memory on average.

The comparison to Compact Tree follows the same trend time-wise (Fig. 8b). Compact Tree clearly outperforms DTREE in terms of bytes per state (Fig. 8e). The use of a Cleary table for the root set is a clear winner.

Figure 8c compares DMC/dtree to SPIN with parallel BFS. Here, we see that DMC/dtree has the edge over SPIN, time-wise. Figure 8f compares DMC/dtree to SPIN with COLLAPSE, but without parallel BFS (these cannot be used simultaneously). Even then, SPIN with COLLAPSE is outperformed by DMC/dtree in all benchmarks.

Comparing the storage components of DMC between themselves (Table 2), we notice all TreeDBS variants compress equally and also equal to LTSmin/TreeDBS. This is expected, as for fixed-length states, the implementations should be equivalent. Furthermore, we see that DTREE loses in terms of bytes per state. The different structure of compression tree is again a likely cause: using the chain of perfectly balanced trees on average results in a less balanced tree than TreeDBS and thus on average a change (via `insert()` or `delta()`) requires more new nodes. This is the price to pay to support variable-length states.

6   Discussion and Conclusion

We presented DTREE, a concurrent variable-length state storage component that stores states in a compression tree. It allows partial reconstruction of states and incremental updates to parts of states *without reconstructing the entire states*. To showcase DTREE, we implemented the DMC Model Checker such that we can expose the functionality of DTREE through the DMC API. We implemented three variable-length state vector models that make full use of the DMC API.

We compare DTREE to other state storage components, such as TreeDBS. In the case of TreeDBS, we *pad* all vectors to the length of the largest vector (manually determined). Here, DTREE is able to perform up to 2.9 times faster than TreeDBS using 29% less memory on average, without the a priori need to manually determine the largest vector. The advantage of DTREE increases as the difference in length between states increases.

To evaluate how much efficiency is lost to gain variable-length support, we compare DMC using DTREE to LTSmin and SPIN using models from the BEEM database with fixed-length states. In this setting, DTREE is actually marginally faster than TreeDBS, but uses 30% more memory. DMC as a whole can only approach the performance of fixed-length state model checker LTSmin, sacrificing 20–23%. It is still outclassed by Compact Tree in terms of bytes per state, which compressed up to 2.3x more than DTREE. In the same tests, DMC with DTREE is faster and provides a higher compression than SPIN with COLLAPSE. Compared to SPIN using COLLAPSE, DTREE is 8.1x faster and uses 6.1x less memory. Even though DMC nor DTREE are particularly optimized for fixed-length complete-state changes, the performance overall is reasonable.

This research is part of the ongoing research towards creating a software model checker for use in a continuous integration pipeline. With the advent of DTREE[1], we are now one step closer.

6.1 Future Work

We have seen that Compact Tree outperforms DTREE for fixed-length states. Compact Tree uses a Cleary Table for its root set. To improve DTREE, we can investigate if we can leverage such a table, since Compact Tree as is uses a 64-bit index and the DMC API currently has only 40 bits available for the state index.

DMC still needs to improve as well. For example, the search core of DMC is a simple parallel BFS, lacking a more sophisticated work-stealing algorithm. Implementing such a feature would improve the performance of DMC as a whole.

We aim to use DMC as the core for our upcoming multi-core software model checker LLMC. The purpose of LLMC is to model check LLVM IR assembly code. To model the stack and heap, DTREE lends itself perfectly. We can then compare the resulting implementation with DIVINE.

Acknowledgements. The author would like to thank Arnd Hartmanns and Jaco van de Pol for their invaluable contributions and Alfons Laarman for discussions on TreeDBS and Compact Tree. This research is sponsored by 3TU Big Software on the Run project (http://www.3tu-bsr.nl/).

References

1. Clarke, E.M., Henzinger, T.A., Veith, H.: Introduction to model checking. In: Clarke, E.M., Henzinger, T.A., Veith, H., Bloem, R. (eds.) Handbook of Model Checking, pp. 1–26. Springer (2018). https://doi.org/10.1007/978-3-319-10575-8_1
2. Kant, G., Laarman, A., Meijer, J., van de Pol, J., Blom, S., van Dijk, T.: LTSmin: high-performance language-independent model checking. In: Baier, C., Tinelli, C. (eds.) TACAS 2015. LNCS, vol. 9035, pp. 692–707. Springer, Heidelberg (2015). https://doi.org/10.1007/978-3-662-46681-0_61

---

[1] The source code of DTREE can be found at https://github.com/bergfi/dtree.

3. Laarman, A., van de Pol, J., Weber, M.: Parallel recursive state compression for free. In: Groce, A., Musuvathi, M. (eds.) SPIN 2011. LNCS, vol. 6823, pp. 38–56. Springer, Heidelberg (2011). https://doi.org/10.1007/978-3-642-22306-8_4
4. Laarman, A.: Optimal compression of combinatorial state spaces, ISSE, vol. 15, no. 3–4, pp. 235–251 (2019). https://doi.org/10.1007/s11334-019-00341-7
5. Laarman, A.W., van de Pol, J.C., Weber, M.: Multi-core LTSmin: marrying modularity and scalability. In: Bobaru, M., Havelund, K., Holzmann, G., Joshi, R. (eds.) Proceedings of the Third International Symposium on NASA Formal Methods, NFM 2011, Pasadena, CA, USA, ser. LNCS, vol. 6617, pp. 506–511. Springer Verlag, Berlin, July 2011. https://doi.org/10.1007/978-3-642-20398-5_40
6. Blom, S., van de Pol, J., Weber, M.: LTSmin: distributed and symbolic reachability. In: Touili, T., Cook, B., Jackson, P. (eds.) CAV 2010. LNCS, vol. 6174, pp. 354–359. Springer, Heidelberg (2010). https://doi.org/10.1007/978-3-642-14295-6_31
7. Blom, S., van de Pol, J.: Symbolic reachability for process algebras with recursive data types. In: Fitzgerald, J.S., Haxthausen, A.E., Yenigun, H. (eds.) ICTAC 2008. LNCS, vol. 5160, pp. 81–95. Springer, Heidelberg (2008). https://doi.org/10.1007/978-3-540-85762-4_6
8. van der Berg, F.I.: Model checking LLVM IR using LTSmin: using relaxed memory model semantics, December 2013. http://essay.utwente.nl/65059/
9. Blom, S., Lisser, B., van de Pol, J., Weber, M.: A database approach to distributed state-space generation. J. Log. Comput. 21(1), 45–62 (2011). https://doi.org/10.1093/logcom/exp004
10. Cleary, J.G.: Compact hash tables using bidirectional linear probing. IEEE Trans. Comput. 33(9), 828–834 (1984). https://doi.org/10.1109/TC.1984.1676499
11. Holzmann, G.J.: The model checker SPIN. IEEE Trans. Software Eng. 23(5), 279–295 (1997)
12. Holzmann, G.J.: State compression in SPIN: recursive indexing and compression training runs (1997)
13. Rockai, P., Still, V., Cerná, I., Barnat, J.: DiVM: model checking with LLVM and graph memory. J. Syst. Softw. 143, 1–13 (2018). https://doi.org/10.1016/j.jss.2018.04.026
14. Lattner, C.: LLVM: An infrastructure for multi-stage optimization. Master's thesis, Computer Science Dept., University of Illinois at Urbana-Champaign, Urbana, IL, December 2002. http://llvm.cs.uiuc.edu
15. Bryant, R.E.: Graph-based algorithms for Boolean function manipulation. IEEE Trans. Comput. 35,(8), 677–691 (1986). https://doi.org/10.1109/TC.1986.1676819
16. Burch, J.R., Clarke, E.M., McMillan, K.L., Dill, D.L.: Sequential circuit verification using symbolic model checking. In: Smith, R.C. (ed.) Proceedings of the 27th ACM/IEEE Design Automation Conference, 24–28 June 1990, Orlando, Florida, USA, pp. 46–51. IEEE Computer Society Press, 1990. https://doi.org/10.1145/123186.123223
17. Jensen, P.G., Larsen, K.G., Srba, J.: PTrie: data structure for compressing and storing sets via prefix sharing. In: Hung, D.V., Kapur, D. (eds.) Theoretical Aspects of Computing - ICTAC 2017-14th International Colloquium, Hanoi, Vietnam, 23–27 October 2017, Proceedings, ser. LNCS, vol. 10580, pp. 248–265. Springer (2017). https://doi.org/10.1007/978-3-319-67729-3_15
18. Pelánek, R.: BEEM: benchmarks for explicit model checkers. In: Bošnački, D., Edelkamp, S. (eds.) SPIN 2007. LNCS, vol. 4595, pp. 263–267. Springer, Heidelberg (2007). https://doi.org/10.1007/978-3-540-73370-6_17
19. Blom, S.C.C., van Dijk, T., Kant, G., Meijer, J., van de Pol, J.C., Weber, M.: LTSmin git repository. https://github.com/utwente-fmt/ltsmin, December 2020

20. Intel® 64 and IA-32 Architectures Software Developer's Manual, 253666th ed., Intel Corporation, Intel Corporation 2200 Mission College Blvd. Santa Clara, CA 95054–1537, September 2016
21. van der Berg, F.I., van de Pol, J.: Concurrent chaining hash maps for software model checking. In: Barrett, C., Yang, J. (eds.) 2019 Formal Methods in Computer Aided Design (FMCAD), ser. Proceedings of the Conference on Formal Methods in Computer-Aided Design (FMCAD) United States, vol. 10, pp. 46–54. IEEE (2019)
22. Michael, M.M., Scott, M.L.: Simple, fast, and practical non-blocking and blocking concurrent queue algorithms. In: Burns, J.E., Moses, Y.(eds.) PODC, pp. 267–275. ACM (1996)
23. van der Berg, F.I., Laarman, A.W.: SpinS: extending LTSmin with Promela through SpinJa. In: 11th International Workshop on Parallel and Distributed Methods in verifiCation, PDMC 2012, London, UK, ser. Electronic Notes in Theoretical Computer Science, Amsterdam. Elsevier, September 2012

Runtime Verification of Generalized Test Tables

Alexander Weigl[1]([⊠])[iD], Mattias Ulbrich[1][iD], Shmuel Tyszberowicz[2][iD],
and Jonas Klamroth[3]

[1] Karlsruhe Institute of Technology (KIT), Karlsruhe, Germany
{weigl,ulbrich}@kit.edu
[2] Afeka Academic College of Engineering, Tel Aviv, Israel
tyshbe@tau.ac.il
[3] FZI Research Center for Information Technology, Karlsruhe, Germany
klamroth@fzi.de

Abstract. Runtime verification allows validation of systems during
their operation by monitoring crucial system properties. It is common to
generate monitors from temporal specifications formulated in languages
like MTL or LTL. However, writing formal specifications might be an
obstacle for practitioners. In this paper we present an approach and a tool
for generating software monitors for reactive systems from a set of Generalized Test Tables (GTTs)—a table-based, user-friendly specification
language specially designed for engineers. The tool is a valuable addition
to the already existing static verifier for GTTs since assumptions made
in specifications can thus be validated at runtime. Moreover, it makes
software and specifications amenable for formal validation that cannot
be verified statically. Moreover, the approach is particularly well-suited
for the specification of workflows as a collection of tables since it supports
dynamic, trigger-based spawning of monitors. The tool produces monitor
code in C++ for tables provided in an existing table definition format.
We show the usefulness of our approach using characteristic examples.

Keywords: Runtime verification · Monitoring · Formal specification

1 Introduction

Motivation. Safety-critical systems are usually validated using testing or static
verification to ensure that they conform to their specification. Testing can usually only cover a small number of possible scenarios, and static verification is
infeasible for many systems. One reason for that is that relevant information may
not yet be available during static verification. Another potential problem is that
the actual static verification engine may require too many resources (in terms

This work was funded by German Research Council (BE 2334/7-2, and UL 433/1-2),
the state Baden-Wuerttemberg via CyberProtect project, and the KIT Alumni Visiting
Grant.

A. Dutle et al. (Eds.): NFM 2021, LNCS 12673, pp. 358–374, 2021.
https://doi.org/10.1007/978-3-030-76384-8_22

of time, memory, or effort needed to come up with suitably strong environment models) to be feasible in practice. Runtime verification (or, synonymously, monitoring) [2], on the other hand, does not suffer from these problems. Monitors are software systems, produced from specifications, that run in parallel to the production code and raise an alarm if the system runs (or potentially runs) into a bad state. They thus provide a sensible alternative to ensure the dependability and reliability of software systems at production time.

The generation of runtime monitors from temporal specifications is a well-studied problem (e.g., for Metric Temporal Logic [13], Bounded Linear Temporal Logic [11], HyperLTL [10]). However, the temporal logics used in these approaches were not originally designed with an engineer developing reactive systems in the field as the intended user. Beckert et al. [4] propose to use *Generalized Test Tables* (GTTs) as a practical temporal specification language for reactive systems (i.e., embedded systems driving cyber-physical systems (CPSs) through a periodically executed program that reads sensors and controls actuators). The specification language picks up specification concepts that practitioners in the engineering field are familiar with, and thus it is particularly user-friendly. By design, they are well-suited for specifying sequential processes.

We present the approach behind the monitor generator tool TTMONITOR which generates efficient runtime monitors code in C++ from GTT specifications. It implements new features (which we describe in this paper) that make it particularly suitable for monitoring analysis for workflows where each process step is specified as an individual test table. Trigger-based mechanisms spawn monitors dynamically to allow this specification technique to work. The tool is part of our formal analysis toolbox for PLC verification code.

Generalized Test Tables. Generalized test tables are a table-based specification language for specifying reactive systems with a focus on practicability and comprehensibility. A reactive system, in the context of this paper, is a piece of software, which is periodically executed: reading input sensor signals and producing output actuator commands. A single repetition of the code is called an I/O cycle. The concept behind GTTs has been derived from concrete test tables—a description language used in industry to formulate test protocols which are written as sequences of concrete sensors and actuators signal values. A GTT is a generalization of a concrete test table in which concrete values (or durations) in table cells may be abstracted into constraints that can represent many values. Hence, a GTT covers not only a single (concrete) test case, but an entire *family of test cases*. Though a GTT thus covers a (possibly infinite) set of concrete behaviors, it keeps its exemplary character since all concrete behaviors are instances of the same ideal workflow description.

Usually a single GTT does not fully specify a system. It rather is a generalized example, covering a certain situation or scenario, and a comprehensive specification requires several tables. It is therefore important that the presented runtime verification approach can efficiently operate on sets of tables. GTTs are well-suited for an incremental specification process, where the specification grows over time as experience on the system behavior is gathered (be it during the design phase or later during testing, or even during production).

GTTs are stateful contract specifications that have assumptions (preconditions) and assertions (postconditions) in every I/O cycle. This distinction in the conditions allows us to distinguish a monitor terminating because of a failed assumption (uncovered case) from a monitor halting because of a failed assertion (specification violation). The contract design of GTTs allows us to distinguish four different modes of a monitor:

- *running*—system and monitor in operation, no violation;
- *extraneous*—the specification does not cover this concrete run;
- *failure*—the monitored run violates the specification;
- *finished*—the monitor has finished, the system continues, but cannot fail this specification any longer.

Contributions. Our contributions in this paper are:

(1) We present an approach by which GTT specifications can be verified dynamically using runtime monitors. It extends an earlier approach that was limited to fewer language constructs. In particular, the presented extensions include row groups, omega repetition, global parameters, and nondeterminism.
(2) We introduce the concept of *Dynamic Monitors*, by which monitors can be restarted, and can have multiple instances running at the same time.
(3) We present an approach for hierarchical combination of monitors. This approach allows adding and removing runtime monitors during operation. The hierarchical combination enables a flexible aggregation of monitor results using a variety of functions.
(4) We provide TTMONITOR, a monitor-generation tool that creates monitors from GTT specifications. The C++ code of the monitor produced by TTMONITOR is highly portable as it does not depend on libraries. The tool sources are publicly available under https://formal.iti.kit.edu/nfm2021.

This work extends and generalizes ideas of generating runtime monitors from GTTs presented by Cha et al. [7], where the approach was tailored to the specific needs of the domain of automated production systems and did not support row groups, omega repetition, global parameters, and nondeterminism.

Outline. In Sect. 2, we briefly explain the syntax and semantics of GTTs. The monitor generation and the supported features are presented in Sect. 3, followed by the application scenarios of these features in Sect. 4. In Sect. 5 we discuss generalizations regarding our approach. Related work is presented in Sect. 6, and we conclude and present further potential optimizations in Sect. 7.

2   Generalized Test Tables

A GTT is a temporal specification in tabular form for a reactive system, such that every I/O cycle corresponds to one row in the table. In principle, the rows

#	ASSUME		ASSERT		☉	
	$T_c[°C]$	$T_b[°C]$	P	B		
0	$(T_c - T_b) > d$	$[10, 60 + d]$	TRUE	FALSE	30s	$\lceil_{[0,1]}$
1	$> T_b, < T_c[-1]$	$> T_b[-1], < 60 + d$	TRUE	FALSE	—	
2	$\leq T_b$	$\leq 60 - d$	FALSE	TRUE	—	$\lceil_{[0,1]}$ −∞
3	$\leq T_b$	$\leq 60 + d$	FALSE	TRUE	—	
4	—	$> 60 - d, \leq 60 + d$	FALSE	FALSE	$[1\text{min}, —]_p$	

Fig. 1. An example GTT for a solar thermal system

are executed from top to bottom, in their natural order, but the specification language possesses means to specify repeated lines or blocks.

A full account on the syntax and semantics of GTTs can be found in [4, 8]; we will briefly summarize it in the following section. The introduction is guided by the concrete example in Fig. 1. The specified system is a solar thermal collector that uses energy of the sunlight to heat water. The system is equipped with an auxiliary gas burner which is activated when the solar energy is not sufficient. The GTT in Fig. 1 specifies how the system should control its water pump (P) and the gas burner (B) in response to the water temperature in the boiler (T_b) and in the collector (T_c).

2.1 Syntactical Elements

Every signal and every actuator variable has its column in a table. Since each table row describes a single step of the behavior, each cell constrains the value of a variable in the corresponding I/O cycle. The set of columns is divided into *assumption columns* and *assertion columns*. The former serve as *preconditions* for the cycle and the latter as *postconditions*, in the sense that all postconditions need to hold after the cycle if the preconditions were true before the cycle. Typically, the input variables of the system are assumption columns as these are generated by a physical environment and thus cannot be influenced by the system. The output variables are usually the assertion columns.

In contrast to concrete test tables, GTTs may contain constraints instead of concrete values in each cell. These constraints describe the set of admissible values for the corresponding cell. Thus GTTs are more expressive than concrete test tables. Syntactically, these constraints are a comma-separated list of Boolean constraints. GTTs support several abbreviations for the constraints. The constraints within a GTT may refer to global parameters which are placeholders for nondeterministically chosen, but fixed values. A system needs to conform to every possible instantiation of a global parameter (in this sense parameters are universally quantified over the entire GTT). The example has a global parameter d that is used to make the specification parametric in the temperature span. For example, the constraint "$[60 - d, 60 + d]$" (in Fig. 1) restricts the boiler temperature T_b to the depicted range and is an abbreviation for $T_b \geq 60 - d$, $T_b \leq 60 + d$ for any arbitrary d. A "don't-care" (—) constraint signals that the value may be chosen arbitrarily. References to values of past I/O cycles can be made using square brackets, e.g., "$< T_c[-1]$" specifies that the collector temperature is strictly decreasing compared to the last cycle. We denote global parameters with lowercase letters to distinguish them from program variables, for which we use uppercase letters. To increase readability, we omit a cell constraint if it is identical to the constraint of the cell directly above.

To make GTTs more expressive than mere sequences of I/O cycles, an individual line or multiple lines (a block) may be annotated with a repetition scheme. The repetition of rows is defined in the special table column DURATION ($\circlearrowright$), and the repetition of blocks is marked by a vertical bar. For example, the duration specification of 30 s in the first row of Fig. 1 states that for the first 30 s the system should adhere to this row. The stated time spans are converted into equivalent numbers of I/O-cycle iterations. For a cycle time of 10 s, the first row is repeated three times, and the last row for at least six times. For the specification of durations, the set of expressions is limited: the cells may contain concrete values, concrete intervals of natural numbers, "—" (nondeterministic, finite repetition) and "$-_\infty$" (infinite repetition). They specify the number of iterations that the respective row (or block) may be repeated.

2.2   Semantics: Table Conformance

The semantics of a GTT as a temporal specification is a set of admissible concrete behaviors. A generalized table T essentially corresponds to the set $B(T)$ of all concrete table expansions in which table rows (and blocks) have been rolled out in accordance to their duration annotations, and all table cells have been replaced with concrete values that satisfy the constraints.

We model a reactive system $S : (I \times \Sigma) \to (\Sigma \times O)$ as a function which takes a signal input in I and an internal state in Σ of the system, and computes the new state and the output in O. Thus, a reactive system is causal and deterministic. An (infinite) trace of S is a sequence $((i_1, o_1), (i_2, o_2), \ldots) \in (I \times O)^\omega$, such that the output values o_k are the result of the repeated application of function S to the input values i_k.

A trace tr of S conforms to T if there exists a concrete table c in the expansion set $B(T)$ such that the i-th element in tr satisfies all assumptions and all assertions in the i-th row of c. A trace violates T if there is no such satisfying witness c, but there exists a table $d \in B(T)$ whose assumptions are satisfied while at least one assertion fails. It is also possible that there is no concrete table for which all assumptions are satisfied by the trace. In this case the trace is not covered by the specification. A system S conforms to a GTT T if every trace of S conforms to T.

Beckert et al. [4] provide a formal definition of GTT conformance as a two-party game between the software system and its environment that also covers cases that we omitted here. In each turn, the environment of the system under test chooses the input values and the system responds with the computed output. A party loses if it emits a value that violates the current assumptions (for the

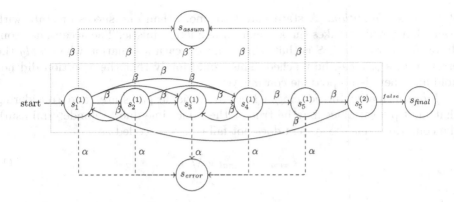

Fig. 2. Sketch of the automaton generated for the GTT of Fig. 1.

environment) or assertions (for the system). This conformance condition can be encoded into an automaton which is described in the following section.

2.3   Automaton Generation

For (static) conformance verification, a GTT is translated into a nondeterministic automaton as described in the following, such that when a trace tr of the system S is accepted by the automaton, it conforms to the GTT. Later this automaton is translated into a transition system encoded by Boolean formulas; see Sect. 3.

Automaton. Figure 2 sketches the generated automaton for the example shown in Fig. 1. A state $s_i^{(k)}$ represents the k-th iteration of the i-th row of the table and expresses that the i-th row is currently a possible step of the test protocol. Hence, if $s_i^{(k)}$ is active, the assumption and assertion of the i-th table row define a valid turn for the challenger and the system in the conformance game. The state s_{error} represents a violation of a row assertion, and the state s_{assum} represents a violation of a row assumption. The state s_{final} represents the end of the table. If this state is reached, the system conforms to the GTT.

There are three kinds of transitions: An α edge from a state $s_i^{(k)}$ to the state s_{error} is triggered if the assumption of the i-th row is satisfied, but the assertion of the same row is violated. A β edge to the state s_{assum} is triggered if the assumption of the i-th row is violated. In this case it does not matter whether the assertion holds or not. A γ edge is taken when both the assumption and the assertion hold, leading to the next possible steps in the test protocol. Note that due to the strong-repeated row group in Fig. 1, the end-of-the-table and thus the final state s_{final} is not reachable. We model this situation by labeling the edge to s_{final} with the contradictory guard *false*.

Acceptance Condition. A state may have more than one successor state with transition γ which makes the automaton nondeterministic. The acceptance condition for a trace $tr \in S$ is that it must never reach a situation where *only* the error state s_{error} can be reached. This would imply that the assertion did not hold and there is no possible continuation.

More formally: Introducing a Boolean variable per state (and considering that multiple variables may be true at the same time due to nondeterminism), the condition that the system does not fail can be encoded as

$$s_{error} \rightarrow s_{final} \vee \bigvee_{i,k} s_i^{(k)} \ . \tag{1}$$

which requires that at least one other state is possible (either a state $s_i^{(k)}$ inside the table or the final state s_{final}) whenever an error has been recognized.

3   Monitor Generation

We now explain how a runtime verification monitor is created from a GTT.

Monitor. A monitor is a software module that runs alongside the monitored reactive system and is executed at the end of each I/O cycle—after the output of the reactive system has been computed. It checks whether the trace (comprising of input, output, and internal state values) observed thus far (i.e., the current system state together with previously observed system states) satisfies the given specification. In the case of a monitor derived from a GTT T, the monitor can report one of four cases:

(1) The trace adheres to the specification, i.e., there is at least one sequence of rows in T such that all assumptions and assertions are satisfied (*running*).
(2) There is no sequence of rows in T such that all trace assumptions are satisfied (*extraneous input*), i.e., the specification does not cover the observed trace.
(3) There is a sequence of rows in T such that all assumptions of the trace are satisfied, but no sequence satisfies all assertions (*failure*).
(4) The trace adheres to the specification for a sequence of rows in T such that the end of T has been reached (*finished*).

The state *finished* is a special case of *running*, but it is particularly interesting since the monitor can idle as it can no longer change its state (in particular it can no longer fail the specification).

Definition 1 (Monitor). *Let $S \colon (I \times \Sigma) \rightarrow (\Sigma \times O)$ be a reactive system with input space I, output space O, and state space Σ. A monitor $\mathcal{M}$ with internal state space Σ_M is a reactive system $\mathcal{M} \colon (I \times O \times \Sigma) \times \Sigma_M \rightarrow \Sigma_M \times \{\text{RUN}, \text{EXTRA}, \text{FAIL}, \text{FIN}\}$ that takes as input the current input, output, and state values of S and returns as output a verdict. The verdict may be RUN (for running), EXTRA (for extraneous), FAIL (for failure), or FIN (for finished).*

From an Automaton to a Monitor. We use the automaton definition from Sect. 2.3 to build a monitor $\mathcal{M}(T)$ from a GTT T that realizes such an automaton. Since the automaton can be nondeterministic, $\mathcal{M}(T)$ needs to consider all possible runs, and hence has to maintain in its state space Σ_M a *set* of current automaton states $\mathbf{S} \subseteq \{s_{error}, s_{assum}, s_{final}, \dots s_k^{(i)} \dots\}$. The automaton construction is suitable for GTTs which do not use global parameters. We derive the verdict $m_T(\mathbf{S})$ of $\mathcal{M}(T)$ from the current automaton states $\mathbf{S}$ as follows:

$$m_T(\mathbf{S}) := \begin{cases} \text{RUN} & : \mathbf{S} \cap \mathbf{S}_{row} \neq \emptyset \\ \text{EXTRA} & : \mathbf{S} = \{s_{assum}\} \vee \mathbf{S} = \emptyset \\ \text{FAIL} & : s_{error} \in \mathbf{S} \wedge \mathbf{S}_{row} \cap \mathbf{S} \neq \emptyset \\ \text{FIN} & : s_{final} \in \mathbf{S} \end{cases} \tag{2}$$

where $\mathbf{S}_{row} = \{s_{final}, \dots s_k^{(i)} \dots\}$ is the set of automaton states representing a table row or the end of the table. If the invariant (1) that encodes conformance to a GTT specification is violated by a system trace, then the verdict function (2) returns FAIL for that trace. In case that the invariant is satisfied for a (finite) trace, the verdict function can make a more fine-grained statement and return one of the three other verdicts, distinguishing between situations in which the specification does not cover the trace (EXTRA), the end of a specification has been reached (FIN), or the trace runs according to the specification (RUN). The monitor construction is designed to maintain conformance (Sect. 2.2).

Proposition 1 (Relation to Conformance). *Let S be a reactive system, T a GTT, and $\mathcal{M}(T)$ the generated monitor. S conforms to T if and only if $\mathcal{M}(T)$ does never produce the verdict FAIL in any I/O cycle step for any possible behavior of S.*

We know from [4] that S conforms to the GTT T if and only if the constructed automaton $\mathcal{A}_T$ (Sect. 2.3) never violates its invariant (1). As the generated monitor $\mathcal{M}(T)$ simulates the execution of the automaton $\mathcal{A}_T$ and the verdict FAIL corresponds to the violation of the invariant, the monitor $\mathcal{M}(T)$ will emit FAIL if and only if a system does not conform to the specification.

Challenges. One challenge of the monitor is to determine the instantiation of the global parameters from the observable system state. In contrast to static conformance verification, where a system needs to adhere to all global parameters' instantiations, the monitor supervises and assesses only the current trace, where the instantiations (along with the input and output values) of the global parameters are determined by the environment and by the system.

In the remainder of this section, we explain how we tackle the following challenges: handling global parameters, especially in combination with a nondeterministic row choice (Sect. 3.1); combining multiple GTTs into a single monitor (Sect. 3.2); restarting after bailing out (Sect. 3.3); and monitoring concurrent events and their effects (Sect. 3.3). These topics have solutions for static verification which cannot be transferred to the case of runtime verification.

3.1 Global Parameters and Nondeterminism

Global parameters within a GTT are universally quantified, which works out fine for static verification which can deal with uninterpreted symbols. But during runtime monitoring, the monitor needs to determine the instantiation of global parameters by observing the current input-output trace. Hence, we need to decide *when* and *to which value* a global parameter is to be bound.

A global parameter may occur in a GTT at an arbitrary position. The first occurrence of a global parameter g could be, for instance, in the constraint $g \operatorname{DIV} 2 = In$ (where "In" is a program variable of the reactive system and DIV denotes integer division). In general, constraints could have zero, one, or multiple solutions for g, hence the value of g may be ambiguous. In our example, the constraint has two solutions for each input value In: $g = 2 * In$ and $g = 2 * In + 1$.

We tackle this problem by introducing a syntactical restriction: the first appearance of a global parameter g needs to be in a binding equation, where g stands alone on one side of the equation. In the above example, the user needs to rewrite the equation, and bound the solution to g explicitly, e.g., "$g = 2 * In$". In Sect. 5 we present two approaches to eliminate this syntactical restriction.

Since time constraints allow rows (and blocks) to be skipped, it cannot be guaranteed that the syntactically first occurrence of a global parameter is evaluated. However, it can be statically ensured that the first evaluation of a global parameter during a run is within a binding equation. Alternatively, this check can also be performed at runtime by the monitor.

Another challenge for global parameters is potential ambiguities induced by nondeterministic tables as multiple rows (automaton states) with different assignments for the same global parameter could be active at the same time and thus force a binding to different values. To resolve this challenge, we use a token-based evaluation of the automaton, where each token represents a possible run of the automaton. Each token carries an assignment of the global parameters together with its current automaton state. A token is always in a single state, and therefore the value bound to a global parameter is unambiguous. If there are multiple possible successor automaton states for a token, the token is duplicated and each copy obtains a different successor state. Because the automaton can be in multiple states, there might be multiple tokens. Furthermore, it is also possible that there are two tokens at the same automaton state with different assignments of the global parameters. Two tokens at the same state with identical assignments can be reduced to a single token as both behave identically.

3.2 Combined Monitors

Since GTTs are designed to describe a set of similar system behaviors, it is often-times not possible to describe the complete system behavior in one table. Hence, the specified behavior of a GTT is only a partial view of the complete system and a more comprehensive specification can be gained by using several GTTs to specify a system. To support such multi-table specifications, we need to support monitoring of several GTTs at the same time. We now show how the generated monitors of GTTs can be stitched together into one combined monitor.

A combined monitor $\mathcal{M}_{T_1,...,T_n}$ is a reactive system which monitors a set $\{T_1,...,T_n\}$ of GTTs by using the monitors $\mathcal{M}(T_i)$ for $1 \leq i \leq n$. The combination essentially runs the monitors in parallel, and the combined monitor state is the tuple of the states of the individual monitors: $\mathbf{S}_{1,...,n} = (\mathbf{S}_1,...,\mathbf{S}_n)$. The most relevant part of the combined monitor is the aggregation function $\overline{m}_{T_1,...,T_n}(\mathbf{S}_{1,...,n})$ which combines the verdicts $m_{T_i}(\mathbf{S}_i)$ of the sub-monitors $\mathcal{M}(T_i)$ (for $1 \leq i \leq n$) into a single verdict $\overline{m}_{T_1,...,T_n}(\mathbf{S}_{1,...,n}) = \mathrm{agg}(m_{T_1}(\mathbf{S}_1),...,m_{T_n}(\mathbf{S}_n))$. There are two canonical aggregation functions: $\mathrm{agg}_\wedge$ and $\mathrm{agg}_\vee$.

For the aggregation, we filter out the *extraneous* results from the sub-monitor verdicts ($\mathrm{filter}_{\mathrm{EXTRA}}(\cdot)$), and then the functions $\mathrm{agg}_\wedge$ and $\mathrm{agg}_\vee$ can be defined as the minimum and the maximum functions with respect to the order FAIL < RUN < FIN on the results. Formally,

$$\mathrm{agg}_\wedge(a_1,...,a_n) = \min(\mathrm{filter}_{\mathrm{EXTRA}}(a_1,...,a_n))$$
$$\mathrm{agg}_\vee(a_1,...,a_n) = \max(\mathrm{filter}_{\mathrm{EXTRA}}(a_1,...,a_n))$$

with the special case that $\max(\emptyset) = \min(\emptyset) = \mathrm{EXTRA}$. The aggregation functions $\mathrm{agg}_\wedge$ and $\mathrm{agg}_\vee$ correspond to the conjunction and disjunction in a three-valued logic with the given order.

The $\mathrm{agg}_\wedge$ function corresponds to the conjunction of the monitors returning RUN if there is no sub-monitor that returns FAIL and at least one monitor is RUN. Similarly, $\mathrm{agg}_\vee$ represents the disjunction returning RUN if at least one sub-monitor signals RUN. The value EXTRA expresses that a monitor has diverged, and this value is ignored in both aggregations.

In general, aggregation functions can be user-defined functions which are fine-tuned for the given tables and the automation system based on gained experience. For example, we allow complex aggregation functions which compute histograms of the given monitor results and aggregate their results based on a given threshold for each category (e.g., a combined monitor indicating RUN implies that at least a given percentage of the sub-monitors are fine (RUN) and the number of errors (FAIL) is below a threshold).

Note that combined monitors themselves can be subject to a combination, which allows the construction of sophisticated combinations. For example, imagine one GTT *emerg* which describes the emergency behavior of a system, and two mutually exclusive GTTs *man* and *auto* covering the manual and automatic operation modes. We can compose a comprehensive specification by logically combining the corresponding monitors for the GTTs, expressing that "*emerg* and *man* or *auto*" should always be satisfied. The corresponding combined monitor is $\mathcal{M}^\wedge(\mathcal{M}_{emerg}, \mathcal{M}^\vee(\mathcal{M}_{man}, \mathcal{M}_{auto}))$.

Performance Considerations. The monitor combination could have been implemented as a single product automaton construction combing all constraints of a set of GTTs. We decided against this product automaton construction, as the implementation effort would be higher and there are no clear performance benefits. States and tokens of and in the product automaton can be saved if the GTTs share initial rows, but this effect is negligible for long-running systems.

On the other hand, if global parameters occur in the GTTs, the approach with several individual monitors (and, hence, a separate token for each GTT) is more flexible as each monitor can consider a separate global parameter binding. Moreover, the approach of combining individual monitors allows the user to include handwritten monitors and supports dynamic monitors (Sect. 3.3).

3.3   Triggered Restarts and Dynamic Monitors

Triggered Restarts. If a monitor $\mathcal{M}$ runs into a situation where its monitored table does not cover the current run, i.e., the assumptions of all currently possible rows are violated, $\mathcal{M}$ does not need to be continued since it cannot recover from that state. Let us call such a monitor *diverging*. Consider a situation where a GTT describes the normal behavior of a system. If an (abnormal) emergency situation has been triggered for the system, the monitor diverges when the abnormal situation occurs since this behavior is not covered by the table. After recovery, it can no longer be used to monitor the system.

This problem was already identified in [7], and a solution which allows a simple and precise monitoring of event-triggered processes has been proposed there. An additional specification can be provided which triggers a restart of a monitor for a GTT. A restart trigger is a condition ϕ on the current state in the constraint language of the table cells. A monitor $\mathcal{M}$ restarts if it has diverged, i.e., once it results in a verdict of EXTRA, and the observed system trace meets ϕ. The restart resets the monitor to its initial state.

Dynamic Monitors. We generalize the idea of restarting further by allowing—beside a restarting condition—a starting condition ψ for a GTT T. Whenever ψ is met by the current system trace, a new instance of the monitor $\mathcal{M}_T$ is created and started. Note that, unlike the restart condition ϕ, the trigger ψ is not bound to another diverged monitor being stuck in the EXTRA state.

Dynamic monitors can be used to compose event-triggered specifications, where the expected system reaction to the event is described. For example, they can be used to specify the flow of work pieces and tracking the correct processing of each work piece in the software of production systems. Whenever a work piece appears at the beginning of the conveyor belt, this event triggers the spawning of a new monitor which monitors that particular work piece. With dynamic monitors, it is not necessary to globally formalize the entire work process chain, but rather one can focus locally on each process step for a single work piece.

A starting condition ψ is evaluated before the execution of the sub-monitors. Therefore, the newly created monitor instances start in the same I/O cycle in which ψ has been satisfied. At the end of a cycle, dynamic monitors which have diverged are discarded to avoid growing memory consumption. As a best practice to keep the memory consumption low, every dynamic monitor should eventually terminate, e.g., the end of specification is reachable.

The concept of dynamic monitors seems to subsume the concept of restarting monitors. But there is a subtle difference: with restarting, there always exists only one monitor instance which can be restarted after it has diverged, whereas a dynamic monitor can have multiple active instances at the same time.

#	ASSUME									ASSERT		⊙
	On	Off	Resume	Set	QuickDecel	QuickAccel	Accel	Brake	Speed	CruiseSpeed	CruiseState	
	BOOL	BOOL	BOOL	BOOL	BOOL	BOOL	BOOL	BOOL	FLOAT	FLOAT	ENUM	
0	FALSE	FALSE	FALSE	—	—	—	—	—		0	OFF	≥ 0
1	TRUE			FALSE					> *SpeedMin*	= *Speed*	ON	1
2	—				FALSE	FALSE	FALSE	FALSE				≥ 0

Restart: *CruiseState = Off*

Fig. 3. Generalized test table for the cruise control system.

4 Application Scenarios

In this section we demonstrate the specification of reactive systems with GTTs and show how the TTMONITOR tool can generate monitors from the GTTs using the presented approach. The chosen examples demonstrate the benefits of the approach in different application contexts for reactive systems. Due to space restrictions, the table input files and monitors generated from them can be found on the companion website.[1]

4.1 Cruise Control System

A cruise control system (CCS) is a driver assistance system found in cars that accurately maintains the speed set by the driver by controlling the throttle-accelerator pedal linkage without driver intervention. If the driver uses the accelerator or the brake pedals, the system releases its control over the velocity. CCSs have already been formally studied [1,12,15]. We follow the specification and Esterel implementation in [19]. There are nine input parameters to the system: *On, Off, Resume, Set, Speed, QuickDeccel, QuickAccel, Accel,* and *Decel.* The CCS returns three output values: the current operation mode (on, off, stand-by, disabled), the current target speed, and the value of the throttle. The GTT in Fig. 3 describes those scenarios in which the CCS is switched on and should maintain the current speed until either the brake or the accelerator pedal are pressed. This monitor becomes obsolete (i.e., it diverges) if the CCS is switched off, and restarts once the system is switched on.

4.2 Linear Regression

Here we demonstrate the feature of global parameter binding. The *Linear Regression* function block implements a commonly needed functionality for implementing CPSs, namely the calibration of sensor values. The evaluated software module origins from [18], where it is used to demonstrate static verification of GTTs using model checking. The state space of this function block, which uses floating point arithmetic, is relatively large and its state transition function relatively complex, limiting the applicability of static verification tools.

Linear Regression maps actual sensor values to a defined range of calibrated values. This mapping is internally represented as a linear interpolation curve

---

[1] https://formal.iti.kit.edu/nfm2021/.

#	ASSUME				ASSERT	⊙
	TPy	TPSet	Mode	X	Y	
0	—	—	Op	—	0	—
1	—	0	Teach	—	0	$[1, to]$
2	y_1	1	Teach	x_1	0	1
3	—	0	Teach	—	0	$[1, to]$
4	y_2	1	Teach	$x_2, \neq x_1$	0	1
5	—	—	Teach	—	0	1
6	—	—	Op	—	$= y_1 + y_2 - y_1/x_2 - x_1(X - x_1)$	—

Fig. 4. Generalized test table of a system which maps sensor values to their physical representation by a taught linear curve. Originally presented in [18].

#	ASSUME					ASSERT						⊙
	CranePos ENUM	CraneWP BOOL	WP@Magazin ENUM	StampState ENUM	WP@Conveyor BOOL	Crane ENUM	Vaccum BOOL	Stamp BOOL	Conv.Belt BOOL	Pusher1 BOOL	Pusher2 BOOL	
0	MAGAZINE	FALSE	METAL_READY	—	—	STOP	—	—	—	—	—	1
1		—				PICKUP	TRUE					$[1, T_1]$
2		TRUE	EMPTY	FREE		STOP						1
3	—		—			MOVE_CW						$[1, T_2]$
4	STAMP					STOP						10
5						RELEASE						5
6						—	FALSE					1
7		FALSE		OCCUPIED				TRUE				1
8	—	—			—	FALSE	FALSE		—			—
9	STAMP	FALSE		READY		PICKUP	TRUE					$[1, T_3]$
10		TRUE		FREE		MOVE_CCW	TRUE					—
11	CONVEYOR					STOP	TRUE					—
12						RELEASE						5
13	—	FALSE				—	FALSE		TRUE	FALSE		1
14						—						T_4
15											TRUE	5

Fig. 5. A GTT for describing the material flow in the PPU plant, which is instantiated when a new work piece appears at the magazine (*WP@Magazin* ≠ EMPTY).

whose parameters are learned during operation. To this end, the function block can be operated in two modes: the calibration mode ("Teach") and the operation mode ("Op"). After learning, the block performs the linear interpolation in the operation mode, mapping the incoming sensor values to values according to the calibrated curve. The system receives the selected mode (*Mode*) and the sensor value input (X), and two additional inputs needed for the calibration: *TPy* for the reference value and *TPSet* to trigger teaching. The system has only a single output Y, which is zero during teaching or for improper reference points. If the reference points are proper values, then the output Y is defined by the linear curve at position X. This behavior is described by the GTT in Fig. 4.

4.3   Conveyor Belt Process

In this scenario we demonstrate the features of dynamic monitors by specifying the material flow inside an automated manufacturing plant. The example is based on the Pick-and-Place-Unit (PPU) developed at the TU Munich [17]. The PPU was developed to demonstrate methods to manage the evolution of long-running hard- and software. More than 20 scenarios have been designed, and they demonstrate a variety of evolution scenarios typical for an automated production system. We use one scenario (scenario number 13) in which the PPU picks up work pieces from a deposit with a crane. If a work piece is metallic, it is transported to the stamp to be engraved. Then the engraved work piece is picked up again and is moved to the conveyor belt, where the work pieces are finally sorted on different ramps. Non-metallic work pieces are not engraved, and are directly moved to the conveyor belt. For optimization, the crane moves non-metallic pieces to the conveyor belt while a metallic piece is being stamped.

Due to the parallel processing (stamping, transporting, and sorting) within the plant, a global specification of the input and output variables is hard to achieve. Instead, we can describe the plant by following the work pieces individually.

Note that the assumptions in Fig. 5 encode the expected physical behavior of the environment. If they are violated, e.g., if a work piece is not detected in time, the monitor raises the signal (*extraneous*), and this should be interpreted as a flag for an error in the environment. One possibility to deal with this is to deliver more explanations why a monitor diverges, as discussed in Sect. 5.

5   Discussion: Generalizations

Counting Repetitions. The automaton for constructing the monitors is generated from a normalized (unrolled) test table. Therefore, a row with a duration $[m, n]$ ends up in an automaton with $n \cdot d$ states, where d denotes the number of unrolled overlying row groups. Basing the evaluation of automata on tokens would allow us to use integer counters in the tokens for counting the repetition of rows and row groups, thus reducing the number of states in the automaton and the code and data size of the monitor. Moreover, we can get rid of the restriction of nonrigid duration constraints and allow the use of state or input variables in the duration column. Their use also enables using a clock time instead of I/O cycle numbers and makes the generated monitors applicable for interactive systems.

Symbolical Representation of Global Parameters. In Sect. 3.1 we restricted the first occurrence of global parameters to a form which describes an unambiguous value to bind. This restriction could be lifted, with a negative impact on the performance, by using a symbolic representation, e.g., a BDD or a CNF formula. Instead of a concrete value, a token would hold a symbolic representation for each global parameter. The constraints of a global parameter in the monitored table cells are added to the token's symbolic representation and limit the value range of the global parameter. The symbolic representation must be satisfiable (describing at least one possible value of the global parameter) during monitoring. Moreover, every monitored constraint needs to be checked symbolically.

A simpler solution can be the use of multiple tokens. Instead of forcing the user to decide on one solution, we create a token for each adhering binding of the global parameters of the equation. Back to the integer division example in Sect. 3.1, we know there are at most two possible solutions, thus we will create zero to two tokens with different assignments. Note, this solution is only possible if the number of solutions is limited and rather small.

Assumptions as Assertions on the Environment. The presented approach reports violated assumptions as extraneous situations and bails out without reporting an error. There are situations in which an assumption violation is an indicator for a serious error occurring in the environment, not only a situation not covered by the specification. In those situation an error should be reported. We observed this in Sect. 4.3, where a disappearing work piece on a conveyor belt is an unexpected event and indicates either a broken sensor or a plant standstill. It needs to be distinguished from a violated assumption for a work piece not covered by the specification. To this end, the specification mechanism can be extended to support more assertion levels than the two presented in this paper.

6   Related Work

The generation of runtime monitors from formal specification is well-studied; see, e.g., [6]. The most closely related topics are the monitoring of reactive systems and the monitoring of engineer-friendly specification languages. Two prominent examples for the latter are LoLA [9] and Copilot [14]. Both are stream-based languages which allow for and claim to be more user-friendly than the underlying temporal logics. Copilot focuses more on the real-time aspect of the created monitors while LoLA can additionally provide statistical measurements for system profiling (rather than pure Boolean verdicts). Both monitoring approaches do not explicitly support dynamic spawning or restarting of monitors.

Bloem et al. [5] propose the construction of *shields*—runtime monitors with the ability to alter the output of the monitored system when a violation is detected. Their monitor construction therefore also requires the synthesis of a reactive system, which computes the alternative correct outputs. They introduce a new notion of k-stabilization which captures the idea that a system can alter the output of a system for k steps, to avoid the violation of given properties.

Bauer et al. [3] present a framework which allows to identify the faulty subcomponent in a reactive system (in addition to monitoring). This is achieved by first monitoring components locally (according to a Timed LTL specification [16]) and then using first order logic to describe the overall system behavior. Thus, it is possible to detect which components may be responsible for an observed error.

7   Conclusion

In this paper we presented an approach for generating runtime monitors from GTTs, which are a table-based specification language for the behavior of reactive systems. In contrast to earlier work, the presented approach can deal with nondeterminism and global parameters in tables. Moreover, we introduced the concept of dynamic monitors which are created/launched at runtime whenever a specified trigger event occurs. They make possible a local specification of parallel and multi-step processes. We show the applicability of the monitoring approach on concrete examples from the domains of automated production systems and embedded controllers. The approach has been implemented in TTMONI-TOR, an open-source tool which generates monitor code in C++ from GTTs specifications.

GTTs have two distinct kinds of constraints: assumptions and assertions. Depending on the type of constraints that fails, a failing trace is reported to either diverge (i.e., the specification does not cover it) or to reveal a flaw in the implementation. This principle can be refined further in future work that will allow the introduction of several different constraint categories. This will allow the monitor to elaborate the nature of failures even further, as feedback to the engineer. For instance, for each hardware component a category could be introduced for the assumptions on its physical response behavior. If a failure is reported in this category, this will directly indicate that the hardware component has failed. Analogously, also for the assertions on software components.

We plan to evaluate our monitor generation approach and the example monitors in simulation and in (real-time) operation in their environment.

References

1. Aghav, J., Tumma, A.: Esterel implementation and validation of cruise controller. In: Computer Science, Engineering and Applications (CCSEA), pp. 128–141 (2011). https://doi.org/10.5121/csit.2011.1214
2. Bartocci, E., Falcone, Y., Francalanza, A., Reger, G.: Introduction to runtime verification. In: Bartocci, E., Falcone, Y. (eds.) Lectures on Runtime Verification. LNCS, vol. 10457, pp. 1–33. Springer, Cham (2018). https://doi.org/10.1007/978-3-319-75632-5_1
3. Bauer, A., Leucker, M., Schallhart, C.: Model-based runtime analysis of distributed reactive systems. In: Australian Software Engineering Conference (ASWEC), pp. 243–252 (2006). https://doi.org/10.1109/ASWEC.2006.36
4. Beckert, B., Cha, S., Ulbrich, M., Vogel-Heuser, B., Weigl, A.: Generalised test tables: a practical specification language for reactive systems. In: Polikarpova, N., Schneider, S. (eds.) IFM 2017. LNCS, vol. 10510, pp. 129–144. Springer, Cham (2017). https://doi.org/10.1007/978-3-319-66845-1_9
5. Bloem, R., Könighofer, B., Könighofer, R., Wang, C.: Shield synthesis: In: Baier, C., Tinelli, C. (eds.) TACAS 2015. LNCS, vol. 9035, pp. 533–548. Springer, Heidelberg (2015). https://doi.org/10.1007/978-3-662-46681-0_51
6. Cassar, I., Francalanza, A., Aceto, L., Ingólfsdóttir, A.: A survey of runtime monitoring instrumentation techniques. In: Francalanza, A., Pace, G.J. (eds.) Proceedings Second International Workshop on Pre- and Post-Deployment Verification Techniques, PrePost@iFM 2017, Torino, Italy, 19 September 2017. EPTCS, vol. 254, pp. 15–28 (2017). https://doi.org/10.4204/EPTCS.254.2
7. Cha, S., Ulewicz, S., Vogel-Heuser, B., Weigl, A., Ulbrich, M., Beckert, B.: Generation of monitoring functions in production automation using test specifications. In: International Conference on Industrial Informatics (INDIN), pp. 339–344. IEEE (2017). https://doi.org/10.1109/INDIN.2017.8104795
8. Cha, S., Weigl, A., Ulbrich, M., Beckert, B., Vogel-Heuser, B.: Applicability of generalized test tables: a case study using the manufacturing system demonstrator xPPU. Automatisierungstechnik **66**(10), 834–848 (2018). https://doi.org/10.1515/auto-2018-0028

9. D'Angelo, B., et al.: LOLA: runtime monitoring of synchronous systems. In: Temporal Representation and Reasoning (TIME), pp. 166–174. IEEE (2005). https://doi.org/10.1109/TIME.2005.26

10. Finkbeiner, B., Hahn, C., Stenger, M., Tentrup, L.: Monitoring hyper properties. Formal Methods Syst. Des. **54**(3), 336–363 (2019). https://doi.org/10.1007/s10703-019-00334-z

11. Finkbeiner, B., Kuhtz, L.: Monitor circuits for LTL with bounded and unbounded future. In: Bensalem, S., Peled, D.A. (eds.) RV 2009. LNCS, vol. 5779, pp. 60–75. Springer, Heidelberg (2009). https://doi.org/10.1007/978-3-642-04694-0_5

12. Heitmeyer, C.L., Kirby, J., Labaw, B.G.: Tools for formal specification, verification, and validation of requirements. In: Conference on Computer Assurance (COMPASS), pp. 35–47 (2009). https://doi.org/10.1109/CMPASS.1997.613206

13. Ho, H.-M., Ouaknine, J., Worrell, J.: Online monitoring of metric temporal logic. In: Bonakdarpour, B., Smolka, S.A. (eds.) RV 2014. LNCS, vol. 8734, pp. 178–192. Springer, Cham (2014). https://doi.org/10.1007/978-3-319-11164-3_15

14. Perez, I., Dedden, F., Goodloe, A.: Copilot 3. Technical report NASA/TM-2020-220587, National Aeronautics and Space Administration (2020)

15. Predut, S., Ipate, F., Gheorghe, M., Campean, F.: Formal modelling of cruise control system using Event-B and Rodin platform. In: High Performance Computing and Communications (HPCC), pp. 1541–1546. IEEE (2018). https://doi.org/10.1109/HPCC/SmartCity/DSS.2018.00253

16. Raskin, J.F.: Logics, automata and classical theories for deciding real time. Ph.D. thesis, Facultés universitaires Notre-Dame de la Paix, Namur (1999)

17. Vogel-Heuser, B., Legat, C., Folmer, J., Feldmann, S.: Researching evolution in industrial plant automation: Scenarios and documentation of the pick and place unit. Technical report, Institute of Automation and Information Systems, Technische Universität München (2014)

18. Weigl, A., et al.: Generalized test tables: a powerful and intuitive specification language for reactive systems. In: Industrial Informatics, (INDIN), pp. 875–882. IEEE (2017). https://doi.org/10.1109/INDIN.2017.8104887

19. Yep, M., Bechet, S.: Esterel cruise controller (2018). https://github.com/ooksei/esterel-cruise-controller/. Accessed 16 Oct 2019

Quasi-Equal Clock Reduction On-the-Fly

Bernd Westphal[✉][iD]

Albert-Ludwigs-Universität Freiburg, Freiburg, Germany
westphal@informatik.uni-freiburg.de

Abstract. For timed automata, there is the notion of quasi-equal clocks. Two clocks are quasi-equal if, in each reachable configuration, they are equal or at least one has value 0. There are approaches to exploit quasi-equality of clocks to speed up reachability checking for timed automata. There is a procedure to detect quasi-equal clocks and a syntactical transformation of networks of timed automata where quasi-equal clocks are encoded by one representative clock and one boolean token per clock.

In this work, we integrate reachability checking for timed automata with an on-the-fly analysis of quasi-equality. Our approach uses a new data-structure that combines Difference Bound Matrices (DBMs) for representative clocks with a vector of boolean tokens and a representation of equivalence classes. Our approach achieves space-savings similar to the syntactical transformation and exploits phase-wise quasi-equality of clocks, where existing approaches only consider quasi-equality in all reachable configurations.

1 Introduction

Space systems often use wireless communication based on Time Division Multiple Access (TDMA) schemes for reliability and efficiency as in, e.g., the RideSharing data aggregation protocol [1,2]. Each participating component usually has a local timer that is most naturally represented in timed models by local clocks. The number of clocks in a model can substantially affect the space and time consumption of model-checking tasks, so a common goal for models of timed systems is to keep the number of clocks low or reduce the number of clocks in a model while preserving the system behaviour.

A number of properties of clocks have been identified that allow us to reduce the number of clocks in a model. The property considered in this article is *quasi-equality*: Two clocks are quasi-equal if and only if, in each reachable model configuration, they are equal or one has value 0. Quasi-equal (but not equal) clocks are in particular observed in protocol designs that employ some kind of time division: Local clocks define cycles, frames, or slots of the time division and each component is responsible for its clocks so clock resets may interleave [12]. Thereby, clocks become unequal but may be quasi-equal. In previous work [11–14] we have developed a source-to-source transformation of descriptions of networks of timed automata. The transformed network reflects all properties of the

---

Supported by the German Research Council (DFG) under grant WE 6198/1-1.

A. Dutle et al. (Eds.): NFM 2021, LNCS 12673, pp. 375–391, 2021.
https://doi.org/10.1007/978-3-030-76384-8_23

original network but only has as many clocks as there are equivalence classes of quasi-equal clocks. A strong advantage of this syntactical approach is that the timed model need not be optimised for model-checking and can naturally model the timed system and thereby ease validation with the protocol engineers (e.g., by simulation, cf. [3]) and limit maintenance effort to one model (as opposed to one model for validation and one for model-checking, obtained following guidelines such as [18,19]). A drawback is that the equivalence classes need to be known a priori and the efficient quasi-equality detection algorithm [15] is sound but not complete.

In this article, we address the question whether the representation of quasi-equal clocks by tokens and representative clocks (as employed in [12]) has a semantical correspondence which allows us to *integrate* detection of quasi-equalities and space-efficient model-checking. To this end, we introduce a new data structure called DBM_T and adapt the classical timed automata model-checking algorithm to the new data structure. The new algorithm avoids the two passes (detection and transformation) and supports the new, more general notion of *local* quasi-equality that has a potential for further space savings.

Related work includes [7,8], where a static analysis of a timed automaton is performed to detect *equal* clocks (which can then be reduced by syntactical substitution). This approach does not support quasi-equality. In the same line of work, [7,8] consider *activity* of clocks (similar to live variables in program analysis); also see, e.g., [4]. Considering activity is orthogonal to our approach. A different branch of research is concerned with minimisations of the number of clocks. The general case (whether there exists a language equivalent timed automaton with fewer clocks than a given one) is undecidable [9]. Guha et al. [10] have shown that a minimal timed bisimilar automaton is effectively constructable, the procedure is expensive in the number of locations and time. Saeedloei et al. [17] minimise under further constraints (same graph, same pattern of clock resets and uses). Our aim is to exploit the quasi-equality of clocks to improve the space consumption of model-checking networks of timed-automata in an integrated algorithm, we do not address minimality of the number of clocks in general.

The paper is structured as follows. Based on preliminaries from Sect. 2, we introduce the new data-structure DBM_T in Sect. 3. In Sects. 4 and 5, we define operations on DBM_T that we use in Sect. 6 to adapt the classical reachability checking algorithm for networks of timed automata to DBM_T. Section 7 reports evaluation results and Sect. 8 concludes.

2   Preliminaries

The definition of the new data-structure of DBM_T relies strongly on the theory of Difference Bound Matrices (DBM), so we need to recall some definitions for self-containedness. The presentation follows [6] and is standard with the exception that we impose some assumptions on zones towards DBMs for convenience. We then briefly recall the syntax and semantics of timed automata, following [16].

2.1   Clocks, Zones, and Difference-Bound-Matrices

Given a finite, non-empty set $X = \{x_0, x_1, \ldots, x_n\}$, $n \geq 0$, of *clocks*, a *clock constraints* (over X) is an expression of the form $\phi = x - y \sim c$ with $\sim \in \{<, \leq\}$ and $c \in \mathbb{Z}$. Assuming a dedicated clock x_0 that always has value 0, clock constraints can express lower and upper bounds on individual clocks. We use $\Phi(X)$ to denote the set of clock constraints and φ to denote subsets of $\Phi(X)$. Functions $\nu : X \to \mathbb{R}_0^+$ are called *valuation* of X.

A *zone* Z is a set of clock constraints, i.e., $Z \subseteq \Phi(X)$. In the following, we assume that for each two clocks x and y there is at most one constraint of the form $x - y \sim c$ in Z, that a zone implies $x \geq 0$ for each clock x, and that a zone includes the constraint $x - x \leq 0$ for each clock $x \in X$. We write $[\![Z]\!]$ to denote the set of valuations that satisfy all constraints in Z, i.e., $[\![Z]\!] = \{\nu \mid \forall \phi \in Z \bullet \nu \models \phi\}$.

Zones can be represented by Difference Bounds Matrices (DBM). The DBM of Z over $X = \{x_0, x_1, \ldots, x_n\}$ is the $(n+1) \times (n+1)$ matrix with $D_{i,j} = (c, \sim)$ if $x_i - x_j \sim c \in Z$ and $D_{i,j} = \infty$ otherwise. We may use D_{x_i, x_j} to denote $D_{i,j}$ and $|D|$ to denote the dimension of the matrix. Figure 2a (on page 5) shows an example DBM that represents the clock valuation $\{x_0 \mapsto 0, x \mapsto 0, y \mapsto 10\}$. We write $[\![D]\!]$ to denote the set of valuations that satisfy all constraints in D, i.e., $[\![D]\!] = \{\nu \mid \forall i, j \bullet D_{i,j} = \infty \vee D_{i,j} = (c, \sim) \wedge \nu \models x_i - x_j \sim c\}$. If D is the DBM of zone Z, then $[\![D]\!] = [\![Z]\!]$. In the following, we assume that DBMs correspond to zones as introduced above, e.g., $D_{x,x} = (0, \leq)$ for all $x \in X$ with the exception that D_{x_0, x_0} may be $(-1, \leq)$ to represent zone Z with $[\![Z]\!] = \emptyset$.

DBM entries are compared as follows. We have $(m, \sim) < \infty$, $(m_1, \sim_1) < (m_2, \sim_2)$ if $m_1 < m_2$, and $(m, <) < (m, \leq)$. Addition of DBM entries is defined as $\infty + b = \infty$ for each DBM entry b, $(m_1, <) + (m_2, \sim) = (m_1 + m_2, <)$, and $(m_1, \leq) + (m_2, \leq) = (m_1 + m_2, \leq)$. It is computable whether any valuation in $[\![D]\!]$ satisfies a clock constraint ϕ, and whether $[\![D_1]\!] \subseteq [\![D_2]\!]$ (then D_2 is said to *subsume* D_1). There are algorithms to compute on DBMs the intersection of $[\![D]\!]$ with a clock constraint, the effect of arbitrary delay (freeing), and the effect of clock resets. There are a notion of *canonicity*, i.e., encoding each zone by exactly one canonical DBM, and canonicity-preserving variants of the algorithms.

2.2   Networks of Timed Automata

A *timed automaton* $\mathcal{A}$ is a tuple $(L, A, X, I, E, \ell_{ini})$ with a finite set of *locations* L (including the *initial location* ℓ_{ini}), a set of *channels* A, and a finite set of clocks X. Each location $\ell \in L$ is assigned a downward-closed *location invariant* $I(\ell) \subseteq \Phi(X)$ and E is a finite set of *edges*. An edge $(\ell, \alpha, \varphi, \varrho, \ell') \in E$ has *source* and *destination* location ℓ and ℓ', a *guard* $\varphi \subseteq \Phi(X)$, an *action* $\alpha \in \{a!, a? \mid a \in A\} \cup \{\tau\}$, and a *reset* $\varrho \subseteq X$. A *network (of timed automata)* $\mathcal{N} = \mathcal{A}_1 \| \ldots \| \mathcal{A}_n$ consists of finitely many automata with pairwise equal channel and clock sets for simplicity (a clock is called local if it is used in location invariants and edges of at most one automaton).

The operational semantics of $\mathcal{N}$ is the transition system $(Conf(\mathcal{N}), \{\xrightarrow{\lambda} \mid \lambda \in \mathbb{R}_0^+ \cup \{\tau\}\}, C_0)$ where $Conf(\mathcal{N})$ is the set of *configurations*. A configuration

$\langle \ell, Z \rangle$ consists of a location vector $\ell \in L_1 \times \cdots \times L_n$ and a zone Z such that $Z \models I(\ell_i)$. Let $Z_0 = Z_{ini}{\uparrow} \wedge I(\ell_0)$, where Z_{ini} implies that each clock $x \in X$ has value 0, and ℓ_0 the vector consisting of all initial locations,. The set of *initial configurations* is $C_0 = \{\langle \ell_0, Z_0 \rangle\}$ if $[\![Z_0]\!] \neq \emptyset$, and $C_0 = \emptyset$ otherwise. There is a *(time abstract) transition* $\langle \ell, Z \rangle \xrightarrow{\tau} \langle \ell', Z' \rangle$ if and only if there are edges $e_i = (\ell_i, \alpha_i, \varphi_i, \varrho_i, \ell'_i) \in E(\mathcal{A}_i)$ and $e_j = (\ell_j, \alpha_j, \varphi_j, \varrho_j, \ell'_j) \in E(\mathcal{A}_j)$, $0 \leq i, j \leq n$, s.t. $Z \models \varphi_i \wedge \varphi_j$, $\ell' = \ell[\ell_i := \ell'_i, \ell_j := \ell'_j]$, and $Z' = Z[\varrho_i \cup \varrho_j]{\uparrow} \wedge I(\ell')$ where either $i = j$ and $\alpha_i = \tau$, or $i \neq j$ and $\alpha_i = a!$ and $\alpha_j = a?$ for some $a \in A$. Edges e_i and e_j are called *enabled* in this case.

A *computation path* (of $\mathcal{N}$) is an initial and consecutive sequence $\langle \ell_0, Z_0 \rangle \xrightarrow{\tau} \langle \ell_1, Z_1 \rangle \xrightarrow{\tau} \ldots \xrightarrow{\tau} \langle \ell_n, Z_n \rangle$, i.e., if $\langle \ell_0, Z_0 \rangle \in C_0$ and $(\langle \ell_i, Z_i \rangle, \langle \ell_{i+1}, Z_{i+1} \rangle) \in \xrightarrow{\tau}$ for all $0 \leq i < n$. A configuration $\langle \ell, Z \rangle$ (or $\langle \ell, \nu \rangle$) is called *reachable* (in $\mathcal{N}$) if and only if there is a computation path with $\langle \ell, Z \rangle = \langle \ell_n, Z_n \rangle$ (or $\nu \in [\![Z]\!]$). We use $Reach(\mathcal{N})$ to denote the set of all reachable configurations of $\mathcal{N}$.

2.3   Quasi-Equal Clocks

To support *local* quasi-equality (not only network-wide), we define global quasi-equality as a special case of quasi-equality in a set of valuations.

Definition 1. *Two clocks $x, y \in X$ are called* quasi-equal *(locally, or phase-wise) in the set of valuations $N \subseteq X \to \mathbb{R}_0^+$ if and only if, for each $\nu \in N$, $\nu \models x = y \vee x = 0 \vee y = 0$. Clocks x and y are called* quasi-equal in network $\mathcal{N}$ *(or network-wide) if and only if x and y are quasi-equal in the all reachable valuations of $\mathcal{N}$. The set of equivalence classes [13] of network-wide quasi-equality is denoted by $\mathcal{EC}_\mathcal{N}$, in the following exclusive of $\{x_0\}$.* ◇

Fig. 1. Clocks x and y are quasi-equal but not equal for $c = 10$.

In Fig. 1, clocks x and y are quasi-equal for $c = 10$ (and unequal otherwise). In Fig. 5 on page 14, clocks x and y are locally but not globally quasi-equal.

3 DBM_T: DBMs with Clock Partitions and Tokens

In this section, we introduce a new data-structure called DBM_T that realises the idea from [11–14] to only store representative clocks for sets of quasi-equal clocks together with boolean tokens that encode whether a clock is equal to the representative or has value 0. While the syntactical transformation of [11–14] has a set of equivalence-classes wrt. quasi-equality as an input, our approach aims at detecting quasi-equality on-the-fly and exploiting phase-wise quasi-equality. To this end, DBM_T consist of a DBM to represent values of representative clocks, a set of sets of quasi-equal clocks, and a vector of boolean tokens.

Definition 2. *A DBMx Q over X is a triple (C, P, T) where $P = X_0, \ldots, X_m$ is a partitioning of X (that is, $X_i \neq \emptyset$, $X_i \cap X_j = \emptyset$ for $i \neq j$, $X_0 \cup \cdots \cup X_m = X$), $T : X \rightarrow \{0,1\}$, and C is a DBM over clocks $\{r_0, \ldots, r_m\}$. We call r_i the representative (clock) of the clocks in X_i and write $[x] = r_i$ for $x \in X_i$.*

We call $T(x)$ the token of x in Q. The token is called positive if and only if $T(x) = 1$ and negative otherwise. In shorthand notation, we write DBM_T as $Q = C, \{\hat{t}_{x_0,1}, \ldots, \hat{t}_{x_0,k_0}\}, \ldots, \{\hat{t}_{x_m,1}, \ldots, \hat{t}_{x_m,k_m}\}$ if $X_i = \{x_{i,1}, \ldots, x_{i,k_i}\}$ and $\hat{t}_x = t_x$ if $T(x) = 1$ and $\hat{t}_x = \bar{t}_x$ if $T(x) = 0$. ◇

$$
\begin{array}{c}
\begin{array}{cccc}
 & x_0 & x & y \\
\begin{array}{c} x_0 \\ x \\ y \end{array} &
\left(\begin{array}{ccc}
(0, \leq) & (0, \leq) & (-10, \leq) \\
(0, \leq) & (0, \leq) & (-10, \leq) \\
(10, \leq) & (10, \leq) & (0, \leq)
\end{array} \right)
\end{array}
\end{array}
\qquad
\left(\begin{array}{cc}
(0, \leq) & (-10, \leq) \\
(10, \leq) & (0, \leq)
\end{array} \right), \{t_{x_0}\}, \{\bar{t}_x, t_y\}
$$

(a) Example DBM D.   (b) Example DBM_T Q.

$$
D(Q) = \left(\begin{array}{ccc}
C_{[x_0],[x_0]} & C_{[x_0],0} & C_{[x_0],[x]} \\
C_{0,[x_0]} & C_{0,0} & C_{0,[x]} \\
C_{[y],[x_0]} & C_{[y],0} & C_{[y],[y]}
\end{array} \right) = \left(\begin{array}{ccc}
(0, \leq) & (0, \leq) & (-10, \leq) \\
(0, \leq) & (0, \leq) & (-10, \leq) \\
(10, \leq) & (10, \leq) & (0, \leq)
\end{array} \right)
$$

(c) The DBM of DBM_T Q.

Fig. 2. DBM and DBM_T examples.

Definition 3. *Let $Q = (C, P, T)$ be a DBM_T with $P = X_0, \ldots, X_m$. Partition X_i from P is called unstable (in Q) if and only if some tokens of clocks in X_i are positive and some negative in T, i.e. if $0 < \sum_{x \in X_i} T(x) < |X_i|$. Otherwise, X_i is called stable. The partition X_i is called strongly stable if and only if all tokens of clocks in X_i are positive, i.e. if. $\sum_{x \in X_i} T(x) = |X_i|$. If X_i is stable but not strongly stable, it is called weakly stable. We call Q stable etc. if and only if all partitions from P are stable.* ◇

Figure 2b shows an example DBM_T in shorthand notation, i.e., we have $P = \{x_0\}, \{x, y\}$ and $T = \{x_0 \mapsto 1, x \mapsto 0, y \mapsto 1\}$. In Q, $X_0 = \{x_0\}$ is strongly stable and $X_1 = \{x, y\}$ is unstable, hence Q is unstable

Definition 4. *Let $Q = (C, P, T)$ be a DBM_T over X. We use $\llbracket Q \rrbracket$ to denote the set of clock valuations where the values of clocks with positive token coincide with the value of their representative in C and where the values of clocks with negative tokens are 0, i.e.*

$$\llbracket Q \rrbracket = \{\nu : X \rightarrow \mathbb{R}_0^+ \mid \exists \nu_0 \in \llbracket C \rrbracket \; \forall x \in X \bullet \nu(x) = \nu_0([x]) \cdot T(x)\}. \qquad ◇$$

DBM$_T$ represent sets of clock valuations just like DBMs. In the following, we define a mapping from DBM$_T$ to DBMs and show that the DBM of a DBM$_T$ represents the same set of clock valuations. Note that the (somewhat unusual) function notation in Definition 5 is introduced to be used in Lemma 4. Figure 2c shows (the computation of) the DBM of DBM$_T$ Q from Fig. 2b.

Definition 5. *Let $Q = (C, P, T)$ be a DBM$_T$ over X. The DBM over X that is point-wise defined as $D(Q)_{x,y} := (f(P,T)(C))_{x,y}$, where*

$$(f(P,T)(C))_{x,y} = \begin{cases} C_{[x],[y]} & , \text{ if } t_x, t_y \\ C_{[x],0} & , \text{ if } t_x, \bar{t}_y \end{cases} \qquad (f(P,T)(C))_{x,y} = \begin{cases} C_{0,[y]} & , \text{ if } \bar{t}_x, t_y \\ C_{0,0} & , \text{ if } \bar{t}_x, \bar{t}_y \end{cases},$$

is called the DBM of Q *and denoted by $D(Q)$.* ◇

Lemma 1. *Let $Q = (C, P, T)$ be a DBM$_T$ over X and $D(Q)$ the DBM of Q.*

1. *For all $\nu \in [\![D(Q)]\!]$, clocks from the same partition and with positive token are equal in ν, i.e., for all X_i from P we have $\forall x, y \in X_i \bullet T(x) = 1 \wedge T(y) = 1 \implies \nu(x) = \nu(y)$.*
2. *For all $\nu \in [\![D(Q)]\!]$, clocks with negative token have value 0 in ν, i.e. $\forall x \in X \bullet T(x) = 0 \implies \nu(x) = 0$.*

Proof. 1. Let $\nu \in [\![D(Q)]\!]$. Then $D(Q)_{i,i} = (0, \leq)$ (cf. Sect. 2.1). Let $x \neq y \in X_i$ and $T(x) = T(y) = 1$. By Definition 5, we have $D(Q)_{x,y} = D_{[x],[y]}$ and $D(Q)_{y,x} = D_{[y],[x]}$. Since x and y are from the same partition, we have $[x] = [y]$ and hence $D_{[x],[y]} = D_{[y],[x]} = (0, \leq)$. Valuation ν satisfies both constraints, $x - y \leq 0$ and $y - x \leq 0$, hence $\nu(x) = \nu(y)$.

2. Let $\nu \in [\![D(Q)]\!]$ and $x \in X$ with $T(x) = 0$. By Definition 5, we have $D(Q)_{x_0,x} = D_{[x_0],0} = (0, \leq) = D_{0,[x_0]} = D(Q)_{x,x_0}$, hence $\nu(x) = \nu(x_0) = 0$. □

Lemma 2. *For each DBM$_T$ Q, $[\![D(Q)]\!] = [\![Q]\!]$.*

Proof. Let $\nu \in [\![D(Q)]\!]$. Construct a valuation ν_0 of the representative clocks as follows. Set $\nu_0(r) = \nu(x)$ if $[x] = r$ and $T(x) = 1$, and set $\nu_0(r) = 0$ otherwise. Valuation ν_0 is well-defined because, by Lemma 1, clocks from the same partition (hence with the same representative) have the same value in ν. For ν_0, we have $\nu(x) = \nu_0([x]) \cdot T(x)$ by construction and by Lemma 1, hence $\nu \in [\![Q]\!]$.

Let $\nu \in [\![Q]\!]$. Then there exists $\nu_0 \in [\![C]\!]$ such that $\nu(x) = \nu_0([x]) \cdot T(x)$. To show $\nu \in [\![D(Q)]\!]$, we have to show $\nu \models D(Q)_{x,y}$ for all $x, y \in X$. Distinguish four cases by the token values:

– If $T(x) = T(y) = 1$, then $D(Q)_{x,y} = C_{[x],[y]}$. The case $C_{[x],[y]} = \infty$ is trivial, hence consider $C_{[x],[y]} = (m, \sim)$. We have $\nu \models x - y \sim m$ iff $\nu(x) - \nu(y) \sim m$ iff $1 \cdot \nu(x) - 1 \cdot \nu(y) \sim m$ iff $\nu_0([x]) - \nu_0([y]) \sim m$ iff $\nu_0 \models [x] - [y] \sim m$. The latter holds because $\nu_0 \in [\![C]\!]$.

– The case $T(x) = 1$ and $T(y) = 0$ follows similarly to the previous one. We have $D(Q)_{x,y} = C_{[x],[x_0]}$ by definition (x is compared to the dedicated clock x_0), and can use $\nu(y) = 0$ from Lemma 1.

– In case $T(x) = T(y) = 0$, we have $D(Q)_{x,y} = C_{[x_0],[x_0]} = (0, \leq)$ and we can use $\nu(x) = \nu(y) = 0$ from Lemma 1. □

In the following, we establish a relation between quasi-equality and DBM_T. As DBM_T include sets of clocks, we are in particular able to represent phase-wise quasi-equality as opposed to network-wide quasi-equality.

Lemma 3. *Let $Q = (C, P, T)$ be a DBM_T and X_i a partition from P. Then all clocks in X_i are quasi-equal in all valuations $\nu \in [\![Q]\!]$.* ◇

Proof. Let $x, y \in X_i$ and $\nu \in [\![Q]\!]$. If $T(x) = T(y) = 1$, then $\nu(x) = \nu_0([x]) = \nu(y)$. If $T(x) = 0$ or $T(y) = 0$, then the value of this clock is 0 in ν. Hence x and y are quasi-equal in ν. □

The following Lemmata 4 and 5 can be seen as a minimality result. It is not surprising that each DBM can be principally represented with a DBM_T by using singletons as partitions, one for each clock. Then the DBM inside the DBM_T is exactly the DBM to be represented. The stronger result here is that for each partitioning of the set of clocks into quasi-equal clocks (in the valuations represented by a DBM), there is an equivalent DBM_T whose dimension is the number of partitions. And if a partitioning P of the set of clocks X is maximal wrt. to quasi-equality, i.e. if there is no partitioning with strictly fewer partitions than P has and with quasi-equal clocks per partition, then there is not for each DBM D over X a DBM_T of size strictly smaller than $|P|$ equivalent to D.

Lemma 4. *Let $X_0, \ldots, X_m$ be a partitioning of the set of clocks X and let D be a DBM s.t. clocks from the same partition are quasi-equal in all valuations of D, i.e. where $\forall 0 \leq i \leq m\ \forall x, y \in X_i\ \forall \nu \in [\![D]\!] \bullet \nu \models x = y \vee x = 0 \vee y = 0$.*
  Then there is a DBM_T $Q = (C, P, T)$ with $|C| = (m + 1)$ and $[\![Q]\!] = [\![D]\!]$. ◇

Proof. Construct a token function $T : X \to \{0, 1\}$ as follows. For each $0 \leq k \leq m$, if for all $x, y \in X_k$ and for all $\nu \in [\![D]\!]$, $\nu(x) = \nu(y)$, then set $T(x) := 1$ for all $x \in X_k$. Otherwise, consider $x \in X_k$ individually. Set $T(x) := 1$ if there is $\nu \in [\![D]\!]$ s.t. $\nu(x) > 0$, and set $T(x) := 0$ otherwise.
  Let C be the DBM of dimension $m + 1$ defined by $f^{-1}(P, T)$, the inverse function of $f(\cdot, \cdot)$ from Definition 5. The inversion is well-defined with the above construction of T and the assumption of quasi-equality as follows. For the case of positive tokens, let $x_1, x_2 \in X_i$ and $y \in X_j$ be clocks with positive token in T. Then $Q_{x_1,y} = Q_{x_2,y}$, because, by construction of T, clocks x_1 and x_2 are equal in all valuations from $[\![D]\!]$ hence they must satisfy the same difference relation to y. The other three cases follow similarly. Then, with $P = X_0, \ldots, X_m$, we have $D(C, P, T) = f(P, T)(f^{-1}(P, T)(D)) = D$, hence $[\![Q]\!] = [\![D]\!]$. □

Lemma 5. *Let $N \subseteq X \to \mathbb{R}_0^+$ be a set of valuations of clocks X and let $X_0, \ldots, X_m$ be a partitioning of X that is maximal wrt. quasi-equality in N (not considering the dedicated partition $X_0 = \{x_0\}$). Let $Q = (C, P, T)$ be a DBM_T with $[\![Q]\!] = N$. Then $|C| \geq m + 1$.* ◇

Proof. Assume $Q = (C, P, T)$ with $[\![Q]\!] = N$ and $|C| < m + 1$. Then we can choose x, y from one partition of P (excluding the dedicated partition X_0) such that $x \in X_{i_1}$ and $y \in X_{i_2}$ with $i_1 \neq i_2$. Since $X_1, \ldots, X_m$ is maximal wrt. quasi-equality in N, there is $\nu \in N$ s.t. $\nu(x) > 0$, $\nu(y) > 0$, and $\nu(x) \neq \nu(y)$.

If we had $T(x) = T(y) = 1$, then for each $\nu' \in [\![Q]\!]$, we had $\nu'(x) = \nu'(y)$, hence $\nu \notin [\![Q]\!]$. If we had, e.g., $T(x) = 0$, then for each $\nu' \in [\![Q]\!]$, we had $\nu'(x) = 0$, hence $\nu \notin [\![Q]\!]$.   □

4   Standard Operations on DBMx

In the following, we define the standard operations for constraint satisfaction, the intersection of DBM_T with a clock constraint, the effect of arbitrary delay (freeing), and the effect of clock resets on DBM_T. We show that applying these operations (except for freeing) on DBM_T and then decoding the DBM_T into a DBM yields the same result as first decoding into a DBM and then applying the standard operation there. Freeing only commutes for strongly stable DBM_T because in an unstable DBM_T the negative tokens enforce that the corresponding clocks have value 0 and not any larger value, which is the effect of freeing.

The valuations encoded by a DBM do not satisfy a constraint ϕ, denoted by $sat(D, \phi) = false$, if and only if $\phi = x - y \sim m$ and $D_{y,x} + (m, \sim) < (0, \leq)$. We write $D \models \phi$ if and only if $sat(D, \phi) = true$. For DBM_T $Q = (C, P, T)$, we define $sat(Q, \phi) := sat(C, \Gamma_Q(\phi))$ using the constraint transformation from Definition 6 below. Both operations are canonically lifted to sets of constraints $\varphi \subseteq \Phi(X)$.

Definition 6. *Let $Q = (C, P, T)$ be a DBM_T over X and $\phi = x - y \sim m \in \Phi(X)$ a clock constraint. Then the Q-transformation of ϕ is defined as follows:*

$$\Gamma_Q(\phi) = \begin{cases} [x] - [y] \sim m & \text{, if } t_x, t_y \\ [x] - [x_0] \sim m & \text{, if } t_x, \bar{t}_y \end{cases} \qquad \Gamma_Q(\phi) = \begin{cases} [x_0] - [y] \sim m & \text{, if } \bar{t}_x, t_y \\ [x_0] - [x_0] \sim m & \text{, if } \bar{t}_x, \bar{t}_y \end{cases},$$

where T provides token values and P representative clocks for clocks X. Sets of clock constraints are Q-transformed element-wise.   ◇

Lemma 6. *For DBM_T Q over X and $\phi \in \Phi(X)$, $D(Q) \models \phi$ iff $Q \models \phi$.*   ◇

Proof. Let $Q = (C, P, T)$ and $\phi = x - y \sim m$. If $T(x) = T(y) = 1$ then $D(Q) \models \phi = false$ iff $D(Q)_{y,x} + (m, \sim) < (0, \leq)$ iff $C_{[y],[x]} + (m, \sim) < (0, \leq)$ iff $C \models \Gamma_Q(\phi) = false$, because $\Gamma_Q(\phi) = [x] - [y] \sim m$. If $T(x) = 0$ and $T(y) = 1$ then $D(Q) \models \phi = false$ iff $C_{[y],0} + (m, \sim) < (0, \leq)$ iff $C \models \Gamma_Q(\phi) = false$, because $\Gamma_Q(\phi) = [x_0] - [y] \sim m$. The other cases follow similarly.   □

A DBM D is subsumed by D' (written $D \subseteq D'$) if and only if $\forall x, y \in X \bullet D_{x,y} \leq D'_{x,y}$. For DBM_T, we say Q' subsumes Q (and write $Q \subseteq Q'$) if and only if $\forall x, y \in X \bullet D(Q)_{x,y} \leq D(Q')_{x,y}$. Note that $D(Q)_{x,y}$ can be computed point-wise, that is, we need not construct the full $D(Q)$.

Lemma 7. *For DBM_T Q, Q' over X, $Q \subseteq Q'$ if and only if $D(Q) \subseteq D(Q')$.* ◇

```
1: if  D_{x,y} + (m,~) < (0,≤)  then
2:      D_{0,0} ← (-1,≤)
3: else if  (m,~) < D_{x,y}  then
4:      D_{x,y} ← (m,~)
5:      for  i,j ∈ {0,...,n}  do
6:          D_{i,j} ← min(D_{i,j}, D_{i,x} + D_{x,j})
7:          D_{i,j} ← min(D_{i,j}, D_{i,y} + D_{y,j})
8:      end for
9: end if
```

Fig. 3. Algorithm $and(D, x - y \sim m)$, $|D| = n + 1$.

Proof. Definition 5.   □

The intersection of a DBM D with a constraint ϕ, written as $D \wedge \varphi$, is defined by the algorithm in Fig. 3. For DBM_T, we define $Q \wedge \phi := C \wedge \Gamma_Q(\phi)$. Both operations are canonically lifted to sets of constraints $\varphi \subseteq \Phi(X)$.

Lemma 8. *For DBM_T Q over X and $\phi \in \Phi(X)$, $D(Q \wedge \phi) = D(Q) \wedge \phi$.* ◇

Proof. Let $\phi = x - y \sim m$. For the case $T(x) = T(y) = 1$, we have $\Gamma_Q(x - y \sim m) = [x] - [y] \sim m$. In Lines 1 and 2 of the algorithm, we check $C_{[x],[y]} + (m, \sim) < (0, \leq)$ in both, $C \wedge \Gamma_Q(\phi)$ and $D(Q) \wedge \phi$, and get the same result. In Line 3, we have $(m, \sim) < C_{[x],[y]}$ iff $(m, \sim) < D(Q)_{x,y}$ and in Line 4, $C'_{[x],[y]} = (m, \sim)$ iff $D(Q)'_{x,y} = (m, \sim)$. Lines 6 and 7 preserve the loop invariant $C'_{[i],[x]} = D(Q)'_{i,x}$ and $C'_{[x],[j]} = D(Q)'_{x,j}$ and $C'_{[i],[j]} = D(Q)'_{i,j}$. Assuming the loop invariant, we have $C'_{[i],[x]} + C'_{[x],[j]} = D(Q)'_{i,x} + D(Q)'_{x,j}$ and

$$\min(C'_{[i],[j]}, D(Q)'_{i,x} + D(Q)'_{x,j}) = \min(D(Q)'_{i,j}, D(Q)'_{i,x} + D(Q)'_{x,j}),$$

hence after Line 6, $C'_{[i],[j]} = D(Q)'_{i,j}$ and similarly for Line 7. The other three cases are argued similarly.   □

The effect of resetting clock x on DBM D, written $reset(D, x)$ (or $D[x := 0]$ for short), is entry-wise defined as follows. $reset(D, x)_{i,j}$ is $D_{i,0}$ if $j = x$, $D_{0,j}$ if $i = x$, and $D_{i,j}$ otherwise. For DBM_T, we define $(C, P, T)[x := 0] = (C, P, T[x := 0])$ if $x \in X_i$, $\sum_{y \neq x \in X_i} T(y) > 0$ and $\nu(x) > 0$ for some $\nu \in [\![Q]\!]$ (∗), and $(C[[x] := 0], P, T[y := 1 \mid y \in X_i])$ otherwise.

Condition (∗) above ensures that, if the representative clock has value 0, then all tokens become positive to avoid weakly unstable DBM_T.

Lemma 9. *For each DBM_T Q over X, $x \in X$, $D(Q[x := 0]) = D(Q)[x := 0]$.*

Proof. For i, j with $i \neq x$ or $j \neq x$, we have $D(Q)[x := 0]_{i,j} = D(Q)_{i,j} = D(Q[x := 0])_{i,j}$ because $Q[x := 0]$ leaves these entries unchanged.

Consider the case $i = x$ and $j = y$. Then $D(Q[x := 0])_{i,j}$ is $b = D(C, P, T')_{i,j}$ with $T' = T[x := 0]$ if $\sum_{z \neq x \in X_i} T(z) > 0$. If $T'(y) = 1$, then $b = C_{0,[y]} = D(Q)_{0,j}$

which is $D(Q)[x := 0]_{i,j}$. If $T'(y) = 0$, then $b = C_{0,0} = D(Q)_{0,0}$ which is $D(Q)[x := 0]_{i,j}$. Otherwise, $b = D(C[x := 0], P, T')_{i,j}$ with $T' = T[X_i := 1]$ where $C[x := 0]_{[x],[y]} = C_{0,[y]}$. If $T[X_i := 1](y) = 1$, then $b = C_{0,[y]} = D(Q)_{0,j} = D(Q)[x := 0]_{i,j}$. If $T[X_i := 1](y) = 0$, then $b = C_{0,0} = D(Q)_{0,0} = D(Q)[x := 0]_{i,j}$. The case $j = x$ and $i = y$ is symmetric. □

Proposition 1. *Let $Q = (C, P, T)$ be a DBM_T over X and $x \in X$. Then $D((C, P, T[x := 0])) = D(Q)[x := 0]$.*

Proof. Reseting x in $D(Q)$ copies over the row and column of the designated clock x_0, $D((C, P, T[x := 0]))$ yields the corresponding entries from the row and column of the (representative of) x_0. □

The following proposition observes that each weakly stable DBM_T has an equivalent strongly stable DBM_T.

Proposition 2. *For DBM_T $Q = (C, P, T)$ with weakly stable partition X_i in P whose representative clock is r, $D(Q) = D((C[r := 0], P, T[X_i := 1]))$.* ◇

Proof. As resets only change DBM entries of x, let $x \in X_i$ and $y \in X$. Then $D(Q)_{x,y} = C_{0,[y]} = C[r := 0]_{[x],[y]} = D((C[r := 0], P, T[X_i := 1]))_{x,y}$. □

The effect of removing upper bounds on clocks (or freeing) in DBM D, written $up(D)$ (or $D\uparrow$ for short), is entry-wise defined as $up(D)_{i,j} = \infty$ if $i > 0$ and $j = 0$, and $D_{i,j}$ otherwise. For DBM_T $Q = (C, P, T)$, we define $up(C, P, T) = (C\uparrow, P, T)$ if Q is strongly stable, and $up(Q) = Q$ otherwise. That is, if Q is not strongly stable, the up operation is effectively the identity.

Lemma 10. *Let Q be a strongly stable DBM_T. Then $D(Q\uparrow) = D(Q)\uparrow$.* ◇

Proof. Let $x \in X \setminus \{x_0\}$. Then $D(Q\uparrow)_{x,0} = Q\uparrow_{[x],[0]]} = C\uparrow_{[x],[0]} = \infty = D(Q)\uparrow_{x,0}$. □

If a DBM_T is not strongly stable, then freeing does not commute with the operation on DBM as illustrated by the network in Fig. 1 with $c = 11$. At time 10, clock x is reset, and then at time 11, clock y is reset, hence x and y are not quasi-equal. This observation matches the intuition of quasi-equality: Quasi-equal clocks are reset at the same point in time, yet not necessarily with the same transition (this would be equality).

Proposition 3. *If DBM_T Q is not strongly stable, $D(Q\uparrow) \neq D(Q)\uparrow$.* ◇

Proof. Let $T(x) = 0$. $D(Q\uparrow)_{x,0} = Q\uparrow_{0,0} = (0, \leq) \neq \infty = D(Q)\uparrow_{x,0}$. □

DBM_T do not have a strong notion of a canonical form in contrast to DBM. For example, for DBM_T $Q = C, \{t_{x_0}\}, \{t_x, \bar{t}_y\}, \{z\}$ with $\nu(x) > \nu(z) > 0$ for all $\nu \in [\![Q]\!]$, we have $D(Q) = D(C, \{t_{x_0}\}, \{t_x\}, \{\bar{t}_y, z\})$. That is, clocks with negative token can be moved from one partition to another without changing the set of represented valuations. The algorithm presented in Sect. 6 does not store multiple encodings of the same set of represented valuations due to the conducted subsumption check. Furthermore, two equal clocks with positive value can be represented by one or two partitions in a DBM_T. The merge operation as introduced in the next section avoids that case in our algorithm by unifying partitions whose representative clock is 0. Before two clocks reach a positive value, they need to have been reset and are unified into one partition then.

5   Splitting and Merging Equivalence Classes

DBM_T cannot be used as a "plug in" replacement in the classical algorithm for reachability checking because the freeing operation on DBM_T does not commute with the operation on DBM. In the following, we introduce a split operation on DBM_T that transforms a given unstable DBM_T into another DBM_T on which freeing can safely be applied. The subsequently introduced merge operation unifies partitions that are equal after a reset. The merge operation is not necessary for correctness but with this operation, our algorithm can achieve space-savings by exploiting phase-wise quasi-equality, where the transformation-based approach only exploits network-wide quasi-equality.

The *split operation* $split(Q, \varphi)$ on DBM_T $Q = (C, P, T)$ wrt. φ is defined as follows. If Q is stable or if no delay is possible from Q under constraint φ, i.e., if there is no $\nu \in [\![D(Q) \wedge \varphi]\!]$ such that $\nu + d \in [\![Q \wedge \varphi]\!]$ with $d > 0$, then $split(Q, \varphi) = Q$. Otherwise, given $P = X_0, \dots, X_m$, let X_i' be $X_i \setminus \{x \in X_i \mid \bar{t}_x\}$ if X_i is unstable in Q, and X_i otherwise. Set $X_{m+1} = \bigcup_{i=1}^{m} X_i \setminus X_i'$. Note that X_{m+1} is not empty, because we assumed at least one unstable partition. Then $split(Q, \varphi) = (C'[r_{m+1} := 0], P', T')$ where C' is an $(m+1) \times (m+1)$ matrix with $C_{i,j}' = C_{i,j}$, $0 \le i, j \le m$, $P' = X_0', \dots, X_m', X_{m+1}$, and $T' = T$.

Lemma 11. *Let Q be a DBM_T over X, $\varphi \subseteq \Phi(X)$, and $\varrho \subseteq X$. Then $D(Q) = D(split(Q, \varphi))$ and $D(split(Q, \varphi)[\varrho := 0]\!\uparrow \wedge \varphi) = D(Q)[\varrho := 0]\!\uparrow \wedge \varphi$.*   ◇

Proof. Let $Q' = split(Q, \varphi)$. The split operation only affects clocks with negative token, so for the clocks with positive tokens, Q' yields the same bounds as copied over from $D(Q)$. For clocks with negative tokens, tokens remains negative and hence $D(Q')$ yields bounds of the dedicated clock.

For the second claim, distinguish two cases. If $Q'[\varrho := 0]$ is strongly stable, Lemmata 10 and 8 apply. If $Q'[\varrho := 0]$ is not strongly stable, then $Q'\!\uparrow = Q'$ by definition and Lemma 8 applies.   □

Note that the split operation as defined above could be called lazy because clocks are kept together in one partition until the network dynamics require a split (by delay in an unstable configuration). A different split operation could group all clocks with negative tokens together as soon as they are reset. Whether a different split operation is more effective in practice needs further research.

The *merge operation* $merge(Q)$ on DBM_T $Q = (C, P, T)$ is defined as follows. Without loss of generality (as we can re-order DBM C and P), assume that $P = \{x_0\}, X_1, \dots, X_k, X_{k+1}, \dots, X_m$ such that $m > k$ and such that partitions

```
1: P ← ∅;
2: W ← {(ℓ₀, Q) | Q = Q₀↑ ∧ I(ℓ₀), Q ≠ ∅};
3: while  (ℓ, Q) ← pick(W)  do                     ▷ empty W terminates loop
4:     if ∀(ℓ, Q') ∈ P : Q ⋢ Q'  then
5:         P ← P ∪ {(ℓ, Q)};
6:         W ← W ∪ {(ℓₛ, Qₛ) | (ℓ, Q) ↝ᵀ (ℓₛ, Q'), Qₛ = Q'↑ ∧ I(ℓₛ), Qₛ ≠ ∅}
7:     end if
8: end while
```

Fig. 4. Reachable configurations computation with DBM_T.

$X_{k+1}, \ldots, X_m$ are exactly those partitions that are stable and whose representative clock gets value 0 in all valuations of C. Then $merge(Q) = (C', P', T')$ where C' is a $(k+1) \times (k+1)$ matrix with $C'_{i,j} = C_{i,j}$, $0 \leq i, j \leq k+1$, $T' = T$, $P' = X_0, \ldots, X_k, (X_{k+1} \cup \cdots \cup X_m)$. Use $merge(Q) = Q$ otherwise.

Lemma 12. *For each DBM_T Q, $D(Q) = D(merge(Q))$.*   ◇

Proof. Consider the entries of $D(Q)$. For partitions $X_0, \ldots, X_k$, the entries in C' are the same as in C, hence $D(Q)$ and $D(merge(Q))$ yield the same bounds. All clocks from partitions $X_{k+1}, \ldots, X_m$ satisfied the same constraints wrt. each other and all other clocks. They continue to do so after merging as we copy over one row and column from C to C' □

6   Putting It All Together

Figure 4 shows an adaptation of the classical algorithm for reachability checking of networks of timed automata for DBM_T. In Line 2, we start with a DBM_T of dimension 2 and all tokens positive because all clocks are equal in the initial configuration by definition. More formally, we use $Q_0 = (C_0, P_0, T_0)$ where $C_0 = \mathbf{0}_{2 \times 2}$ is a 2×2 matrix with all entries being $(0, \leq)$, $P_0 = \{x_0\}, \{x_1, \ldots, x_n\}$, and $T_0(x) = 1$ for each $x \in X$, hence Q_0 is strongly stable. Lemmata 10 and 8 ensure that $D(Q_0)$ is equal to the initial DBM in the classical algorithm. Line 4 conducts the subsumption check on DBM_T, Lemma 7 ensures that the operation corresponds to subsumption check on their DBMs. Line 6 implicitly includes the computation of the set of enabled edges according to their guards, Lemma 8 ensures that the enabledness check is sound on DBM_T.

Given one or two enabled edges, Q' is the effect of taking these edges. We define $(\ell, Q) \overset{\mathcal{T}}{\leadsto} (\ell_s, Q_s)$ if and only if $(C', P', T') = Q \cap \Gamma_Q(\varphi)$, where $\varphi \subseteq \Phi(X)$ is the conjoined guard of the enabled edges, ℓ_s is ℓ updated to the destination locations of the considered edges, and

$$Q_s = merge(split(C', P', T'[\varrho := 0], I(\ell_s))[\varrho := 0])$$

where ϱ is the union of the reset sets of the considered edges. Proposition 1 allows us to reset tokens without resetting representatives (yet). The split operation ensures, by Lemma 11, that the subsequent freeing and intersection with the invariants of the destination location vector has the desired effect. Then the reset operation on the whole DBM_T resets the representative and changes the tokens to all-positive for the weakly stable partitions. The merge operation is not necessary for correctness, yet safe by Lemma 12.

Theorem 1. $\forall \mathcal{N} \; \forall \, (\ell, Q) \in W \; \forall \nu \in [\![D(Q)]\!] \bullet \langle \ell, \nu \rangle \in Reach(\mathcal{N}).$ $\qquad \Diamond$

Proof. By induction over the loop iteration in which a DBM_T is added to W. The induction base is Line 2, where $D(Q)$ the initial D (which is reachable) or empty if C_0, and the loop is skipped. The induction step is Line 6. By induction assumption, there is a reachable $\langle \ell, D \rangle$ corresponding to (ℓ, Q) as picked from W. By Lemma 8, the same sets of edges are found enabled by their guard joint guard φ. Resetting tokens preserves a correspondence by Proposition 1, Lemma 11 ensures that the following freeing and intersection with destination location invariant preserves correspondence. Lemma 12 does not change correspondence, hence $D(Q_s) = (D \wedge \varphi)[\varrho := 0]{\uparrow} \wedge I(\ell_s)$ which is reachable. $\qquad \square$

Theorem 2. $\forall \mathcal{N} \; \forall \, \langle \ell, \nu \rangle \in Reach(\mathcal{N}) \; \exists \, (\ell, Q) \in W@L3 \bullet \nu \in [\![Q]\!].$ $\qquad \Diamond$

Proof. If $\langle \ell, Z \rangle$ is reachable, then the classical algorithm has an execution that adds a corresponding $\langle \ell, D \rangle$ to (properly intialised) W. The pick operation in Fig. 4 can choose corresponding DBM_T from W, and thereby simulate each step of the classical algorithm, yielding a corresponding Q. $\qquad \square$

The following theorem relates our algorithm to the transformation-based approach that exploits network-wide quasi-equality of clocks. The theorem implies that, if there are n equivalence classes of network-wide quasi-equality, then the DBM_T occurring in W during an execution of our algorithm will include DBMs for representative clocks of at most size n, possibly smaller.

Theorem 3. *Let $\mathcal{N}$ be a network over X and EC an equivalence class of (network-wide) quasi-equality. Let $(\ell, (C, P, T))$ be a configuration occurring in W during execution of the algorithm from Fig. 4 without the merge operation. Then for all clocks $x, y \in EC$, there is a partition X_i in P s.t. $x, y \in X_i$.* $\qquad \Diamond$

Proof. In the induction base case, all clocks (except for x_0) are in one partition hence the claim holds. In the induction step, we can assume that the claim holds for (ℓ, Q) as picked from W. Partitions are only changed by the split operation, which operates lazily on unstable partitions, that is, a clock x is only removed from a partition X_i if x has a negative token and a positive delay $d > 0$ is possible. If $y \in X_i$ has a negative token, then it is moved to the same partition as x. If y has a positive token, then the representative has a positive value d' otherwise X_i would not be unstable (by definition of the reset operation on DBM_T). Hence in Q_s, x can have value $d > 0$ and y can have value $d' + d > d$, hence x and y are not quasi-equal, i.e., not in equivalence class EC. $\qquad \square$

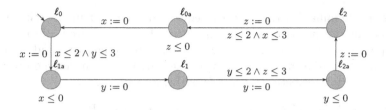

Fig. 5. Illustrative example for equal clock detection [8]; the original does not have locations $\ell_{1a}, \ell_{2a}, \ell_{0a}$ but resets, e.g., x and y on one edge from ℓ_0 to ℓ_1.

Table 1. Evaluation results.

	$\mathcal{N}$	$|\mathcal{N}|$	$|X|$	$|\mathcal{EC}|$	$|\mathcal{T}(\mathcal{N})|$	D	t	C	T	t
1a	TTDA	5	5	1	145	7,105	0.124	1,125	1,015	0.116
1b	[1,2]	6	6	1	341	16,709	0.496	1,364	2,387	0.464
1c		7	7	1	805	65,205	1.612	6,575	7,245	1.532
1d		8	8	1	1,835	148,635	4.696	7,340	16,515	4.500
2a	WFAS	3	2	1	17	153	0.004	68	51	0.004
2b	[3]	4	3	1	28	448	0.012	112	112	0.012
2c		5	4	1	43	1,075	0.016	172	215	0.020
2d		6	5	1	66	2,376	0.032	264	396	0.028
3a	Fig. 1,	2	2	1	4	36	$< 10^{-3}$	16	12	$< 10^{-3}$
3b	$c = 10$	2	3	2	4	64	$< 10^{-3}$	21	16	$< 10^{-3}$
4a	Fig. 1,	2	2	2	3	27	$< 10^{-3}$	22	9	$< 10^{-3}$
4b	$c = 11$	2	3	3	3	48	$< 10^{-3}$	29	12	$< 10^{-3}$
5	Fig. 5 [8]	1	3	3	8	128	$< 10^{-3}$	62	32	$< 10^{-3}$

7   Evaluation

We have prototypically implemented the DBM_T data-structure and the algorithm given in Fig. 4, and included the classical algorithm on DBM for comparison. Table 1 gives results from running the implementation on two well-known case-studies (the TDMA scheduling and message exchange of the Track Topology Data Aggregation (TTDA) [1,2] and the self-monitoring protocol of the Wireless Fire Alarm System (WFAS) [3]), and a selection of artificial benchmarks that we referred to in this article.

Columns '$\mathcal{N}$', '$|\mathcal{N}|$', and '$|X|$' give model name, network size, and the number of clocks in the original system (without dedicated clock x_0), Columns '$\mathcal{EC}$' and '$|\mathcal{T}(\mathcal{N})|$' give the maximum number of equivalence classes of (locally) quasi-equal clocks and the number of reachable configurations. Columns 'D' and 't' give the number of DBM-entries and the runtime (in seconds) with the classical algorithm, and Columns 'C', 'T', 't' give the numbers of DBM-entries and tokens, and the runtime (in seconds) with the new on-the-fly quasi-equal clock reduction. We omit runtimes (indicated by '$< 10^{-3}$') if below the order of microseconds.

For TTDA and WFAS (Rows (1) and (2) in Table 1), we observe the expected savings in the number of DBM-entries: For the larger instances of these networks, the number of DBM-entries goes down by factors of about 20 or 9, respectively. When including the number of tokens (which are, without further optimisations, stored as integers, thus half the size of a DBM entry) we still observe factors of about 9.5 and 5. Regarding verification time, we see some savings with TTDA and WFAS yet much less than for space. To appreciate verification times, recall that the implementation is prototypical and prefers correctness over speed; while space consumption is determined by data structure and algorithm, there is room for improvement in efficiency. Considering the latest figures from the source-to-source transformation approach [12], we see that there are models that reach only 5–10 % of verification time savings (when treating edges as *complex* [12]) and that time savings increase with the number of clocks in the original model, as in our case. A direct comparison to Figures from [12] is not possible because measurements in [12] *exclude* the costs for detection of quasi-equal clocks and the transformation (that are both included in one pass in the new algorithm) and *includes* special and efficiency-relevant treatment of so-called simple edges.

Rows (3) to (4) give the results for our running example from Fig. 1. Depending on the constant c, we obtain one or two equivalence classes ((3a), (4a)), and with another, unrelated clock one equivalence class more ((3b), (4b)). Row (5) shows results from the analysis of Fig. 5. The automaton in Fig. 5 has been derived from a running example of [8] that demonstrates equality of clocks. In our modification, clocks x, y, and z are neither equal nor (globally) quasi-equal, but only locally quasi-equal during certain phases. As expected, we see three different equivalence-classes of quasi-equal clocks over time together with space savings. Neither [8] nor [12] achieve any clock reduction for this model because their equivalence notions are strictly stronger than local quasi-equality.

8   Conclusion

We have shown that the idea to consider representative clocks together with boolean tokens that encode the relation of clocks to the representatives (as used in syntactical transformations for quasi-equal clock reduction) has a direct semantical correspondence in form of DBM_T. Our adaptation of the classical reachability checking algorithm for timed automata to DBM_T allows us to integrate *detection* of quasi-equal clocks with a space-saving *verification*.

If detection is the only goal, the (incomplete) approach of [15] may be more efficient than ours and the syntactical transformation [11] has the advantage that it directly supports all features and strengths of the tool Uppaal [5]. Yet both approaches are limited to network-wide quasi-equality where our algorithm can benefit from phase-wise quasi-equality, and the new algorithm is complete for detection and works in one integrated pass.

Future work includes an extension of our algorithm on DBM_T with a correspondence of the offline partial-order reduction as included in [11–14] in order to also realise the savings in number of configurations that have been observed for models with so-called simple edges (cf. [12]).

References

1. Feo-Arenis, S., Westphal, B.: Formal verification of a parameterized data aggregation protocol. In: Brat, G., Rungta, N., Venet, A. (eds.) NFM 2013. LNCS, vol. 7871, pp. 428–434. Springer, Heidelberg (2013). https://doi.org/10.1007/978-3-642-38088-4_29

2. Feo-Arenis, S., Westphal, B.: Parameterized verification of track topology aggregation protocols. In: Beyer, D., Boreale, M. (eds.) FMOODS/FORTE -2013. LNCS, vol. 7892, pp. 35–49. Springer, Heidelberg (2013). https://doi.org/10.1007/978-3-642-38592-6_4

3. Feo-Arenis, S., Westphal, B., Dietsch, D., Muñiz, M., Andisha, S., Podelski, A.: Ready for testing: ensuring conformance to industrial standards through formal verification. Formal Aspects Comput. **28**(3), 499–527 (2016). https://doi.org/10.1007/s00165-016-0365-3

4. Behrmann, G., Bouyer, P., Fleury, E., Larsen, K.G.: Static guard analysis in timed automata verification. In: Garavel, H., Hatcliff, J. (eds.) TACAS 2003. LNCS, vol. 2619, pp. 254–270. Springer, Heidelberg (2003). https://doi.org/10.1007/3-540-36577-X_18

5. Behrmann, G., David, A., Larsen, K.G.: A tutorial on UPPAAL. In: Bernardo, M., Corradini, F. (eds.) SFM-RT 2004. LNCS, vol. 3185, pp. 200–236. Springer, Heidelberg (2004). https://doi.org/10.1007/978-3-540-30080-9_7

6. Bengtsson, J., Yi, W.: Timed automata: semantics, algorithms and tools. In: Desel, J., Reisig, W., Rozenberg, G. (eds.) ACPN 2003. LNCS, vol. 3098, pp. 87–124. Springer, Heidelberg (2004). https://doi.org/10.1007/978-3-540-27755-2_3

7. Daws, C., Tripakis, S.: Model checking of real-time reachability properties using abstractions. In: Steffen, B. (ed.) TACAS 1998. LNCS, vol. 1384, pp. 313–329. Springer, Heidelberg (1998). https://doi.org/10.1007/BFb0054180

8. Daws, C., Yovine, S.: Reducing the number of clock variables of timed automata. In: RTSS, pp. 73–81. IEEE (1996). https://doi.org/10.1109/REAL.1996.563702

9. Finkel, O.: Undecidable problems about timed automata. In: Asarin, E., Bouyer, P. (eds.) FORMATS 2006. LNCS, vol. 4202, pp. 187–199. Springer, Heidelberg (2006). https://doi.org/10.1007/11867340_14

10. Guha, S., Narayan, C., Arun-Kumar, S.: Reducing clocks in timed automata while preserving bisimulation. In: Baldan, P., Gorla, D. (eds.) CONCUR 2014. LNCS, vol. 8704, pp. 527–543. Springer, Heidelberg (2014). https://doi.org/10.1007/978-3-662-44584-6_36

11. Herrera, C., Westphal, B.: Quasi-equal clock reduction: eliminating assumptions on networks. In: Piterman, N. (ed.) HVC 2015. LNCS, vol. 9434, pp. 173–189. Springer, Cham (2015). https://doi.org/10.1007/978-3-319-26287-1_11

12. Herrera, C., Westphal, B.: The model checking problem in networks with quasi-equal clocks. In: Dyreson, C.E., Hansen, M.R., Hunsberger, L. (eds.) TIME, pp. 21–30. IEEE (2016). https://doi.org/10.1109/TIME.2016.10

13. Herrera, C., Westphal, B., Feo-Arenis, S., Muñiz, M., Podelski, A.: Reducing quasi-equal clocks in networks of timed automata. In: Jurdziński, M., Ničković, D. (eds.) FORMATS 2012. LNCS, vol. 7595, pp. 155–170. Springer, Heidelberg (2012). https://doi.org/10.1007/978-3-642-33365-1_12

14. Herrera, C., Westphal, B., Podelski, A.: Quasi-equal clock reduction: more networks, more queries. In: Ábrahám, E., Havelund, K. (eds.) TACAS 2014. LNCS, vol. 8413, pp. 295–309. Springer, Heidelberg (2014). https://doi.org/10.1007/978-3-642-54862-8_20

15. Muñiz, M., Westphal, B., Podelski, A.: Detecting Quasi-equal Clocks in Timed Automata. In: Braberman, V., Fribourg, L. (eds.) FORMATS 2013. LNCS, vol. 8053, pp. 198–212. Springer, Heidelberg (2013). https://doi.org/10.1007/978-3-642-40229-6_14

16. Olderog, E.R., Dierks, H.: Real-Time Systems - Formal SpecificationandAutomatic Verification. Cambridge University Press, Cambridge (2008)

17. Saeedloei, N., Kluzniak, F.: Clock allocation in timed automata and graph colouring. In: Prandini, M., Deshmukh, J.V. (eds.) HSCC, pp. 71–80. ACM (2018). https://doi.org/10.1145/3178126.3178138

18. Salah, R., Bozga, M., et al.: Compositional Timing Analysis. In: EMSOFT, pp. 39–48. ACM (2009)

19. Waszniowski, L., Hanzalek, Z.: Over-approximate model of multitasking application based on timed automata using only one clock. In: IPDPS, p. 128a. IEEE, April 2005

On the Effectiveness of Signal Rescaling in Hybrid System Falsification

Zhenya Zhang[1]([✉])[ID], Deyun Lyu[1][ID], Paolo Arcaini[2][ID], Lei Ma[1][ID], Ichiro Hasuo[2][ID], and Jianjun Zhao[1]

[1] Kyushu University, Fukuoka, Japan
zhang.zhenya.623@m.kyushu-u.ac.jp
[2] National Institute of Informatics, Tokyo, Japan

Abstract. Hybrid system falsification employs stochastic optimization to search for counterexamples to a system specification in Signal Temporal Logic (STL), guided by quantitative STL robustness. The *scale problem* could arise when the STL formula is composed of sub-formulas concerning signals having different scales (e.g., speed [km/h] and rpm): the performance of falsification could be negatively affected because different scales can mask each other's contribution to robustness. A natural solution consists in rescaling the signals to the same order of magnitude. In this paper, we investigate whether this "basic" approach is always effective, or better rescaling strategies could be devised. Experimental results show that basic rescaling is not always the best strategy, and sometimes "unbalanced" rescalings work better. We investigate the reasons of this, and we identify future research directions based on this observation.

Keywords: Falsification · Signal temporal logic · Scale problem · Rescaling

1 Introduction

Automated formal verification of *hybrid systems* is almost infeasible due to the infinite search spaces given by the physical components. *Falsification* has been proposed as a more practical approach that, rather than attempting to prove the system specification, tries to violate it: given a *model* $\mathcal{M}$ that takes an input signal $\mathbf{u}$ and outputs a signal $\mathcal{M}(\mathbf{u})$, and a temporal logic *specification* φ (usually in Signal Temporal Logic (STL) [5]), the falsification problem consists in finding an input signal $\mathbf{u}$ such that the corresponding output $\mathcal{M}(\mathbf{u})$ violates φ.

This work is supported in part by JSPS KAKENHI Grant No. 20H04168, 19K24348, 19H04086, and JST-Mirai Program Grant No. JPMJMI18BB, Japan. Paolo Arcaini and Ichiro Hasuo are supported by ERATO HASUO Metamathematics for Systems Design Project (No. JPMJER1603), JST.

A. Dutle et al. (Eds.): NFM 2021, LNCS 12673, pp. 392–399, 2021.
https://doi.org/10.1007/978-3-030-76384-8_24

Falsification is usually turned into an optimization problem by exploiting the *robust semantics* of temporal logic formulas [3,5]: instead of the classical Boolean satisfaction relation $\mathbf{v} \models \varphi$, robust semantics assigns a value $[\![\mathbf{v}, \varphi]\!] \in \mathbb{R} \cup \{\infty, -\infty\}$ (i.e., *robustness*) that tells not only whether φ is satisfied or violated (by the sign), but also assesses *how robustly* it is satisfied or violated. Since negative robustness indicates that the specification is violated, the goal of falsification is to minimize the robustness to obtain a negative value. Different optimization-based falsification algorithms have been proposed [7], that employ stochastic optimization approaches, such as *hill-climbing*: they generate inputs with the aim of decreasing robustness, and terminate when they find an input with negative robustness (i.e., a *falsifying input*). Also falsification tools, as Breach [2] and S-TaLiRo [1], are available.

The *scale problem* is a recognized issue in falsification [6,8]. It is due to the computation of robust semantics, namely the way in which the robustness values of different sub-formulas are compared: such computation is problematic in the presence of signals that take values having different order of magnitudes. As a simple example, let's consider the formula $\varphi \equiv \varphi_1 \vee \varphi_2$, with $\varphi_1 \equiv gear < 3$ and $\varphi_2 \equiv speed > 35$. According to the robust semantics, the robustness of φ_1, at a given moment t, is $(3 - gear(t))$, and of φ_2 is $(speed(t) - 35)$; the Boolean connective $\vee$, instead, is interpreted by supremum $\sqcup$. Note that the robustness of φ_1 is always in the order of units, while the robustness of φ_2 is, in general, in the order of tens. Because of this, whenever φ_2 is satisfied, it will almost always *mask* the contribution of φ_1 to the final robustness of φ. The situation is even more frequent if complete formulas with temporal operators (the ones we consider) and their semantics are taken into account. Such a masking effect could be problematic for falsification. Indeed, if the contribution of a signal s_1 to the global robustness is masked by another signal s_2, the falsification algorithm has no guidance, because it does not know how s_1 should be modified to falsify the whole formula.

A naïve solution to the scale problem consists in *rescaling* the signals used in the specification at the same scale; we name such approach as *basic rescaling*. In this paper, we are interested in assessing to what extent such approach is effective, i.e., if applying the basic rescaling leads to optimal falsification results. We perform an empirical evaluation using 2 benchmarks and 12 specifications, showing that the basic rescaling is not always the best strategy; indeed, in some cases, scaling the signals in other ways (e.g., making their orders of magnitude even more different) leads to better falsification results. We do a further analysis of these cases, explaining why this is the case; we then describe how such findings can be used to pave new research directions in falsification.

Paper structure. Sect. 2 provides some necessary background. Sect. 3 introduces the scale problem, and the basic rescaling approach to tackle it. Sect. refsec:experiments presents the experiments we conducted to assess the effectiveness of the basic rescaling, and to discover whether other rescaling strategies are more effective. Finally, Sect. 5 concludes the paper.

2   Preliminary

In this section, we review the falsification framework based on *robust semantics* of temporal logic [3]. Let $T \in \mathbb{R}_+$ be a positive real. An *M-dimensional signal* ($M \in \mathbb{N}$) with a time horizon T is a function $\mathbf{w} \colon [0, T] \to \mathbb{R}^M$. We treat the system model as a black box, i.e., its behaviors are only observed from inputs and their corresponding outputs. Formally, a *system model*, with M-dimensional input and N-dimensional output, is a function $\mathcal{M}$ that takes an input signal $\mathbf{u} \colon [0, T] \to \mathbb{R}^M$ and returns a signal $\mathcal{M}(\mathbf{u}) \colon [0, T] \to \mathbb{R}^N$. Here the common time horizon $T \in \mathbb{R}_+$ is arbitrary.

Definition 1 (STL syntax). We fix a set **Var** of variables. In Signal Temporal Logic (STL), *atomic propositions* and *formulas* are defined as follows, respectively: $\alpha ::\equiv f(x_1, \ldots, x_N) > 0$, and $\varphi ::\equiv \alpha \mid \bot \mid \neg\varphi \mid \varphi \wedge \varphi \mid \varphi \vee \varphi \mid \varphi \, \mathcal{U}_I \, \varphi$. Here f is an N-ary function $f \colon \mathbb{R}^N \to \mathbb{R}$, $x_1, \ldots, x_N \in \mathbf{Var}$, and I is a closed non-singular interval in $\mathbb{R}_{\geq 0}$, i.e. $I = [a, b]$ or $[a, \infty)$ where $a, b \in \mathbb{R}$ and $a < b$. Other common connectives such as $\to, \top, \Box_I$ (always) and $\Diamond_I$ (eventually), are introduced as abbreviations: $\Diamond_I \varphi \equiv \top \, \mathcal{U}_I \, \varphi$ and $\Box_I \varphi \equiv \neg\Diamond_I\neg\varphi$.

Definition 2 (Robust semantics). Let $\mathbf{w} \colon [0, T] \to \mathbb{R}^N$ be an N-dimensional signal, and $t \in [0, T)$. The *t-shift* $\mathbf{w}^t$ of $\mathbf{w}$ is the signal $\mathbf{w}^t \colon [0, T - t] \to \mathbb{R}^N$ defined by $\mathbf{w}^t(t') := \mathbf{w}(t + t')$. Let $\mathbf{w} \colon [0, T] \to \mathbb{R}^{|\mathbf{Var}|}$ be a signal, and φ be an STL formula. We define the *robustness* $[\![\mathbf{w}, \varphi]\!] \in \mathbb{R} \cup \{\infty, -\infty\}$ as follows, by induction on the construction of formulas. $\bigsqcap$ and $\bigsqcup$ denote infimums and supremums of real numbers, respectively. Their binary version $\sqcap$ and $\sqcup$ denote minimum and maximum.

$$[\![\mathbf{w}, f(x_1, \cdots, x_N) > 0]\!] := f\big(\mathbf{w}(0)(x_1), \cdots, \mathbf{w}(0)(x_N)\big)$$
$$[\![\mathbf{w}, \bot]\!] := -\infty \qquad\qquad\qquad [\![\mathbf{w}, \neg\varphi]\!] := -[\![\mathbf{w}, \varphi]\!]$$
$$[\![\mathbf{w}, \varphi_1 \wedge \varphi_2]\!] := [\![\mathbf{w}, \varphi_1]\!] \sqcap [\![\mathbf{w}, \varphi_2]\!] \qquad [\![\mathbf{w}, \varphi_1 \vee \varphi_2]\!] := [\![\mathbf{w}, \varphi_1]\!] \sqcup [\![\mathbf{w}, \varphi_2]\!]$$
$$[\![\mathbf{w}, \varphi_1 \, \mathcal{U}_I \, \varphi_2]\!] := \bigsqcup\nolimits_{t \in I \cap [0,T]} \big([\![\mathbf{w}^t, \varphi_2]\!] \sqcap \bigsqcap\nolimits_{t' \in [0,t)} [\![\mathbf{w}^{t'}, \varphi_1]\!]\big)$$

The original STL semantics is Boolean, given by a binary relation $\models$ between signals and formulas. The robust semantics refines the Boolean one in the following sense: $[\![\mathbf{w}, \varphi]\!] > 0$ implies $\mathbf{w} \models \varphi$, and $[\![\mathbf{w}, \varphi]\!] < 0$ implies $\mathbf{w} \not\models \varphi$, see [5, Prop. 16].

Optimization-Guided Falsification. Falsification can be transformed into an optimization problem by taking the robustness as objective function. The goal of optimization is to minimize the robustness value by varying input signals—once a negative robustness is found, it indicates the existence of a counterexample violating the system specification. To solve the optimization problem, different metaheuristic-based optimization techniques can be used (e.g., CMA-ES, Simulated Annealing), and these have been implemented in state-of-the-art falsification tools such as Breach [2].

3   A Rescaling Approach for Tackling the Scale Problem

The scale problem [6,8] is known to affect the falsification performance. We here shed a light on this problem and present a straightforward solution based on signal rescaling.

Scale Problem. An STL formula is commonly composed of multiple sub-formulas concerning different signals. These signals are likely to have different magnitudes. First of all, different signals can range differently (e.g., *speed* ranges over $[0, 150]$ while *gear* is an integer less than 5). Moreover, the magnitude of a signal may also depend to the use of different measurement units (e.g., *speed* may be measured in km/h, m/s, mph, etc.). The scale problem arises when the robustness of such a formula is computed: the process requires the comparison between robustness values coming from different sub-formulas (see the definition of robust semantics in Definition 2), and so the global robustness may be dominated by only one of the involved signals. As the optimization process in falsification is guided by robustness, the scale problem can pose an influence on the performance of falsification. We show the harmfulness of this issue via an example.

Example 3. Consider an automatic transmission system that outputs *gear* $\in \{1, 2, 3, 4\}$ and *speed* $\in [0, 150]$. A safety property concerning the system is as follows: $\varphi \equiv \Box_I(gear = 4 \to speed > 35)$. φ is equivalent to $\Box_I(\varphi_1 \lor \varphi_2)$ where $\varphi_1 \equiv \neg(gear = 4)$, $\varphi_2 \equiv speed > 35$. Given a signal $\mathbf{w}$ consisting of *speed* and *gear*, the calculation of its robustness consists in computing the infimum of $\{[\![\mathbf{w}^t, \varphi_1 \lor \varphi_2]\!] \mid t \in I\}$. This process is unfolded as follows: (i) for each $t \in I$, compute $[\![\mathbf{w}^t, \varphi_1]\!]$ and $[\![\mathbf{w}^t, \varphi_2]\!]$, and take their maximum as $[\![\mathbf{w}^t, \varphi_1 \lor \varphi_2]\!]$; (ii) obtain $\{[\![\mathbf{w}^t, \varphi_1 \lor \varphi_2]\!] \mid t \in I\}$, and take its infimum as $[\![\mathbf{w}, \varphi]\!]$.

In case $T = \{[\![\mathbf{w}^t, \varphi_1 \lor \varphi_2]\!] \mid t \in I\}$ contains values both from $[\![\mathbf{w}^t, \varphi_1]\!]$ and $[\![\mathbf{w}^t, \varphi_2]\!]$, the infimum of T will almost always be dominated by $[\![\mathbf{w}^t, \varphi_1]\!]$ due to the scale issue of the two signals. This scenario is actually common, especially when φ is not falsified. Hence, the contribution of φ_2 to the final robustness of φ is almost always masked by φ_1. Even worse, $[\![\mathbf{w}^t, \varphi_1]\!]$ changes discretely due to the nature of *gear*, and so does the final robustness $[\![\mathbf{w}, \varphi]\!]$; this means that a small variation of the system input may not result in a change of the final robustness. Such *flat robustness* is problematic for optimization (that has no guidance), and so falsification will likely fail.

Rescaling Approach. Since the scale problem arises because of signals having different magnitudes, a straightforward solution could be to rescale the signals to the same magnitude. We call this approach as *basic rescaling*. For this approach, domain knowledge regarding the ranges $[l, u]$ of each signal is needed for computing the rescaling factor δ. Namely, given an STL formula concerning two signals ranging over $[l_1, u_1]$ and $[l_2, u_2]$, respectively, the *basic* approach for deciding the rescaling factor δ w.r.t. the former signal is $\delta = \frac{u_2 - l_2}{u_1 - l_1}$.

Note that, in our experiments, we will also investigate the use of "unbalanced" scaling factors that rescale the signal in a different way from the basic rescaling (i.e., not at the same order of magnitude), and we will compare their performance.

In our experiments, we use Simulink for the system models. In order to implement the rescaling approach in Simulink, we perform these two steps: (i) we amplify/diminish a selected signal **w** by δ times, by adding a *gain* block to **w** with a parameter δ; (ii) we modify the constants of the STL formula in accordance with the rescaled signals.

4 Experimental Evaluation

We selected two Simulink models used in falsification competitions [4], namely, Automatic Transmission (AT) and Abstract Fuel Control (AFC). Our domain knowledge on the signal ranges of the models is as follows: AT takes throttle $th \in [0, 100]$ and brake $br \in [0, 325]$ as input signals, and gives $gear \in \{1, 2, 3, 4\}$, $speed \in [0, 150]$, and $rpm \in [0, 4500]$ as output signals; AFC takes pedal angle $pa \in [8.8, 70]$ and engine speed $es \in [900, 1100]$ as input signals, and gives controller mode $cm \in \{0, 1, 2\}$ and a scalar $\mu \in [0, 0.25]$ (the performance of the system) as output signals. Note that the ranges for input signals are set by users and thus precise, but the ranges for output signals are reported empirically by sampling. In total, we evaluate 9 specifications for AT and 3 for AFC (see Table 1).

Experiments were conducted using Breach 1.2.13 (with CMA-ES as solver) on an Amazon EC2 c4.large, 2.9 GHz Intel Xeon E5-2666, 2 virtual CPU cores, 4 GB RAM.

Table 1. STL specifications ($\Delta_t(\mathbf{w}) = \mathbf{w}^t - \mathbf{w}$)

Spec. ID	Temporal specification in STL	Spec. ID	Temporal specification in STL
AT1	$\square_{[0,30]} (\Delta_1(speed) < 30 \wedge \Delta_1(rpm) < 3500)$	AT7	$\square_{[0,30]} (gear = 4 \rightarrow speed \geq 35)$
AT2	$\square_{[0,30]} (gear = 4 \rightarrow \Diamond_{[0,5]} (rpm < 4000))$	AT8	$\square_{[0,30]} (speed < 135 \wedge rpm < 4780)$
AT3	$\square_{[0,30]} (\Diamond_{[0,10]} (rpm < 600) \rightarrow gear = 1)$	AT9	$\square_{[0,30]} (th = 0 \vee br = 0) \rightarrow \square_{[0,30]} (speed < 110)$
AT4	$\Diamond_{[10,30]} (speed > 60 \vee rpm < 1000)$	AFC1	$\square_{[11,50]} (cm = 1 \rightarrow \mu < 0.228)$
AT5	$\square_{[0,30]} (\Diamond_{[0,8]} (speed < 130 \wedge rpm < 4750))$	AFC2	$\Diamond_{[0,50]} (pa > 40) \rightarrow \square_{[11,50]} (\mu < 0.225)$
AT6	$\square_{[0,10]} (speed < 50) \vee \Diamond_{[0,30]} (rpm > 2520)$	AFC3	$\Diamond_{[0,50]} (pa > 40) \rightarrow \square_{[11,50]} (\Diamond_{[0,8]} (\mu < 0.06))$

Table 2. Experimental results with different rescaling strategies

δ	AT1			AT2			AT3			AT4			AT5			AT6		
	SR	time	#sim	SR	time	#sim	SR	time	#sim	SR	time	#sim	SR	time	#sim	SR	time	#sim
no-rescaling	2	57.4	44	23	190.9	144.3	9	7.9	6.1	7	49.7	38.3	30	166.4	130.1	7	377.5	280.3
basic	8	152.2	109.1	30	126.5	86.1	30	3.1	2.3	10	24.2	17.8	18	196.2	140.5	13	375.6	269.2
$rpm \times 10^{-3}$	26	103.8	81.7	30	121.5	96.7	18	6.8	5.4	5	14.8	12	10	69.5	55.2	2	452.0	349
$rpm \times 10^{-2}$	12	138.9	105.7	17	203.0	155.2	14	8.2	6.4	3	19.2	15	11	154.3	114.7	13	389.2	273.8
$rpm \times 10^{-1}$	3	114.7	82.3	19	182.3	123.4	13	8.1	6	8	31.7	23.4	30	1.3	1	13	372.4	266
$rpm \times 10^{1}$	4	54.7	41	18	175.8	130.2	17	8.0	6.1	8	26.6	20.1	30	149.2	109.5	5	348.4	244.6

δ	AT7			AT8			AT9			δ	AFC1			AFC2			AFC3		
	SR	time	#sim	SR	time	#sim	SR	time	#sim		SR	time	#sim	SR	time	#sim	SR	time	#sim
no-rescaling	10	137.0	102.7	11	320.5	236.8	22	268.2	209	no-rescaling	4	320.1	234.8	2	487.5	334.5	4	354.6	245.8
basic	28	112.7	84.9	0	-	-	23	192.2	137.5	basic	11	381.7	271.6	30	312.8	225.9	0	-	-
$speed \times 10^{-2}$	29	152.9	122.7	29	326.1	256.7	1	592.4	461	$\mu \times 10^{1}$	11	363.4	254	9	408.0	259.4	11	303.1	215.5
$speed \times 10^{-1}$	23	136.6	108.0	29	296.4	229.1	0	-	-	$\mu \times 10^{2}$	6	387.5	266.2	30	240.3	176.3	4	307.8	197
$speed \times 10^{1}$	10	82.9	62.3	0	-	-	13	388.8	256.2	$\mu \times 10^{3}$	8	405.7	283.9	29	198.7	147.1	1	117.9	78
$speed \times 10^{2}$	8	139.9	94.1	0	-	-	2	139.1	101.5	$\mu \times 10^{4}$	8	467.7	295.9	28	265.9	170.5	2	320.6	228.5

Evaluation. An *experiment* consists in the execution of falsification using a given rescaling strategy (*no-rescaling*, *basic rescaling* as described in Sect. 3, or a different rescaling), over a specification for 30 *trials*, using different seeds. For each experiment, we collect the *success rate (SR)* as the number of trials in which a falsifying input was found, the average execution *time* of the successful trials, and the average number of simulations. Table 2 reports all experimental results[1]. We analyze them using 3 research questions.

RQ1 Does the basic rescaling approach always solve the scale problem?
First, we want to assess the effectiveness of the basic rescaling approach. From Table 2, we observe that in 7 out of 12 cases (AT1, AT2, AT3, AT6, AT7, AFC1, AFC2), the approach does improve the success rate w.r.t. the no-rescaling approach in which the signals are kept in their original order of magnitudes; this is particular evident in AT3. On the other hand, we observe that in some cases there is almost no improvement given by the basic rescaling (as AT4 and AT9) and, in few cases, the basic rescaling approach even diminishes the success rate, as AT5 and AT8: this is an indication that only considering the theoretical ranges of the signals may be not a good strategy, as the concrete robustness values associated to these signals usually have different order of magnitudes.

RQ2 How does the rescaling factor influence the falsification performance?
In the previous RQ, we observed that the basic rescaling is not always effective. In this RQ, we investigate whether other types of rescaling (i.e., not at the same order of magnitude) can lead to better falsification results. From Table 2, we observe that this is the case. In 3 out of 12 cases (AT1, AT5, and AT8), the best falsification result is obtained by an "unbalanced" rescaling strategy. This confirms that the best rescaling is the one that affects the robustness landscape in a way that the falsification algorithm is facilitated. The next RQ provides further analyses that explain such phenomenon.

---

[1] The source code is available at https://github.com/choshina/FalSTAR-NFM.

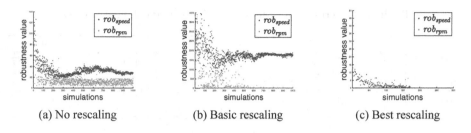

(a) No rescaling   (b) Basic rescaling   (c) Best rescaling

Fig. 1. Comparison of rescaling strategies for AT8

RQ3 Why do "unbalanced" rescalings sometimes improve the performance?
In order to answer this question, we investigate AT8, for which the basic rescaling
does not work at all, while two other unbalanced rescalings work very well. AT8is
$\square_{[0,30]}(\varphi_1 \wedge \varphi_2)$, where $\varphi_1 \equiv speed < 135$ and $\varphi_2 \equiv rpm < 4780$. We run the
falsification algorithm using no-rescaling, basic rescaling, and the best rescaling
strategy (i.e., with *speed* with 10^{-1}), each taking 1000 simulations as timeout.
For each simulation, we calculate values rob_{speed} and rob_{rpm} from the output
signals **w**, as follows:

(i) we obtain $\{[\![\mathbf{w}^t, \varphi_1 \wedge \varphi_2]\!] \mid t \in [0, 30]\}$;
(ii) for each $t \in [0, 30]$, we identify whether $[\![\mathbf{w}^t, \varphi_1 \wedge \varphi_2]\!]$ is given by value
     $[\![\mathbf{w}^t, \varphi_1]\!]$ or $[\![\mathbf{w}^t, \varphi_2]\!]$, and we record $[\![\mathbf{w}^t, \varphi_1]\!]$ in S_{φ_1} or $[\![\mathbf{w}^t, \varphi_2]\!]$ in S_{φ_2},
     accordingly. Then, we assign rob_{speed} as $\bigsqcap S_{\varphi_1}$ and rob_{rpm} as $\bigsqcap S_{\varphi_2}$; if S_{φ_1}
     (or S_{φ_2}) is empty, then rob_{speed} (or rob_{rpm}) is omitted.

In this way, we know, for each sample, which is the signal that contributed
to the final robustness. Figure 1 shows, for the three approaches, rob_{speed} and
rob_{rpm} of each sample. Note that the final robustness of each sample is given by
the minimum between rob_{speed} and rob_{rpm}. In Fig. 1a, we see that *rpm* always
determines the final value, and no falsifying input is found: this shows that, in this
case, falsification driven by *rpm* is not efficient. This is against the assumption of
the basic rescaling that the signals having larger ranges lead to higher robustness
values; indeed, we see from Fig. 1b that the basic rescaling actually worsens the
situation, having the effect of increasing the robustness related to *speed*. From
Fig. 1c, we see that the best rescaling is an unbalanced one, in which the speed
is decreased of one order of magnitude: in this case, the falsification algorithm
is very effective, and finds a falsifying input after 172 simulations.

5   Conclusion and Future Work

We have shown that having signals of different scales in a specification can affect
the falsification effectiveness, because, due to the robust semantics, one signal
can mask the other. We have also shown that the naïve approach that rescales
the signals to the same order of magnitude does not always solve the problem.
Sometimes, "unbalanced" rescalings are better. Future research direction consists

in devising falsification approaches that can automatically find such rescalings, either before or during the search.

References

1. Annpureddy, Y., Liu, C., Fainekos, G., Sankaranarayanan, S.: S-TaLiRo: a tool for temporal logic falsification for hybrid systems. In: Abdulla, P.A., Leino, K.R.M. (eds.) TACAS 2011. LNCS, vol. 6605, pp. 254–257. Springer, Heidelberg (2011). https://doi.org/10.1007/978-3-642-19835-9_21
2. Donzé, A.: Breach, a toolbox for verification and parameter synthesis of hybrid systems. In: Touili, T., Cook, B., Jackson, P. (eds.) CAV 2010. LNCS, vol. 6174, pp. 167–170. Springer, Heidelberg (2010). https://doi.org/10.1007/978-3-642-14295-6_17
3. Donzé, A., Maler, O.: Robust satisfaction of temporal logic over real-valued signals. In: Chatterjee, K., Henzinger, T.A. (eds.) FORMATS 2010. LNCS, vol. 6246, pp. 92–106. Springer, Heidelberg (2010). https://doi.org/10.1007/978-3-642-15297-9_9
4. Ernst, G., et al.: ARCH-COMP 2020 category report: falsification. In: ARCH20. 7th International Workshop on Applied Verification of Continuous and Hybrid Systems (ARCH20). EPiC Series in Computing, vol. 74, pp. 140–152. EasyChair (2020). 10.29007/trr1
5. Fainekos, G.E., Pappas, G.J.: Robustness of temporal logic specifications for continuous-time signals. Theor. Comput. Sci. **410**(42), 4262–4291 (2009)
6. Ferrère, T., Nickovic, D., Donzé, A., Ito, H., Kapinski, J.: Interface-aware signal temporal logic. In: Proceedings of the 22nd ACM International Conference on Hybrid Systems: Computation and Control, HSCC 2019, Montreal, QC, Canada, April 16–18, 2019, pp. 57–66 (2019)
7. Kapinski, J., Deshmukh, J.V., Jin, X., Ito, H., Butts, K.: Simulation-based approaches for verification of embedded control systems: An overview of traditional and advanced modeling, testing, and verification techniques. IEEE Control Syst. **36**(6), 45–64 (2016)
8. Zhang, Z., Hasuo, I., Arcaini, P.: Multi-armed bandits for boolean connectives in hybrid system falsification. In: Dillig, I., Tasiran, S. (eds.) CAV 2019. LNCS, vol. 11561, pp. 401–420. Springer, Cham (2019). https://doi.org/10.1007/978-3-030-25540-4_23

Author Index

Printed in the United States
by Baker & Taylor Publisher Services